HUMAN BEHAVIOR AND THE SOCIAL ENVIRONMENT
SOCIAL SYSTEMS THEORY

SIXTH EDITION

ORREN DALE
Wichita State University

REBECCA SMITH
Middle Tennessee State University

JULIA M. NORLIN
University of Oklahoma

WAYNE A. CHESS
University of Oklahoma

PEARSON

Boston   New York   San Francisco
Mexico City   Montreal   Toronto   London   Madrid   Munich   Paris
Hong Kong   Singapore   Tokyo   Cape Town   Sydney

Senior Series Editor: Patricia Quinlin
Series Editorial Assistant: Carly Czech
Marketing Manager: Wendy Albert
Production Editor: Karen Carter
Editorial Production Service: Holly Crawford
Manufacturing Buyer: Debbie Rossi
Electronic Composition: Publishers' Design and Production Services, Inc.
Photo Researcher: Annie Pickert
Cover Administrator: Joel Gendron

For related titles and support materials, visit our online catalog at www.ablongman.com.

Between the time website information is gathered and then published, it is not unusual for some sites to have closed. Also, the transcription of URLs can result in typographical errors. The publisher would appreciate notification where these errors occur so that they may be corrected in subsequent editions.

Library of Congress Cataloging-in-Publication Data

Dale, Orren
Human behavior and the social environment : social systems theory. — 6th
ed. / Orren Dale . . . [et al.].
         p. cm.
   Includes bibliographical references and index.
   ISBN-13: 978-0-205-61369-4 (alk. paper)
   ISBN-10: 0-205-61369-1
   1. Social service. 2. Social systems. 3. Social systems—Mathematical
models. 4. Human behavior. I. Dale, Orren.

   HV40.H7813 2009
   361.3'2—dc22

                                                                    2008018457

Printed in the United States of America

10 9 8 7 6 5 4 3 2 1   RRD-VA   12 11 10 09 08

Photo Credits: p. 3: IndexOpen; p. 19: IndexOpen; p. 44: IndexOpen; p. 67: National Archives and Records Administration; p. 95: David Buffington/Photodisc/Getty Images; p. 143: IndexOpen; p. 175: David Young-Wolff/PhotoEdit; p. 194: IndexOpen; p. 230: IndexOpen; p. 257: Ariel Skelley/Bettmann/Corbis; p. 293: Michael Moran/Dorling Kindersley; p. 313: IndexOpen; p. 338: IndexOpen; p. 371: Geri Engberg Photography; p. 398: Gail Oskin/AP Images

CONTENTS

PREFACE   ix

PART ONE
OVERVIEW   **1**

  CHAPTER 1
  INTRODUCTION   **3**

    Social Work   3
    The Purpose of Social Work   4
    Theory and Practice in Social Work: Connecting the Dots   5
    The Role of Religion and Spirituality in Social Work   6
    The Relationship of Social Systems Theory to Generalist Practice   7
    Social Systems Theory and Social Work   11
    Social Systems Structure and Function   12
    Social Systems Theory Model   13
    Summary   16
    Glossary   16
    Notes   18

  CHAPTER 2
  A SOCIAL SYSTEMS PERSPECTIVE: THE FOUNDATIONS
  FOR SOCIAL SYSTEMS THEORY   **19**

    The Nature of Theory   19
    Social Systems Perspective   21
    General Systems Theory   23
    Ecological Theory   30
    Functional Theory   31
    Symbolic Interactionism and Role Theory   36
    Summary   40
    Glossary   41
    Notes   42

  CHAPTER 3
  SOCIAL SYSTEMS THEORY: GENERAL FEATURES   **44**

    Definitions   45
    Social Systems Theory   48
    Summary   64
    Glossary   64
    Notes   65

CHAPTER 4
SOCIAL STRATIFICATION, SPIRITUALITY, AND DIVERSITY   67

Introduction   68
Cultural Diversity   70
Social Systems Theory   73
Dimensions of Stratification   78
Conflict and Consensus   81
Conflict, Religion, and Diversity   83
Ethics and Cultural Diversity   85
Summary   89
Glossary   89
Notes   90

PART TWO
THE INDIVIDUAL   93

CHAPTER 5
THE INDIVIDUAL: THEORIES OF PSYCHOLOGY USED BY SOCIAL WORKERS   95

Psychoanalytic/Psychodynamic Theory   96
Behaviorism/Learning Theory   104
Cognitive Development Theory   110
Moral Development Theory   116
Cognitive-Behavioral Theory   124
Humanism   126
Symbolic Interaction Theory   131
Summary   137
Glossary   137
Notes   140

CHAPTER 6
PSYCHOSOCIAL THEORY: A SOCIAL SYSTEMS PERSPECTIVE   143

Focus   144
Assumptions   145
Concepts   145
The Biological Connection   148
Infancy   151
Post Infancy   154
Preschool   156
School   158
Adolescence   161
Early Adulthood   163
Middle Adulthood   165
Late Adulthood   167

Summary   169
Glossary   170
Notes   171

PART THREE
THE SOCIAL GROUP   173

CHAPTER 7
THE SOCIAL GROUP: AN INTRODUCTION   175

Definitions   177
Gemeinschaft and Gesellschaft   178
Natural and Rational Will   179
Primary and Secondary Groups   181
Collections of People, Categories of People, and the Social Group   184
Summary   191
Glossary   191
Notes   192

CHAPTER 8
THE SOCIAL GROUP: THEORETICAL SUPPORT   194

Field Theory   195
Exchange Theory   200
Symbolic Interaction Theory   211
Spirituality and Group Process   225
Summary   226
Glossary   227
Notes   228

CHAPTER 9
THE FAMILY AS A SYSTEM OF ROLES   230

Families as Emergent Structures   230
Structural Family Theory   232
Family Systems Theory   245
Communications/Interactive Theory   250
Summary   254
Glossary   254
Notes   255

CHAPTER 10
THE SOCIAL GROUP AND THE FAMILY: SOCIAL SYSTEMS THEORY   257

The Social Group and the Family   258
Social Systems Theory: Review of General Features   261
Social Systems Theory: The Social Group and the Family   262

Summary   287
Glossary   288
Notes   288

PART FOUR
THE FORMAL ORGANIZATION   291

CHAPTER 11
THE FORMAL ORGANIZATION: AN INTRODUCTION   293

Gemeinschaft and Gesellschaft   294
Definition   295
Organizational Theory and Practice   296
Authority   297
The Weberian Bureaucracy—The Rationalist Position   300
The Human Relations Position   306
Organizational Theory and Social Work Education   308
Summary   310
Glossary   310
Notes   311

CHAPTER 12
THE FORMAL ORGANIZATION: SOCIAL SYSTEMS THEORY   313

Comparisons with the Rationalist and Human Relations Positions   316
The Dialectic   319
Social Systems Theory: Emergence   320
Social Systems Theory: The Functional Requisites   321
Social Systems Theory: The Structural Components   325
Social Systems Theory: Developmental Stages of Formal Organizations   328
Social Systems Theory: Total Quality Management   332
Theories X, Y, and Z   335
Summary   336
Glossary   336
Notes   336

CHAPTER 13
THE FORMAL ORGANIZATION AS A SOCIAL SYSTEM   338

Boundary   340
Suprasystem   341
Interface   343
Input   345
Proposed Output   345
Conversion Operations   346
Output   360

Feedback   362
Summary   366
Glossary   366
Notes   367

PART FIVE
THE COMMUNITY   369

CHAPTER 14
THE COMMUNITY: AN INTRODUCTION   371

Definitions of Community   373
The Ecological Position: Human Ecology   375
The Community Power Position   381
Community Power: The Elitist Position   382
Community Power: The Pluralist Position   386
The Conflict Position   390
Summary   394
Glossary   394
Notes   395

CHAPTER 15
THE COMMUNITY: SOCIAL SYSTEMS THEORY   398

Comparisons with Ecological, Power, and Conflict Positions   400
Social Systems Theory   402
Rural Communities as Adapting Systems   424
Summary   429
Glossary   430
Notes   430

INDEX   433

PREFACE

This, the sixth edition of *Human Behavior and the Social Environment: Social Systems Theory*, continues the emphasis that has characterized the text from the start. Most notably, this edition of the text stresses the application of theory to the full range of social work practice methods. The prime considerations of this text address two elements of social work practice: First, social work practice treats a range of client systems, from the individual to the community. Secondly, social work theories ultimately treat the dynamic interaction between client systems and their social environments.

In each successive edition of the text, we have been concerned with three primary criteria in the selection of theories for inclusion.

1. Our first criterion is the relevance of the theory for social work practice. We have been concerned with relevance rather than theoretical elegance, as our profession demands that our theories address the real world demands of social workers in the field.

2. Our second criterion is the demonstrated validity of the theories for inclusion. In most cases, this can be understood as the empirical validity of the theories as traditionally set forth in the scientific method. However, recent editions of the text have included more materials that elude this criterion. Those theories that address spirituality are less amenable to scientific validation than are theories of behavior, or even cognition. Nonetheless, the last two decades have seen increased interest in spirituality as it affects social work practice, and there is a clear need to develop a critical and theoretical framework for linking spiritual and religious considerations to practice.

3. Our third criterion may seem to be at variance with the second. A set of standards that stresses demonstrated validity would seem to preempt discussion of theories deemed to have failed to meet this test. Why then do we discuss psychoanalytic theory, which has often been pilloried for the failure of the model to demonstrate empirical validity? The reason is that this approach has become so embedded in the language of the profession that it would be hard to function as a social worker in many settings without a basis in psychodynamic concepts. We have noted the criticism of psychoanalysis and other models due to their speculative and unproven assertions, as well as for their inconsistency with certain social work values like empowerment and diversity. Our concern for critical analysis of the contents, and the impact of some theories on our shared vocabulary, convinced us to include some of the content theories that have shaped our professional history.

This edition of the text advances our concern with linking theory and practice. We continue in developing content that "connects the dots" between these traditional elements of the social work educational curriculum.

We have included new and expanded content on cognitive behavioral theory, due to the increasing body of evidence about the effectiveness of cognitive behavioral therapy in various practice applications. In addition, the assessment and treatment of many conditions using cognitive behavioral therapy have advanced the underlying theory, including the recognition that the "unobservable" cognitive events reviled by early behaviorists, such as John B. Watson, are integrally connected with therapeutic interventions targeting behaviors. We regard this as entirely consistent with our view of emotions, cognitions, and behavior as interacting subsystems of the person in the environment.

Related to the augmented content on cognitive behavioral theory, this edition includes additional material on biological subsystems, particularly as they influence psychosocial development theory.

Within our social systems view, we have added new material on complex organizations and community theory as suprasystem influences in the social environment, as well as client systems in their own right for macro practitioners. Additions include theories relative to management and supervision practice derived from McGregor's Theory X and Theory Y, and the managerial Theory Z that extends McGregor's model.

As in earlier editions, we have continued to refine and clarify our conception of social systems as the organizing framework for generalist social work practice. This includes the critical social systems function of feedback, and the interactive dynamics of various systems levels.

It is our goal to provide a comprehensive overview of the theories used at all levels of generalist social work practice. This text can be employed in a one-semester overview of social work theories or with supplemental materials can be expanded to a two-semester application.

We are especially grateful to colleagues, students, and practitioners who have helped us to refine this text and to further our efforts to provide an integrated theoretical foundation for social work practice in the twenty-first century.

PART ONE

OVERVIEW

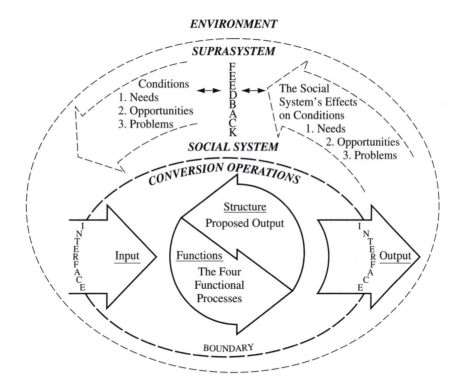

CHAPTER 1

INTRODUCTION

SOCIAL WORK

THE PURPOSE OF SOCIAL WORK

THEORY AND PRACTICE IN SOCIAL WORK:
CONNECTING THE DOTS

THE ROLE OF RELIGION AND SPIRITUALITY
IN SOCIAL WORK

THE RELATIONSHIP OF SOCIAL SYSTEMS
THEORY TO GENERALIST PRACTICE

SOCIAL SYSTEMS THEORY AND SOCIAL WORK

SOCIAL SYSTEMS STRUCTURE AND
FUNCTION

SOCIAL SYSTEMS THEORY MODEL

SUMMARY

GLOSSARY

NOTES

SOCIAL WORK

The *Social Work Dictionary* offers the following definition:

> Social work is the professional activity of helping individuals, groups or communities to enhance or restore their capacity for social functioning and creating societal conditions favorable to this goal.[1]

Our only addition to this definition would be the inclusion of practice with formal organizations.

Social work is a *social* profession. Our area of expert knowledge and the focus of our practice is in the relationships that people have with others. Humans are social beings. Through our relationships with other people we acquire and maintain our distinctive human characteristics.[2]

As we will see later, it is largely through our social relationships with others that we seek a personal state of well-being of becoming all that we are capable of becoming.[3]

Social work is distinguished from other professions in the helping field by its focus on the relationships between people (or other social units, e.g., families) and the social environment in which these relationships take place. The concept of human behavior within the social environment is basic to social work. It means that human behavior can be best understood by considering the reciprocal effects between human behavior and the social context in which the behavior takes place.

Now we can link this question with the first one—"What Is This Book About?" A system is any entity comprised of functionally interdependent parts. The word *functionally* is very important in this definition because it denotes the contribution each part makes to the whole. That the system is social means that the "parts" are humans.

> **SOCIAL SYSTEM**   Any entity comprised of individuals who have functionally interdependent relationships with one another.

Each of the following could be considered a social system—a family, a social group, a formal organization, a community, or a society. Social systems theory offers an explanation as to how these social systems function. The focus of our presentation of social systems theory is not only on how they work, but also on how the social functioning of these social systems can be enhanced.

Social work is about human interdependence and wholeness. This idea of interdependence and wholeness as a way of looking at ourselves and our relationships to others is perhaps best expressed in this excerpt of the work of the great English poet John Donne (1571–1631):

No man is an island, entire of itself;
Every man is a piece of the continent, a
    part of the main;

If a clod be washed away by the sea,
    Europe is the less,
as well as if a promontory were,
as well as if a manor of thy friends or of
    thine own were;
Any man's death diminishes me, because I
    am involved in mankind;
And therefore never send to know for
    whom the bell tolls;
It tolls for thee.

"Devotions XVII"

THE PURPOSE OF SOCIAL WORK

The multiple origins of social work have also given rise to different positions on the purposes of the profession. In 2001, the **Council on Social Work Education** (CSWE, the national body that, among other functions, accredits social work programs) adopted the following statement on the purpose of social work:

The profession of social work is based on the values of service, social and economic justice, dignity and worth of the person, importance of human relationships, and integrity and competence in practice. With these values as defining principles, the purposes of social work are:

- To enhance human well-being and alleviate poverty, oppression, and other forms of social injustice.
- To enhance the social functioning and interactions of individuals, families, groups, organizations, and communities by involving them in accomplishing goals, developing resources, and preventing and alleviating distress.
- To formulate and implement social policies, services, and programs that meet basic human needs and support the development of human capacities.
- To pursue policies, services, and resources through advocacy and social or political actions that promote social and economic justice.
- To develop and use research, knowledge, and skills that advance social work practice.

- To develop and apply practice in the context of diverse cultures.[4]

The academic social work programs across the nation affiliated with CSWE have adopted this purpose statement and are using it in organizing their curricula. This action will have a very important effect on the future direction of the profession.

THEORY AND PRACTICE IN SOCIAL WORK: CONNECTING THE DOTS

This is a book about theories of human behavior, and it is worth our time to take a moment to discuss the role and value of theories in social work. In everyday conversation, many people use the word *theory* in contrast to *practical*, as in "That's nice in theory, but that isn't how it works in real life!" Social work is a practical profession, so what need do we have for theories?

Good theories are intimately tied to their practical applications. The purpose of theory is the prediction and control of events. This is accomplished by using theories to explain the relationship among observed variables. As the world becomes more complicated, we need theories as a road map to understand how things are connected. For a simple example, we observe that some men beat their wives. We observe that many of these men drink a lot of alcohol. It is tempting to conclude that alcohol abuse leads to spouse abuse. That explains the relationship between two observed variables and constitutes a simple theory of wife beating.

Obviously, our alcohol theory is pretty basic and leaves out a lot of other variables. For example, not all men who drink also beat their wives. Moreover, not all men who beat their wives drink. Hmmm, now what? Like so many theories of human behavior, this theory does not account for all of the observed behaviors. In applying theories to human behavior, we almost never get perfect prediction. The gold standard

for any theory is the ability to identify the key variables out of all the myriad possibilities that meet two requirements. A key variable will always predict the behavior, and the behavior will never occur in the absence of that variable. When we have that degree of relationship, we are pretty sure that a cause-and-effect relationship exists between the two variables.

In theories of human behavior, we rarely see clear-cut cause and effect, where one variable alone causes the occurrence of another. Most of the time, theories of human behavior describe contributing variables rather than cause-and-effect relationships. Thus, alcohol abuse might contribute to spouse abuse, but it is neither necessary nor sufficient to cause spouse abuse.

The process of identifying, describing, measuring, and testing the variables and their relationship is the heart of theory building. Our example leads to a conclusion: Good theory building involves careful observation, measurable description, and testing of our hypotheses about the variables we observe. An hypothesis is simply a hunch; based on our observations, we think that we have an idea about which variables contribute to or preclude certain behaviors. We then put that hunch to a test by creating conditions under which we can manipulate the variables and observe the outcome.

In science, the best method for hypothesis testing is to conduct experiments. This is common in the "hard sciences" such as physics and chemistry. In the behavioral sciences, concern for the well-being of the subjects limits our ability to use experimental tests of hypotheses. Imagine the outcry if we took a group of men and randomly had some drink alcohol heavily and some not, then observed the effect on spouse abuse. In addition, the factors involved in human behavior are so subtle and varied that it would be virtually impossible to control them all. As a result, we rely on sample size and statistical methods in many cases to provide the rigor that we lose by not using experiments.

As in the physical sciences, behavioral science gives rise to both grand theories and theories of limited range. The definitions of these terms vary, but the essence is clear. Some theories are useful for a wide range of subjects and situations, such as the notion that behavior is shaped by the positive and negative consequences that follow. This is the so-called "Law of Effect," which is more properly a theory that can generate testable hypotheses. Other theories apply only to a narrow range of subjects or situations. Many theories of limited range exist and have value in social work, and many are in conflict with grand theories that dominate the field.

When we have tested an hypothesis (or a number of related hypotheses) a number of times and the results consistently confirm the expected results, we arrive at a theory. A valid scientific theory then generates new hypotheses that are testable. In this way, science continually challenges its own beliefs. The scientific method, to be effective, must involve open communication of the tests and results. The values of science demand that no theory ever be considered "proven." Some explanations are found to be generally useful, even when they do not strictly describe reality. These useful aggregates are sometimes referred to as "models," which aid our understanding of events without precisely describing them. Useful as models are, it is theory that advances science.

THE ROLE OF RELIGION AND SPIRITUALITY IN SOCIAL WORK

In recent years the subject of spirituality and religion has become more of a focus in social work education and practice. In this book, we make distinctions between spirituality and religion. We treat spirituality as a phenomenon noted primarily at the individual level, while religion is a social institution.

As a social institution, religion performs a variety of functions. Most of these we treat within the discussion of systems theory. Some of the functions of religion, however, deserve and require special attention. In Chapter 4, we treat religion as a major consideration in social diversity and stratification. In general, sociology views religion as an institution that provides a shared, collective way of dealing with the unknowable issues of life. Most world religions have particular value in addressing such disturbing events as death, illness, and trauma. In addition, religion provides a structure to help in the difficult process of making moral choices and acting in an ethical manner.

A key function of religion is promotion of social cohesion, especially in times of distress or in connection with moral issues. We view religion as a set of collective beliefs that are developed and transmitted within the system. In Chapter 4, we note that the intended cohesive effects of religion are concentrated within the system. Recent years have underlined our awareness that while religions are internally cohesive, the relationships between religious groups are often contentious and divisive. The comfort provided by a community of believers is often set against a background of fractious relations between the religious communities in a diverse society. The extreme form of this phenomenon is terrorism based on religious animosity. As we discuss later, it is often difficult to discern when such acts are based on religion, since the religious groups involved also represent different nation-states.

Much of our discussion accepts the distinction Durkheim made between the *sacred* and the *profane* in life. Durkheim regarded the profane as all natural arenas of life. These natural phenomena are known or knowable and are part of what we discuss as the empirical world. The sacred domain consists of things that are beyond the everyday world and consist of ultimately unknowable things. We refer to this sacred realm as spiritual. Religion as an institution is primarily concerned with the realm of the sacred, although some religious functions hedge into the profane world.[5]

As these topics arise throughout this book, it is useful to keep in mind that we view the spiritual realm as identified with the individual. Consequently, spirituality is more personal, flexible, and inclusive as a topic. Many people who regard themselves as spiritual do not identify with an organized religion. Most people who identify themselves as religious consider themselves spiritual. Some may consider that their entire spiritual experience conforms perfectly with the religious belief system to which they belong.

As we move into twenty-first century practice, we are mindful of the pluralistic state of both spirituality and religion. In dealing with religious issues in practice, it is important to remain respectful of diverse perspectives and to remind ourselves that varied and contradictory belief systems represent a practice reality.

THE RELATIONSHIP OF SOCIAL SYSTEMS THEORY TO GENERALIST PRACTICE

Social systems theory forms an important foundation for the eclectic knowledge base of generalist social work practice. Various authors define generalist practice differently, but most agree on the following elements and propositions regarding this approach.

Generalist practice

1. is an integrated approach.
2. utilizes an eclectic knowledge base that is systematically organized.
3. conceptualizes clients in the context of their social and physical environment.
4. is informed and guided by professional values and ethics.
5. seeks to empower clients and promote justice.
6. addresses multiple levels of society.
7. utilizes approaches that share common elements at all system levels.

8. requires that social workers enact a wide range of helping roles.
9. takes place under professional supervision.
10. takes place in the context of formal organizations.
11. relies on critical thinking skills.

Generalist practice may engage systems of any size. Most social problems can be conceptualized from any of a number of perspectives. For example, drug addiction may be understood as a biological process, a personality disorder, a manifestation of disordered family functioning, an outgrowth of one's interaction with peer groups, or as part of a community breakdown. Each of these approaches applies its own theory of limited range to understanding the client and addiction.

Social systems theory provides a connective matrix within which the particular theories applied to each system level that is addressed in generalist practice may be organized into a coherent whole. The characteristics of the connective matrix are dynamic, structural, hierarchical, comprehensive, religious, spiritual, interactional, evaluative, holistic, and functional.

Dynamic.   The social systems approach stresses the dynamic relationship between elements and levels of society. *Dynamic* is a word often used by theorists, and it simply means that the things being studied are in a state of motion. Systems theory originated as an effort to integrate the understanding of living systems in biology. Dynamic features are characteristic of all living things, and many systems we do not think of as alive in the traditional sense display similar properties. In almost all cases, social systems theory seeks to understand the patterns within which this dynamic activity takes place. The system dynamics discussed in this book apply to all sizes and types of social systems. While social movement is complex, it is rarely chaotic. In the process of planned change, it is essential to be able to anticipate the complex relationships between system elements and the consequences that follow when we change any part of the system.

To use the example of addiction once again, the target of intervention is always changing. Addiction itself is viewed as a progressive condition. That is, the nature of the addiction is always evolving. In the early stages, the addict may use drugs for pleasure. Later, the addict may use them to avoid pain. Still later, the addict may use drugs because the lifestyle associated with drugs has been incorporated into the individual's self-identity. In other cases, drug use may be sustained because it has become a source of status or income. The implications of placing a heroin addict on methadone maintenance will address some biological aspects of the condition, but the implications for self-concept, for status, or for economic well-being are also affected, perhaps adversely from the perspective of the client. In generalist practice informed by social systems theory, all such aspects of planned intervention are considered.

Structural. The dynamics of social systems occur within a defined structure. Structure defines the fixed elements of the system. Social systems theory addresses the relationship between structure and dynamic processes. This provides an understanding of the purpose of structure in social systems.

Perhaps no structural feature is more important in social systems than the boundary. Generalist practice demands that the social worker understand the nature of systems boundaries. Understanding the point where one system ends and another begins is crucial to all social work practice. Human beings as biological systems may be understood as being "bounded" by their skin. The "blood-brain barrier" separates the central nervous system and the circulatory system. A family or a gang may be bounded by patterns of behavior and communication. A culture may be bounded by common beliefs and

values. The content may vary, but the concept of boundaries is crucial in grasping holistic functioning. The vocabulary for understanding boundaries, boundary functions and characteristics, and their import in system functioning is developed throughout this text.

Hierarchical. Systems theory addresses the relationships between systems of different sizes. By understanding and applying the concepts and dynamics detailed in this book, the social worker is able to integrate concepts that may at first seem contradictory. Traditionally, social work has identified with the "dual tradition." That perspective conceptualizes problems as both individual issues and manifestations of larger social processes. Social work is unique in its mission to both address the personal and societal aspects of social problems. Herbert Gans famously expressed this apparent duality as the difference between "private troubles and public issues." We believe that social concerns are not one or the other. They are both. Social systems theory equips the generalist practitioner with a framework that incorporates both the personal and the societal aspects of problems, and aids in formulating intervention goals that address both levels.

We use the term *hierarchy* to describe the quality of embeddedness. See Figure 1.1. While this term is familiar, it is in part misleading. A hierarchy often connotes concepts such as power or status. This concept is useful in systems such as bureaucracies and some communities. It is less useful in application to systems such as biosystems or families. We cannot say that the nervous system is more important than

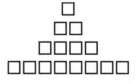

FIGURE 1.1   Hierarchy

the digestive system in the body, for example. A more precise term, *holarchy*, has been coined to describe the concentric organization of social systems into ever larger systems. See Figure 1.2. Each system is composed of smaller systems. Each system in turn is nested in a larger system, and so on. We will introduce specific language to describe this trait in Chapter 3.

Comprehensive. By looking at all levels of social phenomena, social systems theory helps the social worker avoid settling for simplistic explanations for events. In the addiction example, it seems to be true that theories about the biochemical nature of addiction explain a good deal. However, it is also true that theories focused on personality theories also explain certain aspects of the problem. Moreover, there exists a range of models that address addiction as a family process, and still others concerned with peer and community factors. No one level can explain completely the complex social and personal phenomenon we call addiction. It is necessary to develop a perspective within which we can articulate the theories of limited range into a holistic understanding as a foundation for effective generalist intervention.

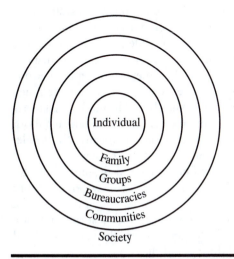

FIGURE 1.2 Holarchy

For many years, those who saw addictions as a personal problem argued with those who saw it as a public policy issue. Should we treat addiction as an illness? Therapists said yes. Should we treat it as a crime? Law enforcement people said yes. Should we interdict drug traffic and keep drugs off the street? The drug czar said yes. Each advocate tended to see their perspective as the "right one" and viewed the others as misguided. Social systems theory creates a critical thinking environment in which each level of explanation has something to offer the practitioner. The practitioner then becomes an agent for a holistic, multimodal approach that addresses the phenomenon of addiction as something that exists at all social levels and may be approached in a coordinated rather than in a disjointed way.

Interactional. Inherent in the social systems model is the idea that social systems interact constantly. This is part and parcel of the dynamic perspective discussed above. The focus of social systems theory is on the interaction between the individual and the environment. The inputs, outputs, and conversion processes discussed in this text constantly bring us to focus on the interpenetration of all levels of society with one another. The flow of energy from the environment into the individual, the process by which the individual converts those inputs, and the flow back into the environment as outputs constantly transforms both the individual and society.

One important implication of interactivity for generalist practice is that it challenges the view of linear causality. In social systems theory, A does not cause B. See Figure 1.3.

This nonlinear way of thinking is crucial in working to empower clients who may see their plight as caused by factors beyond their control. Even in the most hierarchical systems, it can be shown that the actions of those on top of the hierarchy can be influenced by those beneath them. Under the right circumstances, any sys-

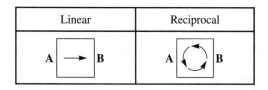

FIGURE 1.3 Linear versus Reciprocal Interaction

tem can be influenced by any other. In applications such as couples counseling, it is important to view partners as both the cause and effect of one another's behavior. It requires discipline to move past viewing one person as the cause of the behavior of another, but we find it is essential in the practical business of empowering clients.

Evaluative Feedback. All systems require information to function properly. Some information confirms that the system is functioning well. Other information informs the system that changes need to be made in the way the system operates. Social work as a profession may be understood as providing both types of crucial feedback to the systems they serve, as well as the systems within which they work. Again, in Chapter 3 and thereafter we will provide a highly developed vocabulary relating to the types and uses of feedback in the social systems approach.

Holistic. Social systems theory places emphasis on the connectedness of social phenomena. It is a hallmark of social systems theory that phenomena are perceived as part of a whole. Many theories in the scientific tradition tend to break things down to discrete elements. This practice, called *reductionism*, assumes that phenomena are no more than the sum of individual parts. Social systems theory requires us to examine things as a whole. Social systems are made up of subsystems and exist within larger systems. In order to be understood, things cannot be re-

duced to a static collection of parts. By assuming this perspective, social systems theory avoids the classic problem of the "Procrustean bed." In ancient Greek mythology, Procrustes was a thief who invited travelers into his home to spend the night. Once the traveler had been wined and dined, he was bedded down in Procrustes's famous bed. This bed was equipped with a device that stretched out the guest to fit the bed if he was too short. If the guest was too tall, the bed had a guillotine that lopped off the excess to make a perfect fit. The analogy to social theory has long been noted. Many theories focus on the facts that fit the model. Theorists are then tempted to lop off facts that don't fit, much like the guillotine. On the other hand, one may be tempted to invent information to "stretch out" the facts that are missing. In this way, observers often persist in using theories of limited range that fail to provide adequate explanation for all the facts without fabricating information to make the situation fit the theory.

Functional. It can be said that social systems theory proposes a functional purpose for all systems. The achievement of a steady state—in which the system functions efficiently, is adapted to the environment, achieves its aims, and provides for its component subsystems—is the optimal function of a system. This state of system well-being provides a universal reference point for all social work practice. Practice demands that we be able to conceptualize our goals—client well-being—across a wide range of system types and sizes. The model used to accomplish this must help us understand both function and dysfunction. Ideally, the model should provide consistent frameworks for understanding functional and dysfunctional dynamics. We believe that systems theory provides such a framework for practice. The four functional requisites for a steady state are described in Chapter 3, and then developed and applied throughout the text.

SOCIAL SYSTEMS THEORY AND SOCIAL WORK

We believe that every profession possesses a culture, and within that culture there will be a shared philosophy or perspective, a worldview. Embedded in this philosophy will be a perception of the purpose served by that profession. Next, the profession's purpose is operationalized by theories or at least an integrated set of concepts. Next, a technology is developed comprised of methods and materials that operationalize these theories and concepts. Finally, this technology is employed in practice. In short, through our curriculum we socialize our students into perspective, introduce them to the relevant theories and concepts, help them learn the technology, and through the practicum, provide the opportunity to employ the technology in a protected and supportive practice environment. This process is summarized in Figure 1.4 in terms of a four-tier approach that links theory to practice.

Tier I: Philosophy/Perspective

Thomas Kuhn, an enormously influential historian, said that two primary requisites are needed for knowledge to advance. The first requirement is a community of scientists. This community must share a common bond and a common scientific perspective. The second requirement is a dominant paradigm. Paradigms serve to orient research and theorizing in a particular area. The assumptions, major concepts, and propositions in an area of study are organized by the controlling paradigm, and the interrelations between these elements can be developed as theories and examined by means of research inquiry. The theories that emerge from the paradigm are empirically testable statements used to explain particular problems, patterns, or behaviors. In the absence of a controlling paradigm, there is little coherence to the development of theory and research. Kuhn

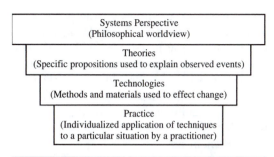

FIGURE 1.4 Construction of Social Systems Theory

is also famous for his observation that major changes occur within a community when there is a paradigm shift from an established perspective to a different point of view.

The social work perspective is comprised of nine **assumptions:**

1. There is an underlying general order in the world.
2. Social ordering is a constant and dynamic process.
3. All human social behavior is *purposive*.
4. All forms of social organization display self-maintaining and development characteristics.
5. All social organizations are greater than the sum of their parts.
6. Well-being is the natural state of all humans and human social organizations. (This assumption serves as the foundation of the **strengths perspective.**)
7. All forms of social organization can be characterized and studied as social systems.
8. The social relationship is the fundamental unit of all social systems.
9. The helping process seen in professional social work is a formalization of a natural social process.

Tier II: Theory

The second level builds from the first and is comprised of a set of concepts and theories that operationalize the purpose of the profession. There are three levels of theory. Limited-range theories are narrow in scope and address the behaviors that are distinctive to a particular class or level of social system. Middle-range theories interrelate two or more of the limited-range theories. Grand theories are broad generalizations that deal with the wide-ranging aspects of social phenomena.

We treat social systems theory as a middle-range theory, having sufficient scope and flexibility to accommodate many narrower-range theories with applications to the various levels of systems within which social workers practice.

Tier III: Technology

The term *technology* is often limited to the consideration of such things as electronics and machines. Our conception refers to technology as the specific methods and materials employed in social work practice. In our view, this practice technology is derived from social systems theory and its related concepts.

Social work practice technologies are often captive to the theories that undergird them. For example, some social work practice approaches are based on problem-focused theories. This may lead to notions such as "if it ain't broke, don't fix it." Such an approach leaves little room for proactive intervention or prevention of problems. The theory limits us to techniques that are reactive, deficit focused, and inconsistent with the professional goals of enhancing human well-being. While problem solving can be a useful tool, it is vital that it be embedded within a larger perspective that emphasizes strengths and positive potential.

Tier IV: Practice

Earlier we discussed the generalist practice model. Practice applications are the point where "the rubber meets the road." Each practitioner

applies the perspective in a unique and personalized fashion. The specific actions of the practitioner represent the realization of the social systems perspective. A generalist practitioner sees the world in dynamic systems terms. Generalist practice is guided by specific theories that are consistent with the systems perspective. Interventions with various systems levels, while specialized, are part of an integrated approach. Specific interventions represent the individualized adaptation each practitioner makes of the model.

SOCIAL SYSTEMS STRUCTURE AND FUNCTION

Two sets of concepts are used in presenting this theory. The first set is structural in nature: it identifies the eight structural elements in all social systems.

Structural Features of Social Systems
- Boundaries
- Suprasystem/Focal System/Subsystem
- Interface
- Proposed Output
- Input
- Conversion Operation
- Output
- Feedback

Each of these structural elements will be discussed and applied at each level of social system discussed in the remainder of this book.

The second set of concepts is functional in nature: it identifies the social functions that must be performed by the system in order for it to survive and grow.

Functional Features of Social Systems
- **Goal Attainment**
- **Adaptation**
- **Integration**
- **Pattern Maintenance**

These four functions were proposed initially by Talcott Parsons. They serve to link systems to their social environments. The functional elements of social systems will be presented in Chapter 2 and applied to each level of social system discussed.

SOCIAL SYSTEMS THEORY MODEL

Think of a **model** as a simplified representation of something of interest. Like most theories, social systems theory is abstract. Constructing a model becomes a way of conveying the critical features of the theory and showing how it can be applied to something real. It is in this sense that a model is abstracted from theory and can be thought of as a feature of technology.

Earlier we indicated that the theory was comprised of eight structural concepts and four functional processes (variables). Figure 1.5, The Social Systems Model, provides a graphic representation of the principal concepts comprising the theory and their relationships to each other. In the parts of the book to follow, we will model systems at the group, family, formal organization, and community levels. Most social workers do not practice at the societal level so this level has been excluded.

To help both in understanding the use of the model and the concepts that comprise it, we will apply it in Chapter 3. Social work programs (schools, departments, etc.) come into existence as the means of preparing professionals to work in agencies that seek to improve the social functioning of individuals, groups, families,

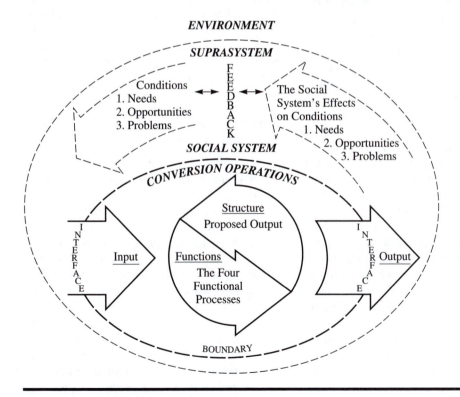

FIGURE 1.5 The Social Systems Model

organizations, and communities. These agencies and those they seek to help are all external to the social work program. Eight concepts comprise the model. The structural elements of social systems theory can be defined as follows.

Boundary. This identifies the border or external limits of the social work program. Typically it serves to identify the social system. Now to the universal characteristics associated with this structure—all social systems have boundaries and perform a boundary-maintaining function. Through boundary-maintaining behaviors, outsiders are distinguished from insiders. This function serves to protect the system from disruptive external influences.

Suprasystem. This is the concept that identifies the specific social context within which the system functions. Suprasystem corresponds to the *social environment* in the phrase *human behavior and the social environment.* The suprasystem is always comprised of specific external social systems that influence and are influenced by the **subject system.**

Subsystem. This is a component element of focal system. Subsystems display all the attributes of a system, but can be located within a larger designated system. For example, a married couple functions as a system and is a subsystem of the total family unit.

Focal System. This is an identified system that is the subject of attention. Designation as a focal system is a matter of the observer's perspective. If a family is the focal system, the siblings are a subsystem and the community is a suprasystem.

Interface. All systems have either formal or informal external relationships that couple the system to those units comprising its suprasystem.

Input. Two classes of input are recognized in social systems theory, signal (task) and maintenance. Signal inputs are those that are processed by the system and result in what will be designated as task outputs.

Conversion Operations. This concept designates the means employed to convert signal inputs to task outputs. These operations are divided in terms of the structural and functional processes employed. The specific structures and functional processes involved will vary by social system. In direct practice terminology, the conversion operation refers to the social work intervention.

Proposed Output. In social systems theory, we operationalize a system's purpose by using the concept of proposed output. In our usage, the concepts of goals and proposed output are synonymous. Goals may be formal or informal, but we hold that all forms of social systems are purposive in their social functioning. We have to be careful here. We are not saying that all who are participants within a social system either fully understand or subscribe to the system's goals. We are saying that the social functioning of the system will evidence purpose. In other words, all social behavior is purposive.

Output. Three classes of output are produced by all social systems:

- *Task outputs* are the actual system outputs that conform to the proposed output. In marriage counseling, a couple whose relationship is strengthened is a task output.
- The term *maintenance outputs* refers to the changes that take place in the maintenance inputs during the conversion process. For example, a social worker who learns new skills in working with the married couple represents maintenance output.
- *Waste* is the residue left from inputs that are used in the conversion process. In marital counseling, waste might consist of interventions that were attempted without the desired effect. In some cases, a couple who fails to achieve proposed changes in the relationship might be considered waste. In another example, ineffective or inappropri-

ate techniques used by the social worker might be considered waste.

Feedback. Feedback answers the question, how successful were we in accomplishing our goals? It is the information generated that permits the system to make adjustments in order to become functionally more efficient and effective. Feedback is always treated as a maintenance input in our presentation of social systems theory. The operations of social systems are cyclical, not linear. We restrict use of the term to information pertaining to the comparison of proposed output and actual output.

It is through feedback that systems are helped to maintain a state of well-being.

Utilizing social systems theory, the cyclical nature of generalist practice is depicted in Figure 1.6. The process is a social one involving, at a minimum, a person in the generalist role and a second person in the client/customer role. This is the **helping system.** It is in this sense that we consider all social workers to be system creators; it is the nature of our profession.

The helping method is conducted in the context of the social work profession's knowledge, values, and skills. Two forms of feedback are evident, task and maintenance. Process feedback

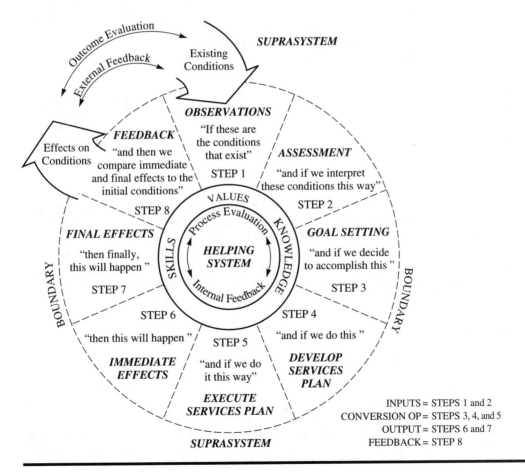

FIGURE 1.6 The Generalist Practice Model

(evaluation) focuses on the extent to which the agreed-upon process features are being followed (the services plan). Outcome evaluation, in its final sense, always represents a comparison of final conditions to beginning conditions. The model always has as its reference point a baseline comprised of the initial conditions. In a manner of speaking, this is a feedback model that is always checking progress against a baseline and a plan as the process moves toward achieving its purpose.

Earlier we made the point that social systems theory should provide a general orientation to practice. For example, in step 1, the generalist will gather data on both the client/customer and that system's social environment. The generalist will focus on strengths, not problems. Next, the worker will move to a more inductive form of reasoning that might suggest use of a narrower-range theory in the specific work with a client system. It is at this point that we envision an interface occurring between the use of social systems theory and theories of limited range.

SUMMARY

In many ways lacking a theory base to its own practice, social work has been affected by its association with medicine, particularly psychiatry. It borrowed heavily from other disciplines, especially psychiatry. Here, psychoanalytic theory was most influential in the profession's forma-

tive years. It is not surprising, given this background, that those whom it served were viewed as people with problems—patients. Practice became problem-oriented and its methods, forms of problem solving. The helping process started with a diagnosis or assessment—a search for and the specification of a problem.

Social work developed specialties before it developed the common features of its practice. Consequently, three significant changes are now under way in the profession. First, the profession is in the process of identifying the knowledge, skills, and values that constitute the foundation for all social work practice. This change is resulting in preparing the generalist practitioner, a person competent to practice at all levels—the individual, group, family, organization, and community.

Second, the purpose of the profession has moved away from its focus on the problems people have to the strengths and capacities they possess. This strengths perspective represents a return to the beliefs in people that characterized those that helped found the profession. Now the purpose of the profession is organized around the capacities of people and the organizations they form to achieve a sense of well-being.

Third, the profession is increasingly relying on its own members for the research and theory building that support its practice. Using both current and longitudinal research, we addressed questions that provided a framework for dealing with generalist practice and the use of social systems theory in the rest of the book.

GLOSSARY

Adaptation   One of the four functional variables in social systems theory. It is conducted externally and facilitates goal attainment.

Administration   A method of indirect practice in social work that is employed to efficiently achieve organizational goals and objectives in a manner that also advances the well-being of organizational members.

Assumption   A belief or supposition that something is true. An example of an assumption in psychoanalytic theory is that there are only two basic psychological motives, sexuality and aggression.

Boundary   A systems concept that defines the border that separates the system from its suprasystem.

Casework   A method of direct practice in social work typically conducted on a face-to-face basis with a client system and focused on improving the client's level of social functioning.

Client system   The ultimate beneficiary of a helping effort. A client system can be an individual, group, family, organization, or community.

Community organization   A method of social work practice that helps individuals, groups, organizations, and other collectives from the same geographic area (community) to deal with shared interests, opportunities, or problems in a manner that enhances their state of well-being.

Concept   A mental construct or idea derived from or associated with a theory, perspective, or model.

Conversion operations   The processes by which a system transforms its inputs into outputs.

Council on Social Work Education (CSWE)   A group of professional social workers, academic institutions, organizations, and agencies that establishes and maintains standards in social work education.

Direct practice   The form of social work practice that involves direct client contact, usually face-to-face, such as casework.

Eclectic   A collection of various theories and practice methods that are differentially employed by a social worker in response to the needs of the client system.

Feedback   The return of information to the system as input. In social systems theory, the term is restricted to information pertaining to the extent that output conforms to proposed output.

Focal system   An identified system that is the subject of attention. Designation as a focal system is a matter of the observer's perspective. If a family is a focal system, the siblings are a subsystem and the community is a suprasystem.

Generalist practice   A form of professional social work practice that can be competently conducted in a variety of settings with client systems of varying size at the several levels of prevention and that utilizes a transferable body of knowledge, values, and skills.

Goal attainment   One of the four functional variables in social systems theory. It is an external function and is synonymous with the concept of task output.

Group work   A method of social work practice that involves a small group of people with common interests who meet regularly in order to work toward their common goals.

Helping system   The social system created by the social worker, which becomes the tool for conducting the helping process.

Indirect practice   The form of social work practice that involves indirect contact with clients. For example, social work administration is conducted on behalf of clients but does not usually involve direct contact with them.

Input   All of the resources, including people, that are required by a social system to accomplish its purposes. Money appropriated to an agency is a vital input.

Integration   One of the four functional variables in social systems theory. It represents an internal function and is synonymous with the concept of maintenance output.

Interface   A boundary segment shared and maintained by two systems, for example, a contract between a school of social work and a child welfare agency through which the agency would provide practicum placements for the school's students.

Macro   A large social system, typically a formal organization or community.

Micro   A small social system, typically a social group or family.

Model   A representation of something real; for example, a social systems model is a representation of a social organization.

Output   The status of signal/task and maintenance inputs following a conversion cycle of a social system.

Pattern maintenance   Protection of a system's core structural patterns, those that provide its unique identity.

Perspective   A way of viewing things broadly so that their relationships and relative importance are understood.

Practice   The process of providing professional assistance to individuals, families, groups, organizations, or communities in an effort to make planned changes designed to move the person/organization toward a state of well-being.

Proposed output   A statement of what a system intends to accomplish. The concept is synonymous with a system's goals and objectives.

Social services   A program of activities provided by social workers and others directed toward the helping of people to meet their needs and/or to enhance their level of social functioning.

Social system   A social entity characterized by individuals or other social units possessing functionally interdependent relationships with each other, for example, a family, agency, or community.

Social systems model   A particular representation of a social system.

Social systems perspective   A set of assumptions on which social systems theory is based.

Social systems theory   A set of assumptions and concepts that seeks to explain the general patterns of behaviors exhibited in the functioning of social systems and how such systems achieve well-being.

Social work   A profession committed to the enhancement of well-being and to the alleviation of poverty and oppression.

Strengths perspective   A manner of approaching practice that focuses on the strengths and capacities of people and the organizations they form to achieve a sense of well-being.

Subject system   The system that is the object of social work practice in which social systems theory is being employed.

Subsystem   A component element of focal system. Subsystems display all the attributes of a system, but can be located within a larger designated system. For example, a married couple functions as a system and is a subsystem of the total family unit.

Suprasystem   That aspect of the social environment to which a subject system is functionally linked; for example, birth families are relevant parts of a family's suprasystem.

Technology   In social work, the application of science to the achievement of its purpose. Included would be the entire body of methods, approaches, materials, and products used to conduct practice.

Theory   A logically derived set of assumptions and concepts used to explain something, for instance, social systems theory.

NOTES

1. Robert L. Barker, *The Social Work Dictionary* (Silver Spring, MD: NASW, 1987), 154.
2. Charles Horton Cooley, *Social Organization* (New York: Charles Scribner & Sons, 1909), 30.
3. Abraham H. Maslow, *The Farther Reaches of Human Nature* (New York: Penguin Books, 1976), 40–51.

4. Council on Social Work Education, "Educational Policy and Accreditation Standards" (Alexandria, VA: Author, 2002), IA.
5. Emile Durkheim, *The Elementary Forms of Religious Life* (New York: Free Press, [1912] 1965).

CHAPTER 2

A SOCIAL SYSTEMS PERSPECTIVE
THE FOUNDATIONS FOR SOCIAL SYSTEMS THEORY

THE NATURE OF THEORY
SOCIAL SYSTEMS PERSPECTIVE
GENERAL SYSTEMS THEORY
ECOLOGICAL THEORY
FUNCTIONAL THEORY

SYMBOLIC INTERACTIONISM AND ROLE
    THEORY
SUMMARY
GLOSSARY
NOTES

THE NATURE OF THEORY

In this book, we have characterized the study of social systems as a "theory." There is dispute among scholars about whether it can properly be considered a theory. It is appropriate for a text of this nature to address this question di-

rectly before proceeding to the substance of our discussion of social systems.

A scientific theory is a set of interrelated concepts, definitions, and statements about relationships that can be tested empirically. The purpose of theory is to increase our understanding of the world by a systematic process of inquiry and validation of knowledge. Robert Merton suggested that scientific knowledge advances best if four conditions are met within the scientific community:

- *Disinterestedness*—belief that the development of knowledge should be distinct from the interests of the scientist; that knowledge should be pursued for its own sake.
- *Communalism*—belief in the value of sharing work among scientists.
- *Organized skepticism*—systematic disposition to challenge the claims of knowledge; a critical posture toward claims that demands objective assessment.
- *Universalism*—systematic agreement on the nature of knowledge and knowledge development (methodology).

Thomas Kuhn speculated that science advances best when subdisciplines have a shared set of theories and methodological assumptions, which he termed *paradigms*. We hold that social systems theory is an application of the general systems paradigm to social phenomena. While it is a high-level theory, it does relate directly to the observed world of social interactions.

There are two essential elements to all scientific theories: concepts and syntax.

- *Concepts* are the fundamental building blocks of scientific theory. They consist of carefully defined abstractions that are drawn from experience. They are abstract rather than concrete and thus are distinguished from facts.
- *Syntax* refers to the relationship among concepts, particularly causal relationships. Statements about the expected relationship between A and B constitute the syntax of a theory and are considered hypotheses when they are subjected to scientific inquiry.

In order to be considered a theory, a set of concepts and syntax must be capable of generating empirically testable hypotheses. For example, the statement that increasing levels of social disorganization will result in increased rates of drug abuse is a syntactical statement of the relationship between social disorganization and suicide, both of which are concepts that would require careful definition.

A theory is more than a single statement about relationships. There are two primary types of statements in a theory. The first is called an *existence statement*. This defines the exact meaning of each concept in the theory. Definitions as such cannot be empirically tested; thus, they must be carefully operationalized for inquiry. In the drug abuse example, the existence statement must define social disorganization and drug abuse in terms that are measurable.

The second type of statement is the *relational statement*. This must specify to some degree the association between two or more defined concepts. These statements can be empirically tested. In the example above, the relational statement is the statement that there is a positive relationship between social disorganization and drug abuse in a population.

Statements can be arranged hierarchically according to both their level of abstraction (an existence consideration) and their degree of truth (a relational consideration). The hierarchy of theoretical knowledge consists of the following:

- *Laws*—the observed regularities in nature
- *Axioms*—knowledge assumed for some purpose to be true
- *Postulates*—essential precursors in a train of reasoning
- *Propositions*—statements derived from a postulate, containing one or more variables subject to proof
- *Empirical generalizations*—summaries of empirical findings
- *Hypotheses*—propositions that are empirically testable

Theories require precise definitions of terms. They also require consensus of usage among scientists. The degree to which there is agreement within a community of scientists on the definitions in a theory is termed the *semantic agreement*. Obviously, if everyone uses a term differently, knowledge building is impaired. Lower-level concepts lend themselves to operational definition, which solves this problem.

The primary opposition to classifying social systems as a theory lies in the level of abstraction of the concepts. High levels of abstraction do not preclude theory development. However, high levels of abstraction may affect what is called the *empirical import* of a theory, that is, the degree to which the concepts in a theory relate to observable realities in the world.

A distinction must be made here between the terms *abstract* and *vague*. Scientific knowledge will not admit vagueness. However, a great deal of our knowledge exists at a medium to high level of abstraction. What Durkheim described as "social facts" constitute the focus of systems theory. These phenomena exist outside the individual acts of units within a system, but are characteristic of the system as a whole. It is our belief that systems concepts and syntax, while highly abstract, have direct empirical referents in the world of the social work practitioner. In addition, the theory serves to provide a connective matrix to the wide range of situations and systems with which social workers are daily engaged.

A second basis for opposing social systems as a theory lies in the varied usage of the key concepts among professionals. Part of the purpose of this book is to move toward consensual usage of terms to permit more systematic knowledge building using systems concepts.

We have attempted in this book to develop carefully the definitions of key systems concepts to allow for consistent usage in the profession. In addition, we have endeavored to define the relationship among these concepts in such a way as to form a foundation for systematic perceptions of social realities. Our goal is the development of systems knowledge that is germane in practice, robust enough to withstand skeptical assessment, and capable of generating testable hypotheses that advance social work knowledge and practice.

SOCIAL SYSTEMS PERSPECTIVE

Chapter 1 introduced the four-tier approach we employed in developing a theory of social systems applicable to generalist practice in social work. Tier I, Philosophy/Perspective, is comprised of nine assumptions. These nine assumptions represent a set of beliefs about human social life and serve as the foundations on which the theory builds. Our position is that all theories, at least in the human and behavioral sciences, start with a set of assumptions about humans and the world in which they live. We believe that the nine assumptions comprising the social systems perspective are widely held by social workers and by social scientists generally.

The order of the following assumptions suggests a hierarchy beginning with an assumption of the existence of a general order and ending with a feature of that order evident in the generalist practice of social work.

1. *There is an underlying intelligible general order in the world to which all matter relates and the existing social order is a subset of the general order.* The search for a general theory of order is based on this assumption, which has two principal and interrelated parts. First, a general or universal order exists. Second, this order is understandable to humans. A value judgment is implied—that seeking an understanding of this general order is desirable.

Science is predicated on this assumption with the scientific method being the approach to the discovery of the various features or characteristics of this order.

2. *Social ordering is a dynamic and constant process that arises out of conditions existing in the general order and the need structure of humans and* *the social organizations and institutions they join to form.* This assumption derives from the first and characterizes the social order as dynamic. The dynamic quality of the social order is to be understood, in part, in light of an ever-changing general order. The forms and common patterns exhibited by all forms of human organization have their origins in (1) the social and physical environment in which they are found and (2) the genetically based need structure found in all humans.

3. *All human social behavior is purposive.* The area of expert knowledge of social work is the social behavior of humans; through this expert knowledge base, social workers help people either individually or within various forms of social organization to improve social functioning. Our approach to knowledge building starts with this assumption—social behavior is purposive behavior and is conducted through social relationships. This assumption holds for the social behavior of an individual as a member of a group, family, formal organization, or **community.** The assumption also applies to each social organization that is a member of a class or level of social organization. For example, we consider social groups and families as a class or level of social organization. This means that each family is a separate and distinct social unit and the behavior of each is purposive.

4. *When fully developed, all forms of social organization display self-maintaining and development characteristics.* Social organizations go through a development process and reach a stage at which they display self-maintaining characteristics. Perhaps a parallel can be drawn to the development and maturation of the human. However, theory development is much more advanced in the area of human growth and development than it is in organizational development.

5. *A social organization, when viewed as a whole, is greater than the sum of its parts.* You cannot understand a social organization through disassembly. The social organization is a whole consisting of parts among which functional relationships exist. A practice example from a social systems perspective is that one does not practice family therapy through individual therapy conducted with each family member. The family is a separate social entity; it is greater than (and different from) the sum of its parts (family members).

6. *Well-being is the natural state of all humans and the various forms of social organization that humans join to form.* Social work practice builds from this assumption. By *natural state*, we mean that the genetic construction of humans provides each individual with the capacity to achieve a state of well-being. This is an individualized state and the assumption is a positive one. A state of well-being is characterized as a healthy or harmonious state that exists between the individual and that person's social environment. This assumption supports the strengths perspective that characterizes the practice of social work. Humanistic theory is particularly helpful in the support of this assumption.

7. *All forms of social organization, when fully developed, can be characterized and studied as social systems.* This assumption is derived from the previous ones and is central to the approach we use for modeling social organizations as social systems. The acceptance of this assumption permits us to seek to understand all forms of social organization from a social systems perspective. It also permits us to start the process of theory development that will help subject these assumptions to scientific study.

8. *The social relationship is the principal structural unit of all social systems.* In this hierarchy of assumptions, we have now moved from an assumption of a general order down to one that identifies the relationship as the key building block in the formation of social systems. Knowledge about the relationship and the ability to use the relationship define the social worker's professional domain.

Social work seeks to improve social functioning as the means of enhancing an individual's sense of well-being. The helping process, therefore, focuses on social relationships, not on the individual as such.

While the relationship affects those who comprise it, the relationship itself cannot be directly discerned by our human senses; you cannot see, touch, smell, taste, or hear a relationship. You know of its existence only by its effects on those who comprise it, that is, by the pattern of coordinated behaviors and responses.

9. *The helping process in generalist practice is a formalization of a natural discovery process that has its origins in how humans observe, feel, think, act, and come to know.*   Humans form relationships with others as a means of meeting their own needs, responding to the needs of others, and adapting to their natural environments. This process is natural and fundamental to human survival. To deal with their environments, humans join together and form social organizations. These can be likened to social tools to do work that no single human can individually accomplish. The profession of social work seeks to understand this basic social process and to use it to advance each person's sense of well-being. The formalization of this natural process is *generalist practice.*

The basic tool of the generalist practitioner is the relationship. This is why we refer to the generalist practitioner as a systems creator. Every practitioner will initiate the helping process by establishing a relationship with the client system. This causes a new system to be created and through the professional use of this new system, the helping process proceeds. Our use of the notion of the practitioner as a systems creator is very similar to what Pincus and Minahan labeled an **action system.**[1]

With the nine assumptions that comprise the social systems perspective serving as a backdrop, we can review the general systems, ecological, functional, and symbolic interaction theories. These four theories have provided most of what we consider to be the conceptual foundations of social systems theory.

Our approach to these lines of theory development starts with the person generally recognized as the major contributor or founder of each specific line of theory. We will also identify what we consider to be the major assumptions and concepts associated with that theory. Finally, we hope to convey that knowledge building is exciting; its aim is to learn more about the world in which we live. For the helping professional, the focus is on understanding why people behave as they do and on developing ways of assisting people to live more personally satisfying and socially useful lives.

GENERAL SYSTEMS THEORY

General systems theory is a theory of order; it has been likened to a science of wholeness. As you will recall, the first assumption identified in our social systems perspective was that there is an underlying intelligible general order in the world to which all matter relates and the existing social order is a subset of the general order. General systems theory proposes to explain why this is so. Its founder was a theoretical biologist, Ludwig von Bertalanffy (1901–1972). Born and educated in Austria, he became dissatisfied with the inability of linear-based, cause-and-effect theories to explain the growth and change he saw in living organisms. It occurred to von Bertalanffy that an explanation of this growth and change might lie in the relationships and interactions among those parts comprising the organism rather than in the parts themselves. In other words, the search for understanding should focus on the order among the parts, not on the parts themselves. This idea revolutionized science. Up to this point, scientists explored largely through a process of reductionism based on a conception of linear causation; that is, they sought an understanding of the whole by understanding all of its parts.

The general systems approach can be illustrated by the old story about the medical school professor who was teaching students about diabetes. As the students walked onto a ward, the professor looked at a patient's chart, then turned to the students and said, "Ladies and Gentlemen, this pancreas was admitted to the hospital two days ago in a diabetic coma." Medicine has long been organized into a series of specialties, each of which addresses a particular body system. By this method of reduction, a doctor can master a great deal of detail about a subject. Obviously, what is lost in this view is an understanding of the patient as a whole human being. Physicians have learned that organs do not function in a vacuum. Diabetes may be affected by mood, diet, drug interactions, and a host of other factors. A systemic perspective helps us understand the patient by understanding the whole person.

The intellectual foundation for general systems theory was set forth by von Bertalanffy in 1928; but it was not until the publication of *General Systems Theory* in 1968 that a complete statement of his theory became generally available.[2] Because of the revolutionary nature of thought in general systems theory, it has taken on the qualities of a social movement for many people.[3] Not only has it caused a rethinking of basic tenets throughout the scientific world, it has also provided a new vocabulary for people in all walks of life; for example, the popular use of terms such as *inputs*, *outputs*, and *feedback*. General systems theory has become more than a theory, it has become a way of thinking—a very broad perspective on the world in which we live. We have adapted this perspective and use it as the foundation for developing a social systems perspective.

The aim of general systems theory is to formulate the principles of organization. The principles must be as applicable to the study of the organizational features of the atom as to the study of the organizational qualities of the universe. Similarly, these same principles must hold for all those studying human behavior, from the psychologist studying the individual to the sociologist studying societal behavior.

Given the complexity and revolutionary nature of von Bertalanffy's thinking, it would be useful to identify some of the concerns he had and some of the assumptions that underlie his position. The concerns expressed by von Bertalanffy parallel concerns by those in social work who are struggling to define generalist practice and its theoretical underpinnings.

The assumption of the existence of a general order serves as a premise for an application of the scientific method, the process of discovery. From this position, the task of science is to seek an understanding of this order. Scientists have gone about this task in modern times by "staking out a territory" and proceeding to investigate that territory through a process of reduction, or reducing the subject matter into ever smaller and more manageable parts; it has been a process of simplification. Some theorists, like von Bertalanffy, found this approach problematic in that it resulted in a growing fragmentation in knowledge-building efforts. Most of us can identify with the insight on this problem expressed by Peter Checkland, a general systems theorist: "Although I usually have difficulty remembering what I did last Tuesday, I have a clear memory of a school science lesson in the 1940s when the chemistry master put into my astonished mind the idea that Nature did not consist of physics, chemistry and biology: these were *arbitrary* divisions, man-made, merely a convenient way of carving up the task of investigating Nature's mysteries."[4] We in social work have done the same thing in our knowledge-building efforts: we have created method categories without agreeing on the knowledge bases that form the foundations of these categories.

In 1973, Bennis and others, commenting on this process of knowledge building by arbitrarily "carving up" a territory, observed, "Perhaps nowhere is the abyss between formal logic and reality more evident than in man's attempt to order knowledge about his own behavior. There are today twenty-four (24) divisions within the

American Psychological Association, and these are presumably logically separable from each other as well as from the subdivisions of sociology, anthropology, political science and psychiatry."[5] In short, general systems theory represents a reaction to the fragmentation that was occurring in scientific thought based on reductive and linear-based reasoning. General systems theory focused on wholeness and causality in interactive rather than in linear terms. Here at last was a way of viewing human behavior that focused on the person and his or her total situation; it was a way of viewing human behavior that the profession of social work had advanced from its professional beginnings.[6] This same concern about fragmentation has given rise to the movement within the profession of social work to identify a common foundation of knowledge, values, and skills to undergird all of practice. By identifying this common foundation, it then becomes possible to think about the generalist practitioner, one who can apply this knowledge to systems of all sizes and to all levels of prevention.

Related to the assumption of a general order is the assumption that a social organization when viewed as a whole, is greater than the sum of its parts. We have adopted this assumption from general systems theory. If indeed this assumption is correct, we introduce a problem when we attempt to understand this whole by taking it apart piece by piece. Even if each part is understood in its entirety, the sum of this understanding does not explain the whole; it is more. In practice terms, if we are confronted with a serious family situation for which help is sought, we make this same mistake by seeking only to understand the individuals who comprise the family. The family is a whole and cannot be understood by understanding only those individuals who comprise it; it is different, it is greater.

Aristotle first framed the argument that the whole is greater than the sum of its parts. Thus, the argument is not new, but for many centuries

it was dismissed. We do not intend to trace this fascinating argument through the history of science; rather, we simply want to note that von Bertalanffy and others have reintroduced the argument in general systems theory.[7] Those in social work who embrace a more holistic approach are advancing this same argument.

Social organizations exhibit features of general order and features that are distinctive to humans as a species. Implicit in this notion is a hierarchy of wholes; each higher level has an ordering that is characteristic of the lower levels, and other features that are distinctive to the higher level.

In the paragraphs that follow, we will identify concepts that have their origins in general systems theory and that help build the foundation for social systems theory.

Emergence

The concept of emergence is helpful for thinking in general systems terms. A whole possesses distinctive **emergent properties**—properties not possessed by the parts comprising the whole.[8] These properties have emerged from the relationships that developed among the parts comprising the whole. In a manner of speaking, they are lost or cease to exist when the whole is separated into parts. A typical example is water. It has solvent properties and a taste not found in the oxygen and hydrogen that combine to form water. A more dramatic example of this notion is life itself. According to the theory of mechanism, life ultimately is reducible to physicochemical events and laws. The contending position is the organismic (systems) one.[9] Life is in an emergent state, one found in the organization of parts, not in the parts themselves.

Love, as expressed in a human relationship (a family), is a familiar and important example of the notion of emergence. Love is not a property of the individual. While love affects the individual, it is a property of a relationship. This basic notion has a variety of practice implications. For example, if in a helping relationship the problems center on properties of a particular relationship, intervention aimed only at the individuals involved is likely to be unsuccessful. The problem and the properties of the problem are elsewhere. In the social systems perspective, we develop this notion of emergence by arguing that the social system cannot be understood except in relationship to its social environment. In other words, properties of this larger whole can only be found and understood by examining the subject system and its relationships with the other social units that comprise its suprasystem.

Open Systems

The concept of **open systems** is fundamental to general systems theory. This concept suggests that systems are dynamically connected to the environments of which they are a part. In other words, an ongoing exchange exists between the subject system and its environment. Figure 2.1 conveys the point by contrasting an open with a **closed system.**

The notion of an open system is a very simple but powerful idea. It encompasses an approach to the study of order that has both internal and external dimensions. To help operationalize *open*, we use the concepts of input and output. When you were in grade school,

one of your early science teachers probably introduced you to the process of photosynthesis. Your teacher sought to link systematically the organic and inorganic parts of the world. He or she described to you how the chlorophyll found in the cells of green plants converts sunlight, water, carbon dioxide, and other elements (inputs) into food for the plant and in the process releases oxygen (output) into the environment. Oxygen in the air then becomes an input that helps sustain animal life. This exemplifies a fundamental form of ordering based on an open-system formulation of exchange. This example also helps to illustrate the interconnectedness of all things as set forth in general systems theory—the output of every system will become an input to another in its environment.

General systems theory holds that all systems should be viewed as open. We take this premise and include it as a component of social systems theory. Simply put, all social systems secure inputs from their environments. These inputs are the necessary resources required for the survival and development of the system itself. The system will then process these inputs, retain some, and release the rest into its environment as outputs.

Three concepts introduced earlier are helpful in thinking about the characteristics of open systems: boundary, interface, and suprasystem. As indicated earlier, every system will possess a boundary. The function of a boundary is to dis-

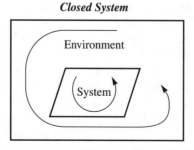

Open System   *Closed System*

FIGURE 2.1   Open and Closed Systems

tinguish the system from its environment and to protect the parts from influences in the environment that might disrupt functioning. A system's boundary will always be permeable in order to permit input/output exchanges with its environment. This is the essence of the concept of an open system. If the boundaries were closed, this would be a closed system. The concept of interface simply means a shared boundary with another system. Systems conduct their input/output exchanges through shared boundaries. In adapting general systems concepts to social systems, we hold that social systems conduct their input/output exchanges with systems in their social environments in purposive ways. Each of the social systems involved in an exchange will possess a boundary and will act purposively. When a pattern exists in these exchanges and when there are mutual expectations involved in the exchange, we label these mutually held expectations in the exchange *interfaces* or *shared segments of boundary.*

For example, think of a computer as a system, one comprised of many parts. Now, if you want a hard copy of something you have processed with your computer, you need a printer. The connection between your computer and printer is called an interface. This connection permits these two systems to communicate; each needs something from the other to produce a hard copy.

The third of these three interdependent concepts related to an open system we have labeled *suprasystem.* Recall that the suprasystem is a larger system of which your subject system is a part. In other words, it is a part of your system's social environment. The suprasystem includes all the other systems with which your subject system has an interface, that is, with which it is functionally linked. All of the agencies, departments, and groups that your social work program works with, for example, in order to educate and graduate students would comprise a suprasystem.

Entropy and Negative Entropy

These two concepts represent opposites and are related to the previously described notions of open systems and closed systems. We are concerned with how growth and development occurs in social systems (negative entropy), and its opposite, how disorganization and the "death" of a system occurs (entropy).

Entropy is a measure of disorder.[10] The origins of the concept are to be found in the second principle of thermodynamics. This principle holds that the general trend of events in nature is toward states of maximum disorder and the leveling down of differences. In practical terms, things wear out, run down, decompose. This is true of all matter—our world, our universe, as well as the house in which we live, and the car that we drive. Entropy, then, refers to a process in which order is lost—in other words, the process of disorganization.

General systems theorists argued that in living things a process of ordering, not disordering, was evident.[11] This reverse process or increase in ordering is called **negative entropy.** In defense of this position von Bertalanffy cited the evolutionary process, the development of ever higher forms of life from the amoeba to the human. We would add that all forms of social organization possess the potential for growth and development (assumption 4—pertaining to the growth and development characteristics of social organizations). For example, think about a close personal or love relationship that you have with another person; this system or social organization had a beginning, and over time it has grown and become more complex and more important. To understand and model this capacity for growth and development, we must look at the conditions or principles that account for this capacity to grow and develop. We might also look at the reverse—how do we account for the disordering process we observe in human relationships?

The premise that people and the systems they form have the capacity for development is central to the purpose of social work. Through the process of development, the state of well-being can be enhanced. We borrow the concept of negative entropy from general systems theory to describe and then to explain how this development occurs.

The concepts we are discussing are both abstract and complex. For us the concepts are no more than a way of thinking about life and about professional practice. For example, marriages that fail and friendships that are lost can also be viewed in terms of being open or closed—exhibiting entropic or negative entropic characteristics. We might add that systems can be equally threatened by becoming too open. This observation leads us to a discussion of the concept of steady state.

Steady State

A crucial concept to be addressed in this section on general systems theory is **steady state.** In practical terms, it can be thought of as the health or well-being of a system. At a more technical level, it pertains to the constancy of a favorable balance of input and output exchanges a system has with its suprasystem.[12] *Favorable balance* refers to a dynamic exchange process in which the balance is in favor of negative entropic forces, those promoting an increase in ordering. In short, if you are paying out more than you are taking in, you are headed for trouble. This point holds whether it is money, love, or anything else that involves an exchange. The point also holds whether we are talking about an individual, a family, an agency, a community, or a nation. For example, both sides of the debate between our two national parties, the Republicans and the Democrats, on the consequences of a growing national debt can be reduced to a fear of the loss of steady state. The collapse of the Soviet Union serves as another example of the loss of steady state at a societal level. Divorce would serve as an example of the loss of steady state at the family level.

The concept of steady state occupies a central place in social systems theory. We use the concept to operationalize the state of well-being. It may be helpful to contrast steady state with a more familiar term, **homeostasis.** Homeostasis is a state of equilibrium produced by a balance of functions and related properties of a system.

Several characteristics of homeostasis are important to keep in mind:

- *Homeostasis* is premised on the notion of a fixed optimum state or balance.
- Deviations from this state are viewed as unbalancing or as evidence of a disordering process.
- The homeostatic state is a dynamic or counterbalancing process.
- The processes resulting in homeostasis are not under the direct or conscious control of the individual.
- The homeostatic process operates through a feedback system with the goal of returning the system to a fixed state.

Theorists have applied the notion of homeostasis as an equilibrium-seeking model to the study of human behavior. For example, in classical psychoanalytic theory, the natural state of the organism is at rest. The primary determinants of behavior are innate sexual and aggressive drives. These drives, when activated, upset an **equilibrium** or homeostatic state. The organism (ego) strives to contain these drives and to restore the organism to a state of equilibrium. In short, homeostasis provides a reactive approach for modeling human social behavior. Steady state, by contrast, offers a proactive approach.

In our presentation of a social systems perspective, we identified the following assumption: When fully developed, all forms of social organization will display self-maintaining and development characteristics. A related assumption is that the natural state of both the individual and all forms of social organization is proactive rather than reactive. Our position is consistent with general systems theory as advanced by von Bertalanffy, who viewed all living organisms as intrinsically active as opposed to passive. "The stimulus (i.e., a change in external conditions) does not cause a process in an otherwise inert system; it only modifies processes in an autonomously active system."[13]

From general systems theory, we have sought to identify key concepts along with some related assumptions that have helped us form a social systems perspective and develop a theory of social systems. While we have borrowed these concepts from general systems theory, we can apply them to individuals and all of the social organizations they join to form other systems. While some of these terms may be new, we encourage you to learn their meanings and the ideas behind them. They are the building blocks for social systems theory.

Equifinality

Equifinality is considered a core premise of general systems theory. This concept refers to the capability of arriving at the same end state by different processes. It can be summarized by the folk saying that "There is more than one way to skin a cat."

Equifinality is one way of assessing the robustness of a system. If a system is blocked in trying to achieve an outcome, there is a tendency to seek alternate pathways to the desired goal. The more persistent and flexible the system is in seeking the goal, the more robust the system is considered to be.

A related concept is **multifinality**, which holds that the same process applied to the same input can result in different outcomes. Taken together, these two concepts suggest that there

is an element of unpredictability to system activities that cannot be reduced to positive certainty. This is sometimes attributed to the inherent uncertainty in living systems.

Holon

The last of the distinctive features of social systems theory to be discussed is the concept of systems as comprised of **holons.** The term was coined by Arthur Koestler to describe the attribute of all systems as being simultaneously oriented outward to the environment and inward toward internal functioning. The word was coined from the Greek word *holos*, meaning whole, combined with the suffix used to designate subatomic particles such as protons and electrons. Koestler likened the holon to Janus, the Roman god of gateways and beginnings. Janus was always depicted with two faces, one facing outward and one inward.[14]

Koestler envisioned the holon as the fundamental unit of any interdependent system. In social systems, an individual is at once a distinct individual and at the same time a part of larger social systems. This dual nature fits well with the systems perspective and with the demands of generalist social work practice. In generalist practice, there is a strong emphasis on understanding the person in the context of the social situation. Much like the concept of the self in symbolic interaction theory, the line between unique individualism and social enmeshment is blurred. Koestler regarded the dichotomy between individual and collective identity as misleading, and felt that the concept of holon captured the fundamental paradox of humans who juggle the demands of individuality and social belonging. The term is used to capture the fact that to be fully human, one must be part of human society. To be part of human society, one must have individual identity.

Koestler elaborated the holon concept by speculating that the holons that make up any system can be understood as intermediate systems. To the extent that a component holon is stable and well organized, it will serve to create a more robust system. Holons were thus depicted much like self-contained units. Koestler believed that systems composed of such units would be more resilient and more easily repaired if damaged. By example, a family is a system composed of individuals. If each individual (holon) in a family is capable of independent functioning as an individual, the well-being of the family system is likely to be enhanced. However, the functioning of the individual family member is not synonymous with the functioning of the family as a whole. By extension, a society made up of functional families is likely to be more functional and robust than one made up of disorganized and poorly functioning families.

Little empirical work has been done on the holon concept. This is due in part to the fact that Koestler was a writer rather than a social scientist. From his writer's perspective, Koestler took a dim view of approaches such as behaviorism that focused on easily observed overt behavior and ignored fundamental human qualities such as spirituality, the will, and activities of the mind.

Understanding human beings and human systems as holons is consistent with the four-problem matrix of Talcott Parsons, who divided essential functions between those that relate to internal processes and maintenance, and those that relate to the demands of the external social world.

ECOLOGICAL THEORY

We have accumulated an immense body of knowledge about matter, and powerful techniques to control and exploit the external world. However, we are grossly ignorant of the effects likely to result from these manipulations; we behave often as if we were the last generation to inhabit the earth.

—*Rene Dubos*

In this quote, Dubos, author of the 1969 Pulitzer Prize winning book *So Human an Animal*, speaks of the perception of a separation of the human race from the rest of the inhabitants of the earth and the possible consequences of that viewpoint.[15] The idea of the human race needing to live in harmony with the physical environment has been the core of Native American culture and its spirituality throughout history. Only recently has concern for the environment invaded the consciousness of U.S. society. In this country there is now a growing awareness that for every wrong that is committed against the environment there is a direct consequence to be paid by us and our future generations. Ecological theory specifically links life to its natural habitat, its environment.[16]

In Part Five, The Community, we review human ecology, particularly that branch that addresses the development of the community. Here our interest is more general and our focus will be on the parent theory. The word *ecology* is derived from the Greek word *oikos* meaning *house* or *place to live in*. Coined in 1873, the term was first applied to plants, later to animals, and more recently to the study of human communities. In its broadest sense, ecology can be defined as the branch of science concerned with the interrelationship between organisms and their environments.

Our special interest in ecological theory stems from the work of a botanist, A. G. Tansley, who introduced the term **ecosystem.** As with von Bertalanffy, Tansley and others associated with the development of ecological theory were dissatisfied with the ability of linear cause-and-effect theories to explain the growth and change in living organisms.[17] From its origins in botany, ecological theory has been applied to the study of all living organisms and in recent years has become important in the study of humans. Currently, ecological theory represents a major school of thought within sociology.

From the beginning, ecological theory has focused on the interdependence that seems to characterize everything sharing the same habitat. Sociologists became interested in ecological theory because it offered a way of examining the effects of environment on social organization and thus it became an approach to the general study of social change. Social work theorists have shown a growing interest in ecological theory or, more particularly, an **ecological perspective.**[18]

Our approach in relating the ecological perspective to the social systems model builds from the ideas advanced by such writers as Duncan and Micklin.[19] Their approaches have helped us in formulating what we have described as the setting factors or influences that affect all forms and sizes of social organizations. You will recall this idea from the second of the nine social systems perspective assumptions: Social ordering is a dynamic and constant process that arises out of conditions existing in the general order and the need structure of humans and the social organizations and institutions they join to form. Ecological theory and an ecosystems way of modeling offer an explanation of this assumption. This explanation is a source of the social work position that human behavior is to be understood within the social environment in which the behavior takes place. Our position on social change is embedded in this assumption. Change is a constant; it is a process and in the most fundamental sense, change is the only reality. Everything is in a state of becoming. The implications of this position are significant in thinking about the generalist practice of social work and understanding human behavior and the social environment. The social environment is in a constant state of change because the larger environment is constantly changing. In short, each is affecting the other and being affected by the other.

FUNCTIONAL THEORY

Functional theory, also called *structural-functionalism*, views society as a complex system of interlocking institutions. The emphasis in functionalism is on the maintenance of social stability, or what we refer to as a *steady state*. Functionalism tends to view the components of society mainly in terms of their contribution to maintaining order. In this regard, functionalism is often criticized as being too static or conservative. Notable functionalists include Emile Durkheim and Talcott Parsons, who are discussed below. Other sociologists take the view that conflict is crucial in promoting needed social changes. These *conflict theorists* include most notably Karl Marx and Herbert Spencer.

Functional theory is more modest in terms of the domain of its concern—society. Through our review of functionalism, we move down to a theory that seeks to explain the behavior of what we earlier called the social order. Society can be thought of as constituting social order at its highest level.

Functional theory represents a line of theory development within sociology. Let us start by distinguishing between two of the social sciences that have the closest connections to social work—psychology and sociology. Psychology is the science of the behavior of organisms, mostly but not exclusively humans.[20] Sociology is the study of human society. While focusing on society, sociologists also study all forms of social organization, including social groups and families.[21]

The term *sociology* was coined by Auguste Comte (1798–1857), a French philosopher who envisioned a new science concerned with the social behavior of humans.[22] The intellectual foundations of this new science were expanded by such contributors as Karl Marx (1818–1883), Max Weber (1864–1920), Herbert Spencer (1820–1903), and Emile Durkheim (1858–1917).[23] A brief review of some of the assumptions held by different theorists should help contrast positions out of which a functionalist theory of society grew. We should also add that sociology is an emerging science. Some of the assumptions that we will summarize are still held by theorists and account for some of the sharp divisions still evident in sociology.

Of these theorists, Karl Marx is probably the most familiar. He assumed that society developed along an evolutionary path and that conflict was the basic societal process that drove development. In his words, "The history of all hitherto existing society is the history of class struggle."[24] According to Marx, society was not to be understood by attention to and understanding the individual. The individual was a product of society.[25] Marx viewed himself as a "scientific socialist."[26] In brief, he held that those who controlled the means of production were the power holders of society. This power differential between those few who controlled the means of production in a society and the masses made violent conflict inevitable.

Max Weber also saw conflict as a central societal process. We will examine his works elsewhere in this book because he, more than any other theorist, has contributed to a theory of power as a central societal process. Here our interest is in identifying some basic assumptions that helped shape the early development of sociology and the functionalist position.

Herbert Spencer, in contrast to Marx and Weber, focused on the individual, not on society, in explaining the social ordering of humans. In many ways he held a psychological view of sociology. Spencer held a basic assumption that society should not be thought of as a separate and distinct entity, as Marx and Weber had suggested. Rather, society was simply the aggregate of the separate individuals that comprised it.[27] From this position, society was like a giant marketplace in which people bargained and entered into relationships with one another. These contractual-like relationships held society together.[28] Like Marx, Spencer held an evolu-

tionary conception of society, but, unlike Marx, the focus was on the individual and the competition of the marketplace. Some individuals were better prepared for the competition for existence than others. Those that were ill prepared did not survive; only the fittest survived. These basic ideas served as the foundation of Social Darwinism and the evolutionary conception of social betterment through competition.[29] For Spencer, a natural order existed that led to human betterment. Government played little role in this natural process.[30]

The origins of functional theory are found in the theories of Emile Durkheim. Earlier in our summary of general systems theory, we introduced the concept of emergence. Simply stated, as individuals come together to meet their needs, the forms of social organization that result possess emergent properties not found in the individuals who comprise them. Durkheim, like Aristotle and many who followed, held that the whole is greater than the sum of its parts. A second assumption derived from Durkheim's position is that human beings are a product of society, an output. Certainly, the individual as a physical being is separate and distinct, but this is not the point. Durkheim argued, as did Cooley and others, that the distinctive features of the human personality are socially acquired.[31] The human personality is formed through the process of **socialization.** This process is conducted, in large part, through social interaction. The humanizing organizations from which the individual acquires a sense of selfhood are the component parts of society. In this sense, the human being is an output of society.

Unlike Spencer, Durkheim argued that the extent to which the individual is integrated into social relationships with others establishes the conditions for that person's survival.[32] Durkheim is probably best known for his study of suicide.[33] Through this research he sought to establish the relationship of the individual to society. He held that the extent that an individual is integrated into society is a determinant of suicide. From his position, a person can be either too little or too greatly integrated into society. The form taken by the act of suicide is related to this position.

Central to Durkheim's position was that societies evolved from simple to more complex forms. Societies over time become more differentiated, more specialized in order to survive and grow. Why should a society progress from a simple to a more complex form? If we consider the society as an open system, it is going to have exchanges with its environment (general systems theory). Next, if we accept the general assumption undergirding ecological theory as earlier presented, society (a social organization) will be affected by changes in population, organizations, the environment, and technology (POET). Change is therefore endemic. The functional differentiation of society is a survival and growth mechanism; it is a way the society seeks steady state (well-being).

Durkheim did not frame his theory in quite the way just described (use of the POET model), but we find his basic position consistent with our presentation of a social systems perspective (assumptions 1–5). Most important, Durkheim's works established what was to become a dominant theoretical position within sociology.

Talcott Parsons (1902–1979) became a leader in the development of functional theory, or what is sometimes referred to as structural-functionalism.[34] While identified with the functional school in sociology, Parsons's early work focused on social action, which he considered the appropriate subject matter of sociology.[35] He was a prolific writer and his writings covered systems as small as an individual in a social situation to society as a whole. Parsons sought to identify a basic pattern of social behavior that would have applications at all levels of social systems. This was the notion behind his concept of social action. In its simplest form, for Parsons, it was comprised of (1) an individual enacting a role, (2) in a social situation, and (3) the orientation of the individual to that situation.[36] By orientation, Parsons referred to the person's motivation and the values that applied. Values were related to the social norms that would be operative and would serve to constrain the range of possible behaviors of the individual in a specified social situation.

Parsons adopted the metaphor of social systems in referring to the various forms of social organization but did not present his works as a theory of social systems, even though one of his major works carried the title *The Social System*.[37] In his later writings, Parsons sought to construct a general theory that would serve to unite the social sciences. Parsons's basic position is summarized as follows:

> Let me start with the proposition that all social systems are organized, in the sense that they are structurally differentiated, about two major axes. When these axes are dichotomized, they define four major "functional problems," with respect to which they differentiate. These four fundamental functional categories apply at all four levels of structural organization. ...[38]

Parsons held that social systems were open systems and were functionally tied to the social environments in which they were found. With this in mind, think of the first of these two axes as vertical, linking the system to its environment. Parsons labeled this as the internal and external axis. Functions associated with this axis mediate relations between the system and what we have defined as the suprasystem. Parsons, consistent with a functionalist orientation, viewed social systems as purposive. Now think of this second or horizontal axis as representing means and ends.

In a next step, Parsons issued a caution and then indicated how these two axes were related:

> These two axes must be considered, not as continua, but as qualitatively differentiated reference categories, however much they may shade into each other. Four main functional problems or dimensions of system structure and process

may be derived from these axes: (1) the external-consummatory reference which I have called "goal-attainment"; (2) the external-instrumental reference which I have elsewhere called "adaptation"; (3) the internal-consummatory reference which I have called "integration"; and, finally, (4) the internal-instrumental reference which I have called "pattern-maintenance and tension-management."[39]

Figure 2.2 diagrams what we have labeled *Parsons's four-problem matrix*. In essence, he has proposed a scheme comprised of four functions of structural organization that can be used for the structural analysis of all social systems.

Goal Attainment.   Starting with the proposition that all social systems exist to satisfy some need, opportunity, or condition existing in the environment, goal attainment is external and an end, or what Parsons labeled a "consummatory" state. Using an earlier example, the students who graduate from your school's program (subject system) and take social work positions in the community represent that system's task output. The employing agencies are external to the system and their act of employing these students represents, from the position of the subject system, goal attainment. Keep in mind that a major

goal of your social work program is the education of competent social workers who will, upon graduation, take professional positions in the field. *Goal attainment* as we are using the term here is not an all-or-nothing state. Think of goal attainment as a variable. Both the social work program and the employing agency want the best possible social workers produced. The actual graduate will be judged by the employing agency, not the social work program and not the graduate herself or himself. To use Parsons's notion of a problem, the subject system must meet minimum expectations of the agencies employing social work graduates or a threat is posed to the well-being of the subject system. We will label this *problem one*. For reasons just explained, goal attainment is an external function, but all of those functions conducted within the system that result in goal attainment are associated with the performance of this function. This is starting to get a bit complicated, but you need to keep this linkage clear as we discuss the other three problems. We will develop these connections in later chapters.

Adaptation.   This function (cell 1) is external and is the means (instrumental) used to achieve goal attainment. Here we have the means–end

	Means/Instrumental	End/Consummatory
External	Adaptation Function Cell 1	Goal-Attainment Function Cell 2
Internal	Pattern-Maintenance Function Cell 3	Integration Function Cell 4

FIGURE 2.2   Parsons's Four-Problem Matrix

connection between cells 1 and 2. General systems theory is again helpful in thinking about this problem. Social systems are by definition proactive as opposed to being reactive. This natural state is one in which the system seeks to act on as well as being acted on.

In being proactive, what is the system attempting to accomplish? In short, the system attempts to adapt its external environment to facilitate goal attainment; this is what we mean by the natural state. How does our mythical social work program seek to do this? Perhaps the most obvious way is in its recruitment of students. The social work program will seek those individuals that possess the qualities that will make them good social workers. The program will then incorporate these features into its admission standards as a means of screening its recruits. Here we have an example of the boundary-maintenance function in terms of its link with the adaptation function.

Perhaps another example will help. The athletic department of our university has a goal of being ranked number one nationally in football. Goal attainment would be to achieve this recognition in a national poll of sports writers and coaches. How is the adaptation function conducted? It is conducted in part by the staff of the athletic department seeking to recruit the best athletes in the country. This is then pursued by attempting to influence the nation's best high school coaches to send their best players to this university to play football, and to offer these athletes scholarships and other incentives (adaptation). The means-end relationship becomes: the more successful we are in recruiting the nation's best athletes (means) the more likely we will be to have players capable of winning all of their games (end). The reverse is also true: if the system is unsuccessful in conducting its adaptation function, goal attainment will be adversely affected as will be the well-being of the system itself. Problem number two is successfully conduct-

ing the adaptation processes that facilitate goal attainment.

Integration.   Integration refers to the coordination of the internal activities of the system. The efficient completion of the system tasks are a crucial part of the conversion operations conducted by the system. The example of the football team can be applied here as well. Once a team has recruited quality players and coaches, integration would consist of conditioning, coaching, and developing game strategies that produce an efficient and winning team. An important element of the integration process in human systems is attending to the morale of the team members and coaches.

Pattern Maintenance (Latency).   This function is represented in cell 3. The variable is internal and is considered a means of accomplishing the integration function. For many, this variable is the most difficult to understand. We explain it this way. Every system will have a hierarchy of patterns that distinguishes its function. As you move down the hierarchy, the patterns of behavior (social functioning) become more important. At or near the bottom are core patterns that must be maintained or the system itself will not survive. In Parsons's presentation, pattern maintenance is the most important of the four functions that a system performs.[40]

An example should help. Let us say that our social work program seeks students who fully subscribe to the profession's code of ethics, and who are bright and emotionally healthy. Presumably the program also seeks faculty who exhibit the same qualities. Now let us suppose that several of the male faculty members are known to be sexually harassing some of the female students. The administration knows about this but has chosen to do nothing. The student victims are reluctant to take action on their own because of the difficulty of proving their case, their embarrassment, and the fear of reprisals. Now let us assume that the values undergirding these codes of behavior are deeply held by the students in this program and the remaining faculty. For them, sexual harassment by the men involved is an inexcusable breach of social work ethics and they believe the violators should be removed and punished, for they are not behaving like professional social workers. Here we have a program pattern that is not being maintained. As a consequence, it is very difficult for faculty and students to feel good about themselves or about the social work program—the means-end relationship between the pattern maintenance and the integration function. The proposition that can be drawn from this example is that unless this pattern is maintained, the system's well-being is threatened.

Now, let us also say that there is another faculty member who is a bit unusual in her dress and manner. While not exhibiting a model of being "mentally healthy," she is perceived as an excellent researcher, but just a fair teacher. Both faculty and students tolerate her "weird" manner. Her behavior is not inconsistent with the core values held by the school, its faculty, and students. Here we have an example of a pattern of behavior within the program that, while troublesome for some, is not a challenge to the basic patterns. In this sense, these patterns do not challenge the well-being of the school and have little effect on the integration function. The fourth problem is performing all of those related functions that assure the pattern-maintenance function is not violated in a manner that will adversely affect performance of the integration function.

We have spent a good bit of time explaining Parsons's four-problem matrix. For us, it represents the basic ideas on which we have built a theory of social systems. Our presentation has greatly simplified Parsons's ideas but in so doing we have started the process of adapting his insights to our presentation of a theory of social systems applicable to the generalist practice of social work.

SYMBOLIC INTERACTIONISM AND ROLE THEORY

Symbolic interactionism is a sociological theory that addresses the interactions between the individual and society. Specifically, this approach is concerned with symbolic communication, such as gestures and language. A major purpose of this approach is to examine the processes by which the naïve individual becomes a functioning member of society. In the symbolic interactionist view, a person becomes fully human only by the continuous process of interaction between the person and the social environment. Symbolic interactionism lays the foundation for all theories of human behavior that focus on communication. Because the implications of this interaction between self and society are so pervasive, we will return to the discussion of symbolic interaction in later discussions of the behavior of individuals, families, and groups.

The term *symbolic interaction* was first used by Herbert Blumer to describe the pioneering work of George Herbert Mead and Charles Horton Cooley.[41] These men emphasized the importance of society in shaping the individual's personality and sense of self. Mead in particular stressed the centrality of language in the socialization process. Language, Mead believed, consisted of the shared symbols by which individuals learned to interpret events and communicate their understanding with others. Mead believed that children become fully human by virtue of the ability to take the role of others and to formulate a system of rules governing social relationships. As the child learns to anticipate the expectations of others, the sense of self emerges. Ultimately, the child learns to observe the behavior of the self in the same way that the child observes the behavior of others.

As the child develops an understanding of social expectations, these are internalized into the emerging self. The lifelong process of gauging social expectations, selecting courses of action, and constantly revising one's understanding of social situations has begun. The sense of self that emerges in this process is distinctive to symbolic interaction. Mead characterized the self as a reflexive process rather than a fixed structure.

Self as Reflexive.   Mead identified the "I" and the "Me" as the two aspects of the self as necessary for the reflexive process to occur. The "I" is the active, spontaneous aspect of the self. The "I" acts and then observes the reactions of others. The reactions of others toward the self are then internalized. By this process, the "Me" is developed over time. The "Me" is composed of the internalized, organized perceptions of the attitudes of others. For example, when a child goes to school for the first time, the "I" might act spontaneously and take a toy away from another child. The teacher scolds the child for taking the toy, and the other child begins to cry. The self observes these reactions and stores the information. Over time, this stored information regarding the attitudes of others forms an organized understanding of the expectations in this situation. The "I" may still want the toy, but the socialized "Me" urges conformity to the social expectations and will do without the toy rather than suffer rebuke.

In time, the child learns to anticipate not only the attitudes of peers, parents, and teachers, but also of more remote others. This process takes place in three stages. In stage 1, the child merely imitates the gestures of others. In stage 2, the child learns to manipulate symbols through language and to act out the roles of others in play. In this stage, the "I" learns to observe and react to the "Me" as if the child were two different people. In this process, called "role taking," the child becomes both the actor and the audience. This is the fundamental dynamic of the reflexive process. At the third level, the child learns symbolically to comprehend the rules of interaction in the form of games. By understanding these rules, the child is able to take the roles of all other participants. In this way,

social rules are incorporated into the self (the "Me"), and it is possible for the child to take part in the complex, coordinated activities that are characteristic of human society.

Ultimately, the developing self produces an image of the "generalized other." This concept refers to a diffuse idea of the societal expectations for the self. This concept is distinct from the expectations of specific significant others, such as parents or peers. The notion of the generalized other becomes the internal representation of the social rules for behavior. This can be understood as the rules or values of a person. The degree to which a person is well socialized depends on how accurately the generalized other model corresponds to actual social reality. Faulty beliefs or models can have serious consequences, as W. I. Thomas made clear in his famous dictum, "Things that are thought to be real are real in their effects."[42]

Throughout life, the self continues as both subject and object. The spontaneous, willing part of the self (the "I") experiences an impulse or desire. This requires a calculation of the impact of this possible action on others in the particular situation (the "definition of the situation"). By imagining the reactions of others, the self selects a role best suited to gain the desired end. Mead believed that each aspect of the self was essential. Without the "I," there would be nothing unique about the individual; we would be mere social automatons. Without the "Me," there could be no responsibility for choices. Organized social interaction would be impossible. The self continues to change throughout life, although Mead believed that earlier experiences were more decisive in formulating the understanding of the generalized other.[43]

Measuring the Self.   For the most part, the major figures of the symbolic interaction movement have focused on the importance of the subjective and dynamic nature of the self. The unknowable aspects of the "I" present major difficulties for empirical researchers. Manford Kuhn sought to overcome this by developing empirical methods for assessing the self. He developed the widely used Twenty Statements Test (TST) to accomplish this.[44] The TST asked the respondent to answer the question "Who am I?" with twenty open-ended responses. The answers to this inquiry were thought to address the "Me" to the exclusion of the more subjective "I." When a subject answers the question with responses such the following, the TST relates to the social aspect of the self:

> I am a mother.
> I am a student.
> I am a Baptist.

It is easy to see these as aspects of the objective "Me." These are referred to as consensual responses, in that a consensus is possible in determining that they are true.

When a subject answers with responses such as the following, the TST is more oriented to the private, internal aspects of self. These responses are referred to as subconsensual:

> I am angry.
> I am worthless.
> I am searching.

These responses are suggestive of a more subjective, dynamic orientation of the self and are characteristic of the "I." Kuhn himself seemed to be less interested in the reflexive self-process and more concerned with the consensual responses.

Dramaturgy.   An interesting outgrowth of symbolic interactionism is found in the work of Erving Goffman, who talked about the social presentation of the self.[45] Elaborating on the performance aspects of the self just described, Goffman sought to analyze behavior as a series of performances, much like what is seen in theater or movies. The individual is presented with social expectations that amount to a "script" for a performance. The person plays a role much like an actor before an audience. Unlike the stage actor who can walk away from the part, the sum of the roles an individual plays in life make up the character of the self. The performance and the actor become one.

Goffman noted that role performances vary when people are "front stage" or "back stage." The snooty clerk in a jewelry store may affect a foreign accent to enhance his or her performance, then drop the accent in dealing with other employees. To some degree, all performances are oriented to an audience that is front stage. The degree to which a person changes character with different audiences can be considered a measure of the degree of personality integration of the individual.

Goffman also noted that people at times sought to indicate to others that there was more to them than could be contained in the role being played. Goffman termed this *role distance*, an effort to show that their identity transcends the performance. A worker in a restaurant who talks about plans to be a writer is distancing from the current role. It is in seeking to distance himself or herself that the individual implies a self different from the performance. It has been suggested that this reflects the distinction Mead makes between the "I" and "Me."

Role Theory.   In this discussion, it is apparent that there is a direct connection between the basic tenets of symbolic interactionism and role theory. Roles, in a sense, involve the internalized rules for proper behavior in a particular situation. Roles provide a structure for the self at the point where the individual intersects with society. Symbolic interactionism envisions an exciting process by which a person from moment to moment assesses situations, takes into account the others in the situation, the rules of society that apply, and then selects a course of action. For this to happen, the person must be part of a set of mutually recognized roles.

For most people, this approach to understanding human behavior is much more consistent with our personal reality than other theoretical views. The behaviorist's view that our behavior is "caused" by a stimulus seems confining. The spontaneity of Mead's "I" is creative without being as primordial as the animalistic id proposed by Freud. What emerges from a careful consideration of the reflexive self is the following:

- Humans are inherently social creatures by nature.
- Social cooperation relies on assessing the situation and the others in the situation.
- Human actions are the product of choice. Our actions are influenced but not determined by the situation.
- Individuals differ in their definitions of situations, and thus individual behavior is never fully predictable.
- There is an essential moral or value component to all behavior. Our calculations are inextricably linked to the imagined impact of our actions on others.
- Even in isolation, individual actions are influenced by social rules by means of the internalized society of the "me."
- All behavior, normal and pathological, emerges through the process of socialization.
- The internal dialog that takes place in all of us is pivotal in understanding the self, human actions, and moral judgment.
- People are responsible for their behavior since it results from choice; yet behavior can be influenced markedly by our primary socialization (as children) and secondary socialization (as adults).
- Some degree of social consensus is needed for us to develop a generalized other. Social fragmentation carries the risk of a corresponding lack of internal reference points for proper behavior.

Roles.   Roles are the basic building blocks of social systems. Roles define the social expectations for occupants of a status, and in so doing serve to link the individual to society. Since the role defines social expectations and social expecta-

tions shape the self, the self can be characterized as the sum of the roles played by an individual. Role theory can be understood both as psychological and social in nature. The network of roles in a society provides a structure within which orderly social interaction can occur.

Viewed from the perspective of symbolic interactionism, it is apparent that the psychology of the self is shaped by the complex of roles we play in life. Our behavior is judged in the context of what we expect of ourselves in a particular situation. The roles played by significant others early in life shape our experience of society in ways that are difficult to change in adulthood. It is possible to understand and intervene in a wide range of human difficulties by understanding the roles one plays, the expectations of those roles, the relative clarity and consistency of role expectations, and the network of significant others with whom we interact in overlapping social roles.

Reference Groups.   When people perform social roles, they do so with an audience in mind. All social behavior is conducted in the context of the expectations of others. This process is called "referencing." Simply, this means that when we act, we refer to someone for approval or disapproval of the action. The person to whom we refer may be real, imaginary, or a generalized other. Our social nature makes it impossible to understand role performance without considering the others whose opinion of our behavior matters to us. The people to whom we appeal for judgments of our behavior are called significant others. We believe that for social workers to understand a client, it is essential for them to also understand those whose judgments are important to the client's self-evaluation.

Work and Family.   The importance of role learning in the family is obvious. The family constitutes what Cooley called a *primary group.* For most of us, the family is central in the development of our sense of the generalized other and hence our enduring values. Our most influential early learning takes place in the family crucible. Family roles evolve over time and provide a fundamental context for the self at every stage of life.

The often neglected area of working life is delineated explicitly in terms of role theory. Many theories of human behavior have some difficulty making the transition from primary groups, such as the family, to secondary groups, such as those in school or work. Role theory provides a well-structured map for assessing both functional and dysfunctional behavior in the workplace. Few theories provide both an explanation of behavior and a repertoire of remedies as does role theory. Role concepts will be developed further in our discussion of the family in Chapter 9.

Role theory and symbolic interaction provide a context for discussing a troublesome concept: normal behavior. As our society becomes ever more diverse, the concept of *normal* has fallen into some disfavor. At one point in our history, there was undoubtedly a "tyranny of normality" that punished nonconforming behavior. Nonetheless, all social systems require some consensus on proper conduct. In our discussion of diversity, we will address the problems that occur for individuals and society when there is intolerance for diversity, as well as when there is insufficient consensus regarding what constitutes proper behavior. Norms, the social expectations for the occupant of a given role, are crucial in understanding this issue. In subsequent chapters, we will attempt to address vexing issues, such as the changing roles of women in our society; the emergence of formerly stigmatized identities such as gays, lesbians, and bisexuals; and our reconceptualization of the roles for persons with disabilities. We believe that role theory is an excellent vehicle for conceptualizing past problems, emerging issues, and possible practice guidelines in these crucial areas of social work practice.

Role theory accomplishes three things that are crucial for social work practice. It defines a structure and context for behavior in a wide range of situations. It requires us to be specific about the role being enacted, the significant others, the expectations, and the consequences for poor performance. Secondly, it distinguishes between the person and the behavior, and assumes that problem behavior is remediable. Finally, it requires of us a careful self-examination about our own expectations, values, and assumptions. The role perspective reminds us that all behavior takes place in a social context and that there is no inherently right or wrong action. The relativism of this approach is uniquely suited to our professional quest to seek to understand without judging.

SUMMARY

In this chapter we summarized Tier I of our four-tier construction that links perspective, theory, technology, and practice. Here we developed a social systems perspective comprised of nine assumptions. This perspective puts forward a set of beliefs on which our presentation of social systems theory builds.

We summarized five lines of theory: general systems, ecological, functional, symbolic interactionism, and role theory. These theories have served to extend and support our social systems perspective. In part, we have also derived our presentation of this perspective from assumptions that we believe serve as foundations for some of these theories.

Just as the assumptions comprising the social systems perspective form a hierarchy of levels of specificity, so do the theories. General systems theory has been likened to a theory of order itself. Ecological theory deals with the ordering of the organic and the inorganic parts of our world. Functional theory deals with the ordering found in society, including its component parts. Symbolic interactionism and role theory are addressed to apply the concepts of functionalism to individuals in society. By virtue of shared norms and internalized expectations, the process of social ordering is injected into the behavior of individual members of society.

Our particular interest has been in the work of Talcott Parsons, a leading functional theorist and his quest for a general theory that would unite the human and behavioral sciences. Central to Parsons's later work was his formulation of what we have chosen to call his four-problem matrix. Simply put, Parsons held that all social systems can be understood as structurally or-ganized around efforts at managing these four problems.

Parsons's work has received considerable criticism, particularly because of what many saw as an inherent conservative bias. Many held that his attention to the ordering processes left little room for understanding social change and processes of disordering. We will be reviewing these criticisms and our approach to the construction of social systems theory in later chapters of this book.

GLOSSARY

Action system   Those with whom the social worker deals in her or his efforts to accomplish the task and achieve the goals of the change effort.

Closed system   A theoretical state in which no external forces are deemed to influence the system.

Community   An inclusive form of social organization that is territorially based and through which most people satisfy their common needs and desires, deal with their common problems, seek means to advance their well-being, and relate to their society.

Ecological perspective   A very general approach for examining systematically the reciprocal relationships between organisms and their environments.

Ecosystem   A systems formulation of the reciprocal relationships between organisms and their environments.

Emergent properties   Characteristics possessed by a social system that are not characteristics of the member components of that system. These so-called new features arise from the relationships that form the system; the whole is greater than the sum of its parts.

Entropy   The disordering process in systems, or a measure of disorder in a system.

Equifinality   Arriving at the same end state by different processes.

Equilibrium   A state of balance or adjustment, typically achieved through opposing actions.

General systems theory   A theory of organization that deals with the formulation and derivation of the principles of all forms of order.

Holon   The fundamental unit of all social systems, comprised of elements that are at once a complete unit and a component part of the larger system.

Homeostasis   A state of equilibrium typically formulated to describe the genetically based adaptive capacities of organisms.

Multifinality   The same process applied to the same input can result in different outcomes.

Negative entropy   The growth and development process in social systems resulting from their capacity to obtain energy inputs from their environments (suprasystems); it is the ordering process in social systems.

Open systems   Systems that engage in exchanges with their environments, which are needed to be mutually deterministic.

Socialization   The process by which individuals acquire and internalize the values, knowledge, skills, and related matters necessary to function successfully as members of a society. In a related sense, it is the more general process by which the individual becomes "humanized."

Steady state   A condition of well-being possessed by a social system and one marked by a continuity of exchanges between the system and its suprasystem.

NOTES

1. Allen Pincus and Anne Minahan, *Social Work Practice: Model and Method* (Itasca, IL: F. E. Peacock, 1973), 61–62.

2. Ludwig von Bertalanffy, *General Systems Theory: Foundations, Development, Applications* (New York: George Braziller, 1968).

3. Ervin Laszlo, *Introduction to Systems Philosophy* (New York: The Free Press, 1972).

4. Peter Checkland, *Systems Thinking, Systems Practice* (New York: John Wiley & Sons, 1981), 4.

5. Warren G. Bennis et al., *Interpersonal Dynamics*, 3rd ed. (Homewood, IL: The Dorsey Press, 1973), v.

6. Mary Richmond, *Social Diagnosis* (New York: Russell Sage Foundation, 1917).

7. von Bertalanffy, *General Systems Theory*, 55.

8. See, for example, the discussion of emergence in F. Kenneth Berrien, *General and Social Systems* (New Brunswick, NJ: Rutgers University Press, 1968), 61–62.

9. von Bertalanffy, *General Systems Theory*, 39–44.

10. See, for example, the discussion of entropy in Ervin Laszlo, *The System's View of the World* (New York: George Braziller, 1972), 34–46.

11. von Bertalanffy, *General Systems Theory*, 39–44.

12. For a useful discussion of steady state in the sense we are using it, see Walter Buckley, *Sociology and Modern Systems Theory* (Englewood Cliffs, NJ: Prentice Hall, 1967), 52–58.

13. Ludwig von Bertalanffy, *Das Gefüge des Lebens* (Leipzig: Teubner, 1937), 133. The point is also found in von Bertalanffy, *General Systems Theory*, 209.

14. Arthur Koestler, *The Ghost in the Machine* (New York: Random House [1955] 1982).

15. Rene J. Dubos, *So Human an Animal* (New York: Scribner, 1968).

16. For an interesting reading on this point, see Al Gore, *Earth in the Balance: Ecology and the Human Spirit* (New York: Penguin, 1993).

17. Otis Dudley Duncan, "From Social Systems to Ecosystem," in *Urban America Conflict and Change*, J. John Palen and Karl H. Flaming, eds., (New York: Holt, Rinehart and Winston, 1972), 4–12; and Michael Micklin, *Population, Environment and Social Organization: Current Issues in Human Ecology* (Hinsdale, IL: The Dryden Press, 1973), 3–19.

18. A helpful introduction to this perspective is contained in Carel B. Germain and Alex Gitterman, "Ecological Perspective," *Encyclopedia of Social Work*, vol. 1, 18th ed. (Silver Spring, MD: National Association of Social Workers, 1987), 488–489. See also Carel Bailey Germain, *Human Behavior in the Social Environment: An Ecological View* (New York: Columbia University Press, 1991). This book uses ecology as a metaphor for purposes of exploring the person–environment relationship.

19. Duncan, *From Social Systems to Ecosystem*; Micklin, *Population, Environment and Social Organization.*

20. *The Encyclopedic Dictionary of Psychology*, 3rd ed. (Guilford, CT: The Dushkin Publishing Group, Author, 1986), 224–227.

21. *The Encyclopedic Dictionary of Sociology*, 3rd ed. (Guilford, CT: The Dushkin Publishing Group, Author, 1986), 279–280.

22. See Nicholas S. Timasheff, *Sociological Theory: Its Nature and Growth* (New York: Random House, 1967), 17–31.

23. See Peter Worsley, ed., *The New Introducing Sociology* (London: Penguin Group, 1992), 1–23 and 420–459.

24. Karl Marx and Friedrich Engels, *The Communist Manifesto*, trans. Samuel Moore and ed. Joseph Katz (New York: Washington Square Press, 1965), 57. The book was originally printed in German and published in 1848.

25. Ibid.

26. Ibid., 21.

27. Timasheff, *Sociological Theory*, 33–43.

28. Ibid.

29. *The Encyclopedic Dictionary of Sociology*, 268–269.

30. Timasheff, *Sociological Theory*, 41–42.

31. Charles Horton Cooley, *Social Organization* (New York: Scribner, 1902).

32. Timasheff, *Sociological Theory*, 109–121.

33. Ibid., 112–115.

34. For a discussion, see *The Encyclopedic Dictionary of Sociology*, 117–118.

35. See Enno Schwanenberg, "On the Meaning of the General Theory of Action," in *Explorations in General Theory in Social Science*, Jan J. Loubser et al., eds., vol. 1 (New York: The Free Press, 1976) 26–45.

36. Timasheff, "Sociological Theory," 240.

37. Talcott Parsons, *The Social System* (Glencoe, IL: The Free Press, 1951).

38. Talcott Parsons, "General Theory in Sociology," in *Sociology Today*, Robert K. Merton, Leonard Broom, and Leonard S. Cottrell, eds. (New York: Basic Books, 1959), 5.

39. Parsons, 6.

40. Talcott Parsons, "An Outline of the Social System," in *Theories of Sociology*, vol. 1, Talcott Parsons, Edward Shils, Kasper D. Naegele, and Jesse R. Pitts, eds. (New York: The Free Press, 1961), 38–39.

41. H. Blumer, *Symbolic Interactionism: Perspective and Method* (Englewood Cliffs, NJ: Prentice Hall, 1969);

G. H. Mead, *Mind, Self and Society* (Chicago: University of Chicago, 1934); and C. H. Cooley, *Human Nature and the Social Order* (New York: Schocken, 1902).

42. W. I. Thomas, *Social Behavior and Personality* (New York: Knopf, 1951).

43. Mead, *Mind, Self and Society.*

44. M. Kuhn and T. McPartland, "An Empirical Investigation of Self Attitudes," *American Sociological Review* 19 (1954): 68–76.

45. E. Goffman, *The Presentation of Self in Everyday Life* (New York: Doubleday, 1959).

CHAPTER 3

SOCIAL SYSTEMS THEORY
GENERAL FEATURES

DEFINITIONS

SOCIAL SYSTEMS THEORY

SUMMARY

GLOSSARY

NOTES

In this chapter we set forth the outlines of the general features of social systems theory. These features are applicable to all system levels addressed by generalist practice and the various forms of advanced practice in social work.

In this approach, we assume the existence of general patterns of behavior exhibited by all social systems at all levels, from the individual to the community. The generalist must understand these patterns in order to practice competently. The model is built on the logic that all social systems, in order to survive and develop, engage in input/output exchanges with their social environments. These exchanges form the basic ordering process that accounts for the relationship between human behavior and the social environment in which it functions. In other words, all social systems affect and are affected by their social environments. The process is cyclical and continuous.

In addition to the general patterns of behavior exhibited by all social systems, distinctive patterns can be seen at each system level—individual, group, family, organization, and community. These distinctive levels are reflected in the way this book is organized. In recognition of these differences, we identify and summarize the limited-range theories that seek to explain these distinctive patterns of behavior at each system level.

DEFINITIONS

Our initial task is to present sets of definitions that will help in understanding the content of this chapter. The first group represents a simple classification scheme of the various social organizations that humans join to form. We would prefer to present a generally recognized typology, but unfortunately none exists.[1] Given this situation, our task has been to create one suited to the purpose of this book.

Our approach focuses on the characteristics that we believe affect the relationships among those who comprise these human groupings. The one characteristic shared by all of the following is the presence of functionally interdependent relationships among the parts of the system.

Keep in mind that when we speak of a part, it might refer to an individual enacting a role in a family system, an administrative unit in a formal organization, or a neighborhood in a community—each is considered a holon. The other characteristics that help differentiate these forms of human groupings are (1) the extent to which expressive (personal) versus **logical** (rational) **actions** dominate; (2) the extent to which relationships among members develop naturally (self-organizing) or are formally constituted;[2] (3) the extent to which the system's purposes are inclusive (broad) or exclusive (narrow); and (4) the extent to which the system's actions are affected by place (location).

First, we offer a definition of the self as a social unit. The subsequent definitions, starting with the social organization, represent the classification of social hierarchies used in this book.

1. **Self**   The individual viewed as the smallest unit of society. The self is a social unit because it functions with internalized social norms and refers its social actions to the society by means of the reflexive process. The individual human being requires a sense of self in order to function as part of a social organization.
2. **Social Organization**   Any social entity comprised of two or more persons/social units who share a purpose, show functionally interdependent and reciprocal relationships, and demonstrate functional and reciprocal relationships with their social environments.
3. **Social Group**   An exclusive, self-organizing form of social organization comprised of two or more members who identify and interact with one another as individuals on a personal basis, possess a shared sense of the group as a social entity, are affected by the group-related actions of members, and whose expressive actions dominate.
4. **Family**   A social group characterized by a shared sense of kinship among its members.
5. **Formal Organization**   A form of social organization deliberately and formally created to achieve relatively specific and delimited goals in which logical actions dominate.
6. **Community**   An inclusive form of social organization that is territorially based and through which most people satisfy their common needs and desires, deal with their common problems, seek means to advance their well-being, and relate to their society.
7. **Society**   A territorially based form of social organization that is the most inclusive and thereby encompasses all other forms.

According to the above definition, a self can be considered a social system. Similarly, all of the subcategories can also be viewed as social systems.

It would make our work easier if each of the classifications were mutually exclusive; they are not. The classifications blend into one another. "Formed" groups are distinguished from self-organizing social groups. For example, a therapeutic group is not self-organizing, it is formed. It shares this characteristic with a formal organization. Depending on the writer and the definition, there can be a large number of types of social groups.[3] The same thing can be said of families and the other levels of social systems. While blending between system levels is a problem, it does not negate the fact that social work education distinguishes different levels of systems.[4] Social systems theory recognizes levels of social systems as well, but its focus is on the general patterns of all systems, not those distinctive to a system level.

We want to add that people often collect at the same location but such aggregates do not necessarily comprise a social organization as defined above. For example, a typical movie audience would not be considered a form of social organization, and thus the social systems theory would not be helpful in examining and predicting the behavior of such an audience. The people attending are there for personal reasons; there is not a shared purpose that links people making them functionally interdependent. In the absence of a shared purpose, no internal or external ordering would result in a sense of wholeness and related purposive behaviors.

Next, we will define concepts that describe the structure of social systems, that is, the interdependent sets of relationships that connect the parts of a social system with one another. In thinking about these concepts, keep in mind assumption 8 of the social systems perspective—the social relationship is the principal structural unit of all social systems. While all social systems are comprised of individuals, the focus is not on the individual; it is on the social relationships carried out between two or more individuals.

Here we search for the common patterns to be modeled and the meanings evidenced by these patterns. Think of social relationships and sets of these relationships as comprising the building blocks of social systems.

First, let us define culture, since all of the other definitions can be usefully thought of as influenced by one's culture.

> **CULTURE**   A set of shared meanings held by a specific group of people and their social systems, which serve as the foundation for their organized way of life.

At the highest level of social organization, the society, all members share a common culture. This culture is transmitted typically through a shared language. Keep in mind that people who share the same culture also attribute meanings to behavior, affect, and objects, as well as to words. While every society will evidence a common culture, **subcultures** will exist as well. A subculture will possess key features of the dominant culture but will possess characteristics distinctive to a subgroup of that society. Subcultures can be identified among those who may reside in particular neighborhoods (Little Italy, China Town), among ethnic groups (Native Americans, African Americans), or among those sharing a common professional interest, such as business or social work.

The concept of subculture is helpful in establishing the notion that whenever people enter into functionally interdependent relationships, sets of shared meanings of those relationships will emerge. These shared meanings serve to support those relationships, thereby giving them stability and predictability over time. The meanings will include, but will not be limited to, those evident in the dominant culture. The most important feature of the subculture will, like the culture itself, be its value base.

> **NORM**   The smallest structural unit of a social system, comprised of the expected behavior of a person enacting a role in a specific interactional situation.

Like all social behaviors, norms are culturally prescribed. An example is when a person extends a hand in an expression of welcome (a behavioral norm in many societies). The counter expected behavior is to extend and grasp the person's hand and shake it. This behavior is usually accompanied by a verbal greeting.

ROLE The principal structural component of a social system representing a culturally determined pattern of behavior expected of an individual in a specified social relationship.

Roles can be thought of as comprised of a loosely configured set of norms. Collectively these norms offer the general prescriptive behavior that an individual enacts while playing a specific role, for example, that of a social worker, mother, friend, and so on.

ROLE RECIPROCITY The behaviors expected in performing the counter role in the conduct of a social relationship.

Role is a relational concept and is to be understood in terms of mutually pursued communication and actions between two or more people. The concept of role reciprocity reflects the notion "that the performance of one role implies and requires the performance of a second role."[5] The mutuality of role performance will evidence three characteristics: (1) certain rights and duties involving two or more roles are recognized and accepted; (2) these roles are located in different status positions; and (3) these roles represent specialized aspects of the same functional process and are directed toward the same or comparable goals.[6] An example is the patterned behaviors between a social worker and a client in a counseling situation. In order to successfully conduct one role, it is necessary to understand the expected behaviors of the counter role. In a practice application, the generalist must not only understand her or his own role but also the role of the client.

STATUS POSITION The location a person occupies in a social system.

A status position is a location in a social system comprised of two or more roles. Using the traditional family as an example, a woman will occupy the role of wife and mother. The reciprocal role to wife is husband and the reciprocal role to mother is child. A social system can be viewed as an interrelated set of positions dedicated to the performance of some shared function. For example, "supervisor of intake" would be a position in a human service agency. Keep in mind that position refers to a location in a social system, it does not refer to a specific person who may currently be in that position.

The person occupying a position in a social system will typically enact more than one role. A position, in fact, can be thought of as a cluster of roles, as reflected in a job description that outlines a series of roles the person is expected to perform. For example, the position of intake supervisor may involve the supervision of five intake workers (one role). The position may also include carrying a small caseload (another role). The job description may also specify that the person holding this position must be a member of the agency's executive committee (still another role). We call this cluster of roles a position.

RELIGION The institutionalized social organizations that promote social cohesion through the transmission of values and beliefs shared by members as they relate to enduring human concerns.

SPIRITUALITY The individual quest of seeking answers to enduring human concerns through means that transcend everyday experience or rational inquiry.

At the societal level, the institution of religion has a pivotal role in formalizing and transmitting values between subsystems and across time. While the value-confirming functions of religious institutions, such as churches, are not the only players in this arena, they have traditionally been among the most influential value-transmission institutions, along with the family. The family, of course, can be seen as a holon component of the value system, operating with the value system endorsed by religious institutions.

At the individual level, we regard pattern maintenance as more a matter of spirituality than of religious institutions. Elsewhere we define spirituality as more personal and less codified than religion. Spiritual concerns for the individual have less to do with regulating patterns of social interaction and more to do with what Parsons would consider internal tension management. At the spiritual level, the individual employs spiritual concerns to address such basic questions as the meaning of life, dealing with death, and the impact of disruptions, such as sickness and trauma. The internal tensions created by these disruptions prompt the spiritual quest. For many people in society, the spiritual answers to these existential questions are nested in a formal religious system.

SOCIAL SYSTEMS THEORY

Our approach to social systems is based on two sets of concepts—four functional and eight structural. The four functional concepts have their origins in Parsons's effort to construct a general theory of social systems, one that would help unite the social and behavioral sciences.[7] We summarized his position in Chapter 2 (see Figure 2.2, Parsons's Four-Problem Matrix). Parsons identified four functional problems confronted by all social systems. Dealing with these common functional problems gives rise to the performance of comparable behavioral patterns or social structures. The four functional problems are (1) adaptation, (2) goal attainment, (3) pattern maintenance, and (4) integration. We have retained the names and the cell structure of the matrix summarized in Figure 2.2. Axis 1 provides the internal-external orientation of system functions. Axis 2 identifies the means-end orientation evident in all social systems.

We want to clarify the meaning Parsons attached to these two axes by using more familiar terms. The profession of social work is distin-

guished by its orientation to practice that holds that the study of human behavior must include the social environment in which it occurs. Think of the internal-external axis identified by Parsons as a way of viewing the linking of the social system to its social environment. Keep in mind the *social* in social work. Social work practice addresses social functioning; the focus is on a relationship. Given this position, we equate human (social) behavior with the social system itself. The internal component of the axis now equates to the social system; the external equates to the social environment in which the social system exists. Organized around this external axis are all of the behaviors that deal with the transactions between the social system and its social environment.

In the social systems perspective, assumption 3 holds that all human social behavior is purposive. The assumption also squares with common sense. We equate the achievement of purpose with the system's end state. The activities we perform represent the means employed to achieve purpose or the end state. This means-end relationship represents the second axis. Every system will engage in those activities required to accomplish its purpose.

This sounds simpler than it is. A group of young children playing together might comprise a social group. These children most likely would have no conception of the purpose of their play—except to have fun. They would also have no idea whatsoever of the relationship between the activities that they perform together and the purpose of their play. Awareness by participants of the means and end is not the issue. At issue is whether a pattern of behavior that evidences a means-end relationship is discernable in social systems at all levels. We hold that such patterns are universal and that under research conditions they can be established.

Now let us return to assumption 6 in the social systems perspective: Well-being is the natural state of all humans and the various forms of social organization that humans join to form.

Social systems theory seeks to operationalize this assumption.

You were introduced to the concept of steady state in our review of general systems theory. In that discussion we equated steady state with well-being. Here we take the next step. In constructing a theory of social systems applicable to the practice of social work, we do not find the notion of "problem" as used by Parsons helpful. First, the concept of problem implies that a solution exists and that one must use a problem-solving methodology to find that solution. In our construction of the theory, *there is no solution;* there are levels of optimization, but there is no final state. Think of steady state in the way Abraham Maslow conceptualized self-actualization—becoming all that one can become.[8] We make a similar application of this idea to social systems—it is a quest without an end.

In general systems theory, you were introduced to the concepts of entropy and negative entropy. Entropy is the disordering process; negative entropy is the reverse, or the process of ordering. Steady state is a state of negative entropy; it is characterized by increasing order. Social systems form through a process of negative entropy. In its early stages, a system is fragile and the process is easily reversed: a disordering process may occur and as a result the system simply may not form or it may lose its

system characteristics. Social systems theory holds that there is a threshold. On the one side, an ordering or growth process is evident (negative entropy). This is steady state. On the other side of this threshold is a disordering process, or entropy. The entropic process, if not reversed, leads to the loss of system status.

Now let us return to the matrix of four cells used by Parsons in his four-problem matrix in Chapter 2. Rather than calling it a problem matrix, we call this matrix the four functional requisites to steady state. Figure 3.1 shows the relationship of these four requisites.

In this construction, goal attainment and integration are both necessary to achieve the threshold identified as steady state. They are dynamic states in that they are constantly varying. Each has a threshold. Since the functions are interdependent, if either drops below the threshold, a disordering process is initiated for the system. Similarly, if both are above the threshold, the ordering process has the synergistic features necessary for steady state.

The four functional concepts represent master functions evident in all social systems. The performance of these functions causes structures to form through which these functions are channeled. In this manner, we identify eight social structures common to all social systems: (1) boundary, (2) suprasystem, (3) interface,

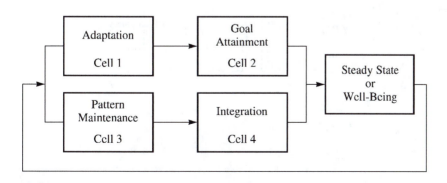

FIGURE 3.1 Steady State: The Four Functional Requisites

(4) input, (5) proposed output, (6) conversion operations, (7) output, and (8) feedback.

Through these eight generic structures, the functional requisites take place. In Figure 1.5, The Social Systems Model, we presented an abbreviated version of the relationships among these eight concepts. A more detailed version is presented in Figure 3.2, Modeling Social Systems Theory. There are two immediate uses of the model. First, it can be used to describe any social system. In other words, the identified structures will be evident in any social system at any level—a social group, family, formal organization, or community. Second, by linking the concepts to one another, the key functional relationships are identified. By modeling selected features of social systems theory, we are able to arrive at universal patterns of behavior and thus explore system dynamics. By so doing, we are using a "technology" derived from the theory.

We have already introduced several of the concepts comprising the system so let us step through the model in summary form. First is the social system and the boundary that identifies it. Outside of this system is its suprasystem. This, as you will recall, is a representation of the key influences external to the social system to which it is functionally linked. Outside the suprasystem is what we label the environment. The concept of environment was introduced to you in Chapter 2 through a review of ecological theory. *Environment* always is changing, thereby influencing the system's suprasystem directly and indirectly. We have not included the environment as one of the structural features. Rather we treat it as a context that has, at this point, an unspecified effect on the social system.

Interface is the concept that links the subject system to its suprasystem. It represents a shared boundary segment between each component of a system's suprasystem. The logic undergirding the construction of the model is that all systems engage in input/output exchanges with their suprasystems. This is how systems survive and develop. The model simply operationalizes this logic through the concepts of

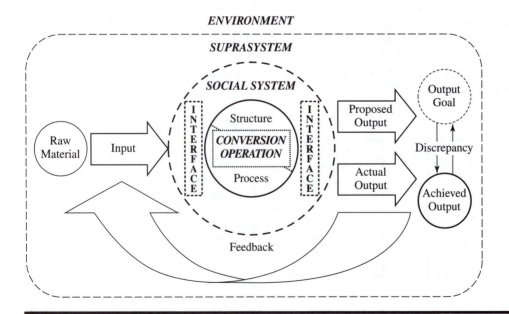

FIGURE 3.2 Modeling Social Systems Theory

input and output. Systems, depending on their function, will have processes to transform their inputs to outputs; we label this process a system's conversion operations.

Conversion operations can be thought of as the master concept. The other seven are secondary concepts that identify supportive structures. You will note in Figure 3.2 that conversion operations are divided into structure and process. The structure portion refers to the social structures through which these processes or functions are performed. The names usually assigned to these structures and their related functions tend to be specific to the social system. For example, the curriculum would be a structural feature in the conversion operations of a social work program. An accompanying process would be teaching. Both structure and process are tied to the functional imperative—goal attainment.

Proposed output is synonymous with the social system's purpose. Keep in mind that purpose is not made explicit in many social systems, such as social groups and families. We can infer purpose by examining the patterns of behavior evidenced by members of a social system. As used here, purpose is most clearly evidenced by examining the actual behaviors of those comprising the system.

Finally, all systems have arrangements for keeping on course. These information subsystems are labeled *feedback*. Here the comparisons of output to proposed output are constantly being made. Internal and external forms of feedback offer information about the integration and goal-attainment functions. These constant comparisons become the way the system helps maintain or enhance steady state. If the feedback is misread or otherwise unheeded, entropy may ensue.

The best way to start modeling the theory is by answering the following question: What accounts for every concept being linked to every other concept? The answer lies in our assumption that all social behavior is purposive. The

system's purpose (proposed output) links all the concepts to each other.

Boundary

Every social system possesses a boundary and exerts energy to maintain its boundary. Here we are examining the relationship between structure and function; they are interdependent concepts. Boundaries simultaneously connect the system to the suprasystem and divide the system from the suprasystem. Boundary serves three major functions:

- It defines and helps to provide a sense of the social system's identity.
- It controls the internal and external exchanges every system has with its environment (suprasystem).
- It provides the overall definition of the roles to be played by those who comprise the system.

With respect to the first function, we consider each social system a social entity, something beyond those individuals and other social units who comprise it. Boundary identifies those organizational features that bind the units together and that create the identity of the system.

We define social systems as being functionally linked to their environments. In using the model, organizations are regarded as open systems so as to depict this functional linkage with their environments. This linkage is always selective so that control of the exchanges between the system and its social environment is of vital importance to its health and well-being. This filtering or control process is treated as a function of boundary. Through those control processes, the boundary shields system members and their relationships from harmful or disruptive external influences. Similarly, boundary-maintaining efforts permit exchanges with those external systems that are deemed functional.

The third function of boundary is to define the roles appropriate to the system. In this same sense, boundary-maintaining behaviors not only serve to provide the overall definition of the appropriate roles, but also help assure that the performance of these roles is in accordance with that definition. As you leave the role of spouse and assume another as student, you are crossing the boundary of one system (the family) and entering into another (the school). While you are the same person, you behave quite differently in each role. In fact, many of the behaviors associated with one role would be completely out of place in the other.

Given the generic nature of the model, the ideas expressed have to be applicable to all systems. Practically speaking, think of boundary as the system performing its gatekeeping function. Remember, boundary is simply the name given to a behavior assumed to represent a universal characteristic of social systems. The behavior will always be enacted by a member or members of the subject system; it is never anything physical.

To further illustrate this idea, assume for a moment a spousal role. You are attending a party and are in a large room with lots of people. You notice from across the room that a person is behaving seductively toward your spouse. The feelings that you have and the actions you and your spouse take exemplify the notion of boundary. For example, you may move toward your spouse and this other person. Your spouse will see you coming and turn toward this intruding stranger, and will say, "I want you to meet my husband/wife; this is _____." The coordinated behavior of you and your spouse serves to define the situation for the intruder, which in turn will normally influence how this person will behave. He or she will recognize the boundary-maintaining behavior and will adjust his or her behavior accordingly. This example may also help to demonstrate the relationship of boundary to pattern maintenance.

Here is another example of boundary maintenance. A mother is attempting to discipline her child when her own mother seeks to intervene on the child's behalf: "Susan, you're much

too hard on Amy. I remember when you. ..." Angrily, Susan interrupts her mother. "Mother, you stay out of this. Amy is my daughter!" Susan is making a boundary-maintenance statement. These words, plus Susan's **affect** (emotion), will probably be sufficient, at least in this instance, to cause Susan's mother to withdraw from a system that does not include her.

Let us assume that Susan and Amy are members of a social system, the Robbins family. In addition to Susan and Amy, there is another child, John. In this example, Susan, her mother Virginia, and the other members of Susan's birth family would constitute another system. Within the Robbins family, Susan is enacting the role of mother, while Amy is in the role of daughter. Susan plays a crucial role in the socialization of Amy, and part of this is accomplished through disciplining Amy when she has done something wrong. Susan will view any external influence that would negate or distort her relationship with Amy as disruptive, and she will attempt to reject or thwart the unwanted influences. This is what we mean by boundary and boundary-maintenance behaviors. In the example of the Robbins family, it is clear that boundary is a social, not a physical, feature of structure.

We have illustrated the concept of boundary as applied to the family viewed as a social system. Let us use two other types of social organizations to illustrate the universality of the concept of boundary: a university and a nation.

In our definition, a university would be considered a formal organization. Given its relatively large size and complexity, the boundary-maintenance function of a university is evident in formally constituted means of determining who are the insiders and outsiders. For example, a university student typically will be issued an identification card and this card in turn must be shown to remove books from the library, obtain tickets to athletic events, and enroll in classes. While the card has a physical existence, it is the social behavior attached to how the card is used

and the meanings that are associated with these behaviors that evidence boundary and the presence of boundary-maintaining behaviors.

When the model is applied to behaviors between nations, we can view the uses of a passport in boundary terms. With a passport, an individual can pass across the boundary separating one country from another. Again, it is the social behaviors that result from the use of a passport that evidence the presence of a boundary. The example of a passport can also be instructive in identifying other functions performed by a boundary. A boundary always serves a filtering or controlling function. In conducting the boundary-maintenance function, representatives of the host system may specify certain temporary roles an individual may enact while in the host system. For example, the person crossing a boundary from one country to another may engage in sightseeing but will be denied the right to work or to vote in that country's elections. Similarly, some people will not be issued a passport because they are deemed to be "undesirable or dangerous," for example, a suspected terrorist.

As you think about these examples, keep in mind the three functions of boundary that are always evident in boundary-maintaining behaviors: (1) boundary defines and helps to provide a sense of the social system's identity; (2) boundary controls the internal and external exchanges that every system has with its suprasystem; and (3) boundary provides the overall definition of the roles to be played by those who comprise the system. These functions will be universally evident in the boundary-maintaining behaviors of all social systems.

From a practice perspective, the concept of boundary can be helpful in identifying the kinds of relationships that comprise a system with which you may be working. If little or no evidence of the boundary-maintenance function exists among family members, this may suggest a weakness of relationships among its members. Also, the form and level that the boundary-

maintenance function takes can be instructive in better understanding some of the key relationships among those involved.

In our previous example, the bluntness and affect associated with Susan's remark "Mother, you stay out of this" may tell you something useful about Susan's relationship with her daughter as well as with her mother. Our only caution would be not to come to any conclusion based on any one comment or set of behaviors. Boundary and boundary-maintenance behaviors should be viewed as distinctive patterns of ongoing relationships, those that help identify and maintain the system by controlling transactions with outsiders. This general pattern of behaviors called boundary maintenance provides useful insights to the helper.

Suprasystem

Every social system has external relationships with individuals, groups, and other social systems that exist in the social environment. Every social system possesses functionally related relationships (social structures) with other external systems. These relationships may be cooperative or conflictual. The point is that the behavior of the subject system is influenced by these external systems, and the nature of this influence must be understood if the system itself is to be understood.

In social systems theory, the concept of suprasystem is used to operationalize the term *social environment* in the phrase *human behavior and the social environment*. Think of the suprasystem as the next larger system of which the subject system is the focal point. The structural components of the suprasystem are always specific. As a practical matter, the suprasystem is comprised of those external individuals, groups, and other social systems that have an identifiable direct and ongoing pattern of relationships with the subject system.

While we will not be modeling a society as a social system in this text, we do consider it a distinctive form of social organization. Society is the most complex social system. All other social systems are components of society and to a lesser or greater degree are functionally related to the society and its culture.

To develop the concept of suprasystem, we will return to our example involving Susan and her mother. Susan, in her role as Amy's mother, was interacting with a vital person in the suprasystem when she warned her own mother, "you stay out of this." Social **interactions** between members of the Robbins family and outsiders constitute suprasystem interactions. Susan's statement can thus be viewed as part of an interaction between a system and its suprasystem. These interactions are mutually determinant. By this we mean that the interaction would have an effect on Susan's mother, on Susan herself, and on the system(s) of which they are a part. In the latter case, let us assume that this interaction helped to define Susan's role toward her mother as well as to further define her own role as Amy's mother. To complete the illustration, let us also assume that this same interaction served to redefine Susan's mother's role both toward Susan and toward Amy, her granddaughter.

Now let us link this interaction between Susan and her mother to our previously defined concepts of society and culture. We are developing the conceptual connection between system, suprasystem, and the larger social environment of which these systems are a part. Here we focus on the society and its culture. Susan did not invent the mother role nor is her instruction of Amy about the roles of child, daughter, and female her own creation. These roles are cultural roles and are widely shared in a given society. Most likely Susan acquired her particular understanding of the role of mother (as well as female and daughter) largely from her own mother.

Thinking of cultural influences on system-suprasystem relationships is helpful in terms of practice applications of the theory. Recall that while culture provides a set of shared meanings for the people who comprise the society, great diversity exists within a culture, including our own. It is useful to think of the U.S. culture as comprised of a general set of shared meanings, and within this general set are more specific subcultures. In the above example, Susan's gender, race, ethnic background, social class, and religious background will affect her conception of herself and her relationships with others. These features will be most evident in what we describe as system-suprasystem relationships. Sensitivity to these diversities is fundamental to the use of social systems theory and to generalist practice.

Interface

Interface is the third of the eight structural concepts that comprise social systems theory. We use interface to connect the first two concepts—boundary and suprasystem. Let us start with the universal structures and associated functions: all social systems will evidence ongoing patterns of interactions with external systems and these interactions will always possess mutually specific characteristics. These mutually specific characteristics are labeled *interface* and should be thought of as a shared boundary between two or more systems.

Earlier, we used an exchange between Susan and her mother to illustrate both boundary maintenance and suprasystem. We will develop this exchange to illustrate our use of the concept of interface. Recall that Susan's statement to her mother was used as an example of boundary maintenance. In effect, Susan was telling her mother that she was interfering and that she had no right to do so. In this statement, Susan was reaffirming (maintaining) her family role vis-à-vis her daughter. In this example, we first wanted to convey the general function of boundary: protecting the subject system from external influences that could be disruptive. This same exchange can also serve as an example of an interface because it represents a specific exchange between representatives of two systems (the Robbins family comprised of Susan, her daughter Amy, and son John, and Susan's birth family comprised of Susan and her two parents, Virginia and James).

In distinguishing between boundary and interface, think of interface as the point where two or more boundaries meet. To some extent, the notion of interface is captured in Roman mythology by Janus, the god of gates and doorways. Recall that Janus has two faces looking in opposite directions. Boundary is an aspect of a system's internal structure, and the boundary-maintaining behaviors are always oriented to these internal needs; it is the face of Janus that looks into the system. Now think of the literal meaning "inter"—between or among. Like the god Janus, it faces in two directions and represents a way of recognizing and dealing with contending interests. Interface defines the specific interactions that take place between a subject system and the specific individuals, groups, and organizations that comprise its suprasystem. The god Janus is an interface in this example. In looking internally, he is evidencing the pattern-maintenance function; looking externally, he is evidencing the adaptation function.

Now, let us continue the interactions between Susan and her mother, Virginia. In response to being told "stay out of this," Virginia is hurt and after a moment of hesitation, says, "Susan, I am sorry; I didn't mean to interfere. You know I love you (referring to the Robbins family members). Look, why don't we go shopping and have lunch? I want to buy Amy and John new fall school clothes." The response is a boundary-maintenance statement from Susan's mother, but one that reaffirms the special relationship between the two families (systems) and their mutual love and need for each other. To conclude this exchange, let us assume that Susan smiles and says, "Mom, I am sorry for being so abrupt. I didn't mean to hurt you. I love you and I know you didn't really mean to interfere.

Lunch sounds great—where shall we go?" The exchange between Susan and her mother provides an example of interface. The boundaries of the two systems are reaffirmed, but more important, features of the agreed-on relationship between the two systems are specified, that is, what is permissible and what is not. Here we make the assumption that Susan and her mother enjoy having lunch together. We also assume that Susan and her children accept as helpful the clothes and other purchases made by Susan's parents. Such purchases could, of course, be treated as interference and be rejected. In such an instance, the behavior would be treated as boundary maintenance.

The concept of interface is applicable to all forms of social organizations when they are treated as social systems. At an international level, the search for an agreement between the United States and other countries seeking arms control, particularly nuclear arms, represents a search for an interface.

It is important to remember that interface refers to formal and informal agreements made between two or more systems to jointly maintain and/or support some aspect of a relationship. The reasons or motivation for doing so may be quite different for each of the parties involved. For example, the United States and Russia would each decide that it was in its own best interest as well as in the best interest of the rest of the world to enter into, and jointly support, an arms agreement. At another level, each may find other advantages to such an agreement; perhaps Russia will find the agreement useful in dealing with China.

Interface, like boundary, is only evident in social behaviors between social units. Interface is only evident in the actual behaviors that link specified social systems with each other. It does not follow that people or organizations always behave toward each other as expected. What can be said is that when there are unexpected behaviors that are deemed threatening, boundary-maintenance behaviors will become evident.

As with all of the concepts comprising the theory, interface is dynamic. Boundaries are always changing, sometimes expanding and sometimes being terminated.

Input

Social systems theory is premised on the position that all forms of social organization are linked to their social environments through input/output exchanges. The concept of input helps us think about this exchange process. Keep in mind that everything contained within a social system was derived from that system's social environment. The concept of input identifies those social structures that permit the inflow of the amounts and types of resources required by the system to function, for example, the admission requirements to your social work program.

We have identified two requirements associated with the development and maintenance of all forms of social systems. First is a set of conditions that exist in the suprasystem that is perceived as an opportunity, need, or problem. Second is an assumption that the perceived opportunity, need, or problem can be best dealt with through some form of collective action. These are the minimum conditions necessary for the creation of a new social system. If the collective actions of those involved meet expectations, the conditions are established for the continuation and development of the social system. If not, a social system will not form or, if formed, will not survive.

The justification for the social system is always external. The social system itself is the means being utilized to satisfy or deal with these external conditions. In short, the social system is always the means for the satisfaction of external conditions. As long as the social system meets minimum expectations for the satisfaction of these external conditions, the basis for continuance exists. Our intention here is to describe this general process, a process that has application to all forms of social organization.

Inputs are required in the creation of a social system. Once formed, the social system must have a continual flow of resources to sustain itself and to perform its functions. Here we return to an earlier assumption that no social system is self-sufficient; to survive it must continually be supplied with external resources. Input/output exchanges between the system and its suprasystem secure these resources.

Signal inputs can be understood as the "raw material" imported into the system for conversion. In the case of a university, the signal input is the entering freshman student. The purpose of the university is to turn the freshman into an educated college graduate. In the case of a family service organization, a troubled family might constitute the signal input, and the goal is to transform the family into one that is healthy and functional. By successfully transforming the freshman or the family, the system accomplishes its goal attainment function.

Maintenance inputs can be understood as the resources required within the system to attain goals. In the case of the university system, maintenance inputs would include libraries and professors. These resources are used to transform the entering freshman into an educated graduate. The family service organization uses trained social workers as maintenance inputs to transform dysfunctional families into functional ones. Maintenance inputs are used by the system to act upon signal inputs for the purpose of goal attainment. The process and structures used by the system to accomplish this are discussed as conversion operations.

The term *signal inputs* is used because of the meaning attached to the word *signal*, a sign or a notification to act. As we will see later on, in large and complex forms of social organization, it is sometimes very difficult to distinguish between signal and maintenance forms of input. For example, in a hospital, patients in a need state would represent signal inputs, and hospital staff would represent maintenance inputs. A sick or injured patient coming into the hospital through the emergency room will signal or activate the system to receive and treat the patient. Particularly in formal social organizations such as a hospital, signal inputs occupy a temporary role. Also, the boundary-maintenance function of the subject system essentially assigns and defines the role. To help identify signal and maintenance inputs, each will wear a "uniform," for instance, a patient will be in a hospital gown and the nursing staff will be in their special uniforms.

In a practice application of this model, client systems always constitute the signal inputs. The generalist worker and all of the other resources required to accomplish the helping effort are designated as maintenance inputs. In more precise terms, signal inputs are represented by the client system and the condition or situation for which the client system is seeking help. All other resources to be used in the helping relationship would be classified as maintenance inputs. Recall that in the theory, every system performs a boundary-maintenance function. In the example of the hospital, the emergency room staff will first provide an assessment of the person's condition and, based on that assessment, decide what needs to be done. One possible action would be to admit the person to the hospital. This assessment represents a boundary-maintenance function, and the decision to admit would cause the person to be treated as a signal input. Conceptually speaking, we can say that the intake function in all human service agencies is also a boundary-maintenance function, the purpose of which is to screen for signal inputs. Also, if a person is admitted into the system, the assessment process specifies the role the person is expected to play, for example, client, patient, or consumer. The input process is also designed to help the person in the new role understand the counter roles (for example, doctor, nurse, and social worker) that he or she will likely encounter.

The hospital example applies the concept of input to an existing form of social system. The notion of input also applies to the creation of new forms of social relationships. Rather than a hospital, let us use the example of a family counseling center. This is also an existing social system, but by discussing a case, we will see how new social systems are, as a professional activity, consciously formed.

Proposed Output

Proposed output is the concept used to operationalize the purpose of a social system. Proposed outputs always have their origins in conditions existing in the suprasystem and represent a specification of how these conditions will be altered by actions taken by the social system.

We will now illustrate a way of operationalizing a system's purpose. Social systems theory assumes an underlying order. To help describe this ordering we use a "soft" form of technology called logic modeling. We are in no way saying that all those people who may comprise a social system actually and consciously engage in such a rational process. Some may, most will not. What we are saying is that if the actual behaviors of those comprising a social system were fully known, they would exhibit an underlying pattern or order similar to the one we are about to discuss. The pattern would be an informal one and would have a great deal of looseness to it, but it would exhibit purposiveness. We are also saying that in a professional helping process, the generalist does engage in this logical process.

The approach that we used to operationalize proposed output is called a **hierarchy of outcomes** and is comprised of four concepts—**purpose, goals, objectives,** and **activities.** The approach and the associated definitions are displayed in Figure 3.3.

The hierarchy is distinguished by an increasing level of specificity. The first three levels deal with a future state of conditions in the suprasystem. The fourth level, *Activities*, is not a future state, but rather how the future state

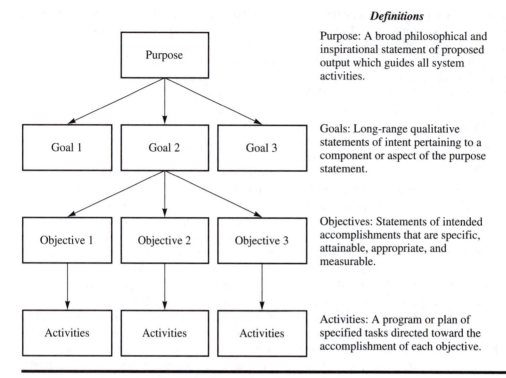

Purpose: A broad philosophical and inspirational statement of proposed output which guides all system activities.

Goals: Long-range qualitative statements of intent pertaining to a component or aspect of the purpose statement.

Objectives: Statements of intended accomplishments that are specific, attainable, appropriate, and measurable.

Activities: A program or plan of specified tasks directed toward the accomplishment of each objective.

FIGURE 3.3   Proposed Output as Hierarchy of Outcomes

specified by each of the objectives is to be achieved. As used here, activities are the means employed to pursue purpose.

We are introducing features of the means-end axis of the four functional requisites. In an application of this hierarchy to the generalist practice of social work, the goals and objectives would be found in step 3 of our generalist practice model (Figure 1.6) and the activities would be incorporated in step 4 (*Services Plan*).

In thinking about a practice application of this hierarchy, always keep in mind the generalist practice model in Figure 1.6 and the purpose of social work. In every practice application, the hierarchy of outcomes will have its origins in how the enhancement of human well-being is to be accomplished.

Conversion Operations

Conversion operations is the name given to the concept that embodies the structural arrangements systems have for transforming their inputs into outputs. We will start our discussion of conversion operations by reminding you of one of the assumptions comprising the social systems perspective: All human social behavior is purposive. Identifying and describing purposiveness becomes the key for developing the concept of conversion operations. Our discussion will be organized under the subheadings of structure and functions.

Structure.   In earlier sections, we discussed boundary, interface, inputs, and proposed output. Each of these concepts pertains to a specialized aspect of the system's structure. In this section we will build on these earlier discussions involving structure, but our focus will be on the internal features of structure involved in the conversion of inputs to outputs.

The concept of **structure** refers to the patterns, formal or informal, that affect and give direction to social functioning within the system and between the system and its suprasystem. Included in structure are roles, goals, service plans, space, and ties with other systems in the social environment. All of these structural components are derived from social systems theory.

A focus on social relationships is central to the theory. The structure of the social system is comprised of these relationships. In introducing this chapter, we provided definitions of some key terms needed to describe social structure, for example, norms, roles, and positions. Remember, a role is merely a concept used to describe an identifiable and relatively stable set of expected behaviors; it is not to be confused with the individual as such.

To understand the concept of role, let us turn for a moment to the insights on human behavior offered by Shakespeare.

> All the world's a stage,
> And all the men and women merely
>   players;
> They have their exits and their entrances,
> And one man in his time plays many
>   parts . . .
> *As You Like It*, Act 2, Scene 7

In the first line, if we were to substitute *suprasystem* for *stage* we would be getting close to our conception of the interplay between a system and its suprasystem. The stage and its props help shape the behaviors of those on stage and the perceptions held by the audience of what is happening. The reference in the second line to players suggests a script. The notion of a script is very close to what we mean by the structure of a social system. This structure guides and shapes human social functioning. Finally, *"parts"* as used by Shakespeare is essentially what we mean by *roles*. Each script will contain many roles, and in life people play many different roles in many different scripts (social systems).

We should add that our notions of structure and role are far more dynamic and much less tightly drawn than indicated in the preceding passage. What does not come through in this passage is how much each of us is shaped by the events that surround us, and how we play and innovate and thus shape the roles we are given to play. Later we will use the concept of function to illustrate what we mean by *play* and *shape the social roles we are given*.

In the previous section we discussed proposed output. The concept operationalizes the system's purpose. There are two main classes of proposed output, task and maintenance. These two forms are derived from the essence of social systems theory—that goal attainment and integration are the two outcomes that determine the system's steady state (well-being). Similarly, these two forms of proposed output determine the two classes of inputs—signal (task) and maintenance—and the structures (and functions) of conversion operations.

Functions.   The term **function** refers to the various activities and tasks associated with carrying out a service's plan. The service's plan itself would represent structure. Whereas the term *structure* is used to designate all of the features that represent the underlying order guiding social behaviors, the concept of *functions* refers to the behaviors themselves.

Structure is always anticipatory, whereas functions are always the meanings attached to actual behaviors. Both structure and function are sets of meanings. Structure represents the normative expectations of those about to be involved in an interactional situation, or in retrospect what was expected to occur. Functions are the meanings attached to the behaviors, that is, the words and emotions (affect) actually exchanged by those participating in the exchange or affected by it. Just as there are behavioral expectations associated with role performance, so there are expectations about the affect. The display of appropriate affect in carrying out a role has special significance for those in the helping professions. If a client does not display affect appropriate to the role in a specific interactional situation, it is a possible indication of an emotional problem. The concept of structure helps you think about what might be expected in behaviors and affect in a given interactional situation. Your set of expectations then becomes the basis for drawing comparisons between what might have been expected and what actually occurred.

To explain these concepts as linked with the generalist practice model, let us refer again to Figure 1.6. Structure is most clearly evident in steps 3 (*Goal Setting*) and 4 (*Develop Services Plan*). In these two steps the practitioner is developing the structure that will guide the helping effort. As a student, you are socialized into a way of conducting your practice—this is the notion of structure. How you actually conduct your practice with a specific client is an example of (social) functioning. The reference point is always "how you are supposed to do it." In the practice model, step 5, *Execute Services Plan*, deals with the concept of function. We draw this distinction in the model because the actual behaviors only approximate the expected behaviors. Drawing this distinction also becomes a way of understanding why (social) structure is always changing.

This section on conversion operations and the section on proposed output are the heart of this chapter. Here we link our social systems theory to the generalist practice of social work. The next component of the structural features of the theory is output.

Output

Input was defined as the set of structures associated with control of the inflow of resources required for system functioning. Output identifies those social structures associated with the release of task outputs to the suprasystem. Together these concepts are used in the theory to describe the exchange relationships that all systems have with their suprasystems. Social systems theory recognizes three classifications of output: (1) **task outputs**, (2) **maintenance outputs**, and (3) **waste**.

Task outputs are signal inputs that, following a cycle of conversion operations, are released to a system's suprasystem. The social structures are those that are involved in this release. In the simplest forms of systems, this can be a set of norms contained within at least two reciprocal roles. The departure might be a person leaving a friendship group and moving away. The set of behaviors might include a final dinner together, hugs, goodbyes, and promises to write.

Case Example. Our subject system is the Arnold family, consisting of Bill, twenty-three, Sarah, nineteen, and their only child, Donnie, age two. The couple has been married three years. Because of Sarah's physical abuse of Donnie, the court placed Donnie temporarily in a foster home and referred his parents to the Westwood Child & Family Center for assessment and assistance. Pat Gray, a social work practicum student, is assigned the case.

The system boundary develops around the three people who comprise this emerging helping system: Pat Gray, the social worker, and Donnie's parents, Bill and Sarah Arnold. Each of these system members, as part of his or her role, exhibits boundary-maintaining behaviors.

Ms. Gray utilizes a strengths perspective in assessing the couple. Family issues include financial stress, low self-esteem of the parents, and physical abuse of the child. In an application of social systems theory, the Arnolds, with their family issues, are identified as the signal input, while Ms. Gray, with her professional knowledge and skills, and the agency resources constitute the maintenance input.

The task of the helping system is to shape a hierarchy of outcomes (mutual goals) within the social structure of the systems conversion operation (the therapeutic intervention). The proposed outputs include reduction of financial stress, increase in self-esteem, and a safe environment for the child. A contract is initiated between Ms. Gray and the Arnolds outlining the steps necessary to meet the proposed outputs. These steps comprise the service plan or intervention to be completed by the helping system.

When the Arnolds meet their service plan objectives, they will be converted from signal inputs to task outputs. That is, the proposed goal will be achieved. Ms. Gray's increased knowledge, job satisfaction, and the well-being of the agency represent task output. Figure 3.4 illustrates the application of social systems theory to this case example.

Waste is used in its literal sense—an inefficient and/or ineffective use of a resource, a resource that did not contribute in the expected manner to either a task or maintenance output. As used in social systems theory, it becomes a way of accounting for all of the inputs into a system.

Examples of waste might be a treatment approach that is ineffective in helping the family change. Suppose a client is referred to a parent education program, and in the course of treatment, the client became hostile and dropped out. The decision to drop out would represent

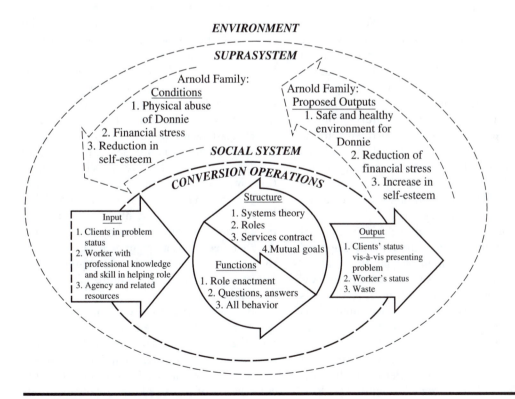

FIGURE 3.4   The Helping System: The Arnold Family

waste for the system. Even if the client resumed treatment and concluded successfully, the ineffective program would represent wasted effort and resources in the conversion effort.

Feedback

The final systems concept to be reviewed in this chapter is feedback. Earlier, the point was made that each concept comprising the theory is a representation of some characteristic of all social systems within their suprasystems. We make the assumption that all such systems have ongoing functional relationships with other individuals, groups, and agencies that comprise their suprasystems. These relationships are deemed to be cyclical and mutually determinant, as opposed to being linear in nature. In other words, the relationship is like a loop with the return segment of the loop back to the subject organization labeled *feedback*. Feedback provides the necessary information to answer the question, To what extent does output conform to proposed output? Not only do we make the assumption that all forms of social organization have information exchanges of the type described, but that through this information exchange, the system makes adjustments and is able to maintain its functional fit with its suprasystem. If this information exchange is impeded, distorted, or ignored, it becomes problematic to the system and unless corrected can lead to the loss of steady state.

Our use of the concept of feedback contains three key features. First, the concept is applied only to a system's output; second, the information generated is always in reference to the system's proposed output; and third, feedback is always considered a maintenance input—it is used to strengthen the system, that is, to help maintain steady state.

Feedback is always evaluative in nature and pertains to the differences between what was proposed and what actually happened. Frequently, the analogy of a furnace's thermostat is used to illustrate feedback. The thermostat is a heat-sensing device typically located in an area requiring a desired temperature. A person sets the thermostat at the desired temperature level. When the surrounding temperature drops below the desired level, an electrical contact is made which in turn causes the furnace to turn on. The furnace continues to warm the space to the desired level. Once the air surrounding the thermostat reaches the desired level, the electrical contact is broken, which automatically turns the furnace off. The output of the furnace is heat, the proposed output is a predetermined room temperature. The thermostat measures output against what is intended. Once the intended heat level is reached, it signals the system that for the moment its job is done and so its output of heat ceases. The thermostat is a sensor used to determine desired conditions. Once these conditions have been reached, it sends information (input) back to the system. Based on this input, the furnace ceases its work, at least temporarily. The example of the thermostat is helpful both in explaining the concept of feedback and in drawing the contrast between a physical and a social process. Certainly the physical process of maintaining a desired functional relationship between the furnace and its environment is a more precise one than can usually be accomplished between social organizations and their environments.

The use of the thermostat is also helpful in illustrating how feedback influences system inputs. In the case of the thermostat, it determines whether electricity, an input, will be supplied to the system. In the case of a social process, the influence on inputs is much more subtle, informal, and complicated.

Social systems theory distinguishes two types of outputs, maintenance and task; therefore, there will be two levels of feedback. Maintenance feedback is internal and deals with the status of the system itself and results from the comparison of proposed maintenance outputs with actual maintenance outputs. This information evidences the integration function and the contribution it makes to steady state. Task feedback is external and deals with the status of relationships between the system and its suprasystem. Here, proposed task outputs are compared with actual task outputs. This information pertains to the goal-attainment function and the contribution it makes to steady state.

Feedback is categorized as **positive** or **negative**. Over time, we have revised our presentation of this important systems concept. The idea of feedback as a device to correct system operations is derived from the work of mathematician Norbert Wiener, who first conceptualized the field of cybernetics. In mathematics, negative feedback refers to a decrease in the direction or amount of something being measured, while positive refers to an increase in the amount or direction of something being measured. In mathematics, a person who begins a diet and loses weight is receiving negative feedback. That is, their weight is going down. For the dieter, that is positive news, but it comes by way of negative feedback. The alternative of going on a diet and gaining weight is too horrible to discuss here.

Wiener's work in the field of cybernetics was inspired by his assignment during World War II to develop an antiaircraft gun that was self-aiming. Wiener relied on tracking the target, firing on it, and then measuring the results. If you fire and hit the target, the feedback confirms your aim. If you fire and miss, you seek feedback. If you have accurate feedback, each time you fire you ought to be able to get closer to the target. This is a type of negative feedback (the magnitude of error is decreasing) as mathematicians use the term. In Wiener's model, the gun corrects each error by analyzing feedback data, until the target is finally hit. Wiener used this basic notion of self-correcting systems to develop cybernetic machines, an early type of robotics using computers. The feedback loop is a central feature of cybernetics and of all living systems models.

In social work, we employ the same concept, but have come to reverse the terminology. Positive feedback in social work is most often used to designate data that confirm we are on the right track. Our dieter cuts down the calories with the goal of weight loss. After two weeks, she has lost five pounds (actual results may vary), and she would certainly consider this as positive feedback. If, on the other hand, she had lost no weight, that would be received as negative feedback. For the purposes of our discussion, the definitions of the mathematicians are counter to our intuition, and potentially confusing. Therefore, we propose the following usage. Positive feedback is defined as feedback that confirms the current operation of the system. Negative feedback is feedback that seeks to correct or adjust the current operation of the system.

Accurate feedback data on client system operations are essential for generalist social work practice. If we engage a client in treatment for low self-esteem, we create an action system with the client to change his or her state of well-being. If we use a program of medication, diet, exercise, and therapy to work with the client, it is essential that we complete the feedback loop to determine the effects of our treatment system elements. If the self-esteem score goes down, we would consider that negative feedback.

Social work practice requires us to demonstrate the value of the interventions we undertake with clients. We make extensive use of data to examine the effects of our interventions on client systems. Feedback data, however accurate, are more valuable when we have an accurate picture of the client system behavior before we began intervention. This is referred to as *baseline data*. The use of client histories, initial assessments, and other types of data allows us to refine and make better use of feedback data in assessing client progress and in improving practice methods. It is an important part of professional education to learn new methods and tools to improve the precision and reliability of the feedback data we collect. As illustrated in Figure

1.6, the feedback loop in step 8 allows us to compare the immediate and final effects to the initial conditions noted in our baseline data. Without clear assessments, statements of our goals, and precise feedback information, we will find ourselves, like Wiener's gunners, taking a shot in the dark.

SUMMARY

In the preceding pages we provided an in-depth presentation of the four functional and eight structural concepts that comprise social systems theory. We employed a model to help explain the relationships of these concepts to the theory. If the theory works as intended, the model can be applied to any social system as a way of describing its key structural features. Social systems theory offers an explanation as to how the system maintains steady state. The modeling of the system also helps to explain, in structural terms, how this occurs. Steady state is dynamic, and through feedback, information pertaining to the performance of the integration and goal-attainment functions is supplied to the system. This information is fed back as either negative or positive feedback.

Our presentation of the theory has been cast in practice rather than research terms. To test the theory, one would have to set up the necessary controls, and select measures of the dependent variable and the independent variables, along with specifying the questions to be tested. We conducted our own studies of job satisfaction and job stress with this in mind. Our hope is that others will find this presentation of the theory sufficiently useful to subject its basic propositions to testing. In the meantime, our primary focus will be on developing the practice relevance of the theory.

GLOSSARY

Activity An organized set of intended or actual actions that takes place in social systems and constitutes the means to obtain the proposed output.

Affect The feelings or emotion expressed by a person and observed and interpreted by others.

Community An inclusive form of social organization that is territorially based and through which most people satisfy their common needs and desires, deal with their common problems, seek means to advance their well-being, and relate to their society.

Culture A set of shared meanings held by a specified group of people that serves as the social foundations for their organized way of life.

Family A social group characterized by an actual or perceived sense of kinship among its members.

Formal organization A form of social organization deliberately and formally created to achieve relatively specific and delimited goals in which logical actions are dominant.

Function To perform a set of activities or tasks. In social systems theory, functioning is part of conversion operations and occurs within the social structure of the system.

Goal A proposed future state to be achieved through the pursuit of functionally related activities. Within a hierarchy of outcomes, goals represent long-range qualitative statements of intent pertaining to a component or aspect of the purpose statement.

Hierarchy of outcomes An approach to formulating proposed output in the social systems model.

Interactions Reciprocal actions, those that are mutually determined. As used here, interactions and social functioning are considered synonymous.

Logical actions Types of actions (behaviors) that are reasoned as opposed to being personally or spontaneously enacted.

Maintenance inputs Inputs that sustain and enhance the system and that, following a cycle of system activities, may be designated as maintenance outputs.

Maintenance outputs The designation of maintenance inputs following a cycle of a system's conversion actions.

Negative feedback Feedback that seeks to correct or adjust the current operation of the system.

Norm The usual behavior associated with role enactment in a prescribed interactional situation.

Objectives In a hierarchy of outcomes, those statements of intended accomplishment derived from a specific goal. These statements are specific, attainable, and measurable.

Positive feedback Feedback that confirms the current operation of the system.

Proposed output A statement of what a system intends to accomplish, a system's goals and objectives, for example.

Purpose A broad philosophical and inspirational statement of proposed output, which guides all practice (system) activities.

Religion The institutionalized social organizations that promote social cohesion through the transmission of values and beliefs shared by members as they relate to enduring human concerns.

Role A structural component of a social system comprised of functionally integrated sets of norms. The term represents the expected behaviors of the persons enacting the prescribed roles.

Role reciprocity A mutuality of exchange in pursuit of shared purpose. The exchange will evidence three characteristics: (1) certain rights and duties involving two or more roles are recognized and accepted; (2) these roles are located in different status positions; and (3) these roles represent specialized aspects of the same functional process and are directed toward the same or comparable goals.

Self The individual viewed as the smallest unit of society. The self is a social unit because it functions with internalized social norms and refers its social actions to the society by means of the reflexive process. The individual human being requires a sense of self in order to function as part of a social organization.

Signal inputs Inputs that the system processes and that become task outputs.

Social group An exclusive, self-organizing form of social organization comprised of two or more members who identify and interact with one another on a personal basis as individuals, possess a shared sense of the group as a social entity, are affected by the group-related actions of members, and in which expressive actions dominate.

Social organization Any social entity comprised of two or more persons or social units who share a purpose and who show functionally interdependent and reciprocal relationships. The social organization itself has functional and reciprocal relationships with its social environment.

Society The most inclusive territorially based form of social organization, which dominates all other forms.

Spirituality The individual quest of seeking answers to enduring human concerns through means that transcend everyday experience or rational inquiry.

Status position A location in a social system comprised of two or more roles.

Structure (social) The relatively stable sets of expectations on which interactions are based.

Subculture A component of a larger culture shared by a subgroup of that culture.

Task outputs Signal inputs following a cycle of a system's conversion operations.

Waste The inefficient, ineffective, or inappropriate use of inputs.

NOTES

1. For those interested in a review of approaches to a classification, see, for example, W. Richard Scott, *Organizations: Rational, Natural and Open Systems* (Englewood Cliffs, NJ: Prentice Hall, 1981), 28–53.

2. For a discussion of the notion of self-organizing, see J. B. Probst, "Some Cybernetic Principles for the Design, Control and Development of Social Systems," *Cybernetics and Systems, 16,* no. 2–3 (1985): 171–180.

3. For an example, see Gerald Corey and Marianne . S. Corey, *Groups: Process and Practice* (Belmont, CA: Wadsworth, 1977), 5–8.

4. Council on Social Work Education, "Curriculum Policy Statement for Baccalaureate Degree Programs in Social Work Education" (New York: Author), B5.7.7.

5. Alvin L. Bertrand, *Social Organization: A General Systems and Role Theory Perspective* (Philadelphia: F.A. David Co., 1972), 38.

6. Ibid.

7. Talcott Parsons, "General Theory in Sociology," *Sociology Today*, eds. Robert K. Merton, Leonard Broom, and Leonard S. Cottrell, Jr. (New York: Basic Books, 1959), 3–38.

8. See, for example, Abraham H. Maslow, *The Farther Reaches of Human Nature* (New York: Penguin Books, 1976).

CHAPTER 4

SOCIAL STRATIFICATION, SPIRITUALITY, AND DIVERSITY

INTRODUCTION
CULTURAL DIVERSITY
SOCIAL SYSTEMS THEORY
DIMENSIONS OF STRATIFICATION
CONFLICT AND CONSENSUS

CONFLICT, RELIGION, AND DIVERSITY
ETHICS AND CULTURALDIVERSITY
SUMMARY
GLOSSARY
NOTES

INTRODUCTION

Culture Wars: How the West Won

The roots of our discussion of diversity reach down to the philosophical systems of thought that undergird Western culture. Why is the Western world in such a position of power and influence today? We propose two reasons: science and democracy.

Western science, with its emphasis on the mastery of nature, has produced tools and technology that have allowed the West to bulldoze other cultures. The Europeans rolled over North America, South America, and Africa in less than a century. Ancient cultures vanished as Europeans equipped with unprecedented war machines enslaved one continent and all but exterminated the peoples of two others. The vast reaches of the Pacific saw one island culture after another taken over by European influence. The Europeans were on a roll, and they showed little evidence of concern about the impact of economic and cultural imperialism on what quickly became subject societies.

Even civilizations with thousands of years of history, with imperial traditions of their own, wilted in the face of Western techno-power. India became a British colony. Much of China and other parts of Asia were assimilated into the empires of Britain, France, Spain, and Portugal. Although scale and distance prevented the total assimilation of most Asian cultures, Western hegemony was established. It is our belief that most of the success of the West in competition with other cultures resulted from the ability to project force based on science and technology.

The other factor favoring the West was democracy. The principles of the Enlightenment challenged authority and opened society to the talents of a wide range of people. These skills and insights then could be recognized and developed. The Enlightenment attitude of "question authority" created a climate that allowed new knowledge to flourish. Flourish it did, despite the efforts of autocrats to compel orthodoxy. The political expression of this philosophy was democracy, which recognized the value of the individual rather than the state or the plutocrats. Democracy created a more open system, and the products of science flooded this open system. The root of science, positivism, directed people's thoughts toward the natural world. During the Enlightenment, the "perfectibility of Man" (sic) was at hand.

As the Enlightenment gained momentum, the successes of the explorers and conquerors cemented Western certainty about not only its technological but also its moral superiority. The whole discipline of anthropology came about to help understand and administer the conquered "primitive peoples." As we consider the modern issue of diversity, we can begin with the question, What was lost in the process as the European steamroller vanquished the cultures of the world? Was Western culture superior in all respects, or only in technology and administration? How can our history inform our consideration of how best to understand human behavior in the pluralistic context of the modern world? First, let us examine the Western tradition a little more closely by looking at the system of thought that emerged from the Enlightenment.

Modernism: Mastering Nature

"Modernism" isn't modern; rather, it is a term applied to the evolution of thought that occurred with the rise of the Industrial Revolution. In the modernist view, so to speak, "the truth is out there." It was possible for human beings to discover the truths of nature. In the preindustrial world, social organization was perceived to be static, autocratic, and provincial. Modernism attempted to apply more dynamic and open approaches to the interpretation of social events, past and present. For example, the term *modernism* applied to scriptural study seeks to replace a literal view of the Bible with an effort to apply concepts of science and critical research to Biblical interpretation.

Modernism as an approach emerged in different fields of study, in different places, and at different times during industrialization. The central tenets of modernism were present in varying degrees depending on the time, place, and application. Generally, modernism could be understood to involve *rationalism* as a perspective. The great thinkers of the Enlightenment were all advocates of rational assessment rather than the feudal practice of relying on tradition and dogma. This perspective gave rise to a method of rational inquiry called *science*. Scientism may seem obvious as a perspective in our time, but it conflicted, sometimes violently, with traditionalist views.

The conflict of science and tradition is illustrated by the famous case of Galileo, who was tried for heresy and condemned to death for his scientific discussions of astronomy. Galileo, whose death sentence was later commuted to life under house arrest, was guilty of advocating views that conflicted with traditional church dogma and authority. The Catholic Church reversed its condemnation of Galileo in 1992, more than three hundred years after his death.

Humanism is another feature of modernism. This use of the term applies to an emphasis on human achievement and perspectives, asserting that the potential for truth and virtue resides in humans, not only in God. *Democracy* was another tenet of the modernists. It followed their view that humans were capable of self-governance, rather than reliance on divinely ordained monarchial rule. *Individualism* in the modernist tradition focused on the importance of the individual rather than the social whole. The origin of ethics and values was held to be within the individual human being. *Romanticism* was the final major feature of modernism. This usage of the term differs from current connotations. Romanticism referred to a literary style derived from the Romans, stressing adventure, nature, and unexpected incidents. The current usage evolved from the romantic literature in which love became an individual emotional adventure, rather than the somewhat dreary, feudal arrangements surrounding marriage.[1]

Modernism laid a foundation for a worldview that was predicated on the idea of progress. Whereas the feudal age was static, modernists believed that through science and reason constant improvement in society is possible. Modernism also asserted a view of universality according to which nature everywhere operates on the same laws. In contrast to the mystical views of the time, these laws were open to human discovery and understanding. By extension, the scientific perspective applied to social sciences, and the quest for the natural laws governing human behavior. Finally, the modernist perspective promotes a view of the world as *regular* and *predictable* using the natural laws. This point of view came to be applied to human enterprises as well as to the natural sciences.[2]

Postmodernism: A Philosophy Fragmentation

Postmodernism refers to a period that is usually identified as starting the 1970s as a reaction to the widespread social unrest and technological innovations in communication in the previous decade.[3] The 1960s were characterized by unrest, cynicism about social institutions, social fragmentation, polarization of political views, an emphasis on subjectivity, challenges to social organization, and increasing emphasis on social divisions rather than common social identity. In this climate, challenges to the rather upbeat views of modernity were inevitable. Belief in science as producing only positive outcomes was challenged. Confidence about social progress was replaced by suspicion of those in authority. The anxious views taken of the social protestors by those in power reciprocated this mistrust.

The rational objectivity of science is challenged by the postmodern view that all knowledge is contextual and subjective. Where modernism stresses clarity, order, reason, and consensus, postmodernism emphasizes difference, particularity, and irregularities in the recognition of differences among people. Postmodern thought addresses the concept of diversity without superiority. By use of eclectic perspectives, inclusiveness of competing views, and elaboration rather than reduction, postmodernism emphasizes diversity as a competition of equally valid perspectives. No one view is seen as having a monopoly on the truth. In fact, postmodernism sees the quest for knowledge and the quest for power as synonymous.

In social systems terms, postmodernism can be understood two ways. As an entropic process, it is moving away from unified social organization. As a neg-entropic process, it promotes social order by identifying competing internal interests and encouraging social patterns that have less tension and higher levels of integration. In what might be considered a triumph of postmodern relativism, the value of this perspective probably depends on your point of view.

Feudal dogmatism sought to create order by compelling social orthodoxy. Modernism sought to bring order by discovering objective truths that do not rely on values or context. Postmodernism sees the realm of ideas as an arena of competition, with differing understandings of the truth. The debate over which perspective best defines the terms for understanding social conditions is a power struggle that will determine policies and practices in the future.

CULTURAL DIVERSITY

In our discussion of diversity, we are focusing on what is termed *cultural diversity*. We characterize the issue as cultural diversity rather than *racial*, *ethnic*, or some other type of diversity because we are focused on the social processes that develop as those members of diverse groups relate to one another and to society. In selecting this perspective, we are choosing to address not the trait as such, but rather the culture that grows up around a shared sense of identity. In this view, the African American community is not defined by skin color or by heritage. Rather, it is defined by the common values, beliefs, and norms shared by those who identify with this group.

The definition of culture has varied widely in the social sciences. Almost all disciplines use the term, and there is only loose consensus on the meaning. We prefer the definition offered by Kroeber and Kluckhon after they reviewed almost 160 definitions found in the social science literature. Their search covered sociology, anthropology, psychology, psychiatry, and other disciplines besides social work. They concluded that

> **Culture** consists of patterns, explicit and implicit, of and for behavior acquired by symbols, constituting the distinctive achievements of human groups. Including their embodiments in artifacts: the essential core of culture consists of the traditional (i.e., the historically derived and selected) ideas and especially their attached values.[4]

This definition coincides with the essential features of social systems as seen through the perspective of symbolic interactionism. The values that are attached to the behaviors are of paramount importance. The implicit and explicit aspects of culture are also important in this understanding of the term, corresponding to external and internal system functions.

Culture as defined is the encompassing view of social patterns that are acquired as opposed to innate. Innate functions are presumed to be universal. In our discussion, the focus is on subsystems within the culture. Like culture, *subculture* is a term widely used without careful explication. The term has been used because it symbolizes two crucial social processes: the relationship of subsystems to each other and the relationship of subsystems to the whole. Gordon defined **subculture** as follows:

> A subdivision of a national culture composed of a number of factorable social situations such as class status, ethnic background, regional and rural v. urban residence and religious affiliations but forming in their combination a functional unity, which has an integrated impact on the participating individual.[5]

To this, we would add only that the impact of subculture is not unidirectional. As the subculture has impact on the individual, so is the subculture itself shaped by the aggregated inputs of its members. These collective movements shape culture by group consensus. There is also notable influence from what might be called *cultural stars*. Stars are individuals whose prominence and identification with a particular group has the power to modify the collective cultural impression of a group. In our time, Martin Luther King might be regarded as a prime example of a cultural star—one whose eloquence, courage, and commitment defined a movement and a social group. It is by collective action and occasional charismatic influence that social perceptions change. These perceptions are then incorporated into the dynamic between the subculture and the culture.

Subcultures function as systems in the same manner as cultures do. The larger culture simply forms the suprasystem for the subculture, with the attendant dynamics that we call **boundary effects**. The organization of cultures functions as a holarchy, with each subculture embedded in the next larger cultural system. Some subcultures exist at the same hierarchical level. These "peer cultures" are not embedded one within the other. Rather, each has its own transactions with the environment, and each is a part of the environment of the other. For example, in the nineteenth century, Irish and Italian immigrants to American cities were distinct groups with about the same status in the American culture. They interacted with one another at the boundary, but each was embedded in the larger American culture. Although comparable in level, the content of these cultures varied. The shared meanings of the suprasystem provide the unifying element in this case.

Social work practice today embraces a perspective called *cultural relativity*. This premise suggests that all human behavior be assessed first in context of culture. There is no presumption of a cross-cultural standard for proper behavior. Some biological phenomena are universal, and these are not addressed by social systems theory. For example, the need for sleep is universal, not cultural.

As we discussed in relation to modernism and postmodernism, Western medicine relies on a scientific, universalistic view of health and disease. While this works well for biological conditions such as cancer, it does not work well with behaviors at the symbolic level. The use of a concept like psychopathology in psychiatry implies a universal view in which symptoms such as hallucinations are indicative of illness, no matter who has those symptoms. In the positivistic view of science, a hallucination is a distorted perceptual process always indicative of illness. From the standpoint of a Native American on a vision quest, hallucinations are a normal and desirable part of the experience. In the relativistic view, a hallucination is expected and admired. The cultural conceit that one can view all behavior from a single universal cultural perspective has produced obvious culture clash in providing mental health services to minority populations. Not surprisingly, some adaptations have been noted as our sensitivity to cultural differences grows. Even in psychiatry, the DSM IV has begun to include materials that suggest some recognition of cultural relativism.

Anthropologist Franz Boas defined the study of anthropology as concerned with historically created diversities in human culture. Boas felt that it was the province of psychology to address universal human nature. This we would call a *universalistic quest*, and it is one that psychology long since abandoned. Social work is more aligned with the anthropological view of relativism than the scientific quest for universalism on this point. The classical statement summarizing cultural relativism comes from a student of Boas, Ruth Benedict. She defined cultural relativity as "the coexisting and equally valid patterns of life which mankind (sic) has created for itself from the raw materials of existence."[6] This definition also conforms to our view of social systems. The "raw materials" of which Benedict spoke we consider to be the environmental inputs used by the cultural subsystems. The culture that evolves performs the pattern maintenance and tension reduction functions posited by Parsons.

In our discussion, we characterize the subcultures and their relation to the larger culture. We will use the term **minority culture** to describe the subculture and **dominant culture** to describe the "national" culture defined by Gordon. We use the term *minority culture* for two reasons. First, in most cases, the subculture is a numerical minority within the larger system. For example, Native Americans as a minority culture represent about 2 percent of the total national population. Secondly, this is the term currently used widely in policy contexts to define disadvantaged groups in society. For example, the standard Equal Employment Opportunity (EEO) program language refers to "minority applicants" for a job. These "protected minorities" may be numerically superior, as is the case for women in this country. The term *dominant culture* has disagreeable connotations for some people. In our use, we define the dominant culture in terms of power. The dominant culture is comprised of the group that has the power to coerce the behavioral compliance of those not in that group. Thus, while white,

heterosexual men might be a minority in number, the cultural views identified by this elite subculture provide the foundations for the dominant culture. The term *dominant culture* describes this very important quality of having the power to compel behavior.

Subcultures function as elements of the culture. Consequently, subcultures are subject to both entropic and neg-entropic processes. Therefore, we would expect to see ongoing adaptive changes at work in subcultures. If the dominant culture has the power to compel behavior, it is expected that adaptation of minority subcultures would be toward conformity to dominant cultural norms. The term used for this process is *cultural integration*. This is the process by which a fragmented culture becomes whole or entire. There are three elements of cultural integration:

- Logical, emotional, or esthetic consistency among groups
- Congruence of cultural norms with behavior
- Critical or functional interdependence of subcultures

The pressure toward cultural integration is historically identified as the "melting pot" model. As different cultures entered the country, they became "Americanized" in language, values, and behavior. Their old cultural identity was subordinated to the new and in time tended to be lost. To a small degree, the assimilated cultures influenced the dominant culture, but only in limited ways. Minority cultures lacked the power to compel and thus relied only on the power to attract. This has been likened to "seasoning" the melting pot.

The counterforce to cultural integration is *cultural differentiation*. Subcultures differentiate from the dominant culture for one of two reasons. In the first case, the subculture is denied full admission to the dominant culture by boundary protection devices. In the example of slavery, a host of laws, practices, and norms grew up that excluded slaves from white culture. The norms and institutions persisted after the laws were expunged. Isolated by force, the African American community developed a culture that was significantly differentiated from the dominant culture. As forces for cultural integration grew, more and more of the boundaries formerly impermeable to African Americans were penetrated. Nonetheless, a perceptibly different cultural pattern persisted among even those African Americans who had access to fuller membership in the dominant culture. One historical example is instructive. As the civil rights movement (a cultural integration process) gained influence in the 1960s, the initial goal was racial integration. Some groups within the African American movement then began to advocate for Black Separatism, including a "return to Africa" movement. This was the same goal advocated by Segregationists after the Civil War, a policy that resulted in the creation of Liberia. In this instance, it is clear that it was not the goal itself that was significant, but the different meanings that this goal had to the two cultures. In this case, the African American culture had split into two subcultures, the so-called militants and the moderates. As Piven and Cloward were to note later, racial integration was not a matter of physically intermingling the races, but of equality of opportunity in gaining goals desired by both groups. The goal is not to create an emulsified society of intermingled neighborhoods. That was not the desire of either group. Rather, opportunity to gain access to desired goals and the freedom to choose a residence or job were the issue.[7]

SOCIAL SYSTEMS THEORY

Social systems theory provides a useful framework for the consideration of social diversity. Let us begin with the proposition that in a homogeneous society (a purely hypothetical construct) there would be no hierarchy. In all known societies, including many animal societies, the existence of "pecking order" hierarchies is evident. This suggests that a power hierarchy serves some essential function since it is a universal feature of organized societies. In sociology, the organization of a society into hierarchical groups in such a way that there is inequality in the distribution of goods, services, or prerogatives is termed *social stratification*. The process by which groups are assigned stratified social status is the primary concern in discussing diversity. We will consider diversity primarily in the context of this process of social stratification. In our discussion, it will be necessary to distinguish between what Robert Merton called *manifest* and *latent functions*.[8] Merton is a functional theorist, and his views on social functions are consistent for the most part with the major concepts of Talcott Parsons whom we discussed earlier.

Manifest functions are the openly stated conscious functions of a social system. They involve the intended and recognized consequences of a social action. For example, the manifest function of police work is to enforce the law and apprehend criminals. In so doing, the police enforce the norms of a social group by punishing those who violate the expectations of proper behavior. From the standpoint of the dominant culture, police functions are necessary and noble services provided by officers whose job entails physical risks.

Latent functions are unconscious, covert, or unstated functions performed by a social system. These may reflect hidden purposes of a social system. Latent functions may be intended or unintended. Many times, latent functions go unrecognized. The tendency to overlook latent functions is more pronounced among those who are fully socialized into the system. Marginal people or groups may, by virtue of experience and perspective, have a keener perception of latent functions. A latent function of the police system may be to limit the freedom of movement of certain minorities by questioning them about possible criminal intent when they venture into areas where their presence creates apprehension in the members of the dominant culture. In African American communities, the issue of racial profiling becomes a transparent code word for this latent function. The mocking characterization by African Americans of being arrested for "DWB," meaning Driving While Black, makes the point. The simple fact of being Black can be treated as criminal by those charged with law enforcement.

The Function of Dysfunction

Not everything that occurs in a system serves either manifest or latent functions. There are some actions by a social system that do not accomplish the desired functions or which have no identified functions. A familiar example for welfare clients is the legendary bureaucratic inefficiency of many agencies designed to serve the needy. A benign explanation for bureaucratic inefficiency is that it is simply an inevitable artifact of the size and complexity of the system, a **dysfunction.** However, we must be cautious in assuming that all apparent dysfunction is benign. Sometimes dysfunction is a masquerade for a latent function. Those who are poorly served by a malfunctioning system are likely to suspect that inefficiency represents a latent function of the system. Inefficiency, they argue, is a way to deny benefits and services to which people are entitled. Rude treatment, seemingly a dysfunction in a human services agency, may actually serve the latent function of "punishing" the undeserving for seeking assistance. There is an old saying that goes "never assume malice when ignorance is sufficient explanation." In the case of system functions, however, it has been often noted that those who suffer at the hands of the system are willing to believe the worst about the motives of those in power.

Open and Closed Systems

The social hierarchy may be relatively closed or open. The degree of system openness pertains both to the types of interaction between the system and the environment, and to transactions that occur within the system structure itself. It is important to remind yourself that the definition of system and environment are relative. If we consider American society as the focal system, then the African American community is a subsystem. If we consider the African American community as a system, then the American culture is the environment.

Racial unrest could be considered an adaptive struggle against an unjust system. This might be the view of a militant Malcolm X, who was involved in the goal attainment activity of seeking justice for African Americans. Viewed from the larger society, racial unrest could be seen as an internal problem of integration (keeping people content), or of pattern maintenance and tension management (maintaining the status quo).

The sanctions employed by a society to control members may range from mild verbal reproof to cruelty and death. Manifest social functions usually have formal structures and processes that are intended to facilitate goal attainment. Latent functions often rely on informal or hidden processes to accomplish the goal. Thus, there will be no written policy that says that a police officer should single out African Americans for interrogation. The norm develops as a product of being socialized into a relatively closed system. Similarly, there is no requirement that a welfare official be gruff and insensitive, but for many clients it might seem that they come straight from a training program in rudeness.

Boundary Effect

When we consider diversity from the standpoint of social systems theory, turbulence at the interface becomes a central concern. In the discussion of the family as a system of roles, we addressed this concept briefly. Recall that according to systems theory, one characteristic of a system is that it is defined by a boundary. In social systems, we can say that the nature of transactions that occur within the boundaries of a system are different in qualitative and quantitative ways from those that take place between systems. A system ceases to be a system if the boundary does not define the nature of transactions. This is the **boundary effect**. We described two ways this occurs.

First, there is *energy loss* in conducting transactions across an interface. The most common form of energy in social systems is communication. In the consideration of communication between two different cultures, the effect is obvious in practice. The experience of interacting with people from different cultures requires more energy than does interaction with people from one's own culture. The effort expended in conveying nuances of meaning when language barriers exist is an obvious instance. The information carried in communication is diminished as it crosses the interface.

Time spent in interaction with people from other cultures requires the sort of effort and vigilance we recall from childhood, when the norms and rules of behavior were new to us. Developing *cultural competency*, which is the process we are describing, requires effort and dedication. By the time one becomes acculturated, the effort is no longer required. At that point, we can say that we have entered into the other culture, and the boundary effect no longer applies.

The second aspect of the boundary effect is that *information is distorted* in the process of crossing the interface. In person-to-person communication, a woman might say to a man, "You are a big boy now." Her meaning is that he is moving up in the world and is becoming one of the controlling elite. He, being sensitive about his weight, interprets the remark as a derogatory reference. A man might say to his wife, "We ought to do something for fun." Her reply is "Are you saying that I am no fun to be with?" This common type of distortion observed in family therapy is amplified by the boundary effect. There are many stories like the one of the American manufacturer who sought to market detergent in another country, but in that country the name of the product was translated as a slang name for sex organs. The marketing campaign was not a great success.

A third aspect of the boundary effect is *political significance*. This aspect is more pronounced in subcultural interactions. In the example above, we noted that, even in families with close ties and a common culture, communication distortion is easy to observe. Distortion caused by language differences is also easily observed. In many cases, we are considering subcultural differences. In such cases, the language is common to both groups. However, the nature of symbolic language allows such subtle shifts in meaning that it is quite common that words and symbols have dramatically different resonances for different subcultures. In Winston Churchill's famous observation, "The United States and Great Britain are two nations divided by a common language."

Two familiar examples illustrate this point. A male boss walks in to talk to a group of women whom he supervises. Trying to be breezy, he says, "Okay, girls, listen up." Of course, any woman in the group who is sensitive about the oppression of women in a male-dominated culture is going to take offense. The seemingly innocuous term *girls* has taken on subcultural significance to some of those in this oppressed group. The familiar example of the white man calling an African American man a "boy" has the same effect. Both of these examples are now so widely cited that they no longer constitute a subcultural meaning. They are part of the shared cultural perception of political meanings. Nonetheless, there are still instances of people who use such terms. Dissatisfaction over the use of the term *ladies* as an instrument of oppression of women, conjuring up for some a past characterized by sex role dichotomy, or the term *handicapped* to describe persons with disabilities are other examples of linguistic oppression. The point to be underlined here is that words and gestures carry different connotations to different subcultures not simply due to miscommunication, but based on the belief that certain practices have the latent goal of oppression.

The discussion under this third point can all be summarized as "political correctness." It is hard to find a place in the current literature where the term *PC* is not used negatively. The reason is not hard to fathom. As soon as a term is identified as carrying a social control message, sensitivity to its use increases. As sensitivity increases, those who seek to exercise control shift to other terms. Those who are oppressed by a term may seek to promote other terms that do not have the latent function of "keeping them in their place." Thus, the evolution of neologisms that seek to displace culturally pejorative phrases continues.

Minority Status as a Holon

In Chapter 2, we discussed the concept of holon proposed by Arthur Koestler. You will recall that the term *holon* refers to the process of a system that is simultaneously oriented both inward toward system processes and outward to the environment. When we use the term *holon* to describe this orientation, it stresses the importance of both internal and environmental processes for system survival. One of the places this concept is most important is in considering the difficulties encountered by minorities who are functioning in the environment of a majority culture.

In a complex culture, those in a minority status are called upon to develop a dual identity. The minority person must learn to function in the dominant culture as do all members of that culture. In addition, minority persons must learn

to function as a member of their minority culture.[9] The more widely the norms of the two cultures vary, the greater will be the strain on the minority individual. In addition, some cultural identities bear a burden of stigma that increases the difficulty of transactions with the dominant culture. Finally, some cultural memberships are clandestine in nature, and this adds yet a further burden.

We have discussed elsewhere the fact that our industrial society confronts most people with two rather conflicting social contexts. The family of origin is a nurturing context in which the developing person is socialized to the culture and within which the sense of self is developed. As the person encounters the wider environment in school, work, and other contexts, the primary role relationships of the family are replaced by secondary role relationships that are more structured, rational, and impersonal. The family of origin serves as the proximate representation of the culture. If one is born into a minority culture, the values and socialization process of the family will be at some variance from the larger culture. In cases of racial, ethnic, or religious minority culture, the contrast between the minority/family culture and the dominant culture are overt.

For racial minorities, Billingsley observed that our culture requires individuals to develop two distinctive identities.[10] They must first develop a sense of self within the family and minority culture. Assuming that the minority culture is structured around accepted norms, this process is no different than in nonminority cultures. As the minority child develops, the self encounters the larger world of the dominant culture. A distinct sense of self as a minority person in a dominant culture must be developed. If the racial identity of the self is stigmatized in that culture, or if role ascription severely limits the roles available to the minority person in the dominant culture, it is to be expected that the interface between the dominant and minority cultures will be turbulent. The tension between the subcultures is replicated in the social self of the minority person.

We accept the common view that those in the dominant culture have a less acute sense of the social strain imposed by a stratified system of racial subcultures. Since the sanctions imposed by society are more severe for minority persons, this is to be expected. When members of the dominant culture violate the norms of the society, they can also become quickly socialized to a previously invisible reality. This is the case in interracial marriage, which typically results in the marital pair taking the identity of the minority partner.

In circumstances such as those experienced by gays, lesbians, and bisexuals, the child may experience a sense of alienation early in life. Sex role socialization begins almost immediately in our culture. The vehicle for this socialization is the family. Most families prepare their children for the sex role behavior expected by the culture. Many gays, lesbians, and bisexuals report experiencing a sense of minority sexual orientation well before puberty. Many also keep the feelings secret, since they conflict with role expectations. This secrecy creates internal tension for the developing child and complicates the nurturing relationship with the family. At some point in development, the child becomes aware that there are others who share their feelings and orientation. If the family of origin accepts this sexual awareness, the primary relationships can be maintained with modified expectations. If the family rejects the emerging self-awareness of the child, the relationship with the family is strained. The developing person may look elsewhere for relationships that nurture this newly emerged sense of self.

Since the social systems of gays, lesbians, and bisexuals are quite varied in formality, structure, and social acceptance, there is no settled normative process for the development of a sense of self among sexual lifestyle minorities. The culture of sexual lifestyle minorities is in a rapidly developing state. These groups have made dramatic progress in removing the stigma of minority sexual orientation and in gaining institutional recognition in the larger society. Nonetheless, examples abound that make it clear that there is resistance in the dominant culture to full acceptance of minority sexual lifestyles. The disastrous "Don't ask—don't tell" policy adopted in the United States military regarding sexual orientation is illustrative of the cultural ambivalence regarding this subcultural group.

Cultural infusion, the process of gaining access to positions where decisions are made, is a strategy for addressing this problem. It is in the nature of subsystems to find a steady state where communication and interaction are stress free. If such a group is all white and all male, it is much easier to revert to sexist and racist language than it would be if women and minorities were present. In Goffman's phrase, the presence of representatives of oppressed groups in decision environments keeps these from becoming "backstage" settings.[11] However, the society seeking to maintain a steady state can be quite resourceful. Decisions may be made outside the formally recognized processes. The formal settings of decision making, as we know, are not necessarily the place where the real action is. If men have backstage business discussions at a golf course and then bring these decisions to the boardroom, it is not surprising that the women and minorities excluded from the golf club will clamor to get in.

The implications of this discussion do not lead to a reassuring conclusion. It is human nature to associate with those who are like us. It is easy, it is efficient, and it feels right. This tendency leads to subgrouping. It is the nature of systems to seek a steady state. One way of accomplishing this is through social stratification. As Gouldner noted, the way that inequality remains in stratified societies is by way of coercion.[12]

One subtle means of coercion is through language. Language also provides a medium of resistance. It is part of the mission of social workers always to be willing to live with the discomfort and strain of seeking to understand a culture different from their own. We believe that it is possible, even essential, for a professional to be trained for cultural competence. This means that there is a goal that women and men; different races; and different ethnicities, religions, and classes can relate constructively. A diverse society does not mean a compartmentalized society. The better angels of our nature call us to seek cultural competence and to promote cultural competence as a value in society. The looming alternative is a balkanization of society that promotes only widening gaps between groups and a state of permanent mistrust and hostility.

DIMENSIONS OF STRATIFICATION

In this chapter, we consider the impact of social diversity on human behavior and social systems. We regard diversity as a matter of social stratification. Further, we believe that from the standpoint of social systems theory, there are both advantages and disadvantages to stratification. This might sound strange in the context of social work practice, since the connotations of stratification usually conjure up images of inequality and oppression. We will address this as we progress in this chapter, but for now be assured that we fully subscribe to the values of social work regarding inequality and oppression. Here, we attempt to answer the troublesome question: Why is there stratification in every known human society? Only by understanding the phenomenon from a theoretical perspective can we hope to address it in social work practice.

At various points in this book, we have said that social systems must accomplish two seemingly incompatible tasks. They must adapt to a constantly changing environment, and they must maintain continuity of social structures and processes. In other words, all systems must

both change and remain constant. These conflicting needs produce internal tensions that must be managed by the system.

As we have noted, Talcott Parsons and functionalist theory have been criticized for having a bias toward maintaining the steady state of a system. Parsons termed this function "pattern maintenance and tension reduction." It is worthwhile to keep this criticism in mind and to contrast the functional perspective with conflict theory as we discuss stratification.

Parsons identified two primary dimensions along which social stratification takes place. We discussed these in connection with role theory, but let us review them briefly in relation to diversity and stratification. Parsons maintained that positions or roles are assigned by society in one of two primary ways: ascription or achievement.

Ascription refers to roles that an individual is assigned on the basis of some attribute over which the person has no control. Generally the assignment takes place at birth, as with attributes such as gender, race, and ethnicity. Some ascribed roles occur later, as with aging. Accidents or diseases that result in disability may also occur at any time. **Ascribed status** is usually presumed by society to be permanent. It is characteristic of ascribed roles that the individual can do little or nothing to alter social status. While the attributes on which ascription is based are often physical, the greater significance derives from the social meanings attached to the role by society and by the role incumbent.

Achievement refers to roles that a person occupies as a result of individual actions. Occupations are prime examples of achieved status, as are such things as parenthood, homeownership, and so forth. **Achieved status** is not necessarily positive. Such attributes as drug addict, prostitute, or traitor are examples of achieved status positions.

In most cases, access to desirable achieved status positions is related to the ascribed positions into which one is born or forced by events.

If one is ascribed low status by virtue of race, it will limit the opportunities to achieve high-status positions. The reverse is also true. If one is "high born," moving into high-achievement status may be relatively easy. It has been observed that the measure of a person in society is more a matter of what one overcomes than what one achieves. Malcolm X, for example, observed that he was prevented by his race (ascribed status) from being able to become a lawyer (achieved status). By contrast, in a Democratic Party convention keynote speech, Ann Richards said of President George Bush that "he was born on third base and thinks he hit a triple." Bush, of course, was born to a wealthy and politically connected family. That presumably made his ascent to high-achieved status relatively easy. Often the view of social outsiders is that those on the inside succeed despite showing little talent or effort.

A **stigma** (from the Greek word for a mark or a brand) is any attribute that discredits or disqualifies a person from full social acceptance. The term is widely used to describe any social status deemed undesirable by a culture. In the work of Goffman, stigma takes on a more specific meaning. Goffman characterized a stigma as producing a "spoiled identity." The stigmatized individual had to develop specialized social skills to deal with the social signficance attached to the stigma.[13]

Goffman distinguished three types of stigma:

- **Abominations of the body.**   This includes physical deformities, limitations, or other identifiable characteristics. Stigma here is based on observable physical deviations from the norm. The historical tendency to characterize a person with physical abnormalities as a "freak," served to create a damaged social identity for the affected person and with it a permanently inferior social status.

- **Blemishes of character.**   This includes persons with mental illness, addicts, and criminals. By lumping together all members of this class, a delimited social status was created that allowed society to treat all members of the group the same. For example, treating a criminal who sells a joint to a friend in the same way one would treat a drug kingpin diminishes the distinction between the behaviors of the two. Such categories usually form a social fear of the threat posed by the stigmatized group behavior.

- **Tribal stigma.**   This stigma is based on race, religion, or ethnicity. Membership in these groups creates a stereotypical social impression that does not allow for individual differences. Social mobility is impaired and individuality is submerged. For the most part, this is the type of stigma discussed in this chapter. Tribal bias reduces people to subhuman status. The manifest function of stigma is to ostracize or limit the impact of the stigmatized person or group. The latent function of stigma is to consolidate the community around existing values and beliefs regarding the shared belief system.[14]

It is a measure of the degree of a society's open versus closed structure as to how difficult it is to escape status ascription. In caste systems, such as India or South Africa before the end of apartheid, being assigned to a caste on the basis of race meant virtually no social mobility was possible. Attempts to challenge the entrenched systems were met with severe sanctions, up to and including death. In caste systems, the process of coercion as described by Gouldner is manifest.[15] The rules were enforced by existing structures, such as courts and prisons. In the United States, there is no manifest racial caste system. Nonetheless, there is racism and a very real process of ascription. This is referred to legally as a difference between de jure ("in law") and de facto ("in actuality") segregation.

After the emancipation of slaves, the manifest function of oppression became latent. The enforcement of the latent caste system fell to groups like the Ku Klux Klan, whose "invisible empire" was often populated by people who had high-status positions in the visible social order.

Later, as the normative support for the Klan eroded, the process of enforcing racist norms became increasingly a latent function. No manifest laws or rules now exist to enforce racial ascription. Many manifest laws do exist to constrain discriminatory acts, a prime example being the Equal Employment Opportunity (EEO) program. However, the very existence of EEO programs signals that the latent processes of racism still exist.

When a society becomes stratified on the basis of ascription, access to achieved roles is blocked for low-status members. Despite lack of access to achieved status, low-status people still aspire to the rewards a society offers. Again we turn to Merton's view of stratification and status. Merton proposed the "anomie theory" of social deviance.

In Merton's work, *conformity* meant behaving in accord with norms whether you liked it or not. *Innovation* was a matter of finding new ways to the goal when you were blocked by society. This may include criminal means like being a drug dealer. *Ritualism* referred to "going through the motions," as seen in bureaucrats who follow procedure with no real commitment to the goals. *Retreatism* is exemplified by the dropout who rejects both the system rules and its rewards, such as hermits. *Rebellion* refers to the outsider who seeks new goals and new means, like the hippies who rejected materialism and the work ethic in favor of "doing your own thing."[16]

In Table 4.1, we can imagine a middle-class conformist who abides by middle-class norms, does what he is supposed to, and is rewarded by society. By contrast, one who does not conform is a deviant. Here we understand deviance as a response to social conditions, not a result of some biological or psychological flaw in the person. Those who are in high-ascribed status positions will have easy access to achievement opportunities like education, jobs, and so forth. This group tends to succeed because they understand the system, and those who control the

system are comfortable with them. Those in the middle tend to conform most rigorously to norms of behavior and attitude. The "sensible middle"—beloved of politicians—accepts and expects that they and others will behave in "appropriate" ways. Part of the reason that those in the middle conform is that their status relies on continuous validation by others. Unlike those with great wealth, they are not permitted eccentricities, so they have more to lose by misbehavior. Those in the lower-social strata have less investment in social norms, since they do not have status or possessions to lose. Thus, an unemployed minority male in the inner city, with no hope of ever improving his life in the legitimate system, is a better candidate to resort to crime, drugs, or dropout behavior than is an employed middle-class white male.

For low-status people like Malcolm Little, also known as Malcolm (X), and later Malcolm Shabazz, education and jobs were not likely to be forthcoming. Malcolm thus turned to "innovative" activities in crime to gain the opportunity denied him in regular society. Merton's perspective is interesting: it suggests that even a person such as Malcolm, denied opportunity and identity in a racist society, still shares in the cultural desire for material success and believes that hard work is the way to achieve material success. In effect, Malcolm was partly socialized by society. His frustration at unequal opportunity then led to a dramatic revision in his concept of himself, his race, and society. In Merton's terms, this led him from criminal "innovation" as a young man to rebellion later in life. His goal became changing the social structure as it affected his people. Malcolm's story is even more tragically inspiring when we note that his personal growth continued as he developed his Islamic faith. Ultimately, he came to transcend his culture and experience and developed a belief in universal human equality.[17]

It is apparent that those who are denied opportunity in the legitimate social structure become a threat to the continuation of the system.

TABLE 4.1   Merton's Modes of Individual Adaptation Table

MODE	INSTITUTIONALIZED MEANS (HARD WORK)	SOCIAL GOAL (WEALTH)
Conformity	Positive	Positive
Innovation	Negative	Positive
Ritualism	Positive	Negative
Retreatism	Negative	Negative
Rebellion	Positive/Negative	Positive/Negative

Source: Merton, *Social Theory and Social Structure*, p. 194.

Note: Positive means acceptance. *Negative* means rejection. *Positive/Negative* indicates replacement with new means and goals.

It is in the interest of system stability to get as many people as possible to conform. If whole groups of people become convinced that both the goals of the system and the accepted means to those goals are out of reach, then rebellion is no longer a personal act. It then becomes a social problem of system continuity. In the functionalist view, the optimum course for society is to make constant, incremental adjustments in order to satisfy all four functional system prerequisites. A key problem from the systems perspective is that once some group in society no longer sees itself as part of the larger society, the goals of the two systems diverge, and a competition for resources in the environment ensues.

CONFLICT AND CONSENSUS

As we have already discussed, there are two major theoretical points of view that deal with continuity and change. Functionalism is identified with the importance of maintaining social stability. **Conflict theory** is focused on the inevitability of change and the tensions that are produced by change. In considering social diversity from this perspective, it is clear that diversity is not an issue until it produces conflict within a system. When a system is confronted with conflict, processes are engaged that seek to return it to the steady state. When the steady state produces unbearable tension within the system, conflict arises between the elements of the system.

The Wrong Crowd.   Diversity in the American system adds an additional dimension to the differential opportunity model discussed previously. Edwin Sutherland, one of the first to address the problem of deviance, proposed differential association as an explanation for social deviance. Sutherland, after rejecting simpler solutions of the time, concluded that people will engage in criminal behavior when the opportunity is present and when their associations with others provides them with the skills to conduct criminal acts and the social approval for these acts. When a person's associations with those who have criminal skills and criminal inclinations are more important than their associations with those who favor noncriminal (normal) behavior, the person will tend to commit criminal acts.

The importance of this influence by association was based on four factors:

- *Frequency.* How often do you have contact?
- *Duration.* How long do contacts last?
- *Priority.* How important is the association?
- *Intensity.* What is the significance of the contact?[18]

Sutherland's model is usually understood as a cultural transmission model of deviance. It can be applied to many deviant behaviors not considered criminal in the familiar sense. The abolitionists who operated the "underground railroad" for runaway slaves were deviant in the culture of their time. They had a secret order, learned the skills of smuggling slaves to the North, and came to value their relationships with like-minded people more than the approval of the slave-holding society. While an antislavery Quaker helping free the slaves may not seem criminal now, it was at the time. Similarly, draft resisters in the era of the Vietnam War formed associations to protest the war, attack the selective service system, and change social policies. Those who opposed this effort saw this group as unquestionably criminal and seditious. Those in the resistance saw themselves as humanists. Our point is that the communications within the abolitionists and the prowar or antiwar groups would be easier and more comfortable than they would be with the opposing camp. The tendency is for like-minded individuals to talk to one another, not to those with different goals. This is sometimes referred to as "preaching to the choir." Today, this same phenomenon can be observed in talking about a subject like gay rights. Those who favor gay rights will communicate more easily with others of the same view. Those opposed will do likewise. As levels of social conflict occur, the tendency is for each group to more aggressively demonize opposing points of view. This disinclination of conflicting groups to communicate effectively with one another has sometimes been characterized as "a dialogue of the deaf."

Irreconcilable Differences. A functionalist or systems perspective might lead one to see compromise as the most adaptive response for a social system. In the conflict view, it may seem more valuable to press for increasing polarity on contentious issues. When one group in a society sees their position as one on which there is no compromise, this polarization tendency is most notable. In the 1988 presidential campaign, Gerald Ford declared himself a moderate on

abortion. Both sides of the issue howled that there could be no such thing. Some issues confront society with all-or-nothing choices that recall the old adage that "You can't cross a chasm in two small jumps." Slavery was such an issue. The legacy still plagues our society.

Parsons saw social progress taking place gradually through four stages. As noted elsewhere, Parsons is interpreted as an advocate of the status quo rather than progress. Thus, we can infer that this is an incremental model that tends to conserve as much as possible of the existing social structure. This is often referred to in political rhetoric as responsible social change. It can also serve the latent function of delaying or denying social change to excluded groups, such as occurred in the civil rights era.

- **Differentiation** (complexity of society). Society grows more complex, as occurred with the move from agrarian to industrial economic organization. Stratification increases as differentiation progresses. This reflects the negentropic process we have discussed regarding systems theory. Differentiation is a high-energy phase of social development, with a good deal of tension within the system.

- **Adaptive upgrading** (increased specialization). Role specialization increases. Men become external factory workers and women take on more expressive or nurturing functions. Specializations like worker, manager, and other service roles emerge. Society moves to more organic solidarity, with greater degrees of interdependence and less independence.

- **Inclusion** (bringing outsiders in). Elaboration of the elite power structure to include greater numbers of lower-status persons. Women and minorities reenter the decision arena. Evolution of a more egalitarian social order emerges.

- **Value generation.** Developing an inclusive value orientation to supplant the narrower and conflicting value systems of competing subcultures. In the melting pot mode, this amounted to creating an American value system out of the multiple immigrant cultural systems. A value system that is nonsexist, nonracist, and inclusive would be the ideal for this outcome.[19]

As Parsons discussed this process, he made clear that it is not automatic. Social progress is not a given, nor is it epigenetic in nature. Conflict theorists pose a less sanguine view. Marx saw social change as revolutionary rather than evolutionary. Coser saw progress developing only out of conflict.[20] As subcultures are assimilated into a society, the "border effect" clashes subside, but sometimes only at the cost of lives and treasure.

We turn now to a consideration of how social work can serve two masters: society and the oppressed. How do we fight injustice when the concept of justice is culturally relative? Who is to say what pace of social change is best? Are we on the side of the system, or the persons excluded by the system? What do we do when several oppressed groups seek the same resources or different goals? The Code of Ethics attempts to set out value-based behaviors that help us through the wilderness of a diverse and evolving society.

CONFLICT, RELIGION, AND DIVERSITY

Religion has been a central factor in the history of social conflict. While Marx and the communist system he inspired portrayed most social conflict as class warfare between the rich and the poor, the modern world is witness to religious strife as a primary factor in worldwide conflict. Elsewhere we discuss the role of religion as being paradoxical. Within any religious system, the goal of religious beliefs is to promote solidarity within the group, formulate and transmit shared values that enhance pattern maintenance, and codify belief systems in order to have them conform to other system activities. When internal dissent grows within a religion, a frequent result is schism. Since the spiritual claims upon which religions rest are by their nature unprovable by natural means, the resolution of religious differences is often accomplished by means of either separation or force.

The systemic functions of religion between groups are different from the internal function. Historically, the clashes between world religions have been savage, long lasting, and inconclusive. While religion provides a coordinating internal function for groups of believers, the between group relations are largely a matter of boundary protection and competition for resources in the suprasystem.

The history of social conflict around religious themes is prodigious. The outstanding example is the Crusades of the eleventh to thirteenth century. This ongoing endeavor sought to recapture Jerusalem from the "Saracens" or Muslims. As warriors were pressed into service against the Muslims, they also took time to murder Jews and Eastern Orthodox Christians on their way to the Middle East. The Crusades left one of the great lasting legacies of religious enmity. Even today the word *Crusader* is invoked by Muslims to characterize what was perceived as a brutal invasion by foreigners. The word *Crusade* resonates with Muslims in much the way that the Arabic word *jihad* is felt by Christians.

The Inquisition was an organized effort to enforce conformity to religious beliefs. Instituted in Spain to seek out Muslims and Jews who had supposedly converted to Christianity but who supposedly continued to practice their former religions in secret, the Inquisition was a tool of the monarchy supported by the Papacy. The use of torture to "inquire" into the religious beliefs of the victims became legendary.

World history has other examples virtually without number of extreme measures taken to oppress populations on the basis of religion. The burning of heretics such as Joan of Arc, the persecution of unorthodox beliefs such as those held by Galileo about his heliocentric theory, the genocide prosecuted against the Jews by a

German Christian regime under Hitler, the history of "the Sword and the Book" in which Spain sent missionaries and conquistadores to the New World to convert the Native Americans, the long-standing conflict between Hindus and Muslims on the Indian subcontinent that flares periodically into religious warfare and has resulted in the partition of India and Pakistan, and many more.

Less brutal but nonetheless important examples of religious intragroup and intergroup conflict can be found. Political and religious beliefs, nominally separated in the United States, have often been interwoven on important issues. Religion was invoked as a basis for rallying racial oppression in the creation of the Ku Klux Klan. The place of prayer in school has resulted in conflicting views among various religious groups. Conflicting values about issues such as abortion, birth control, and capital punishment are often cloaked in discussions about religious beliefs and employ religious documents to support the truth of a particular value position. Often, of course, the same documents are used by both sides to support a position.

What pattern can be drawn from the welter of examples briefly presented here? Several principles emerge. First, conflict and oppression on the basis of religious beliefs or membership are a continuing real problem in our society. Second, the function of religious belief systems and institutions differs depending on whether you are considering the internal instrumental function of pattern maintenance (stability) or the external function of goal attainment. Goal attainment functions, particularly among proselytic religions, are more likely to produce overt conflict and violence. Third, the ostensibly religious functions of a system are often performed in service of nonreligious elements of society. Two brief examples, one familiar, one probably not, will be used to illustrate this point.

Most of us are familiar with Max Weber's phrase, "the Protestant Ethic" that he used to describe the social value of hard work and self-reliance. Weber believed that these values, necessary to the development of a successful capitalist economic system, were given legitimacy by resort to the ideas of the Reformation, and were tied to dozens of scriptural references for support. These ideas were inconsistent with notions of greed and seeking maximum profit for minimum work. The Protestant Ethic ennobled hard work, which had sometimes been considered a curse. By embracing religious foundations for the "spirit of capitalism," the individual virtues of hard work and commercial interest were transformed into societal values ideally suited to the needs of the economic subsystems of society. This process of fusing the "sacred and profane" elements of society illustrates the principle that many subsystem functions can be viewed as holons, in this case addressing both a religious value system and an economic reality.[21]

An interesting contrast is the current school of thought called *Juche*, a nominal religion developed in North Korea under Kim Il Sung beginning in the 1950s. Juche, Korean for "self-reliance," is founded along the lines of Soviet Stalinism. It dictates that individuals are responsible for the state, and that the state should be independent from outside influences. Over time, it has been developed as doctrine that individuals may attain spiritual immortality by proper devotion to the state and Juche. Claiming more than 23 million adherents, Juche seems a clear example of the blurring of secular state interests with religious auspice. By appropriating religious language and imagery, the political leader becomes the "Great Leader" whose function is codified in the Juche faith and to whom the adherents owe both religious and political allegiance.

While Weber found that emerging capitalism had enlisted selected parts of the Christian tradition to support the secular needs of the state, the founders of Juche created a religious institution out of whole cloth to support the needs of the state. The Protestant Ethic has been important in forming social attitudes that support laissez faire capitalism, and have been important in focusing resistance to social welfare programs that seem to some to undermine individual responsibility and initiative. Juche, rather than citing existing religious traditions to support the state (many extant Eastern religions lack anything directly comparable to the individualistic Protestant Ethic), has created an institution to support the function of the communist party.

These two contrasting approaches both take advantage of what seems to be an innate human need for systems that transcend the mundane aspects of daily life. Current estimates suggest that Christianity, Islam, and Hinduism together claim more than 3 billion followers. The fourth largest group identified in world statistics is composed of the nonreligious, including atheists, agnostics and secular groups. It is clear that people "voting with their feet" find value in the spiritual/religious experience. It is equally clear that the beliefs and values that unite religious communities also set the stage for conflict between groups. In our view, the spiritual nature of human beings arises at the individual, intuitive nature, and is shaped by the religious systems that exist and compete in the individual's social environment. An understanding of the importance of human spirituality, the nature and complex functions of organized religion, and the secular uses of religion is important in grasping the development of human character and social institutions.

ETHICS AND CULTURAL DIVERSITY

The nature and complexity of cultural diversity make it difficult to determine the best way to address diversity from a professional perspective. We believe that there is no universal ethical standard (*summum bonum*) to guide us here. **Ethics** constitute a code for conduct. If there is

no universal standard, we engage our responsibilities from a normative basis. The norms of the profession rest on six core values set out in the preamble to the NASW Code of Ethics:

- Service
- Social justice
- Dignity and worth of the person
- Importance of human relationships
- Integrity
- Competence[22]

The ethical principles prescribe the behavior expected of social workers based on these values. This space does not permit a full examination of these behavioral prescriptions. It is possible to generalize about the thrust of the ethical principles set forth in the preamble. Social workers are expected to be devoted to others, to concentrate services to the vulnerable and oppressed groups in society, to pursue social change by challenging injustice, to promote social understanding and acceptance of diversity, and to promote universal equal participation in society by all groups and individuals.

In pursuit of these goals, the social worker is expected to demonstrate respect for all people, to understand human relationships as a vehicle for change, to behave honestly and responsibly, and to continually improve practice knowledge and competence. In our reading of the ethical principles—and the code overall—the thrust of the prescribed activities is toward social change. The goals are grounded in a belief in universal equality. The goals speak of equality of opportunity rather than outcome, a kind of process orientation that implies "leveling the playing field" in order for all people to achieve according to their ability. Stated in the abstract, most of these principles share the manifest goals of the dominant culture. The subtleties of these goals and the institutional resistance to change that they provoke are crucial. If social workers are to achieve these ethical objectives, they must master the subtleties of the system.

The Code of Ethics also speaks directly to the issue of cultural competence and social diversity in Section 1:05:

Cultural Competence and Social Diversity

(a) Social workers should understand culture and its function in human behavior and society, recognizing the strengths that exist in all cultures.

(b) Social workers should have a knowledge base on their client's cultures and be able to demonstrate competence in the provision of services that are sensitive to the client's cultures and to the differences among people and cultural groups.

(c) Social workers should obtain education about and seek to understand the nature of social diversity and oppression with respect to race, ethnicity, national origin, color, sex, sexual orientation, age, marital status, political belief, religion and mental or physical disability.[23]

We have addressed the fact that social stratification occurs on the basis of many different attributes of cultural groups. There is no scientific way to identify which dimensions should be given priorities. The NASW ethical perspective emerged as part of a political process that identified eleven dimensions of diversity. Many of the dimensions that follow are not mutually exclusive.

1. *Race* is a complex dimension of diversity. The existence of injustice based on perceived race is a historical fact. Race, as a biological fact, changes as society changes. The biological distinctions between races have altered due to racial mixing. While biological bases for stratification are weakening, institutional racism continues. Segregationists feared this reality, which they sneeringly called "mongrelization" of the races because it would blur the lines that allowed for racial coercion. The so-called "Tiger Woods factor" illustrates our point that it is not race per se that defines stratification. You may recall that golfer Tiger Woods, when asked how it felt to be the first Black winner of a major golf tournament, deflected the question by identify-

ing himself as a "Cablanasian," his own personal mixture of Caucasian, Black, Native American, and Asian ancestry. This response angered some minority groups, who saw Woods as the sort of cultural star who could elevate the social status of a minority group. Woods's insistence on his individual heritage diluted the collective agenda of groups seeking to advance social recognition of minorities as groups.

2. *Ethnicity* (from the Greek *ethnos* for "nation") refers to groups characterized by various traits. These include language, national or geographic origin, customs, religion, and race. This comes closest to our view of subcultures, since it includes normative groups whose shared sense of identity cuts across various dimensions used for classification. In the United States, this would include such groups as Swedes, Jews, Muslims, African Americans, Indians, Mexican Americans, and so forth. In each case, ethnic group membership might involve a complex of traits shared by members.

3. *National origin* refers to the nation of birth. However, national origin may continue as a dimension of stratification for many generations if distinctive subcultures persist. The melting-pot model originally addressed the goal of subsuming groups of differing national origin into a common American identity. The melting-pot approach was much more successful in addressing differences of national origin than in addressing race.

4. *Color* would seem to be synonymous with race. However, anthropologists have noted that color in many parts of the world is a basis for social stratification even within identifiable racial groups. For example, immigrants to the United States from Southern European countries had darker skin than the Northern Europeans. The Southern Europeans were relegated to a lower social status. In the complex society of multiracial and multicultural New Orleans in the 1950s, African American social gatherings sometimes imposed the "brown paper bag test." For people whose skin was darker than the grocery bag, admission was denied. The principle at work was that in a racist dominant culture, even within minority racial groups, the darker skin hues were a basis for discrimination. The "Black Pride" movement addressed this feature of oppression by celebrating the achievements of people of color.

5. *Sex*, as used here, refers to gender. In twentieth century America, women began to recognize their shared oppressed status. Women as an oppressed group faced a unique challenge. Unlike racial groups, women were truly integrated into American culture. Women shared the social status of their husbands and fathers. They lived in the same cities, neighborhoods, and homes. The "consciousness raising" that took place in trying to alert women to the hidden practices of employment discrimination, violence against women, vulnerability to poverty, and related issues was complex. One problem was that high-status women did not easily accept their shared status with poor women of different ethnic groups. We consider this as the primary example of a latent group. Women had social concerns in common, but the organization of society obscured their commonalities. Pattern maintenance activities by the dominant culture (and here we include women who identified with the sexist status quo) sought to stigmatize feminist women as lesbians, bra burners, man haters, or worse. The enormous discrepancies in the condition of women made shared identity and collective action difficult.

6. *Sexual orientation* refers to the sexual partners to whom one is attracted or with whom one has sexual intimacy. This minority culture consists of *gays*, a term usually referring to men but sometimes used to refer to both men and women; lesbians, women whose partners of choice are other women; and bisexuals, who have sexual interest or activity with both men

and women. This group is excluded on the basis of orientation or activity. This culture based on behavior is different from the other dimensions of oppression identified thus far. Sexual orientation has been more stigmatized than other minority cultures. The ability to conceal one's sexual orientation to escape social stigma creates unique problems with this group. Many high-status members of this group historically remained "in the closet," protecting their social status by distancing themselves from the minority community. Many gay people had same-sex relationships, but did not identify with the subculture. The process of "outing," in which a person's minority sexual orientation is made public against the person's will, is a form of social activism that has produced great controversy. As a value issue, outing violates individual preference in favor of group interests, which tends to violate one of the dominant culture beliefs regarding the primacy of the individual.[24]

7. *Age* addresses the social vulnerability of the older person. Old age carries with it increasing risk of disease or infirmity, frequent loss of occupational status, and loss of both intimate partners and many family roles. In a dominant culture that places a high value on economic productivity, old people become less productive and hence less valued. The weakening of family networks has produced the view that nuclear families must choose between child care and care of aging parents. Americans are living longer and healthier lives, extending productivity but also increasing the economic burdens of geriatric illness. People tend to make highly disproportionate demands on the health care system in the last years of life, to cite but one problematic example. Health concerns and poverty are the two factors that most unite this minority culture. As with gender, intragroup differences have made the development of a subcultural identity for the aging difficult. Strangely, a great deal of stigma has been attached to aging, even though it is a universal process.

8. *Marital status* has been mentioned relative to gender. Marriage is the preferred dominant culture institution for providing intimate relationships (not merely sex) and caring for children. Marital status has served to obscure sexual discrimination against women. Until late in the twentieth century, marital status virtually indemnified men from responsibility for sexual, physical, or emotional violence against women. The positives of marriage have to do with its recognized status in society, its productivity in child raising, as a unit of consumption, and as an adaptable system for providing a context of emotional and nurturing relationships. Sexual orientation minorities have sought recognition of their relationships as marital in nature or at least equivalent in terms of social benefits linked to marriage. The dominant culture has been relatively intolerant in allowing variations in the structure of marriage. The notable exception is increasing acceptance of divorce and the virtual institutionalization of a pattern of serial marriage.

9. *Political belief* is identified as a basis for discrimination since the open political system is culturally valued. Earlier we described the democratic principles as one of the advantages of modern Western society. There is a constant tendency to redefine the rules of politics to the advantage of one group or another. Most often, the direction of this change is toward pattern maintenance, since those who make the rules are insiders with the most to gain from the status quo. Political discrimination has most often been directed against economic change movements, such as socialism, or social change movements, such as the civil rights voter registration movement. Episodes such as the McCarthyism of the 1950s demonstrate that when the dominant culture perceives a threat to its existence or stability, it will take extreme actions that violate cultural values. This process usually involves demonizing the target of discrimination.

10. *Religion* requires little discussion in this context. Religious freedom is a founding principle of the dominant culture. Religious oppression tends to occur when religious practice involves some activity not seen in the dominant culture as a legitimate spiritual issue. Examples have included Mormon polygamy, which resulted in oppression and violence. Ultimately, this practice had to be foregone for the Church of the Latter-Day Saints to be accepted into the dominant culture. African American churches were frequent targets of violence in the civil rights movement since these churches were the focus of political as well as spiritual activities. Synagogues are periodic targets of hate violence. The use of hallucinogens in the Native American Church resulted in challenges as to whether the NAC was a true church. Pacifist churches, such as the Mennonites and Quakers, have an on-again, off-again degree of acceptance depending on current political conditions. Since spirituality is a universal consideration in human society, religious institutions can be expected to always present some conflicts between dominant and minority religious views. We regard it as evident that religious tolerance is not a given in the dominant culture, but always an expression that requires protection.

11. *Mental or physical disability* is a complex issue as it relates to equal opportunity. Physical or mental conditions requiring consideration conflict with two dominant cultural values. The first is equality and the second is self-reliance. The law requires "reasonable accommodation" of the needs of people with disabilities. Accommodations, reasonable or not, place some burden on others. Accommodations may also carry the implication that the person with a disability enjoys advantages denied the person who is able-bodied. Cultural stars, such as the disabled physicist Stephen Hawking or the schizophrenic mathematician John Forbes Nash, Jr., have two effects: they increase awareness of the potentials of persons with disabilities, but they also may produce unrealistic expectations and demands that serve the latent function of encouraging continued discrimination against this group. Spirited debate continues regarding who should be considered disabled. The stigma attached to this group, the absence of a common condition or circumstance, and economic implications for the system combine to make this a difficult issue of social justice.

Poverty

The poor are not included in this listing of vulnerable groups. Poverty is addressed in the NASW's general ethical principles, along with unemployment and discrimination. Whatever the basis of discrimination, poverty is the frequent result. No matter what theory of human behavior one embraces, the impact of poverty is catastrophic. Social work addresses poverty as both process and outcome. Programs such as income maintenance and health care provide relief to the poor. Social services aid the poor in becoming self-reliant participants in the system. It is common to observe bogus theories that attempt to explain human traits that are more easily understood as products of poverty. It is our view that poverty does not constitute a culture, but that it is the artifact of cultural processes of injustice and discrimination. People who are free to choose may align themselves with whatever beliefs and social arrangements they wish. If social arrangements are imposed on people to their detriment, social workers are ethically compelled to challenge the social processes that perpetuate the system.

SUMMARY

In this chapter, we discussed the issue of cultural diversity from a social systems perspective. Diversity is understood from the standpoint of culture as a "social fact." The objective facts of difference are less important than the degree to which those who share a common trait come together to form a cultural identity. The philosophy of modernism forms the foundation for a scientific worldview. Postmodernism sees the world in terms of cultures that are different but equally valid. The result is cultural relativism, which requires that all behavior be seen and understood as taking place in a specific cultural context.

Functionalism stresses the forces that maintain stability in a culture. Conflict theory stresses the tensions that result from difference and the processes that arise to deal with those tensions.

All societies tend to create hierarchies of social status based on individual traits. Society is differentiated on a wide range of attributes. Selecting which of those attributes to target is a philosophical or political problem and is addressed in the context of social work ethics.

The ethical code seems to incline toward the definition of social work functions as an agent of change rather than of stability. There are clear ethical and value commitments to the oppressed groups at lower social strata.

GLOSSARY

Achieved status   A social position or role to which one is assigned on the basis of individual acts and abilities; it may be positive or negative.

Adaptive upgrading   In functional theory, the process of increasing role specialization as a society becomes more organic and less mechanical.

Ascribed status   A social position or role to which one is assigned on the basis of traits over which the individual has no control.

Boundary effect   The turbulence created at the interface between two systems or subsystems. This effect results in energy loss and distortion in intersystem transactions.

Closed system   A system in which boundaries are relatively impermeable. In society, it usually connotes a system of rigid stratification or social hierarchy.

Conflict theory   The sociological view that maintains that conflict between social subsystems is natural and inevitable. In this view, progress only occurs as an outgrowth of conflict.

Culture The pattern of beliefs, values, norms, and goals accepted by a social group.

Differentiation In functional theory, the first stage in the evolution of a society, in which the society moves to a more complex or organic mode of interdependency subsystems.

Dominant culture The group in society that has the means to enforce its values or expectations on minority cultures.

Dysfunction An activity within a system that serves no purpose, whether manifest or latent.

Ethics A code of conduct for a group based on the shared values of the group.

Functionalism A sociological perspective that views society as an organic whole made up of interrelated parts. Functionalism is usually interpreted as advocating system stability and gradual, incremental changes.

Inclusion In functional theory, the process of opening the system structure to formerly excluded individuals or groups.

Infusion The process of a minority culture gaining access to the decision-making positions of a dominant culture.

Latent function The informal and often hidden functions of a system. Informal functions may lack formal structure or defined processes. For example, a latent function of education may be to provide respite to parents from the duties of child care.

Manifest function The formal and culturally accepted functions of a system usually with recognized structures for accomplishing the function. For example, the manifest function of public education is to teach children.

Minority culture The groups in society whose values, beliefs, and goals differ from the dominant culture.

Modernism The philosophical school that advocates rationality and science, among other features. Modernism emerged as the worldview of the Industrial Revolution and Western industrial culture.

Open system A system that allows relatively easy movement across system borders. In society, it usually connotes a condition of easy social mobility.

Postmodernism The worldview that emerged in the 1960s and 1970s, seeing cultural perspectives as different but equally valid. Based on subjectivity rather than objective science, this is the basis of cultural relativity.

Stigma A social response to specific traits of an individual or group. Stigma assigns the stigmatized person or group to a lower-social status, termed a "spoiled identity."

Stratification The organization of a society into a status hierarchy, with a disproportionate distribution of social benefits and costs to the various strata.

Subculture A group within a larger culture whose beliefs, values, norms, and goals differ in some degree from those of the larger dominant culture.

Value generation The final stage of functional system development, in which tolerant and inclusive value systems are developed for behavior.

Values The perspective of an individual or group regarding what conditions are good or worthwhile.

NOTES

1. Shirley Zimmerman, *Family Policy: Constructed Solutions to Family Problems* (Thousand Oaks, CA: Sage, 2001).

2. David Elkind, *Ties That Stress: The New Family Imbalance* (Cambridge, MA: Harvard University Press, 1994).

3. W. Doherty, *Postmodernism and Family Theory* (St. Paul, MN: University of Minnesota Family Services, 1997).

4. A. L. Kroeber and C. Kluckhon, "Culture: A Critical Review of Concepts and Definitions," *Papers of the Peabody Museum of American Archeology and Ethnology* 47:1(1952): 181.

5. M. M. Gordon, "The Concept of the Sub-Culture and Its Application," *Social Forces*, vol. 26 (1947): 40.

6. R. Benedict, *Patterns of Culture* (London: Routledge, 1935), 278.

7. R. Piven and R. Cloward, *Regulating the Poor: The Functions of Public Welfare* (New York: Vintage, 1993, updated).

8. R. Merton, *Social Theory and Social Structure* (Glencoe, IL: Free Press, 1968).

9. A. Billingsley, *Black Families in White America* (New York: Simon & Schuster, 1988).

10. Ibid.

11. E. Goffman, *Behavior in Public Places: Notes on Social Organization of Gatherings* (Glencoe, IL: Free Press, 1963).

12. A. Gouldner, "The Norm of Reciprocity," *American Sociological Review* 25 (April 1964): 161–177.

13. E. Goffman, *Stigma: Notes on the Management of a Spoiled Identity* (Englewood Cliffs, NJ: Prentice-Hall, 1963).

14. Ibid.

15. Gouldner, "The Norm of Reciprocity," 161–177.

16. Merton, *Social Theory and Social Structure*.

17. Alex Haley, *The Autobiography of Malcolm X* (New York: Ballantine, 1992).

18. D. Sutherland and D. Cressey, *Principles of Criminology*, 10th ed. (Philadelphia: Lippincott, 1978).

19. T. Parsons, "General Theory in Sociology." In R. Merton, L. Broom, and L. Cottrell, eds., *Sociology Today* (New York: Basic Books, 1959).

20. L. Coser, *The Functions of Social Conflict* (New York: Free Press, 1956).

21. Max Weber, *The Protestant Ethic and the Spirit of Capitalism* (New York: Scribner's Press, 1958).

22. National Association of Social Workers, *Code of Ethics* (Washington, DC: NASW Press, 1996).

23. Ibid.

24. H. Gochros and J. Gochros, *The Sexually Oppressed* (New York: Association Press, 1997).

PART TWO

THE INDIVIDUAL

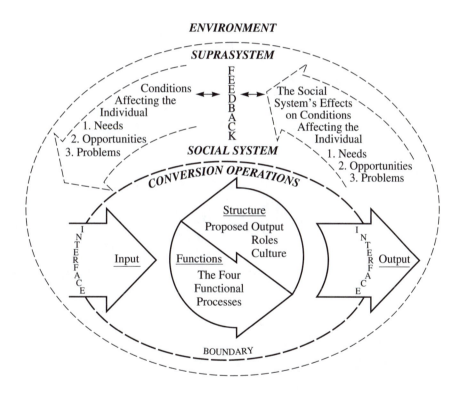

CHAPTER 5

THE INDIVIDUAL
THEORIES OF PSYCHOLOGY
USED BY SOCIAL WORKERS

PSYCHOANALYTIC/PSYCHODYNAMIC THEORY

BEHAVIORISM/LEARNING THEORY

COGNITIVE DEVELOPMENT THEORY

MORAL DEVELOPMENT THEORY

COGNITIVE-BEHAVIORAL THEORY

HUMANISM

SYMBOLIC INTERACTION THEORY

SUMMARY

GLOSSARY

NOTES

In this chapter, we review theories relevant to the generalist practice of social work as well as to advanced forms of direct practice. We have identified the assumption that the individual should be viewed as both the cause and the effect of all forms of human association. While this book examines in detail these reciprocal effects, an understanding of the individual as a separate and distinct human personality is crucial in all forms of social work practice. From our perspective, the individual in a role is always a member of a social system. Each of us has a physical, psychological, spiritual, and social existence. We are each a whole, and it is the interplay of these four subsystems that comprises the complete human experience.

A useful place to start our review of psychological theory and its interface with sociology is to draw a distinction between the two disciplines. Recall that both of these social sciences, like all other sciences, grew out of the study of philosophy. We humans have always been curious and have sought to understand the world around us as well as the purpose of human existence. As our knowledge increased, there was a movement toward the development of specialty areas of inquiry; sociology and psychology are two of the many domains of science that have evolved over the centuries.

Sociology is a science of human social organization and social processes. The focus has tended to be macro, with primary attention given to human societies. The word "*sociology*" was coined by Auguste Comte (1798–1857) as he sought to define a new social science. The tie between this new science and the older physical sciences is evidenced by his reference to sociology as "social physics."[1]

Psychology is a science of human and animal behavior. While the focus of psychology is on human behavior, the study of lower forms of animal life has been critically important in the development of this field.[2] For many psychologists, the study of lower and simpler forms of

animal life has important implications in understanding human behavior.

In organizing our approach, a decision had to be made about which psychological theories to include and how to classify them. A myriad of theories exists with no widely accepted classification system. Our approach was guided by a judgment as to the practice utility of these theories and their usefulness in terms of the development of social systems theory.

We have categorized the theories to be reviewed in this chapter as follows: (1) psychoanalytic/psychodynamic, (2) behaviorism/learning, (3) cognitive development, (4) moral development, (5) cognitive-behavioral theory, (6) humanism, and (7) symbolic interactionism. It is important to distinguish between a line of theory development and a particular theorist. Suffice it to say that within any of the above classifications there will, in most instances, be a number of different theorists, each with a particular area of emphasis or interest. In presenting each of these lines of theory development, we will provide an introduction including some brief historical data about the leading theorist(s), a statement of focus, and an identification of key assumptions and concepts. Then through a summary, we will identify its implications in the use of the social systems perspective and its contribution to the practice of social work.[3]

PSYCHOANALYTIC/PSYCHODYNAMIC THEORY

We start our discussion with psychoanalytic theory for two reasons: the historical importance of psychoanalytic theory and the critical impact this line of theory development has had on the profession of social work. Sigmund Freud was one of the last century's greatest thinkers, and for many years psychoanalytic theory was the dominating influence in psychology. Psychoanalytic theory greatly influenced the development of the behavioral and social sciences generally, and in Western culture specifically.

Social work was in a very formative stage of development when psychoanalytic theory impacted psychology and psychiatry in this country. The influence was particularly strong in social casework, the dominant practice method in social work for much of its history.[4] Psychoanalytic theory provided social work with a theoretical base to practice, and the role of the psychoanalyst/psychiatrist was one to emulate.

We have labeled this section *Psychoanalytic/ Psychodynamic Theory*, and for the most part, we will be organizing content around the theory as it was developed by Freud. As with other theories, there are a number of variations; most of the important ones were developed by students and colleagues of Freud. This general cluster of theories is frequently referred to as psychodynamic theory. **Psychodynamic** simply refers to cognitive, emotional, and motivational processes that consciously and unconsciously affect one's behavior. Before proceeding, we should also note that **psychoanalysis** is the method of treatment based on psychoanalytic theory.

Sigmund Freud (1856–1939) is the acknowledged founder of psychoanalytic theory. He was born in Freiberg, Moravia. At the age of four, he and his family moved to Vienna where he spent all but the last year of his life. Educated as a physician, his interest was research, particularly in the area of neurology. His fascination with the problem of hysteria eventually led to the development of psychoanalytic theory.[5]

Several things are important in tracking the development of psychoanalytic theory. First, its founder, Freud, was a physician, not a social scientist. His training was in the physical sciences as was his orientation as a researcher. Second, he lived and practiced in Vienna during the latter part of the nineteenth and beginning of the twentieth centuries. The historical and cultural influences of this time affected his theory de-

velopment. Third, Freud's theory building was grounded in his direct practice with patients who were largely women drawn from the middle and upper classes. In short, his theory was developed largely from clinical sources rather than from experimentation. His subjects were troubled people, not the mentally healthy.

Focus

Psychoanalysis can be categorized as a general theory of individual behavior due to its scope. It is a comprehensive theory dealing with intrapsychic determinants of behavior (motivation), psychopathology, and the treatment of psychopathology. There is little in the way of psychological behavior that cannot be explained by this theory.

Assumptions

The following five assumptions are those that we consider to be fundamental to this line of theory development.

1. The primary determinants of behavior arise from sexual and aggressive drives.
2. Behavior stems from unconscious determinants.
3. Development is in accordance with the epigenetic principle and is associated with sexual maturation.
4. All behavior is purposive.
5. Behavior is in accordance with the "pleasure principle," the maximization of pleasure and minimization of pain.

In thinking about the assumptions undergirding psychoanalytic theory, we would like to again emphasize that Freud was a physician and his education was in the physical sciences. It is also important to keep in mind the state of science in the latter part of the 1800s. Freud was also influenced, like many of the other scientists of his time, by the work of Charles Darwin and the process of natural selection.[6]

Evolutionary theory is based on the assumption that natural laws exist that apply to all forms of life. Unlike humanists, evolutionists are concerned with what humans have in common with all life forms; humans are animals and will exhibit patterns of behavior and development based on natural laws. For example, psychoanalytic theory incorporates the epigenetic development principle. The basic notion is borrowed from embryology and holds that organisms develop from an undifferentiated mass (fertilized egg) through a series of fixed stages to a mature state. These stages are separate and distinct, and no stage is ever skipped. Difficulties in one stage will tend to have adverse developmental consequences in subsequent stages. The latter point becomes especially important if the problem in development at a particular stage occurs early in that stage. For example, the organism's heart will be the first organ to form and function, followed shortly by the brain and spinal cord. Difficulties affecting the development of the heart and central nervous system, especially early in the development of either stage, will have severe consequences to the developing fetus.

Freud extended the epigenetic principle to the psychosexual development of the human and postulated five stages of development.[7] Other theorists operating from the same assumption have advanced additional stages. For example, Erikson's developmental theory has eight stages[8] and Newman and Newman have eleven, spanning the "prenatal to very old age."[9] It should be noted that as theorists have added stages they have also addressed the interplay between the individual as a physical and psychological being and the individual's social environment. In so doing, they have narrowed the gap between so-called psychological and sociological theories of human behavior.

Freudian, or what might be termed classical, psychoanalytic theory, assumes the existence of unconscious determinants of behavior.

The unconscious can be likened to a life force composed of sexual and aggressive impulses. In fact, all behavior is assumed to have its origins in these animal-like instinctive impulses.[10]

Concepts

Freud was interested in the psychic determinants of behavior. Our review of the key concepts of psychoanalytic theory will be organized under the five structural categories of these determinants. The five areas are (1) levels of consciousness, (2) structures of the mind, (3) stages of development, (4) dynamics, and (5) well-being.

Levels of Consciousness.   Freud was interested in what he called a study of personality. His emphasis was on hidden or unknown factors in personality development and human behavior. This led him and his colleagues to develop an elaborate model of the psyche, which proposed a number of strictures and processes that remain the focus of controversy today. Freud identified three levels of thought: unconscious, preconscious, and conscious.

Unconscious.   It may be fairly stated that the primary area of interest for Freud was the unconscious. The **unconscious** is the seat of innate, primal forces that are present at birth. These instinctual forces provide the driving force that motivates the behavior of the individual.

The primary unconscious energy of the personality Freud termed the *libido* (Latin for "desire"). This is the energy of what Freud considered the life force. In his early writing, Freud considered the libido to be mainly sexual. Later, he revised the concept so that libido became associated with all the life instincts.

By the end of the First World War, Freud was appalled at the scope of the death and devastation. He became convinced that human nature could not be explained solely by a life energy. He posited another instinctual force, which has come to be called the *death instinct* or *thanatos* (Greek for "death"). Freud himself never gave a specific name to these impulses. The death instincts were presumed to alternate with the life instinct in personality dynamics. Libido gave rise to love and social behaviors. Thanatos gave rise to aggression and sadistic behaviors. These innate impulses could alternate, fuse, or neutralize one another.

While the instincts of libido and thanatos are unconscious, they come to expression in the conscious processes of the ego and the superego.

Conscious.   While the instincts operate at the unconscious level, the ability of the personality to perceive and experience external reality takes place in the **conscious**. The ego is mainly conscious and guides the purposeful acts of the personality. The effects of the unconscious instincts are not available to the conscious self.

The ability of the personality to make choices based on perception and information is a manifestation of consciousness. While emotions are present in the conscious mind, the distinctive part of consciousness is rational thought.

When instinctual impulses become too uncomfortable for the conscious mind, awareness of these impulses is **repressed.** Repression is defined as the process of forcing thoughts out of conscious awareness and back into the unconscious whence they arose. Repression becomes the fundamental notion in Freud's concept of ego defense mechanisms.

Preconscious.   Between the unconscious and the conscious mind, there lay a zone Freud called the **preconscious**. Material in the preconscious can be called into consciousness without special effort. It may be as simple as focusing awareness in the proper area. Unlike repressed material, preconscious material need not be composed of emotionally laden thoughts. Repressed material tends to be available only with the aid of dream interpretation, hypnosis, or free association.

Structures of the Mind.   In his later work, Freud moved from his discussion of consciousness to a more structured view of the psyche. To the confusion of some, the concepts of the unconscious, preconscious, and conscious mind evolved into the personality structures, which Freud called the *id* (Latin for "it"), the *ego* (Latin for "self"), and the *superego* (Latin for "Over Self"). As Hall described this development of theory, "In the mentally healthy person, these three systems form a unified and harmonious organization. By working together they enable the individual to carry on efficient and satisfying transactions with his environment. The purpose of these transactions is the fulfillment of man's basic needs and desires. Conversely, when these three systems of the personality are at odds with one another, the person is said to be maladjusted. He is dissatisfied with himself and the world, and his efficiency is reduced."[11]

Id.   The **id** contains one's inherited instinctual urges. It is the primitive, unconscious part of the human personality, driven by the pleasure principle. The concept of id is understood in terms of biological and evolutionary origins. The id is comprised of aggressive and sexual impulses. These impulses are to be understood in terms of their survival purposes, that is, perpetuation of the species through survival and reproduction.

Ego.   The **ego** arises from the id due to socialization. While drawing its energy from the id, the ego is guided by the reality principle, the recognition of the behavioral demands of the external world. The notion of the ego in psychoanalytic theory contains the recognition that a person has the capacity to think, to learn, to reason, and to adjust behaviors to the social environment. This cognitive capacity represents an important building block used by later theorists.

Superego.   The **superego** is the third of the three subsystems comprising the mind's structure. It can be likened to an incorporation within the person of parental attitudes and more generally of existing cultural standards. Sometimes the superego is likened to one's conscience. The superego chastises the ego for doing things deemed wrong. In another sense, the superego can be likened to an *ego ideal*, a standard or conception of what the person can become with effort. The superego does give evidence of attention to the environmental effects on the individual and the evolution of a morality system that impacts on behavior.

Interplay The ego is the mediator between the id and the superego, pushed from both sides but guided by its own logic and sense of reality. The ego may be strong or weak, and here the practice implications most clearly emerge. Freud also developed a series of concepts dealing with the means used by the ego to defend against the impulses of the id and the unrealistic expectations of the superego. These he termed **defense mechanisms.** Much of human behavior can be viewed as defensive in nature. There is a struggle among one's more basal, primitive impulses; unrealistically high expectations for one's self; and an ever-changing environment.

Alexander and Ross summarize Freud's structure of the mind and the interplay of the id, ego, and superego as follows:

> The id is the original powerhouse of the mental apparatus; it contains the inherited instinctive forces which at birth are not yet organized into a coordinated system. The ego is conceived as a product of development which consists in the adaptation of the inherited instinctive drives to one another and to the environment. The superego . . . represents the incorporation of parental attitudes which are determined by the existing cultural standards. After maturation, the ego becomes the dynamic center of behavior. . . . The ego's function . . . is to carry out . . . coordinated rational behavior and is aimed at maintaining a constant condition . . . within the organism. . . . In satisfying biological needs and in defending the organism against excessive external stimulation, the ego performs its homeostatic tasks with the help of four basic faculties: (1) internal perception of instinctive needs, (2) external perception of existing conditions upon which the gratification of subjective needs depends, (3) the integrative faculty by which the ego coordinates instinctive urges with one another and with the requirements of the super-

ego and adapts them to environmental conditions, and (4) the executive faculty by which it controls voluntary behavior.[12]

Stages of Development. A key assumption in psychoanalytic theory is that development is consistent with the epigenetic principle. The concept of developmental stages in psychoanalytic theory is based on the contention that human sexuality develops in fixed stages and that these stages provide a foundation for the psychological development of the human. The focus in psychoanalytic theory is psychosexual development, not physical, psychological, or psychosocial development. The attachment of libido to a specific part of the body results in the creation of an erogenous zone or an area that, when stimulated, elicits highly pleasurable feelings. In short, classical psychoanalytic theory holds that there is a specific sequence in the development of erogenous zones. This general development pattern is merely part of the comprehensive maturational process guided by innate, biological factors.

Freud identified five stages in this development sequence: (1) oral, (2) anal, (3) phallic, (4) latency, and (5) genital.[13]

Oral Stage. The **oral stage** covers the period from birth to about eighteen months of age. Initiated by the sucking reflex, the infant not only feeds but also derives pleasure from the sucking process itself. The newborn has no conception of self or others, but the development of this vital social process is started through the taking of nourishment. The oral period is of fundamental importance to the infant's development. Here a relationship prototype begins that will have significance throughout life: the nourishing, caring, and protection offered by a mother or mother surrogate. In accordance with the epigenetic principle, problems in this stage of development have severe implications for subsequent stages and the general development of the human personality.

Anal Stage.   Next in sequence is the **anal stage.** It starts around the eighteenth month and lasts until the child is about three years old. Now the anal region becomes energized with libido and the infant turns his or her attention to the pleasures associated with bowel movements and the fecal products produced. Guided by id impulses, the child will express pleasure by handling and smearing his or her feces. The parents, of course, are less than enamored of this expression of pleasure and the socialization struggle starts in earnest.

The anal period coincides with the infant's growing capacity to differentiate himself or herself from the rest of the world. The infant's mother and other caregivers become objects in their own right. They become sources of pleasure and sometimes pain. Up to this point the infant has little control over life, but through the eroticism associated with the anal area, things begin to change. The young child now has something important to control, bowel movements. An important struggle develops, one that is deemed to have far-reaching implications in terms of the child's development. On the one hand, there are the id-related impulses associated with the pleasure of bowel movements and the play with feces; and on the other, there are the child's parents who are likely to have some distaste for anal matters. They will soon seek to impose their views on behavior on their child. Thus, toilet training will start.

The parents are far too powerful and the child will lose in the resulting struggle. Sometimes the problems associated with this period are essentially resolved. Sometimes they are not, and this leaves scars on the developing personality. The progressive development through these life stages is marred by problems, and the ego capacities or defenses are weakened. The ego acquires new and more sophisticated and effective defense mechanisms for successfully dealing with the special problems posed in each stage of psychosexual development. To the extent that this is not the case, the ego will have

growing difficulties contending with the ongoing battle between the id and the evolving superego.

Phallic Stage.   The **phallic stage,** sometimes termed the **Oedipal stage,** starts at around age three and lasts until age six or so. At this time, the genital area becomes the important erogenous zone. Freud and many of his followers gave greater theoretical attention to the problems confronting the boy during this period than the girl. According to Freud, the young boy takes ever greater interest in his penis and the pleasure it gives him. The boy also takes an interest in the sexual equipment of others, both boys and girls. Now, more than earlier, psychological development takes a somewhat different track for males and females.[14]

Freud's use of the Oedipal complex that confronts boys at this time is instructive. Typically the boy's mother is his first love object; she has been his primary caregiver and he feels pleasure in her presence. His pleasure should not be thought of as an adult form of sexuality, but is nevertheless sexual in character. The young boy may want to continue to sleep with his mother but will be told "you're getting too big—you need to sleep in your own bed." What is not entirely clear to the child in this logic is why his father can sleep with his mother but he cannot. But, as with the struggle in the anal stage, the child is destined to lose this battle also. To make a long story short, the boy wishes to possess his mother but cannot. His father is the rival for his mother's love. Both his father's size and cultural prohibitions will make the boy's battle a lost cause. Important from a developmental perspective is the crisis created by the boy's sexual strivings for his mother and the reality that he cannot have her. Many aggressive and sexual fantasies plague the young boy. He must learn to deal with this crisis and typically does so by repressing these feelings, that is, by burying them in his unconscious. At the same time, helping the child is a constantly growing superego, the internalization of parental and cultural prohibitions.

The young girl goes through similar experiences, but her attachment is to her father or his surrogate. Like her male counterpart, she experiences competitive feelings toward the parent of the same sex. In the case of the young girl, this period is often referred to as comprising the **Electra complex.**

Latency Stage. The next stage is one of comparative quiet and is labeled the **latency stage.** By now, the normally developing child has acquired a good ego-based defense structure and the power of the id-related aggressive and sexual impulses have become latent. This stage typically coincides with the start of school and lasts until puberty. Temporarily freed from the impulses of the id, the child can direct his or her energies outward toward the world. Typically, this is a time of learning and mastery.

Genital Stage. The latency period comes to an abrupt halt with the onset of puberty. For girls, this is roughly at age eleven and for boys puberty begins at about thirteen. The individual has entered the genital stage. Sexual feelings swell inside, but now both the girl and the boy are prepared in terms of their physical equipment to find a release for their sexual impulses. But the problem is more complicated; not only are cultural and social barriers to be confronted but also past and repressed feelings as well. The ego's defense mechanisms are severely tested. From a psychoanalytic and developmental theory perspective, this is a difficult, perhaps the most difficult, period in a person's life.

According to Freudian thought, the **genital phase** is the final stage in psychosexual development. The adolescent must deal with the reawakened Oedipal and Electra impulses. It is a difficult time for both the adolescent and the family. Typically the resolution is accomplished by the selection of a permanent sexual partner, marriage, and movement away from parents.

In classical psychoanalytic theory, the early years are the formative ones. The basic personality is formed early. Freud had little to say about adult experiences; these experiences are deemed to have little effect on the person's basic personality structure. However, life's stresses and strains will tend to stir up earlier, unresolved conflicts, which may tax the individual's defense mechanisms. Regression to an earlier developmental stage can occur.

The strength and capacities of these defense mechanisms are to be understood in terms of the previously mentioned life stages. As evidenced by Freud's clinical practice, some of these problems can be disabling, resulting in the development of neuroses or psychoses.

Dynamics. Central to psychoanalytic theory is the notion of a life force, energy of genetic origin that takes the form of instinctual sexual and aggressive impulses; these forces are constantly striving for expression. This force in humans results in the structuring of the mind into the id, ego, and superego. The basic maturational sequence that guides all animal development also affects this life force. In other words, the dynamics of human behavior have their origins in these sexual and aggressive drives, but their expression in behavior is modified by the interplay of the id, ego, and superego, and by the psychosexual stage of one's development.

Well-being. Psychoanalytic theory has its origins in the study of mentally troubled people. No central concept exists that deals with a state of health or well-being. However, two related concepts pertain to the direction, conservation, and management of psychic energy: the pleasure principle and the reality principle.

Pleasure Principle. In formulating psychoanalytic theory, Freud advanced the **pleasure principle,** which he considered to be of genetic origin. Simply stated, the principle holds that organisms seek pleasure and avoid pain by the immediate discharge of their instinctive drives and tension states.

Reality Principle. Controlling the pleasure principle is the **reality principle.** Just as the pleasure principle guides the behavior of the id, the reality principle guides the behavior of the ego. The ego comprehends the demands and expectations of the environment. The reality principle is based on the recognition of the demands of the real world and of the fact that one's behavior needs to be adjusted to this reality. In effect, the ego finds ways of postponing the immediate forms of gratification related to the pleasure principle in order to deal with the constraints imposed by those with which one has to get along.

A typical example used to illustrate these contending principles is the behavior of the young child. The youngster seeks immediate gratification of impulses. The child soon learns that this pursuit of instant gratification can lead to serious problems with parents. Parents, in turn, are very powerful and can discipline in ways that are quite unpleasant. Here the adventuresome child learns about reality. As ego is strengthened, the reality principle gains dominance, but not control, over the pleasure principle.

Well-being, in a manner of speaking, is a state of equilibrium. The internal drives based on the pleasure principle are countered by the ego's adaptive arrangements, which in turn are based on the reality principle. These two principles and their opposing actions are reflective of the homeostatic conception of well-being embodied in psychoanalytic theory.

Psychoanalysis and Religion

There has long been tension between established religious views and many behavioral scientists. Freud was a notable cause of such tensions. He interpreted doctrines and rituals in terms of his own theory. One of the criticisms of Freud has been that he extended his principles, derived from the study of pathological people, to the arena of world religion.

Freud scorned religion as the universal neurosis of mankind. In his view, religion served to provide an escape from fear and uncertainty, particularly in relation to death. Many religious beliefs, including belief in God, Freud understood as projections of family life onto a cosmic stage. Freud used his notion of the mind to dismiss religious belief as a neurotic security blanket.

Not all members of the analytic school were as cynical as Freud. Carl Jung is frequently identified as one of the major twentieth-century figures in psychiatry who was most open to spirituality in the human experience. The broader outlines of Jungian theory are well known. Those that are usually related to spirituality have to do with the collective unconscious and the numinous.

Jung believed that the collective unconscious, most notably the archetypes, were part of a shared human memory. According to Jung, the archetypes provided a transpersonal means of adapting to a personal environment. Jung has inspired continuing spiritual inquiry into the nature of the collective unconscious, even crossing over into the realm of investigations into possible genetic means of transmitting such experiences.

Jung viewed the numinous as a change in consciousness due to an encounter with spiritual power. He posited that an encounter with the numinous might be positive or negative, depending on the character of the person. He felt a damaged psyche might distort the numinous, turning the experience into something dangerous or evil. Jung accepted that humans have an instinct toward wholeness and that this is enhanced by healthy encounters with the numinous.

Alfred Adler developed a theory that presented a positive view of self-transcendence. Adler was a contemporary of Jung and an early colleague of Freud. Adler believed that much of human behavior was motivated by the drive to overcome inferiority and gain power. In Adler's view, people compensated for the sense of inferiority in various ways. As the person matured, Adler believed that the striving for personal superiority and power gave way to an advanced social interest. At the highest levels, this self-transcendence led the individual to seek social improvement and strive for the betterment of all humanity. This principle of self-transcendence, while not as overtly spiritual as Jung's speculations, was entirely consistent with the idea of submerging the self into the collective welfare of society or humanity as a whole.

Summary and Implications

In this section, we have sought to present an outline of the major features of psychoanalytic theory. It is a rich and historically important line of theory development. Our review only has touched on what we consider to be its core features. For many, modern psychoanalytic theory is still the theory of choice, particularly for those engaged in long-term individual psychotherapy.

It should be noted that much of psychoanalytic theory has been faulted for two different shortcomings. First, the theory is largely speculative and has little empirical evidence to support the major propositions. Related to this concern is the fact that the treatment principles derived from the theory have had little evidence of effectiveness despite many years of application.

A second area of contention has to do with some of the assumptions of the model that are seen to be damaging to some groups in society. Feminist theory is sharply critical of some of the allegedly misogynistic elements of psychoanalysis, including the inherent assumption that female personality development is inferior to that of males due to incomplete repression in the phallic phase. It is also easily inferred that persons of gay/lesbian orientation demonstrate perversion of the normal libidinal development posited by the model. Many critics feel that the model is limited by unexamined cultural and environmental influences. This deficit is complicated by the absence of empirical studies that might have corrected and refined the assumptions of the model.

The tie between psychoanalytic theory and the social systems theory is indirect and historical. It is indirect in the sense that the life stage development model to be presented later has its origins in psychoanalytic theory. It is historical in that Freud's works have influenced most of the other theories presented in this book, particularly humanistic theory and field theory. Most important, psychoanalytic theory is derived from a fundamentally different set of assumptions than social systems theory. Psychoanalytic theory focuses on assumptions about the individual and the internal determinants of behavior. Social systems theory stems from assumptions about order and the external determinants of human behavior.[15] Earlier, we mentioned the importance of psychoanalytic theory in the development of the casework method in social work. While this influence has been diminishing over the decades, psychosocial theory, a derivative of psychoanalytic theory, remains very influential.

BEHAVIORISM/LEARNING THEORY

The second general line of theory development we will track is behaviorism and learning theory. For our current purpose, we are considering behaviorism and learning theory to be essentially synonymous. We find it useful to view the development of this line of thinking as a response, in part, to psychoanalytic theory. For example, psychoanalysis was concerned with the internal determinants of behavior, the aggressive and sexual impulses comprising the id. Behaviorism is concerned with manifest behavior. A behavior is a fact and thus a point of departure for attempting to explain it. For the behaviorist, the determinants are to be found in the external situation of the person, not in the person's inner life.

As with each line of theory development, there is a problem in labeling the line of inquiry and then deciding what to include and what to omit. This is particularly true for what we are choosing to label behaviorism and learning theory. Daniel Robinson aptly described the issue.

> There is no doubt that the behaviorist perspective has been the dominant one in modern psychology, at least in the English speaking world, for the past thirty years. Despite the monolithic expression it has been given by its several influential spokesmen, it is a highly varied and shifting perspective. Behaviorism is not a single ism standing in defense of a short list of propositions. It is more a "culture" within psychology than a "school," more a habit of thought than a system. It is therefore, with caution that one goes about saying what behaviorism is.[16]

What was true about the importance and diversity of behaviorism in 1979, when Robinson wrote these words, is at least equally true today. In the past several decades, behaviorism has also become a dominant influence in social work, a part of a general move within the profession toward a more scientific approach to practice.

In the beginning, behaviorism was devoted to building a scientific psychology by using the traditional methods and procedures employed in the physical sciences. John Watson (1878–1958), who can be termed the father of American behaviorism, sought to rid psychology of its preoccupation with subjective theorizing.

Watson was born in a rural area of South Carolina near the town of Greenville. He attended Freeman University and went on to do graduate work at the University of Chicago, finishing his doctorate in 1903. Watson then took a teaching position at Johns Hopkins University, where he did his most important work. Watson led what is sometimes referred to as the behavioral revolt in psychology. His position was very clear: there was no place in psychology for the study of consciousness through introspection and other such methods.[17] He believed that psychology should drop from its vocabulary such concepts as consciousness, the unconscious, mind, need, goal, and emotion, and

most, if not all, the concepts noted in the previous section on psychoanalytic theory. Psychology should, according to Watson, focus its effort on the understanding, prediction, and control of behavior.[18]

Modern behaviorism has its clearest origins in the work of the Russian physiologist Ivan Pavlov (1849–1936). Pavlov was fifty years of age when he began his now famous work. Dogs salivate when food touches their tongue, a process that facilitates the digestion of food. Pavlov observed that his dogs would also salivate prior to the presentation of food, apparently stimulated by the footsteps of those coming to feed them. In short, a physiologically or internally based reflex to food was being triggered or elicited by a stimulus having no intrinsic relationship to the food—the footsteps.

Pavlov's experiment involved placing a dog in a harness in a darkened room. A light would be flashed on and seconds later food powder would be placed in the dog's mouth. The dog would salivate as the food powder touched the tongue. This would be repeated several times. Pavlov found that the light alone would eventually produce salivation. This serves as an example of the classical conditioned response experiment. Food placed on the dog's tongue represents an **unconditioned stimulus (US).** The light that preceded the feeding was a **conditioned stimulus (CS).** The salivation in response to the food was the **unconditioned reflex (UR).** The salivation linked to the presence of the light, but in the absence of food, constituted the **conditioned reflex (CR).** Pavlov identified an elemental form of stimulus–response learning.[19]

Watson built on the work of Pavlov and founded what we are referring to as the behaviorist tradition in modern-day psychology. As is the case with each of the other major theories, Watson is just one of many writers who has made contributions. Others include Edward Thorndike, John Dollard, Clark Hull, B. F. Skinner, and Albert Bandura, to mention but a few.[20]

Watson was an environmentalist and his position is clearly evident in the following famous quote:

> Give me a dozen healthy infants, well formed and my own specified world to bring them up in and I'll guarantee to take any one at random and train him to become any type of specialist I might select—doctor, lawyer, artist, merchant, chief, and yes, even beggar-man and thief, regardless of his talents, penchants, tendencies, abilities, vocations, and race of his ancestors.[21]

Watson understood that he was overstating his position, but nevertheless the quote conveys well his firm and, some would say, radical environmental position.

Focus

The focus of this line of theory development is on how behavior is influenced or regulated by environmental conditions. **Radical** or stimulus–response **(S–R) behaviorism** views environmental control as acting directly on the individual's behavior. **Methodological** or stimulus–organism–response **(S–O–R) behaviorism** views environmental–behavioral relationships as being mediated by the individual's symbolic or cognitive processes. **Behavior modification** is the application of this line of theory to the resolution of human problems.

Assumptions

Different behaviorists will start with different assumptions. Our interest here is in identifying areas of general agreement. We are particularly interested in presenting the assumptions that distinguish behaviorism from other major lines of theory development.

1. There is continuity of the species. Functional relationships between animal behavior and the environment also hold for human beings.

2. The conditions of the environment are the primary determinants of animal and human behavior.

3. The procedures of natural science (for example, systematic observation and experiment) are the best way to understand behavior-environment relationships.

4. Both normal and abnormal behaviors are the product of behavior-environment relationships and can be modified by the manipulation of these relationships.

5. The individual's "personality" is the sum of acquired behaviors and learned behavioral-environment relations.

Behaviorism shares with psychoanalytic theory the premise that the study of humans starts with the recognition that humans are animals. Consequently, experiments performed on animals have applications to humans, for example, Pavlov's work with dogs.

In many ways, the remaining assumptions are the antithesis of positions held in psychoanalytic theory. In psychoanalytic theory, the personality is formed largely by internal, psychic determinants and the interplay between the id, ego, and superego. Environmental determinants of behavior are given little attention. Behaviorists hold that the causation of behavior is not to be found in internal states of the individual (the unconscious), but in the person's external environment. Behaviorists, in the tradition of Watson and Skinner, feel that attention to such internal states retards rather than advances the scientific study of behavior.

Behaviorists do not assume that human behavior is shaped by life stages that follow the epigenetic principle. They hold that the environment shapes behavior in a continuous manner. From this position, behaviorists offer a process model rather than a stage model in formulating their theory.

Behaviorist theory emphasizes that the human is a reactive creature, reacting to stimuli located in the environment. This helps explain the assumption that the human personality is the sum of learned behaviors.

Concepts

The assumptions undergirding behaviorism are reflected in a large number of concepts. We will summarize those we consider most important. Before doing so, we want to draw a distinction between two important lines of thinking within the behaviorist framework. Earlier we noted the work of Pavlov and Watson. Their work was described as being in the **classical conditioning** tradition within behaviorism. Here we used the stimulus–response experiment and concepts such as unconditioned stimulus (US) and conditioned stimulus (CS). A second line of investigation, best demonstrated by the work of B. F. Skinner, is known as **operant conditioning.** In classical conditioning, responses are automatically elicited by known stimuli. The focus in operant conditioning is on the response and its consequences, not the antecedent stimulus. Skinner held that behavior is shaped and controlled by its consequences.[22] In this formulation, what stimulated the behavior in the first instance is not the central issue. It is what follows the behavior that influences its continuance or discontinuance. In short, behavior is determined by its consequences.

Reinforcement.   We described classical (respondent) conditioning as following the S–R paradigm (Stimulus–Response). In that model, a response is triggered (elicited) by a stimulus. Note that the behavior is innate. The learning that takes place refers to linking a new stimulus to elicit the old response.

In operant conditioning, the behavior precedes the stimulus. Therefore, the paradigm is expressed as R–S (Response–Stimulus).

Whereas respondent conditioning is passive, operant conditioning is active. Rather than learning to attach old behavior to new stimuli, operant conditioning allows the development of new and complex behaviors.

Here is how it works. The organism (human or animal) first emits a behavior. This behavior is followed by some event (stimulus) in the environment. This stimulus will determine the probability that the behavior is emitted again in similar circumstances. If the stimulus is reinforcing, the behavior becomes more likely in the future. If the stimulus is punishing, the behavior becomes less likely. For example, an infant is in a crib. The infant is hungry. The infant begins to cry. The response of crying results in the mother coming to nurse the infant. Assuming that the infant likes the response, it is more likely that the next time the infant is hungry in a crib, it will cry. The only confusing thing in this paradigm is language: it seems odd that we call the behavior a "response" when it comes before the stimulus. This is only an artifact of the classical conditioning paradigm.

Any stimulus that increases the probability of a behavior occurring again is called **reinforcement.** If we introduce a reinforcing stimulus, it is called **positive reinforcement.** If we take away an aversive stimulus, it is called **negative reinforcement.** This about our example. The mother nursing the crying child is a positive reinforcement for crying (giving something good). If the child has a wet diaper and the mother removes it, this is called negative reinforcement (taking away something bad).

The key is that all reinforcement increases the probability of the behavior that it follows. The terms *positive* and *negative* here refer only to whether we add or take away a stimulus. Refer to Figure 5.1.

Reinforcement Schedules.   Operant behavior is influenced not only by the type of reinforcer, but also by the schedule on which reinforcement is delivered. There are several types of **reinforcement schedules.**

> *Continuous:*   If individuals receive reinforcement every time they act a certain way, the schedule is continuous. Continuous

Effects on Behavior

	Reinforcement (Increase)	Punishment (Decrease)
Positive (Add)	Positive Reinforcement	Positive Punishment
Negative (Remove)	Negative Reinforcement	Negative Punishment

Modification to Environment

FIGURE 5.1   Effects on Behavior—Positive and Negative Reinforcement

schedules produce rapid learning, but extinction of the behavior is also rapid if the behavior is not reinforced.

Interval: In this schedule, reinforcement comes after the passage of time. For example, a child gets an allowance once a week. This is a fixed-interval schedule. If the child gets the allowance sometimes daily, sometimes weekly, or sometimes monthly, it is a variable interval schedule. Note that the reinforcer is tied to time, not to behavior. Interval schedules produce lower rates of behavior, with a marked "plateau" of reduced behavior frequency after the reinforcer is delivered each time.

Ratio: Ratio schedules present the reinforcer after a certain number of behaviors have occurred. If we pay workers for every ten widgets they make, this is a fixed-ratio schedule. If they are paid after five, then ten, then four widgets, and so on, this is a variable ratio schedule. Variable ratio schedules produce high and stable rates of behavior.

Complex: Complex schedules blend features of interval and ratio schedules in

order to gain some of the advantages of each.

Extinction: Extinction schedules result in the elimination of the behavior due to nonreinforcement. Spontaneous recovery is noted after the passage of time following termination of reinforcement.

Punishment.   **Punishment** refers to a class of stimuli that decrease the probability of the behavior (response) that they follow. Punishing stimuli are aversive to the organism. Thus, when punishment follows a behavior, it decreases the probability of the behavior.

For example, the infant crying in the crib prompts the mother to come in and spank the child. This punishment decreases the likelihood of crying in the future under these circumstances.

As with reinforcement, punishment may consist of either presenting or withdrawing a stimulus. When the crying baby is presented with a spanking, it is positive punishment. If the baby cries while nursing and then the mother stops nursing, it is negative punishment.

It has been noted that positive punishment such as spanking results in a generalized effect on behavior. The child will learn in time to avoid not only the punished behavior, but the punishing person as well. This is called stimulus generalization. In addition, some positive punishment results in a fear pattern called the *activation response*. Activation creates fear or anxiety—emotional states that impair precise learning. For example, a parent who slaps a child may be punishing a behavior, but also creates a state of anxious arousal that takes time to dissipate, and during that time, all learning is impaired. Nathan Azrin, among others, noted that severe punishment can be highly effective. For some subjects, severe punishment lowers the rate of the behavior to zero and keeps it there for virtually indefinite periods. Azrin also noted that punishment does not teach new behavior; it serves only to reduce or eliminate behavior.[23] For these and other reasons, we cannot consider reinforcement and punishment as merely mirror images of one another.

A less traumatic way to way to eliminate behavior is by withholding reinforcement. This procedure deprives the subject of the opportunity to earn reinforcement, hence it is a "time out" from positive reinforcement. No activation syndrome is noted in the use of this procedure.

Extinction occurs when we cease to reinforce a behavior that was previously being reinforced. For example, if a child has tantrums to gain the positive reinforcement of parental attention, eliminating parental attention will result in operant extinction of the tantrum behavior. In many cases, extinguished behavior recurs for noapparent reason after a period of time has elapsed. This is called "spontaneous recovery." For example, the tantruming child may cease the behavior when the parents withdraw their attention. After a few weeks, the tantrum behavior is likely to reappear. For this reason, it is useful to instruct clients on the spontaneous recovery phenomenon so that they do not revert to giving attention to the undesired behavior.

Note that we are here briefly describing operant extinction. It should be noted that extinction is also present in classical conditioning.

When Pavlov conditioned the dogs to salivate at the sound of a bell or the flash of a light, he did so by pairing the food powder with the conditioned stimulus. If he repeatedly used the conditioned stimulus (the bell) and did not present the food powder, after a time the conditioned reflex of salivation would be extinguished.

This respondent conditioning might at first seem a laboratory curiosity with little social work significance. However, we must point out that important human responses, such as anxiety, are respondent in nature. Some suspect that we may develop anxiety by classical pairing of anxiety-provoking stimuli, such as noise, pain, or discomfort, with other objects. By training people to a response such as relaxation in response to anxiety-provoking stimuli, such as snakes, it is possible to desensitize people to previously crippling fearful stimuli. This procedure, called systematic desensitization, is thought to be at the root of many successful counseling techniques, which may make use of it without being aware of it.

Modeling. Bandura was instrumental in expanding behavioral learning theory beyond the work of the classical and operant models. Bandura noted that people and animals learn not only by direct experience, but also vicariously. When subjects observe the consequences of behavior to others, the behavior of the observers is affected by the consequences they observe occurring to others.[24]

Modeling, or vicarious learning, seems to obey the same general principles as operant learning already described. Modeling differs in that it is clearly social to some degree. For example, the degree to which a human observer changes behavior after watching the consequences to another will depend in part on the situation and in part on the degree to which the subject and the model are thought to be similar.

Modeling may also take the form of verbal modeling. We tend to think of models as those we observe in action. However, when we describe to a child a situation in which "nice lit-tle boys get to have a dessert after dinner, but sassy little boys do not," we are modeling be-havior and consequences at an abstract level. Bandura noted that when our verbal depictions conflict with observed consequences, we believe what we see more than what we are told.[25] Like-wise, if we emulate the behavior of a model who receives rewards for working hard, but we are not rewarded for hard work, our behavior is guided by the direct consequences rather than the modeled learning.

Extinction.   **Extinction** occurs when a previ-ously reinforced behavior is no longer followed by its prior consequences. Behaviors that are extinguished are reduced to their baseline or natural level of occurrence. In practical terms, if a child throws a temper tantrum to secure parental attention and the parents consistently withdraw their attention from the child when this occurs, the tantrum behavior will fade or be extinguished. The behavior is not being rewarded, therefore it is extinguished. **Spon-taneous recovery** is a related concept, which holds that an extinguished behavior can sponta-neously reappear under circumstances similar to those in which the behavior was originally reinforced.

Generalization and Discrimination.   **Gener-alization** is the term applied to the process whereby a response generalizes across a class of stimuli. An example would be a young child who says "da da" when her father appears. Here the word *da da* has been reinforced and she has thus made the association between the words and her father. The child may then say "da da" when any adult male appears; the stimulus has been generalized to a class of stimuli—adult males.

   Discrimination is the opposite process to generalization. It is the ability to respond only to an individual case from a class of stimuli; thus, the child says "da da" only when her fa-ther appears.

Shaping.   **Shaping,** as used in operant condi-tioning, is a method for establishing new behav-iors. The notion of shaping, or successive approximation, helps convey the position that conditioning typically occurs through a gradual process rather than all at once. A desired behav-ior can be achieved through a series of steps, with each step representing progress toward achievement of the sought-after behavior. For example, teaching a son or daughter to catch a ball typically involves shaping. All of those behaviors that will lead to the ability to catch a ball are reinforced. Verbal cues and reinforcers might include: "Keep your eye on the ball when daddy tosses it . . . That a girl . . . Remember to keep your eye on the ball . . . Now put your glove hand out in front . . . That was good . . . You almost caught it that time . . . Don't close your eyes . . . There, you're doing real good . . . You're going to become daddy's ball player," and so on.

COGNITIVE DEVELOPMENT THEORY

Cognitive development as an approach is sig-nificantly different from cognitive-behavioral theory. Cognition means to know. Thus, **cog-nitive development theory** development per-tains to the steps involved in deriving meaning from experience; how do we come to know?

   While a number of theorists have made contributions to this line of thinking, none is better known and more highly respected than Jean Piaget (1896–1980). Born in Switzerland, Piaget, like Darwin, showed talent as a natural-ist while still a child. Indicative of his talent and potential, Piaget published an article at the age of ten on an albino sparrow he had observed in a park. Piaget's observation skill as a naturalist was to serve him well later on in his work with children and how they learn.

   As a young man, Piaget went to the Sor-bonne in Paris where he worked in the labora-tory of Alfred Binet. Binet was conducting studies there on the nature of intelligence. In his work, Piaget sought to understand how children arrive at their answers to problems, how they reason. Just as the behaviorists hold that human behavior is shaped by environmental influences, the cognitive development theorists hold that knowing is shaped by the interaction between the individual and the environment.

Focus

This is a theory of human development focused on cognitive processes. In this sense, it is a narrower-range theory than those addressing a wider range of development processes, for example, psychoanalytic theory.

Assumptions

As with other lines of theory development, not all theorists in a given category are going to operate from the same set of assumptions. Our interest is in identifying those that appear central to a given line of theory development. For us, the following four assumptions form the foundation of this theory:

1. Cognitive development occurs in a fixed sequence.
2. Cognitive development displays continuity, with each stage building on the preceding stage and representing ever more comprehensive and more complex ways of thinking.
3. Cognitive development is not governed by either internal maturation or external teaching but rather by the person through his or her own activities.
4. Cognitive structures are created, developed, and modified by the interaction of the person and his or her environment.

We find these assumptions to be consistent with those comprising social systems theory. Particularly helpful is the position taken with respect to the interplay between the individual and the environment in the development of cognitive structures. While it is important to note that cognition is assumed to develop through a series of fixed and invariant stages, Piaget did not hold that these stages were genetically determined.[26] While cognitive development is considered a stage theory, Piaget was by no means a strict maturationist.

Cognitive development theorists assume that people of different ages think differently. The position is tied to stages of development. The central idea is that children think differently than do adults. At this point, it should prove useful to the reader for us to contrast assumptions made by cognitive development theorists and those undergirding other lines of theory development. Central to psychoanalytic theory is the assumption that development is governed principally by a genetically based maturation cycle. At each stage, the individual is confronted with stimuli that have internal origins, but these influences on the personality are shaped more or less by environmental experience. A diametrically opposing position is held by the behaviorist. The maturationally based explanation is rejected and personality development is grounded in a set of learned behaviors. Cognitive development theorists in the tradition of Piaget hold that cognitive development is essentially a spontaneous process in which children build their own cognitive structures through their own experiences. This proposition holds special interest for us. A proactive position is taken in seeking to understand human behavior. The interaction between a human being and the environment is an active one. The natural state is one in which the child is actively exploring the environment. In so doing, the child is constantly building new cognitive structures and elaborating on older ones as a means of comprehending and coping with the environment. Piaget was a constructivist and held that knowledge was constantly building based on its interaction with reality, resulting in continuous creativity.[27]

Concepts

A number of important concepts build from the assumptions of cognitive development theory. The most important are those that identify the four developmental periods. Before describing these, we will present Piaget's notion of stage and summarize some of the other key concepts associated with cognitive development.

Stage.   A **stage** is a developmental level typically conceptualized in terms of epigenetic theory (the structural elaboration of the unstructured egg as opposed to the growth of a preformed individual). More generally, the notion of stage is linked to a basic organizational scheme that is distinctive in its own right; it is more complex than the previous stage but less complex than the next higher stage. A **stage theory** is one that employs stages as a fundamental organizing scheme in explaining growth and development. For example, cognitive development is a stage theory, behaviorism is not.

In cognitive development theory as advanced by Piaget, the distinctiveness of a stage is evidenced by the following qualities:

1. The mode of thinking is qualitatively different at each stage.
2. Each stage is internally organized; it is a whole unto itself.
3. The individual progresses through stages in a progressive and invariant way. No stage is skipped.
4. Each higher stage builds on and integrates with the next lower stage in a hierarchical manner; the stages are vertically as well as horizontally integrated.
5. The stages are characteristic of all humankind. They are not culturally based and thus, the same stages would be evident in all cultures.

Schema.   A **schema** is a diagram or outlines. The concept of schema is used in cognitive development theory to denote the existence of a structure or representation of reality in memory. In social systems theory, the concept of schema would be labeled as a structural feature, a guide to action that would be called forth in a specific interactional situation. In cognitive development theory, the first schemata are tied to inborn reflexes. In this sense, schemata have their origins in a reactive stance of the child, such as the sucking reflex that occurs when the infant's lips are touched. Building on the reflex are a host of associated experiences on which the child builds his or her own action schemata. The proactive posture in social development thus becomes evident.

Assimilation.   **Assimilation** refers to the integration of new experiences and objects into an existing schema. For example, if the reader had been introduced earlier to the social systems perspective, the social systems theory and model would already have been assimilated into an existing schema. In a matter of speaking, the new information would simply help flesh out and elaborate on an existing frame of reference.

Accommodation.   To accommodate means to adjust in order to accomplish a fit. Some new experiences or pieces of information simply do not fit into an existing schema or previous sets of related experiences. These new and novel experiences require the construction of new schemata, or, more likely, the modification of existing schemata. This process is referred to as **accommodation.** To extend the example noted earlier, if you have not had any previous experience in systems thinking, the content in this book will involve some accommodation process on your part. The content is not only new, but also involves a different kind of thinking. Thus, it cannot simply be assimilated into existing cognitive structures. The task is more difficult and involves an expenditure of more energy when new and different structures are being developed.

Organization.   **Organization** as used here refers to a tendency to seek and build order.

According to the cognitive development theory, the individual will always tend to seek coherence in schemata (that is, to systematize observations and data in the development of cognitive structures). Piaget only made very sparing use of biological concepts in his work. He viewed the tendencies of assimilation, accommodation, and organization as biological tendencies apparent in all organisms. Thus, according to Piaget, the propensity to create order and for behavior to evidence this underlying ordering process is genetically determined.

According to systems theory, if the content is new and accommodation takes place, it will be followed by a reordering of relevant structures. This is the "aha" (it is finally making sense to me) phenomenon. For many students unfamiliar with systems thinking, the first part of the semester is a struggle as they attempt to fit the systems theory and perspective into their usual way of thinking. Then something appears to happen quite spontaneously—a light goes on.

The notions of assimilation, accommodation, and organization identify a general approach to ordering employed by Piaget. In Chapter 2, we identified an assumption of the existence of a general ordering phenomenon. Piaget specified in detail the ordering processes he proposed as an explanation for cognitive development. Stated differently, human beings seek order. Disorder is uncomfortable and, sometimes, frightening. Recall that Maslow identified safety and security needs as the second level of needs following only physiological needs in relative importance. These safety needs include the need for structure and order.[28] People are self-organizing both in terms of their own thinking and in the various groupings that they form. Piaget gives us some clues about this basic ordering process as it is developed in the cognitive structures of humans.

Piaget's Four Stages.

Piaget did not tie his stages to specific ages, believing that considerable variation occurs in the age at which chil-dren enter a given developmental stage.[29] The suggested ages are offered only as a general point of orientation.

Sensorimotor Intelligence (Birth to Eighteen Months of Age). As suggested by the phrase **sensorimotor intelligence,** development at this stage centers on sensory and motor schemata. The importance of sucking and its relationship to the taking in of nourishment and the related social experiences with caregivers is clearly evident in this developmental stage. Sucking is just one of the reflexes being developed. In addition, motor skills are rapidly developing, impacting on cognitive schemata. In thinking about this stage, it is important to recognize the physical action basis for the development of these cognitive structures.

Piaget identified six substages occurring within stage I: (1) reflexes, such as sucking; (2) primary circular reactions, which are successful cycles of action (beginnings of memory); (3) secondary circular reactions; (4) coordination of secondary schemata; (5) tertiary circular reactions; and (6) beginnings of thought.[30]

Piaget used the concept of **circular reaction** to describe learning activities in which the infant attempts to repeat an action (the circular action) that first occurred by chance. An example would be the infant's hand coming in contact with the mouth. The hand drops and the child tries (initially unsuccessfully) to repeat the movement. This is an attempt at coordinating two separate motor schemata—an arm movement and sucking. Piaget describes primary, secondary, and tertiary circular reactions, each involving a greater differentiation in sensorimotor actions.

In a secondary circular reaction, the child chances onto external events. An example would be a child who has caused a rattling sound in the crib. Interested in the noise, the child strikes to repeat the action. Tertiary circular reactions represent a further development of schemata. In tertiary circular reactions, the child experiments with different actions, each with a different outcome. For example, a child is sitting in her highchair playing with several objects. She pushes one off, watching it fall to the floor. She pushes another, again watching it fall. She then takes another object, leans over the chair, and drops the article to the floor. She repeats the action but from a different angle, again watching the relationships between different moves and different outcomes. The schema is becoming ever more differentiated through her circular actions.

The sensorimotor stage builds on the genetically based reflex actions with which the infant is equipped at birth. Chance happenings resulting from these sensorimotor actions start a pattern of increasing elaboration (schemata). Very early on, the child demonstrates a learning or memory capacity through the repetition and elaboration of various sensorimotor-based actions. This stage ends (roughly at eighteen months of age) when a new capacity emerges, one that will separate the child from all other life forms: language.

Preoperational Thought (Eighteen Months of Age to the Early School Years, Ages Six to Eight). The notion of operations, as used by Piaget, refers to a transformation that is carried out in thought rather than in a physical action. In adult terms, one can become angry and strike the offending person; or, one can become angry, think about striking the person, and decide on another course of action. Thinking about such events involves a representation of a situation and taking or not taking action based on the contemplation of a variety of possibilities and their respective consequences. Thinking, as just described, is a very complex set of operations. A child, according to Piaget, moves through a series of stages prior to achieving this kind of complex thought process.

With the term **preoperational thought,** Piaget identified a transition between sensorimotor and operational thought. In the sensorimotor period, the child's mental development

is concerned with the immediate environment. Initially, it is with explorations involving her or his own body. Later in this period, it broadens to include the child's immediate environment. Critically important in stage I is the child's growing capacity to distinguish between self and environment. The child, through the elaboration of schemata, gains a growing sense of time, space, causality, and object permanence.

Early in life, things exist for the infant only to the extent that they occur within the perceptive field. In other words, the infant does not have a schema of a permanent object. Such schemata develop as a consequence of experience (learning) and maturational development. Piaget described this phenomena of object permanence in experimenting with his own seven-month-old child:

> At the time of his feeding I show him the bottle, he extends his hand to take it, but at that moment, I hide it behind my arm. If he sees one end sticking out he kicks and screams and gives every indication of wanting to have it. If, however, the bottle is completely hidden and nothing sticks out, he stops crying and acts for all we know as if the bottle no longer existed, as if it had been dissolved and absorbed into my arm.[31]

The notion of object permanence is particularly helpful in differentiating between stage I and stage II, in which the child becomes able to comprehend the existence of objects (including people) even though they may not be immediately present. For example, mother exists for the infant even though she is at work. Even more important, the child has learned that she or he is also an object.

In stage II, a new form of thinking arises, one based on symbolic representations. Schemata based on sensorimotor representation must now accommodate new experiences. A reordering of thinking takes place (organization) in which symbolic structures gain dominance. During this time (the reordering of schemata), the child's thinking is illogical. It does not make much sense from an adult's perspective.

The child in stage II is rapidly learning that all of the objects in her or his environment have names. Importantly, the child learns that she or he, too, has a name. In this way, the child's development of selfhood rapidly develops.

In the preoperational thought stage, the child is learning many words and their meanings. At this point in development, the child is moving from single words to combinations of two or three words and then on to sentences. The child's verbalizations are reflective of the increasingly more complex thought structures that are forming.

Children at this stage are starting to use these symbols and their meanings as an early form of thinking. During this time, the child is imitating others and engaging in a variety of imaginary activities. The child's knowledge and skill-building schemata are very much tied to perceptions of her or his own direct experiences with things in the world.

Concrete Operational Thought (Age Seven to Early Adolescence, Ages Eleven to Thirteen). This period of **concrete operational thought** coincides with the early school years and is marked by a rapid development of cognitive abilities. At the age of six or seven, the child's cognitive schemes start to evidence the organization associated with thinking on a symbolic level. Prior to this time, the child's thinking has been essentially unsystematic and lacking a common thread of logic. It is important to remember that developmentally the child's first symbols are based in motor actions not in linguistics. In the stage of concrete operations, the child begins to internalize physical actions as mental actions (operations). At this stage, children are able to formulate classes or categories of objects. For example, a child at this stage would be able to sort a series of blocks of varying sizes and colors easily when asked to do so. The child at the preoperational level would need to physically com-

pare the blocks in order to determine relative size. Now the child is able to keep the sorting schemes in her or his head and mentally make the comparisons. Behaviorally, the child at this concrete operational level will be able to coordinate thinking and acting much more rapidly and successfully than her or his counterpart at the preoperational level of thought.

Coinciding with concrete operational thought is a movement from egocentrism to a concern for others. At the first substage of the sensorimotor stage, the infant moves toward self-identification. Here the infant begins the separation of self from the experienced environment. This has occurred in normal development by the time the level of preoperational thought has been reached. At the preoperations stage, the child is the center of her or his universe. Here we have solitary and imaginary play taking place. While a child may play in the presence of others, it is not until the child achieves the level of concrete operations that she or he has the cognitive capacities to fully take the actions of others into her or his thoughts and actions. Now the child has the mental capacities to engage with others in game play. At this stage, cognitive and social development are rapidly occurring with each acting on the other. From a symbolic interaction position, the child is now developing the capacity of taking the role of another. The child is learning to look at things from another person's point of view.

Piaget, through his research and theory building, sought to map the development of mental capabilities. His work is of great consequence to educators. In thinking about his work and its implications, keep in mind the assumption upon which his theory builds. Cognitive development occurs through the child's own activities. In short, children are born inquisitive and they learn in part through their interactions with others in their social environments. They are proactive. The teaching-learning environment is fundamental. The period of concrete operations is critically important in developing a child's thirst for knowledge.

Formal Operational Thought (Adolescence through Adulthood).   The final stage of cognitive development Piaget labeled **formal operational thought.** This stage starts around age eleven, coinciding essentially with adolescence, and continues throughout adulthood. It is important to recognize that cognitive development does not stop at adolescence, but develops throughout one's life. The person in this stage has the cognitive equipment to lead a full and productive life. While Piaget posited four stages of development, it does not follow that all people progress to the fourth, that of formal operations.

In contrast to concrete operations, the person at the formal operations stage can deal abstractly with the logic of things. At this level of reasoning, the person develops the capacity to reason along multiple lines so that in any given situation the person is able to deal with all contingencies. The point has now been reached at which thinking becomes detached from the here and now. The individual now has the capacity for reflective thinking and the contemplation of future states under various sets of circumstances.

Piaget believed that one achieves the formal operations level of cognitive capacity through social interactions with others. People learn through their interactions with others of differing points of view and other ways of thinking. This open-system formulation is fully consistent with social systems theory.[32]

Piaget's work has implications for many other lines of theory development as well as for the various forms of professional practice such as social work. For example, symbolic interaction theory, which will be reviewed in Part Three, is premised, in part, on a level of cognitive capacity that permits one to mentally play one's own role and the role of others. We commonly and casually refer to this as thinking about an upcoming situation. This capacity exists at the level of formal operations. Symbolic

interaction also assumes a well-developed reflective and introspective capability in developing a sense of selfhood.

Summary

Social systems theory operationalizes a perspective on the ordering of human relationships. This ordering can be applied to a relationship comprised of two people or to a society as a whole. In all instances, the order being described is social and ultimately exists in the minds of those enacting social roles. Structure, as order, is never anything physical. It is always social. Cognitive development theory supplies an approach to the study of the mental structures and processes. In so doing, it helps to inform social systems theory and its applications to practice.

We have taken the position that the individual derives her or his sense of humanness and selfhood through interactions with others. Piaget and others in this intellectual tradition help link cognitive and social development; cognitive development is a social process, as is selfhood.

In the past couple of decades, cognitive development theory has had growing importance in social work; this has been particularly true in work involving children and adolescents, and in brief (time-limited) forms of helping. A growing number of social workers now employ cognitive therapy in their work with a wide variety of clients.[33] As with behaviorism, the growing interest in cognitive development theory seems tied to a general move toward a scientific base for practice.

MORAL DEVELOPMENT THEORY

Morality, the role of values, and the relationship of cognitive states involving moral issues and behavior have been differentially approached within different lines of theory development. As we introduce this section, distinguishing between the concepts of values, morals, and ethics should be useful.

A value is a principle, standard, or quality viewed as worthwhile. We consider a value to be a shared meaning as to what is desirable and undesirable in social life. For example, in this society, the importance of work is stressed. The societal value can be stated as follows: "To work is good, not to work is bad."

Moral refers to the judgments made about what is right and wrong in human conduct and character. Morals constitute a reasoned code of what is right and wrong that grows out of larger societal values and pertains to interpersonal relationships—for example, being fair, honest, and just.

Ethics is the study of moral choices and also refers to the codified values and morals of a profession. Ethics deal with the conduct or specific moral choices made by a person within a situation involving relationships with others. For example, the National Association of Social Workers' Code of Ethics provides the practitioner with a guide to professional conduct with clients.

In moral development theory, we are interested in the stages humans go through in developing their sense of what is right and wrong.[34] Because values and ethics form the foundations of generalist and advanced forms of practice, we will be examining the development of this reasoning capacity at all levels of relationships, from the interpersonal to the societal.

Earlier in this chapter, we provided a brief summary of psychoanalytic theory. While moral development is not a primary issue in this line of theory, the matter is contained in Freud's concept of the superego. Recall that the superego corresponds to one's conscience. According to Freud, an individual's behavior is viewed in terms of the ego's capacity to deal with the demands of the id and the superego. Given its attention to the superego, psychoanalytic theory offers an approach to the study of moral reasoning and ethical behavior.

The issue of morality and learned behavior has not been a central focus of behaviorism, at least by early writers. Skinner wrote:

In an operant analysis of the stimulus control of verbal behavior, we can identify the referent of abstract terms, but terms like "morality" and "justice" raise an additional problem. It can be solved by recognizing that the behavior we call moral or just is a product of special kinds of social contingencies arranged by governments, religions, economic systems and ethical groups. We need to analyze those contingencies if we are to build a world in which people behave morally and justly, and a first step in that direction is to dismiss morality and justice as personal possessions.[35]

As with psychoanalytic theory and behaviorist theory, humanistic theory does not give primary attention to moral development. However, Abraham Maslow did consider moral behavior and its relationship to human needs in his basic formulation of a hierarchy of human needs. The contribution Maslow made is the linkage he established between need satisfaction and one's value system. He summarized his argument as follows:

The Instinctoid Nature of Basic Needs, constitute for me the foundation of a system of intrinsic human values, human goods that validate themselves, that are intrinsically good and desirable and that need no further justification. This is a hierarchy of values which are to be found in the very essence of human nature itself. These are not only wanted and desired by all human beings, but also needed in the sense that they are necessary to avoid illness and psychopathology.[36]

Clearly, a well-established line of theory development in psychology dealing with moral development is lacking. While not neglected, this content tends to be incorporated into theories of a broader range. For us, the clearest line of theory pertaining to moral development is to be found in the work of Lawrence Kohlberg.[37] We need at the onset to acknowledge that

Kohlberg's work builds on and extends the work done by Piaget.

Lawrence Kohlberg was born in Bronxville, New York, in 1927. He attended Andover Academy in Massachusetts. Kohlberg, after a period of work on behalf of the Israeli cause, enrolled at the University of Chicago, completing his baccalaureate degree in one year. During his graduate education in psychology at the University of Chicago, he became familiar with Piaget's work. Kohlberg's interest was in the moral reasoning of children. This became the subject of his doctoral dissertation. His methodology was patterned after the work of Piaget and involved the interviewing of children and adolescents on moral issues. Kohlberg received his doctorate in 1958. He stayed on and taught at the University of Chicago before becoming a professor of education at Harvard.

Focus

As indicated by its title, moral development is a stage theory; it is linked to one's general cognitive development, but focuses on those processes associated with the development of moral reasoning and the ethical basis of behavior. It is a stage theory of narrow range.

Assumptions

Given the closeness of moral development and cognitive development, the same general assumptions are shared by these two lines of theory development. We have identified the following particular assumptions of moral development theory:

1. The progressive stages of human maturation are associated with capacities for progressively higher stages of moral reasoning.
2. Once the major moral premise of a person is understood, the solution to moral problems confronted by that person can be derived through laws of thought.

3. A link exists between moral reasoning and ethical behavior.
4. There is a greater tie between moral reasoning and ethical actions at higher than at lower stages of moral development.

Like Piaget, Kohlberg is not a strict maturationist. By this we mean that Kohlberg does not believe that the stages of moral development he postulated are the direct result of maturation. While associated with human maturational processes, they depend on a child's thinking about and experiencing, within a social context, moral problems. In short, moral development is a social process linked to the general physical, psychological, social, and spiritual development of the individual.

Given the narrow range of moral development theory, the assumptions are more specific and are approaching researchable propositions. Kohlberg and others have done a significant amount of research in recent years. The focus of our presentation and space limitations do not permit a review of this research; however, it has been well documented by others.[38] Our interest is in the presentation of the basic outlines of this theory and in linking it to social systems theory and the practice applications in social work.

Concepts

Moral development theory shares many of the same concepts summarized earlier in our review of cognitive development theory. Our interest in this section will be with the six stages of moral development identified by Kohlberg. Like Piaget, Kohlberg developed his theory by interviewing children, initially those between the ages of ten and sixteen. Later, he expanded his research to include adults. Kohlberg was interested in how children think; more specifically, in how they mentally deal with moral issues and moral dilemmas. He sought to understand the pattern of thoughts that led to their conclusions. Given this approach, it is difficult to separate his theory from the methodology employed.

His assumption was that children at different stages of moral development would use qualitatively different forms of reasoning in dealing with the dilemmas. A typical approach would be to provide the child with a dilemma and then, in an interview, probe the child's reasoning. Based on the reasoning evidenced, a scoring guide would place the child at a particular stage of moral reasoning. The ethical dilemma that follows is one of the more famous posed by Kohlberg. It is entitled "Heinz Steals the Drug."

> In Europe, a woman was near death from a special kind of cancer. There was one drug that the doctors thought might save her. It was a form of radium that a druggist in the same town had recently discovered. The drug was expensive to make, but the druggist was charging ten times what the drug cost him to make. He paid $200 for the radium and charged $2,000 for a small dose of the drug. The sick woman's husband, Heinz, went to everyone he knew to borrow the money, but he could only get together about $1,000 which is half of what it cost. He told the druggist that his wife was dying and asked him to sell it cheaper or let him pay later. But the druggist said: "No, I discovered the drug and I'm going to make money from it." So Heinz got desperate and broke into the man's store to steal the drug for his wife. Should the husband have done that?[39]

Kohlberg's model of moral development was comprised of three levels, with each level consisting of two stages, for a total of six.

Level I: Preconventional Morality
Stage 1. Here the logic is based on whether the behavior should be rewarded or punished. The orientation reflects a perception of what is right or wrong. There is little middle ground, reflecting the child's concrete operations mode of thinking. In short, good behavior is rewarded

and bad behavior is punished. Stealing is bad; therefore, since Heinz stole and thus did something bad, he should be punished. The issue is clear-cut for the child operating at stage 1: there are no mitigating circumstances.

For children at this stage, rules exist externally to them. These rules are fixed and one obeys them to avoid punishment. In Kohlberg's use of **preconventional morality,** he noted that the thinking that resulted from the logic used had not been internalized. The child does not yet possess a personal sense of the notion of conventional (customary or nominative) standards.

Stage 2. In this egocentric stage, the central concern is: What is there to be gained? Here a self-interest orientation is evidenced. The child has gained an understanding that people hold different views and do things for different reasons. Again the child has not formed her or his own conception of right and wrong but does recognize that there is no single view. Reflecting the self-interest orientation of this stage, the child's thinking will tend to reflect egocentrism. What was in it for Heinz? Perhaps the end justified the means employed.

Level II: Conventional Morality.   While level I rests on an egocentric sense of fairness linked to individual need, level II evidences a logic based on fairness that incorporates shared conventions. Similar to level I, the moral reasoning at this level still has external rules and **conventional morality** as its reference.

Stage 3.   The concern of stage 3 is approval, particularly of those in authority, such as parents, teachers, and God. Children who tend to give stage 3 responses are usually entering adolescence. While their orientation is widening, they are very much concerned with the approval of others. In the case of Heinz's dilemma, they identify with his intention of saving his wife's life and his lack of options. They also tend to view the druggist as selfish and bad. Of the two, it is the druggist who is wrong and should be punished.

Stage 4.   In this stage, the child displays a growing concern about and respect for authority and the best interest of society. The young person is now evidencing a societal perspective. While morality is still external, the young person senses that the good of the individual is tied to the good of all; maintaining order is important. With respect to Heinz, the child experiences sympathy for his wish to save his wife, but this is tempered by the view that what he did was wrong. The moral reasoning of this stage reflects a belief in the need to rule by law. There would be anarchy if we all were guided by what we personally considered right and wrong as opposed to a common set of rules applicable to all regardless of the merit of individual motives.

Level III: Postconventional Morality.   In Kohlberg's hierarchy of moral reasoning, **postconventional morality** represents the highest or most advanced level of thought. Movement is away from a morality based in convention to one tied to the individual's own system of values and moral standards.

Stage 5.   In stage 5, the child recognizes that an orderly society is not necessarily a just society. In this stage, the reasoning becomes sensitive to an individual's rights but within a larger framework that seeks to advance the well-being of all. In a manner of speaking, the child has a new perspective on what is meant by "improving the quality of life" and is concerned with how this might be accomplished for the benefit of all.

In the Heinz dilemma, respondents incorporating stage 5 thinking seek to weigh the moral and legal issues involved. On the one hand, moral judgment holds that life is more important than property. On the other, the contention is that social control binds us to live and behave within the law. If a law is not just, there

are ways to change it using democratic processes. In fact, we have a responsibility to seek these changes in order to improve the quality of life of all. In the case of Heinz, any judgment should consider his act within a broad social perspective. Both Heinz and the druggist have reasons for their actions. While there is a recognized need to hold Heinz responsible for his illegal act, the level of punishment should fully consider the reasons for his act.

Stage 6.   Kohlberg's final stage is one that recognizes a system of ethical principles that apply to all people in all cultures. The principles of justice are viewed as universal; they apply to all humankind irrespective of gender, color, national origin, sexual orientation, or physical or mental condition.

The civil rights movement, the women's movement, the gay-lesbian movement, and the worldwide human rights movement all have relevance to the moral reasoning evident in stage 6. Martin Luther King's work and dedication to civil rights, and the life and work of Mahatma Gandhi, are frequently used as examples to illustrate the moral right and responsibility to perform acts of civil disobedience. Social justice justifies the challenge of laws that are deemed immoral and hurtful.[40]

Gender-Related Differences.   The work of Carol Gilligan is particularly important.[41] In *In a Different Voice*, she examines possible gender differences and the development of psychological theory. Lawrence Kohlberg was a teacher, friend, and colleague of Gilligan's. Her work particularly reflects issues related to Kohlberg's theory of moral development.

To help develop her position, Gilligan used responses to Heinz's predicament. For our review, we will illustrate gender differences by examining the responses of two very bright and articulate children, Jake and Amy, both eleven. While arriving at similar conclusions, the logic they used was quite different. Consistent with the dilemma as constructed by Kohlberg, Jake focused on the conflict between the value of life versus property.

> For one thing, a human life is worth more than money, and if the druggist only makes $1,000, he is still going to live, but if Heinz doesn't steal the drug, his wife is going to die. (Why is life worth more than money?) Because the druggist can get a thousand dollars later from rich people with cancer, but Heinz can't get his wife again. (Why not?) Because people are all different and so you couldn't get Heinz's wife again.[42]

Jake developed his logical thinking in math, which he indicated was "the only thing that is totally logical."[43] He also took the law and the possible actions of the judge into account, all from the above position. He reasoned that laws are human creations and thus contain errors based on unforeseen circumstances. In this case, while Heinz did break the law, the judge should be as lenient as possible, recognizing Heinz's motive, the value of life over property. In Kohlberg's rating system, Jake's responses would be level II (conventional morality), a mixture of stages 3 and 4.

Amy's response as to whether Heinz should steal the drug involved a different logic and was more tentative.

> Well, I don't think so. I think there might be other ways besides stealing it, like if he could borrow the money or make a loan or something, but he really shouldn't steal the drug—but his wife shouldn't die either.[44]

Amy was then asked why she felt that Heinz should not steal the drug. Her reply did not consider either property or law but rather the effect that the theft could have on the relationship between Heinz and his wife.

> If he stole the drug, he might save his wife then, but if he did, he might have to go to jail, and then his wife might get sicker again, and he couldn't get more of the drug, and it might not

be good. So, they should really just talk it out and find some other way to make the money.[45]

Amy's moral reasoning builds on the human relationships involved. She views society as bound together through systems of human relationships, not as an institutionalized system of rules and laws. The solution to this problem is to be found in a natural set of human relationships based on mutual understanding and mutual respect. Amy reasoned, "If Heinz and the druggist had talked it out long enough, they could reach something besides stealing."[46]

Given Kohlberg's rating scale and definition of stages, Amy appears to be a full stage lower in development than Jake. Is the logic of Jake superior to, or just different from, the logic used by Amy? They do look at the world, at least through this dilemma, differently. For Jake, the dilemma is one of life versus property rights and an imperfectly written law. Amy sees it as a breakdown in human relationships. The means for resolution is the relationship; it is both the means and the end.

For us, Gilligan's thoughtful work provides another way of examining structural patterns of interaction having relevance to the social systems theory. Her work suggests that patterns of thinking might be gender-related. Differences in thinking patterns may be helpful in exploring women's issues as they pertain to forms of discrimination and oppression. These differences in thinking may operate very subtly but to the detriment of women in societies dominated by men. Gilligan developed her reasoning by comparing a hierarchical stage model evident in cognitive and moral development with a web. She framed women's issues as follows:

> The reason women's experience has been so difficult to decipher or even discern is that a shift in the imagery of relationships gives rise to a problem of interpretation. The images of hierarchy and web, drawn from the texts of men's and women's fantasies and thoughts, convey different ways of structuring relationships and are associated with different views of morality and self.[47]

Faith and Spirituality Development

Wilber developed what he termed a "Spectrum Model" of spiritual development that is grounded in the stages of cognitive development proposed by Piaget. Wilber focused on the evolutionary development of a spiritual way of experiencing the world. The model is eclectic and inclusive, drawing from psychological, social, and religious paradigms.

Viewed as a developmental sequence, Wilber's spiritual development model shows the influence of Piaget. Wilber proposed the following stages:

1. Sensori-physical: body-oriented awareness
2. Preoperations: fantasy-emotional centeredness
3. Late Preoperational: symbolic representational thinking
4. Concrete Operations: autonomous but conformist
5. Formal Operational: sophisticated rationality
6. Vision Logic: holistic inclusivity
7. Psychic: communion with the world
8. Subtle: communion with divinity
9. Formlessness: no separation
10. Nondual: the union of the ultimate and the ordinary[48]

He organized his system into a holarchy, as discussed in our earlier references to Koestler. Each successive stage subsumes the earlier stage, and each stage is construed as a holon: it addresses the inner contents of all previous stages, but is oriented outward also to the next stage of development. It can be visualized as resembling the concentric growth rings of a tree, with the growing edge analogous to the cambium located in the outermost ring at any stage.

In Wilber's view, the physical self, cognition, emotion, and morality are all components of the development of the self as a holistic, ultimately spiritual creature. Fixation at lower stages of spiritual development may occur due to environmental or spiritual obstacles. Wilber's view is emphatically systemic in nature, incorporating biological, psychological, social, and spiritual models.

Similarly, Fowler postulated a developmental model of faith that follows the stage sequence of Piaget. Fowler envisioned faith as an organizing schema within the person that aids coping with social developmental tasks, formulating self-concept around social relationships, understanding existential issues such as the place of the self in relation to the universal, and dealing with morality.[49]

Operating from a largely Christian frame of reference, Fowler's stages of faith development demonstrate more influence from social institutions, and are more representative of what we have referred to as religious rather than spiritual considerations. The stages are generally consistent with a development away from conforming belief systems and in the direction of independent judgment in the manner of Kohlberg's moral model.

Neither Wilber nor Fowler offered truly epigenetic models, since both allowed for alterations in the hierarchy due to personality or circumstance. Clearly, Wilber's model is more mystical in its orientation and moves further in expanding spiritual development beyond the moral development processes set forth by Kohlberg.

Summary

The work of Piaget suggests that cognitive development occurs in a fixed sequence. The progression is hierarchical and results in an ever more complex and differentiated set of structures. At the level of formal operations, the individual is able to think conceptually and symbolically, and is thus freed of thinking based on direct experience. The individual now possesses the mental capacities for both retrospective and future thinking, not only about self and others but also about all forms of human groupings, and thus can plan and work toward building a better world.

Piaget also advanced the notion that cognitive development is a social process, one that is dependent on interactions with others. We find cognitive development theory useful, not only because it supports the view that selfhood is an ongoing social process, but also because it suggests that this occurs in fixed stages. Within social systems theory, this offers a structural dimension that incorporates the notion of life stages.

Kohlberg builds on the foundation of cognitive theory by charting moral development. Our interest in moral development is threefold. First, the profession of social work is grounded in a set of values and moral reasoning that focuses on an individual's right to be self-determined and to be allowed to achieve his or her well-being. This is the foundation on which the professional helping relationship and the profession's use of the service contract builds. Kohlberg's work helps extend the reasoning on which the social work values of self-determination, potentiality, human worth and dignity, and others rest. At a more general level, the profession of social work is devoted to a set of moral principles that apply to all and have as their purpose an improvement in the well-being of all people. This is the profession's highest statement of purpose. Again, Kohlberg's moral development theory helps operationalize the notion of social process by linking it to the highest level of moral reasoning and the involvement of a set of moral principles.

Second, while both cognitive and moral development theory are classified as psychological theories, individual development is recognized as a social process. This view, presented in cognitive and moral development theory, is for us one-sided and linear in its orientation. The impact that the individual as a psychological being has on the groups in which she or he is a member is not examined. The cyclical impact of the individual and the social environment is not addressed. The use of these two theories within the framework provided by social systems theory becomes a way of incorporating these reciprocal and dynamic influences.

For example, we hold that the various groups that humans form evolve into group cultures, which include value systems. These value systems, especially in families, become reference points that affect the moral development of group members. This interplay between group (family) members and the individual members, particularly children, is especially important. We will be examining these relationships in Part Three, The Social Group.

Social systems theory also employs a four-functional-requisite paradigm to explain well-being. Pattern maintenance is one of the four requisite functions comprising this paradigm. Kohlberg's work on moral development theory is helpful in thinking about the pattern-maintenance function. Recall that the function pertains to the maintenance of the core or most vital patterns of behavior that distinguish the social system from others. In reviewing this function, we mentioned that all systems possess a hierarchy of interactional patterns with those at the core being the ones that are most important to maintain. If those patterns are violated, the system risks losing steady state and ceasing to exist. In most groups, this core pattern will be interlaced with mutually shared moral values, for example, trust, confidentiality, fidelity, honesty, justice, and respect, to mention but a few. The thinking and research performed by Kohlberg and others in this tradition help us understand why these patterns are of such fundamental importance in the maintenance and development of the social system.

Third and finally, the concept of moral development may explain the differences in thought in different people. We are especially interested in the differences in the development of moral thought that may be gender-related.

It should be noted that critics have observed that Kohlberg's theory addresses moral thought.

His theory does not deal with moral actions as such. This focus on cognition rather than behavior makes it difficult to validate the theory empirically.

Wilber extended cognitive development into the realm of faith and spirituality, proposing a ten-stage model. He viewed spirituality as the highest stage of the holarchically organized self. Fowler's developmental model of faith is patterned closely on Piaget's stages. Both Wilber and Fowler discussed the environmental factors that may impede self-actualization.

COGNITIVE-BEHAVIORAL THEORY

An important extension of the behavioral learning model is what is referred to as **cognitive-behavioral theory.** This approach extends the behavioral model by considering cognitive (mental) events in addition to behaviors.

Some of the most promising developments in the therapeutic application of human behavior theory have come in the synthesis of behavioral learning theory and cognitive theory. Despite the apparent contradiction between the extreme empiricism of behaviorists such as Watson and Skinner and the rationalism of the cognitive theorists, the emerging field of cognitive behavioral therapy has enjoyed success in a number of treatment applications. Arnold Lazarus, a pioneer in behavioral therapy, long said that there has always been a cognitive component to the various behavior therapies.[50] The theory that supports cognitive behavioral therapy is not fully developed, and seems to arise inductively from the practical application of the two schools of thought to therapeutic work.

The basic idea of cognitive behavioral therapy and its emerging theory base is that a person's thoughts (cognitions), emotions (feelings), and behaviors all interact. Much attention has been paid to the impact of flawed thinking on the person's emotions. Seligman observed that the fleeting automatic thoughts a person has in response to outside events do much to determine faulty behavioral responses.[51] For example, a person who lacks self-confidence might interpret every remark as a criticism. When a friend says, "Hi" and asks where you have been, your automatic thought might be that the friend thinks you have been goofing off. You then begin to stutter and apologize, and this behavior leads your friend to be irritated and angry. In cognitive behavioral therapy, one approach would be to identify the automatic thought, and by changing that thought change the ensuing behavior.

Seligman is also among those who have noted that a thought process (or habit) called *learned helplessness* may account for many behavioral problems. Learned helplessness is a mindset that exists when a person comes to believe that they have no control over events or their own life. It is believed that people with this thought style may be more prone to mood disorders, notably depression.[52] *Attribution theory*, an approach developed by Abramson that concerns itself with the thought processes that go with interpreting events in our lives, called this trait an "explanatory style." Her belief is that if we change the explanations that people give to events, we can change their behavior. This approach is a type of what is called *reframing.*[53]

Attribution theory and the learned helplessness model have slightly different interpretations of how thinking errors result in persistent behavior problems, but they share broad similarities. Attribution theory suggests that people locate the cause of their problems internally, in effect blaming themselves. Seligman's hopelessness model suggests three factors that produce dysfunctional thought leading to behavior problems:

- *Personal.* People with problems see themselves as the cause ("I am just stupid!").
- *Permanent.* People with problems see the problems as unchangeable ("My life is hopeless!").

- *Pervasive.*   People with problems see the problem as contaminating their entire life ("My divorce has ruined everything for me!").

Albert Ellis and Aaron Beck have made important contributions to this approach, which has direct treatment implications. In cognitive-behavioral theory, ideas such as self-concept are seen as important antecedents to overt behavior. For example, if a person thinks of himself as unattractive, his behavior in meeting an attractive woman might be influenced by that thought.[54]

Ellis has diagrammed the cognitive-behavioral sequence as follows:

	Activating Event →	Underlying Belief →	Consequences
Problem	Meet attractive person	"I am ugly"	Avoid communication
Treatment	Meet attractive person	"I am handsome"	Approach the person

Ellis calls this approach **Rational Emotive Therapy**.

The concept of **"self-talk,"** an internal dialog, is important here. For example, if a person says to himself, "I am ugly, she will not like me," he is unlikely to approach an attractive woman. Thus, his behavior of avoiding interaction makes it impossible to dispute the self-concept. Cognitive-behavioral theory extends the concepts of behaviorism by disputing or contradicting negative self-talk. By rehearsing positive self-talk, the subsequent behavior in social situations can be altered.

The cognitive-behavioral model has demonstrated its practical applicability and is consistent with the traditional social work emphasis on the person-in-the-environment perspective. The synthesis of empirical rigor and the subjective mental events such as self-talk have produced some of the most promising practice

results of any of the theories discussed in this chapter.

The work in cognitive behavioral theory development continues, currently stressing the effect of thinking on emotions and behavior. Marsha Linehan applied an approach called dialectical behavior therapy (DBT) to the treatment of borderline personality disorders.[55] Dialectical behavior therapy is a complex approach that draws on cognitive and behavioral theory to address the emotional volatility of clients with borderline personality disorders. An interesting feature of DBT is that borderline personality disorder is characterized by a seriously flawed thinking style called "splitting," in which the client is unable to think of people except in either/or, black or white, ways. To the these clients, people are good or evil, for us or against us, with no gray areas. In DBT, the therapist works to gain control of the volatile emotions; then this increased emotional control in turn allows the client to develop more nuanced and effective styles of thought. This presages other approaches in which the cause-and-effect interactions between thoughts, feelings, and behaviors can be more effectively modeled and worked with. Linehan's approach employs reframing, engagement, self-talk, group support, and supportive confrontation.

Ongoing research and clinical application may lead to other connections between thoughts, feelings, and behavior. Arnold Lazarus noted the centrality of what is called "mindfulness," the ability to attend closely to one's own ongoing thought processes.[56] This is a central element of meditation in many Eastern religious and philosophical practices. For future researchers, the focus on mindfulness may lead to the integration of cognitive-behavioral theory with the ancient theories of behavior linked to Buddhism and Hinduism. By moving toward the inclusion of other cultural traditions and theories, we are anticipating the broader humanism discussed in the next section.

HUMANISM

In **humanistic theory** we find support for the focus on strengths and the orientation toward the human potential that is incorporated in a social systems perspective to practice. Humanism is sometimes referred to as the "third force" in modern psychology.[57] A review of the notion of the third force may be helpful in distinguishing this line of theory development. Briefly stated, psychoanalytic theory and behaviorism represent the two forces that historically have been most influential in psychology. These same two lines of theory development have dominated approaches used by professional helpers, including social workers. The third force, humanism, represents an alternative way of understanding human behavior.

Humanism seeks to rectify some perceived deficiencies in both the psychoanalytic and behavioral approaches. Among the concerns that prompted the humanists to come up with their third force, the following are notable.

- *Determinism.* Both psychoanalysis and behaviorism reject the notion that human choice is possible. Psychoanalysis proposes that behavior is determined by a combination of instinctive drives, unconscious processes, and early developmental events. Behaviorism asserts that behavior is determined solely by consequences and that neither human thought nor free will play a role.
- *Reductionism.* Both the psychoanalysts and the behaviorists stress that human behavior can be understood in the same way we understand the behavior of animals. Neither makes allowance for uniquely human potential or positive motivations.
- *Pathology.* Psychoanalysis is focused on pathological behavior and has little to contribute to models of healthy human development and behavior. Analysts tend to focus on problems, as in the old joke that says "the analytic patient who comes to treatment early is

anxious, if he comes late he is resisting, and if he comes on time he is compulsive."

- *Limited Focus.* Radical behaviorism dogmatically rejects any role for human thought or for any other aspect of human experience that is not directly observable. This results in occasionally cumbersome inventions that force nonbehavioral concepts, such as "thought" into theoretical straitjackets.
- *Value Deficiency.* Neither of the two classical approaches provides an adequate framework for "valuing the client" and respecting client uniqueness, life experience, and choice.

The third force focuses on the "humanness" of mankind and the wholeness of the individual as opposed to some particular feature of the individual such as cognitive development.[58] In a sense, humanism is as much a way of thinking as it is a distinctive line of theory development. Perhaps because it is less dogmatic than psychoanalytic or behaviorist theories, many professional helpers have adopted it as a general guide to practice.

Many writers and theorists are identified with humanistic theory, including Carl Rogers, Gordon Allport, Charlotte Buhler, and Abraham Maslow. We will focus our attention on the contributions of Abraham Maslow. Born in Brooklyn, New York, Abraham Maslow (1908–1970) was well informed in both psychoanalytic and behaviorist theories. Maslow's concern about the deficiencies in these theories led to his formulation of a humanistic theory.

Assumptions

Humanistic psychology focuses on wholeness and is congruent with the assumptions contained in the social systems perspective. The central contribution of humanism to these assumptions is its attention to human potential, growth, and its proactive formulation of human behavior. Earlier we identified the following assumption: Well-being is the natural state of all humans and the various types of social organizations that humans join to form. This assumption borrows heavily from humanistic theory, particularly the work of Maslow. What we have done is simply extended this idea to all the forms of human groupings that individuals join to form.

The focus in humanism is on the distinctiveness of humankind. Perhaps the central theme linking theorists of this tradition is the assumption that humans have an inner drive directing them toward self-fulfillment, which is sometimes referred to as the "human potential movement." Maslow's theory of the hierarchy of needs is perhaps the clearest presentation of a human drive toward fulfillment, the need to become self-actualized.[59]

Humanism in the tradition of Maslow asserts that a psychology of human behavior should be developed by the study of the healthiest of humankind. Through the study of those who were self-actualized, Maslow fashioned his need theory.[60] Consistent with this view of a drive toward self-actualization, Maslow assumed that one's inner nature is good, or at least neutral. Humanism also stresses the individualistic nature of the human; each person is unique. Specifically, Maslow held that the understanding of human behavior starts with the acceptance of an essentially biologically based inner nature and of the fact that each person's inner nature is part unique and part species-wide.[61]

Concepts

A brief review of some of the central concepts used by Maslow in formulating his need theory should prove useful in demonstrating their tie to a social systems perspective.

Need. The concept of **need** pertains to an internal stimulus of genetic origin, a source of motivation directed toward the survival and development of the human. For Maslow, need represents a central organizing concept, one that he uses to identify the distinctive qualities of humankind. Given the genetic basis of human needs, for Maslow these needs provide the foundation for a "system of intrinsic values."[62] He postulated a hierarchy of needs that forms the foundation for a hierarchy of values; these values constitute the essence of human nature. Needs and the means through which needs are satisfied become the medium for individual development, but even more important, for the development of humankind itself.

Hierarchy of Needs. Maslow identifies five need levels: survival, safety and security, social belonging, self-esteem, and self-actualization. These needs are arranged in a hierarchy from those that are most basic and related to satisfaction of survival imperatives (such as food) to self-actualization (the realization of one's unique potential). In conceptualizing this need structure, Maslow viewed these needs as instinct remnants with the lowest-level needs (survival-level needs) being most like instincts. At each higher level, the needs are less like instincts; by this, Maslow meant that they were more easily overcome by adverse environmental conditions.

The lower-level needs in the hierarchy are labeled *basic* or *deficiency needs* and include survival, safety and security, social belonging, and self-esteem. Self-actualization is called a *meta* need. Meta or growth needs transcend the basic needs of the individual and deal with the capacity of the person to become all that he or she can be.

Prepotency Principle. A critical feature of Maslow's hierarchy of needs is what he called the prepotency relationship among the need levels. A phrase synonymous with **prepotency** would be *gaining dominance.* Maslow contended that once a lower-level need is essentially satisfied, the need loses its power to motivate the individual and the next higher need level gains dominance, or becomes prepotent.[63] Once all deficiency needs are essentially satisfied, the need for self-actualization gains dominance. The five need levels identified by Maslow and the notion of prepotency are illustrated in Figure 5.2.

Survival Needs. The needs comprising this level are based on the physiological requirements of the human body. These needs include the need for food, water, air, sex, and rest, among others. Sex is included as a **survival-level need** in the sense that the continuation of the species depends on reproduction. In accordance with the prepotency principle, once the survival-level needs are satisfied, they lose their dominance in shaping behavior. Hunger is often used to illustrate a survival-level need; that is, the degree of its intensity is lost once hunger is satisfied. Thus, a person who is truly hungry is dominated by the need; it is all the person can think about. However, once the hunger and related survival needs are satisfied, the need loses its dominance. The person then is said to be "refractory" to food as a stimulus. Hunger is then replaced by a higher-level need.

Maslow is helpful in formulating an approach to the study of the behavior of both the individual and society. In short, Maslow argued that need satisfaction should be treated as a basic human right. In its essence, the argument is that to become truly human, these needs must be satisfied. It is a societal responsibility to create arrangements that facilitate the satisfaction of these needs. While this point is peripheral to our main discussion, we do want to call your attention to this aspect of Maslow's argument. We also want to make the observation that the provision of social welfare services appears to incorporate a priority hierarchy similar to the one proposed by Maslow. For example, the provision of public assistance programs is basically aimed at meeting the survival-level needs of eligible recipients for food, clothing, and shelter. These needs are met before social belonging needs are met. We will have more to say about the usefulness of Maslow's ideas in a later section of this book when we deal with an application of social systems theory to the community.

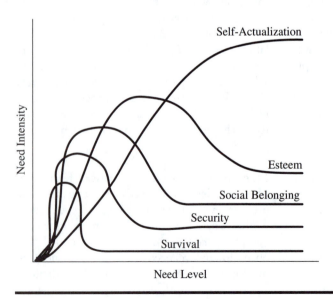

FIGURE 5.2 Maslow's Prepotency Principle

Safety and Security Needs.   Once survival-level needs are satisfied, the individual becomes conscious of the need for personal safety and the protection of his or her belongings; these needs become prepotent. When people are frightened, much of their behavior can be seen as efforts aimed at seeking a safe and secure environment. While not as dominating as survival needs, the pursuit of **safety and security needs** can account for important aspects of a person's behavior.

It is important to note that Maslow did not relate his need theory to age levels or to maturational stages. In other words, the young child or the old person may each be seeking to satisfy his or her respective survival or safety needs. Similarly, just as one may progress up the need hierarchy, so can one progress down.

Maslow also extended the need for safety and security to include the human need for orderliness and predictability. Here again we find a theorist arguing the existence of a human need for order and a propensity to create order. We have found this idea of Maslow's a useful one, and it is incorporated into our perspective. Simply put, humans both seek and create order. We are system creators; it is part of our nature.

Belongingness and Love Needs.   The need to belong, to be loved, becomes prepotent once safety and security needs are largely satisfied. It is important to distinguish between one's sexual needs and love. Sex is a physiological need; love is a relationship need. In its healthiest expression, sexual intimacy occurs within a loving relationship.

Maslow's contention that **belongingness and love needs** are genetically based and therefore universal among humans has been helpful. For us, this position offers further theoretical support for the need to look at human behavior within a social context. To become human one must enter into relationships with others. Only through other people can our need for a sense of belongingness and love be satisfied. In Part Three, The Social Group, we build on Maslow's contention by arguing that the social group offers the primary vehicle through which our sense of self, our sense of humanness, is both acquired and supported throughout life.

Esteem Needs.   The notion of esteem as used by Maslow includes both self-respect and respect from others. This need becomes prepotent once love and belongingness needs have largely been satisfied. The concept of **esteem needs** is essentially synonymous with the idea of mastery and a sense of competency. In other words, it is not enough to be loved and to possess a sense of belonging; one needs to feel good about oneself in order to possess self-esteem.

Esteem needs, along with those needs lower in the hierarchy, are classified as basic or deficiency needs. From the humanist position, one is not truly human if one's esteem needs are not met. Maslow's definition of basic needs helps us think about the implications for generalist practice.

Self-Actualization Needs.   There is a qualitative break between self-esteem and **self-actualization needs.** Self-actualization needs are growth needs.[64] Because of major environmental barriers, few people ever completely fulfill their potential. Much of Maslow's later works are concerned with self-actualization. His list of "being" values includes, among others, wholeness, completion, beauty, truth, uniqueness, and self-sufficiency.

Self-actualization needs are highly individualized and personalized and cannot be satisfied by others in the same way lower-level needs can be. The person must feel that satisfaction is accomplished largely from his or her own efforts. Maslow's need hierarchy can also be viewed as a dependence-independence continuum. This notion of a continuum reduces the emphasis on the prepotency principle but retains some of the key ideas embodied in Maslow's work. The notion of a continuum is in keeping with some of the more recent research seeking to operationalize Maslow's work.[65] Figure 5.3 illustrates Maslow's hierarchy of needs as well as the related notion of a dependence-independence continuum.

Late in his life, Maslow began to explore the concept of transcendent motives that are of a higher order than self-actualization. Transcendent motives, much like the ideas of Adler, suggest that at the point of maximum individual development, the individual begins to generalize development to the society rather than the self. The "peak experiences" of self-actualization become more frequent and may become such a feature of the personality that the person experiences revelation and insight.[66]

Humanistic psychology and Maslow's need theory in particular have contributed significantly to our social systems perspective. Humanistic theory stresses the distinctive features of the individual as opposed to qualities that

may be found in other forms of animal life. While we support the supposition that common patterns of ordering exist in all life, this is not the subject matter of the social systems perspective or of social systems theory. We are more concerned with those patterns that distinguish human forms of social organization. In the most fundamental sense, these features are found in the individuals who comprise such organizations. Employing the previously discussed concept of emergence, these qualities possessed by all humans account for the special ordering features possessed by the various classes of social organization, such as, for example, the family.

We find Maslow's contention of a hierarchy of human needs a useful concept. For us, whether these needs are of genetic origin or deeply rooted in culture is not central. What is central is a dynamic conception of human behavior and one that has a positive developmental thrust—self-actualization. These qualities, aside from their conceptual utility, provide a firm ideological

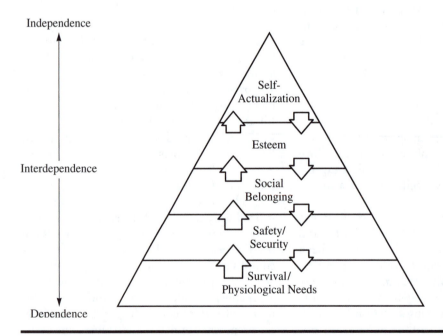

FIGURE 5.3   Maslow's Hierarchy of Needs

foundation for a professional practice aimed at improving human well-being. In this sense we incorporate the general notion of a positive thrust toward growth and development that helps establish the use of a strengths perspective in the generalist practice of social work.

SYMBOLIC INTERACTION THEORY

We have already introduced symbolic interaction briefly in Chapter 2. An understanding of symbolic interaction has important applications at various levels of human behavior, including the individual. In understanding the interrelationships of the individual, roles, and societies, the following brief definitions might be useful:

Key Symbolic Interaction Concepts

- *Symbol.* A sign for which a shared meaning exists in society. Examples include words, meanings, gestures, marks, and body postures.
- *Social Interaction.* An exchange of meanings (symbols) typically occurring between two or more individuals enacting functionally related roles and upon which some form of coordinated behavior typically results.
- *Object.* A person or thing that is assigned meaning on the basis of ongoing activity. Objects are defined by the purpose or goal-directed activity of the self.
- *Act.* A unit of behavior related to a purpose. Acts are cyclical, the end of one act being the start of another. Acts form chains that are intrinsic to the social system.
- *Social Act.* The smallest functional unit of a social relationship. Social acts involve taking the role of at least one other person and coordination with that other person.
- *Role.* A position within a social system to which expectations and norms are attached. Roles guide but do not determine behavior in the symbolic interaction view. Roles provide structure within a system, and sets of

roles are functionally directed toward common goals.
- *Situation.* The physical and social context within which social acts occur. Situations influence acts, and acts in turn alter the situation. All social behavior is "situated," that is, defined in part by the context in which it occurs.
- *Self.* The objectification of one's existence. The self exists as a reflexive interaction between the "I," the subjective aspect, and the "Me," the internalized expectations of the society. Both "I" and "Me" are conscious aspects of the self.
- *Other.* A person with whom the self interacts. The other may be real or imagined. The other may be a collective (generalized other) representing the perceived expectations of some group. Significant others are those whose expectations matter in the formation of the self-concept.
- *Conversation of Gestures.* Simple human interaction in the form of behaviors that communicate without the need for language. Touching, feeding, or signaling, such as waving, are examples. Gestures form the foundation for symbolic communication.

Stages of Selfhood

Symbolic interactionism is not usually presented as a stage model. Mead identified three stages in the development of symbolic communication. However, he did not apply these to development past early childhood. Chess has developed a perspective that relates the emergence of symbolic interaction to the other theories of human behavior discussed in this chapter.

We believe that the understanding of the self as a social unit is an important contribution of symbolic interaction. We also believe that this perspective fits perfectly with the social orientation of our profession. In the following discussion, we identify the sequences through which the self develops. We do not intend this as an epigenetic model. Particularly in its later phases, the emergence of self is characterized by a plasticity and connection to the environment that makes fixed stages impossible.

Stage I: Prelanguage (Ages Birth to Eighteen Months).   In this earliest stage of development of the self, the infant interacts with the environment primarily by means of gestures. Gestural interaction, as Mead noted, lacks the richness and flexibility of symbolic interaction. Nonetheless, it provides the foundation for the development of language and with that the fully social self. At this stage, we can consider the infant no more than a "proto-self"—literally, the first or original self.[67]

Prelanguage interaction for the infant is limited in scope. The infant learns to "take the role" of others by direct interaction. The inputs from others are of a direct, sensual nature. Examples of such sensory data include feeding, warmth, stroking, and sounds, such as cooing and baby talk. This corresponds to the sensorimotor intelligence described by Piaget. The caregiver is a source of positive reinforcement, much in the manner posited by behaviorists. The infant's sense of self is inextricably bound up with the caregiver and begins to individuate only as language and related cognitive abilities emerge. This enmeshment with the other is discussed extensively by John Bowlby as "attachment."[68]

Characteristic of stage theories is the fact that the events in early stages influence the later developmental events. As we will discuss at length in the next chapter, the experiences of the prelanguage stage form the foundation of the infant's emotional orientation to the world and to self. Erikson discussed this conflict as "trust versus mistrust."[69] If the transactions with the caregiver are safe and nurturing, the infant is predisposed to a trusting and optimistic view of the world. If the caregiver is unreliable, hurtful, or distant, the emergence of self will be distorted by mistrust, fear, and low regard for the importance of the self. There are thought to be identifiable adult personality traits that are vestiges of the early life conflicts and their resolution. A familiar example is the compulsive behaviors of some adults, which is described as "anal-retentive" in psychoanalytic theory.

The experiences of the prelanguage phase generate the emotional substrate of the self. This primal emotional orientation emerges before language skills. It is thus not accessible to memory by the usual conversational means. This fact does much to explain the unique character of verbal therapeutic encounters between clients and their therapists. In many modes of therapy, we observe a strong focus on helping clients learn to talk about feelings. This is important because the experiences of the proto-self in infancy are stored without language. Memories are experienced directly as recalled feelings, often chaotic and confused. Freud characterized such feelings as repressed. We believe that these primal experiences are simply stored in this preverbal format. Reliance on reason or verbal skills to adduce them is useless. Hypnosis, especially as practiced by Milton Erickson, was shown to aid clients in accessing this confusing, pre-articulate jumble of important memories.[70] Learning from Erickson's example, communications-based approaches, such as neurolinguistic programming theory, suggest that our choice of language rests on a primitive emotional and sensory foundation that offers insight into the proto-self for trained practitioners. If we understand the process of expressing primal feelings as a skill, we can work with clients to impose language retroactively on the experiences of the proto-self. This greatly simplifies the cumbersome processes used by analysts to access early life experiences.

You will note that this stage of development corresponds with the stage in Kohlberg's work during which there is no moral sense in the infant.[71] For this reason, we can say that there is no "right or wrong" about feelings, they simply are. We note also that it is inappropriate for an adult to act on feelings in the way a child does.

For an adult, acting on feelings without regard to others is narcissistic, since the adult has the capacity to understand behavior as a social act.

Stage 2: Role Playing (Ages Eighteen Months to Four Years). During this stage, the child makes dramatic advances in language skills. By the age of eighteen months, a child typically has a vocabulary of three to fifty words. At age three, the child's vocabulary may exceed 2,000 words. By age four, the child's language skills will be well developed.[72]

During this stage, the child faces multiple tasks: going through toilet training, developing a sense of autonomy and differentiating from the caregiver, beginning to develop moral judgment, and developing preoperational thought processes. The development of preoperational thought, with its growing capacity for the use of language, holds the greatest importance for our consideration of the self.

At this stage, Freud noted the beginnings of the superego. The superego results from the introjection of parental attitudes. The processes of the superego are not conscious; therefore, the messages sent from the superego to the ego are imprecise in nature. These messages are interpreted by the ego as neurotic anxiety. Our view is that this process is not dynamically unconscious, but simply an artifact of the child's developing language and cognitive capacities. We believe one can understand a child having good feelings and bad feelings about the self without recourse to constructs such as ego ideal, repression, neurosis, and so on.

The key process involved in stage 2 of the socialization process is called "play."[73] At this stage, the child's universe has expanded both cognitively and in fact. Words now have symbolic meanings, not just emotional connotations. "Mom" refers to the known caregiver, "go" refers to leaving, and so forth. The child is capable of imaginary play. This play greatly enlarges the world and involves taking the role of others.

Consider the behavior of a typical two-year-old girl. At this age, she can play house, and alternate in taking the voice of the mother, father, and the self. She can engage in imaginary play and experiment with different social possibilities. This process produces a repertoire of potential roles that are incorporated into the child's self.

The child learns to play out roles with herself as the object. She learns to imagine whether Mom sees her as "good" or "bad." In time she can learn to distinguish that it is her behavior, not her self, that is being judged. This moral component to behavior is fundamental to the development of a social self. At this stage, the focus is on the role, not on the interactions between the roles. Much of the play of the child is solitary, but the imagination of the child is engaged in learning to view herself from the standpoint of others. This carries with it the quality of primitive moral judgment, since the child constantly experiences actions as having good or bad consequences for her.

The child at this stage is learning to regard herself as a social object. In so doing, she attempts to anticipate the social consequences of behavior. Symbolic interaction theory does not consider all behaviors as social acts. Only when actions are undertaken in the considered context of others does behavior become social. It is more than wordplay to say that at this stage the child is moving from mere behavior into the realm of social action. In this process, she becomes more than an organism; she becomes a social self whose every conscious act will soon be social in nature.

By considering the social consequences of behavior through play, the child is developing a proactive self. She assigns meanings to her acts based on the reactions of others. She behaves in ways that she anticipates will produce desired consequences. The consequences that concern the developing child are mainly social and become more so as she moves to subsequent stages of development.

Stage 3: Game Play (Ages Four to Twelve).
This is a stage of rapid learning. The child is
exposed to a widening world upon leaving home
and going to school. The primacy of the caregiver role is supplanted by a world of adults who
are more numerous and less intimate. The child
encounters a system of age peers. The rules of
social interaction grow more complex.

The changes in the external environment
are paralleled by cognitive changes. The child
develops the capacity first for preoperational
thought, then for concrete operations. Moral
thought grows past the focus on the direct rewards and punishments that accrue to behaviors. While in stage 2, the child focused on one
role at a time; in stage 3, the child is able to conceptualize a variety of individuals in a network
of functionally related roles. Social activity requires that the child be able to take into consideration all the key roles of a system at one time
and to understand the rules that connect the different roles. This complex conceptualization of
the social system can be likened to mapping.

Mead used the concept of "games" to describe this more complex orientation.[74] Let us
consider a ten-year-old boy who plays soccer as
an example to illustrate Mead's point. In playing
soccer, the child occupies one role. From his
perspective, he must consider the organization
and relationship of the two teams in the game.
He must anticipate how each role will be played.
He must anticipate how his teammates will react
when he is attacking, and how the other team
will react on defense. He must anticipate and
seek to counter the defenses of the goalkeeper.
In the process, he is no doubt anticipating the
reaction and judgment of his coach, his parents,
and the spectators. He understands not only the
role of others, but also the rules that define the
relationships between those others. It is a complex world, and he has developed complex cognitive skills to map it. He has learned to imagine
his performance of his roles from the perspective of various others and to make a judgment
of that performance as a social act.

As he learns to enact his role, the child will
no doubt make many mistakes. It is here that he
develops skill in "defining the situation" as a social context. If he defines the game as a place to
demonstrate skill, it has one meaning. If he defines it as a place to make friends, it has another.
As we have noted, all human social action requires that the actor define the situation. That
is, we give meaning to all the actions and possible actions in a situation. This constant process
of assessment and judgment becomes so automatic that we are scarcely aware of it in familiar
social situations. In novel circumstances, we can
quickly become preoccupied with this activity.
We must recall that for the stage 3 child, many
of the situations an adult might consider routine are still novel. Thus, the level of vigilance
required in social definitions is quite high. Our
soccer player might define his actions on the
field as meeting the expectations of his parents
to "be a good sport." It might involve his
coach's desire to "be a winner." Or, his peers
might call on him to maintain a mocking role
distance from "the silly game." In fact, he will
likely consider all these perspectives and more,
including the explicit rules of the game itself.
The implicit social rules are of much greater
import over time.

In the soccer example, a child reacts to
many "others." He is able to create a notion of
the generalized other to guide his social actions.
This allows him to imagine how "they" think
about his play. The spectators at the game are a
simple type of generalized other. In fact, our
soccer player may imagine a remote, abstract
generalized other that need not be present to be
important in defining a situation. This ability to
consider the rules, the others (including those
not physically present), and the self constitute
the beginnings of systems-oriented thought.
This ability to conceptualize the self, others,
rules, goals, and reactions as part of the system
as a whole is a uniquely human achievement.
This ability accounts in large part for our great
success as a species. If this capacity does not de-

velop, serious social complications are almost certain. A person who, like a stage 1 child, continues to act in unsocialized ways on the basis of emotional impulses will certainly run afoul of the social order. A great deal of social work practice has to do with helping clients whose early experiences have failed to prepare them to function as a coordinated part of an intricate social system. Clients with mental illnesses, such as schizophrenia, may lack the ability to form the abstract understanding of rules needed for complex social behavior. In skilled social work practice, these rules may be rendered more concrete so that the client may develop better understanding and thus more autonomy in society.

Stage 4: Selfhood Stabilization (Ages Twelve through Thirty-Five). In this stage, the self addresses the crucial task of selfhood stabilization. Selfhood is a process that continues throughout life. Our sense of self is different at eighteen from what it is at thirty-five. The reflexive process of selfhood is dynamic and incessant. It is never really at rest. Nonetheless, the self does achieve a relative steady state. This steady state we have described as a state of well-being. The self continues to define new and changing situations, adjust behavior to these new demands, and alter the sense of self as a process. However, in this stage the process is one of morphostasis (maintaining the system) rather than morphogenesis (creating the system). The adjustments in the self are usually minor, barring major upheaval in a person's circumstances.

Adolescence defines the early part of this stage. A major task of selfhood is achievement of a sexual identity in this stage. Our adult identity is closely bound up with our sexuality. Sexual identity is importantly influenced by anatomy and physiology, but the greater significance for the self comes from social meanings.

Hormonal changes affect mood, among other things, in ways that lie beneath the threshold of the self. Powerful and unfamiliar emotions are characteristic of adolescence. The

social meaning assigned to these sensations is crucial. If society defines sexuality as base and distasteful, the feelings experienced by the adolescent cannot remain unaffected. If the feelings are seen as normal and positive, this can also be incorporated into the self-concept. Feelings of sexual attraction that are not "normal" in a society pose particular dangers for the emerging self-concept of gay, lesbian, or bisexual persons. Social work has long sought to promote a social normalization of attitudes toward these common variations in sexual orientation.

Stage 4 corresponds to Piaget's notion of the development of formal operations. In the previous stage, concrete operations, logic was tied to tangible phenomena. Now, logic is freed to deal with abstract concepts that have no simple counterpart in the physical world. The logical and systematic nature of thought now can address factors such as love, justice, and meaning without being tied to specifics in direct experience. This ability, in turn, makes possible higher levels of abstract moral reasoning, which relate to concepts such as justice and are capable of transcending the social conventions of one's own life. In essence, one becomes truly freed to think and judge as an individual. This ability to transcend social rules requires that one first have the ability to understand them. Kohlberg, as we have noted, felt that most people never were able to arrive at this transcendent level of morality, which is mute testimony to the power of social conformity.[75]

The biological and social consequence of sexual maturity is the potential for the self to form new relationships and create a family system. Historically, this was linked to the important function of having and caring for children. Much of modern morality has emerged from the efforts of the social system to protect the vital function of procreation. Modern society has realized much greater flexibility in the forms and structures of families. Gochros and Gochros discuss the reproductive bias, which has long defined normal sexual identity as that "which could conceivably result in a socially approved pregnancy." Not all people are linked to or defined by procreation-based values, and this has been a source of conflict in defining social rules.[76] This has produced predictable complications for people whose definitions of self differ from those prescribed by social convention. As we will discuss in connection with social stratification and diversity, our complex society has created a range of generalized others and social models to which people may refer as they stabilize their adult sense of self. While this creates more freedom, it also creates more tension within the social system.

Another vital social task that occurs during this phase is occupational choice. Many theories pay little attention to this issue, although it occupies a prominent place in defining our self and our place in the social order. Occupational choice is interlaced with the family of origin and cannot be ignored in the process of selecting a life partner. In our society, occupation is the prime determinant of economic well-being. Success in developing a stable adult self, with the ability to coordinate social relations, cooperate with others, and engage in sustained, goal-directed activities are major determinants of the quality of life an individual will enjoy. For most people, work life is structured into more formally defined roles and rules than family life. For that reason, some people derive a safer and more stable sense of self from their work than from their families. In clinical observation, it has frequently been noted that when a person begins to fail in social tasks, "the job is the last to go." The clear expectations and definitions of roles at work probably account for this phenomenon. Certainly we know that entry into the workplace and retirement from one's career represent events of enormous importance in self-definition, stability, and self-esteem.

Stage 5: Selfhood Fulfillment (Thirty-Five and Beyond).   This stage might more accurately be defined as "the pursuit of fulfillment." This con-veys a sense of the process and some of the Sisyphean flavor of selfhood. Sisyphus, you recall, was the ancient Greek mythical figure who cheated death and was condemned by the gods to roll a stone up a hill for all eternity, only to have it roll back and so begin the task anew. The business of selfhood is similarly unending. Selfhood is not a static state. For the self to exist as a system, continuous application of energy is required to maintain order and structure. This process does not end with maturity, but continues throughout life.

In this stage, the self is increasingly future oriented. The self is usually established, but the pursuit of goals continues. Interruptions in the steady state of the self (having children, occupational crises, wars, illness, loss of loved ones, children leaving home, and so forth) represent real issues. Some external crises may represent major threats to the steady state of the adult self-system. Failure to achieve a stable sense of self earlier in life, of course, aggravates these risks.

In some views, the late stages of life may be understood as the triumph of entropic processes over negative entropy. Inevitably, we die. To some degree, we may begin to disintegrate as a self before we die. Our cognitive powers dim. Our physical self begins to fail. We withdraw from major life roles such as work, parenthood, friendship, and so on. It is not surprising that many gerontologists advocate that the older adult maintain a high level of social involvement to forestall this entropic process of disintegration with society. The future-oriented self knows this, and this knowledge is often basic to the pursuit of fulfillment. Irvin Yalom, as an existentialist, identified four universal existential issues that all adults must address:[77]

- Meaning of life
- Aloneness
- Freedom and responsibility
- Death

The meaning of life is certainly a symbolic issue and derives from the total experience of one's life. The search for meaning is a familiar existential theme and is entirely consonant with a symbolic interactional view. This quest, together with the reality of death, forms the foundation for the spiritual quest humans face.

Aloneness seems contrary to a social interactional view. However, we feel that it is quite consistent with symbolic interactionism to say that people live life in a social milieu so that personal identity and social context cannot be distinguished. As one confronts death, it is an intensely personal experience. We have no social network of those who have experienced it. Death is an ultimate act we must face alone, and our social nature recoils. In our society, where life is generally good, death is viewed as something to be feared. In other times and other places, death may be seen as a liberation. It is a topic not often discussed in our society. Our society treats death the way Victorian society treated sex: we know it is there, but nice people don't discuss it.

Freedom and responsibility also pose interesting questions for the adult self. If we have lived life trying to figure out the views of others, were we ever really free? If we behave so as to gain rewards and acceptance, can we say that we are responsible for our actions? Are we, after all, determined by our context?

In the next chapter, we discuss Erik Erikson and his view of generativity. In this view, the last stages of life gain meaning as the self seeks to make a creative contribution that will outlast physical existence. This meaning may be found in the nature of spirituality, children, inventions, social justice, ideas, or help for others. For adults with healthy selfhood, the importance of the self does not end with death.

SUMMARY

In this chapter, we reviewed seven theories that relate to individual behavior and development. Each stresses different aspects of behavior. Each is important to the field of social work, and each informs social systems theory in a somewhat different way. Psychoanalysis stresses innate drives and unconscious processes. Behaviorism considers behavior as a product of environmental stimuli. Humanism addresses unique human characteristics and potentials. Cognitive and moral development theories suggest that people do not all think alike. Social workers should be alert to the implications of this reasoning. Social work practice in all of its forms is premised on relationships. Symbolic interaction theory illustrates the inseparable linkages between the development of self and the relationship with others. In this section, we described the evolution of the self in stages and linked those stages with the descriptions of various aspects of human development provided by other approaches. The sequence of these stages is diagrammed in Figure 6.1 at the end of the next chapter.

GLOSSARY

Accommodation In cognitive development theory, the construction of new schemata or modification of existing schemata to adjust to new experiences or information.

Anal stage The second of the five psychosexual stages associated with psychoanalytic theory.

Assimilation In cognitive development theory, the fitting of new experiences and objects into an existing schema.

Behavior modification/therapy The treatment of problem behaviors usually employing operant conditioning procedures.

Belongingness and love needs This third need level of Maslow becomes prepotent when safety and security needs are largely satisfied. This need is typified by affiliation, intimacy, caring, loving.

Circular reaction In cognitive development theory, the term used to describe each learning activity in which infants attempt to repeat an action that first occurred by chance.

Classical conditioning   A basic paradigm in experimental psychology that emphasizes the learning of associations between environmental events or stimuli.

Cognitive-behavioral theory   The extension of behavioral learning principles to include cognitive events (thoughts).

Cognitive development theory   Theory pertaining to the steps involved in deriving meaning from experience.

Concrete operational thought   The third of Piaget's four cognitive stages. This stage starts at about age six and ends in early adolescence.

Conditioned reflex (CR)   In classical conditioning, the response evoked by a stimulus as a consequence of repeated association.

Conditioned stimulus (CS)   In classical conditioning, the stimulus that produces the response as a consequence of repeated and systematic association.

Conscious   The individual's capacity to experience cognitively and emotionally what is going on in the environment and to process and act in accordance with this information.

Conventional morality   The second level of Kohlberg's moral development theory. The moral reasoning is based on a sense of fairness that incorporates shared conventions.

Defense mechanism   In psychoanalytic theory, the means used by the ego to defend against impulses of the id and the unrealistic expectations of the superego.

Discrimination   In behaviorism, the ability to respond only to an individual case from a set of stimuli.

Ego   In psychoanalytic theory, the part of the mental structure that has been socialized and experiences and interprets reality.

Electra complex   In psychoanalytic theory, this concept is the counterpart of the Oedipal complex. The daughter possesses an unconscious incestuous desire for her father along with animosity toward her mother.

Esteem needs   The fourth of Maslow's need levels is concerned with our need for self-respect and respect from others. This need level dominates after the social belonging and love needs are largely satisfied.

Extinction   The assumption that behaviors that are not reinforced will reduce to their baseline or natural level of occurrence.

Formal operational thought   The fourth of Piaget's cognitive stages. Adult capacities of reasoning, abstraction, and symbolization emerge. This stage begins at adolescence and continues through adulthood.

Generalization   In operant conditioning, the process in which a response generalizes across a class of stimuli.

Genital stage   The fifth and final stage in psychoanalytic theory.

Humanistic theory   A major branch of modern psychology called the "third force" (the other two forces being psychoanalysis and behaviorism). This psychological approach views humans as having a natural tendency toward actualization, growth, and a fulfillment of basic potential. It views basic human nature as positive.

Id   In psychoanalytic theory, the primitive part of the mental apparatus that contains inherited instinctual urges.

Latency stage   The fourth of the five psychosexual stages in psychoanalytic theory.

Methodological (S–O–R) behaviorism   The theory that environmental–behavioral relationships are mediated by an individual's symbolic or cognitive processes.

Need   An internal state of an individual pertaining to requirements for a state of well-being, for example, an internal motivational state.

Negative reinforcement   The removal of an averse stimulus.

Oedipal stage   Alternative language for the phallic stage of development among males in psychoanalytic theory.

Operant conditioning   The position that behavior is determined by its consequences.

Oral stage   The first of the five psychosexual stages in development identified in psychoanalytic theory.

Organization   In cognitive development theory, the tendency to seek and build order.

Phallic stage   The third of the five psychosexual stages of development in psychoanalytic theory.

Pleasure principle   Freud's principle of psychoanalytic theory that holds that organisms seek pleasure and avoid pain by the immediate discharge of their instinctive drives and tension states.

Positive reinforcer A stimulus that increases the possibility that an antecedent behavior will occur again.

Postconventional morality The third level of Kohlberg's hierarchy of moral development.

Preconscious Thoughts and content that are not in the person's awareness but, unlike the unconscious, can be recalled by the individual when needed.

Preconventional morality The first level of development in Kohlberg's theory of moral development.

Preoperational thought The second of Piaget's four cognitive stages. This stage occurs from approximately eighteen months of age and ends during the early school years.

Prepotency A concept related to Maslow's need theory. This concept simply means that a lower-level need dominates our attention and motivates us until it is satisfied, then the next higher need level becomes prepotent.

Psychoanalysis The method of treatment is based on psychoanalytic theory.

Psychodynamic Cognitive, emotional, and motivational processes that consciously and unconsciously affect one's behavior.

Punishment The method of ending a given behavior by the addition of an unpleasant stimulus.

Radical (S–R) behaviorism The theory that environmental control acts directly on behavior.

Rational-Emotive-Therapy Ellis's specific application of cognitive-behavioral principles to include subjective events.

Reality principle In psychoanalytic theory, the recognition of the behavioral demands of the real world. The ego learns and finds ways of postponing the immediate forms of gratification related to the pleasure principle.

Reinforcement A stimulus that increases the probability that a specified antecedent behavior will occur again.

Reinforcement schedules The timing structures employed to increase the probability of a desired behavior occurring. Schedules include continuous reinforcement, fixed-ratio schedule, and variable-ratio schedule, among others.

Repression The manner, according to Freud, in which animal-like aggressive and sexual impulses are "forgotten" by an individual. These impulses then become part of the person's unconscious.

Safety and security needs The second of Maslow's five need levels, these needs dominate or become prepotent after survival needs have been met. Individuals at this need level are concerned with personal safety, protection of belongings, orderliness, and predictability.

Schema In cognitive development theory, a perceived representation of reality in memory.

Self-actualization needs The growth, meta, or being needs that are qualitatively different from Maslow's four lower or basic need levels. These being needs are highly individualized, personalized, and internalized. Few individuals become truly self-actualized.

Self-talk Internal dialogue composed of unuttered thoughts.

Sensorimotor intelligence The first of Piaget's four cognitive stages. This stage is from birth to eighteen months of age. Development centers on sensory and motor schemes.

Shaping The concept of reinforcing all behaviors that lead to a desired end behavior.

Spectrum Model Wilber's stage model of spirituality based on cognitive developmental principles.

Spontaneous recovery The concept that extinguished behaviors can reappear under circumstances similar to those that originally reinforced the behaviors.

Stage A developmental level tied to epigenetic theory.

Stage theory A classification of theories organized around maturational development, that is, a fixed sequence of stages.

Superego In psychoanalytic theory, the part of the mental structure likened to one's conscience. The superego contains a person's parental attitudes and cultural standards.

Survival-level need The most basic human needs according to Maslow, these needs constitute the first of five need levels. These needs include, among others, food, water, air, sex, and rest.

Unconditioned reflex (UR) In classical conditioning, a physiologically or internally based response to an unconditioned stimulus.

Unconditioned stimulus (US) In classical conditioning, the stimulus that evokes the unconditioned response, for example, a stimulus that produces a response prior to a learning opportunity.

Unconscious   In psychoanalytic theory, this concept is synonymous with life force and includes sexual and aggressive impulses that are animal-like inorigin, including desires, wishes, and experiences that are frightening or unacceptable to the individual.

NOTES

1. See *The Encyclopedic Dictionary of Sociology*, 3rd ed. (Guilford, CT: The Dushkin Publishing Group, 1986), 279.

2. *The Encyclopedic Dictionary of Psychology*, 3rd ed. (Guilford, CT: The Dushkin Publishing Group, 1986), 224–227.

3. For a brief but helpful summary of these lines of theory development, see Joyce O. Beckett and Harriette C. Johnson, "Human Development," *Encyclopedia of Social Work*, vol. 2 (Washington DC: NASW Press, 1995), 1385–1404.

4. For a general review, see Donald Brieland, "Social Work Practice: History and Evolution," *Encyclopedia of Social Work*, vol. 3 (Washington DC: NASW Press, 1995), 2247–2258.

5. Freud's early work in hysteria was done in collaboration with Josef Breuer and resulted in the publication in 1895 of *Studies in Hysteria*. Later, Breuer disassociated himself from Freud, from psychoanalytic theory, and from what came to be known as the practice of psychoanalysis.

6. Charles Darwin, *The Origin of Species* (New York: Modern Library, 1859).

7. See, for example, Sigmund Freud (1920), *A General Introduction to Psychoanalysis*, J. Riviere, trans. (New York: Washington Square Press, 1965).

8. Erik H. Erikson, *Childhood and Society*, 2nd ed. (New York: W. W. Norton, 1963).

9. Barbara M. Newman and Philip R. Newman, *Development Through Life: A Psychosocial Approach*, 6th ed. (New York: Brooks/Cole, 1995).

10. See, for example, Sigmund Freud, *Instincts and their Vicissitudes*, J. Riviere, trans. Collected Papers, vol. IV (New York: Basic Books, 1959).

11. C. Hall, *A Primer of Freudian Psychology* (New York: Mentor, 1954).

12. F. Alexander and H. Ross, eds., *Dynamic Psychiatry* (Chicago, IL: University of Chicago Press, 1952), 9–10.

13. Sigmund Freud, "New Introductory Lectures on Psychoanalysis." In J. Strachey, ed., *The Standard Edition of the Complete Psychological Works of Sigmund Freud*, vol. 22 (London: Hogarth Press, 1964).

14. See, for example, Sigmund Freud, "Female Sexuality," J. Strachey, trans., *Collected Papers*, vol. V (New York: Basic Books, 1959).

15. Measures of influence can be either positive or negative. For an interesting example of the latter, see E. F. Torrey, *Freudian Fraud: The Malignant Effects of Freud's Theory on American Thought and Culture* (New York: Harper Collins, 1992).

16. Daniel N. Robinson, *Systems of Modern Psychology* (New York: Columbia University Press, 1979), 93.

17. See particularly John B. Watson, "Psychology as the Behaviorist Views it," *Psychological Review*, vol. 1, no. 2 (April 1994): 248.

18. Ibid.

19. For a review, see Ivan P. Pavlov, *Conditional Reflexes*, G. V. Ansev, trans. (London: Oxford University Press, 1964).

20. For discussions of their works, see Edwin G. Boring, *A History of Experimental Psychology* (New York: Appleton-Century-Crofts, 1957).

21. John B. Watson, *Behaviorism* (New York: W. W. Norton, 1970), 104.

22. B. F. Skinner, *The Behavior of Organisms* (Englewood Cliffs, NJ: Prentice Hall, 1938), 20–21.

23. Nathan Azrin and W. C. Holz in W. K. Honig, *Operant Behavior: Areas of Research and Application* (Englewood Cliffs, NJ: Prentice Hall, 1966).

24. Albert Bandura and Richard Walters, *Social Learning and Personality Development* (New York: Holt, Rinehart & Winston, 1963).

25. Ibid.

26. For a discussion of this relationship, see Jean Piaget, "Piaget's Theory," in *Handbook of Child Psychology*, Paul H. Mussen, ed., 4th ed. (New York: John Wiley & Sons, 1983), 103–128.

27. Ibid.

28. Abraham H. Maslow, *Motivation and Personality*, 2nd ed. (New York: Harper and Row, 1970), 35–58.

29. Piaget, "Piaget's Theory," 109–112.

30. For a convenient and easily understood summary of Piaget's stage model, see Ruth M. Beard, *An Outline of Piaget's Developmental Psychology for Students and Teachers* (New York: Basic Books, 1969).

31. Ibid., 49.

32. Jean Piaget, *The Psychology of Intelligence* (London: Routledge & Kegan, 1950), 53.

33. For a review of cognitive theory and its development in social work, see Edmund Sherman, "Cognitive Therapy," *Encyclopedia of Social Work*, vol. 1 (Silver Spring: MD: National Association of Social Workers, 1987), 288–291.

34. For a social work application, see Diane de Anda, "Adolescents," *Encyclopedia of Social Work*, vol. 1 (Silver Spring, MD: National Association of Social Workers, 1987), 288–291.

35. B. F. Skinner, *About Behaviorism* (New York: Alfred A. Knopf, 1974), 244.

36. Maslow, *Motivation and Personality*, XIII.

37. For example, see Lawrence Kohlberg, "Development of Moral Character and Moral Ideology," M. L. Hoffman and L. W. Hoffman, eds., *Review of Child Development Research*, vol. 1 (New York: Russell Sage Foundation, 1964).

38. See, for example, John C. Gibbs and Keith E. Widaman, *Social Intelligence: Measuring the Development of Sociomoral Reflections* (Englewood Cliffs, NJ: Prentice Hall, 1982).

39. Lawrence Kohlberg, "The Development of Children's Orientations Toward a Moral Order: 1 Sequence in the Development of Moral Thought," *Human Development*, vol. 6 (1963): 19.

40. Lawrence Kohlberg, *Essays on Moral Development*, vol. 1 (New York: Harper and Row, 1981), 43.

41. Carol Gilligan, *In a Different Voice* (Cambridge, MA: Harvard University Press, 1982).

42. Ibid., 26.

43. Ibid.

44. Ibid., 29.

45. Ibid., 28.

46. Ibid., 62.

47. Ibid., 72.

48. Ken Wilber, *Sex, Ecology, Spirituality: The Spirit of Evolution* (Boston: Shambhala, 1995).

49. James Fowler, *Stages of Faith: The Psychology of Human Development and the Quest for Meaning* (San Francisco: Harper & Row, 1981).

50. Arnold A. Lazarus, *Brief but Comprehensive Psychotherapy: The Multimodal Way* (New York: Springer, 1997).

51. Ibid.

52. M. Seligman. *Helplessness: On Depression, Development, and Death* (San Francisco: W.H. Freeman, 1975).

53. L. Abramson, M. Seligman, and J. Teasdale. "Learned Helplessness in Humans: Critique and Reformulation." *Journal of Abnormal Psychology*, Vol 87 (1978): pp 49–74.

54. K. Dobson (Ed.), *Handbook of Cognitive-Behavioral Therapies* (New York: Guilford Press, 1988).

55. M. Linehan and L. Dimeff. "DBT in a Nutshell," *California Psychologist*, Vol 34 (2001): 10–14. Also see M. M. Linehan, *Understanding Borderline Personality Disorder: The Dialectic Approach* (New York: Guilford Press, 1995.)

56. Francis Turner. *Social Work Treatment: Interlocking Theoretical Approaches.* New York: Free Press, 1996.

57. See, for example, Frank Goble, *The Third Force* (New York: Grossman, 1970); and Daniel N. Robinson, *Systems of Modern Psychology* (New York: Columbia University Press, 1979).

58. Ibid.

59. Abraham H. Maslow, *Motivation and Personality*, 2nd ed. (New York: Harper and Row, 1970), 35–58.

60. Ibid., 149–180.

61. Ibid., 35–38.

62. Ibid., xiii.

63. Ibid., 36–38.

64. For particular attention to the notion of self-actualization, see Abraham H. Maslow, *The Farther Reaches of Human Nature* (New York: Penguin Books, 1976).

65. See particularly Clayton P. Alderfer, *Existence, Relatedness and Growth* (New York: The Free Press, 1972); and Wayne A. Chess and Julia Norlin, "Toward a Theory and Methodology for Need Assessment: Experiences under Title XX" (Norman, OK: School of Social Work, 1978).

66. A Maslow, *Religions, Values, and Peak-Experiences* (New York: Viking Press, 1973).

67. George H. Mead, *Mind, Self, and Society* (Chicago: University of Chicago Press, 1934).

68. J. Bowlby, *Separation* (New York: Basic Books, 1973).

69. E. Erickson, *Childhood and Society.*

70. J. Zeig, *Experiencing Erickson: An Introduction to the Man and His Work* (New York: Brunner/Mazel, 1993).

71. Kohlberg, "The Development of Children's Orientations Toward a Moral Order," 19.

72. Barbara Newman and Phillip Newman, *Development Through Life: A Psychosocial Perspective*, 6th ed. (Pacific Grove, CA: Brooks/Cole, 1995).

73. Mead, *Mind, Self, and Society.*

74. Ibid.

75. Kohlberg, *Essays on Moral Development.*

76. H. Gochros, J. Gochros, and J. Fischer, *Helping the Sexually Oppressed* (Englewood Cliffs, NJ: Prentice Hall, 1986).

77. Irvin Yalom, *Existential Pyschotherapy* (New York: Basic Books, 1980).

CHAPTER 6

PSYCHOSOCIAL THEORY
A SOCIAL SYSTEMS PERSPECTIVE

FOCUS

ASSUMPTIONS

CONCEPTS

THE BIOLOGICAL CONNECTION

INFANCY

POST INFANCY

PRESCHOOL

SCHOOL

ADOLESCENCE

EARLY ADULTHOOD

MIDDLE ADULTHOOD

LATE ADULTHOOD

SUMMARY

GLOSSARY

NOTES

In the previous chapter we provided an overview of several important lines of theory development now being used by practicing social workers. In this chapter we add another, psychosocial theory. According to our research, psychosocial and social systems are the two theoretical para-digms currently dominating the practice of social work.[1]

We have indicated how theories of limited range can be incorporated within the larger framework provided by social systems theory. Our effort in this chapter is to summarize psychosocial theory. In doing so, we will add content from social systems theory to extend the social dimensions of the theory. In short, psychosocial theory has its origins in psychoanalytical theory and builds from the psychosexual features of that theory. In this sense, both are classified as stage theories, but psychosocial theory incorporates content on the social influences of development at each stage. Of special importance to social work, psychosocial theory extends the number of life stages so that the entire life span is covered. By so doing, psychosocial theory has taken on considerable importance in the client assessment phase of social work practice. *The Social Work Dictionary* does not offer an entry on psychosocial theory but does define "psychosocial development theory." We consider the two to be synonymous, with the notion of development simply incorporating the concept of life stage. *The Social Work Dictionary* provides the following definition:

> The concepts delineated by Erik Erikson and others to describe the various stages, life tasks, and challenges that every person experiences throughout the life cycle. The phases and life tasks, defined elsewhere in this dictionary, are trust versus mistrust, autonomy versus shame and doubt, initiative versus guilt, industry versus inferiority, identity versus role confusion, intimacy versus isolation, generativity versus stagnation, and integrity versus despair. Some other psychosocial theorists describe different ages and life tasks.[2]

As indicated in this definition, the chief architect of this line of theory development is Erik Erikson. In a manner of speaking, he is to psychosocial theory what Freud is to psychoanalytic theory. So while there are a number of contributors to this line of theory development, our review will focus mainly on the work of Erikson.[3]

Erik Erikson was born in Frankfurt, Germany, in 1902. Being of Jewish descent, he fled Germany with the rise of Nazism and settled in Boston. While in Germany, he studied under and was psychoanalyzed by Anna Freud, Sigmund Freud's daughter. Erikson's interest was in children and he became Boston's first child psychoanalyst.

His psychosocial theory can be distinguished from the more classical psychoanalytic theory in two important ways. First, psychosocial theory focuses on the ego, not the id. While the id and the presence of unconscious determinants of behavior are acknowledged, consciousness and the role of ego are stressed; in short, psychosocial theory is an ego, not an id, psychology. Second, the stages encompass the life span and focus on the interplay between the distinctive features of the stage and the psychological, social, and cultural experiences associated with each life stage. Erikson acknowledged the importance of sexual maturation, but his stage formulation is a psychosocial rather than a psychosexual one.[4]

Many, if not most, psychological theories help us understand our individuality. Psychosocial theory helps us examine the common patterns of behavior that provide the foundations on which our individuality emerges and develops, stage by stage.

FOCUS

In relative terms, psychosocial theory is of narrow, or limited, range, at least in comparison to psychoanalytic theory. The dominant organizing schemes are life-stage and internal (psycho) and external (social) determinants of behavior (the psychosocial crisis). As originally formed, the focus of this theory is the individual. We will expand on this focus by emphasizing an open-system formulation, one that views the individual in proactive rather than reactive terms. In so doing, we maintain more of a dual focus, the individual and the social environment. Through the use of social systems theory, we will show how each acts on the other and how each is affected by the other.

ASSUMPTIONS

Given the origins of psychosocial theory, many of the assumptions deemed central to psychoanalytic theory should also apply. This is not entirely the case. Erikson did not dwell on such notions as the unconscious, id drives, or the continuity of humans with the animal kingdom. His focus is on consciousness, the ego, and the interplay of internal and external determinants of an individual's behavior. The following assumptions are central for this presentation of psychosocial theory:

1. Stages of development over the life span of the individual are distinguishable—from conception to the end of life; these stages are universal.
2. These stages are linked to the more general maturational process and occur in an invariant sequence.
3. Each developmental stage is affected by the previous stage in a cyclical fashion.
4. The whole person must be understood, and the whole is comprised of the physical, psychological, social, and spiritual dimensions.
5. An understanding of a person's behavior must specifically consider the social context in which it occurs as well as the life stage.
6. The ego or self develops and changes over the life span, and a sense of selfhood can be considered an outcome related to each life stage.[5]

The assumptions build on and expand the more general assumptions previously identified with the social systems perspective (see Chapter 2). Through psychosocial theory, we will examine an approach that helps us understand the sources of personality organization.

CONCEPTS

Within the framework provided by social systems theory, three organizing concepts will be used to present psychosocial theory: (1) life stage, (2) psychosocial crises, and (3) developmental activities.

Stage, as you will recall from the definition given previously, refers to a developmental level. **Life stage** as used in psychosocial theory means the same thing as stage. Theorists vary in the number of stages identified and the labels they attach to each stage. Table 6.1 compares the stages used by Freud in psychoanalytic theory with the approach used by Erikson.

Of the three organizing concepts, life stage is the most important and serves as the basis for presenting much of the content of psychosocial theory in this chapter. Utilizing social systems theory, the individual emerges from each life stage a different or at least a changed person. In essence, the difference results primarily from the resolution of the psychosocial crisis associated with the life stage.[6]

The notion of **psychosocial crisis** has its origins in Erikson's work and is the concept used to designate the tension state that develops between the person and his or her social environment in each life stage. We suggest that you think of this concept as a particular way of operationalizing the basic notion of human behavior and the social environment. This theory holds that in each stage of development the person experiences sets of internally based needs. These needs are associated with the maturational process. The person also possesses certain developmental capacities and experiences to cope with and satisfy these needs.

Corresponding sets of expectations, interpersonal and social, confront the person externally. While serving to drive the developmental process, these expectations are beyond, or at least different from, the capabilities and experiences currently possessed by the individual. The interplay of these conflicting expectations, desires, and demands creates the psychosocial crisis. The idea of a crisis is a very helpful and powerful one in offering an explanation of a wide range of human behavior. Erikson, however, cautioned against viewing a crisis as

TABLE 6.1   Life Stages: Psychosocial Theory

STAGE DESIGNATION	APPROXIMATE AGES	PSYCHOANALYTIC	PSYCHOSOCIAL CRISES
1. Infancy	birth–18 months	Oral	Basic Trust versus Basic Mistrust
2. Post Infancy	18 months to 3	Anal	Autonomy versus Shame and Doubt
3. Preschool	3–6	Phallic (Oedipal)	Initiative versus Guilt
4. School	6–12	Latency	Industry versus Inferiority
5. Adolescence	12–20	Genital	Identity versus Role Confusion
6. Early Adulthood	20–35	—	Intimacy versus Isolation
7. Middle Adulthood	35–65	—	Generativity versus Stagnation
8. Late Adulthood	65–death	—	Ego Integrity versus Despair

negative; it is merely the natural state of tension associated with the different sets of expectations and coping capacities of each life stage.

Erikson, building on the insights of Freud, identified a psychosocial crisis associated with each psychosexual stage.[7] His designation was in the form of a **polarity** evidencing what he viewed as the central developmental issue and the outcome parameters for dealing with the issue. By polarity, we mean that the resolution of the psychosocial crisis of each stage will result in an individual's possessing personality (self) features falling somewhere between the two opposing poles. For example, in stage 2 (post infancy) the psychosocial crisis is autonomy versus shame and doubt. Recall that Freud designated this as the anal period. The youngster at this age is gaining an early sense of self and finds pleasure with her or his own body products. The child also is now at the maturational level that permits a growing amount of control over bowel and bladder movements. This is one of the few areas in which the youngster is able to exercise control. The child's parents or their surrogates also have ideas of how, where, and under what circumstances bowel and bladder functions are to be performed. Here we have the classical conflict between the internally based needs of the child and the external societal demands for compliance with normative standards. The societal agents charged with this responsibility are the child's parents. While a difficult time for both

child and parents, the crisis will be resolved and with mutual effects. With respect to the child, the stage will impact in terms of some combination of an internalized sense of autonomy, or shame and doubt.

The resolution of a psychosocial crisis is not inalterable. In psychosocial theory, the effect is registered in the ego or what we prefer to call one's sense of **selfhood.** Consider the development of selfhood as a process. Psychosocial theory provides a way of examining this process from the perspective of a life stage. Within this context, think of the resolution of a psychosocial crisis as resulting in the acquisition of new or modified features of one's self. For example, in post infancy, a child may gain a sense of personal autonomy, but with some minor feelings of shame and doubt. This sense of autonomy then provides a structural feature of selfhood that future experiences will build on or undermine. Subsequent life experiences can both contribute to the further development of this aspect of selfhood derived from the resolution of the psychosocial crisis, or distract from it, resulting in a reduced sense of personal autonomy and an increase in self-doubt.

Erikson clearly recognized the cyclical and mutually deterministic effects of social intervention. For example, he spoke of the importance of parents' confidence in themselves in their parenting roles.[8] This sense of **self-efficacy** in the parenting role, according to

Erikson, is transmitted to the child and has meaning. The child's response will tend to be confirming to the parents. We believe the reverse is also true, particularly in very young children. If the parents are anxious and unsure in their parenting roles, the child will mirror this anxiousness and uncertainty. In this scenario, the child's behavior tends to confirm the parents' perceptions of themselves, and they continue to feel uncertain and anxious.

Some digression is indicated at this point to emphasize the importance of the notion of reciprocal and mutually deterministic effects in the formulation of psychosocial theory. It is useful to keep in mind that the theory describes a social process, but from the viewpoint of individual development. So just as the child struggling with the crisis of autonomy versus shame and doubt will be affected by the behavior of his or her caregivers, so will the caregivers be affected by the behavior of the child. These effects are then transmitted back to the child; it is a mutually shaping and ongoing process both within and between each life stage.

Perhaps an example drawn from our own research can help develop the point. As a general proposition, we believe that the social worker's own sense of personal confidence in his or her professional role is a key determinant in the outcome of his or her work with clients. It is the same dynamic as parents' feeling confident in their roles. If a worker is anxious and unsure of her- or himself in the helping role, we believe this is communicated to the client with adverse effects on both the helper and client roles. Again, each affects the other in an ongoing way. Our own research on this phenomenon to date has concentrated on these effects on the worker. Our findings suggest that perceptions of competence have a buffering effect against burnout and are positively correlated with feelings of job satisfaction.[9] Our contention is that a cyclical and mutually deterministic conception of life-stage development is more useful than one based in linear reasoning.

We wish to make one further observation prior to concluding this summary of the notion of a psychosocial crisis. A major criticism of Freud's work, for some, was that it was biased in terms of gender, race, class, culture, and other factors. Erikson understood this criticism and it explains in part his avid interest in anthropology and the other social sciences. He wished to formulate his ideas in a manner that would reduce such biases.[10] Keep in mind that much has changed since Erikson produced his important work over forty-five years ago.

We find Erikson's designations of the psychosocial crisis at each life stage of great help, and representative of the magnitude of his many insights into human behavior. The specific designations of these stages are affected by cultural expectations and as such can be viewed as most representative of western and industrialized societies in the 1950s. Also, these societies have been dominated by males and so the labeling of psychosocial crises will be influenced by this dominance. This does not diminish the importance of or the existence of the so-called crisis, it merely acknowledges that there is great diversity in our world and this diversity is constantly changing, as are social expectations.

In psychosocial theory, the label *developmental task* is frequently used to describe what we refer to as activities in social systems theory. Thus, for our purposes, developmental tasks and **developmental activities** refer to the same thing. Our use of the concept of activity has been described in our discussion of a hierarchy of outcomes.

In psychosocial theory, universal sets of activities (developmental tasks) take place within social systems. These are the means the system employs to deal with the psychosocial crisis at each life stage. A positive resolution of the psychosocial crisis is the implicit goal for each life stage. Recall that in the hierarchy of outcomes, activities are derived from goals and objectives. They are the selected means to be employed by the system to achieve its goal.

The power and the usefulness of psychosocial theory is in the identification of a universal set of developmental activities employed at each life stage for dealing with the psychosocial crisis. These developmental activities are institutionalized into sets of roles associated with each life stage, for example, the typical family roles of mother, father, and child. These role sets then provide the basic structure through which the developmental activities are played out. It is useful to view these activities as part of a natural ordering that occurs between the person and his or her social environment at each life stage. This natural ordering is derived from a combination of the genetic equipment possessed by each human, the maturational development of the human, and the cultural expectations associated with each society.[11] Again, while there will be variations of these activities within different cultures, these variations are within the so-called natural order; the order itself should be treated as a given. For example, all human infants require care arrangements or they will not survive. Every society will institutionalize arrangements for the care of the very young; these arrangements, for example, the nurturing role, constitute the natural ordering associated with dealing with the crisis of basic trust versus basic mistrust.

As with all the major concepts being defined, the notion of activities has its origins in the insights of Freud. Toilet training offers a familiar example of what we mean by a set of developmental activities. These activities are typically engaged in during the post infancy stage and, in part, serve as a means for dealing with the crisis of autonomy versus shame and doubt. Other sets of activities exist as well; another example would be language training and development. A central point to remember is that these activities are social and take place between the individual and others playing a central, or at least a significant, role in the development process. It is this social process that we model as a social system, for instance, a family.

The concept of activities serves to identify core patterns of behavior that are distinctive to each life stage and serve as a medium through which the psychosocial crisis is mediated. The performance of these activities involves learning and the involvement of ever more complex cognitive states. Part of this learning involves the development of the ego or what we call the self. These cognitive patterns and the related sense of selfhood are elaborated on stage by stage.

The work of Hamacheck is of interest here.[12] He formulated, by stage, behavioral expressions related to the polarity identified in each stage, for example, autonomy versus shame and doubt. People deemed to have a sense of autonomy "like to make their own decisions, particularly about matters important to them." In contrast, those who possess a sense of shame and doubt about themselves "prefer being told what to do rather than make their own decisions."[13]

In the sections ahead we will be discussing each of the life stages identified by Erikson using the organizing schemes noted earlier.

THE BIOLOGICAL CONNECTION

The person as a system is comprised of a number of subsystems that interact to create a functional whole. The biological subsystems within the person determine many of the timetables of development and maturation. This is especially true in the earlier phases of development. In looking at human development, it is apparent that many of the emerging social skills are keyed to underlying biological processes. The relationship between biological subsystems and behavior is not the focus of this book, but it needs to be noted as we open our discussion of psychosocial theory.

There are three important considerations about biology to keep in mind in studying human behavior: causation, genetics, and evolution.

Causation.   One consideration is the causation of behavior. The reductionist view holds that the behavior of complex systems can be grasped by understanding the elements that make up the system. For example, if we wish to understand pain and the influence of pain avoidance on human learning, we can attempt to do so by understanding the neurological processes involved in producing the sensation of pain. As we discussed regarding holism, this ignores the fact that the emergent properties of pain in the human experience suggest that pain to a human being may be more than a sensation. It is an innate trait of human beings to attribute meaning to the pain and to try to understand its causes. The mere sensation of pain as a biological phenomenon is unlikely to produce a full understanding of pain as a causal influence on behavior. Causation has to do not only with biomechanisms, but also with the process of attribution of meaning to the sensation and its perceived causes.

Genetics.   A second consideration about biology as a factor in social behavior is genetics. Genes are located within all the cells of one's body and contain the hereditary information of each individual. They are the units that determine the limits of a person's characteristics—both physical and mental. Genetic transmission of information is the central mechanism of species continuity. It is assumed to be the basis for the process of natural selection by which adaptive traits emerge and flourish, and maladaptive traits are allowed to die out. Genetic information creates the template for epigenetic development, the "road map" that guides the development of each member of a species. The genetic road map defines the common course of a life span's existence for a species; within that developmental map, each individual may take a unique course, but only insofar as it stays within the boundaries defined by genetics. A man may exercise and make himself strong, but he cannot exceed the

genetic potential of the species to become a horse.

It is a hallmark of human beings that we have a weaker repertoire of reflexes and instincts than do lower species. Unlike the monarch butterfly, we cannot migrate across half a world armed only with inherited navigational skills. However, our compensation seems to be that each individual human being has the ability to learn and store a vast amount of information over the course of a single lifetime. We can do this because of our unique brain and nervous system. Our ability to learn and communicate information imbued our species with the ability to adapt rapidly to changing environmental conditions.

Human beings require a long period of vulnerable childhood and dedicated parenting in order to grow to an age where the formidable human ability to adjust and learn activates. Our ability to adjust individually to local conditions is a great survival talent, but it is nonetheless constrained by the limits of our genetic potential. As we shall see, human adaptability within a life span is an advantage purchased at the cost of stability; if we adapt too quickly to change, we may find ourselves exposed to environmental conditions that pose a risk to our individual and collective survival. For example, the rapid growth of our ability to shape our own physical environment through technology may pose a threat to our survival through nuclear war, pollution, climate change, or even genetic tinkering.

The influence of the environment and circumstance can diminish the level of trait expression, but cannot add to the genetically determined potential of the individual. There are two broad areas of interest that may constitute exceptions to this principle: science and faith. Recent advances in genetics have made it possible to physically alter the genetic materials that define human potential. While still a very new and uncertain technology, it is clear that genetic engineering will be an arena of feverish research interest in the near future. The other factor that bids to free human potential from its genetic constraints is faith. History is full of stories of miracle healing of conditions that seem to be cured by faith, willpower, or some other agency beyond normal human experience. Since genetic engineering is so new, and these mystical experiences are so idiosyncratic, we will confine our discussion to a general template that defines human development as driven in part by the encoding in DNA, and maximized or limited by the varied environments the person encounters over a lifetime.

Evolution.   The third consideration regarding biology as a factor in social behavior is closely related to genetics: It is the theory of evolution. Evolution is a theory of how changes in species arise due to adaptation to the environment—a process of natural selection that eliminated less well adapted species over time. Evolution was the BIG idea of the nineteenth century, and remains a source of controversy today. Almost all life sciences, including the behavioral sciences, have been molded to a considerable degree by evolutionary theory. While some approaches to evolution have been flawed, natural selection has become a cornerstone of the life sciences.

In part due to the theory of evolution, we recognize that change comes in two different time frames: evolutionary time and the single life span. Evolutionary change relies on genetic mutation and subsequent natural selection in a process that may play out over eons. Genes may mutate in an instant, but nature is patient in sorting out the results of the changes. The span of a single life is over in the blink of an eye in evolutionary time, but it defines our human experience. We carry within us the genetic legacy of our evolution, and the adapted ability to think and react to the vicissitudes of our own life. Our theories must account for both of these processes.

Evolutionary change is slow and widespread, thus relatively stable. Individual adaptation is rapid and volatile, and carries with it the risk of the unknown. We believe that humans have developed cultural systems that serve in part to slow the rapid pace of change. The changes made possible with the technology devised by the human brain produce changes at a revolutionary pace. The "disconnect" between the evolutionary pace of biological change and the revolutionary pace of human technology can produce potentially catastrophic events. We surmise that an unrecognized value of cultural systems is to moderate the headlong pace of change made possible by human innovation.

There are several broadly accepted principles that describe development as a clearly biological process. Examples include the *cephalo-caudal* development pattern. This simply means that development begins and proceeds most rapidly at the head, and proceeds to the "tail," or feet of the embryo. Another example is the *proximo-distal* developmental pattern. In this process, the embryo develops from its center toward the extremities. It also seems to be true that innate behaviors that have survival value such as the sucking reflex emerge early according to internal cues, and become dormant when their utility phase has passed. Other developmental patterns include the progression from vegetative (life-supporting) functions to executive (voluntary behavior) functions.

Some innate instinctual complexes such as the activation syndrome (the so-called "flight or fight" response) are instinctual, but can be evoked throughout life by certain environmental conditions. The activation syndrome emerged as a response to a life-threatening stimulus. In modern life, less dangerous threats trigger this response, resulting in nonspecific anxiety. This instinct in the original environment of adaptedness served a survival purpose. The response persists, but the new environment has few mortal threats, and the result is a vestigial response that produces a great deal of needless suffering.

For more complex behaviors, the principle that is most often invoked is called the *epigenetic development principle*. Epigenesis is defined as the emergence of new developmental features in a pattern that is fixed and invariant. That is, the properties of the organism emerge in the same sequence, and the sequence cannot be changed. Stages cannot be skipped in this model. The speed of the process, or the degree to which full potential is achieved at each stage, may vary according to how well the environment supports the new attribute. The sequence of emergence itself is immutable, as determined by genetic encoding.

The example that is often used to illustrate this epigenesis is the growth of the oak tree. The full developmental potential of the oak tree is contained in the seed. When the seed is planted, the growth of the tree follows a preordained course. First it sends out a root, then it sprouts, then it grows, flowers, and germinates. The process may be weak or robust depending on the environment, but the sequence is always the same. It is generally believed that this principle applies best to biological traits, and less well to social and learned behaviors, which are far more variable and responsive to environmental conditions.

As we turn to Erikson's theory of psychosocial development, we must keep in mind that the idea of universal stages of development common to all human beings is based on the biological substrate of our humanity. The influence of these biological processes is often obscured in the complex social and physical environments we occupy, but their influence recurs in a variety of manifestations, from aggression to fear, from addiction to obesity, and in one's continuing quest to master both one's environment and one's body.

INFANCY

In introducing infancy as a life stage, two points are particularly noteworthy. First, while this stage starts at birth, development begins at the point of conception. There is also more to this prenatal development process than the genetic contribution of the two partners. Research findings focusing on prenatal development suggest that the mother's psychological, physical, and social well-being are critically important to the developing fetus, and thus the use of drugs or smoking by the mother affects the fetus.[14]

Second, at birth the infant is far more advanced in development than is generally understood and thus early social experiences are more important than many parents realize. Freud and Erikson both recognized the importance of the early developmental stages, with infancy being perhaps the most influential of all. This position is in accordance with the epigenetic principle, and it also makes sense from the position of psychosocial theory. If the general proposition is accepted that humanness is socially acquired, then it follows that the infant's early experiences with other humans are critical. Here the parental roles, particularly that of the mother or the primary caregiver, are critical. Here a context is formed to deal with the psychosocial crisis.

Psychosocial Crisis: Basic Trust versus Basic Mistrust

The family is the prototype social organization and is found in one form or another in all societies. While the family performs many functions, none is more important than the care and protection of children. Whether it is a traditional nuclear family, a single-parent family, an extended family, a foster family, or any of the other varied forms, the family provides the social environment in which the **basic trust versus mistrust** crisis is played out. As developed in this book, the family becomes the primary social system for dealing with this crisis. In systems language, the infant and her or his parents in their parental roles become the primary inputs to the system.

The term *basic*, as in *basic need*, used by Erikson, is instructive. The infant at this stage is entirely helpless; she or he would perish if not for the care and protection provided by other humans. The infant, while being of the animal kingdom, is also quite a different and special kind of animal. This distinctiveness is to be found, in large part, in her or his social nature and the cognitive capacities that provide the basis for developing this social (human) nature. The medium for developing this capacity is the relationship; it is the primary way in which all humans functionally link themselves with others. The most fundamental relationship is with the primary caregiver, the person(s) who assumes the initial "mothering" or nurturing role. Since this relationship is the first, it becomes the prototype for future relationships. *Trust* as used here has several related meanings, such as confidence, reliability, predictability, and dependability. *Basic* means fundamental, the core or essence of trust. Recall that at birth the child is only equipped with a few genetically based capacities, for example, sucking. Cognitive development theory is instructive here for it is through the maturation of the sensory and motor functions that learning proceeds. The infant can taste, feel, see, hear, and smell, but most important, she or he can learn and attribute meaning to these early sensory and motor experiences. Basic trust or mistrust is a meaning that is learned and one that is attributed to a relationship. In the vocabulary of systems theory, a sense of trust or mistrust is an output of this stage; it is an attribute of the self and this attribute becomes an input for the next stage.

Developmental Activities

In psychoanalytic theory this is the oral stage. Most writers, including Erikson in the psychosocial tradition, acknowledge the importance of the infant's mouth during this formative period. The sucking response is part of the genetic equipment with which the infant begins life. Not only is the mouth used for taking in nourishment, it is through the mouth that the infant starts exploring the world.

Erikson, building on Freud's work, noted that while the mouth and oral activity is important, the infant's other sensory equipment is similarly important. Not only is the infant taking food in through the mouth, but also much more is being taken in via the eyes, ears, nose, and other organs.[15] Again, cognitive development theory is helpful in grasping the structures of thought occurring at this time via the sensory and motor systems.

During the initial phase of this eighteen-month period, much of the family's activities are centered around feeding, holding, changing diapers, bathing, and otherwise attending to the physiological needs of the infant. When these activities are carried out, the infant deals with the crisis of basic trust versus mistrust. In the language of systems theory, these activities comprise the interaction portion of the system's conversion operations.

Recall that the infant is born with essentially a clean slate; there is no sense of self, of mother, of father, or anything or anyone else in the world. Most of these meanings are learned, and through activities with others, become part of the infant's growing sense of personhood. In this sense they are social experiences. The infant is hungry and is fed. How the infant is fed creates the social experiences. The food fulfills a need and is thus pleasurable. Being held close to the parent's warm body and being rocked is also pleasurable. These experiences become linked as the cognitive structures evolve, and out of these social activities a sense of trust or mistrust forms.

The infant comes to recognize her or his mother and other family members and, through their caring responses to her or his needs, experiences pleasure, comfort, and a general sense of well-being in their presence. A relationship, and a vital one, is under way. To the extent that the infant's needs are satisfied physiologically and socially, a sense of trust of others develops. To the extent that needs are not satisfied or that there is an inconsistent pattern, a sense of mistrust evolves.

Keep in mind that while psychosocial theory focuses on the interplay of internal and social experiences, the infant is learning about the world from her or his own experiences as well. So while the early experiences of the infant with family members is critical, the total environment that the child experiences is similarly important. It needs to be safe and stimulating. The child learns by and through the richness and diversity of this environment.

While the focus of psychosocial theory is on the individual, most of the experiences dealt with are social, so the effects are, from a social systems perspective, reciprocal and mutually deterministic. To illustrate these ideas, we will use the Jones family. Barbara and Sam were married while in college and both worked awhile before deciding to have children. They were both twenty-seven when they learned that Barbara was pregnant. Not only were Barbara and Sam delighted with the news, but both sets of parents and other family members were as well. Quickly Barbara became the center of attention of family members and friends. There was much talk, particularly among the women, about the pregnancy, visits to the obstetrician, and their own experiences while pregnant. Sam wanted, to the greatest extent possible, to share the birthing experience with Barbara. He attended the birthing classes with Barbara and both prepared for their future parenting roles. Thus there was an intensive socialization process under way long before Ann's birth. Not only were Barbara and Sam being prepared for their parental roles, but also all four of their parents were working through their own feelings about being grandparents; Ann was the first grandchild on both sides of the family. In short, both the social system and the key aspects of its suprasystem were in line with and supportive of the new addition to the system.

What has been depicted is a very supportive, if not ideal, environment for the birth of Ann. Extensive preparations had been made so that Barbara would be with Ann during the critical first few months of her life. While Sam's company did not have paternity leave, he did use three weeks of vacation time to stay home with Barbara and Ann. Ann had her own room and

Barbara took three months' leave from her job. She decided not to breast-feed Ann. In part this was so that both she and Sam could share feeding and otherwise caring for Ann.

Barbara and Sam enjoyed holding, rocking, and constantly talking to Ann. Ann, in return, would smile and coo in response to the attention she was receiving. There were difficult as well as good times, but the care she was given was consistent and loving. Barbara and Sam had been well prepared and were confident in their parenting roles.

Barbara's return to work was especially difficult. She felt guilty about Ann being in a nursery day-care program. However, the decision to return to work was her own and fully supported by Sam. The Joneses' routine and lifestyle were significantly altered by Ann. For example, the couple had to get up two hours earlier so that Ann could be dropped off at day care. The partying with friends on weekends came to an end, as well as the intimate dinners and special vacations they had enjoyed together. The roles of the Joneses were both different and more complicated as a consequence of Ann's birth. Barbara and Sam were becoming different people as they assumed their parenting roles. The social system known as the Joneses was different. Why? Because it had added a new member and had adopted new goals pertaining to the raising of Ann.

Ann was confronted with the crisis of basic trust versus basic mistrust. Her parents were also dealing with a psychosocial crisis associated with the life stage of early adulthood—intimacy versus isolation. These crises were played out within the social system that was the Jones family—Barbara and Sam in their parental roles and Ann as their infant daughter.

Erikson made the point that the resolution of the crisis always falls somewhere between the two poles. In Ann's case, she experienced both feelings of trust and distrust, with the sense of trust dominating. Importantly, one cannot know trust without some sense of distrust. Ann, as she grows older, will need to know when she can trust and when she cannot trust. Erikson put it as follows: "the human infant must experience a goodly measure of mistrust in order to trust discerningly."[16]

Before leaving our discussion of Ann's infancy stage, it is important for us to remind you again that we are seeking to describe a line of theory development from the perspective of health and well-being. Given that Ann is a healthy baby, cared for by loving, competent, healthy, and economically secure parents, the chances are that she is going to develop into a healthy, stable adult. Many children are born into far less advantageous circumstances; some will be unwanted, others will be born to very young, poor, inexperienced parents. Others will not have parents at all. Some will not survive, but all who do, in accordance with this line of theory, will be faced with solving the psychosocial crisis of basic trust versus basic mistrust.

Perhaps surprisingly, and in spite of all the environmental problems, most of these infants will, like Ann, solve the crisis on the positive side. The key for successful resolution is in both the richness of the environmental circumstances and the quality of the relationships with key caretakers. Perhaps a useful way of viewing this is from the social systems perspective that there is a natural ordering and that problems arise when there is substantial deviation from this ordering. Finally, it is the natural ordering of developmental activities associated with the psychosocial crises that constitutes the conversion operations of the social system. In an application of the social systems model to a family, the cycle can correspond to the life stage, or, at a micro level, to a social act within the framework of a specific life stage, such as an episode dealing with the potty training of Ann.

POST INFANCY

Freud labeled this the anal stage because, through the maturational process, the child now has gained control of the sphincter muscles. This level of control is important to both the child and to his or her caregivers. For the child, it is the beginning of a sense of personhood, a state of existence independent of others in the environment. During the first eighteen months of life, the infant existed largely by taking things in, not only through the mouth but also through all of the senses. Mental capacities were rapidly developing through the maturation of sensorimotor systems. This first stage was labeled sensorimotor intelligence by Piaget and establishes the cognitive foundations for the next stage of development—preoperational thought.

Erikson's contribution to psychosocial theory was the recognition that a range of developmental changes affect the child during this period of post infancy. Freud recognized and focused on the sexual maturation and its effects. Certainly the child was interested in and at times preoccupied with bladder and bowel functions. However, much more was happening, according to Erikson. During this post infancy period, the child is becoming mobile and is learning to speak. Through language and the associated imagery, the child begins the process of understanding her- or himself as possessing a separate and distinct existence.

Psychosocial Crisis: Autonomy versus Shame and Doubt

The recognition of the struggle of developing a sense of **autonomy,** of separateness, led Erikson to define the psychosocial crisis of this stage as **autonomy versus shame and doubt.** Recall that this is the stage of "the terrible twos." The normally developing child is willful and quick to say no—even when no means yes! Not only is the child grasping some of the implications of the control she or he has over her or his body, but also the impact that words have on others—especially "NO!" Being repeatedly told no! in a demanding voice by a two-year-old is, for many parents, a provocation—an invitation to "show the little critter who is boss." Unappreciated in such circumstances is the fact that the child and parent simply don't think the same way. For the child, the immediate situation is all there is; there is no comprehension of the implications of "*no*" in the same sense that it is understood by the adult. The child has been repeatedly told no—don't do this, don't do that—no!—no! At this point of development the child has learned the word *no* and at least some of its implications. It is, in the mind of the child, a very powerful word, far more powerful than the word *yes*. It is a beginning way that the child has of experiencing her or his own individuality—of becoming autonomous.

Parents are society's agents for the socialization of the young. For some, we would hope only a few, the provocativeness of the child at this age is evident of something bad inside, perhaps evil; their task is to rid the child of this "badness." This can be likened to "breaking the will" of the child. While there may be many ways of doing this, one is to shame, to humiliate, to humble the child for his or her wrongdoings.[17]

Developmental Activities

The activities of each lower stage serve as the foundation for activities of the next higher one. Critical in infancy was the development of trusting relationships and sensorimotor skills, and the beginning differentiation of selfhood.

While each child has her or his own developmental pattern, most children around the age of one are standing alone and starting to take their first few steps.[18] In the stage of post infancy, the child starts by taking a few awkward, hesitant steps; by the end of this stage, she or he is running and jumping—in constant motion. The dominant theme underlying the activity patterns of this stage is the growing capacity of the child for self-care. In recognition of this growing capacity, sets of societal expectations are reflected in the parenting role. Youngsters of this age are expected to become

more mobile and so this becomes evident in the behavior of parents. Much of family life at this stage is linked to activities helping the child become more mobile, to feed herself or himself, to develop toilet habits, to communicate her or his needs and wishes, to generally adopt the behavior society expects of post infancy. Importantly, many of the activities of this age are social—the child is learning how to become a person. Much of this is being accomplished through language development.

At the point of entry into this stage (eighteen months of age), most children will have a vocabulary of just a few words (roughly three to thirty). By the time they are ready for the next stage, their vocabulary will consist of approximately 1,000 words. The child is not only rapidly learning new words, but he or she is also developing a sense of selfhood as well. The child takes in the world through the imitation of others, particularly parents and others having significance to the child. The post infancy period is also the time when the child starts engaging in solitary play. The child lives in part in an imaginary world. Through this imaginary world, the child plays out what is happening around him or her. Here he or she plays house; in so doing the child is playing out what his or her understanding is of the role of mother, father, as well as his or her own role. Typically, the child will play all of the parts, including his or her own. In effect, the child is learning the roles of others by playing them. The work of Piaget is helpful here in understanding what is going on in the mind of the child. This is the stage of preoperational thought, learning by doing, by experiencing.

Let us turn to the Joneses and to Ann who is now three years old. She is the "apple of her daddy's eye" and a source of great pride for Barbara and for both sets of grandparents. Ann attends day care at the Children's Center, a program provided for the employees of the Midtown Mental Health Center, her mother's place of employment. Barbara was anxious for Ann to be with children from a variety of cultural and socioeconomic backgrounds. Center patients, staff, and neighborhood residents all use the Children's Center. Given that the mental health center serves a low-income clientele, the children in day care are literally from every imaginable background.

In this scenario, the day-care center becomes an important part of the suprasystem for the Joneses. Ann spends over forty hours a week in day care, almost as much of her waking hours as she spends with her parents. Both Barbara and Sam initially had ambivalent feelings about the amount of time Ann spent in day care; Barbara had particular difficulty with day care, feeling somehow that she was compromising her relationship with Ann by not staying home "like a real mommy." Contributing to her feelings was her knowledge that Verna, Sam's mother, felt that her place was in the home taking care of Ann and her husband. Barbara understood her sensitivity around this point; nevertheless, each time they visited Sam's parents, she had the sense that Verna was searching for evidence that Ann was somehow being adversely affected by her day-care experiences (a new feature in the interface between the Joneses and Sam's parents).

All the evidence was to the contrary. Ann looked forward to day care and, while the pace was hectic, all things seemed to be going well with the Joneses. According to Barbara, Ann was easy to toilet train. She had established bowel control by the time she was eighteen months old and by twenty-four months seldom wet herself. Sam likened Ann's stubborn streak to Barbara, saying they appeared to be "out of the same mold." This stubbornness, evidenced by Ann's saying, and sometimes screaming No! and stamping her little foot, reached a high point when she was about thirty months old and has since diminished. Barbara and Sam, for the most part, didn't react to these outbursts by Ann. They were firm in their dealings with her and when things became tense, would simply put

Ann on a chair telling her that when she settled down she could join the family again—"in the meantime—stay put!" In their private times together thinking about how difficult Ann could be, they would console each other by saying, "this too will pass."

While acknowledging their ups and downs, Barbara and Sam were feeling quite good about themselves and particularly about how well Ann was progressing. They reminded each other of their earlier decision not to have children. In Barbara's words: "While I love my work and I love being Sam's wife, Ann has given me something special. In a crazy way, by being a mother I think I now know what being a woman really is about."

The point we wish to emphasize in the example is the cyclical and interactive effects that family members have on one another in terms of life-stage development. Not only is Ann dealing with a psychosocial crisis (autonomy versus shame and doubt), but also are her parents (intimacy versus isolation) and grandparents (generativity versus stagnation). Each is having an effect on the other, but Ann, as the first child and grandchild, is, for the moment, a focal point.

PRESCHOOL

The third life stage corresponds to what Freud designated as the phallic or Oedipal stage. Recall that in psychoanalytic theory, as a result of the process of sexual maturation, the sexual energy that was focused in the anal area shifts at this stage to the genitals. Youngsters, as they grow older, are curious about all parts of the body; now this curiosity centers on their genitals and the genitals of others. This interest is heightened by the pleasure associated with the manipulation of these special body parts. Frequently, the child's parents are not as enthusiastic about this genital play as is the child, often saying, "Quit that!" "That's not nice!" "Good little girls (boys) don't play with themselves!" and other admonitions. Some of the parental admonitions to the young at this age are both frightening and bizarre, for example, references to castration. It is small wonder that the psychosocial crisis of this age deals with initiative and guilt.

Erikson, as he did at each stage, looked for a broader scheme than simply the sexual one for characterizing the stage. The youngster at three is now quite mobile and, having shed diapers, is much more in control of her or his movements. The child seems anxious to test the limits of these new capacities. In a way, the child feels there are no limits: "I am Superman (woman)." Sometimes, and to the consternation of parents, the child is like a perpetual motion machine.

Psychosocial Crisis: Initiative versus Guilt

Erikson was a bit uncomfortable with the notion of initiative as he sought to frame this crisis. The polarity, according to Erikson, is initiative and guilt.[19] It is useful to think of guilt as associated with or as an adverse consequence of the initiative. The relationships among the crises of the stages are important to keep in mind. The previous crisis dealt with autonomy versus shame and doubt. Here we make the assumption that eventually a positive resolution of this crisis was reached. The child, with this developing sense of autonomy, is now testing out his or her capacities and "the sky is the limit." The problem is that there *are* limits and the child will discover that he or she is not Superman or Superwoman, that he or she cannot fly, and that dad or mom has already been spoken for. The key in resolving the crisis is to maintain the spirit of initiative and for the child not to have an overwhelming sense of guilt over the excesses that characterize the initiatives undertaken.

Given the systems perspective being applied, the resolution is a system outcome, the key system again being the child's family. In other words, the task outcome of this stage will be a sense of selfhood possessed by the child as it pertains to a ratio of feeling **initiative versus guilt.**

Developmental Activities

At this time, much is going on with the child physically, cognitively, and socially. In some sense, initiatives are occurring in each of these areas. Similarly, sets of developmental activities are associated with each of the areas. Cognitively, this is the period that Piaget labeled *preoperational thought.* Learning is still very much linked to the here and now. This is important because one of the things the youngster is learning is gender.

Ann, in our Jones family, has had many reminders of her gender from all of the important people around her: "Ann is Daddy's girl"; "Ann, good little girls don't do that"; "Ann, pretty is as pretty does"; "Ann is such a beautiful little girl." Ann, who is now five, has her mother as a role model for what *female* as well as *mother* means. She has also observed, with more than a casual interest, the experiences of tenderness and love between her father and mother. With this in mind she announces that she too is going to marry Daddy when she gets big. Simply stated, to understand sex as gender is to learn what *male* and *female* both mean. Complicating this understanding is the fact that sex roles are constantly changing. Ann's gender role is not a given; it is something that she will learn. It is a meaning that she will acquire and which will shift and change throughout her life. It will be influenced by her age, her race, the social class of her family, and generally by the normative standards evident in the Jones family and by other groups (systems) of which she will be a member.

The point here is that a host of activities take place between the youngster and her or his caretaker that result in the acquisition of a perception of gender. This perception is a vital part of the acquisition and development of a sense of self. These activities, for the most part, occur within the family and the acquisition of the gender dimension of self can be usefully viewed as a system outcome.

Fortunately for Ann, both of her parents are confident in their respective sex roles and so she has had good role models for both. Ann, while not comprehending the genital basis of gender, does understand that, like her mother, she has a vagina and later, when she gets "big," she will have breasts like her mother. Her dad, like all males, has a penis. Barbara and Sam enjoyed and at times were amused at Ann's questions dealing with sexual matters, such as why females have a vagina and males a penis. Her questions were answered in a matter-of-fact and simple way and this seemed to satisfy Ann, at least until she could think of the next question. Barbara and Sam understood that Ann had no real comprehension of the genital basis of sex at this stage of her development. They also knew, or at least hoped, that in a few years Ann would be asking them some of these same questions again.

In concluding this discussion on activities, we call your attention to the moral development occurring at this time. The earlier discussions of the superego in psychoanalytic theory and moral development theory are pertinent here. The child at the preschool stage has a sense of what is right and wrong, at least within the framework provided by his or her caregivers. Recall that children at the preschool stage would be at what Kohlberg labeled *level I*, the preconventional level of moral development. This stage is marked by the child seeing rules as fixed and absolute. These rules are, in a sense, handed down by adults and other "absolute" authorities. Within this context it is useful to consider the sense of guilt that children can develop at this stage when told they are bad and should be punished. Again, it is important to remember that the young child and the adult do not think in the same way. Parents need to be alert to and sensitive to these differences.

SCHOOL

The stage we designate as school corresponds generally to the time the child is in the elementary or grade school (between the ages of six and twelve). Freud labels this the latency period, essentially a quiet and dormant period in terms of psychosexual development. Although it may be quiet in terms of sexual maturation, it is anything but quiet with respect to the cognitive development taking place. This stage ends with the onset of puberty at approximately age twelve, a bit earlier for most females and a bit later for most males.

Psychosocial Crisis: Industry versus Inferiority

This is a busy time for children, a time when they start preparing for life as an adult more formally. Erikson observed that children in all cultures receive some systematic instruction during this period.[20] While many children have been in day care and thus away from their families during the day, school is different. It tends to be more formal and more evaluative in nature. There are tests, grades, "passes," and "failures"; it is for most children a more competitive environment than they have previously experienced. In most instances, children find themselves in classes organized by age and its associated expectations. Children are compared with one another and children compare themselves with others as well. For most children, it is a difficult as well as an exciting and challenging time. Industry is expected and rewarded, lack of industry is not, but is nevertheless labeled; a child may be called "slow," "lazy," or "a problem," for example. The outcome of this stage will be an aspect of selfhood containing some ratio of feelings of industry and inferiority.

The child, by entering school, has also entered a major new social system. In the Jones family, Ann was Ann, the daughter of Barbara and Sam Jones. Now she takes on a more differentiated role, Ann the student. She is one of fifteen students in her class and one of 225 in her school, Monroe Elementary School. She is faced with a different arena in which to compete for attention and recognition; it is less personal and more formal than her family system.

The outcome of the psychosocial crisis of **industry versus inferiority** is now somewhat more problematic, in part because more social systems affect or produce the outcome. The two principal ones for all are the family and the school, but there are others as well—the church, neighborhood, and school friendship groups would serve as examples. While for most children the family remains the dominant influence, the school is rapidly gaining in importance. There are also other factors that will impact on the outcome of this crisis, factors over which Barbara and Sam as well as Ann have little control. An example would be the quality of the school program, the competence and sensitivity of the teacher, the equipment, the supplies, and the teaching and learning environment available to the child. On a more general level would be the richness and diversity of the school system itself. Examples would include specialty programs available in athletics, music, and the arts. Other cultural features include the diversity of students and faculty in terms of gender, race, religion, social class, and disability to which the child is exposed, and how the social system deals with these differences.

Developmental Activities

With each higher life stage, the number of social systems involved in dealing with the psychosocial crisis increases. Similarly, greater structural differentiation tends to occur within the social systems themselves. As these systems become more structurally differentiated, the child is called on to master an ever greater number of roles and their associated sets of activities. The child will do better at some than at others. For example, one of your authors recalls a son coming home from second grade excited about what he had accomplished in school that day; he was first in his class! On inquiry, it turned out that he was the fastest runner in his class. His parents had hoped that he might have been "number one" in arithmetic or at least in spelling but they did not indicate their disappointment. However, for the youngster and his friends, being the fastest runner in his class was by far a greater achievement.

During the school stage, the child evolves from what Piaget labeled as preoperational to using concrete operational thought. Through cognitive development, the child gains the mental capacities to deal with an ever more stimulating and complex environment. In part, it will be through the new cognitive capacities that the child will either be helped or hindered in dealing with the crisis of industry versus inferiority in this society.

The child's cognitive development will affect both the child's intellectual and social capacities. In earlier stages the child acquired a sense of personal autonomy and initiative on which this stage builds. As a part of this development, the child acquired a personal sense of selfhood, including gender and some knowledge of the key roles played by others in his or her life, for example, mother, father, grandparent, other family members, and day-care teacher. This knowledge has largely been accumulated through the process of imitation and identification. The knowledge of these roles has been experienced as they relate to the child. The child's level of cognitive development is now permitting the child to mentally take on the role of others in much more complex and interactive forms of problem-solving or goal-related activities.

To illustrate the basic notions involved, we pick up with Ann who is now eleven and a sixth-grader at Monroe Elementary School. Our focal system will be a new social group, a girls' basketball team. The developmental activities that will be illustrated are those associated with learning a team sport. We will be interested in how, through game play, Ann will develop additional capacities to think representationally and, more generally, how the team experience will help her deal with the psychosocial crisis of this age.

Ann and her two best friends, Susie and Wendy, decided to join the school's newly formed girls' basketball team. Like both of her parents, she is physically well coordinated and assertive. By joining the team, Ann gets a first-hand lesson in interdependence. In this regard, she soon finds that her personal goals must be subordinated to those of the team. With the assistance of her coach, Ms. Bacon, she begins to understand her role on the team (Ann plays a guard position) in relationship to the roles (positions) played by her teammates. Ann is assertive like her mother, and loves to try to steal the ball from the opposing team. While supportive of her assertiveness, Ann's coach cautions Ann against taking frequent risks to steal the ball from opponents because, in so doing, her position on defense is left unguarded. Through coaching and game play, Ann learns the game and her role vis-à-vis the roles of other team members. Ann's cognitive stage (the beginning of formal operational thought) now allows her to mentally take on the role of others in ever more complex ways. She is able to explore representationally (mentally) the possible outcomes of her actions in relationship to total team play. Ann discovers that some times are more opportune than others to make steal attempts without jeopardizing her team's defense. In short, Ann is learning to mentally and simultaneously take the roles of all her team members, and those of the opponents, as well as her own, into consideration before she makes an attempt to steal the ball. She mentally becomes able to anticipate the actions of others before they occur and by so doing, adjust her own actions.

Ann's teammates, who themselves are gaining skill in mentally taking on the roles of oth-ers, begin to adjust to Ann's assertive style of play as she adjusts to theirs. By the end of the season, the team has greatly improved. One by one, Ann's coach instituted specific defense and offense strategies. The coach was aware of the girls' expanding ability to think representationally and utilized this as new and more complex plays were introduced.

The experiences Ann had in playing her first year of competitive sports assisted her in the resolution of the psychosocial crisis of industry versus inferiority. She learned through basketball and a variety of other social experiences to work cooperatively with others toward a team goal, even with those girls that she did not especially like. Here she recalls Ms. Bacon's frequent reminder, "Remember, girls, it's teamwork that wins games."

As she developed her athletic skills through basketball, Ann also gained a greater mastery over her own body. She also learned how to lose as well as to win as a "good sport." Self-evaluation in a situation occupies a great deal of the school-age child's thinking and Ann's coach was mindful of this as she worked with the girls. Similar to the leader of a therapeutic group, the coach guides the development of a group culture. A sense of cohesion is developed that will assist each member in gaining a sense of personal competence necessary to the development of self-efficacy. This confidence in oneself, in turn, is vital to the resolution of the crisis of industry versus inferiority.

Both Barbara and Sam attended Ann's games. They marveled at how fast she was growing up. Their presence helped Ann and she would cast a glance to the stands after making either a bad or a good play. She also looked to her coach for reactions to both her good and bad plays. Ann was finding another important female role model in her life, Ms. Bacon. Ann's friendships with her two special friends, Susie and Wendy, also grew. These friendships were about to take on even more importance as Ann enters adolescence.

ADOLESCENCE

In classical psychoanalytic theory, this period is labeled genital, and ends the process of psychosexual maturation; the individual at this stage is physiologically capable of sexual reproduction. In accord with the psychoanalytic position, the latency period ends with an infusion of sexual energy marking the onset of the genital stage. More dramatically than the previous stages, the individual enters the stage as one person and completes it as another; the girl becomes a woman, and the boy, a man.

Erikson, as with the other stages, recognized the importance of sexuality. But much more is going on. While the young person may be physiologically capable of sexual reproduction, there is more to adulthood than sexual capacity. The adolescent is continuing to seek a definition of self. At least for a little while, this process is going to be complicated by the rapidly occurring physical changes as well as the growing intensity of sexual impulses. Young women and young men need to adjust to their new bodies. Changes are also occurring cognitively; this is the stage of formal operations. For those who reach this stage, a whole new and important set of cognitive capacities are available to deal with the psychosocial crisis.

Psychosocial Crisis: Identity versus Role Confusion

Many, if not most, writers who deal with the period of adolescence treat it as a period of great change and turmoil. The child enters this period, and after eight or so years, emerges with an identity as an adult, ready to take her or his place in society. This stage can be usefully viewed as a period of transformation from childhood to adulthood. The medium of the transformation is, for most people, the social group. While the family remains important, the peer group now plays a key role.[21]

Cooley's observations on "the looking glass self" are helpful in contemplating the psychosocial crisis of adolescence.[22] An identity is being sought; the sense of identity that had evolved largely through the socialization efforts occurring within the family no longer fits the rapidly developing and changing teenager. A new identity is needed. This is the stage of life in which the adolescent spends a good bit of time in front of the mirror checking on the physical changes taking place in his or her body; in many ways, the adolescent is also searching for an identity in the mirror—Who am I?

As suggested by Cooley, the adolescent searches particularly for an identity within the peer group. Erikson spoke to the propensity of young people of this age to join together.

> Young people can also be remarkably clannish, and cruel in their exclusion of all those who are "different," in skin color or cultural background, in tastes and gifts, and often in such petty aspects of dress and gesture as have been temporarily selected as *the* signs of an in-grouper or out-grouper. It is important to understand (which does not mean condone or participate in) such intolerance as a defense against a sense of identity confusion. For adolescents not only help one another temporarily through much discomfort by forming cliques and by stereotyping themselves, their ideals, and their enemies; they also perversely test each other's capacity to pledge fidelity.[23]

Some psychosocial theorists, notably Barbara M. Newman and Philip R. Newman, have given additional attention to the role of the group in the search for personal identity. Building on the work of Erikson, they proposed that adolescence be divided into two periods, early and later adolescence.[24] The psychosocial crisis of early adolescence in their scheme is labeled "group identity versus alienation."[25] The point they developed is that the search for personal identity by the adolescent involves two steps. First is the development of a group identity (the peer group). The so-called group identity then provides the framework for the second step, the acquisition of a personal sense of identity (self).

Developmental Activities

The developmental activities through which the psychosocial crisis is played out include a number of social systems, the family, the peer group, the school, and the job, to mention but a few. In each, the adolescent plays a role. Each of these systems has its own set of goals which, as we have pointed out before, is the source of the role and the activities associated with playing that role. The problem is that the goals of some of these systems are in conflict with others. The clearest example for most young people is the goals of the family versus the goals of their peer group. When conflicts arise between the goals of two or more systems and an individual is playing a role in each of the systems, some level of role conflict inevitably results. For the adolescent as well as others, this situation gives special meaning to the expression "being between a rock and a hard place." For most young people of this age, the solution involves an emancipation from the family as a necessary condition for solving the crisis of identity versus role confusion.

We now pick up with Ann and the Jones family again. Ann is seventeen, living at home, and is a senior at Midtown High School. She serves as vice-president of her senior class, is a member of the Thespians Club and the school's basketball team, and works weekends as a cashier at Wal-Mart. Ann has dated since the age of fifteen, having had a couple of what she describes as "steady relationships," but is not involved in one at the moment. In sixth grade she developed a strong friendship with two other members of the basketball team, Susie and Wendy. Their friendship has persisted and intensified; they still refer to themselves as the "Fearsome Threesome." The name developed as a consequence of their "fearsome" behavior on the basketball court.

Barbara and Sam are now forty-five. In addition to Ann, they have a son, Paul, thirteen. Both sets of their parents are alive and enjoying good health. Barbara and Sam own their home

and financially, as Barbara puts it, "We are able to make ends meet." Except for Sam's experience with drugs early in the marriage, the marriage has worked for both of them.

While at times "bumpy," there has been nothing of great consequence in Ann's experiences as a teenager. Ann received a car for her sixteenth birthday. She was disappointed that it wasn't new, especially since both Susie and Wendy had received new cars from their folks on their sixteenth birthdays. There were also family difficulties over a boy that Ann had dated. This problem was centered around Sam, who did not like the fact that the fellow drove a motorcycle and wore an earring. Simply put, and in Sam's words, "I just don't like and don't trust the kid. I can't imagine what Ann sees in him!" Barbara was far less concerned about the relationship than her husband and, for the most part, mediated the problem between the two. Barbara's role shifted as Ann grew into a young woman. While still "Mom," to Ann she was also a friend and, at least to some extent, a confidant.

Barbara and Sam had the usual aspirations and worries about Ann; a special concern was drugs. It was generally acknowledged that drugs were a major problem in high school. Drugs, premarital sexual relations, and moral and ethical matters generally were topics of conversation between Ann and her mother. Ann did try marijuana although she has as yet not admitted it to her mother. In discussing the matter with Susie and Wendy, she observed, "You know, neither Mom nor Dad has ever asked me if I had tried drugs. I know where they are and I really appreciate the way they have handled this." Ann's own explanation is that she can get on her own high. In Ann's words, "Basketball is a high for me."

Ann is well on her way to a successful resolution of the crisis of **identity versus role confusion.** She has been popular in high school and received honorable mention for all-state guard as a member of the school's basketball team. She is confident in her role as a woman and, while not as yet having a sexual relationship with a man, feels that she doesn't have any "hangups" about sex.

Ann feels as though she has been something of a disappointment to her family as a student. While considered a solid B student, she knows that her mother was "straight A." Compounding the problem is Ann's ambivalence about what kind of career she wants and even if she wants to go on to college. While her parents have been supportive of her dilemma, she knows it is troubling to them. In this regard, she is not likely to easily forget her dad's terse remark, "You know, you can't make a living playing basketball." She does know that she needs to get away from home, to be on her own. Most of her friends are making plans for college, but she is not sure she is ready for college. She likes work, but hasn't found anything that she finds especially rewarding. Ann does like to travel, but to travel, one needs money and she has none.

EARLY ADULTHOOD

One of Erikson's most significant contributions to psychosocial theory was the addition of separate stages for adulthood. He was the first Freudian to do so. This attention to adulthood as well as to ego functions helped to establish psychosocial theory and to distinguish it from psychoanalytic theory.

Through a satisfactory resolution of the identity versus role confusion crisis, the young adult is now prepared to assume his or her place in society. This typically includes the selection of a mate and a job. This selection process contains the challenges for dealing with the crisis of this stage.

The Psychosocial Crisis: Intimacy versus Isolation

The adolescent, particularly during the early years of the stage, is absorbed in the search for identity. Erikson believed that a sense of personal identity is a prerequisite for intimacy. By intimacy, Erikson is referring to the capacity for giving oneself to a relationship in a full sense of mutuality. It takes a strong personal identity to do so; the danger is the loss of self in this process. The risk of a loss of identity in an intimate relationship with another becomes a core issue in this crisis.

Erikson related an incident in which Freud was asked what the normal adult should be able to do well. Freud's answer was a simple one— "Lieben und arbeiten" (to love and to work).[26] This, for Erikson, gets at the heart of the crisis that must be dealt with at this age. He observed:

> It pays to ponder on this simple formula; it gets deeper as you think about it. For when Freud said "love" he meant "genital" love, and genital "love"; when he said love *and* work, he meant a general work-productiveness which would not preoccupy the individual to the extent that he loses his right or capacity to be a genital and a loving being. Thus we may ponder, but we cannot improve on "the professor's" formula.[27]

In accordance with psychosocial theory, to become truly human, one must be capable of loving. This means giving oneself to another, who gives himself or herself to you, and doing so without either losing his or her own identity. There is still another part; to be able to give oneself to work and to do so without losing one's sense of personal identity, and still possess the ability to maintain the loving relationship. The risks are considerable, but that is the nature of the psychosocial crisis of this age. How many times have you heard, or perhaps said to yourself, "I am not ready to make this commitment"?

In developing systems theory, we have integrated some of the concepts borrowed from Abraham Maslow. Here Maslow's notion of a hierarchy of needs is instructive.[28] He contended that once survival and safety needs are satisfied, belongingness and love needs become dominant. While these needs will be addressed in a number of different ways, each will involve relationships with others. The most important and powerful of these will be through an intimate and continuous relationship with another person.[29]

Both Maslow and Erikson distinguished between the sexual expression of love in an intimate and love relationship and the sexual act in terms of a reproductive or recreational function. The former is involved in dealing with the crisis of **intimacy versus isolation,** while the latter is considered a negative way of dealing with the same crisis. Erikson posits the problem in this stage as the inability or unwillingness to enter and remain committed to an intimate relationship. The consequence is a growing sense of isolation and thus the diminishment of the potential of selfhood. While Erikson may be correct, an alternative position would hold that his conception is time and/or culture bound; there may be alternative ways of addressing intimacy needs.

Developmental Activities

While there are many sets of developmental activities to be mastered by the young adult, according to Erikson the two most important are in the domains of selecting a partner and choosing a career. In some instances, one's career and one's partnership coincide; for increasing numbers of young adults, both men and women, they are separate systems. The two domains, in turn, involve new major social systems; the family is one, the second is work, usually in the role of an employee.

We will return to the Joneses in order to develop the concept of activities as they are applied at this age. Our focus this time will be on Barbara at the age of thirty-five. Recall that Barbara and Sam are the same age. Ann is now seven and Paul is a vigorous three-year-old. In psychosocial development terms, we have a family of four with three different life-stage crises providing the dynamics of family life. The principal social system in which these crises will be played out is the same for each, the family. The

particular suprasystems having importance will be determined by the specific family cycle or social act being modeled.

We pick up with Barbara on the date of her and Sam's fourteenth wedding anniversary. It is a Saturday night. The kids are in bed and she is alone. Sam lost his job at the Biosk Corporation when it was taken over by a larger company. After a period of unemployment, Sam recently found a job as a salesman with another steel company. The job requires a great deal of travel, something neither he nor Barbara likes. She is thinking back to their tenth anniversary and remembering that Sam had missed that date also, again because of his job. She is feeling a bit sorry for herself when the phone rings. It is Sam calling from Peoria. That afternoon, a dozen red roses arrived from Sam, and at least for that moment, it made her day. Sam was also thinking about missing their tenth anniversary and now says, "Look, I have to be in Chicago on Monday. Why don't you meet me there and we will take a couple of days and celebrate our anniversary." Sam is always surprising Barbara and she loves him for it. He continues, "I have already talked to Mom and she will take care of the kids. I know you have time coming at work. We haven't been to Chicago together since school—let's do it." After some protest that they can't afford it, Barbara agrees and adds, "Sam, I really do miss you. Where will I meet you?— the same place?"

After hanging up from Sam she smiles, and thinks back over the past fourteen years. Barbara is now a supervisor at the mental health center. She enjoys her administrative duties but, at least for the moment, has given up her aspirations to become a director of a mental health center. She reflects on the birth of Ann and Paul and how complicated life became, and on her eventual decision to be a wife and mother first, and to place her career second. She thinks to herself "something had to be first, at least for now; but, Sam owes me one. We have had a good marriage. He has been good for me and I know I have been good for him. I do miss him; I can hardly wait to get to Chicago."

Barbara then calls Sam's folks to confirm the babysitting arrangements. After completing the call, she decides to go on to bed; it has been a busy and complicated day. She stops and checks on Ann and Paul, who are asleep. "What a couple of little angels," she thinks and she smiles, "it has been a good life."

The point we are seeking to develop here is the successful resolution that Barbara has made to the psychosocial crisis of intimacy versus isolation. She has experienced good and bad times in her marriage and in her life. She has continued to develop personally and still enjoys an intimate and loving relationship with Sam. We highlight the latter point because for Erikson and many others in this tradition, a mature and satisfying sexual relationship is a primary measure of one's successfully solving this crisis.[30]

MIDDLE ADULTHOOD

For Erikson, the middle years of adulthood are of central importance, at least as important as any of the other life stages. Here the generations are linked in an evolutionary manner. The middle adult years prepare individuals of the next generation for their place in society. Here also is that period in which individuals who are successfully dealing with the crisis of this stage, are seeking ways of making our world a better place.

Psychosocial Crisis: Generativity versus Stagnation

The age span comprising this stage is thirty years, from age thirty-five to age sixty-five, the longest of all the stages. It covers for most people the most productive years of their lives. The notion of generativity denotes personal growth that evidences a sense of mutuality toward humankind while stagnation refers to a lack of such growth and a developing sense of personal

impoverishment. A sense of generativity is typically experienced through work, civic activities, help of others, and through the raising and guidance of children. Erikson gave special attention to the latter area, the raising and guidance of children. He did not, however, restrict the notion of generativity to the raising of one's own children, but to the general effort made by one generation for the betterment of life for the next.[31] The tie made by Erikson between the crisis of the previous stage, intimacy versus isolation, and this stage is important. Through achieving a sense of intimacy, one is able to maintain a sense of personal identity yet become a part of a larger whole. The larger whole is the sense of mutuality with another person. A strong sense of intimacy includes the ability to recognize and be responsive to the needs of another, as well as the ability to give and receive. It is a state of maturity in which one is able to continue growing by giving.[32] By so doing, the foundation is set for the next stage of development.

Again Maslow and need theory is helpful. Through the satisfaction of one's social belonging and love needs, a still higher level of need satisfaction becomes dominant, the need for a sense of self-esteem.

> Satisfaction of the self-esteem need leads to feelings of self-confidence, worth, strength, capability, and adequacy, of being useful and necessary in the world. But thwarting of these needs produces feelings of inferiority, of weakness, and of helplessness. These feelings in turn give rise to either basic discouragement or else compensatory or neurotic trends.[33]

Recall from our earlier review of need theory that Maslow held that needs are of genetic origin.[34] While Maslow did not posit a life-stage link with his hierarchy of needs, he did recognize a tie between the satisfaction of higher need levels and age. Simply put, he concluded that a maturity associated with age and experience was necessary in order to progress to the highest level in his hierarchy.[35] In describing the need for a sense of self-esteem, he broadens the concern to include a sense of autonomy and freedom.

Here we wish to digress a moment and expand on the notion of generativity by further noting Maslow's ideas. We do so because of the worldwide changes that are occurring as people of the world, particularly those enslaved, seek greater freedom and independence.

Maslow was not sure whether the need for a sense of independence and freedom was part of the need for personal esteem, that is, whether it was a universal need at this level in the hierarchy.[36] Maslow raised this issue some fifty years ago. While we still do not know the answer, his concern then has a prophetic quality.

While in its fullest sense, generativity deals with a sense of mutuality with all humanity, a sense of responsibility for others, it, too, according to Erikson, has a negative aspect: stagnation.[37]

Developmental Activities

The notion of domains of life is useful in thinking about this stage of life and the activities associated with dealing with the crisis of **generativity versus stagnation.** For most people, the domains would include the family and the rearing of children, work, the church, and community service, among others.

To deal positively with the crisis of this stage, the individual must feel good about her- or himself, and her or his life situation. Some useful research has been performed in this area. It is also the general area in which we have done much of our research. For example, some interesting work has been done on life satisfaction and problems with marriage, parent-child relationships, and work. A finding of interest is that happiness in marriage is consistently related to overall happiness and life satisfaction.[38] Our own research supports this position, especially the relationship between marital satisfaction and job satisfaction. A particularly interesting finding in our study of job satisfaction among child welfare workers was the strong relationship

between marital satisfaction and job satisfaction. In fact, marital satisfaction was the single strongest predictor of job satisfaction.[39] Simply put, those workers who were feeling good about their marriages were feeling good about their jobs and vice versa. Our research design did not permit us to determine the specific relationships involved, but we assume they are interactive. On the negative side, our research suggests there is a relationship between marital satisfaction and the susceptibility to job burnout.[40] Thus, while the crisis of generativity versus stagnation is played out in several domains of activities, these domains appear to be closely linked.

For purposes of our example, Barbara and Sam are now fifty-eight years old. Ann is divorced, is rearing two children alone, and lives in Dallas. Like her mother, she too is a social worker. Paul has not married; he is an architect, loves his work, and lives in San Francisco. Barbara and Sam moved to Chicago over ten years ago primarily because of unusual job opportunities for both of them. Also, Chicago was one of their favorite towns; it was where they went to school, fell in love, and married. Sam is district sales manager of a steel company; Barbara did realize her ambition and is now executive director of the North Care Mental Health Center. Both of Sam's parents have died as has Barbara's father. Her mother is still vigorous, but did move close to the Joneses "just to be close to family."

Barbara and Sam have just finished meeting with their attorney after having made some changes in their will. Trust funds have been set up for both of their grandchildren to help with their educations. They have also set up a small trust for their church, and Barbara has set up one for the school of social work she attended. Driving back home Barbara remarks, "We have had a good life, I just hope that Ann and Paul have as good a life. I so worry about Ann and the kids. She would be so much better if she would let us help more." Sam laughs and reminds Barbara of the difficulties she had with his mother. He goes on to reassure her that Ann and the grandchildren seem quite happy. He adds, "You know that Ann is a lot like you. She is going to do it her way."

Later that evening, still taking stock of their lives, Sam asks, "Next to the kids and our life, what is the thing that you have done that has given you the most pleasure?" Barbara smiles, saying, "That's not hard. I really have enjoyed my job and the people at the center. We are like a big family and, believe me, are really making life better for our clients. I am especially proud of our new day-care program for the children of staff and our clients. I remember how important the Children's Center was for me after we had Ann. Did I tell you that they have asked me to chair a state task force to see if we can get state funding for this service? One of my ambitions is to see it made possible for every mental health center to develop a day-care program for children for both staff and clients. I don't think there is anything I have done that has been more appreciated by staff than starting this program. Can you imagine the research opportunities that it could open up?"

Barbara and Sam continue to grow and, as they do, their attention is starting to shift and to broaden. While concerned about their own children and grandchildren, they are increasingly thinking about other children and other people generally; they are wondering how their own lives can be used to make the world just a little better. Also, by establishing trusts for their grandchildren, their church, and Barbara's school, they are insuring some continuity of their contributions after they are gone.

LATE ADULTHOOD

Late adulthood completes the life cycle according to Erikson. It starts at roughly the time the person enters retirement (of whatever sort) and ends with death. At the time Erikson wrote, there was a very modest amount of scientific lit-erature dealing with old age. To some extent, this meagerness of literature may reflect a society that placed relatively little value on its elderly. Old people, in a manner of speaking, were considered to have made their contribution and were "put out to pasture." There would be a physical decline and the inevitable death; What more is there to say?

Erikson did not share such a conception of later adulthood. For him, it was an important time of life. It was a time for reflection and a time for putting it all together as well as a time for a continuing contribution.[41] Other psychosocial theorists, noting the increasing length of life and related changes, have added one or more additional stages to the life span.[42]

Psychosocial Crisis: Ego Integrity versus Despair

Erikson connected the first life stage (trust) with the last (integrity) by offering a dictionary definition of trust—"the assured reliance on another's integrity."[43] The cycle is thus completed. The healthy child should not fear life if her or his elders have achieved a sufficient sense of personal integrity so as not to fear death.[44]

In recent years, the scientific literature on the sociology and the psychology of aging has increased significantly. Similarly, there is a growing interest in schools of social work and in other professional schools in the issues of death and dying. Many schools, in fact, offer courses on the subject of dying. Our interest here is only to call your attention to the growing importance of this final life stage in terms of knowledge building, research, and as a field of practice. We believe this field will undergo rapid professionalization in the years ahead and become a major growth area for professional social work. Why? Among other reasons, our society is rapidly aging and seniors are becoming a powerful political force. More important, it is a critical life stage; people are living longer, are in better health longer, and are becoming economically more secure. Enormous opportunities exist for improving the well-being of this segment of our population so they, in turn, can contribute further to society. In short, the issue is how to help people in this stage of their life achieve a sense of **ego integrity.**

Integrity is not easily achieved. It requires a favorable ratio of successes in dealing with each of life's stages. Poetically, Erikson put it in the following way: "Only in him who in some way has taken care of things and people and has adapted himself to the triumphs and disappointments adherent to being, the originator of others or the generator of products and ideas—only in him may gradually ripen the fruit of these seven stages."[45] As the person grows older, he or she develops a sense of his or her own mortality. For most people, this meaning starts evolving during middle adulthood and pressures them to successfully deal with the crisis of generativity versus stagnation; they are confronting the fact that time is running out. There is not time to start over, no "trying to get it right the next time." This realization accounts for the despair and the fear of death in many.

Conversely, for those who have been fortunate enough to have "ripened the fruit" of the previous seven stages, an opportunity is offered for a final quest—true wisdom and self-actualization.

Developmental Activities

With retirement, with the death of one's parents and some colleagues and friends, there is a reduction in the support systems through which one plays out this final psychosocial crisis. Another handicap also exists: the role definition held by society of being old. For it is through the societal roles a person is given that the crisis is confronted. As indicated, in ours and many other western and industrialized societies, the role of being an "old person" has essentially been a negative one. This is now changing and part of the credit for this goes to people like Erikson and others who see the potential for contributions to be made at this stage of life.[46]

For many people, retirement offers a whole new set of opportunities. Where there had been children, they are now grown, as are the grandchildren. This is the time of great-grandchildren and somewhat less of a responsibility than there was in being a grandparent. Increasing numbers of retired people can travel and volunteer their time. In short, this stage provides a time of choice, a time of greater control over one's life. This is also the time in which one contemplates and evaluates the past and prepares for death. In this latter case, society is recognizing the importance of choice over how one dies. Death is the final experience. It needs to be handled in a dignified, caring, and sensitive way. The rapid growth of hospice programs in recent years is an expression of a recognition of the growing importance of death as a life event, as a completion of the life cycle over which the terminally ill person exercises control.

We now visit the Joneses for a final time. Barbara is now eighty-four and, while still living independently, has been informed that she has terminal cancer. Sam died three years earlier from a heart attack. Ann did remarry and had a third child whom she nicknamed Wendy, after her own lifelong friend. Ann returned to Midtown and, following in her mother's footsteps, became and is currently director of the Midtown Mental Health Center.

After retiring, Barbara became an active volunteer. In addition to her church, she served on the advisory body to her school of social work, serving eight years as chair. She also was very active in the mental health movement, both at the state and national levels. For two years, she served as secretary for the American Alliance for the Mentally Ill. Throughout her professional life, Barbara had two special areas of interest, children's programs and programs for the seriously and persistently mentally ill.

Upon learning of her terminal cancer, Barbara started making final preparations for her death. She sold the house in which she and Sam had spent so many happy years, and moved back to Midtown to be close to Ann. While Paul never married, he was always attentive to his parents. He remains in San Francisco with a thriving practice as an architect. Since learning of his mother's illness, he visits her monthly.

Barbara accepted Sam's death. He had two previous heart attacks and so the final one came as no surprise. While death is always hard to accept, especially when it comes to one so dear, Sam's own acceptance of his coming death helped. At times they would reminisce about their times together, both good and bad. He would still tell her, "You are still one hell of a woman and I love you." Sam continued to surprise Barbara with red roses. She still has pressed in her Bible the final rose Sam gave her. Barbara is tired, at peace, and she misses Sam.

Barbara and Sam met and satisfactorily resolved each of their life crises on the positive side. As they contemplated their eventual deaths, Sam often said to Barbara, "At least in a small way, Barbara, the world is a little better place for our having been here."

Spirituality and Psychosocial Theory

Erikson, unlike many other theorists, paid attention to religious beliefs as a major influence on the developing person. Erikson considered religion primarily in the social context, as a matter of social convention and as a consideration in selecting reference groups. There is little in his work that attempts to assess the spiritual or mystical elements of any particular belief system.

In regard to generativity, Erikson addresses the question of self-transcendence. In his early work, this focused on the question of having and raising children. Over time this was elaborated to issues of making contributions to society that will outlive the person. The considerations he raised in this regard were largely material rather than spiritual.

Only in the final stage, integrity versus despair, does Erikson seem to give primacy to

spiritual considerations. The question of the meaning of life, considered in the personal and epigenetic context, is his sole consideration. There is nothing prescriptive or preferential in Erikson to suggest that development of a spiritual orientation at this stage offers developmental advantages. He clearly suggests that stagnation in the previous stage, a preoccupation with the material, is dysfunctional. The failure to find integrative meaning and the resultant despair seem to be essentially individual developmental issues addressed by the person. The degree to which the social context supports and guides spiritual development is more implied than explicit.

SUMMARY

In this chapter, we provided an outline of psychosocial theory from a social systems perspective. Building primarily on the work of Erikson, we reviewed eight life stages. Each stage is treated in outcome terms. The psychosocial crisis of each stage results in a change and, it is hoped, a further positive development of one's sense of selfhood. The crisis is primarily played out in a series of developmental activities associated with the societal role assigned to each of these life stages. The role provides the structure through which the developmental activities take place. The role is always associated with other roles within the various systems' activities during the stage. For most people, the family is the dominant system. Each individual brings her or his own genetic and experiential background into each life stage. This is played out against and in accordance with cultural expectations and within a series of different social systems, each with its own suprasystem. The result, in every instance, is a unique human personality. Throughout this chapter we pointed out the linkages among the theories presented in Part Two, The Individual. A comparison chart of stage theories is presented in Figure 6.1.

FIGURE 6.1 Stage Theories Comparison Chart

PSYCHOSEXUAL STAGES (FREUD)	PSYCHOSOCIAL STAGES (ERIKSON)	COGNITIVE STAGES (PIAGET)	MORAL STAGES (KOHLBERG)	SELFHOOD STAGES (CHESS)
Genital (13+)	Integrity versus Despair (60+)	Formal Operations (12+)	Postconventional (16+)	Selfhood Realization (36+)
	Generativity versus Stagnation (25–60)			
	Intimacy versus Isolation (19–25)			Selfhood Construction (12–35)
	Identity versus Alienation (12–18)		Conventional (10–16)	
Latency (6–12)	Industry versus Inferiority (5–12)	Concrete Operations (7–12)		Game Playing (4–12)
Phallic (3–5)	Initiative versus Guilt (3–5)	Preoperational Thought (2–7)	Preconventional (4–10)	
Anal (1–2)	Autonomy versus Shame and Doubt (1–2)			Role Playing (1.5–4)
			Premoral Stage (0–4)	
Oral (0–1)	Trust versus Mistrust (0–1)	Sensorimotor Intelligence (0-2)		Prelanguage (0–1.5)

GLOSSARY _____

Autonomy The ability to think and act independently.

Autonomy versus shame and doubt The psychosocial crisis associated with the post-infancy life stage. Resolution leads to either a sense of self-control and freedom or an overwhelming sense of self-doubt.

Basic trust versus basic mistrust The psychosocial crisis associated with the life stage of infancy. The infant, through the relationship with the primary caregiver, develops a fundamental sense of confidence in others, or a sense of unpredictability, fear, and basic mistrust, which affects his or her perception of self.

Developmental activities The means employed by an individual to deal with the psychosocial crisis at each life stage.

Ego integrity versus despair The psychosocial crisis associated with late adulthood, the completion of the life cycle. Ego integrity conveys a final sense of wholeness or completeness of self. Death holds no fear. Despair, the counterpart, represents the recognition that death is near but the sense of personal wholeness has not and will not be achieved. Death is therefore feared.

Generativity versus stagnation The psychosocial crisis associated with the middle adulthood life stage. Generativity, the positive resolution, deals with a sense of mutuality toward all, of continuing to grow through giving. Stagnation, the negative pole, is a lack of growth, a sense of personal impoverishment.

Identity versus role confusion The psychosocial crisis of adolescence. This is the stage of life in which important psychosocial and psychological change is taking place. The crisis deals with the search for a personal identity.

Industry versus inferiority The psychosocial crisis of the school-age life stage is resolved through a sense of pride and accomplishment (positive) or through a negative self-evaluation and sense of incompetence.

Initiative versus guilt The psychosocial crisis of the preschool stage. The crisis deals with the motiva-

tional thrust behind every social act and the meaning assigned by the child to this motivation.

Intimacy versus isolation The psychosocial crisis of early adulthood. A positive resolution results in the ability to give of oneself to a relationship in a full sense of mutuality without fearing the loss of oneself in the process. A negative resolution is the diminishment of the potential of selfhood as one remains psychologically distant from others.

Life stage A developmental level that corresponds to a period of life. In psychosocial theory, each life stage is associated with a psychosocial crisis that must be resolved.

Polarity The resolution of the psychosocial crisis of each stage will result in an individual possessing personality (self) features falling somewhere between the positive and negative poles.

Psychosocial crisis The natural state of tension resulting from the different sets of expectations and coping capacities associated with each life stage.

Self-efficacy The development of the self's competence in a specified area of social functioning, for example, in the parenting role.

Selfhood A process that continues throughout life and is impacted by the resolution of the psychosocial crisis of each life stage.

NOTES

1. This is an ongoing research effort involving the authors and Dr. Srinika Jayaratne. For information dealing with methodology and implications to social work, see, for example, Srinika Jayaratne et al., "A Comparison of Job Satisfaction, Burnout and Turnover Among Workers in Child Welfare, Community Mental Health, Family Service and Health Settings," *Social Work*, vol. 29. no. 5 (September–October 1984): 448–453 and "Private and Agency Practitioners: Some Data and Observations," *Social Service Review*, vol. 62 (June 1988): 324–336.

2. *The Social Work Dictionary* (Silver Spring, MD: National Association of Social Workers, 1987), 130.

3. See particularly, Erik Erikson, *Childhood and Society*, 2nd ed. (New York: W. W. Norton, 1963). This

is Erikson's most important work and contains the most comprehensive presentation of his theory.

4. Ibid., 15–18.

5. Ibid., 247–274. Erikson labels the chapter dealing with the life stages as "The Eight Stages of Man." For consistency purposes, it is useful to treat the eight psychosocial crises identified by Erikson as constituting his designation of the eight stages that comprise psychosocial theory. In other words, the psychosocial crisis of the stage is also the name given to the stage itself.

6. Ibid. The position we are adopting here is consistent, in our opinion, with the one advanced by Erikson. He identified a series of ego qualities associated with a favorable outcome for each of the life stages.

For example, a person favorably resolving the psychosocial crisis of initiative versus guilt would exhibit the ego quality of purposiveness.

7. See Chapter 4 for a review of the stages employed by Freud in psychoanalytic theory.

8. Ibid., 247. For a further development of this point, also see Erik Erikson, "Identity and the Life Cycle," *Psychological Issues*, vol. 1, no. 1 (New York: International Universities Press, 1954), 64.

9. For a review of this research and the model used, see particularly Srinika Jayaratne and Wayne Chess, "Job Stress, Job Deficit, Emotional Support and Competence: Their Relationship to Burnout," *The Journal of Applied Social Sciences*, vol. 10, no. 2 (Spring/Summer 1986): 135–155 and Srinika Jayaratne, David Himle, and Wayne A. Chess, "Dealing with Work Stress and Strain: Is the Perception of Support More Important Than Its Use?" *The Journal of Applied Behavioral Science*, vol. 24, no. 22 (1988): 191–202.

10. Erikson, *Childhood and Society*, 11–19.

11. Robert J. Havighurst, *Developmental Tasks and Education*, 3rd ed. (New York: David McKay, 1972), 2.

12. Dan E. Hamacheck, "Evaluating Self-Concept and Ego Development Within Erikson's Psychosocial Framework: A Formulation," *Journal of Counseling and Development*, vol. 66 (April 1988): 354–360.

13. Ibid., 366.

14. The literature in this area is extensive and growing. For example, see S. K. Clarren and D. W. Smith, "The Fetal Alcohol Syndrome," *New England Journal of Medicine*, vol. 298 (1978): 1063–1067. See also Barbara M. Newman and Philip R. Newman, *Development Through Life: A Psychosocial Approach*, 6th ed. (New York: Brooks/Cole, 1995), 167.

15. Erikson, *Childhood and Society*, 72–80.

16. Erik Erikson, "Reflections on Dr. Borg's Life Cycle," *Daedalus*, 105 (1976): 23.

17. Erikson, *Childhood and Society*, 252–253.

18. For a useful introduction to the charting of the maturational process, see A. Gesell, *The Embryology of Behavior* (New York: Harper and Row, 1945).

19. Erikson, *Childhood and Society*, 255.

20. Ibid., 259.

21. Ibid., 261.

22. Charles H. Cooley, *Human Nature and the Social Order* (Glencoe, IL: The Free Press, 1956), 184.

23. Erikson, *Childhood and Society*, 262.

24. Barbara M. Newman and Philip R. Newman, *Development Through Life: A Psychosocial Approach*, 404–515.

25. Ibid., 448–451.

26. Erikson, *Childhood and Society*, 265.

27. Ibid.

28. Abraham Maslow, *Motivation and Personality*, 2nd ed. (New York: Harper and Row, 1970), 35–95.

29. Ibid.

30. Erikson, *Childhood and Society*, 265.

31. Ibid., 266–268.

32. Ibid.

33. Maslow, *Motivation and Personality*, 45.

34. Ibid., 77–95.

35. Ibid., 150.

36. Ibid., 45.

37. Erikson, *Childhood and Society*, 267.

38. See, for example, Gerald Burin, Joseph Veroff, and Sheila Feld, *Americans View Their Mental Health* (New York: Basic Books, 1960); and J. Veroff, E. Douvan, and R. Hulka, *The Inner American: A Self-Portrait from 1957 to 1976* (New York: Basic Books, 1981).

39. Wayne A. Chess and Julia M. Norlin, *Child Abuse and Neglect in Oklahoma: A Study of the Department of Human Services Programs Aimed at Identifying, Controlling and Preventing Child Abuse and Neglect* (Norman, OK: The University of Oklahoma, 1981), III, 70–79.

40. Ibid.

41. Erikson, *Childhood and Society*, 268–269.

42. For an interesting discussion and for someone who has written extensively in the area, see Bernice Neugarten, ed., *Age or Need: Public Policies for Older People* (Beverly Hills, CA: Sage, 1982).

43. Erikson, *Childhood and Society*, 269.

44. Ibid.

45. Ibid., 268.

46. Ruth E. Dunkle and Theresa Norgard, "Aging Overview," *Encyclopedia of Social Work*, vol. 1 (Washington, DC: NASW Press, 1995), 142–153.

PART THREE

THE SOCIAL GROUP

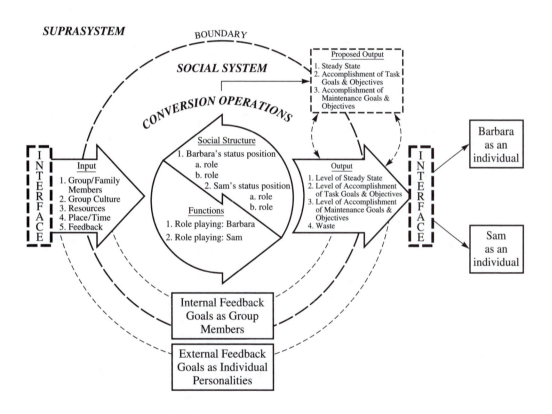

CHAPTER 7

THE SOCIAL GROUP
AN INTRODUCTION

DEFINITIONS

GEMEINSCHAFT AND GESELLSCHAFT

NATURAL AND RATIONAL WILL

PRIMARY AND SECONDARY GROUPS

COLLECTIONS OF PEOPLE, CATEGORIES OF
PEOPLE, AND THE SOCIAL GROUP

SUMMARY

GLOSSARY

NOTES

In this book, the social systems perspective presented here is a framework for developing a large-scale map of the social behavior landscape. Think of this map as social systems theory, a general theory for understanding the behavior of individuals, groups, families, formal organizations, and communities. Within this large map, we sometimes need more specific theories that deal with specific types of behavior. Social systems theory is suited for use of such theories.

In fact, it should guide us to the more effective use of what we will refer to as theories of limited range, including theories of individual behavior. However, our focus here is social: we believe this to be a proper perspective for the profession, and a solid foundation for effective social work practice.

One of the assumptions comprising the social systems perspective reads: Social ordering is a dynamic and constant process that arises out of conditions existing in the general order and the need structure of humans and the social organizations and institutions they join to form (see Chapter 2, assumption 2). We build from this assumption by taking the position that the distinctive features in human relationships are rooted in the basic interdependence of individuals. Humans have survived as a species because of their ability to join with each other as a means of satisfying their own needs and of dealing with the problems and opportunities posed by their physical and social environments. The extension of this assumption, the interdependence of humans and the interactions they have with their environments, forms the premise for social systems theory.

Embedded in the notion of the interdependence of humans and their social environments is the assumed social or gregarious nature of people. This observation is certainly not a new one. For example, several centuries before the birth of Christ, Aristotle wrote, "Man is by Nature a social animal. Anyone who either cannot lead the common life or is so self-sufficient as not to need to, and therefore does not partake of society is either a beast or a god."[1]

What is meant by social nature and how is this nature expressed? There are no conclusive answers to these questions and the search encompasses much of the subject matter of psychology and sociology. What can be described are the lines of debate and inquiry in the pursuit of answers to these questions. Particularly important is the information on theory development that contributes to social systems theory. We have already reviewed some of these theories in terms of the contribution they have made to the general features of social systems theory. In that review, we summarized the work of Abraham Maslow. Maslow clearly addresses the issue of the social nature of humans in his need theory.[2]

According to Maslow, belongingness and love needs represent basic needs and become dominant when the individual's physiological and safety needs have been satisfied.[3] Human interdependence and cooperation become the chief means through which survival and safety needs are addressed. Once these needs are satisfied, the pursuit of belongingness needs and love needs takes on a different character. Human association is no longer a means, it becomes an end in itself. In other words, a sense of belonging or love can only be obtained from other humans. Thus, association through social groups becomes both an end in itself and a means for achieving the satisfaction of social needs.

Many theorists reject the notion that human social behavior is genetically based. For some theorists, notably behaviorists, social behaviors are learned behaviors. For us, the argument as to whether social behavior is genetically based or learned is not central to our current purpose. What is important is recognition that it does exist and that it helps to account for our ability as a species to exist and, if numbers are an indication, to prosper. Sometimes it seems that we get caught up in negatives—our inhumanities. Examples of such behaviors abound, as a reading of any newspaper will attest. What we lose sight of sometimes is our basic humanity. We have a social nature, an ability to conceive of others as well as ourselves as individuals, to have feelings toward others, and to enter into relationships with them for the pursuit of shared purposes.

The social group and the family provide us with the clearest source of insights into our social behavior, our distinctive human qualities. In social systems theory, we consider the family a special kind of social group. In a later chapter, we will be reviewing practice theories that apply to the social group and others that apply to the family. For now we are interested in the generic level of the social group. Our position is that the social group is the first level of social organization. In a sense, the social group is the building block on which all larger, more complex forms of social organization depend. We will start the inquiry by reviewing our definition of the social group.

DEFINITIONS

Earlier we offered a simple classification of social organization, including the definition of the **social group:**

> **SOCIAL   GROUP** An   exclusive,   self-organizing form of social organization comprised of two or more members who identify and interact with one another on a personal basis as individuals, possess a shared sense of the group as a social entity, are affected by the group-related actions of members, and in which expressive actions dominate.

Based on this definition, our interest is in identifying the distinguishing features of the social group. These features help to differentiate the social group from other forms of social organization. We will be exploring these characteristics because of the implications they have when social systems theory is applied to a social group.

We consider six characteristics possessed by the social group to be particularly important.

1. *Size.*   The minimum group size is specified but the maximum is not. As a form of social organization, the social group is small. The upper limit in size is constrained by the person-to-person nature of interactions that all group members must have with one another. If this person-to-person feature is lost, in terms of the definition, the organization ceases to be a social group.

2. *Goal structure.*   The social group is characterized by minimum levels of role differentiation. Interaction among members is essentially person-to-person, and as total personalities rather than in narrowly defined roles. As a consequence, the goal structure of the group tends to be implicit rather than explicit; that is, the goals are derived essentially from the needs, such as social belonging and love, of those persons comprising the group. The goal structure derives from the informal and personal nature of the relationships that dominate in social groups.

3. *Identity.*   All members share a common group identity and perceive the group as a whole. This unity is most clearly expressed by the use of "we" when reference is made to group-related activities. Critically, the social group has a key effect on the selfhood possessed by its individual members. Because the group is relatively undifferentiated, members relate to each other as human personalities and thereby contribute to the development, maintenance, and enhancement of their sense of selfhood.

4. *Effect on individual behavior.*   The social group performs significant socialization and social control functions for its members. In short, every social group possesses a distinctive subculture, which includes a normative system that influences the group-related behavior of its members. These group norms are adopted, in part, by members (internalized) and become part of the individual's own value system.

5. *Self-organizing.*   The relationships among group members and the resulting interactions have their origins in the internal or natural state of the members. In this sense, social groups are self-organizing. The group-related actions are driven primarily by emotional as opposed to reasoned factors. Thus, relationships in social groups serve as an end in and of themselves as opposed to being instrumental or a means to some other end. This self-organizing feature of social groups helps distinguish what we label a **natural group** from a **formed group.** Formed groups are consciously constructed to perform some group-related task.

6. *Exclusive.*   The social group is the most exclusive of all forms of social organization. The family serves as an example of the social group that is most exclusive. The notion of exclusiveness is useful in thinking about the relative stability potential of the group and the corresponding stability of patterns important in the socialization of its members.

The family is the prototype social group, but our definition includes a large number of familiar groups, including the play group of the child, the teenage club (or gang), the friendship group of the adult, and the activity group. All of these groups are included in the definition to the extent that the relationships among group members conform to the definition. For example, if the primary purpose of an activity group such as a bowling club is to teach people to bowl or to earn money for the club through tournament winnings, the group would not fit the definition. In this instance, instruction or earning money would have taken primacy over human association. Therefore, groups formed specifically to achieve what we have earlier defined as task goals would not be included in the definition of social groups. Among these formed groups would be task-oriented committees, athletic teams, therapeutic groups, work project teams, and quality circles. We consider the distinction made between social or natural groups and formed groups to be important, primarily because of the differential impact these groups have on their members, that is, the contribution they make to the continued socialization of members.

In Part One we used examples of natural and formed groups. Relative to knowledge building, we consider the social group the locus for theory construction. Through our understanding of the social group, we learn how to apply this knowledge and utilize these implications in the forming of a helping relationship. In other words, we consider the helping system in social work a formed group. Its critical features are derived from our understanding of what we have defined as the social group.

The conceptual foundation for the definition of the social group as used in this chapter is found in the writings of Ferdinand Toennies and Charles Horton Cooley, among others. Because of the importance of the ideas introduced by Toennies and Cooley, selected features of their ideas will be reviewed in the following sections. We are also indebted to them because their ideas on the characteristics of social relationships served as the cornerstone for the clas-

sification of social organizations used in this book. Toennies and Cooley are also helpful in our effort to distinguish between natural and formed groups while showing how the former instructs us in the latter.

GEMEINSCHAFT AND GESELLSCHAFT

Writing in the latter part of the 1880s, Ferdinand Toennies (1855–1936), a German sociologist and philosopher, developed the concepts of Gemeinschaft and Gesellschaft to contrast two basic types of social relationships.[4] Toennies used these concepts to describe what he viewed as qualitatively different relationships among people in traditional and predominantly rural societies versus those in more modern and industrialized societies.

Gemeinschaft characterizes personal relationships that are entered into and enjoyed for their own sake. Such relationships evolve naturally and actions are spontaneous (as opposed to being deliberated on) and **cathected** (invested with emotional energy). These relationships are characterized as intimate, traditional, and informal. The prototype Gemeinschaft relationship would be that existing between family members. Gemeinschaft relationships dominate in what we have defined as the social group.

Gesellschaft relationships are entered into as a means toward some end. Such relationships are characterized by rational considerations and are calculated as the best means for achieving a determined end. These relationships are contractual, impersonal, voluntary, and limited.

The prototype Gesellschaft relationship is that between a buyer and seller. For example, an individual enters into a contractual relationship (means) with a real estate agent for the purpose of selling a home (end). Given the definition of Gesellschaft, we assume that the person wishing to sell the house would seek an agent possessing the skill, knowledge, experience, and other qualities associated with being a good real estate salesperson. Any personal or Gemeinschaft features that might develop in that relationship would be secondary to its primary purpose—selling the house. This distinction between means and ends is fundamental in understanding the differences between these two types of relationships. In contrast to a social group, a formed group is one that is characterized by Gesellschaft relationships.

Bear in mind that Toennies was attempting to develop two analytically pure models for examining social relationships. He was living during a period of rapid change resulting from the effects of industrialization and urbanization and was interested in the human effects of these changes. In short, Toennies observed that as social life became more complex and society more differentiated, a corresponding shift appeared to be occurring from Gemeinschaft to Gesellschaft types of relationships. As a practical matter, though, it should be understood that all human relationships will have Gemeinschaft and Gesellschaft qualities. In most instances, one or the other will tend to dominate and thus distinguish a particular social organization. Gemeinschaft qualities are considered to dominate Gesellschaft features in social groups. This is not to say that in a given instance a social group might not evolve into a form of social organization in which Gesellschaft relationships dominate; however, if that occurs, it ceases to be what is here defined as a social group and becomes something else, for example, a formal organization or a formed group.

NATURAL AND RATIONAL WILL

From time to time in the chapters ahead we will refer to the Gemeinschaft and Gesellschaft features of relationships. Because of the importance of these two types of relationships, it is helpful to tie these concepts to Toennies's search for a deeper explanation of human behavior. He introduced his inquiry as follows:

"What, why, and how do thinking humans will and want? The simple and most general answer is: they want to attain an end and seek the most appropriate means of attaining it."[5] How do humans will and want? In addressing the question, Toennies identified two contrasting types of will; one he labeled **natural**, the other **rational**.[6]

Natural will is linked to the essence or underlying character of the person. In its most elementary or simplest form, it is expressed in the direct, naive, honest, and emotional acts of the child. For a child, the explanation for an action might be, "I did it because I wanted to." For an adult, an explanation of an act based in natural will would be, "It felt like the right thing to do."

Rational will is a contemplated choice, one in which the alternatives are weighed and a decision is made as to the best means of achieving a specified end.

As in the case of the related concepts of Gemeinschaft and Gesellschaft, Toennies formulated two ideal or pure forms of will. Like their relationship counterparts, these two conceptions of will can be viewed as contrasting points on a continuum that is used to examine how human choices that underlie social behavior are made and exercised.

Natural will is the older of the two, having its origins in the very nature of men and women. It was subsequently developed in the cultural patterns that have evolved within societies over the centuries of human association. In a sense, natural will represents a collective wisdom passed from generation to generation; it is incorporated in the individual through the general socialization process. This form of will embodies a sense of tradition. Rational will is of more recent origin and is associated, in part, with the growing complexity of social life. It can be argued that rational and natural will have a common origin in an internal state of the human.

Natural will, as evident in overt behavior such as an act of affection, is a relatively direct expression of this so-called natural state. In contrast, rational will is affected more by a reasoned assessment of the social, political, and physical environment, and a judgment of the possible effects of actions on the person's own goals, for example, when a woman makes a decision to pursue a professional career. Here the decision often results from a conscious consideration of the money to be earned, the status of the profession among one's peers, and the market demand for such professionals. In contrast would be the woman who simply assumes that as an adult she will marry, bear children, and take care of a home, her children, and her husband. In the latter instance, the reasoning would be that this is the way it has always been, and always will be; therefore, it is right.

Recall that Toennies was writing in the latter part of the nineteenth century and was contemplating the effects of the rapid urbanization and industrialization of human association and the structure of society. During this time, people were becoming more mobile, the family was changing from an extended to a nuclear form, and people were increasingly dependent on jobs for their livelihood. People were less likely to know one another, yet they were growing more interdependent. The conditions were thus established for new forms of association among people; these new forms of relationships Toennies labeled Gesellschaft. Because of their contractual and temporal features, these new forms of relationships seemed more functionally suited to the needs of people in a rapidly changing, mobile, and industrially based society.

We again return to the essence of Toennies's question—How do humans will and want? Let us attempt a reply by using the popular expression "Where there's a will, there's a way." The expression is helpful on two counts: first, it introduces the notion of the relative intensity of will or the degree of human determination (motivation); and second, the expression again addresses the relationship between means and ends. *Will* becomes that which is needed or desired, the end state, or in systems language, the proposed outcome. *Way* becomes the means

for achieving the end state, or in systems terms, the structure or approach to be used.

When the notion of intensity of human determination (will) is combined with the relationships between means and ends, two different courses of actions become possible. First, given a relatively fixed association between means and ends, any given action will require a particular level of intensity of will for the specified action to take place. An analogy would be flipping a switch—it's either on or off, the action either took place or it did not. In the second instance, no fixed relationship is perceived to exist between the means and the end. Here one might assume a more complex set of possible actions in which various levels of human determination become associated with different means to achieve the desired end state, for example, How badly do you want it? or, If you want it badly enough, you will figure out a way to get it.

In part, the means-ends relationships undergird the distinction made by Toennies between natural and rational will. For example, in very stable and tradition-bound societies, there are relatively fixed ways of doing things, clearly established means for achieving a specified end—"This is the way we have always done it." In less traditional or modern (open) societies, more options are available to secure an end state. Simply put, natural will is associated with the relatively fixed connections between means and ends and rational will with those situations in which alternative means are available to secure a given want.

It would be useful to pause at this point and identify some of the contributions made by Toennies that have aided our definition and conceptualization of the social group. Here Toennies's use of the social relationship to contrast the origins of human actions (will) and the expression and purpose of will in human association is useful. According to Toennies, the patterned social relationships that define the social group result from natural will and are an expression of the mutual dependence humans have on one another and on their environment. This natural dependence is manifested and fulfilled by mutual performance—nothing more, nothing less. Here, in its strictest sense, is the purest example of the origin of relationships that result in the forming of social groups.

Using Toennies's concepts and our definition, the social group arises out of those human needs associated with the expression of natural will, and the resulting relationships are Gemeinschaft in nature. The intimacy, the sentiments, the person-to-person nature of the relationships among group members have as their central function the affirmation of each person's existence as a human being. In this sense, these Gemeinschaft relationships serve as both a means and an end. Later in this section we will be building on Toennies's concepts of natural will and Gemeinschaft to establish the position that the social group is the medium through which each person develops a personal identity.

In other words, the Gemeinschaft relationship form rooted in natural will is the primary medium of socialization in the young. Through Gemeinschaft forms of relationships, an individual's sense of selfhood is initially developed. Gesellschaft types of relationships have their impact later in development.

One final point needs to be made before moving on, and that pertains to Toennies's use of the term **mutuality.**[7] Mutuality means holding the same feelings toward each other. This feature of mutuality, the sharing of sentiments, characterizes or is a condition of a Gemeinschaft relationship. We point this out because the concept of mutuality is a necessary condition for a professional helping relationship. Toennies's work represents one of the origins of this concept as applied to a therapeutic or helping relationship. The client and worker share a common or mutual sense of and respect for each other as human beings. Through this mutuality, the worker and client are able to achieve a common definition of the problem, a

course of action to be followed, and a goal to be achieved. Recall also that the concept of mutuality includes the provision that the relationship can achieve its mutual intention only through mutual performance. Forming the professional relationship, which is essentially Gesellschaft by its contractual nature, incorporates Gemeinschaft features as necessary conditions for the achievement of its goals. This notion of mutuality as used by Toennies serves as an example of how knowledge gained in the study of natural groups has applications to formed groups, such as the professional helping relationship.

PRIMARY AND SECONDARY GROUPS

Primary and secondary groups can be usefully categorized by the types of relationships that link people together. Simply stated, Gemeinschaft relationships dominate in primary groups while Gesellschaft dominate in secondary groups. In the pages ahead our interest will be in primary groups and the forms they take. It is in Part Four, The Formal Organization, that we focus on the so-called secondary groups.

The term **primary group** was coined by Charles Horton Cooley (1864–1929), an American social psychologist, and appeared in his first major work, *Human Nature and the Social Order.*[8] As with Toennies, Cooley developed an evolutionary conception of social organization. Like other social scientists of their time, both were influenced by the rapid social changes associated with the industrial revolution, urbanization, bureaucratization, and centralization. Unlike Toennies, Cooley focused his attention at the individual level, being interested in how the individual's personality was formed and in the general interplay between society and the individual. Cooley's evolutionary point of view followed two channels, the hereditary or physical origins and the social origins of human nature. He was strongly influenced by Charles Darwin in his evolutionary views of the "physical channel in human development,"[9] but it was his reasoning and the conceptual development of the social origins of human nature for which we are more indebted. Also to be noted was Cooley's focus on the wholeness of the human physical, spiritual, and social spheres; each comprises a part of the whole. In introducing you to the notion of wholeness and order, we used the words of the poet John Donne, "No man is an island, entire of itself." Cooley introduced his idea of wholeness when applied to the human mind and social organization in a somewhat similar and thoughtful way.

> Mind is an organic whole made up of cooperating individualities, in somewhat the same way that the music of an orchestra is made up of divergent but related sounds. No one would think it necessary or reasonable to divide the music into two kinds, that made by the whole and that of particular instruments, and no more are there two kinds of mind, the social mind and the individual mind. When we study the social mind we merely fix our attention on larger aspects and relations rather than to the narrower ones of ordinary psychology.[10]

Cooley's sense of wholeness and the relationship of the individual to society is fully consistent with the systems notions being developed in this chapter, and in this sense, we view Cooley's work as making a significant contribution to modern systems thinking.

Cooley's conceptualization has provided a useful point of departure for the development of our approach in defining and modeling the social group. Of central importance is Cooley's contention that the primary group provides the medium through which the human personality is formed and subsequently supported. In short, his position is that the primary group comprises the individual's earliest form of human association, typically the family or its surrogate. Through this primary group association the infant learns those specific behaviors, values, and other attributes that constitute humanness. In a larger sense, the child is able to learn and exchange meanings through the acquisition of language. Through language the child is able to form a sense of those around him or her and to evolve a sense of self. While the process of the child's development of language was not described in any definitive sense by Cooley, he viewed the process as an internalization of members of the group through some form of psychological or image representation. Out of these representations, the child is able to differentiate external objects, people, and things, as well as an evolving sense of selfhood. The family is just one of the primary groups that constitute the social mediums through which the child and later the adult acquire humanness and a sense of self. While Cooley stressed the importance of the family in providing the critical primary-group experience, it is just one of the many group experiences through which the human is socialized and through which personal development takes place throughout life. Cooley summarized his position as follows:

> It is the nature which is developed and expressed in those simple, face to face groups that are somewhat alike in all societies; groups of the family, the playground, and the neighborhood. In the essential similarity of these is to be found the basis, in experience, for similar ideas and sentiments in the human mind. In these, everywhere human nature comes into existence. Man does not have it at birth; he cannot acquire it except through fellowship, and it decays in isolation.[11]

Cooley's general thesis of the primary group and its relationship to personality formation has served as a useful point of departure for many writers. We generally agree with the thesis, and it has assisted us in developing our definition of the social group. Cooley's writings also serve as an important foundation for other assumptions we make about the social group and its function. These assumptions are as follows:

1. The social group is a universal form of social organization and is thus found in all societies and throughout recorded history.

2. The social group derives its basic character and form from the individuals who comprise it; but as a social entity, it is not explainable in terms of the sum of its members. It is more. It possesses emergent properties that become evident only through the relationships people have with one another.

3. Individuals derive their essential and common attributes of humanness through participation in social groups. In other words, the social group is the primary medium through which the socialization process occurs.

4. Humanness is both socially acquired and supported. It is a dynamic state of being and must be sustained by social interactions throughout the life cycle.

5. The uniqueness of the human personality results from a dynamic interplay of its physical, spiritual, psychological, and social components. It is the constantly changing social context in which social functioning takes place that gives rise to the uniqueness of the individual and those social systems comprised of individuals.

Cooley, as much as any other theorist, has contributed to our view that one's identity is dynamic; it is a social process and it is lifelong. How does this social process take place? We will share with you in Chapter 7 how various theorists view this process. For now think of the process of identity formation as being dialectic in nature. The term *dialectic* developed in the works of G. F. W. Hegel (1770–1831), who proposed a logic based on the form of an argument.[12] In the Hegelian dialectic, a thesis is presented, it is countered by an equally plausible antithesis, and the result is a synthesis that represents a temporary reconciliation of the two opposing arguments.

The term *dialectic* is closely related to *dialogue* in its origins, and the idea of dialogue or conversation is woven throughout much of the theory we shall be discussing. The fact that human identity as we understand it cannot arise in any except a social context is central to social systems theory. The equally fundamental notion is that human identity is never accomplished: it is constantly in the process of development. Each unique experience alters us, in ways great and small, so that we are always in the process of becoming.

Perhaps the most famous example of this dialectical or interactive process is found in the "looking glass self" proposed by Charles H. Cooley.[13] Cooley maintained that the person comes to self-understanding by internalizing the ideas about how she or he is perceived by others. In a given situation, the person acts, observes the reaction of others, and then forms a judgment of the self based on what the self thinks that others think. Thus, it is not so much the actions of the self (theses), or the reactions of others (antitheses), but the conceptions one holds about the reactions of others (syntheses), which form the foundation of self-concept. The following example should help:

The Dialectic: A "Joke"

1. Thesis: Actions by Self
"I am funny and my friends will enjoy this joke." The story is a crude one and is followed by a "belch" that accentuates the punch line.
2. Antithesis: Reaction by the Group
The group of friends listen to the story. At the conclusion they share glances and then politely laugh.
3. Synthesis: Self-Judgment
"I am disgusting."

In the above example, it might have been just as easy for the self to have internalized the judgment "I am funny," which would have led to a very different self-concept and a very different perception of the acceptability of belching in social situations. In this instance, the self assigned a meaning to the response of the others, including the exchange of glances. The dynamic in terms of Cooley's "looking glass self" becomes "I am what you think I am." For us, the use of a **dialectic** in thinking about the process of socialization and formation of self is very useful. As a critical thinking tool, it takes something very complex and reduces it to its essence. We will be developing the use of a dialectic as a critical thinking tool in Chapter 10 when we review some of the specific social psychology theories having application in working with groups and families.

COLLECTIONS OF PEOPLE, CATEGORIES OF PEOPLE, AND THE SOCIAL GROUP

Our interest in Part Three is the social group and the further exploration of the power of Gemeinschaft relationships in affecting group behavior and in socializing the individual members of the group. We also want to identify how the power of the Gemeinschaft relationship is harnessed by various types of formed groups. As an introduction, we will first distinguish our notion of the social group from other types of **collections of people.**

Collections of People

By *collections* we merely want to note that individuals do gather at the same place at the same time, but do not interact with one another except in the most casual manner, for example, asking another person for directions. A vast range of such collections occur, a horde of shoppers in a mall, people attending a theater or rock concert, or passengers on an airplane. Sometimes the incidental gathering of people at the same place and at the same time can result in the conditions out of which social groups form. For example, a gathering of people on an elevator are in close proximity, but they do not constitute a group. Should this same collection of people be trapped in the elevator and forced to

interact in order to manage an escape, they could quickly turn into a group. Or, if someone became ill on the elevator, a group dynamic might quickly emerge. The failure of such a dynamic to emerge in cases of criminal assaults in public places is the stuff of urban legends about impersonal human groupings in modern life. While all collections of people are potential groups, the conditions that generate group interactions are complex and difficult to predict.

Categories of People

The term *category* is used to describe a number of people who have something in common, but who do not interact and are not necessarily in the same place at the same time. **Categories of people** are of crucial importance in social work practice, since many of the things defined as common to categories include social problems. Categories such as unwed mother, ethnic minority, Asian American, working poor, gay males, or physically challenged teenagers are commonly identified targets of social policies and programs. It is important to remember that such people do not constitute a group solely on the basis of fitting into the category. A support group for the physically challenged may not work if the members refuse to identify with the group. It is often the case that a group dynamic is difficult to develop when the common trait of members is one stigmatized in society.

The emergence of a social group out of a collection of people is powerfully evoked in this famous passage from *The Grapes of Wrath*, John Steinbeck's wrenching portrayal of the migration of dust bowl farmers from Oklahoma to California in the Great Depression:

> The cars of the migrant people crawled out of the side roads onto the great cross-country highway, and they took the migrant way west. In the daylight they scuttled like bugs to the westward; and as the dark caught them, they clustered like bugs near to shelter and water. And because they were lonely and perplexed, because they had all

come from a place of sadness and worry and defeat, and because they were all going to a new mysterious place, they huddled together; they talked together; they shared their lives, their food, and the things they hoped for in the new country. ... Every night a world created, complete with furniture friends made, and enemies established; a world complete with braggarts and with cowards, with quiet men, with humble men, with kindly maneuver night relationships that make a world, established; and every morning the world torn down like a circus.

At first the families were timid in the building and tumbling worlds, but gradually the technique of building worlds became their technique. Then leaders emerged, then laws were made, then codes came into being.[14]

Formed versus Natural Groups

The distinction between formed and natural groups is important in social work and represents the foundation for the emergence of social group work as a practice method in social work.[15] We seek to employ the understanding we gain from natural groups in formed groups.

Toseland and Rivas are helpful in distinguishing between formed and natural groups. They defined natural groups as "groups that come together spontaneously on the basis of naturally occurring events, interpersonal attraction, or the mutually perceived needs of members."[16] Such groups include, among others, families, family surrogates, peer groups, friendship groups, street gangs, and cliques. Natural groups lack, and do not require, formal sponsorship or artificial support. This type of group is not planned per se, nor is it constructed by any person or group in a deliberate sense. Natural groups tend to have long developmental histories, and these histories involve the evaluation of group roles over time, with resultant complications in the social exchanges that take place within the group. The natural group arises as an adaptation to conditions in the social environment. The internal structure of the group is not

imposed, but develops over time. Toseland and Rivas's definition of natural groups is very similar to our definition of the social group and what Cooley described as the primary group.

In contrast, formed groups are defined as "those groups that come together through some outside influence or intervention."[17] These groups do not usually exist without some outside sponsorship or affiliation. Formed groups are typically convened for a specific purpose. Examples include classroom groups, work groups, therapy groups, treatment teams, committees, clubs, and athletic teams. The internal role structure of such groups is simpler, since such groups often do not develop over long periods of time in the manner of natural groups. While these groups are limited by the same requirement of face-to-face interaction required of all groups, members may be confined to a narrower spectrum of roles within which group interaction takes place. While the variety of functions served by formed groups makes generalizations difficult, the same basic processes found in families and natural groups are assumed to be at play in formed groups, although these dynamics may be more constrained than in natural groups. Thus, basic human needs, instincts, emotions, drives for status, control, affection, and the rest will exist in these groups as surely as they do in families, although we can expect them to manifest themselves differently.

Core affiliations, which shape individual identity over time, tend to arise more often in natural groups, particularly the family. This is no doubt due to various factors: the status of the family in the larger society, the fact that it is our first social exposure, the variety of roles offered, the length of time one spends in the family, and the malleability of the family form may all account for this. Nonetheless, formed groups also can and do influence identity, particularly what has been termed the "situated identity" of daily interactions. The more recent the group membership, the more marginal our standing in the group, and the lower the status of the group are all factors that diminish the influence of the group on personal identity.

Task versus Treatment Groups

While **task** and **treatment groups** are both formed groups, the distinction between task and treatment groups has special importance for social workers. Toseland and Rivas made a number of comparisons and contrasts that are useful in preparing for our discussion of groups. In the distinction drawn between formed and natural groups and between task and treatment groups, we see how our understanding of the dynamics of natural groups is systematically employed in forming treatment groups. The distinction drawn between task and treatment groups by Toseland and Rivas can be summarized as follows:

Task versus Treatment Group Traits

- Bonding in treatment groups is based on member's personal need; in task groups it is based on the common task to be completed
- Roles in treatment develop via interaction; in task groups they may be assigned
- Communication pattern in treatment groups is open; in task it is focused on the task
- Procedures in treatment groups vary from formal to informal; in task groups there is a formal agenda and rules
- Composition in treatment groups is based on common concerns, problems or characteristics; in task groups it is based on needed talents, expertise or division of labor
- Self-disclosure in treatment groups is expected to be high; in task groups it is expected to be low
- Confidentiality in treatment groups requires that group proceedings are usually private and confined to the group; in task groups proceedings may be private but are frequently open to the public
- Evaluation in treatment groups is based on members meeting treatment goals; in task

groups it is based on successful task accomplishment[18]

The types of treatment groups include educational groups, growth groups, remediation (treatment) groups, and socialization groups. The variables within each type are subject to change, but the entire class of treatment groups is more similar to what we have defined as social groups than the counterpart task groups.

The distinctions between task and treatment groups as drawn by Toseland and Rivas follow, to a considerable extent, the distinctions between groups in which Gemeinschaft and Gesellschaft relationships dominate. Gemeinschaft relationships among members will dominate in treatment groups, while Gesellschaft relationships will dominate in task groups. In terms of social systems theory, members of treatment groups are largely concerned with the requisite functions of pattern maintenance and integration, while task groups are more concerned with the functions of adaptation and goal attainment. Keep in mind that all four functions must be performed to maintain steady state.

Stages in Group Development

In Part Two, you were introduced to theories dealing with the life-stage development of the individual. Group theorists have used the notion of stage to formulate stages of group development. The variety of groups makes it difficult to develop a stage model that addresses all possible groups. The relative importance of stages, the duration of stages, and the intensity of interaction in each stage may all vary with the group type. Nonetheless, it is important to remember that as the group develops a collective history, roles, interactions, needs, and perceptions may change, sometimes dramatically. A group at point A is not the same as that group at point B. How great a difference there is may vary, but there will be a difference.

We will now discuss some of the member needs that shift during the life of a group. As a rough sequence, consider the famous formulation offered by Tuckman, which defined the stages of groups this way:

1. *Forming*—the planning phase, when the factors which generate initial group cohesion are identified, and group purposes are defined. This may be a very formal or a very intuitive process.
2. *Storming*—the process of sorting out initial perceptions, relationships, hierarchies, and expectations. Power issues often emerge here, as do conflicting expectations and personal agendas.
3. *Norming*—developing a stabilized set of behavioral expectations for members in the group, establishing operating procedures, preparing to get the "work" of the group done.
4. *Performing*—the working phase, with relationships agreed upon and standards set, the task of the group or the needs of the members occupy the creative energies of the group.[19]

Tuckman's catchy formulation captures most of the essential elements in stage models of groups. It serves as a pragmatic reminder that trying to "force the agenda" may well distort or delay the group's need for a natural progression. Recall, however, that the length, intensity, and relative value of each stage may vary widely. Some groups may storm indefinitely; others may move quickly to the performance mode. Moreover, while it is clear that stages exist in some form, the question of their fixed, invariant sequence remains open.

A slightly more formal and more complete formulation of stages was offered by Klein, whose work on groups has influenced many group practitioners and theorists. Klein proposed the following stages:

1. *Orientation*—establishing the purpose of the group and introduction of members.

2. *Resistance*—individual members defending against perceived threats in the group process.
3. *Negotiation*—establishing the rules and norms of the group, seeking consensus on key issues.
4. *Intimacy*—group functioning with a degree of perceived safety for members, bonding accomplished among members, identification with the group and its purposes.
5. *Termination*—disengagement from the group, finishing the work of the group, cleaning up loose ends, attaining emotional and task closure.[20]

Group interaction can be expected to vary with the stage of the group. The relative focus of the group on the group as a whole, on individual members, or on the context and purpose of the group will vary across time, and to some degree with the circumstances of the group. Termination, in particular, is variable since the sensitivity of the group task, the degree of members' self-disclosure, members' prior personal histories of loss, and the status of the group make termination in some cases a powerful experience; in other cases, it is ceremonial.

In-Groups and Out-Groups

The frequently used terms of *in-* and *out-*, in relation to groups, can be instructive as we introduce the notion of group behaviors. Up to this point, our focus has been essentially internal, the formation and classification of groups. Now we turn to a discussion of relationships among groups. Generalists, as well as those seeking to practice in an advanced form of social work, must understand relationships among groups. As an introduction to the general notions involved, the idea of **in-groups** and **out-groups** takes on special meaning at the neighborhood level, in conflicts between street gangs. This same violence occurs between rival groups at all system levels, for example, in instances of "ethnic cleansing."

Since a major purpose of groups is to satisfy belonging needs, it is crucially important to define a boundary that delineates membership. The process of membership has a dual character. One must be chosen by others for membership, and one must choose to belong. In-groups are defined as those social groupings in which the individual feels at home. The group shares some common interests, some shared expectations, and some norms, which render behavior more predictable among group members. In-groups are very similar to what we have labeled the social groups or natural groups. Out-groups are defined as those social groupings in which the individual does not feel a sense of belonging. These definitions are focused on the individual member. Although other members of the group must similarly be comfortable with the individual as a member, these judgments are made on the group level. Likewise, out-group status requires some consensus among members that the individual does not qualify for in-group status.

In-group and out-group status accounts for many of the invisible boundaries that characterize human behavior in complex social systems. The transactions across the boundaries from in-group to out-group are systematically different from the transactions that occur within these boundaries. The greater the difference in the normative structures and member characteristics of two groups, the greater will be the likelihood of what has been called "turbulence at the interface." The potential for miscommunication and defensiveness is much greater when communicating across as opposed to within group boundaries. That miscommunication takes two forms: information loss and information distortion.

Information loss occurs when the differences between the groups is significant, so that messages "encoded" for one group require significant "decoding" for another. In a literal ex-

ample, if a person from one culture is speaking to a person from another culture, even simple communications require some exertion. A tourist may ask a local in a small village where he can get brunch, but the local may have no concept of such a meal. The local person is puzzled, the tourist frustrated. The tourist then simplifies his request, asking where he can get something to eat. The local gives directions to a nearby spot. The spot turns out to be a grocery store. The tourist either buys something there or goes away hungry, grousing to himself that these people are uncivilized. In this case, *uncivilized* means that the locals do not share the same vocabulary and expectations as those of the in-group with which the tourist identifies. The local, meanwhile, is puzzled or amused at the notion of eating a meal in the middle of the morning, if even that much information got through in the confusion. In diagrammatic form, communication across the invisible boundary between the in-group and out-group might be depicted as in Figure 7.1.

Information distortion is sometimes more problematic, because parties may think that they have in fact communicated when they have not. A famous example is a white man socialized in a society in which being called a "good ole' boy" is a compliment. This man, in meeting a black man of his same age, asks about where to go to

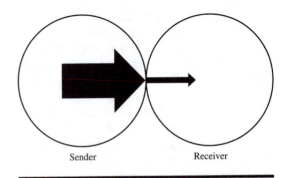

Sender   Receiver

FIGURE 7.1   Information Loss between In-Group and Out-Group Members

hear good music. He addresses the black man, asking, "Where do you boys go for a good time?" The white man in this example (dated though it may seem in this day and age) assumes that he and the black man are members of the same in-group, young males. He encodes his message as a casual inquiry between equals. The black man, of course, is socialized to a different culture, in which being called "boy" in any form is a racial insult. The black man responds, saying, "Do you see any boys here, Cowboy?" "Cowboy" in this context may be an insult, as the tone would surely convey. The white man goes away convinced that black men are overly sensitive and irrational. The black man is confirmed in his own opinion that white men are callous racists.

The care that must be taken to guard against distortion in the encoding and decoding process requires energy, and becomes another reason that people choose to operate within the confines of in-groups rather than expend the effort and take the risks of communicating across the boundaries that define such systems. Figure 7.2 provides a graphic representation of information distortion across a well-defined interface.

In human society, of course, human beings are constantly involved in a wide range of col-lectivities, categories, and groups. Our identity shifts more or less constantly, since we identify ourselves in large part on the basis of the shifting social context. The process of selecting which group membership defines us in a given context is an ongoing one, and led to social psychologist Lou Zurcher defining our identity as a "mutable self."[21]

The sociologist Georg Simmel (1858–1918) devoted a great deal of attention to the issue of identity and group membership. One of his famous books poses the question *How is Society Possible?* The number of group memberships and their often conflicting requirements explain the difficulty of reciprocal relations across the often invisible boundaries of group identity. Simmel used the phrase "the web of group affiliations" to denote this complex inter-weaving of social influences, individual perception, and reciprocal interaction. Simmel's theories profoundly influenced the American schools of sociology, important among them, the symbolic interactionalists.[22] Simmel stressed the problem of how we can accurately perceive others in social interactions, and how the characteristics of our self fit in with the structures and requirements of society.

This line of inquiry, in which the fluctuations in personal identity were the focus, led ultimately to the formulation of what is called the "fundamental attribution error." This concept may be summarized as an assertion that in the study of human behavior, the tendency is to place too much importance on individual personality (or character), while neglecting the situational variables that mold our behavior in various contexts. One of the most important of these influences is the subjective group membership we hold at any given moment. An example might help illustrate this point.

Remember the scene from lots of old western movies in which the bad guy was being held in jail, and the men of the town were at the saloon drinking. At first the saloon may be the

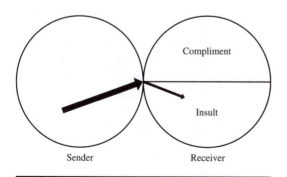

Compliment

Insult

Sender   Receiver

FIGURE 7.2 Information Distortion between In-Group and Out-Group Members

scene of a collectivity, a bunch of guys drinking more or less in isolation. Then conversation starts, and the collectivity begins to identify some common concerns, having to do with the fact that the West would be better off without riffraff such as the outlaw being held in jail. Soon a leader emerges, a group norm—the Code of the West—is invoked, and the group sets off with the common goal of hanging the varmint from the highest tree.

When they get to the jailhouse, the sheriff faces an angry mob (which now is a group) and tries to talk them out of what they are about to do. He may try several tactics. Often, the sheriff calls out the leader of the group, on the assumption that the group norms were developed under the spell of his influence. When the sheriff shoots the leader, or humiliates him, the others identify with this outcome, decide they don't like it, and go away muttering. Or, the sheriff may begin to call out the names of individuals in the mob, and remind them of other group affiliations they hold. He will ask one mobster how he can face his children having done this. He will ask another how he can ever go to church again and pose as a Christian. Yet another might be asked what his mother would think to see him drunk and murderous. At the same time, the sheriff may attack the bonds that hold the mob together. He frequently notes that "the whiskey is doing the talking," thus diminishing the attractiveness of mob membership, or he may say that the leader is merely using them for his own purposes, thus sowing doubt about the true unity of concern shared by mob members.

In this scenario, the web of affiliations described by Simmel is invoked to break down identification with a current group.[23] The mob identity in this case is called the *manifest affiliation*. The manifest affiliation determines the behavior and attitudes in the situation. All other potential group identities are termed *latent affiliations*. Latent affiliations do not define identity in the situation, but may be invoked in a variety of ways. In group therapy, one of the most useful purposes of group membership is to test out possible courses of action against all possible latent identities, using other members for feedback.

Religion and Spirituality in Groups

Religion and spirituality enter into group process in various ways. Few theories of group behavior take full account of these considerations as a part of group dynamics. The primary influence is found at the level of the individual members as subsystems in the group under the auspices of the agency or institutional suprasystem that convenes the group.

At the subsystem level, the degree of personal spirituality of the members of a group will have marked influence. Groups that are composed of members who range from preoperational spirituality (fantasy and emotional) to the vision logic or causal levels are unlikely to have coherence. Spirituality in the formation or conduct of a group is a factor that few group theorists or practitioners address. Yalom addressed levels of emotional maturity, but it is mainly in his later work on existentialism that this is fully developed. His important book on group psychotherapy pays little attention to spirituality in group process.

At the level of individual members, more attention is usually paid to member religious beliefs than to the level of member spirituality. Religious beliefs will often be assessed and accounted for as personality variables. For example, a group therapist might take an inflexible religious belief system as an indicator of personal dogmatism. Taking account of religious beliefs as opposed to spiritual level is more commonly observed. A group of people with strong but conflicting religious viewpoints might be expected to produce little group coherence and high, irresolvable levels of conflict. Unless religious belief is the focus of the group, it is likely to produce unforeseen complications in group process.

At the level of the suprasystem, the nature of the responsible agency is likely to have obvious impact on the gestalt of members coming into the group. For instance, a group for young women with unwanted pregnancies might be perceived very differently if the group is under the auspices of Catholic Social Services than if the group is under the auspices of Planned Parenthood. The known (or assumed) beliefs of a sponsoring agency create an expectation that may be implicit in members, and like all group process this implicit consideration must be identified and made explicit if the group is to function effectively.

SUMMARY

Chapter 7 introduces Part Three, The Social Group. In Chapter 3, Social Systems Theory: General Features, we shared with you the reasoning for including the family and the social group in the same system level. In this chapter, we started by describing some of the characteristics of the social group. We then introduced the concepts of Gemeinschaft and Gesellschaft for purposes of distinguishing the social group from other system levels. Gemeinschaft relationships characterize the social group. This type of relationship, in our usage, has its origins in the genetic structure of humans. We humans have a social nature that is the core determinant of the societies we build and perpetuate. The social group and that special form, the family, constitute the building blocks of such societies.

We further differentiated the social group through Cooley's use of the term *primary group*. Through the use of the primary group, we established the position that our humanness is acquired and developed throughout life by our participation in social groups, particularly the family. The social group represents the medium through which much of the socialization process occurs. It is also the primary medium through which our own sense of selfhood is developed and sustained.

The social group is further distinguished by contrasting formed and what are frequently called natural groups. In our usage, social groups, primary groups, and natural groups are synonymous. The contrast between formed and natural is helpful to identify a mixed or bridging classification of social systems. For current purposes, think of the formed group as possessing a mix of Gemeinschaft and Gesellschaft relationships.

Next we divide formed groups into two general classifications—task groups and treatment groups. Through this discussion we defined generalist practice, in fact, all social work practice, as constituting a "treatment" group. In short, the concept of treatment groups makes use of our understanding of the behaviors of social groups and applies this understanding to the helping system, for example, in the generalist practice of social work.

We concluded this chapter with a review of the notions of in-groups and out-groups. Here we focused on intergroup relationships. While focused on social groups, the basic dynamics involved have relevance at all system levels.

GLOSSARY

Categories of people   People who share a common characteristic but who are not necessarily in the same place at the same time and do not evidence personal relationships, for example, the "working poor."

Cathected   An adjective describing a relationship or an object invested with emotional energy (feeling).

Collections of people   Individuals who converge at the same place and at the same time but essentially without relationships with one another.

Dialectic   A dialogue in which a position is set forth—the thesis. This thesis is challenged by a counterthesis and is resolved by a synthesis of the two. This establishes the thesis for the next cycle of the dialogue.

Formed group   A group that is consciously created to perform tasks as the means to accomplish a goal.

Gemeinschaft   A type of relationship that is informal, personal, and entered into for its own sake (as opposed to a Gesellschaft relationship).

Gesellschaft   A type of relationship that is formal, impersonal, contractual, and entered into as a means to another end (as opposed to a Gemeinschaft relationship).

In-group   A group designation that highlights the group's strong beliefs, values, attitudes, and exclusionary behaviors toward out-group members, that is, those not designated as in-group members. The contrasting group is known as the out-group.

Mutuality   A sense of being mutual; two or more people holding comparable feelings toward each other. Within a helping relationship, it is the capacity of the worker and client to experience a sense of being mutual.

Natural group   A group that is self-organizing as opposed to being consciously created. The fact that natural groups are self-organizing is based primarily in the genetic structure of the human not in external circumstances. Natural groups and social groups are synonymous.

Natural will   As used here, a view held by Toennies

of human volition based in one's basic (inherited) nature.

Out-group   See In-group.

Primary groups   Groups that form naturally and are based on the affiliation needs of humans. They are primary groups in the sense that they are most important and the first form taken in human associations. *Primary groups, social groups,* and *natural groups* are synonymous terms.

Rational will   As used by Toennies, a form of human volition linked to a reasoning capacity, which ties choices of action to the possible consequences of those actions. See Natural will.

Secondary groups   A loose categorization of all forms of human groups not considered primary. See Primary groups.

Social group   An exclusive, self-organizing form of social organization comprised of two or more members who identify and interact with one another on a personal basis as individuals, possess a shared sense of the group as a social entity, are affected by the group-related actions of members, and in which expressive actions dominate.

Task group   A formed, as distinguished from natural, group.

Treatment group   A group formed for purposes of conducting treatment, or more generally, the helping system in work with clients or customers.

NOTES

1. Aristotle, *Politics,* c. 328 B.C. in *The World's Great Thinkers* (New York: Random House, 1947), 91.
2. Abraham H. Maslow, *Motivation and Personality,* 2nd ed. (New York: Harper and Row, 1970), 77–95.
3. Ibid.
4. Ferdinand Toennies, *Community and Society,* ed. and trans. Charles P. Loomis (Lansing, MI: Michigan State University Press, 1957), 247–259.
5. Ibid., 247.
6. Ibid.
7. Ibid., 247–259.
8. Charles Horton Cooley, *Human Nature and the Social Order,* rev. ed. (New York: Charles Scribner's Sons, 1922), 32.
9. Ibid., 23–25.
10. Charles Horton Cooley, *Social Organization* (New York: Charles Scribner's Sons, 1909), 3.
11. Ibid., 30.
12. For a review of the logic, see G. W. F. Hegel, "Philosophical History," in *The World's Great Thinkers: Man and the State, The Political Philosophers* (New York: Random House, 1947), 405–483.
13. Cooley, *Human Nature and the Social Order,* 23.
14. John Steinbeck, *The Grapes of Wrath* (New York: Harper, 1939), 264.
15. See, for example, Janice H. Schapler and Maeda J. Galensky, "Group Practice Overview," *Encyclopedia of Social Work,* vol. 2 (Washington, DC: NASW, 1995), 1129–1142.
16. R. Toseland and R. Rivas, *An Introduction to Group Work Practice* (New York: Macmillan, 1984), 14.
17. Ibid.
18. Ibid., 16.

19. See B. Tuckman, "Developmental Sequences in Small Groups," *Psychological Bulletin* (1967) 63: 384–389.

20. Alan Klein, *Effective Group Work* (New York: Association Press, 1972).

21. Lou Zurcher, *The Mutable Self: A Self Concept for Social Change* (Beverly Hills, CA: Sage, 1977).

22. For a review of Simmel's work, including excerpts from *How Is Society Possible?*, see Kurt H. Wolff, ed. and trans., *The Sociology of Georg Simmel* (New York: The Free Press, 1950).

23. Ibid.

CHAPTER 8

THE SOCIAL GROUP
THEORETICAL SUPPORT

FIELD THEORY   SUMMARY
EXCHANGE THEORY   GLOSSARY
SYMBOLIC INTERACTION THEORY   NOTES
SPIRITUALITY AND GROUP PROCESS

Our interest in this chapter is in identifying those lines of theory that have helped in the development of social systems theory and its application to the social group. In the previous chapter, we noted that the social group, for us, is the building block for the more complex forms of social organization, such as the formal organization and the community. So just as the individual is the component from which the social group is formed, so is the social group the component out of which higher, more complex types of social organization are formed.

From the beginnings of social work, the group has been an area of professional concern, but practice has been hindered by the lack of a united theoretical approach.[1] Only in the past decade has a consensus been forming that social systems theory provides the conceptual foundations for work with groups. Janice H. Schopler and Maeda J. Galinsky, writing in the 1995 edition of the *Encyclopedia of Social Work*, put it thusly:

> Social work practice with groups is guided by a view of groups as social systems. Although other theoretical perspectives, such as psychoanalytic theory, existential theory, learning theory, field theory and social exchange theory, have influenced the development of group work models, all the major formulations of social group work rely on concepts from social systems theory to describe group functioning.[2]

We concur with this position, but would add that to support generalist practice, social systems theory needs to be presented as a general theory with special applications to work with social groups and families. In developing the distinctive features of social systems theory applied to groups and families, we have found three lines of theory development helpful—field, exchange, and symbolic interaction. We find the foundations of these theories compatible with social systems theory and believe many will find these more narrow-range, or what are sometimes called limited-range, theories helpful to use within the framework provided by social systems theory.

In the pages ahead, we will be summarizing field, exchange, and symbolic interaction theory. In doing so we will identify the major theorist(s) associated with each, the basic assumptions on which each theory builds, and each theory's key concepts.

We will start our review with field theory. More so than most psychological theories (those focusing on the individual), field theory focuses on the individual within the social environment. By so doing, field theory serves as a useful bridge between theories that focus on the individual and those that focus on social groups and the behavior of individuals within them.

FIELD THEORY

In a memorial address at the 1947 convention of the American Psychological Association,

Tolman summed up the contributions of Kurt Lewin (1890–1947) by noting, "Freud, the clinician and Lewin, the experimentalist—these are the two men whose names will stand out before all others in the history of our psychological era."[3]

Lewin is not classified as a general or social systems theorist; his quest might be best described as the "purification" of psychology. He believed that each science seeks to purify its own concepts and in so doing tends to segregate itself from the others. So, according to Lewin, any idea of a unification of all sciences through the development of a general (systems) theory was wishful thinking. Lewin's contribution to our effort at forming a social systems theory stems from the fact that he was one of the earliest psychologists to hold that human behavior could be usefully studied only by viewing the individual in an environmental context. More important, he supplied the concepts and the experimental approaches to undertake studies from this perspective. Lewin's mark on the behavioral sciences is still seen in the familiarity of some of his concepts and the related terms he coined, for example, *group dynamics, sensitivity training, life space,* and *action research.*[4] His commitment to the importance of theory in knowledge building and the application of that knowledge to the problems of everyday life is perhaps best reflected in his often-quoted remark, "There is nothing so practical as a good theory."[5]

Lewin was deeply influenced as a student and a young scholar by **gestalt psychology,** and the development of his holistic approach to the study of human behavior bears its mark. Our interest in Lewin's work stems not only from his attention to the study of human behavior in an environmental context, but also from the extensive research he and his students accomplished in support of this contention. Lewin thus became one of the first theorists to provide empirical support for a social systems perspective on the study of social organizations.

While best known as a psychologist, Lewin held that it is possible to construct a general social psychological theory that would apply to the study of the group, family, formal organizations, and the community, as well as the individual.[6] His development of field theory was premised in part on this assumption. Thus, Lewin's work can be usefully viewed as a precursor to social systems theory.

Lewin's quest for a general theory for psychology was associated with his search for a branch of mathematics that would provide the precision needed to express and test his various constructs. The best known of his mathematical expressions is $B = F(P,E)$ or B (behavior) equals F (the function) of P (the person) and the E (environment).[7] Lewin assumed the person and the environment to be an interdependent whole. This whole becomes the **life space** (LSp) of the person. Mathematically, it is expressed as $B = F(P,E) = F(LSp)$. According to Lewin, "The task of explaining behavior then becomes identical with (1) finding a scientific representation of the life space (LSp) and (2) determining the function (F) which links the behavior to the life space. This function F is what one usually calls a law."[8]

We cite Lewin's mathematical expression because it embodies the central point developed in this book: Human behavior or the behavior of any social organization is to be understood in terms of its function and the reciprocal relations it has with its social environment. For us, field theory supports the contention that social organizations can be viewed as open systems, and that the behavior of any social system can be understood in terms of the interplay between the system and its suprasystem.

Unlike Freud and many other theorists, Lewin did not search for behavioral determinants in the individual's past, genetic legacy, or capacity to learn and reason. Behavior, according to Lewin, depends not on the past or the future but the here and now, or in his terms, "the pres-

ent field." This is not to say that unconscious determinants cannot be contained in the present field. What is central, though, is the person's current situation. This is the point at which professional intervention becomes focused.

Assumptions

Lewin's work helped us in formulating several of the assumptions introduced in Chapter 2, A Social Systems Perspective. While he is best remembered as a psychologist, his concept of the field as a behavioral determinant also applied to the various groups that individuals join to form. We are not suggesting that Lewin's field theory shares all of the same assumptions that undergird the social systems perspective. Rather, we are saying that Lewin's work helped us in formulating a social systems perspective. Field theory also helped us develop our assumption pertaining to the cause-and-effect relationship between the individual and the group. It was unfortunate that Lewin died so young (at age fifty-six) because in the years immediately preceding his death, his interest was focusing on groups and larger systems and their effects on those who comprise them. Even so, his research in field theory offers avenues for investigating social systems features.

Concepts

In the development of field theory, Lewin developed a series of concepts and definitions that are instructive as well as relevant in forming social systems theory. Included are such familiar concepts as field, needs, goals, tensions, tension systems, and equilibrium.

Field. For our present purposes, *field* and *life space* can be considered synonymous. The field is the environment in which the individual or other social unit is located and in which they are related behaviorally. Field theory holds that the individual (and other social units) cannot be conceived apart from the environment.[9] Another useful way of thinking about field is as that environment which serves as the source for observational data pertaining to social systems.

More so than any other line of theory development, field theory and the notion of field helped us in constructing our notion of suprasystem. Like field, suprasystem is the larger context that includes the subject system and serves as the source for observational data.

To present a more serious example, when a woman is considering a divorce, she must take into account the impact of this decision on a number of group-affiliated identities. What will a divorce mean to her as a mother? What will be the effect on her children? What will her parents think of her action? What will her parents-in-law think? What will her boss think of her? What will her minister and church friends think? What changes will this make in her relationship with other women? With men? Which of the friends she made as a married woman will desert her?

Kurt Lewin would characterize this dilemma in terms of the "hodological space" occupied by this woman.[10] The term *hodological* is derived from the Greek word for pathway, the analogy being that the interior landscape of the life space is navigated much like traveling winding paths through natural obstacles. Each zone of the life space is loaded with social significance, and each zone is different. Moreover, from moment to moment, the woman dwells in a different part of the life space. At one moment she may be dreamily contemplating the pleasures of freedom offered by divorce, when a telephone call from her mother-in-law snaps her abruptly into a different identity, in which the idea of divorce is laden with anxiety and guilt. For such a woman, a group in which she can safely explore alternatives from the standpoint of each of these "nested social identities" would be useful indeed. Lewin might depict such a **life space** as seen in Figure 8.1, with a plus sign (+) indicating positive zones and a minus sign (–) indicating painful or negative zones.[11]

Needs. Lewin distinguished two categories of human needs: genuine and quasi needs.[12] **Genuine needs** have their clearest origins in an inner state of the individual and can be likened to what Abraham Maslow called physiological

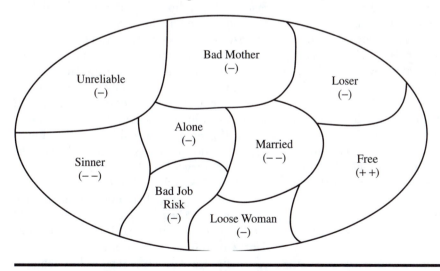

FIGURE 8.1 Positive and Negative Life-Space Zones

or survival-level needs, such as hunger.[13] **Quasi needs,** on the other hand, are derived from sources external to the person and pertain to specific intentions of the individual. Quasi needs have their roots in genuine needs but are of a secondary order. For example, hunger is a basic need; deciding what to have for dinner to satisfy that need, or in which restaurant to dine, would serve as an example of a quasi need. In other words, the decision or the intention of an individual to do something causes a quasi need to be created. By their nature, quasi needs are much more frequently experienced and are less stable than genuine needs.

In our view, it is useful to think about genuine needs as having their origins in the genetic structure of humans. Quasi needs, on the other hand, are affected in their expression by the field and by the larger culture of which the person is a part. Of interest is Lewin's theoretical position that the tension or energy patterns behind quasi needs and genuine needs are identical. Therefore, according to this position, a need of any order exists only when it upsets an equilibrium within the person. In other words, being hungry becomes motivational only when it disturbs a person's inner state and results in the creation of a tension system, which, in turn, causes the individual to take actions to restore equilibrium. Lewin's formulation simplifies the study of needs as sources of motivation by holding a universal explanation of how need satisfaction takes place.[14]

Lewin's concept of needs provides a way of thinking about human motivation and possible linkages between internal and external sources of motivation (the distinction drawn between genuine and quasi needs). Lewin's work and that done by Maslow have shaped our way of thinking about the role played by needs in social systems theory.

Goals. In Lewin's formulation, needs arise out of a sense of disequilibrium within the life space and serve to energize, organize, and focus behavior. While we do not share Lewin's conception of an equilibrium theory as a way of viewing the origins of human actions (preferring the more dynamic concept of steady state), his general thesis is important, particularly his attention to the role played by goals. In this formulation, goals are viewed as the correspondents of needs—genuine or quasi. Similarly, the achievement of a goal is essentially equivalent to need satisfaction. While Lewin used the term *goal* in a much broader sense than it is used in social systems theory, the underlying point is the same. In both instances, goals are end states that serve an organizing function for those seeking their accomplishment. From this position, it matters little whether the goal is as narrowly conceived as being on time for an appointment, or as broad as wanting to become a good social worker. The underlying dynamics are essentially equivalent. In both instances, the goals represent end states that serve to organize; that is, they provide an order to those behaviors needed to achieve the end state.

Tensions. With the foregoing features of field theory serving as background, we found Lewin's theory of psychological tensions helpful in developing the outcome orientation that characterizes social systems theory. These so-called tensions energize the person with respect to the pursuit of goals. In Lewin's formulation, these same processes can be assumed to operate in groups and in other forms of social organization as well as within the individual.

At this point, it would be useful to introduce the notion of psychological tensions through a story told of Lewin.[15] He was said to be constantly searching through everyday experiences for insights to better understand human behavior and to help in the construction of field theory. The story goes that Lewin and his students would frequently meet in a cafe and discuss their ideas over coffee and rolls. On one of these occasions, and after several hours of discussion, one of the group members had to leave and so asked for the check. Although the waiter had not kept a written record, he made his calculation quickly and presented the group with an exact bill. Lewin observed this and after about a half hour called the waiter over and asked him to produce the bill again. The annoyed waiter replied, "I don't know any longer what you people ordered, you paid your bill."[16] It was as though a state of tension had existed in the mind of this waiter that helped him keep track of his transactions with the group. Once he had completed his service, this tension state dissipated and was directed elsewhere, to another group of customers.

In the previous example, one can envision a whole series of related activities that comprised the waiter's relationship with this group; that is, consistent with his role as a waiter, he engaged in an ordered set of activities with these customers. These activities culminated in a final event, the rendering of a check and payment. Here the goal was the receipt of payment. Lewin was intrigued with what he had observed, and this experience eventually led to the famous studies of tension systems conducted by Zeigarnik.[17] Done under Lewin's supervision, these studies constituted a test of the proposition that an individual's intention to accomplish a specific task corresponds to the creation of a psychological state within the person, a **tension system,** and that the need to discharge this tension results in goal-directed activity until the task has been completed. According to Lewin's thesis, the adoption of a goal causes a person to create a system or an ordered set of behaviors to be engaged in until the goal is achieved. To the extent that the goal remains unfulfilled, it will maintain an influence over the person's thoughts and behaviors. Once fulfilled, the tension is released and the energy becomes available for other actions—the need has been satisfied. We find this general notion helpful and believe the concept of what Lewin called a tension system has appropriate applications to all forms of social organization.

Bluma Zeigarnik, one of Lewin's students, conducted her famous studies between 1924 and 1926. She was concerned with the effects on the person of unfinished tasks. Much like the question raised by the story of the waiter, at issue was whether a person under experimental conditions would be more likely to remember an unfinished or a finished task. Here the proposition was that person would more likely remember the unfinished task because the tension system created by its adoption would not have been released, and the need would remain unsatisfied. This proposition was supported under many different conditions and variations.[18] Other researchers have conducted similar or related studies that corroborated these findings.[19] The so-called **Zeigarnik effect,** the preferential recall of uncompleted tasks, has served as empirical support for Lewin's contention that a correlation exists between the release of the tension state and the satisfaction of a need. This finding has served as a cornerstone for research and theory building up to the present time. For example, the Freudian proposition that slips of the tongue and dreams are manifestations of unconscious tension states seeking discharge is viewed as pertaining to this same phenomenon. These findings, while focused on the individual and that person's life space, take on greater significance with Lewin's contention that the group and other forms of social organization could be studied as social entities utilizing the principles and concepts underlying field theory.[20]

Field theory has served a useful transition function in moving from contributions made to social systems theory derived from psychological theories to social psychological theories. First, field theory is an open-system formulation, one that views the individual in relationship to a social environment; indeed, Lewin extended this basic formulation to various forms of social organization, such as the family, an agency, or a community. The behavior of each is to be understood as a function of a field of forces.

Second, Lewin established a linkage between the concepts of needs (human motivation), goals (human purpose), and tension systems (energized patterns of activities directed toward goal achievement) that we have found helpful and have generalized as part of social systems theory. Specifically, this linkage helped us develop the functional orientation of the theory. Also, the linkage of tension systems to goals helped us conceive of the social system operating in natural cycles, with each cycle related to a goal state.

Third, Lewin undertook the task of subjecting his various concepts to empirical investigation. While our current interest is not in examining the research in support of social systems theory, the effort made by Lewin is noteworthy and awaits further attention.

EXCHANGE THEORY

Central to social systems theory is the notion that all forms of social organization are comprised of interacting and interdependent parts. In developing a theory of social systems relevant to practice with groups and families, it is insufficient simply to assume that the components are interactive and interdependent. The question is, why are they so? Perhaps an even more fundamental question is, how does social interaction get started? While there are no final answers to such questions, **exchange theory** offers an avenue of explanation that we have found useful. It is also one of the oldest theories of social behavior and perhaps the most straightforward. This latter characteristic makes it particularly appealing to students who are searching for the relevance of theory to practice.

Toennies can again be helpful in setting forth the conceptual foundations of exchange theory. In drawing the distinction between natural and rational will and the resulting Gemeinschaft and Gesellschaft forms of relationships, he observed:

However, when I become conscious of my most urgent needs and find that I can neither satisfy them of my own volition nor out of natural relation, this means that I must do something to satisfy my need; that is, engage in free activity which is bound only by the requirement or possibly conditioned by the need but not by consideration for other people. Soon I perceived that I must work on other people in order to influence them to deliver or give something to me which I need . . . However, as a rule when one is not receiving something in a Gemeinschaft-like relationship, such as from within the family, one must earn or buy it by labor, service or money. . . . I now enter or have already entered into a social relationship, but it is of a different kind. Its prototype is barter or exchange.[21]

As suggested by Toennies, exchange theory appears to have its clearest application in the explanation of social organizations in which Gesellschaft relationships dominate. Our position is, however, that every social organization possesses both Gemeinschaft and Gesellschaft features and that exchange theory has applications to all forms of social organization possessing system features.

Exchange theory has its conceptual foundations in the needs that humans have for one another, with exchange being the medium through which need satisfaction occurs. Because of the recurring nature of many human needs (e.g., survival, safety, and social needs), individuals have an incentive to stabilize and perpetuate those exchange arrangements that are deemed mutually satisfying, useful, or otherwise necessary. Simply put, this process of stabilizing and providing continuity to these relationships results in the formation of social systems. From this perspective, the basic notions of the universality of human needs and the process of social exchange offer an important avenue for the explanation of human behavior.

Social systems theory has a functional orientation. By this we mean that a social system can be understood by examining its effects on other social systems and vice versa. Recall that systems theory is premised on output and input exchanges between systems. That is to say, the task output of every system represents an input to other systems in its suprasystem. We believe that exchange theory offers a useful way of describing these output–input relationships, by treating them as a form of exchange. Similarly, by examining these exchange arrangements and their effects on each other we can better understand why social systems behave as they do and can construct a model that incorporates these behaviors.

In exchange theory, things possessing value are exchanged between the participating parties. These things can range from goods and services to sentiments and emotional supports. It does not follow that identical items are exchanged, only that the items are considered to have comparable value based on the perceptions held by those involved. The processes of exchange should not be thought of as a precise, conscious calculation of the value of this versus that. In some instances, this may be the case (e.g., the purchase of an object from a store), but what is being described is a much more general, imprecise, social process in which human emotional as well as logical considerations are involved in the assignment of worth.

The following example should help develop some of the basic notions behind exchange theory. On the first day of class, June Edwards and Margaret Rabovsky, along with about thirty other students, were in the process of introducing themselves. The professor had suggested that in their introductions, each take a moment to share with others why they are seeking a career in social work, what their current employment status is, if any, and what kind of professional position they will seek upon graduation. In introducing herself, Margaret indicated that she was from out of state and, while not currently employed, will need to find a part-

time job to help meet school expenses. She explained that in her hometown of Columbus, Ohio, she had served as a volunteer at a school for the mentally handicapped and hoped eventually to work professionally with physically and mentally handicapped children.

After class, June sought Margaret out and explained that she was currently working part time as a recreation aide at a children's convalescence center and that she understood there was an opening for another part-time aide. "It only pays minimum wage, but the staff is real nice and the kids are great. If you're interested, I can tell you who to call." "Am I!" was Margaret's response. She went on to say that she was recently divorced and while not getting assistance from her former husband, she was being helped by her parents. "I am temporarily living with them and they are helping with tuition and books until I can get back on my feet." Margaret thanked June for the job lead and was anxious to know more about the work. It was getting close to noon and June said, "What are you doing for lunch? If you're not busy, we can talk about the job."

In the above example, we have a group of strangers meeting in their first social work class. Given their mutual interest in social work and the classes they are going to take together, it seems inevitable that friendships will evolve among many of them. At issue is how social interaction is started in the first instance—what is the starting mechanism? Obviously there are a myriad of ways, but according to exchange theory there is a foundation principle—the person initiating the interaction gives something of value to another. The general expectation then is that the recipient will respond with something of comparable value. In a sense, the recipient returns something of comparable value to stay out of debt. Exchange theorists are not suggesting that the people engaging in social interaction are necessarily conscious about the notion of exchange in these terms. What they are saying is that an examination of human interaction suggests that social exchange is a basic dynamic. In our example, June offers Margaret information about a possible job, a very helpful and courteous act. Margaret gratefully acknowledges the important information by thanking June. Margaret's acknowledgment made June feel good about herself and glad that she had taken the time to share the job information.

From the standpoint of exchange theory, June, in supplying the information to Margaret, would hold an expectation that it would be gratefully or at least courteously received. In short, there was the expectation that Margaret would respond, and the response would have value to June. In this instance, the grateful response by Margaret fulfilled June's expectation and confirmed her own sense of being a helpful and caring person. Margaret increased the value of her response to June by sharing information about her recent divorce and the role her parents are playing in helping Margaret to reorient her life. Margaret did not have to add anything about her personal life in her response to a stranger. By doing so, she further confirmed the value of June's information and in effect invited another response. June found Margaret's response confirming to her own sense of selfhood but also started to form a "first impression" of Margaret; it was a positive impression of someone she might want to get to know better. She may have thought to herself, Margaret seems to be an awfully nice person; it would be helpful if she could get a job out at the center. I bet the kids would love her.

The two did have lunch together. In the course of their conversation June shared more about the job with Margaret. In the exchange, each began sharing a bit more about themselves. The next day they sat next to each other in class and Margaret said that she had called the center for a job interview. What we have in the interactions between June and Margaret is the possible start of a personal friendship, a two-person

group. If one does form, we would refer to it as a natural group. Its origins are found in the social needs all people have for one another. Such a group would conform to our definition: An exclusive, self-organizing form of social organization comprised of two or more members who identify and interact with one another on a personal basis as individuals, possess a shared sense of the group as a social entity, are affected by the group-related actions of members, and in which expressive (natural) actions dominate.

Conversations such as the ones between June and Margaret are commonplace and occur throughout our lifetimes. Sometimes they are represented by a single exchange, some are continued on a casual basis, and a few result in the formation of a group. We are interested in exchange theory because it offers an explanation of how social organizations form, one having a very wide application, and, perhaps equally important, it also offers an explanation of why they don't form. For example, in the above exchange, consider what might have happened if Margaret's response had not met June's expectation, if it was not gratefully received—"A recreation aide, I'm not that hard up yet, but thanks!" Such a response would depreciate not only the value of June's information but also June herself, as she works as a recreation aide. We can surmise, based on this latter exchange, that the two would not have had lunch together. We might also guess that June would not be particularly interested in sitting next to Margaret in class.

The position being developed here is that social exchange can be viewed as representing a universal principle undergirding social life. It thus offers a framework for examining human social behavior at all levels. Here we need to be careful; we are not suggesting that the notion of exchange can explain all social behavior—far from it. What we are saying is that the notion of social exchange can be a useful and beginning building block for the study of social behavior. How does interaction lead to the kind of social relationships that comprise social groups? Exchange theory offers a way to help answer that question.

Before moving on, one additional point needs to be made. While our interest is in identifying the patterns common to the various forms of social organization, we are all individuals and as such we are all different from one another in special ways. The science of psychology helps us understand these individual differences. June and Margaret are distinct human personalities. June sought Margaret out to talk with her. She did not have to do this; it was a voluntary act on her part. Margaret responded in a positive and enthusiastic manner. Again, this was a voluntary response on Margaret's part. Here we are not concerned with a psychological understanding of June or Margaret. Our focus instead is in understanding the interaction or the social exchange between them. People make choices in what they do and what they don't do, whom they associate with, and whom they do not associate with. They choose among alternatives based on expected benefits related to their own needs, past experiences, and the range of options they believe are open to them. In short, people choose among alternative courses of action as they perceive them. The phrase *as they perceive them* is critical because it represents an appraisal of what is of value to them.

With our example of June and Margaret serving as a background, let us examine some of the ideas of those who have set forth the basic tenets of exchange theory. Perhaps more than any other social scientist, George C. Homans is associated with the development of and current interest in exchange theory.[22] His approach to formulating exchange theory borrows heavily from behaviorist principles. Unlike many of his colleagues in sociology, Homans's interest was in the small group as opposed to the large and more complex types of social organization. Homans felt that understanding the more elementary forms of social organization would help in understanding the more complex forms—large formal organizations and societies. In other words, he believed that investigations of the small group could be used to understand the behaviors of people and other social units in larger forms of social organization. Even more basic, Homans held that psychological generalizations are an important component of sociological explanations. Operating from this perspective, he frequently reminded his colleagues that no human form of social organization exists that is not comprised of individuals, and therefore, sociological analysis should always consider individuals and their fundamental patterns of behavior.[23] This position by Homans is similar to the one we hold that accounts for the basic organization of this book.

One of the criticisms of exchange theory is its vocabulary, for example, *costs*, *benefits*, *rewards*, and so on. Many find the approach troublesome because it sounds as though an economic model is being used as a major explanation for social behavior. Homans commented on this general reluctance by his colleagues to acknowledge the importance of exchange in the development of sociological theory:

> In our unguarded moments we sociologists find words like "reward" and "costs" slipping into what we say. Human nature will break in upon even our most elaborate theories. But we seldom let it have its way with us and follow up systematically with what these words imply. Of all our many "approaches" to social behavior the one that sees it as an economy is the most neglected, and yet it is the one we use every moment of our lives—except when we write sociology.[24]

Assumptions

In the construction of theory in the social sciences, we hold that there will always be a set of assumptions that comprise a perspective of that part of social life the theorist seeks to explain. Sometimes the theorist will make these assumptions explicit, sometimes not. The following are assumptions associated with Homans's view of exchange theory. They are derived from central propositions set forth by Homans.[25]

1. Human social behavior can be understood as an exchange among people of things possessing value. These "things" can be material or symbolic, for example, goods, services, or sentiments.
2. The provision of something of value from one person to another, when accepted by the other (the initiation of a relationship), creates an obligation to reciprocate. The provision of something of value in return completes the first cycle of the exchange transaction.
3. The exchange process, once initiated, tends toward a balance—the things exchanged possess similar value as perceived by those involved in the exchange. In short, the balance in terms of relative value becomes the central force in maintaining the equilibrium of the social interaction. Social organization is formed and maintained through such a process.
4. An exchange always involves both a cost and a reward to each person. Derived from this is the related assumption that the relationship will be continued as long as the perceived costs of the exchange over time do not exceed its rewards, or that a more advantageous alternative is not available.
5. Dynamically, each person in the exchange seeks to maximize his or her return (reward less costs will equal the return).

According to Homans, these general assumptions about exchange are the basis for the development of social structure in groups. Based on these assumptions, it becomes possible to derive more specific researchable proposi-

tions as to how people behave in social groups. For example, in assumption 3, we would assume that each group member will see that no one group member derives a disproportionate amount of profit (value-satisfaction) from the group. In other words, the group will tend toward a dynamic state of balance characterized by a sense of equity or fairness in the exchanges among group members.

Before proceeding, we want to comment on the criticism that exchange theory appears to be based on an economic conception of social behavior. The use of costs, rewards, and benefits are certainly key concepts in economic theory and perhaps more useful words can be found to describe the dynamics of social exchange. For us, it appears more likely that economic theory has its origins in the fundamental patterns undergirding exchange relationships among humans, for example, bartering. In short, the reverse seems more likely the case: economic theory has its origins in basic human patterns of exchange and represents an attempt to rationalize exchange relationships and their dynamics, which extend beyond individuals to ever larger social systems.

Reductionist and linear thinking traps also need to be avoided. Our interest in this chapter is in the social group and the search is for a line of theory development that will help us better understand how social groups form and grow. We believe that social exchange theory can be useful in this regard. We will also be using the notion of exchange as we examine the behaviors of larger and more complex forms of social systems, for example, the formal organization. Forms of exchange in such social systems are not merely the extension of the forms of exchange found in social groups; these larger forms of social organization possess emergent features that will affect the dynamics of exchange. We will discuss this at greater length later.

It is useful to conceive of exchange theory as encompassing a wide range and multiple forms of exchange—from simple to complex. Also it is important not to limit the notion of exchange to only one set of activities, but rather to view it as a core event or set of events frequently associated with a range of supporting or related activities.

Another more complex example can help develop this point. Susan and Bob are in marital counseling because of increasing interpersonal and sexual difficulties. Susan complains that she gets little pleasure out of their sexual relationship and since she has gone to work, there have been increased interpersonal difficulties between her and Bob. These difficulties seem to center on routine household duties. Bob indicates that their sexual relationship was quite good until recently, or at least as far as he was concerned. Now, he complains that Susan is always finding excuses, "She is too tired, has a headache—it's just one excuse after another." Bob also complains that many of their arguments start over simple things "like who does what around the house—and then it's downhill from there—we end up screaming at each other."

Bob and Susan married when she was a sophomore and he was a senior in college. Upon graduating, Bob found an excellent position as an accountant. Susan quit school to become a housewife. The first two years of marriage were fine, with Susan staying home, taking care of the house, and generally supporting her husband's career. She then became restless and generally bored, and finally decided to go back to school to complete her social work education. Following graduation, she took a professional position in a child protective agency. Just as she was feeling better as a person, troubles started to increase with Bob. While on the surface supportive of her return to school and the pursuit of a career, he became annoyed at the demands her job placed on their home and personal life. For example, Susan occasionally had to respond during evenings and weekends to emergencies that arose in her work. Also, Bob complained about the TV dinners and the fact that the house was always a mess. Susan, in turn, complained that Bob had promised to help more around the house after she returned to work, but in effect he still expected her to prepare meals and do most of the housework.

As their personal tensions developed, she found their sexual relationship less and less satisfying. She also felt that Bob was becoming more demanding sexually, and explained, "this has turned me off." From an exchange theory perspective, Susan and Bob's earlier relationship was typified by an exchange in which Susan's needs for economic and emotional security were provided by Bob. In exchange, she met his sexual and esteem needs through her supportive role as a wife and sexual partner. For a couple of years there was a balance in this exchange. But as Susan became more self-confident and economically self-sufficient through her educational and professional achievements, the balance shifted, and the economic and emotional security provided by Bob became less important (possessed less value). Also, Susan found less pleasure in attempting to satisfy Bob sexually, feeling that he was far less attentive to her sexual needs than she was to his. What was happening was that their personal and situational needs changed, and there was not a corresponding shift in the way they responded to each other's needs. Unless Susan and Bob are able to adjust to each other's needs and establish a new working balance in this exchange, their marriage is likely to end in divorce.

The example makes several points. First, exchange relationships can become quite complex, forming a core around which many related activities revolve. Second, exchange relationships are dynamic in the same sense as the social organizations of which they are a part; these relationships are constantly changing, constantly developing. Once focused, there is a strain toward balance in the exchanges but there are counterstrains toward imbalance. Finally, and as suggested by Homans, social exchange has both its costs and its rewards. In our example, Susan is beginning to sense that the costs of her relationship are exceeding the rewards. The same thing is happening to Bob. Their marriage is in danger, which has resulted in their mutual recognition of the need for help in the form of marital counseling. In the language of social systems theory, steady state is being threatened.

Concepts

While a large number of concepts are associated with exchange theory, Peter Blau introduced four that we consider particularly important: (1) transaction, (2) differentiation, (3) stabilization, and (4) organization.[26] Blau employed these concepts to describe processes that form generic stages in the development of social systems.

Unlike Homans, who concentrated his attention on the small group and simple levels of social organization, Blau focused on larger and more formally constituted social organizations.[27] While Gesellschaft types of relationships tend to dominate in such structures, we have found his writings helpful and applicable to the social group.

Transaction.   This concept was used by Blau to describe the initiating phase of a social relationship. This phase can be viewed as having its origins in the needs of the individual; through interactions with others, need fulfillment occurs. In the most fundamental sense, exchange is rooted in self-interest—a person initiates interaction by giving something to another with the expectation of getting something needed in return. In an absolute sense, it is not necessary to assume any cultural or normative supports for the **transaction** process. In other words, human interdependence is so fundamental to human survival that exchange becomes a medium for dealing with survival issues. We can view culture as developing in part out of this basic human interdependence

through the mechanism of exchange. A general cultural norm of reciprocity is supportive of exchange. We will be treating reciprocity as does Gouldner, that is, as a universal norm evident in one form or another in all cultures and throughout recorded history.[28] The norm of reciprocity is reflected in such biblical assertions as "Do unto others as you would have them do unto you." While we will be focusing on the positive features of exchange as an approach to explaining social organization, a negative side must be acknowledged, exemplified in the familiar saying, "An eye for an eye and a tooth for a tooth."

The premise supporting the transaction phase is that the initiating person hopes that the offer of something of value to another will be accepted and thereby create a sense of obligation on the other to return something of comparable value. Each person is satisfying the other through an exchange, and through this process a social structure is created that will serve as a guide for subsequent exchanges. It should be noted that if the receiving person does not respond, or offers something of less than the expected value, the relationship is likely not to get started in the first instance, or at least will be off to a shaky start. If the receiving person does respond and offers something of comparable value in return, then the expectations of the initiating person are fulfilled. Given the success of the first transaction, the conditions are established on which subsequent exchanges can occur. Here, we have the possible start of a social group, whether it be two, three, ten, or more people.

Something new is being created. Its unifying force is the relationship that binds those participants together in an interdependent way. Those participating in the exchanges are in effect producing something of use to the other. A subtlety is involved, and it is seen most clearly in social groups, those in which Gemeinschaft features dominate. The exchange transactions among members create a level of interdependence that takes on a separate character. Not only do the members involved in exchange transactions derive something of value through their relationships with one another, but they also obtain something of value from a new entity being formed—a group; a synergic effect occurs. It should be noted that during this initial transaction phase, the relationships among those participating in the exchange are very fragile. Our earlier example of June and Margaret was intended to illustrate the transaction phase of social exchange.

Olsen, in reviewing Blau's work, identified three principles associated with the transaction phase:

1. The greater the probability that a potential exchange transaction will prove rewarding (benefits equal or greater than costs) to an actor, the more likely one is to initiate it.
2. The greater an actor's obligations to reciprocate for benefits previously received from another, the more likely that actor is to complete an exchange transaction.
3. An exchange relationship will be perpetuated as long as it proves rewarding to the participants, they have no other more attractive alternatives, and their needs and goals remain unsatisfied.[29]

The reader can safely make the assumption that in real life, few exchanges get beyond the transaction phase on their way to a social group.

Differentiation.   The notion of power plays a central role in the way Blau conceptualized social exchange.[30] Given the premise that humans depend on one another for the satisfaction of a variety of different needs, exchange theory becomes a way of conceptualizing the dynamics of this interdependence. Blau made the point that the relative dependence people have on one another can be viewed in terms of the influence or power people have over one

another. In other words, "Your need of what I have (your dependence on me) represents my power over you." Similarly, "What you have that I need (my dependence on you) represents your power over me." Assuming that the individuals entering into an exchange do so voluntarily, the transaction phase of the exchange process is marked by a balance. Here *balance* refers to the perceptions held by those involved in the exchange that the exchange is fair; that is, what the person is receiving through the exchange (relationship) is at least equal to what he or she is giving. If this were not the case, the exchange would not have been entered into in the first place, or if an initial exchange proves disappointing from a balance perspective, it would not be continued.

Olsen is helpful in developing the notion of balance from a power perspective. From this position, social exchange can be treated as a balanced reciprocal influence characterized by (1) voluntariness—each individual chooses to participate or not to participate in the exchange; (2) stability—a stable pattern of exchange develops and persists over time; (3) equity—each participant perceives a sense of equality in relation to the other person(s) involved in the exchange; and (4) distributive justice—at any given time, the balance between what is given and received may not be equal, but over time it will even out.[31]

Given the changing needs of people and the differential access individuals have to resources, there is always a possibility that the exchange transaction will evolve from a balanced reciprocal influence to an unbalanced one. In keeping with the name given this process, the exchange transactions will tend to become differentiated relative to the power possessed by each member over others involved in the exchange. Blau made the point as follows:

> By supplying services in demand to others, a person establishes power over them. If he regularly renders needed services they cannot readily obtain elsewhere, others become dependent on and obligated to him for these services, and

unless they can furnish other benefits to him that produce interdependence by making him equally dependent on them, their unilateral dependence obligates them to comply with his request lest he ceases to continue to meet their needs.[32]

When an exchange becomes unbalanced, or loses one or more of the previously defined characteristics of balance, one of several things may occur. Given other alternative sources of need satisfaction, the most likely outcome is that the exchange is terminated—"We just couldn't make it work." Perhaps of greater theoretical interest are those relationships that continue in some unbalanced form.

The notion of balance (or what we choose to call steady state) suggests stability. Becoming unbalanced indicates instability. Thus, inquiry, based on a social power perspective, into unbalanced forms of exchange becomes a way of investigating destabilizing forces in social groups. For example, when one member of a group becomes more powerful than the other(s), for whatever reason, and the one(s) with lesser power remain(s) dependent on the more powerful one, the conditions exist for a coercive or exploitive relationship to develop. If this should occur, conflict is likely to result. An example is a woman who is physically abused by her husband. From an exchange perspective, the relationship may initially have been in balance, with both enjoying the friendship, love, sexual behavior, and so on, of the other. But let us say that the husband, through his work, has had opportunities for other friendships and liaisons with other women. Because of this, these resources from his wife lose some of their value to him. She, in turn, by being confined to the house and not working, becomes more dependent on him but possesses diminished resources for exchange. Simply put, the exchanges become unbalanced. Tensions increase between the two, finally resulting in the husband physically assaulting his wife. The wife, who is without a job and without other family, is essentially without options. To call the police or to seek

help is, from an exchange perspective, to place herself in even greater jeopardy, that is, to risk the loss of economic security and whatever is left of the personal relationship with her husband. As we know from our own practices and from newspaper accounts, the woman's situation becomes desperate, sometimes resulting in desperate actions.

Once an exchange transaction becomes unbalanced, Olsen suggested there will be a tendency on the part of the more powerful individual to maintain and otherwise to take advantage of the weaker one(s). The point here is that by capitalizing on the advantage, the more powerful individual secures his or her advantage and avoids the added costs of a balanced exchange. In this connection, Olsen stated the principle involved as follows:

> To the extent that a relationship becomes unbalanced as a result of power differentiation and cannot be rebalanced in some manner, it will be transformed from reciprocal influence exchange to coercive control exertion.[33]

Before leaving the **differentiation** process as set forth by Blau and Olsen, we want to remind the reader of our preference for treating power as only one dimension of differentiation. Also, that differentiation can be usefully treated as a phase in group development, one that will characterize development of all social groups as they move toward stabilization. Our position is that as the patterns of exchange become ongoing, role differentiation is an inevitable feature of the exchange process. Each person brings something to the group that is exchanged with that brought by others. A series of expectations develop among those comprising the exchange. These sets of mutual expectations become the normative features of the roles comprising the exchange relationship. In a balanced reciprocal exchange, the values of these role features are essentially equivalent. Each person in the group is different in the sense that she or he brings something valued by other group members. In exchange terms, she or he gives something of her- or himself to another and in return receives something of comparable, or perhaps of greater, value.

Stabilization. The third process in exchange theory is aptly named and refers to those developments that seek to firm up the exchange transaction and to limit the destabilizing forces —power inequities, for example, that come into play. Given previously stated properties and principles underlying exchange, the assumption is that all exchange relationships surviving the first two stages of development will move toward stabilization. Olsen summarized three principal ways by which **stabilization** occurs: development of (1) mutual trust, (2) shared norms, and (3) leadership.[34]

Given the dominance of self-interest in the first or transaction phase, and the potential for power differentiation in the second phase, it stands to reason that the stabilization phase of an exchange relationship would be associated with the development of mutual trust. At this point, it is useful to draw a distinction between mutual trust as it might be developed in Gesellschaft as opposed to Gemeinschaft groups. In Gesellschaft relationships, the exchange represents a means for achieving some end. In other words, the exchange is dominated by logic in the sense that there is a calculation of the means and ends and a decision is made. An almost infinite number of such relationships is possible. They can involve a single transaction and thus be very short term (e.g., buying an item at a garage sale), or they can involve multiple exchanges and last a lifetime (e.g., services received from the family physician).

Here an observation is in order about the transaction phase—the greater the value of that being exchanged, the greater the likelihood of some formal specification of the details of the exchange. For example, in a garage sale, money is likely to be exchanged for the item. There are no guarantees and no objective standard exists for measuring the value of the object, such as

an old glass. Here individuals only enter into the exchange if they each agree on the value of the item. On the other hand, if an apartment is being leased (exchanged for money), there is a likelihood of a much more elaborate and formalized set of conditions surrounding the exchange; in most instances, there will be papers signed by the two parties that set forth in detail the rights and duties of each. In short, in Gesellschaft relationships in which items of significant value are involved, the matter of mutual trust tends to be dealt with by an explication of the conditions and terms of the exchange agreement. This agreement is then evidenced by a signed contract. If a disagreement should later arise, the signed contract becomes the basis for resolution or of a subsequent legal action. The growing use of prenuptial agreements is another example in which Gesellschaft as well as Gemeinschaft features exist in the exchange relationship at the level of the social group.

In Gemeinschaft relationships, the exchange serves as an end in itself as opposed to being a means to an end. This distinction is important in understanding the dynamics involved, particularly as they pertain to the stabilization phase. Given this distinction, the notion of a formal contract specifying the conditions and terms of the exchange is antithetical to a Gemeinschaft relationship. In other words, exchanges involving relationships possessing significant Gemeinschaft features are likely to be much more open, vague, and perhaps risky. For example, in a developing friendship group, what is being exchanged is some part of the self. As a consequence, the early transaction phase is likely to be characterized by low-risk forms of exchange. If in the differentiation phase the exchange is becoming unbalanced and is taking on coercive features, one can cut one's losses and get out.

It would seem to follow that in an exchange in which Gemeinschaft relationships dominate, there would be a tendency for such exchanges to start at a low-risk level. It would also follow that such exchanges (e.g., the satisfaction of social belonging needs) would tend to be recurring in nature. Therefore, mutual trust would tend to develop over time through the process of mutuality in need fulfillment. This process would tend to be associated over time with ever greater risks being taken by the parties involved in the exchange.

A practice example would be a counseling relationship with a client unable to pay a fee, or at least a full fee. From an exchange perspective, the client would be expected to be very cautious in the transactional phase. Mutual testing-out would take place, with the client being especially wary because of having so little to offer in the exchange. Given the inability to pay a fee, the client also runs the risk of becoming involved in a coercive type of relationship, especially if the client is a nonvoluntary one, for example, a client sent to the agency by the court because of child abuse. Given this situation, one should expect a good bit of testing out, with mutual trust developing slowly.

At a more general level, Blau commented on the development of mutual trust as a feature of the stabilization process.

> By discharging their obligations for services rendered, if only to provide inducements for the supply of more assistance, individuals demonstrate their trustworthiness, and the gradual expansion of mutual service is accompanied by a parallel growth of mutual trust. Hence processes of social exchange, which may originate in pure self-interest, generate trust in social relations through their current and gradual expanding character.[35]

Olsen identified three norms central in the stabilization process: (1) reciprocity, (2) fairness, and (3) distributive justice.[36] A number of sociologists have identified the notion of reciprocity as central to all forms of social systems; for example, Simmel noted "the reciprocity of service and return service" and that "all contacts among men rest on the schema of giving and returning equivalence."[37] Some authors would consider fairness and distributive justice features of a general norm of reciprocity.[38] But for our current purposes, it is useful to consider fairness and distributive justice as norms in their own right. Reciprocity means a mutual exchange. The key notion is *mutual*, and by this the exchange is bound and judged by whether what was given and what was received have comparable value. It is a norm in the sense that the meaning of reciprocity has been internalized, and thus one is morally obliged to return to the giver something of equivalent value.

The notion of fairness in exchange, while similar to reciprocity, is not so much grounded in the idea of mutuality as it is to some objective measure of equity. In this sense, the exchange would be in keeping with some established measure of equivalence and would be seen as such by an impartial third party.

The point is that once an exchange is enacted and deemed beneficial, conflicting forces come into play. On the one hand, through the differentiation process, the possibility exists for one or more of the participants to seek an advantage and gain control in the relationship. While holding certain advantages for the more powerful person, the disadvantage is the instability that the imbalance introduces. Stabilizing forces come into play through mutually satisfying exchanges and the development of mutual trust. And, as we just pointed out, the sharing of such norms as reciprocity and fairness facilitates the stabilization process in exchange. The norm of distributive justice mentioned earlier refers to a shared belief held by those participating in the exchange that, while the exchanges that take place day by day may not be equivalent, they will balance out in the long term.

An example here would be the husband who works and supports his wife while she pursues her graduate education in social work. The bargain they have is that once she gets her degree and obtains a professional position, she will support him as he goes back for his master's degree in elementary education. Here the exchange is unbalanced to one side for a period of time and then unbalanced to the other side for another period. But in the longer term, the couple mutually benefits—there has been distributive justice.

Exchange theorists assume that the stabilization phase in the development of social relationships is accompanied by the evolution of leadership roles. In the discussion of the differentiation phase, the tendency for an exchange relationship to become unbalanced was noted. This unbalancing was viewed as a result of the greater power one person has over the other(s) in the exchange relationship. Countering this unbalancing threat is the tendency by members involved in the exchange to assume leadership and follower roles. By this we mean that an influence structure will emerge in which certain people will be recognized for the usefulness of their ideas or behaviors in facilitating the exchange process and its outcomes. In the social group, this is an informal process. As we will see later, in the formal organization, the influence structure will have both formal and informal features. At this point, it is important to recognize that leadership, whether formally or informally established, is a social process, and as such, its effects are only evident in the behavior of the people involved. In other words, leadership only works if the lead is followed, if others are influenced and behave in the expected manner. Here the notion of legitimacy is important and simply means that the leadership actions being exercised are followed. That is to say, by following the leader's suggestions, members legitimate or confirm the role of the leader. In relationship to the exchange process, the leadership function focuses on securing the kind of conditions that stabilize exchange transactions, such as guarding against the development of power inequities. Olsen stated the principle as follows:

> Exchange relationships become stabilized through time to the extent that they develop mutual trust, shared norms and legitimate leadership.[39]

Organization. The final concept to be discussed Blau labeled *organization*. While our primary interest in exchange theory is in the explanation offered as to how groups form, Blau intended his theory to have explanatory value for the total process of social organization.[40] In this sense, exchange theory could be viewed as a general theory. Organization, in Blau's view, becomes an outcome of exchange interactions and thus the fourth and final stage of the process. In social systems theory, the counterpart of this phase is when a social system initially achieves steady state. At this point, the functional interdependence of the parts has been established and there is evidence of recurring and stabilized patterns of interaction; that is, an ordering process is evident. The concept of organization is less well developed by Blau than the other three and as a consequence has less utility for our immediate purposes.

In this section, we have summarized the key assumptions, concepts, and principles of exchange theory. In so doing, we have sought to identify a line of theory development having application to social groups and other levels of social systems as well. For us, the exchange paradigm is useful in thinking about how relationships form and how social organizations develop. The paradigm also has utility in viewing suprasystem/social system relationships. Social systems theory builds from a functional conception of social organization; through forms of input–output exchange, systems relate to other systems that comprise their suprasystems. Exchange theory offers an avenue for exploring and developing this notion of exchange both internally and between the system and its suprasystem.

SYMBOLIC INTERACTION THEORY

In summarizing exchange theory, we were interested in offering an explanation as to how groups form and develop. Now we turn to a line of theory that helps us understand the dynamics of communication.

As with the other theories reviewed, there is no such thing as *a* theory of **symbolic**

interaction; it is more useful to think of a general line of theory development referred to as symbolic interaction. A number of theorists have made contributions to this line of reasoning. The two best known and most important are Charles Horton Cooley and George Herbert Mead. We also want to note at this point that several major social work theorists made important contributions to the development of the theory of symbolic interaction. Best known among these contributors was Jane Addams.[41]

Earlier we cited the distinctions between primary and secondary groups. Recall that Cooley contended that through the medium of primary groups, particularly the family, the individual acquired her or his distinctive human characteristics.[42] Also, through such groups, these human qualities are supported and developed throughout the life cycle. Cooley's efforts at explaining this position laid the intellectual foundations for the theory of symbolic interaction. While Cooley's contributions are of great importance, the acknowledged founder of the theory was George Herbert Mead.[43] Mead did not term his theory symbolic interaction, but rather *social behaviorism*. His choice of words is instructive. Mead found behaviorist theory of great help as he sought to understand and account for the social behavior of humans. His concern, though, was with its narrowness, its strict attention to directly observable behavior. Mead held that the individual possessed an inner life and an emotional or affective dimension to existence that was not adequately addressed by behaviorism. In many ways, a strict behavioral orientation is like paying attention only to that part of an iceberg showing above the water, the part that is directly observable. Symbolic interaction theory, while incorporating much of the social learning features of behaviorism, also addresses the inner life of the individual, what we might term the antecedents of behavior. Using the analogy of the iceberg, we must attend to what lies both above and below the surface.

The most comprehensive presentation of Mead's work is to be found in *Mind, Self, and Society*.[44] The book was published in 1934, three years after his death. It is based on class notes assembled by his students at the University of Chicago.

Assumptions

The assumptions that form the foundations to the theory of symbolic interaction extend those that comprise our social systems perspective.[45]

1. The distinctiveness of humans derives primarily from their capacity to observe, think, communicate or share their thoughts with others, and to act in accord with their thinking. This assumption holds that only humans possess this capacity of linking, observing, thinking, feeling, communicating, and doing. This assumption helps establish the foundation for our conception of generalist practice.

2. Selfhood, the ability of the person to conceive of her- or himself as an object, is socially acquired, supported, and developed throughout life. While the capacity to develop a sense of selfhood is genetically based, the self has no antecedent existence within the organism.

3. The capacity to think and to communicate is based on the ability to learn, retain, and purposively use an enormous amount of information. This information is in the form of conventional meanings attached to **symbols.** The notion of symbols is nothing more than a name (e.g., a dictionary meaning given to something real or imagined). The systematic structuring of these symbols by people sharing the same general culture is what we refer to as language, for example, the English language.

4. The relationship of observing, thinking, feeling, and acting is dynamic and cyclical. Human social behavior is a social process in which the individual (self) initiates an action and by both the consciousness (awareness) of self and of others, controls and modifies that action through to completion. That is to say, the social act is modified or adjusted as it is being carried out by the person. This is accomplished by the person (self) constantly interpreting the reactions and behaviors of those actually comprising or otherwise exerting an effect on the social interaction. A specification of this process within the framework of social work knowledge, skills, and values, we call the generalist practice of social work.

5. The proactive foundation (motivational source) for human social behavior comes from the capacity to think symbolically, to imagine future states, and to take action in pursuit of such imagined states. It is therefore assumed that the human has the capacity to form in her or his mind future states of existence, and to share these states with others for purposes of mobilizing mutual or social action required to pursue such states. In ordinary terms, we refer to this as thinking.

6. Just as the individual possesses the capacity to contemplate future states, so do the various social organizations that humans join to form. This capacity accounts for the proactive nature of all forms of social organizations—the family, the formal organization, the community, and society.

Symbolic interaction theory makes use of a series of concepts, many with familiar names but very specialized meanings. Resting on the assumptions just noted, these concepts and their interrelationships form the building blocks of the theory. In the paragraphs ahead we will summarize the more important of these concepts.

Symbol. A symbol is something, typically a word, that represents something else. A word such as *tree* serves as a name of something that has existence in our environment. There is common agreement in our society, and among those who use the English language, on the meaning

of *tree*. As a consequence, we can communicate with one another about trees. The word *tall* is also a symbol but is of a somewhat different order. It does not describe a specific entity but rather a characteristic of some entity. For example, one would not say, There is a tall. Rather the symbol *tall* helps to describe something, a tall tree, a tall woman, a tall building, and so forth. We have evolved, and continue to evolve, an extensive set of symbols in order to communicate with each other. Importantly, symbols are meanings assigned not only to sounds (words), but also to marks, gestures, facial expressions, and body movements (language).

The fact of the matter is that we humans have assigned symbols to every aspect of our physical, social, psychological, and spiritual environments. By so doing, we can communicate with one another about everything imaginable. According to symbolic interactionists, humans construct a representation of reality through their language. From this position, humans relate to one another primarily in terms of these commonly shared meanings. In the most fundamental sense, social interaction becomes symbolic interaction.

More so than most other theorists dealing with human behavior, the symbolic interactionist ties language, and more generally symbolic exchanges, to behavior. Given this tie and the importance of language, one starts to get a different perspective on those who are handicapped in their capacity to learn and to communicate. We are not referring only to those who may be mentally and physically impaired, but also to all those who have limited learning (educational) opportunities or experiences.

Socialization. The concept of **socialization** means to become social and by extension to become like other people who share the same culture. Simply put, to become socialized is to become human. More technically, socialization refers to the social process through which individuals learn and internalize the values, beliefs, attitudes, knowledge, skills, and behaviors of their society. One learns to use symbols personally and socially in and through the socialization process.

Most people think of socialization in terms of the very young. Perhaps the trials and tribulations of parents attempting to toilet train their spirited two-year-old gets across the general idea. People in our society use a toilet to dispose of their body wastes. It is a learned behavior and most parents take the task of toilet training their young quite seriously. The example of toilet training is instructive in understanding the state of tension that inevitably exists between an individual's natural strivings and the relentless and powerful forces of socialization. Examples are the protests and tantrums of a child not wanting to go to bed, or the later pressures felt by many young women and men from their families to "settle down" and get married.

In symbolic interaction theory, the process of socialization is lifelong. The key notion is that the symbols of one's culture are learned, internalized, and become the basis for who we become and what we do as social beings. For example, whether born into an American, African, or Asian family, the infant arrives with essentially the same genetic capacities. While we may all be very much alike and in this sense equal at birth, we are subjected to quite different social experiences throughout the remainder of our lives. These experiences shape us in very real ways and from the symbolic interactionist point of view, we become a product (an output) of these experiences. In other words, the same infant raised in three different families, in three different cultures (social environments) would have become three quite different persons. Similarly, gender and its meanings will be different in each culture and to some extent within each family. A female raised in three different families and in three different cultures would have become three quite different women. Just as one learns to become a physician or a social worker,

so does one learn how to be white versus black, a woman versus a man, American versus Japanese, and so on. We do not wish to downplay the biological and physiological differences among people. We only wish to say that through the process of socialization, we attribute different meanings to these differences. These meanings are also constantly changing; the meaning of being a woman today is far different for most people than it was twenty or fifty years ago. For example, the sense of selfhood of the women reading this book today is likely to be quite different from that held by their own mothers or grandmothers. Similarly, their daughters and granddaughters will view themselves in their gender roles quite differently.

The point we wish to make is that one's genetic heritage is not a central issue in symbolic interaction theory. Rather there is an acknowledgment that one's genetic heritage sets some broad and important parameters for development. What is central is the social environment in which we are raised. This social environment is given meaning as a symbolic environment and in turn defines who we are and shapes our perceptions of reality throughout life. Just as this social environment is constantly changing, so will our socialization be continuous and change our conception of who we are throughout life. For example, your conception of yourself as a woman or man at twenty-five is likely to be quite different from what it will be at thirty-five, at fifty, and at seventy-five. In part, this is because in our culture we view people differently at different stages in life. These cultural differences affect the views we hold of ourselves at different stages in our development.

Socialization is a form of social learning. It is social in the sense of it being a part of an interactional process. The process is also cyclical and its effects mutual. The process starts at birth; the relationship that is initiated is frequently referred to as bonding. In the traditional family, the parents have acquired, in their own socialization process, notions of their respective parental roles. They enact these roles with respect to the newly born infant. They hold, caress, feed, talk, soothe, and otherwise respond to the multiple needs of their infant. They also respond to the child's cries, smiles, noises, and movements as a "parent." In so doing, they are learning and developing the parenting role with respect to their infant. To put this another way, both the parents and their child are being socialized into their respective roles. This is what we mean by being mutual and cyclical. The mother responds, the child responds, the child's response shapes the mother's next response, and so on. Each acts on the other; each is affected by the other.

Symbolic interactionists hold that socialization is essentially a cognitive process.[46] This being the case, early socialization depends on the acquisition of language. To become socialized in the sense we are defining the concept, the infant must develop a capacity for self-reference. By this we mean the infant must distinguish between herself or himself and all other matter. This process is active during the first couple of years of life. Mead suggested that this takes place through a two-stage process. First is the play stage. Here the child plays at being another, for example, mother, father; the play is initially focused on significant (and interesting) people in the child's social environment. Second is the game stage, the beginning of group activity and group ordering.

In the play stage, socialization is occurring in the sense of learning roles, those that are critical in the life situation of the very young child. These roles are learned by taking on and playing the role, for example, of mother. In so doing, the child will typically then enact two roles, her mother's and her own. In this play stage, the young child is in the process of differentiating between herself and others; she is developing a sense of selfhood by playing at roles. To put this another way, she is evolving a

sense of self by practicing her own role in reference to counter roles, those of mother, father, sister, and so forth. The key process is one of imitation.

The second stage in this socialization process is much more complicated. In the first stage, the child plays both parts; saying something in one character and responding in the other. It is essentially a private form of play. The second stage is social in that it involves others. Mead put it this way: "If we contrast play with the situation in an organized game, we note the essential difference that the child who plays in a game must be ready to take the attitude of everyone else involved in that game, and that these different roles must have a definite relationship to each other."[47] It is in the structural relationships among game players that the child must have a sense of herself and all the other players. Cognitively, the structural ordering is much more complex in game play than in individual play. The child must evolve a more differentiated sense of self to participate in a game than is needed at the play stage. Clearly it is within the family (or its substitute) and small play groups that the child learns of herself or himself and others. It is here that the sense of social ordering and one's relationships in that order has it origins. It is also in this capacity for sensing order that one evolves an ever more complex and differentiated sense of selfhood.

Self.   As evident in our discussion, socialization and self are closely related concepts.[48] In the theory of symbolic interaction, the **self** is created and developed throughout life via the socialization process. Socialization, in turn, takes place through social interaction. Let us pause a moment here and summarize the relationships among self, socialization, and social interaction. We have defined socialization as the social process through which individuals learn about and internalize the values, beliefs, attitudes, knowledge, and behaviors of their society.

A social relationship is a cognitive and affective connection between two or more people in which each takes the other(s) into account in his or her thoughts and in relevant aspects of behavior. The extent and level of this connection is associated with the specific roles being enacted in the relationships, for example, mother–daughter or social worker–client.

Now in our definition of socialization we used the term *internalize;* we internalize values, beliefs, attitudes, and so on. To internalize means to adopt, to take on, or in symbolic interaction theory, to incorporate into one's self. The first step in the socialization process becomes developing a self; it is this self that is socialized throughout life. Recall that in symbolic interaction theory, an assumption is made that at birth we do not have a residual self that is a part of our genetic heritage that then grows and develops like other parts of our body. What we do have is a brain that permits us to sense, to learn, to think, to feel, and to take others into consideration in a state of self-consciousness and then to act in accord with this state. This capacity of being able to evolve a state of consciousness of one-self and others the symbolic interactionists label *self.*

We have described the self as a process originating very early within the larger socialization process. Symbolic interactionists also use the concept of self as an outcome. The distinction is important in terms of the use we make of it in social systems theory, particularly as applied to the social group. At one level, we can think of examining the socialization process at any point in time. The self can be thought of as the sense of selfhood that exists at that point. An analogy would be a movie that we interrupt to examine a frame. In this sense, the self is an outcome, effect, or product of the process up to that time. Social groups, particularly the family, are vital in the socialization process, particularly in a child's early development. Just as we might stop a movie and examine an individual frame,

so we can examine a family at any point in time in terms of its effects on the development of self in any or all of its members. To help develop this point, we will return to Cooley. In discussing the role of the primary (social) group in developing a sense of selfhood, he noted:

> By primary groups, I mean those characterized by intimate face-to-face associations and cooperation. They are primary in several senses, but chiefly in that they are fundamental in forming the social nature and ideals of the individual.[49]

In a way, we are modeling this process described by Cooley when we apply the systems model to a social group. At any point, a task output of the group will be the sense of selfhood possessed by its individual members that can be attributed to the interactions within the group. We will be developing this idea throughout Part Three of this book.

Now let's return to our description of the concept of self. To start, we will build on the insights provided by Cooley. An approach for thinking about the social origins of self is found in his well-known looking glass self referred to earlier.[50]

> As we see our face, figure and dress in the glass, and are interested in them because they are ours, and pleased or otherwise with them according as they do or do not answer to what we should like them to be; so in imagination we perceive in another's mind some thought of our appearance, manners, aims, deeds, character, friends, and so on, and are variously affected by it.
>
> A self-idea of this sort seems to have three principal elements: the imagination of our appearance to the other person; the imagination of his judgment of that appearance, and some sort of self-feeling, such as pride or mortification. The comparison with a looking glass hardly suggests the second element, the imagined judgment, which is quite essential.
>
> The thing that moves us to pride or shame is not the mere mechanical reflection of ourselves,

but an imputed sentiment, the imagined effect of this reflection upon another's mind. This is evident from the fact that the character and weight of that other, in whose mind we see ourselves, makes all the difference with our feeling.[51]

We are all familiar with the extent to which we are influenced by the feelings of others, especially those very close to us. Cooley, however, is suggesting something much more basic, a way of thinking about how our sense of selfhood arises in the first place. For the moment, let us explore a bit more the basic notion of a looking glass self. Simply put, the sense of self is derived as follows: I am what I think you think I am. From this perspective, the self is acquired externally as opposed to arising internally. It is acquired from others who have formed a conception of the individual as a person. Obviously, this is not a direct transfer but a perception of a perception, or in the words used earlier: I am what I think you think I am. Several features of this position are critical in the socialization process: (1) the sense of self is socially acquired, it is a learning outcome; (2) selfhood is acquired from multiple sources, not one, and these multiple sources have different valences (power) in the formulation process; (3) just as there is no single source from which the notion of selfhood evolves, the same sources can convey different and conflicting meanings to the person at different times (for example, Do as I say, not as I do); and (4) the notion of selfhood is based on a social process and that process is active throughout one's life. In other words, the conception of self is dynamic, always in a state of becoming. Given this dynamic character, the process must be supported throughout life or a loss of a sense of selfhood occurs.

The notion of the looking glass self should be thought of only as a starting place for exploring how our sense of selfhood is developed and sustained. Most of us feel that we have much more of an integrated and stable sense of

ourselves than is suggested by Cooley's analogy. On the other hand, think of the times we have said to ourselves or heard others say, I feel myself pulled in a hundred directions, I've got to get myself together, or I've got to find myself.

A number of scholars have built on Cooley's work, but none have made more of a contribution than George Herbert Mead. In thinking of self, his ideas of the "I and the me" are very useful.[52] It is important to keep in mind that Mead is not suggesting that "I" and "me" are structures within the brain, nor that the self is a physical entity located somewhere within the body. The self is a state of consciousness in which the individual is able to conceive of herself or himself as a separate and distinct person. The symbolic interactionists refer to this state of consciousness as the capacity to view oneself as a social object.

Mead's use of the I and me is simply an analytic device by which one is able to think about the self as both a process and an effect of the process. Simply stated, the I and the me comprise the self. An example of the basic notion involved would be, I wonder what he thinks of me. In this sentence, the I and me comprise the two components of self. Here the I designates the subject phase of the process, the me, the object phase. The I is that sense of self as perceived by the individual, it is always in memory and represents an historical sense of self. This perception of the I held by the other, from the view of the I, constitutes the me in the phrase—I wonder what he thinks of me. In this sense, the me results from taking the role of the other and evaluating the action of the I within the framework of the relationship. The process in which the self evolves is not linear, it is cyclical and mutually deterministic. This sounds more complicated than it is. The point is that selfhood is a process. At any stage in this process, the person has a sense of self. This sense of self is designated as the I. The person in any social relationship has both a sense of self (the I component) and a particular sense of how another person may view her or him. This sense of another's view is accomplished by taking on the role of this other person. The actual interactions that take place between the two people involved in the relationship will be affected by these prior perceptions.

At the completion of what we will designate a social act (the completion of a cycle of activities within a social relationship), there will be an evaluation of what occurred. This is the feedback loop. Included in this evaluation will be a personal evaluation of the role you played as viewed by the person in the other role; this is the me part of the self. This impression is then merged into the self as a me within a specific role. This impression similarly affects the I part of the self if the relationship is a significant one. Finally, this merged sense of the I and me will form a foundation for the next encounter in this social relationship (an updated sense of self). In some relationships, this process is a very conscious one, in others it is not. In other words, you leave an impression with the other person and that person leaves one with you. Your perception of the other person's impressions of you is termed the me in that role. That impression of yourself will in turn affect your own more general impression of your self.

Each of us is involved in many relationships of varied consequence. What we have done is to isolate an example of an interaction in which the individual thought, I wonder what he thinks of me. This was done to illustrate the self as a process. Our sense of selfhood is affected in an ongoing way by a great number of social relationships with each having somewhat of a different effect.

While the I and me are useful in examining the process of self-development, we all intuitively know that we are more than the sum of our social relationships. We do not bend and change with each new relationship. The self has, in most people, great stability. Mead's use of the

notion of the generalized other is helpful in thinking about this stability.

> The organized community or social group which gives to the individual his unity of self may be called "the generalized other."[53]

Early in life, this so-called generalized other is a composite sense of who we are as derived from the key people in our social environments—parents, other family members, and others with whom we have significant relationships. Through these people, we learn about life and about ourselves. In the popular parlance, these people have served as role models.

Freud's use of the term *superego* is somewhat akin to Mead's use of the term *generalized other*, that part of the self that serves as a conscience and sets ethical standards for behavior. Early in life, we learn from others general patterns of what is right and what is wrong from society's view. A value system and moral code cut across various roles that we play within our particular culture. This value system and morality is internalized and becomes part of our sense of self. So, just as we may be affected in our behavior by specific others in our social environments, so will we be constrained by a generalized other. For the moment think of the I part of our self being constrained and influenced by both generalized and specific others, with the generalized others being something like our conscience. Again, caution is indicated: while stable for most people, conceptions of what is right and wrong also change. The caution is that each of us will be guided by a generalized other. There is no single generalized other and for each of us this other also changes and develops throughout life.

Now let us pause in our development of the concepts and through use of an example integrate the concepts of symbol, socialization, and self. We have indicated that the development of a sense of self or selfhood is a part of the socialization process that we all have experienced. This process, at least in the early years, is most typically carried out through a social group, the family. Just as a child learns the names of all kinds of things, so does she learn her own name.

For our example, let us call her Ann. All members of the family will use the same designation when communicating with her. She learns this designation (symbol) through repetition and reinforcement in the same manner that she learns the names of other objects in her environment. But there is far more to the process than merely learning her name. In referring to her, family members and others will convey a variety of related meanings attached to Ann and her behaviors: Ann's Daddy's girl, Mama loves Ann, Ann, no! Ann wet her pants, Ann's been bad, and so on. Again, the messages are many and frequently evaluative in terms of what Ann should do and not do. Ann develops a sense of selfhood essentially derived from the meanings held of Ann by people who care for her and on whom she depends, those with whom she has a relationship.

Early in Ann's life (and in the socialization process), the sense of self is relatively undifferentiated. As she grows into adulthood, she will acquire many different roles, and her sense of self will become more complex. She will view herself as Ann the woman, Ann the friend, Ann the student, and so on. In conceptualizing the socialization process of self, the distinctions made between **ascribed** and **achieved roles** are important to grasp. An ascribed role is assigned to the person by others as a consequence of the person possessing a particular attribute. These assigned roles are normative and drawn from society itself. Typically, these ascribed roles pertain to such things as a person's gender, age, race, or condition, such as handicapped, and life stage (a child). An achieved role, as suggested by the term itself, is attained, presumably by the individual involved. Examples of an achieved role would be a social worker, a college grad, a

"mover and shaker," and so on. While conceptually both ascribed and achieved roles represent locations or structural positions in a social system, the concepts are helpful in understanding the process of socialization itself.

For example, Ann's conception of self will be strongly influenced by being female, a child, white, and from a middle-class family. She will be responded to because prior cultural definitions exist for each of these ascribed roles, and the significant people in her life are, for the most part, going to apply these meanings to her. For example, Good little girls don't sit that way, Good little girls don't sass their mothers, Pretty is as pretty does. Especially in the early years of life, Ann, through her behavior, will be evaluated in terms of cultural norms or standards, that is, what good little girls should be like. She will learn something of what is expected in being a child, or in being a girl, in terms of how her own behavior corresponds to the standards of these ascribed roles held by her parents and others significant to her. In short, she acquires a sense of selfhood but one that is substantially affected by prevailing norms, particularly those applying to the roles ascribed to Ann. She will develop a sense of self, become an individual different from anybody else. But, and this is frequently not understood, she will be much more alike than different from other white women of her age. Why? Because she has been socialized into these key roles. The associated values, beliefs, and ways of behaving have become internalized and are like a second nature to her.

Let's return to Ann's early socialization process. Ann, like any very young child, is entirely dependent on her parents to meet all of her needs—food, shelter, safety, love. She has been born or has otherwise come into a particular family or set of caregivers. The point is that, so far, Ann has not had much say in her life and what happens to her. Her parents are very powerful, and she quickly learns lessons about what happens when she obeys and disobeys her parents. In general terms, obedient behavior is rewarded while disobedient behavior is not. In fact, depending on the level of disobedience, her misbehavior can result in various forms of punishment. Most children, but certainly not all, learn that life is a lot easier if they behave. In learning to behave, it becomes necessary for the child to have a conception of self, to be able to treat her- or himself as an object, and to symbolically imagine her or his behavior in terms of all the applicable dos and don'ts. Assuming some reasonable level of parental consistency in these dos and don'ts and the resultant actions, Ann can imagine how her parents or others are going to behave toward her in an ever larger number of circumstances. By this symbolic representation of herself and all those relevant to her, she can symbolically try out a great range of behaviors in her mind. By so doing, she gains an ever larger sense of control over herself and others. In other words, Ann will learn how to think about herself in a large number of circumstances. By playing the role of others, she can anticipate the likely consequences of a proposed action and decide whether or not to do it—"I'd better not do it, mother will be furious and she will ground me for a month."

It also should be acknowledged at this point that no single, comprehensive, unified culture exists. Rather, there exists a general set of widely held meanings that provide a sufficient unity and integration so that people sharing the same culture can communicate meaningfully with each other. The concept of culture should be viewed as dynamic, constantly changing, and constantly developing. The implications of the socialization process stem from these features; there is no single track that each person follows in terms of becoming socialized. There is, instead, great diversity in the transmission process, especially in a relatively open society such as ours. Given the pluralistic nature of U.S. culture, it is useful to think of each family, each social group, as having its own subculture.

While drawn from and having much in common with the wider culture, it has its own unique features.

Using Ann as an example again, let us assume that she was born into a very religious family, each family member's role being highly prescribed within the definitions set by a certain denomination (Baptist, Catholic, Methodist, Presbyterian, or so on). Also, for illustrative purposes, let us assume that the family is middle-class, urban, and Midwestern. The point is that each of these features of the family, particularly its religious and class background, contributes to the development of specific aspects of a subculture that distinguish this family as a social group from all other families. Here subculture represents a set of meanings derived from the larger culture but possesses its own distinguishing qualities. In our example, Ann's initial learning about and experiences with the wider culture will be through the special filter (subculture) of her own family. What she will learn as she grows older, meets other people, participates in other groups, attends school, and so on, is that not everybody thinks alike; or, from a symbolic interactionist position, not everyone attaches the same meaning to symbols. In short, Ann will receive mixed messages about all that surrounds her—everything from what is right and what is wrong to who she is. Developing and maintaining a sense of self is no easy task. It is no wonder that children as well as adults experience problems in this process. Some of these problems become severe and, as members of the helping professions understand, require professional assistance.

Situation. From a symbolic interactionist point of view, all behavior occurs within some larger context; this context is called the **situation.** Every situation has many features, including time, location, physical objects, and as we will see in a moment, roles. All of these features are interrelated and hold a meaning for the person who is involved in forming a definition of a specified situation. In other words, all social behavior derives from an individual's definition of the situation in which he or she will be interacting with others.[54] Through the process of socialization, each person acquires a vast repertoire of situations that he or she has experienced, heard about, read about, seen acted out on television, or simply imagined. This storehouse of memories provides the source of definitions that the person uses in any given social circumstance. Critical to this notion of situation is the attendant concept of self. In terms of defining a situation, the major consideration is how the individuals doing the defining determine the roles they are to play and how those roles should be enacted within a given situation. In short, the defined situation is a major determinant of behavior.

Given this general approach to the understanding of human behavior, the coordination of social behavior depends in large part on the sharing of comparable definitions of the situation by those who will be interacting with each other. Conceptually, these common definitions result from the common experiences, the common learning, and the use of common symbols during the process of socialization. If a group of people who do not know each other are assembled, with each holding a different definition of the situation in which they are involved, a degree of socially awkward behavior might well result. What if the assembled people held such diverse definitions of the situations as a cocktail party, a funeral, a committee meeting, and a wedding reception? If you were in such a situation and had understood the situation to be a cocktail party to raise money for a politician, you would probably be wondering where the bar and hors d'oeuvres were located. Your preliminary definition would probably be shaken if the person standing next to you appeared somewhat puzzled and inquired where he might find the body of the deceased.

Central to the notion of situation are the roles required in the defined situation. A person's definition of the situation establishes, at least in general terms, the role he or she is to play and the roles to be played by other people involved in the same situation. This formulation suggests an approach for understanding the social coordination evident in social life. In developing this position, it is important not to assign a narrow conception to the notion of situation, for example, a wedding or a specific meeting. Rather, situation should be thought of as a focal point or a point of orientation for a variety and usually an ongoing set of social interactions. Using the notion of a point of orientation, every situation will have a goal to which the various social interactions pertain. For example, a family's evening meal would be a situation. For most families, it occurs at a typical time and place, and the roles of all family members as they pertain to this situation are mutually understood. Situations become linked for the individual, but the person's precise role in any given situation is derived from his or her definition of that situation.

For most adults, the situations they face are familiar ones. This is not to say that all situations are accurately defined or are routine. Life is full of surprises—some good, some bad. A surprise is a defined situation that turns out to have some novel features, that is, people not behaving in the expected way.

An example of how situations are typically linked might be helpful. Barbara and Sam Jones have been married for five years. They live in a three-room apartment and both hold professional positions. Barbara is a generalist social worker at the Midtown Mental Health Center, and Sam is an accountant for the Biosk Corporation, a large steel-making firm. The example starts with the alarm going off at 7:00 A.M. Sam is positioned to turn off the alarm (part of his role). The first situation to be faced is getting ready for work—showering, using the bathroom, deciding what to wear, dressing, and so on. Given that Barbara and Sam have been married several years, the chances are that their early morning routines are well established. They share a common definition of the situation and each knows what to expect from the other, that is, each knows the other's role and each expects that role to be carried out in the expected manner. Given the common definition of the situation, they take turns using the bathroom, showering, accessing the clothes closet, and there is small talk about the day past and the events likely to occur in the day ahead.

Soon they move from their bedroom to the kitchen, and the situation changes and becomes organized around having breakfast. Again, this situation has a definition, and their respective roles are mutually understood and carried out. Someone sets the table, someone prepares the food, someone brings in the paper, feeds and lets the pets out, and so on. If either Barbara or Sam should not carry out a role in the expected manner (satisfactorily), a point of tension between the two may arise—"Sam, have you fed the dog?" "Barbara, cool it! I'll feed the damn dog when I finish the paper!"

Once breakfast is concluded, the two start preparing for their respective work situations. Again, the transition is likely to be relatively smooth, with both taking on different roles or modifying their roles, each suited to their definition of the situation about to unfold. They move out of their roles in the social group known as Barbara and Sam—the Joneses—into their roles in larger and formally constituted social organizations, for example, Midtown Mental Health Center and Biosk Corporation. Conceptually, when Barbara and Sam move out of their respective spousal roles, the roles in the social group known as the Joneses remain dormant until the two reactivate them through their mutual entry into another situation, when they return to their apartment that evening or if they meet for lunch.

For Barbara, the transition from the role of wife to the role of generalist social worker occurs almost automatically as she bids good-bye to her husband and enters the mental health center. Again, it is a familiar situation; she knows generally what to expect in terms of how people will play their roles and how she will play hers. As she moves toward her own office, she picks up additional clues that help her define the upcoming situation, for example, remarks from the secretary or colleagues, seeing a familiar client anxiously waiting to see her, or noticing yesterday's unanswered telephone calls. Typically, there are continuities to situations that greatly facilitate the process of definition. As in the case of Barbara, it is almost as if she had stepped out of her social work role at the end of the previous work day and stepped back into it at the start of the next work day with little or no loss of continuity. It is useful to think of the individual as playing only one role at a time, but possessing great skill in moving in and out of roles as the situation dictates.

The point illustrated in the example of Barbara and Sam is that most situations confronting people are familiar, and over time people gain a pretty good idea of how they fit in. In other words, they have an overall grasp of each situation, of how all roles are generally enacted. Situations flow from one to another, and people ad just to the appropriate roles naturally and almost automatically. Importantly, social behavior is to be understood as influenced by the person's definition of the situation and the definition means not only understanding one's own role but also having a general understanding of all of the roles that are active and pertinent to the defined situation. In this sense and in his or her own mind, the individual acts out his or her own role as well as the roles of others in the process of defining the situation. While roles are the most critical feature in defining the situation, there are other important components that shape behaviors (e.g., time, space, physical features).

Not all situations confronted by people in social life are familiar and routine. Also, even seemingly routine situations have surprises. What the symbolic interactionists are suggesting is a general approach for understanding social behavior. Inherent in their position is a formulation of how the human memory functions. They suggest that the individual does not, so to speak, memorize bits and pieces of information that are somehow recalled and reassembled as needed; more likely, memory involves the retention of larger and at least loosely ordered information. In addition, the ordering of the retained material probably contains some reference to the individual as a self (a social object) so that the memory has what might be termed a behavioral orientation. The issue of the structure of memory is not central here; what is central from this theoretical perspective is that the individual's definition of the situation provides the orientation that results in that person's behavior. In the course of interactions occurring within that situation, the individual constantly receives feedback as to how successfully or appropriately she or he is playing her or his role in relation to the goal of that situation. Again, this process in most instances is subtle, and adjustments are made automatically. At other times, the process may be anything but automatic and subtle. Rather than socially coordinated behavior associated with a stable relationship, conflict may arise, which leads to redefined and restructured roles or perhaps the termination of a relationship, for example, termination of a social group—a divorce in the case of the Joneses.

Social Act. The **social act** is the final concept to be reviewed in this section. We have left it for last because it serves a useful integrating function in helping to summarize the theory of symbolic interaction. The social act also is helpful in operationalizing the notion of conversion operations as used in the social systems model, particularly when applied to the social group.

Symbolic interactionists, along with many other students of human behavior, have sought approaches at the micro level for examining social behavior. Needed was a means for examining behavior that would preserve its wholeness qualities, but at the same time permit the identification of a unit of interaction that could serve as the building block for the larger study of the process of social interaction and social organization. Among social interactionists, this unit of behavior is labeled the *social act.*[55]

Earlier we used Sam and Barbara to illustrate the notion of situation as the context that defines roles and provides direction for social interaction. We described a continuous stream of behaviors starting with waking in the morning. While on the surface it appears as though the couple is involved in a continuing stream of activities, sometimes with each other, sometimes with others, and sometimes alone, on closer inspection, the stream of activities appears much more like a series of episodes of behavior joined like links in a chain. There is evidence of purposiveness of behavior both within an individual link (having breakfast) as well as with the total chain of events for the day.

The social act can be viewed as an episode or link in an ongoing chain of social behaviors.[56] Recognizing that much of social behavior is routine, the notion of the social act can be helpful in seeking understanding of the larger process of social interaction and social organization. The social act, at a minimum, will involve two people enacting separate but reciprocal roles, and it will have both a discernible beginning and a discernible end. The social act, as it is conducted in a social group, will possess a cyclical quality. By this we mean the act is not linear, but circular in form. The end state of the act is not a final state but an intermediate one; it serves to conclude one set of interactions, but in so doing, sets the conditions or starting point for the next cycle.

For example, two friends (a social group) meet for lunch. Upon seeing the other, one says, "Hi, how has it been going?" The other responds similarly and they may shake hands or embrace momentarily. Here we have the start of a social act. They have lunch together, conduct their business or just enjoy each other's company. The episode concludes with the two parting—"Great lunch, see you later." Each then goes his or her own way with the likelihood that each will be involved in a series of such episodes each day. The use of an initial greeting and a good-bye in the example shows that the social act assumes a beginning and ending phase. The ending phase "Great lunch, see you later" shows that the ending phase contains within it the conditions for the next cycle. The next cycle could occur in an hour, a day, a week, a month, or a year or more. The point being made is that the connection in social relationships that links social acts in the form of an ongoing relationship is essentially time independent. By this we mean that the relationship doesn't have a physical structure to it, rather it has a mental one. This relationship and the respective roles within the relationship exist in the minds of the two people involved. If they are close friends, they will think of each other while they are apart. In thinking of each other, each will play themselves as well as the role of the other—"I was thinking about you last night."

A social act will always occur in a specified situation. In other words, the interactions will occur in a specific context. This context will provide additional clues to the participants' roles and also how the roles are to be carried out. In our example, the social act took place at noon in a restaurant. Time, spacial arrangements, the presence of other people, and the purpose of the meeting will all help shape the interactions that will take place. In social systems theory, the roles, the situation, all of the conditions that will affect interactions are features of the structural components of conversion operations. The actual behaviors that

transpire between the two friends having lunch can be labeled interactions or the function being performed.

To extend the above example, let us assume that the two friends are of the opposite sex; not only are they good friends but they also have a sexual relationship with each other. They are both lawyers and are employed by competing law firms. In the lunch setting, their roles were shaped by that situation; if they happened to be facing each other in the courtroom, their roles would be shaped by a different situation. Similarly, if they were spending the night together, that setting would shape their respective roles. In the example, we are dealing with the same two people, but they play quite different roles with each other depending on the situation and its definition. If their relationship is stable, the chances are that they will move in and out and switch roles quite naturally.

In describing the above relationship, we used the word *stable*. In the language of the theory, the relationship (group) would be in steady state. Each of the two individuals has a good sense of self and possesses the capacity in the relationship to take on his or her own role and the role of the other as well. In this sense, each would be sensitive to the interest and needs of the other and take the other into consideration in his or her own role enactments. This capacity of being able to act by taking into consideration the role of the other is sometimes referred to as mutuality. It is, as we indicated earlier, an important capacity to possess in working with clients in formed groups.

To conclude this discussion of the social act, we will elaborate a bit more on the dynamics of the interactions involved. First, there will be a communication (symbol/meaning) sent by the one initiating the interaction—"Hi, how has it been going?" This communication is based on a definition of the situation, the role to be played toward the other and the other person's role toward the sender. The greeting contains within it an expectation of the type of response to be returned. The initiating person makes the assumption that the other person has defined the situation and the role he or she is to play in a similar or compatible fashion. If the communication is received by the other in the expected way and the expected response is sent, then the social act is well under way. The interaction will continue but with the same dynamics playing. If a communication is sent but not received in the intended way, we have the start of a communication problem. The response made in return is not confirming, which in turn will affect the next communication to be sent, and so forth.

Again the notions of the I and me are useful in understanding the basic dynamics involved in the social act. The message being sent is coming from the I. As the message is being sent, it will be interpreted and modified based on how it sounds to the me who is taking the role of the other. Most of the time, what we say coincides with what we thought we were going to say. At other times it does not. In such instances we may say to ourselves—"I can't believe I said that." Also, we have all made slips of the tongue. The point here is that we are never quite sure what we are saying until we actually say it. An evaluative process is involved that includes the self and that part of the self that takes the role of the other.

The social act is concluded as the individuals move on to their next set of activities. Consciously or unconsciously, an evaluative activity is associated with the closure. The evaluation includes taking the role of the other and examining one's performance from that perspective. That evaluation is taken in and in some small way affects the self and the conditions for the next cycle.

SPIRITUALITY AND GROUP PROCESS

Martin Buber was a philosopher, social activist, and writer. His masterwork is *I and Thou*, a discussion of human relationships in a spiritual context.[57] For our purposes, we include Buber's work in the discussion of groups because it represents a kind of ideal type for human interaction, the essence of group process, going far beyond what we have discussed thus far as gemeinschaft relationships.

In Buber's work, the "I" is a subject, a being who is engaged with the world in one of two ways. In an I-It relationship, the subject is engaged with others as objects. The I-It relationship views the world as consisting of knowable things, including people, and it is in the I-It mode that people are studied, analyzed, and described.[58]

Buber's ideal is the "I-Thou" relationship in which each person is whole, and the relationship is mutually affirming.[59] In loving relationships, the "I-Thou" respect each other's "unity of being" and interact with respect, caring, commitment, and responsibility. Buber regarded God as the Eternal Thou. In the I-Thou relationship with God, there is no intervening purpose other than to experience the other. Thus, each I can speak (experience) directly the Eternal Thou. God cannot be studied or analyzed, only experienced. The Eternal Thou is, in the truest mystical sense, unknowable. The Eternal Thou (God) is known only as an absolute entity that gives unity to all being. In addition, the loss of self-consciousness in an I-Thou relationship suggests the submergence of the ego in an authentic I-Thou encounter.

Current accepted group theory has a good deal of the I-It component, in which the client is an object of assessment, diagnosis, and manipulation (therapy) toward a desired end. Objectification of the client and the group is inherent in most models of group process that stress achievement of a determined outcome. The promotion of I-Thou relationships between members of formed groups must be taken as an idealized goal, although it may have heuristic value as we search for improved ways to optimize human interaction. The I-Eternal Thou relationship of each member of the group impacts the individual's functioning within the group and may impact the outcome of group process, especially if the group is sponsored by faith-based services.

SUMMARY

In this chapter, we introduced lines of theory development that, when placed within the framework provided by social systems theory, have helped us specify the distinctive features of social groups. While we noted the absence of general agreement on a theory of social groups, we believe the existing theories can be helpful to the practitioner. We concentrated our review in this chapter on three theories: field, social exchange, and symbolic interaction.

Field theory shares with practice theory in social work the paradigm of understanding human behavior in the social environment. Field theory was also constructed with the idea that it would have application to the study of human behavior at all system levels. In this sense we treat field theory as one of the precursors to social systems theory. Field theory has particular relevance to the study of social groups because of Lewin's contention that groups and families, like an individual, can only be understood in the context of their social environment, that is, within a field of systems determinants.

Exchange theory offers insights into a variety of forms of human association. The theory also summarizes a great deal of common sense and offers an explanation of much that occurs in one's everyday life experiences. Its relatively straightforward qualities suggested that it would be a good place to start an explanation of the relationships between human behavior and the social environment. Simply put, the link between humans and their social environments can be understood as a form of exchange—You have something I need and I have something you need, so let's get together. Certainly much of human behavior is far more complex than is suggested by this statement, but it does offer a useful starting place.

Exchange theory is more helpful in understanding the development of relationships within social organizations than between them. Nevertheless, the metaphor of exchange is useful in understanding relationships both within and between social organizations. In the latter case, exchange offers a way of explicating what we mean when we speak of the functional qualities of the model. In short, social organizations produce things that possess value to others in their social environments (suprasystems). These things are termed outputs and are exchanged for those inputs needed by the system to continue the exchange process.

Symbolic interaction theory helps convey what we mean by the interplay between structure and interactions. Central in this construction are the concepts of self, situation, and social act. In symbolic interaction, self is the ability to see oneself as a whole, as an object in a social situation. We know and generally understand our own roles in life as well as those played by others. We can, by taking on our own roles as well as those of others, contemplate or imagine our behavior with others in advance of actual interactions. As humans we have the capacity to think and to imagine as well as to act. In fact, the latter is to be understood or conditioned by the former. From this perspective, social interaction is symbolic interaction.

For us, the single most helpful contribution of symbolic interaction theory is the explanation offered of how the self is formed and how it develops throughout life. In short, the sense of selfhood is a social outcome and most clearly one associated with the social group. This insight gives the social group its distinctive feature. Conceptually speaking, the person is both a signal and maintenance input to the social group. The task output of every social group affects our sense of selfhood. Through the social group, particularly the family, the sense of self is both developed and supported throughout life.

We concluded our review of symbolic interaction by summarizing what is meant by the social act. The social act provides the analytic tool for examining social interaction. At the micro level, the social act operationalizes the concept of conversion operations as we use it in the social systems model. In a manner of speaking, the social act is the counterpart of a cycle of social interactions or functions that we are seeking to model in the social group.

GLOSSARY

Achieved role   A role that has been earned or is recognized as a consequence of meeting certain requirements, as distinguished from an ascribed role. The role of professional social worker is an achieved role, that is, it is achieved as a consequence of meeting certain requirements.

Ascribed role   A role that has been assigned and is not related to something consciously sought by the individual. Typically an ascribed role pertains to a characteristic possessed by the individual, for example, color, gender, or age. The role of woman is an ascribed role.

Differentiation   A social process of increased specification usually related to or derived from the pursuit of some shared goal (purpose). Also, the second stage of exchange as used in exchange theory.

Exchange theory   A social psychological theory that accounts for social organization by an exchange process.

Genuine needs   In field theory, a motivational state based on internal (natural) determinants and related to the maintenance of the person's well-being, for example, hunger.

Gestalt theory   A line of theory development that emphasizes a holistic approach for understanding human behavior.

Life space   The concept employed by Kurt Lewin that includes the person and his or her environment as an interdependent whole.

Quasi needs   In field theory, need states that develop as a consequence of genuine needs; they are the equivalent of the specific intentions of an individual.

Self   An individual's perception of herself or himself. The perception is socially acquired. Self is roughly equivalent to the notion of personhood or ego. The concept represents the ability of an individual to perceive of her- or himself as a separate and distinct social entity, that is, an object.

Situation   The larger context in which human behavior takes place and in which reciprocal influences exist between the individual and a relevant environment. The concept is associated with the theory of symbolic interaction and is roughly equivalent to the notion of suprasystem as used in this book.

Social act   The smallest unit of interaction occurring within an ongoing social relationship (symbolic interaction theory).

Socialization   The process by which the individual learns to think and act in accord with prevailing norms, for example, cultural expectations.

Stabilization   The third stage of development of social organization in exchange theory.

Symbol   A sign for which a shared meaning exists within a society. Typical symbols include, among others, words, gestures, marks, and body posturing.

Symbolic interaction theory   A social psychological theory that accounts for social interaction and the development of social organization through an exchange of meanings as symbols. In the most fundamental sense, the notion of self is an acquired meaning. Reality, the perception of the real world, in effect is a system of meanings that is socially acquired and supported.

Tension system   The psychic energy associated with a need state within a psychological field (field theory).

Transaction   The initial developmental stage or level in exchange theory. Premised in self-interest, exchange is sought by providing something of value to another with the expectation that something needed by the person initiating the exchange will be offered in return.

Zeigarnik effect   In field theory, the preferential recall of uncompleted tasks.

NOTES

1. See Charles D. Garvin, "Group Theory and Research," vol. 1, in *Encyclopedia of Social Work* (New York: NASW, 1987), 682–696.

2. Janice H. Schopler and Maeda J. Galinsky, "Group Practice Overview," *Encyclopedia of Social Work*, vol. 2 (Washington, DC: NASW, 1995), 1133.

3. Alfred J. Marrow, *The Practical Theorist* (New York: Basic Books, 1969), ix.

4. See, for example, Kurt Lewin, "Experiments in Social Space," *Harvard Education Review*, 9 (1939): 21–22.

5. Marrow, *The Practical Theorist*.

6. Ibid., 166.

7. Kurt Lewin, "Behavior and Development as a Function of the Total Situation," *Manual of Child Psychology*, ed. Leonard Carmichael, 2nd ed. (New York: John Wiley & Sons, 1954), 918–919.

8. Ibid., 919.

9. Sylvia Hazelman MacCall, "A Comparative Study of the System of Lewin and Hoffka with Special Reference to Memory Phenomena," *Contributions to Psychological Theory*, vol. II, no. 1 (Durham, NC: Duke University Press, 1939), 12–14.

10. Kurt Lewin, *Principles of Topological Psychology* (New York: McGraw-Hill, 1936).

11. Ibid.

12. Ibid., 946–948.

13. Abraham H. Maslow, *Motivation and Personality*, 2nd ed. (New York: Harper and Row, 1970), 35–38.

14. Kurt Lewin, *Field Theory in Social Science*, ed. Dorwin Cartwright (New York: Harper Brothers, 1951), 274–297.

15. Marrow, *The Practical Theorist*, 26–28.

16. Ibid., 27.

17. Ibid., 40–47.

18. Ibid.

19. Joseph de Rivera, ed., *Field Theory as Social Science: Contributions of Lewin's Berlin Group* (New York: Gardner Press, 1976), 49–150.

20. Ibid., 144–146.

21. Ferdinand Toennies, *Fundamental Concepts of Sociology* (Gemeinschaft und Gesellschaft) trans. and ed. Charles P. Loomis (New York: American Book Co., 1940), 19–20.

22. Robert L. Hamblin and John H. Kunkel, eds., *Behavioral Theory in Sociology: Essays in Honor of George C. Homans* (New Brunswick, NJ: Transaction Books, 1977).

23. Weldon T. Johnson, "Exchange Theory in Perspective: The Promise of George C. Homans," in Hamblin and Kunkel, eds., *Behavioral Theory in Sociology: Essays in Honor of George C. Homans* (New Brunswick, NJ: Transaction Books, 1977), 78.

24. George C. Homans, "Social Behaviors as Exchange," *The American Journal of Sociology*, 63 (May 1958): 606.

25. Ibid.

26. Peter M. Blau, *Exchange and Power in Social Life* (New York: John Wiley & Sons, 1964).

27. Ibid.

28. Alvin W. Gouldner, "The Norm of Reciprocity," *American Sociological Review*, 25 (April 1960): 161–178.

29. Marvin E. Olsen, *The Process of Social Organization: Power in Social Systems*, 2nd ed. (New York, Holt, Rinehart and Winston, 1978), 93.

30. Blau, *Exchange and Power*, 116.

31. Olsen, *Process*, 94.

32. Blau, *Exchange and Power*, 118.

33. Olsen, *Process*, 95.

34. Ibid., 96.

35. Blau, *Exchange and Power*, 94.

36. Olsen, *Process*, 96–97.

37. Georg Simmel, *The Sociology of Georg Simmel*, trans. and ed. Kurt H. Wolff (Glencoe, IL: Free Press, 1950), 387.

38. Gouldner, "Norm of Reciprocity."

39. Olsen, *Process*, 97.

40. Blau, *Exchange and Power*.

41. Mary Jo Dugan and Michael Hills, eds., *Women and Symbolic Interaction* (Boston: Allen & Unwin, 1987), 3–15.

42. Charles Horton Cooley, *Social Organization* (Glencoe, IL: The Free Press, 1909), 23–31.

43. See, for example, Anselm Strauss, ed., *The Social Psychology of George Herbert Mead* (Chicago: The University of Chicago Press, 1956), iv–xvi.

44. George Herbert Mead, *Mind, Self, and Society* (Chicago: University of Chicago Press, 1934).

45. The assumptions are made by the authors and have no single source. Symbolic interaction has its

foundations in the philosophy of pragmatism and is associated with the thinking of Charles Peirce, John Dewey, and George Herbert Mead. For an interesting review of the origins of symbolic interaction, see Hans Joas, *G. H. Mead: A Contemporary Reexamination of His Thought* (Cambridge, MA: The MIT Press, 1985), 33–63.

46. Mead, *Mind, Self and Society*, 135–226.

47. Ibid, 151.

48. For a discussion, see John P. Hewitt, *Self and Society: A Symbolic Interactionist Social Psychology*, 3rd ed. (Boston: Allyn and Bacon, 1984), 91–143.

49. Charles Horton Cooley, *Social Organization* (New York: Scribner, 1902), 184.

50. Charles Horton Cooley, *Human Nature and the Social Order* (Glencoe, IL: The Free Press, 1956), 23.

51. Ibid.

52. Mead, *Mind, Self and Society*, 173–281.

53. Ibid., 154.

54. For a development of this idea, see Johnathan H. Turner, *A Theory of Social Interaction* (Stanford, CA: Stanford University Press, 1988).

55. Hewitt, *Self and Society*, 65–70.

56. Ibid.

57. Martin Buber, *I and Thou* (translated by R. G. Smith), (Edinburgh: T&T Clark, 1957).

58. Ibid.

59. Ibid.

CHAPTER 9

THE FAMILY AS A SYSTEM OF ROLES

FAMILIES AS EMERGENT STRUCTURES

STRUCTURAL FAMILY THEORY

FAMILY SYSTEMS THEORY

COMMUNICATIONS/INTERACTIVE THEORY

SUMMARY

GLOSSARY

NOTES

FAMILIES AS EMERGENT STRUCTURES

In the previous two chapters, we introduced the social group and the main lines of theory development that inform practice with this level of social system, particularly the family. In this chapter, we will focus on the development of family theory that employs the system paradigm. In our judgment, practice theory is much more advanced in work with families than in the more general area of work with groups. Our special interest in reviewing family theory is the contribution it has made to our development of social systems theory and those distinctive features of the theory that apply to social groups.

In our earlier review of social groups, we highlighted the concept of social roles. Roles, as we indicated, are the essential foundation for an understanding of a good deal of the behavior we observe in human social systems. The structured patterns of interactions that emerge in informal interactions can be traced to the dynamics of role interactions. When people interact in systems over time, the role dynamic becomes a part of both the structure and the function that define the position. As we shall see, some theories posit that structure and function in systems interactions are actually two sides of the same coin.

Roles are social in nature: they require at least two participants in order to come into being. The fundamental social unit, then, is the dyad. Social systems are made up of these dyads in constant interaction. In some cases, as we discussed, when a person is fully socialized, his or her behavior takes on a social character by interaction with an internalized "generalized other" even when he or she is alone.

Our next step is to apply this understanding of role-based behavior to the activities of more complex systems. In this chapter, we begin by discussing social systems theory as applied to what Cooley referred to as primary groups.[1] These groups, characterized by their relatively small size and face-to-face character, represent the next step up from the dyadic focus on reciprocal social roles. The family is characterized in each of the theories presented here as a system of social roles. Each theory has its own perspective, but each stresses system dynamics rather than individual personality as a requisite for understanding the family. Each of these theories also builds on the symbolic interactional idea of a self divided into a subjective and objective component. The logic model presented earlier will help in understanding how these elements come together in a coherent whole. The theories presented will help you understand some of the common problems observed in families. We have given particular attention to Bowen's approach, which emphasizes the process by which emotional processes distort and disrupt family interactions.[2] The basic unit

of analysis for our discussion is the social role, and we will consider the family as a role set.

The family is a social system of profound importance in understanding human behavior. Structurally, the family is a small group. Functionally, the family is expected to complete a staggering array of tasks: providing intimacy for the marital pair, socializing the children, providing shelter, serving as an economic unit of both production and consumption, providing social and emotional support, and a host of others. In form, families vary so widely that we have to be cautious in our use of the term. The family, as outlined in the theories that follow, begins as a dyad and progresses into almost limitless forms. To say that the family begins as a dyad is itself a simplification: the original pair typically begins the new family already embedded in a multigenerational family context whose web of influence is subtle but unmistakable.

The nuclear family, as we tend to think of it today, is a relatively modern invention. The idea of a mating pair who represent a socially bounded system that is economically and socially self-reliant, sexually exclusive, and has a contract with the state that allows exclusive franchise to have and raise children, would in various cultures and at various times have seemed strange. Indeed, what we now call the traditional family has long been called by sociologists the "rump" or "unstable" family.[3]

We hear the family referred to often as a social institution. However, the family as we most often see it today does not meet some of the traditional requirements of an institution. Let us make one point to illustrate this fact. Institutions are social organizations that persist over time, and whose structure and functions endure beyond the tenure of any one role incumbent in the social position. In the modern family, couples contract to form a social unit for the possible creation or accession of children, the evolution of the family over the period of child development, and the progression of the original pair into old age and death. At no point in this progress does the nuclear family have a living role model present within the family boundaries who can model the roles expected at each stage in family life. The mating pair may use their parents as models, but the parents, in most instances, live some distance away and are at a different stage of development. The pair must have and raise children without the close social support that might be available in a tribe, an extended family, or a commune. When the children mature and leave the home, the "empty nest" poses a new developmental challenge to the couple, again without close support or accessible role models. The death of the first partner then leaves the surviving partner with a lonely and unsupported role, disconnected from the remains of the family.

This grim perspective is offered merely as a counterweight to the notion that the family is a secure and enduring social institution. The modern family is small (most often composed of no more than two generations), mobile, adaptive, economically focused, and frighteningly vulnerable to misfortunes that might befall the adult pair. In a major sense, it is a creation of the industrial revolution: this cataclysmic social change severed families from the land, made multigenerational extended families obsolete, and created a new social unit. This new unit was able to move to where jobs were available, relied on a sex role dichotomy to assure that the men met the economic needs and the women met the nurturing needs, and in the process created role sets and social norms, which are today under wide-scale assault as repressive, outmoded, and unworkable.

The Industrial Revolution, which produced the modern nuclear family, is four hundred years old. Today, we face the prospect of what Daniel Bell called the postindustrial society.[4] The nuclear family, still new in historical terms, is already outmoded. The modern family may have multiple forms. We know that serial monogamy has emerged as a competitor to the traditional nuclear family, even though mores

and values have not fully validated this form of social organization. Marriage is no longer a requisite for socially sanctioned childbearing. Childbearing is no longer an automatically expected product of social coupling. Same-sex couples may now seek social sanction to raise children. Sex occurs outside any social sanctioning process. The state has produced a quasi-familial childraising system called foster care, paying people to raise children, thus creating an industry. Child care, a private enterprise industry has arisen to take over the child care for families that require both adult members to work outside the home. For a whole economic class of people, the single-parent (which means *single-mother* in most cases) family is normative.

With all these changes and more, the models of family life are understandably strained today. Nonetheless, the family remains a social system of crucial importance. If it had no other significance, it would still be important because social myths persist that define it as important. As W. I. Thomas once said, "things that are thought to be real are real in their effects."[5] The effects of the mutable family on modern life are crucial, and our models strain to keep up with reality as we are propelled inexorably and at what seems an ever accelerating pace into the future.

With this discussion as a caveat, we attempt now to present three important systemic theories that focus on family dynamics. It is easy to read these theories as benighted and unaware of the contemporary complexities and variations of family life as social work practitioners encounter it. Nonetheless, the system dynamics of small groups that are multigenerational, multitasked, and multistructural present a necessary and useful view of the evolution of the family as we observe it in the twenty-first century.

STRUCTURAL FAMILY THEORY

One of the most influential theories of the family was developed by a family therapist named Salvador Minuchin.[6] Minuchin called his approach structural family treatment, and indeed much of the appeal of the model comes from its ability to help us visualize the family structures that arise as a result of repeated patterns of interaction.

Minuchin and **structural family theory** have a colorful history, and it is clear in reading that history that Minuchin is comfortable with the type of conflict he feels is an essential part of family interaction. He was born in Argentina, and trained as a physician and psychiatrist. His specialty was child psychiatry, although he twice took time out from his practice to serve in the Israeli army during times of war. In his early work, Minuchin was motivated to provide services to low-income minority families in Philadelphia. His work with these families involved aggressive treatment in which the family members were asked to enact in treatment the issues that produced problems in the home. Minuchin quickly recognized the cultural barriers to communication that arose between educated, middle-class therapists and poor and uneducated families functioning in the demanding inner-city environment. Minuchin recruited and trained paraprofessional counselors who understood the culture and were able to mediate across the boundaries of culture and experience, which limited communication in the treatment settings.

Minuchin came to believe that child psychiatry could not be practiced outside the context of the family. He took this belief with him when he became director of the Philadelphia Child Guidance Clinic, which became one of the most influential centers for innovative family therapy in the world. As he began to apply the treatment methods he developed to other types of families, he encountered resistance and criticism from other psychiatrists. As he said pointedly, he got no "flack" for his methods when they were used with poor, inner-city black families, but the ideas of systemic family therapy applied to middle-class families excited all sorts of professional resistance. Minuchin's trademark confrontive treatment style and systemic ideas placed him in constant conflict with the American Psychiatric Association, whose efforts to call him to account

were greeted by Minuchin's refusal to meet and answer their concerns.[7]

Minuchin's views were, to say the least, at a variance with traditional views of individual psychopathology and its treatment. His views were much more in line with the ideas of Talcott Parsons, already discussed in Chapter 2. The influence of Parsons on structural family theory is evident in this passage noted by Nichols and Schwartz:[8]

> That the [nuclear family] is itself a subsystem of a larger system is of course a sociological commonplace. But to break it in turn down into subsystems is a less familiar way of looking at it. Yet we will treat the family in this way, and say that, in certain crucially important respects, the very young child does not participate in, is not fully a "member" of his whole family, but only of a subsystem of it, the mother-child subsystem. The marriage pair constitute another subsystem as may, for certain purposes, also the child with all his siblings, all the males in the family, all the females, etc. In fact, any combination of two or more members as differentiated from one or more other members may be treated as a social system of the family as a whole.[9]

The family system as Minuchin described it is made up of four different subsystems: (1) spousal, (2) parental, (3) parent–child, and (4) sibling. The subsystems themselves are a product of what Minuchin calls the "invisible set of functional demands that organizes the way in which the family members interact. Repeated transactions establish patterns of how, when, and to whom to relate, and these patterns underpin the system."[10]

Structural family theory consists of three primary constructs: (1) structure, (2) subsystem, and (3) boundaries. It is obvious that these constructs developed from the same sources as the social systems theory we have been discussing throughout.

Nichols and Schwartz quite accurately characterized the impact of Minuchin's theory as "allowing the therapist to see what he is looking at."[11] The underlying structure of the family, as with many social systems, is confusing at first. The use of the theory to infer structures from observed behavior is a major product of this conceptually elegant approach. Few applications of the systems perspective have a more direct practical payoff to social workers than the understanding of family structure through the prism of structural family theory.

Structure refers to the organized pattern in which families interact. As we have alluded to earlier, the pattern is related to role positions within the role set. The term *structure* here seems to imply a rather static understanding of the family, but this is far from the case. Structures can be understood more as grooves worn down by repeated family transactions. These grooves tend to delimit how, when, and with whom the family members interact. The patterns are thematic rather than literal; that is, there is a persistent quality to structured communication rather than specific content or ritualized enactment.

For example, the oldest son in a family wants to go out with friends. The mother says no, but the father then intervenes and says yes. Repeated in various contexts over time, this creates a family structure that defines the mother as negative and controlling, the father as tolerant and supportive. This in turn delimits the other possible role enactments between the mother–son and father–son role sets. At the extreme of this cycle, it becomes impossible for any of the members to escape the role trap and have the mother enact the role of the supportive and tolerant parent, or the father set limits and enact the controlling role.

Part of the family structure relates to rules. Rules may be overt or covert, but the covert rules are far more influential in family functioning than the overt rules. For instance, a rule that is overtly stated might be: We do not allow the use of drugs in this house. This rule is apparently clear, and compliance or sanction would seem to present few problems. However, if the overt rule is accompanied by a covert rule,

such as, You can use drugs, but don't let anyone see you, or You can use drugs, but don't get so screwed up that it is obvious, then the rules produce a pattern of secretiveness commonly seen in chemically dependent families. The clinical axiom, "You are as sick as your secrets," comes from this pattern. A related clinical expression is the famous line, "A secret is something that everyone knows but nobody talks about." By making a covert rule overt, the distorting influence on the family system is diminished, simply because the family does not have to behave in a manner incongruent with the socially expressed reality.

Structural family theory makes it clear that all families operate under both **universal** and **idiosyncratic constraints.** Perhaps the most obvious example of a universal constraint is the need shared by all families for some form of control hierarchy. In most cases, the parents exercise control over the children, and in many cases, one parent exercises power more often than, or differently from, the other. This example carries within it an implicit oversimplification: for example, in large numbers of modern families, there may be many parental roles enacted. In a family of divorce, the children may relate to both families: one has the custodial parent and a stepparent, the other has a noncustodial parent and stepparent with whom the children interact during visitation. Often grandparents, other family members, friends, professional caretakers, and so forth may exercise some part of the parental function within this blended-family context.

An idiosyncratic restraint is one that is unique to the individual family circumstances. For example, in a family with an alcoholic father, the father may take part in the family power hierarchy only when he has been drinking. When he is sober, he might be withdrawn and ineffective in family functioning, and when he is hung over he may be treated by the mother and children as another one of the children. Addiction, mental illness, single parenthood, and a host of other factors commonly encountered in social work practice give rise to idiosyncratic constraints that affect families in ways similar enough to present recognizable patterns, but still variable enough to elude being considered universal.

The roles in this type of family system are **reciprocal** and **complementary.** Role reciprocity was discussed earlier, and involves the fact that the enactment of each role in the family tends to evoke responsive behaviors in other members. Such patterns are considered reciprocal rather than causal, since it cannot be determined in fact which person acted and which person reacted. Each is both cause and effect to the other. One of the most predictable responses to an attempt to intervene in a problematic family pattern is that the members of a role set will attempt to characterize a problem in terms of "who started it." The role of the reactor is generally felt to be less blameworthy than the behavior of the actor who started it. Whatever "it" is in the family pattern, the trap of trying to figure out who started it is one that a social worker employing the structural model is generally well advised to avoid.

Complementary roles are those in which the actions of one member of the set are different from but fit together with the actions of another member (see Figure 9.1). For example, if the wife in a marriage is a personable extrovert who tells funny stories, her husband's complementary role would be to function as an appreciative listener. As parents, the father might be cold and demanding of the children, the mother might be warm and nurturing. The contrasting type of role relationship is termed **symmetrical.** In symmetrical relations, both a wife and her husband may have careers as social workers, may take the same role as supportive nurturer to their children, and so on.

The view of some theorists is that the interdependent "fit" of the complementary role set makes this style more stable. The symmetrical role pattern is seen as inherently competitive, therefore less stable. Within the family, it is clear that if the parents are to be the controlling members, the children must take the role of being controlled. If one parent is more powerful than the other, the complementary role set must be accepted by both partners or conflict will result. If children seek to control the parents rather than accepting being controlled, family conflict is likely to result.

Repeated transactions over time foster mutual expectations within members of the family role set. These expectations in turn become determinants of a family pattern, and may become so automatic that the causes of the pattern are forgotten. If a family becomes accustomed to constant complaints on the part of a father about the demands of his job, the burdens of his roles, and the behavior of other family members, it may result in the mother becoming distant and unconcerned. If the father should seek therapy and be diagnosed as depressed, he may become dependent on outside support for nurturance, and the family pattern would tend to perpetuate itself even while the father pursues individual treatment for his own needs. The

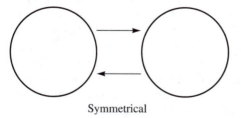
Symmetrical

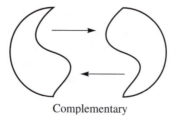
Complementary

FIGURE 9.1   Symmetrical and Complementary Relationships

label applied to the problem may determine the paradigm from which it is viewed, and therefore may become a matter of paramount concern. If the complaining father is seen in family context, his problems might be understood as artifacts of poor role complementarity. If he is seen as an individual, the depression might be understood as his personal problem, with little to do with the family dynamics. While the principle of equifinality would suggest that intervention from either perspective could be expected to impact the family system, the skilled social worker would want to be alert to the system dynamics and capitalize on the changes in the father in order to foster adaptive changes in the family.

As will be discussed later in regard to the communications/interactive approach, the structures of the family are **epiphenomenal** in nature. That is, what we observe in the interactional behavior of family members gives clues to the underlying structure of the family, but does not in itself constitute that structure. The pattern of interpersonal transactions can be difficult to determine, and discernment requires practice. Practice alone, however, does not preclude the need for a model for understanding the phenomena being observed. In structural theory, the impetus is to observe the repeated patterns of interaction that produce enduring family structures that are resistant to change. Individual observations are the stuff of intervention, but in order to be meaningful, they must be organized according to some conceptual schema that captures the elusive family structure.

The patterns within a family may be thematic rather than phenomenal, and various themes may be present within a single transaction. Take the example of a father and a teenage son who have been close and friendly until the son begins to date a girl of whom the father disapproves. The son and the father begin to argue, the son refuses to do as his father wishes, and continues to see his girlfriend despite being prohibited to do so by his father. The father and son may actually come to blows, and the mother is ineffective in her attempts to defuse the conflict. The manifest theme in such a family would be the conflict between the father and son. However, also present is the fact that this relationship is much more intense and presumably more meaningful to both than is either party's relationship to the mother in this context. Different family systems theorists might view the phenomena of this family differently, based on the hypotheses generated by the theory. For our purposes here, it is sufficient to say that a social worker who saw the conflict as indicative of no relationship between father and son would miss the important point that this relationship is intensely important to both. The interpretations and interventions undertaken might be based on the view that this is a power struggle (need theme), a role accession crisis (interactional theme), a distraction from relationship problems between the parents (interactional theme), or based on sexual competition between father and son (instinctual theme). As we can readily recognize, there is no single way to "connect the dots" we observe in the specific phenomena of family interaction. The theory one would use for intervention in the example described would be of importance in determining the meaning of what we observe, and the direction our intervention should take.

Family Subsystems

The structures that evolve in families are formed in order to carry out the various functions required of the family. Individual members' behavior aligns them with other members in various subsystem arrangements, which accomplish the varying and sometimes conflicting functions of the family. One of the most dramatic contrasts between the individualistic and systemic views of behavior can be found in the shifting formation of family subsystems. For example, family members are constantly engaging and disengaging from others in the role set as circumstances require. Each member of the family not only plays multiple roles, but is engaged in differing role sets within and between these roles. The social worker who attempts to assess and work with the family while viewing it as a collection of individuals rather than as a collection of roles will find this type of assessment prohibitively difficult.

It is first necessary to describe the four subsystems identified by Minuchin and his associates in the structural family therapy school. As we discuss each of these subsystems, keep in mind the systems model discussed earlier, and also bear in mind that some of the subsystem coalitions described are overt, while others are covert. A subsystem of teenage siblings may be overt and obvious, while a subsystem between a parent and a child in coalition against the other parent may be covert in the extreme. All subsystems are fleeting—they appear and recede in response to situations, shifting constantly in a manner Lewin characterized as the "rubber map" of identity.[12]

It is also important to keep in mind that the subsystems are composed of interacting roles. If we confuse the person with the role, it becomes difficult to assess problems. For example, in the first two subsystems, spousal and parental, the people are the same in both subsystems. The roles played by the two people are often quite different depending on which role is manifest in a given situation. For example, the role of husband may be quite different from the role of father, even though they are different facets of the same person. A couple that argues over parenting issues, then allows those differences to affect their affection and respect for each other as spouses, is not maintaining the boundary between the two subsystems.

Spousal Subsystem. The spousal subsystem is the first to appear in the developmental history of a family. The system is formed when two people come together for the express purpose of creating a family. One of the chief functions of the spousal pair is intimacy, and seeking the status that our culture recognizes as, among other things, legitimating intimate sexual behavior. Other functions include important economic factors, since the spousal pair enjoys certain economic advantages such as inheritance, co-insurance, and property privileges.

Minuchin discussed this process in the context of heterosexual pairs, since this is obviously the most familiar and accepted pairing in our culture. A reading of Minuchin reveals little difficulty in applying this definition to same-sex pairs, although it is apparent that in our culture, such couples experience considerable obstacles in proceeding to subsequent stages that involve the accession of children to the family system. In addition, the granting of the economic status afforded to heterosexual pairs is still largely withheld from same-sex pairs in this culture. A significant symbolic fact is that few civil or religious ceremonies are available to same-sex couples to signal the transformation of the spousal pair from individuals to a recognized social standing as a couple. Other cultural variations on the heterosexual pair could be noted. There are groups, many of historical interest, who practiced group marriage, communal living, or polygamy. The structural family therapy model is more strained in addressing these arrangements than it is in addressing the same-sex pair.

Minuchin believed that complementarity and accommodation were important ingredients for the spousal subsystem. Complementarity referred to the assignment of roles to each spouse that were mutually supportive, yet respected the individuality of each. This lock-and-key type of role set is akin to the rationale that has been in long use for the assignment of dichotomous sex roles to men and women in this society. Several theorists have noted that exaggerated role complementarity, of the type that characterizes some gender role expectations in segments of our society, limits individual initiative and freedom. The most obvious example is the idea that a woman's place is in the home. This has led to some criticism of the notion of role complementarity among feminist theorists. We believe that the descriptive nature of role complementarity is useful if it is not taken as a prescriptive statement about how role responsibilities and privileges should be assigned on a cultural basis. Each spouse has different, yet interdependent responsibilities.

Accommodation refers to the fact that there is an ongoing process of compromise between the needs of each spouse, each giving something at times, getting something at other times. Accommodation implies that the adjustments within the role set are relatively minor, as opposed to a redefinition of a role or norm. The permanence of the role set was emphasized earlier in the concept of distributive justice which states, as you recall from exchange theory, that over a long period, rewards and costs in a relationship even out. This view dictates that once the spousal subsystem perceives itself as a family, the exchange of rewards and costs in the relationship takes place in the context of a long-term family commitment. Thus, when a couple is dating, each may calculate the reward potential of the relationship on the basis of what happens in a single evening, a single week, or a month. That calculation, addressed elsewhere in the discussion of exchange theory, is very different when the relationship is viewed as a lifetime commitment. For example, a man who values beauty in a woman might regard an unattractive woman as unsuitable as a date, but suitable as a potential spouse if she has the qualities he associates with being a good mother to his children. Likewise, a woman might find a man exciting and fun as a date, but too unstable to serve as her economic partner in a committed spousal relationship.

The balance between individual needs and spousal system needs reflects an internal system boundary that secures the identity of the two individuals. The individuals themselves are defined by a boundary that identifies them as a couple, protects them from outside forces, and preserves a pattern of interaction within the relationship that is unique and different from any that takes place across the boundary.

The internal boundary defines roles and protects individual identity. Each spouse is allowed a sphere of personal activity. The outer boundary protects the pair from such things as cross-generational influence from the parents of each spouse, or from peers, social institutions, and other suprasystem manifestations. The outer boundaries are symbolized by rituals such as marriage, by laws, by mores, by custom, and by the individual idiosyncrasies of the spousal pair.

As we shall see in the next section, the spousal system boundary also protects against violation by the children of the family. This second type of protection is also intergenerational in nature. However, in our culture the boundaries against intrusion by children are more idiosyncratic than are the boundaries that protect the pair from society at large. Thus, a social worker might expect more boundary definition problems due to intrusion by children, since these issues are not as well codified in the social scripts of the culture. Simply put, the individual pair develops more of its own style with regard to parenting responsibilities, and "making it up as you go along" leaves the system open to more possibilities for error.

The spousal subsystem in structural family theory, then, has internal and external boundaries, an expectation of permanence, important intimate and economic functions, and provides the foundation for the second-stage family function of reproduction and childraising. Despite the fact that human beings have been at the process of mating and childraising for a long time, it goes without saying that boundary violations can occur with some regularity. For example, parents who may be struggling with issues of role loss meddle in the lives of the spousal pair and try to impose their own values and wishes. Old friends may seek to invade the spousal system to protect their investment in one or the other partner as emotional support.

It must be said that social agencies (notably child welfare agencies, but there are others) are in the wholesale business of invading the life space of the spousal pair and usurping their legitimate prerogative. To the extent that a spousal pair deviates from social norms, the boundaries that protect them are weaker and more permeable. We have already referred to same-sex couples and the problems they often encounter in family formation. Unmarried couples, although more tolerated now than in the past, invite boundary violations much more readily than married couples due to their lack of legitimating ritual. Many physically challenged couples can recount horror stories about how their perceived differences from the norm provide a pretext for boundary violations of various types, and from various social sectors. Poverty often forces arrangements that bring extended families and others into close living proximity, and these factors represent a constant threat to the boundaries that define the spousal pair as unique. The workplace, particularly in the form of such industries as migrant farm labor, impose enormous burdens on spousal pairs who must travel and work under circumstances that often fail to reflect basic human dignity, let alone respect the system identity of the spousal pair.

Divorce, an increasingly common phenomenon in our society, must be understood to have a changing and important impact on the way we define the spousal subsystem. In making a spousal commitment to the family, we ask that individuals begin to calculate the cost–benefit ratio of the relationship within a lifelong time frame. Thus, when after ten years of marriage, a husband tells his wife he is going to divorce her, she may feel that her decision to work while he went to college and medical school will not pay the distributive justice rewards she had expected at the time of commitment. It is increasingly common in this age of accessible, non-stigmatizing divorce for individuals to calculate not only the distributive reward prospects of a commitment, but also the short-term risks thereof. This calculation, admittedly more complex, is changing our societal view of marriage, and it has been said that in fact the cultural norm is now serial monogamy. An old cartoon in a familiar magazine illustrated this with a starry-eyed bride leaving the church with her groom to whom she said, "Darling, how romantic, our first wedding." While this is presently a norm violation of the wedding ceremony, it may not be in the near future. As sex roles become more symmetrical in society, it is perhaps some compensation for the increased probability that the long-term distributive justice rewards expected of a marriage are less frequently realized.

Parental Subsystem.   With the accession of children to the family, the spousal system becomes a subsystem of the new family structure. The same people are involved as were in the spousal subsystem, but the functional focus has changed to childraising. We will note the difference between the two subsystems by calling the spousal system members the husband and wife, and the parental subsystem members the mother and father.

The parental subsystem focuses on the care and socialization of the children. The husband and wife form the executive system for the family. In functional families, if the parents do not exercise this executive authority, the system is believed to be at risk. As in the spousal subsystem noted earlier, the internal boundaries in the parental subsystem define the differential allocation of executive authority between the husband and wife (rarely are the two roles perfectly symmetrical, but in adapted families they reflect a mutual accommodation).

The addition of children to the family, of course, requires adjustments in the operation of the spousal subsystem. The crisis of role accession (having a child) may mean that certain freedoms, privileges, and practices of the pre-childbearing spousal system may be lost. There will certainly be the addition of many new role responsibilities, and the accommodation arrived at in the spousal stage must now be renegotiated in earnest. It is important for social workers to keep in mind that in working with couples, one role set may be manifest in a given situation, but the other is always latently present. Thus, if a couple had a good pre-childbearing relationship, and then the mother invests most of her nurturing energy in the newborn baby, it would be naive to expect that the husband in the spousal subsystem will remain unaffected. The systems principle is clear: changes in one part of the system produce changes throughout the system. Clients often find it helpful and clarifying to conceptualize their frictions as husband and wife as artifacts of new demands made on them as mother and father. It should also be noted that the birth of a new baby is frequently the occasion for renewed assaults on the boundaries of the family system by parents (now grandparents) and others, offering advice, criticism, and help whether or not it is requested.

The internal boundaries within the system must, as the children grow, struggle with the paradoxical parenting requirements. The children are to be nourished, cherished, and protected, and at the same time they are to be encouraged to become autonomous and self-reliant. The delicate balance of forces within the family is tested with each new developmental challenge, and with each additional child entering the family system. The demands and conflicts inherent in the parenting function can be expected to affect the foundation relationship that exists between husband and wife.

With the advent of children into the family system, each spousal partner automatically becomes part of two subsystems: spousal and parental. These are sometimes so close that they become isomorphic concepts for the spouse/

parents. Role confusion may result, with a lack of clarity about which role is primary. Different theories abound in this area, and we must carefully evaluate practice theory and personal values before we attempt social work practice in this delicate area of family functioning.

Parent-Child Subsystem.   In addition to the roles of spouse and parent, each adult also becomes involved in the parent-child subsystem. The functional role of this subsystem is the care and socialization of, and the provision of autonomy to, the child. The relationships here quickly become more complex, and they test the internal boundaries of both the spousal and parental subsystems. Each individual parent has a relationship with the child, which forms a parental subsystem that is intergenerational in nature. The parents together have a relationship with the child in which the two of them function as a single unit (imagine the baby picture with mom and dad smiling happily at the newborn, united in their parental bliss). As more children come along, each parent has a relationship with each child, the parental system has a relationship with each child, and the children as we shall see have a relationship with each other. Each forms a type of subsystem. Each is influenced by the others, but each is unique. As the climate in each subsystem changes, it can also be expected to have ramifications for the nonparenting relationship between the spousal pair of husband and wife. To picture this, it is easier to imagine the family with children a little older, say a boy ten, a girl twelve, and a boy sixteen. We diagram some of the parent-child subsystem possibilities in Figure 9.2.

Sibling Subsystem.   The sibling subsystem comes into being with the birth or addition of a second child. The children have their own functional needs apart from the parents. These include the need for autonomy and relationships with peers, a need to test reality, and so on. Testing skills and exploring self-concept are

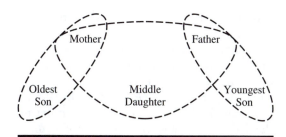

FIGURE 9.2   Parent–Child Subsystems

two subsystem functions. Sullivan talked about an important developmental concept not often discussed elsewhere, which is important among the subsystems of children, both within and without the family.[13] The concept is termed **isophilia,** which literally means self-love. In this context, it means learning to love someone much like yourself, which is viewed as a step toward learning to love those more different. By loving other kids, one learns to love in a way much different from loving those parents on whom you depend, and who are regarded as vastly different from the self.

Since the executive authority of the parents may interfere, sibling subsystems are often more open than other systems. In addition, at certain stages in development, many kids develop friendships that render permeable the system boundaries of the family. Latency-age kids, for example, often enjoy sleepovers, moving back and forth between homes and developing pseudo-sibling relationships with age peers. More complex things happen as children become adolescents and begin dating, and the relationships between siblings and others form the foundation for in-law relationships later. Each developmental stage has the effect of blurring family boundaries. Nonetheless, many sibling subsystems develop a very clear function and pattern within a family, and it is distinct from outside relationships.

In cases of family dysfunction, the sibling subsystem may perform many stabilizing functions. Sibling support has been anecdotally demonstrated to be important in cases of incest,

domestic violence, substance abuse, and other pathological disruptions of the family. Of course, sibling abuse, be it emotional, physical, or sexual, is also part of the pattern of dysfunction in some families.

The sibling subsystem must be understood in the context of the increasingly common **blended family.** When divorce occurs, children are often exposed to new family systems (whether or not a legal remarriage ensues). Siblings from quite different family cultures governed by different idiosyncratic rules (both implicit and explicit) must learn how to function in a complex system forged of two, and in some cases more, already well-established elements. Often this process takes place with only minimal parental guidance, since the parents are struggling with issues in the spousal subsystem. Moreover, many parents may not choose to consciously acknowledge problems among siblings, for obvious defensive reasons. While a full discussion of this complex and important issue is beyond the scope of this book, it is crucial that social workers recognize the important role of communication in the establishment of roles and boundaries in blended family systems. Obviously, included in this issue is the concern with foster care homes, which have all the issues of blended families, along with the further complication of role conflict for parents and instability for the child or children. Attention to both the obvious and the subtle tensions in these situations is essential to effective social work practice with these systems.

Family System Boundaries

The concept of system boundaries is crucial in structural family theory. The boundaries are important because, like covert rules, they must be inferred from observed interactions. In biology, boundaries are living membranes that simultaneously connect and divide systems. Like their physical counterparts, social system boundaries allow some things to pass, while some things are blocked. In family systems and in groups, the focus of concern is interpersonal communication across boundaries.

As discussed in Chapter 2, Koestler summarized the linking-separating functions of boundaries in the term *holon*.[14] He likened a holon to the Roman god Janus, who was always depicted as having two faces. (The month January is so named because it faces back into the old year and forward into the new.) The holonic boundary faces inward into the system and outward toward the suprasystem. By its nature, the process of restricting inputs defines the system. Although the boundaries of systems limit access, they must be permeable to some degree or the system will not be viable.

An important system concept is sometimes described as turbulence at the interface. The interface where two boundaries meet in a family or between a family and the suprasystem is characterized by two importance effects on communication. The two factors, **distortion** and **information loss,** are graphically displayed in Figure 9.3.

Distortion at the interface is caused by a simple but easily overlooked fact: the interactions that take place within a boundary are different from those that take place across a boundary; the differences may be quantitative or qualitative. That is, the communication within a system tends to be of a different type than communications that take place across a boundary; the differences may be quantitative or qualitative. That is, the communication within a system tends to be of a different type than communications that take place across boundaries. In addition, in some systems, communications within boundaries are more frequent than those that occur across boundaries. Either pattern may serve to define the system. For example, in the spousal subsystem during the dating phase, it is common to develop nicknames for each other, to develop secret words to describe private activities such as lovemaking, and in general to have a different vocal tone and expression when talking to the system partner. This tendency is so common that most keen observers can begin to tell when a friend is smitten simply by the way the friend talks (or doesn't talk) about the partner.

In the same way, family communication can become so idiosyncratic in some dysfunctional families that the style of communication becomes almost encoded, a totally private language. This accounts in part for the fact that so many of the family theorists were first drawn to this field by way of communications, and the widespread early interest in the patterns of communication in severely disturbed families such as those with schizophrenic members. This early theorizing went so far as to suggest that poor communication caused schizophrenia, a notion not generally accepted now. However, it is clear to even a casual observer that styles and patterns of family communication, not merely content, differ when the family boundary is breached by, say, a visitor. For example, having the preacher to dinner strains the normal

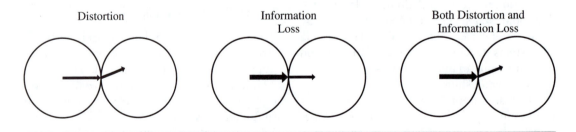

FIGURE 9.3   Distortion and Information Loss across the Interface

patterns of family communication in order to accommodate this temporary visitor.

When two families, each with its own private style of communication, try to communicate, there is considerable risk of distortion and misunderstanding. Commonly, when two families get together for the first time because their children are engaged, the boundary collision between the two private systems can be spectacular to behold. Each time a counselor enters into this realm of private communication, precautions must be taken to guard against misunderstanding based on the predispositions that we each bring to the understanding of others.

The second phenomenon that occurs at the communication interface between two systems is loss of information. It requires more energy to cross a boundary than to communicate within a boundary. Thus, we are trying to communicate with someone who does not share our useful vocabulary (this is very different from our formal intellectual vocabulary). We find making ourselves understood much more difficult. An obvious example is communicating with someone who does not speak English. In this case, we know we are not communicating. More subtle and more to the point is what happens when a family member tries to talk to a counselor about incest. The family has usually embedded the event in rules (don't talk) and encryptions (euphemistic words or expressions for forbidden acts) so that the effort on the part of a client to simply get the experience into words in a different setting is exhausting.

The private rules that operate within a family, and the ways these differ when nonfamily members are present, give insights into the patterns and processes of the family. A comedian underlined this point when he joked, "Last week I went over to visit some friends. They told me to make myself at home, so I got into my underwear and started watching TV."

A colleague tells the story of moving to Hawaii, where some of the local people of Polynesian ancestry advised him after several visits

to his home that it was offensive when he asked if he could get them something. The assumption on their part was that if they were welcome in the home and wanted something, they would either ask or go get it for themselves.

Social workers communicate across boundaries of race, economic class, gender, sexual preference, physical challenge, and sometimes unimaginable personal experiences that define boundaries whose existence they must always seek to identify and overcome. Many families in oppressed groups, and many with idiosyncratic dysfunction, develop intensely personal ways of communicating, which are bounded to protect from outside intervention. This protective function does not go into abeyance simply because our intentions are good. The natural protective function of family boundaries represents a crucial challenge to social workers in overcoming both information distortion and information loss. Practice requires energy and patience in establishing accurate communication that does not violate the safety needs of the client family system. We will explore these issues from a slightly different perspective in the next section.

Family Structure Mapping.   In order to visualize the inferred structure in family systems, we have developed a series of conventions to depict family structures. These depictions help illustrate some of the structure and dynamics in structural family theory. Figure 9.4 depicts a

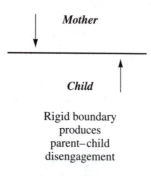

Mother

Child

Rigid boundary
produces
parent–child
disengagement

FIGURE 9.4   Parent–Child Disengagement

rigid family boundary between mother and child. In such a system, a closed-system dynamic emerges, and the ability of the system to accommodate or adapt to others is impaired. Rigid boundaries are resistant to transactions, produce both distortion and information loss, and result in a condition termed **disengagement.** Disengagement is the social isolation that results from the absence of needed social transactions between family members.

In Figure 9.5, we see the depiction of **clear boundaries** between mother and child. Clear boundaries are the hallmark of functional families. They provide definition of the spheres of personal autonomy for family members, and still allow for needed transactions between members in order to fulfill family functions.

In Figure 9.6, we see the symbolic depiction of a **diffuse boundary.** The diffuse boundary fails to protect the autonomy of the respective family members, producing confusion over identity and control. This results in a system too open to outside influence, and incapable of developing an internal structure that provides a sense of distinct identity. This lack of clear personal identity is termed **enmeshment.**

In Figure 9.7, conflict between the mother and father is depicted. This conflict, if it becomes a pattern over time, results in the creation of a rigid boundary. The chronically conflictual interaction pattern produces a family structurally adapted to conflict. This rigid boundary thus produces disengagement between the spouses, and may require the development of some compensatory means of fulfilling the natural functions of the spousal subsystem. If this conflict is resolved by each parent meeting the frustrated spousal system needs through overinvolvement with a child, the result could be enmeshment in the parent-child subsystems. This is also depicted in Figure 9.7.

In Figure 9.8, we see the depiction of a **coalition.** A coalition represents intergenerational enmeshment, usually as a means of conflict avoidance or to compensate for unmet

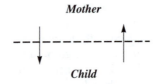

Clear boundary
produces normal-
functioning
parent–child
subsystem

FIGURE 9.5 Normal-Functioning Parent–Child Subsystem

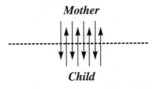

Diffuse boundary
produces
enmeshment in
parent–child
subsystem

FIGURE 9.6 Enmeshment in Parent–Child Subsystem

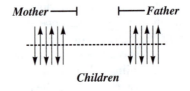

Conflict between mother and father
produces disengagement within
parental subsystem and enmeshment
of the parent–child subsystem

FIGURE 9.7 Disengagement within Parental Subsystem and Enmeshment of the Parent–Child Subsystem

needs in the appropriate subsystem. In the diagram, the mother and child are engaged in a coalition (which is covert) against the father. The mother is enmeshed with the child and disengaged from the father. Minuchin and Nichols regarded this as "the signature arrangement of the troubled middle-class family."[15] The mother-child coalition substitutes for the closeness missing in the spousal subsystem. This arrangement might be expected to arise as a dysfunctional means of coping with the conflict depicted in Figure 9.7.

In Figure 9.9, we see the depiction of **detouring.** Detouring refers to redirecting a conflicted relationship to implicate a third member of the family. Similar to Bowen's concept of triangulation, this is a form of tension reduction seen in the ego defense mechanism termed **displacement.** This is similar to the concept of scapegoating when the feelings directed toward the child are hostile, although the detour may take the less obvious form of being overly solicitous about a child as a means of meeting unmet spousal needs.

In Figure 9.10, we present the symbols used to depict involvement and overinvolvement. These symbols reflect the frequency and intensity of transactions between family members. Overinvolvement carries the implied risk of enmeshment, although at various points in the life of a family, overinvolvement, as with a sick child, may be required. If the pattern persists past the point at which a stressor such as illness demands overinvolvement, it may perpetuate itself as a dysfunctional structure.

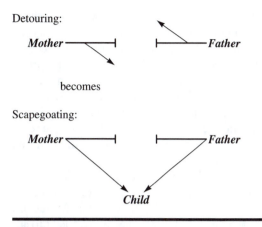

Detouring:

becomes

Scapegoating:

FIGURE 9.9   Detouring and Scapegoating

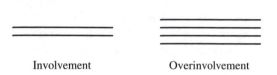

Involvement   Overinvolvement

FIGURE 9.10   Involvement and Overinvolvement

The symbolic depictions, or maps, developed in structural family theory are aids in assessing family processes. We have used only a few of the symbols to illustrate how they are used to depict family functions. A wide range of depictions is possible, all of them illustrating the basic system principle that families are living systems that are constantly changing and adapting their internal functions as a means of adapting to external demands or stressors. We have not addressed the practice implications of this approach, since that is beyond the scope of this book. However, it is apparent that this approach to understanding family structure and functions has immediate practice implications.

FAMILY SYSTEMS THEORY

Family systems theory is a development of the work of Murray Bowen.[16] Like Minuchin, Bowen was trained as a psychiatrist, and became

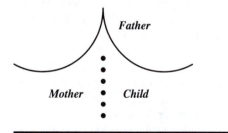

FIGURE 9.8   Coalition

interested in the puzzles posed by schizophrenic communication. Bowen's early research focused on the mother–child relationship in schizophrenia, and on what Bowen termed the *symbiotic relationship* between the two. Bowen came to feel that the pattern of shifts from closeness to distance in this relationship, keyed to the internal emotional states of the participants, was crucial in understanding the early schizophrenic experience.

Bowen is generally credited with developing the most inclusive approach to understanding the behavior of families. Unlike Minuchin, Bowen expanded his perspective to take into account the internal states of the family members as a precursor to the study of interactional patterns. Bowen, in the course of his theoretical development, came to posit that the patterns of interpersonal behavior were closely tied to, if not determined by, the balance of intellectual and emotional processes within the individual family members. While this belief strays somewhat from our focus on the observable realm of interpersonal behavior, in Bowen's theory there is virtually an isomorphic relationship between intrapersonal and interpersonal patterns. As we shall see, it is far from clear which is the chicken and which the egg in this intricate relationship.

Bowenian family systems theory is rich in concepts that bridge the study of individual and interpersonal behavior. We will concentrate here on the major concepts as they amplify the structural emphasis found in the work of Minuchin.

Bowen's focus of study is on the nuclear family, but he came to believe that the processes of the nuclear family could not be separated from those of the extended, multigenerational family system. The family in this schema is understood as an emotional system, and the nature of emotional influence is such that long dead or physically absent members are still very much present in the ongoing family emotional system.[17] The influences of one generation are passed on in complex ways to subsequent generations, influencing interpersonal behavior in profound ways.

Differentiation

The most important single concept in family systems theory is the idea of the **differentiation** of the self. In Bowen's early work, he used this phrase to describe the development of boundaries between the self and others. In this usage, the term clearly refers to what we would call a boundary issue in the development of self-concept. Undifferentiated individuals have little autonomous identity, and are vulnerable to a kind of emotional contagion found in dysfunctional families.

In his later work, and in a usage Bowen came to prefer, differentiation refers to a distinction between the intellectual and emotional processes in the individual. The individual's inability to distinguish between thinking and feeling produces a tendency to deal with emotional needs by becoming enmeshed with others. Thus, the social pattern of differentiation Bowen observed early came to be understood as a social response to the internal confusion between thoughts and feelings.[18] Bowen was very clear about where he stood on the issue of internal differentiation: the inability to gain rational control over one's emotions produced both personal and social distress in life. The emotions of the undifferentiated person flood the field, making it impossible to think clearly about problems and issues.

The undifferentiated, emotional person tends to be unable to learn from experience, and thus becomes trapped in a pattern of behavior that is reactive, rigid, and marked by a dependence on others for emotional well-being. This definition is close indeed to the currently popular concept of codependency, a condition first noted in alcoholic families where one spouse relies on the other for feelings of value and well-being. In some cases, the individual simply fuses his or her identity with the other, echoing emotions without reflection. Just as rigidly, some individuals develop a fixed pattern of counter-conformity in which they reject anything proposed by the other. A clinical axiom for this type of behavior is: "180 degrees from sick is still sick."

By contrast, the rational, differentiated person is capable of learning from experience. This makes it possible to be more flexible, more adaptable to changing social situations, and more self-sufficient. Such individuals are able to be in emotionally intimate contact with others without becoming reflexively shaped by the emotions of the other. Family systems theory emphasizes that the differentiated person is able to have and experience emotions; they are simply not dominated by the emotional impulse. Such a person is able to gain some internal state that holds these two vital processes in balance.

Differentiation as a social phenomenon can be understood as the process of gaining at least partial self-control and autonomy in order to lift oneself out of the emotional chaos of the family. The term "adaptive level of functioning" was coined to describe the individual's ability to function under conditions of stress. This might be understood as self-control, which is the process of gaining rational control of behavior situations in which there is a perceived need to react emotionally.[19]

Differentiation, then, focuses our attention on the emotional aspects of the family system. The model proposes that a balance between the two processes is possible and desirable in order to improve the adaptive capacity of both the individual and the family systems. This model stands in stark contrast to some therapeutic models, which seem to imply that rational consideration is somehow inauthentic or artificial. It opens up the family therapy process to the possibility that the use of reason, analysis, and self-awareness offers important tools for alleviating family dysfunction.

Triangles

The family systems model proposes that the basic social unit—the dyad—does all right until it is placed under stress. Under stress, the undifferentiated dyad seeks to distance members from each other. The members then seek relief from the emotional tension by reaching out and involving a third party in the stressful situation. The emotional immaturity characteristic of undifferentiated individuals is thus temporarily relieved. However, the involvement of a third party complicates the effective resolution of the tensions within the original dyad.

Examples of **triangulation** are easy to cite. When two people who are dating have a fight, one of the pair may seek out a friend for consolation. In some cases, a vulnerable third party may offer to intercede when he or she perceives the distress of one of the original dyad. Any time we find ourselves complaining to a friend about someone else, we should remember that the resolution of the tension cannot take place without actually addressing the person concerned. Whenever there is tension, it is likely that the script being disclosed will cast one person (almost always the one to whom you are listening) as the victim. When we are being thus addressed it should be clear that we are being invited to rescue the speaker.

In transactional analysis, a related therapeutic system that employs an internalized family model in explaining social behavior, this process is called the victim–persecutor–rescuer triad. The script in place has clear role expectations, and the pressure to rescue the victim can be considerable. It should be noted, however, that these are roles and not people. The actors in the roles may change, but the pattern dynamic is likely to persist. A victim once rescued may simply go on to require rescue again. Triangulation of a third person into the script prevents direct confrontation and resolution of the tension. In this regard, both structural and family systems theories stress that the ability to recognize the conflict-avoidance patterns present in families is essential in order to assist the family in developing more effective tension-reduction strategies. Such intervention, of course, requires that the social worker have attained sufficient self-differentiation so as not to be drawn into the conflict as a rescuer and thus perpetuate the problematic pattern.

Nuclear Family Emotional Process

This phrase is used to describe the pattern Bowen labeled the "undifferentiated family ego mass."[20] In this process, the lack of internal boundaries within the family makes individual autonomy impossible, and the undifferentiated family members resolve their emotional needs by fusion with other family members, until in extreme cases everyone in the family feels everyone else's feelings. This is different from empathy as described earlier. Empathy involves the conscious ability of a differentiated person to understand the feelings of the other. In this environment of emotional fusion, the members feel each other's emotions as their own. The fusion tends to produce reactive (self-protective) emotional distance, which excites the undifferentiated need for more fusion. As one person pulls away, the other is panicked and tries more desperately to pull the person back in. Other system responses are for one of the members to become dysfunctional or sick, for open conflict to emerge, or for one or more of the children to become scapegoats.

Family Projection Process

In this pattern, tensions between undifferentiated parents result in one parent seeking to meet emotional needs by projecting anxiety about adequacy onto a child, becoming overinvolved with the child, and thus stifling the child's own striving for autonomy and clear boundaries. This is similar to Minuchin's de-

touring process.[21] Whether the bond formed is cooperative or conflictual, it is fused in nature. The anxious projection by the involved parent is supported by the disengaged parent, since the pattern serves to distract both adults from the primary disturbance in the spousal pair. The ultimate effect on the child is debilitating, which then requires more parental concern and perpetuates the pattern.

Multigenerational Transmission Process

In undifferentiated families, the child who is most involved in the family dysfunction tends to become less differentiated than the parents. The child who is most detached may attain higher levels of differentiation. As the child grows to adulthood, the tendency is to seek out partners at the same level of personal differentiation. This leads, in time, to either gradual deterioration or gradual improvement in terms of differentiation over generations. The implication is that in family development it is healthy to distance oneself from unhealthy families, and healthy to engage oneself in healthy families.

The view that individual pathology is a progression of system activity over generations is a dramatic extension of the individual psychopathology model. The cascade of indirect interpersonal influence down to the current generation has major implications for social programming, as well as for therapeutic intervention in families.

In order to help conceptualize the multigenerational structure of families, Bowen developed his genogram conventions to display family origins. This approach does not display the dynamics of family interactions as clearly as the structural family diagrams of Minuchin, but it does highlight the events and relationships in previous generations and distal family members, which Bowen believed could impact all members of the family via the multigenerational transmission process. The conventions employed by Bowen are depicted in Figure 9.11.

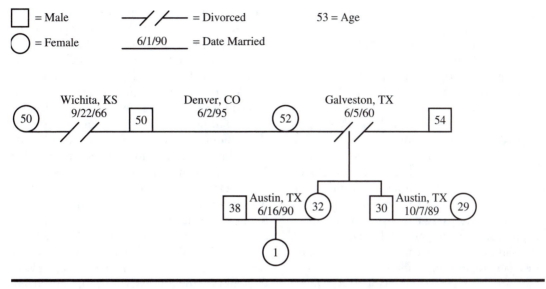

FIGURE 9.11   Genogram with Conventions Noted

Emotional Cutoff

In order to escape the emotional fusion in the undifferentiated family ego mass, children may seek to escape family influence by physically moving away, by severing emotional ties, or by seeking to protect themselves from family patterns by bringing outside third parties in as protection. The emotional cutoff, although superficially it may seem to be a good adjustment to a dysfunctional family, may itself be crippling. In our discussion of differentiation, we noted that 180 degrees from sick is still sick. This applies to the cutoff as well. The energy required to maintain physical or emotional distance may be more usefully applied to work on differentiation. The trauma many adult children of dysfunctional families experience in such things as going home for holidays, attendance at family rituals, and so forth is ample testimony to the unresolved issues that still tie up adaptive energy, and may await transmission in the multigenerational process to the next generation.

Societal Emotional Process

This concept is of particular interest to students of social systems theory. Not long before his death, Bowen discussed the fact that the societal system had emotional issues and content. As the ambient level of social anxiety increases, this angst is transmitted to the family systems. This differs in some way from models that hold that the family is an element of the societal, and that the addictive influence of the elements creates the emotional climate in society at large. Bowen's concept is more in keeping with the reciprocal, nonlinear influence model we have been describing in connection with social systems theory. While the mechanism of transmission of societal emotions is unclear, it hearkens back to the work of Durkheim, who found in the abstract social processes of anomie the origins of the intensely personal act of suicide.[22]

In our times, the direct intrusion of the larger society into the family setting by way of radio, television, and other mass media is undeniable.

The impact of these intrusions is a source of controversy among social critics. Our model suggests, however, that we cannot understand this development toward the "global village" using only linear, cause-and-effect models. Families affect and are affected by the larger culture, and these effects must include the complex emotional issues to which family systems theory directs our attention.

The structural theory we have discussed emphasizes the rules and structures developed in families by repeated patterns of transaction. Family systems theory stresses the family as an irrational emotional system, balanced by a more adaptive, rational potential in human systems.

The family as we see it thus far is a structure etched by repetition, made up of a system of emotions, and in tension with a system of thought. We turn now to a model that explores the channels by which the various elements of the family system are linked—the communications/interactive approach.

COMMUNICATIONS/INTERACTIVE THEORY

The communication/interactive theory of family functioning developed originally on the West Coast, and, unlike the models discussed thus far, involved the contributions of a number of theorists. A remarkable group of pioneers was organized around the Mental Research Institute organized by Don Jackson and the Schizophrenia Project headed by Gregory Bateson.[23] Influenced by diverse considerations such as the brilliant hypnotherapy of Milton Erickson, the cybernetic models originated by Norbert Weiner, and the mathematical philosophy of Bertrand Russell and Albert North Whitehead, not to mention the influence of anthropologist Margaret Mead, the two Palo Alto schools became a creative force in the development of both theoretical models and therapeutic practice approaches. The processes described in this approach have important similarities to the structural and systems approaches, but several unique features posited here are important to understanding family functioning and social work practice with families by both the generalist and those in advanced practice with families.

A core concept developed in this school of thought is that all behavior has communication value. The understanding of communication in this school moves well beyond the realm of symbolic verbal behavior discussed by Mead.[24] Indeed, in a famous phrase, Virginia Satir said, "One cannot not communicate."[25] Silence, withdrawal, and avoidance are all forms of communication when they take place in a social context. Moreover, communication thus defined was quickly understood as the social matrix in which all psychotherapeutic activity takes place. Communication processes, in turn, were all understood to be central in the construction of reality both in individuals and in family systems.

Nichols and Schwartz among others have pointed out that the communications/interactive approach summarized here has perhaps the best claim among the many contenders for being the originator of family therapy as we understand that field today.[26] In fact, the pioneering work in this area has become fundamental to the approaches discussed thus far. We take the study of this group out of historical order only because we must understand the communications processes in relation to the rules and structures posited by Minuchin and the rational–emotional dichotomy proposed by Bowen before the subtleties of communication dynamics can be appreciated.

Communications/interactive theory is markedly systemic in nature. In this model, the family is viewed as a living system, and interpersonal communication is understood as the mechanism by which that system regulates itself and seeks to maintain steady state. Some of the apparently quirky aspects of family behavior are more easily understood if this system-maintenance aspect of communication is clearly acknowledged.

Central to the development of this approach was the pioneering integrative work of Gregory Bateson. Bateson, like both Minuchin and Bowen, was interested in the problem of schizophrenic communication.[27] Influenced by the importance of feedback in Weiner's cybernetic model, Bateson examined family communication with the goal of understanding the family as a self-regulating system, even when the system appeared to be functioning poorly.[28]

Metacommunications

In order to understand the nuances of family communication, it is imperative that communication be understood as a multilevel phenomenon. Satir defined **metacommunication** as the sending of a message about a message.[29] Metacommunication informs the receiver of communication about how the message is to be taken. The metamessages may be verbal or nonverbal, implicit or explicit. Commonly in families, the metacommunications of concern are nonverbal and implicit in nature.

Metacommunications are epiphenomenal in nature. That is, they derive their significance from the fact that they provide a context that allows us to interpret more fully the phenomena of overt communication. Satir shared the axiomatic belief of those in the communications school that all behavior is communication. In a sense, behavior contextualizes communication and enriches or alters its meaning.

Metacommunication may consist of facial expressions, tone of voice, body posture, gestures, and choice of wording. When these metamessages are compatible with the expressed content of the message, communication is said to be **congruent.** When the metamessages contradict some aspect of the expressed content, the communication is said to be **incongruent.** Incongruent communications have the effect of creating uncertainty in the receiver about the meaning of the communication.

In one example, a man approaches a female acquaintance and says, "You really look great today." If the metamessages are congruent, the communication may be considered feedback to the woman regarding her appearance. However, if the tone is sarcastic, the opposite may be true. If the tone is leering, the message may be taken as a sexual overture. If the situation is such that both parties to the communication know that the woman is hung over from a night of heavy drinking, it may be taken as affirmation that her condition is not apparent to observers. The range of nuances in communication is formidable and varies with the setting, the nature of the relationship, the extent to which the two parties have a mutual understanding of the metacommunications system, and so forth.

Another type of message incongruity occurs when the emotional tone of the sender does not match the verbal content of the message. This is a common occurrence in family treatment. For example, a wife in treatment may complain that her husband does not care for her any longer. At this, the husband gets red in the face and shouts at his wife, "You know I love you." The manifest message is that he cares for her, but the metamessage throws that meaning into doubt. A variation on this interaction occurs when a husband tells his wife he is worried about their relationship, and she responds by saying, "I love you as much as I ever did." The doubting husband cannot tell whether to take this as affirmation of her devotion or acknowledgment that she not only cares little for him now, she may never have cared for him in the past.

In a climate of concern about sexual harassment, overt and verbal metacommunications are often used in situations in which nonverbal communication would have sufficed in the past. For instance, in the previous example, if the woman were applying for a job, the man interviewing her may say, "You really look great today," then recognize the possible misconstruction of that message by the receiver as a sexual proposition. The man then might say, "I just mean that I think your dress is becoming. Nothing more." This disavowal of any possible misunderstanding may clarify the message, but it may also serve to call attention to the possible sexual construction of his remark. It is apparent, in this example, that a good deal of communication about sex is laden with metacommunications.

One purpose of metacommunication in some situations is that it allows the sender to deny responsibility for the message if the message is not taken as intended. A famous example is a man asking a woman if she would like to go look at the sunset. The intent may be for the woman to agree, with the purpose being to seek privacy for a romantic interlude. If the woman is agreeable, she might say, "Sure, I think sunsets are romantic," signaling her understanding and agreement. If she says, "No thanks, sunsets are boring," the response refutes the romantic overture without making the refusal explicit. If the man persists and asks again, the woman may say, "Look, I don't want to look at the sunset, and I don't want to have anything to do with you." The man may then attempt to save face by denying the metacommunication and claiming responsibility only for the overt message. His response might be, "Gee, don't get huffy. I just meant that you might like to see the view." This strategic retreat from the metamessage may fool no one, but the woman's explication of his metamessage leaves him no other choice except to accept responsibility for the entire communication. For this reason, a great deal of communications therapy with families involves making implicit messages explicit and encouraging family members to take full responsibility for the messages they send.

Another common example of metacommunication is humor. If a woman is making racist jokes and is confronted by someone who is offended, she may take refuge from responsibility by saying, "I was only joking. Don't be so touchy." If the jokes are tolerated, that may then be taken as confirmation that the receiver shares the racist sentiment, jokes or not. The essence of many types of humor lies in the multilevel qualities of human communication.

Double Bind Communication

Double bind communication builds on the multilevel nature of human communication noted above. Occurring most commonly in a complementary relationship, the double bind has six characteristics.

1. Two or more persons, one of whom is designated the "victim"
2. Repeated experience
3. A primary negative injunction
4. A secondary injunction conflicting with the first, and occurring at a higher level of abstraction, and like the first accompanied by punishments or signals that threaten survival
5. A tertiary negative injunction that prohibits the victim from escaping the field
6. Finally, the complete set of ingredients is no longer necessary when the victim has learned to perceive his or her universe in double bind patterns. Almost any part of the double bind sequence may then be sufficient to precipitate panic or rage. The pattern of conflicting injunctions may even be taken over by hallucinatory voices.[30]

An illustration of the famous double bind communication is offered as follows: a mother and a child are involved in a long-term ambivalent relationship, with the child identified as the victim. Over time, the mother regularly tells the child verbally, "Come to mother," the words being accompanied by holding the arms open as if to receive the child. As the child approaches in response to this message, the mother is seen to tense up, and her body language and expression indicate rejection. The child, seeing this second, more abstract message, which contradicts the verbal message, stops. Seeing the child stop, the mother then says, "What's the matter, don't you love your mother?" The child, by virtue of social inexperience, is unable to articulate the bind, and unable to make sense of the contradictory commands. By virtue of the child's status as a dependent, she or he is unable to leave the field, and thus must remain in the double bind environment.

This scenario, repeated in multiple forms and different settings, comes to define the entire context of the mother-child relationship: anxious, ambivalent, and punitive. In the end, any contact with the mother, any accusation about being unloving, and perhaps any reference to the mother may be enough to trigger the double bind response of anxiety, anger, and fear.

The emphasis on the pattern of responses over multiple repetitions echoes the structural family therapy belief that structures emerge in response to repeated patterns of interaction. No single incident of such paradoxical communication could in itself be considered to create a double bind. In addition, if the child does submit to the bind, no bind exists. The message sent by the mother need not automatically be accepted by the child, even though in many situations the child will lack the skills needed to escape the bind. Nonetheless, the situation is interactional despite the fact that much of the power resides with the mother in this instance.

The structure that emerges in this scenario is detrimental both to the development of the individual victim and to the functioning of the family. When communication cannot be relied on to provide effective feedback on behavior, the result is ambiguity over time, which leads to an entropic disintegration of internal and social boundaries of the self.

The double bind theory illustrates clearly the principle of pattern repetition that, over time, produces an internal family structure. In this case, the structure is counterproductive for all participants and for the system as a whole. In other cases, repeated patterns of family interac-tion may produce adaptive structures, such as mutual affirmation and support. Most theorists agree that while the double bind theory is a fascinating insight into one of the more corrosive effects of communication dysfunction, the more valuable contribution from this school is the concept of metacommunications.

Family Homeostasis

Viewed in systemic perspective, by far the most important realization arising from the study of the communications/interactive approach is the complexity of communication. This in turn is instructive in considering the feedback mechanisms that exist to regulate family homeostasis, which is referred to in social systems theory as *steady state*.

An essential aspect of metacommunication in families is that all messages have both command and report aspects. This is reflective of the reciprocal nature of the role structure that underlies interpersonal communication. In each interaction, the message sender offers information to the other about the sender. The same communication also carries a signal about the behavior that is expected or required (depending on the relationship) of the receiver.

Messages that disturb the equilibrium of the family are met with various types of resistance. This fact is important to social workers, since therapeutic change in a dysfunctional family will be resisted just as strongly as would a disruptive change. Therefore, when the family develops a structured pattern of behavior over time that limits its ability to function, attempts at changing this pattern will be resisted even if some members of the family profess a wish to change. A familiar example is the family of an alcoholic in denial. The family is frozen in the structures produced by repeated denial of the problem.

An example would be a wife who works at two jobs to make ends meet because her alcoholic husband cannot keep a steady job. By asking the wife, who is overperforming in her role, to change behaviors and confront the alcohol problem, we induce a crisis in the family. Confronting the underperforming husband, the wife may find that any change in his drinking challenges her role as the real head of the household. In order to protect homeostasis, even a dysfunctional homeostasis, the two partners in the complementary relationship may engage in subtle and complex maneuvers to sabotage the changes. Thus, the wife may become angry and critical of her husband's attendance at Alcoholics Anonymous, and tell him she liked it better when he was drinking, because at least then he was at home.

This type of example has long made it clear that changes in one part of a family system must be accompanied by work with the others in the role set, lest the tendency to seek steady state assert itself and undermine therapeutic gains by the identified client. The client, in this view, is not necessarily the most dysfunctional person in the family. Satir stated it well: "the symptom bearer in the family is not necessarily the sickest, merely the weakest."[31]

Communication is essential in providing the family with feedback in order to monitor system performance. Clear, unambiguous communication is the best feedback channel. The communications/interactive theory makes it obvious that interpersonal communication is often ambiguous, sometimes internally contradictory, and may serve various purposes within a system. Clarification of role issues and family problems necessitates an understanding of interpersonal communication as multilevel, multipurpose, and situated.

SUMMARY

In this chapter, we discussed the family and its developing forms in the context of social systems theory. The family can be viewed as a social invention that responds to the emerging needs of a society, in this case, the Industrial Revolution and economic necessity.

Structural family theory emphasizes three main theoretical concepts relevant to systemic thought. Structure is defined as the enduring aspects of a family that result from patterns of interaction repeated over time. Subsystems, which are derived from Parsons and Bales, stress the functional subdivision of the family in a way that cuts across the traditional personalistic view of families. Boundaries are needed to define subsystems and are inferred from the observation of interactional patterns.

Family systems theory stresses the emotional aspects of the family system and contrasts emotional and intellectual processes by means of a crucial process called differentiation. We viewed the family system from a multigenerational perspective as a system embedded in a dynamic suprasystem. We then emphasized the anxiety-management function of the family, with particular reference to the process of triangulation.

Communications/interactive theory addresses the crucial importance of communication in providing feedback on family adaptation and subsystem performance. We can explore communication as a situated, multilevel process with implications for social work practice. The family will tend to seek a homeostatic steady state, and this tendency may produce resistance to attempts to therapeutically induce change in the system. We concluded by noting the universally communicative aspects of all behavior.

GLOSSARY

Accommodation   Relatively minor adjustments in attitudes and behavior made in response to the needs of others in a role set.

Blended families   Families whose spouses and children are united following death or divorce into a single system.

Clear boundary A boundary that defines differences between members of a role set, allowing communication while at the same time defining an area of individual autonomy for each member.

Coalition As used here, a form of intergenerational enmeshment, usually as a means of conflict avoidance.

Complementary roles Roles within a role set that differ in function but whose distinctive features are mutually supportive of others in the role set.

Congruent messages Messages that have the same or consistent meanings at all possible levels of abstraction.

Detouring As used here, a redirecting of a conflicted relationship to implicate another member of the family.

Differentiation (1) The existence of effective boundaries between the self and others. (2) A clear delineation between emotional and intellectual processes within the person, with preference given to intellectual processes as determinants of behavior.

Diffuse boundary A boundary that offers only imprecise delineation for the participants in a role set, with ill-defined autonomy and risk of enmeshment.

Disengagement Social or emotional detachment from another person.

Displacement A defense mechanism in psychoanalytic theory by which anxiety is reduced through the transfer of feelings or thoughts from an unacceptable to a more acceptable thought or feeling.

Distortion Unplanned interference with the meaning or goal of a message, resulting from resistance in crossing a systems interface.

Double bind communication A seriously flawed pattern of communication that consists of incongruent messages repeated over time, without the opportunity for escape or confrontation, resulting in anxiety, dysfunction, or madness in the designated victim.

Enmeshment Overinvolvement with another, resulting in loss of clear identity, a result of diffuse boundaries.

Epiphenomenal Manifest family social structures, but not the underlying structure of the family.

Idiosyncratic constraint Factors that influence the family structure and function on an individual or case-by-case basis.

Incongruent messages Messages that carry different meanings and/or intentions at different levels of abstraction.

Information loss Reduction in the message value of a communication as a result of energy expended in crossing a systems interface.

Isophilia Literally, this means self-love. It is used here to explain a function of the sibling subsystem. While children learn to love someone much like themselves (a sibling), they take a step toward learning to love those who are more different.

Metacommunication (1) A multilevel communication; (2) communication about communication, an epiphenomenal factor in communication; (3) an abstract message that contradicts a more overt message.

Reciprocal roles Elements in a role set; interactive and mutually defining positions within a social situation in which norms are referential to one another.

Structural family theory An influential theory of the family developed by Salvador Minuchin.

Structure A relatively permanent pattern of family interaction that defines and limits internal family processes, and that results from frequently repeated patterns of interaction over time.

Symmetrical roles Roles within a role set whose functions are the same or similar, and which operate in a cooperative fashion chosen by both participants.

Triangulation Reduction of tension within a dyad by involving a third person to be the target of the enmeshed anxiety of the dyadic pair.

Universal constraint A factor that influences structure in all families, for example, the need for an executive hierarchy.

NOTES

1. Charles H. Cooley, *Human Nature and the Social Order* (New York: Scribner's Sons, 1902).

2. Murray Bowen, *Family Psychotherapy* (New York: Norton, 1988).

3. See, for a discussion, R. Federico, *Sociology* (Menlo Park: Addison-Wesley, 1975), 286.

4. Daniel Bell, *The Coming of Post-Industrial Society: A Venture Into Social Forecasting* (New York: Basic Books, 1973).

5. W. I. Thomas, *Social Behavior and Personality: Contributions of W. I. Thomas to Theory and Social Research* (New York: Social Science Research Council, 1951).

6. Salvador Minuchin, *Families and Family Therapy* (Boston: Harvard University Press, 1974).

7. See M. Nichols and R. Schwartz, *Family Therapy: Concepts and Methods* (New York: The Free Press, 1995), 211.

8. Ibid., 97.

9. For a context, see Talcott Parsons and R. Bales, *Family Socialization and Interaction Process* (New York: The Free Press, 1955).

10. Minuchin, *Families and Family Therapy*, 215.

11. Nichols and Schwartz, *Family Therapy*, 209.

12. Kurt Lewin, *Principles of Sociological Psychology* (New York: McGraw Hill, 1936).

13. H. S. Sullivan, *The Interpersonal Theory of Psychiatry* (New York: Norton, 1953).

14. A. Koestler, *Janus: A Summing Up* (New York: Random House, 1978).

15. Salvador Minuchin and M. Nichols, *Family Healing: Tales of Hope and Renewal* (Boston: Harvard University Press, 1974), 121.

16. Murray Bowen, *Family Psychotherapy* (New York: Norton, 1988).

17. Ibid.

18. Ibid.

19. P. G. Guerin, L. Fay, S. Burden, and J. Kautto, in M. Nichols and R. Schwartz, *Family Therapy: Concepts and Methods* (Boston: Allyn and Bacon, 1994).

20. Murray Bowen, *Family Psychotherapy* (New York, Norton, 1988).

21. Salvador Minuchin, "Structural Family Therapy," in *Handbook of Family Therapy*, vol. II, A. Gruman and D. Kniskern, eds. (New York: Bruner/Mazel, 1991).

22. E. Durkheim, *Suicide*, trans. J. Spaulding and G. Simpson (New York: The Free Press, 1951).

23. P. Watzlawick, L. Beavin, and D. Jackson, *Pragmatics of Human Communication* (New York: Norton, 1967). For a general review, also see A. Gruman and D. Kniskern, eds., *Handbook of Family Therapy* (New York: Bruner/Mazel, 1991).

24. G. H. Mead, *Mind, Self and Society* (Chicago: University of Chicago, 1934).

25. Virginia Satir, *Conjoint Family Therapy* (Palo Alto, CA: Science and Behavior Books, 1964).

26. M. Nichols and R. Schwartz, *Family Therapy: Concepts and Methods* (New York: The Free Press, 1995).

27. Gregory Bateson, D. Jackson, J. Haley, and J. Weakland, "Toward a Theory of Schizophrenia," *Behavioral Science*, 1 (1956): 251–264.

28. N. Weiner, *Cybernetics* (Cambridge: MIT Press, 1961).

29. Virginia Satir, "The Family as a Treatment Unit," in *Changing Families*, J. Haley, ed. (New York: Gruen & Stratton, 1971).

30. Gregory Bateson, D. Jackson, J. Haley, and J. Weakland, "A Note on the Double-Bind," *Family Process*, 2 (1963): 154–161.

31. Satir, "The Family as a Treatment Unit."

CHAPTER 10

THE SOCIAL GROUP AND THE FAMILY
SOCIAL SYSTEMS THEORY

THE SOCIAL GROUP AND THE FAMILY

SOCIAL SYSTEMS THEORY: REVIEW OF GENERAL
FEATURES

SOCIAL SYSTEMS THEORY: THE SOCIAL GROUP
AND THE FAMILY

SUMMARY

GLOSSARY

NOTES

You have been introduced to two opposing ways of viewing and seeking understanding of human behavior: the **individualistic** and the **situated.** The first, and for many people the more familiar of the two, is the individualistic. Here the emphasis is on the person and the factors that account for the regularities in the individual's behavior. It was in Part Two, The Individual, that we reviewed theories based on this approach.

One important part of this approach is personality theory, which focuses on the relatively enduring patterns of behavior exhibited by a person over time and across a range of situations. Often, the person is understood in terms of a developmental process, which stresses the continuity of existence from birth to death. This developmental perspective we refer to as the **ontogenetic** perspective. Ontogenesis refers to the creation of the self. Such an approach emphasizes the themes and processes that make the person unique and identifiable to self and others. Often such models of individual development are organized as a series of stages. Freud had his familiar five stages of psychosexual development, Piaget his stages of cognitive development, Kohlberg his stages of moral development, and Erikson his stages of psychosocial development.[1] Stage models often focus on the fixed, emergent pattern of development, termed *epigenesis*. These models have much to offer students of individual behavior, and their study offers many useful insights to social work practitioners.

The second, or situated, approach views and seeks understanding of human behavior in the context of the social environment. This is the approach taken in this book. As developed in social systems theory, the approach taken at the group and family level has a twin focus: the individual as a member of a social system and the social system itself. In both instances, the focus includes the immediate social situation and *the meanings the person attaches to that social situation.* It is a social psychological, rather than a psychological, view of human and organizational behavior. This view is rooted in the social systems perspective outlined in Chapter 2. To help prepare you for this way of examining behavior, we have introduced several social psychological theories and their principal theorists. We have included field, exchange, and symbolic interaction theory.

While all have been helpful, the theory of symbolic interaction has been particularly useful in our formulation of the distinctive features of social systems theory when applied to the group. In part, this stems from the importance that symbolic interaction theory gives to the immediate situation. By so doing, the theory adds a time dimension to what is meant in social work by human behavior and the social environment.

As viewed by the theory of symbolic interaction and by social systems theory, situations are characterized by their social nature, by their variability, and by the fact that each situation differs in its objective makeup, and more important, in the way the situation is defined by the participants of the group. In short, the process of behaving requires that the person, as a group member, actively define or give meaning to the situation. In this approach, the subjective meaning of situations has as much weight as the objective realities. (This helps account for cultural differences in the way individuals encounter the same objective situations.)

This so-called situated perspective stresses the elastic nature of human behavior, the active, defining role of the mind when applied at the group level. This approach takes as its study the interactional dynamics that occur among people, not the individual him- or herself. It is informed by what sociologists call the fundamental attribution error. This principle states that much of social science tends to place too much emphasis on the importance of the person (personality) and too little emphasis on the situation as it influences human behavior.

THE SOCIAL GROUP AND THE FAMILY

We have included the family as a special form of social group and have distinguished between the social group as a natural/primary group and the myriad types of formed/secondary groups. In introducing social systems theory at the level of the social group, we hold that families are arguably the most crucial of human social organizations, and they, along with other social groups, represent the most elemental form of social organization. Group theory can be viewed as a natural extension of family theory. While there are important limitations on this perspective, indeed, it can be and has been widely asserted that group behavior is in large part a reenactment of family dynamics to which individuals were exposed early in life. Families and groups represent building blocks on which a conception of larger and more complex social organizations can, at least in part, be based.

The survival of our species, it has been noted often, has been assured by our uniquely human capacity for social cooperation that is flexible, adaptive, and complex. Much of this social cooperation is learned within the family. This adaptive capacity takes place within the span of a human life, rather than across generations. These qualities have allowed human beings to overcome major obstacles and threats in the environment, and to compete as a species with others that are faster, more powerful, or possessed of keener senses. Complex and coordinated human interaction represents a distinctive human evolutionary advantage in adapting to constantly changing conditions in the world. Human interaction is different from cooperative behavior in other species. Cooperative behavior in other species is primarily instinctual in nature and is thus far less capable of rapid adaptation to changing conditions that challenge survival of other species. This social cooperation is our most defining human trait.

The distinctive features of social systems theory applied to social groups and families build from the special characteristics of this level of social system. In starting our introduction of the theory, we will review briefly these characteristics. Earlier we offered a simple classification of social organization. Included was the following definition of the social group:

SOCIAL GROUP An exclusive, self-organizing form of social organization of two or more members who identify and interact with one another on a personal basis as individuals, possess a shared sense of the group as a social entity, are affected by the group-related actions of members, and in which expressive (natural) actions dominate.

We identified six characteristics of the social group to be particularly important.

1. *Size.* The minimum group size (two) is specified, but the maximum is not. As a form of social organization, the social group is small. The upper limit in size is constrained by the necessity of person-to-person interactions among group members. If the person-to-person feature is lost, the organization ceases to be a social group in our terms.

To illustrate the complexity of the interaction potential in small groups, consider the following table by Kephart, which enumerates the number of potential interactions (dyads, triads, and so forth) among group members as the size of the social group increases. As the data suggest, the upper limit on the small group size that permits full member interaction is quite low.[2]

GROUP SIZE	POTENTIAL RELATIONSHIPS
2	1
3	6
4	25
5	90
6	301
7	966

2. *Goal structure.* Two principal types of goals are found in all social groups. The first is what group theorists label the **affiliative;** the goal is to belong to and be recognized by others as a group member. In terms of systems theory, think of the affiliative goal structure as essentially the same as a maintenance goal.

The second goal structure is labeled **achievement** by group theorists; the goal is to accomplish some external goal that is held in common by group members. In systems theory, the achievement goal structure is equated with task goals.

The affiliative-oriented social group is characterized by minimum levels of role differentiation. Interaction among members is essentially person-to-person, and as total personalities rather than in terms of tightly partitioned delineations of individuals. As a consequence, the goal structure of the group tends to be implicit rather than explicit. That is, the goals are derived essentially from the needs, such as social belonging and love, of those individuals comprising the group. This type of group is more oriented to internal feedback among members regarding acceptance by others in the group. Structure is more fluid, and rules are often implicit. Leadership is defined by consensus of the group. In terms of the requisite functions, all four will be performed, but pattern-maintenance and integration functions dominate.

Achievement-oriented groups will have somewhat higher levels of role differentiation than do affiliative groups. Leadership roles tend to be more explicit and delineated, and based on expertise in the areas required for goal attainment. Role hierarchies are more explicit, and the patterns of interaction may be more delimited. This type of group goal structure is more oriented to feedback from the suprasystem on goal attainment. This type of social group overlaps with what we have earlier defined as a formed or task group. The goal-attainment and adaptation functions are particularly evident and important in social groups evidencing an achievement goal structure.

3. *Identity.*   All members share a common group identity and perceive the group as a whole. This unity is most clearly expressed by the notion of "we" when reference is made to group-related activities. In addition, the social group has an effect on the selfhood possessed by the individual members. That is, the self-concepts of the members in varying degrees are influenced by membership in the group. Perhaps more than any other theorist, Charles Cooley linked the development of one's personal identity to experience gained within the primary (social) group.[3] Humans are members of many

primary as well as secondary groups. All groups will have some effect on the development and maintenance of a person's identity.

The notion of identity or what is referred to as the selfhood in the theory of symbolic interaction represents a critically important characteristic of this level of social system. We develop this point in social systems theory by holding that the effect on selfhood is always one of the task outcomes of this level of social system.

4. *Effect on individual behavior.*   The social group performs significant socialization as well as social control functions for its members. In short, every social group possesses a distinctive subculture, which includes a normative structure that influences the group-related behavior of its members. The group norms are adopted, in part, by members (internalized) and become a part of the individual's sense of self.

The focus on feedback from the suprasystem makes the achievement-oriented group more tolerant of behavioral diversity, insofar as that diversity contributes to goal attainment. When the goal is belonging, as in the affiliation group, the tolerance for deviance is lower and the pressure for conformity is higher, reflecting the dominance of the pattern-maintenance and integration functions. The famous concept of **deviance credit** is applicable here. Deviance credit refers to a group's tolerance for members' deviation from expected behavior. If a group is goal oriented, such as a basketball team oriented to winning, members who have talents essential to goal achievement may be permitted to deviate. A player with valuable skills may be allowed to skip practice, have orange hair, and ignore coaches. Players of lesser ability will be expected to conform more closely to group norms for behavior.

Some families are focused more on member achievement than others, and such families may grant deviance credit to successful members (success may be in the form of beauty, intelligence, talent, or other qualities). A family oriented to affiliation would be expected to have less openness to deviance, and require conformity in career selection, marital partners, and so forth.

5. *Self-organizing versus external organizing.* In affiliation-oriented groups, the relationships among group members and the resulting interactions have their origins in the internal or natural state of the members. In this sense, social groups are self-organizing. The group-related actions are driven primarily by emotional as opposed to reasoned factors. Thus, relationships in a social group serve as ends in and of themselves as well as the means. This probably sounds complicated, but think of this characteristic in terms of the distinction between Gemeinschaft and Gesellschaft relationships. In their pure form, the relationships among group members are Gemeinschaft—they are entered into and enjoyed for their own sake. In this sense, they are both means and ends. These relationships typically involve the participants across a number of loosely partitioned roles, and are thus concerned with the whole person rather than a person in a limited role. These relationships are characterized as innate, traditional, and informal.

In social systems theory, we incorporate this basic notion by holding that the individual can be understood as both a signal/task input and a maintenance input to the group. Next, the individual as a group member will always represent a key feature of the group's suprasystem in that person's roles outside the group. Finally, the individual group member, as a human personality, will always be a feature of the group's task output.

6. *Exclusiveness.* The concept of Gemeinschaft is also helpful in understanding the exclusiveness characteristic of social groups. These relationships are personal; the need for such relationships arises inside the individual and is part of that person's social nature. Given the power and the time required to sustain such relationships, most people are only involved in a relatively few such groups; the central one for most people is the family or its surrogate. This is not to deny that many people participate in large numbers of formed or secondary groups, they do; but our interest is in the social group and why it is so exclusive and, in relative terms, so powerful in its potential effect on the selfhood of group members.

Earlier we introduced you to the distinction between in-groups and out-groups. The exclusiveness is evidenced in this distinction and in the intensity with which the group sometimes performs the boundary-maintaining function. While thinking about the intensity that is sometimes evident in protecting the group's exclusiveness, remember that an attack on the group can be perceived as a personal attack. An example here would be a man who responds to an insult to his brother as if it were an insult to him directly.

SOCIAL SYSTEMS THEORY: REVIEW OF GENERAL FEATURES

With the previous content serving as background, we will start our discussion with a summary of the general features of social systems theory and thus seek to couple Parts One and Three. Social systems theory is derived from a social systems perspective, which in turn has its conceptual roots in general systems, ecological, functional, and humanistic theory. Using a four-tier approach—(1) perspective, (2) theory, (3) technology, and (4) practice—we link theory to practice in social work. By employing this four-tier approach, we are able to offer a consistent language, set of concepts, and propositions that link theory to practice.

In short, social systems theory seeks to explain well-being. Recall that the purpose of the profession of social work is the advancement of human well-being. Borrowing from general systems theory, we equate steady state with well-being. General systems theory is a theory of order with entropy representing the disordering process and negative entropy the ordering process. Steady state is evidenced by the dominance of the ordering process. Social systems theory holds that all systems will evidence both entropic and negative entropic processes. Social systems are in constant change. As a consequence, some disordering process always occurs in adapting to change while reordering occurs to accommodate change. On balance, to maintain steady state, the ordering process dominates. If the disordering process becomes dominant and irreversible, steady state is lost and the system ceases to exist. Conceptually speaking, there is no final level or ultimate steady state (well-being).

Borrowing from functional theory and the work of Talcott Parsons, steady state depends on the successful performance of four required functions: (1) adaptation, (2) goal attainment, (3) pattern maintenance, and (4) integration.[4] The relationship of the four functional requisites to steady state is depicted in Figure 3.1, Steady State: The Four Functional Requisites. In systems theory, steady state becomes the dependent variable, with two independent variables, goal attainment and integration. In using systems theory as a foundation for generalist social work practice, the challenge is to maintain steady state while advancing social progress.

In the performance of the four requisite functions, eight structures emerge that are common to all social systems. Think of social structures as recurring patterns of behavior on which the interdependence of the parts comprising the system depend. The eight structures are labeled (1) boundary, (2) suprasystem, (3) interface, (4) input, (5) proposed output, (6) conversion operations, (7) output, and (8) feedback.

SOCIAL SYSTEMS THEORY: THE SOCIAL GROUP AND THE FAMILY

In approaching the construction of the theory, we will organize our discussion by the functional requirements and by the eight social structures that emerge in performing these four functions.

The Four Functional Requisites

Figure 10.1, The Social Group/Family: Modeling Steady State, will serve as an introduction to our summary of the part played by the functional requisites. Keep in mind the assumption that all social systems, and thus all social groups, are purposive in their behavior. Simply put, they seek to survive and develop; to do so they must perform the four functional requisites as displayed in Figure 10.1.

The graphic is organized to illustrate how the social group as a social system seeks to achieve, maintain, and advance steady state or the well-being of the group. The rectangle on the far right of the graphic depicts the group's steady state or level of well-being at any point in time. Steady state is a variable. This simply means that it varies from one moment to another. In social systems theory, steady state is the dependent variable, that is, what the theory seeks to explain.

Moving to the left we find the two independent variables—goal attainment and integration. Recall that goal attainment and integration represent end states. Earlier in this chapter we noted that all social groups will evidence two principal types of goal structures, affiliative and achievement. In our construction of social systems theory, achievement goals equate to goal attainment (the task output). Goal attainment is external and refers to needs or conditions existing in other social units external to the group. Conceptually speaking, goal attainment corresponds to the development and maintenance of

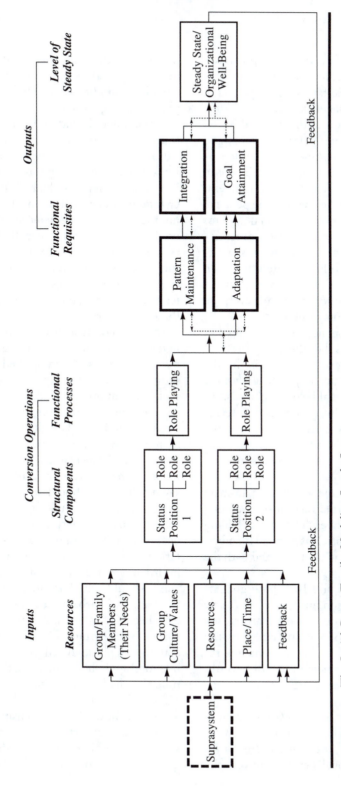

FIGURE 10.1 The Social Group/Family: Modeling Steady State

263

the sense of selfhood of each group member. Recall that each group member has an existence external to the group itself, that is, the person in his or her nongroup member role.

We introduced you to this basic idea earlier while discussing family systems theory and such concepts as enmeshment and codependency. In both instances, problems in group behavior arise that affect the development, maintenance, and enhancement of the personal identity of group members. In social systems theory, there is a constant interplay between social units in the suprasystem and the system itself. Each affects the other. These effects can contribute positively at the group level in the sense of personal autonomy, or the reverse, a loss of personal autonomy (selfhood).

Integration corresponds to what group theorists have described as the affiliative goal structure. These goals have their origin in the internal need states of humans, particularly what Maslow labeled the social belonging needs.[5] In social systems theory, integration is an internal function and is characterized as the state that represents functional coordination and the satisfaction of the needs of the system's internal components.

The optimal outcome sought is an ultimate alignment of the internal relationships among group members, with each member feeling good about her- or himself as a group member, her or his relationship with others, and with the group as a whole.

As indicated in Figure 10.1, both goal attainment and integration must be satisfactorily performed for the group to maintain steady state. Contributing to goal attainment is the adaptation function. It has an instrumental relationship to goal attainment or, in other words, serves as a means—as an instrument to accomplish goal attainment.

For many people the word *adapt* is narrowly defined, being essentially viewed as one way. In other words, *to adapt* essentially means *to get along*. Used in a personal sense, it conveys the notion that the individual needs to change in order to get along with others. An example would be a mother's advice to her son: "Johnny, you are going to have to learn to get along." The point here is that for many people the notion of adaptation suggests that the external situation (suprasystem) is not subject to change; it is taken as a given. From this definition, it is the individual, group, family, and so on, that must change in order to accomplish the fit. This is not the meaning of the concept of adaptation as used in social systems theory. Building from the assumptions in exchange theory, we hold that the system's adaptation actions are proactive; the initial actions focus on the modification of features (other systems) of its suprasystem. If these efforts prove unsuccessful, only then will the system modify its behavior in order to facilitate goal attainment, or, if necessary, change or modify its goals. At an applied level, the assumption is that the adaptive behaviors of most social organizations include changes within and between the organization and other organizations and individuals in its environment. For example, gays and lesbians may identify mainstream social expectations about sexual behavior as being oppressive. Rather than merely saying that they should adapt in order to get along, this model would suggest that proactive steps to change society by social action and education may improve mutual adaptation. Adaptation actions in social groups are typically informal rather than formal. The following example should help illustrate the basic idea.

Sam and Barbara are college students and have been dating for several months; they constitute a social group. They find themselves becoming deeply involved emotionally in their relationship. In both instances, this was the first time they had found themselves so intimately and deeply involved with another person. Both were a bit shaken by the intensity of their relationship and uncertain about what it meant. What they did know was that they wanted to spend as much time with each other as possible.

Complicating their personal relationship was their different religious backgrounds. Barbara came from a devout Catholic family while Sam's family was Methodist. Sam's family was active in their church but would not be considered deeply religious. Sam had relatively little interest in the church and had not attended church regularly since leaving home to go to college.

In contemplating their relationship and its future, Sam suggested to Barbara that she move in with him. Although she and Sam had been having sexual relations, the idea of moving in with Sam came as something of a shock. For Barbara, their sexual relationship was one thing, but living together was quite another. Foremost in her mind was the visibility this would give to their relationship and what her parents would say. After talking about the proposed living arrangement and working through her own feelings, Barbara consented and moved in. Conceptually, we can say the goals of the system included the satisfaction of the couple's respective social belonging and love needs (affiliative goals) and the development of their sense of selfhood (achievement goals). In this connection, they each felt that the relationship was good for them in terms of making them better people—the goal-attainment function.

The problem of adaptation can be treated as the manipulation of the suprasystem in a manner that facilitates goal attainment. Simply put, the problem was getting their respective families (and friends) to accept and be supportive of their relationship and living arrangement. All of the activities that Barbara and Sam engaged in vis-à-vis their respective parents to obtain acceptance of their new relationship would be treated as adaptation. Keep in mind that these activities are occurring with people external to them. We say that these efforts represent performance of the adaptation function.

We have stressed the input/output exchanges each system has with its suprasystem. The situation being confronted by the couple can illustrate this relationship. To develop the

connection between adaptation and input, let us assume that both Sam's and Barbara's parents have been helping them meet the costs of their education. Now, the lack of acceptance of this relationship by either or both sets of parents could affect the money available to meet the couple's living and college expenses (maintenance inputs). Given the above definition, their efforts to gain parental acceptance of their relationship now involve both money and emotional support. If their efforts to solve the problem of adaptation prove unsuccessful (parents' withdrawal of financial support), either Sam or Barbara, or perhaps both, may have to quit school and go to work. The other option would be to heed the position of their parents and again live apart, or, depending on the extent of the pressure, terminate their relationship. In both instances, coping with the adaptation problem will play a key role in dealing with their goal-attainment problem (securing parental acceptance of their relationship is the means for sustaining and developing their personal relationship and their own sense of personal well-being).

The example was selected because it helps illustrate the proactive stance that we attribute to this feature of how a system maintains steady state. The example is not intended to indicate that in each and every group there will be very active efforts made to adapt its environment in terms of facilitating goal attainment; nor does it follow that every group successfully solves the problem of adaptation. The concept identifies an ever-present issue that must be addressed continuously and successfully if the system is to maintain steady state.

Pattern maintenance as depicted in Figure 10.1 is an internal function and has an instrumental relationship to performance of the integration function. Of the four requisite functions, it is the most important. While all four are necessary to maintain steady state, pattern maintenance is the most vulnerable to disruption in successfully performing the integration function. If this occurs, steady state is threatened.

Pattern maintenance as used in theory construction is premised on the assumption that each social system will possess a hierarchy of relationship patterns. These patterns will vary in terms of their relative importance to the preservation and to the development of the system itself.

Just as individuals possess a value system that influences their behavior, so do the groupings that individuals join to form, such as a social group or family. Simply put, selected values will be shared by the members of the group and they support specific behavior patterns. In effect, these values become group values and they in turn will affect interactions between group members and between group and nongroup members. In the latter instances, some of these behaviors between group members and nongroup members would be evident in performing the boundary-maintenance function. Boundary-maintaining behaviors can, in selected instances, be useful in identifying efforts at dealing with the problem of pattern maintenance.

To help illustrate the pattern-maintenance function, we will develop the example involving our couple (the social group) comprised of Barbara and Sam.

Barbara and Sam vowed to each other that the other would be their only sexual partner as long as they were together. The value involved was the rightness of being each other's only sexual partner. This agreement became a shared value and one that they both considered fundamental to their personal relationship and later on to their marriage. In this instance, the pattern-maintenance function would include all of those efforts made by the couple to guard against any violation of this aspect (pattern) of their relationship. Here the assumption is made that this agreement is so important to them that any violation of it would likely result in the inability to successfully accomplish the integration function. "I can't feel good about myself or about us knowing that you slept with _____."

Exchange theory can be useful in conceptualizing the notion of pattern maintenance as a problem to be contended with in helping to successfully accomplish the integration function. In our presentation of the core concepts and assumptions in exchange theory, we identified four processes and likened the first three to stages in group development—transaction, differentiation, and stabilization. You recall that the stabilization phase is evidenced by the presence of mutual trust, shared norms, and the development of legitimate leadership. We hold that a social group, as we have defined it, comes into existence only during the stabilization phase. The earlier stages might be referred to as presocial group status. Finally, we hold that in the formation of the social group, not all of the shared norms or the features of mutual trust are of equal importance or of the same order; these relationship features exist in a hierarchy of relative importance. The norms, trust levels, and leadership forms vary by group and particularly by the goals that guide group behavior. Those norms and their undergirding values deemed central to the pursuit of the group's goals constitute the pattern that must be maintained. The following examples may prove helpful in identifying the notion of core values.

For our neighborhood gang, the Trojans, a core value is that, regardless of the price paid, no Trojan gang member ever "rats" or "narcs" to the police on another member (turns informer). To turn in another group member would constitute the most fundamental violation of trust and would destroy the gang.

A group of high school girls, the Thumpers, vow that no member will ever accept a date from another's boyfriend. Again, to do so would represent a fundamental violation of trust that might well lead to the dissolution of the group itself.

Every social system is comprised of individuals, and so we assume that some level of tension between group and personal goals is inevitable. Just as there is an assumed affinity that draws group members together (performing the integration function, based in part on social belonging needs), so is there an assumed movement in the opposite direction in which members seek greater autonomy and control over their own lives (goal-attainment function). It is useful to think of the pattern-maintenance function as addressing, in part, the tension that inevitably arises between the demands of performing the integration and goal-attainment functions. Successful management of this tension is required to achieve, maintain, and advance steady state.

Moving back to Figure 10.1, it is the performance of the four requisite functions that causes the eight social structures to emerge and to provide stability to the social functioning of the group. These eight structures and their related functions are depicted under the heading of *Conversion Operations* and would be evident in the two status positions and their associated roles. The performance of role is labeled *Role Playing*. Our attempt in this graphic is to depict a generic social group. For example, position 1 could be represented by Barbara and position 2 by Sam. Only these roles are included to help illustrate the idea that in social groups there tends to be little role differentiation. For example, role 1 in each case might include being each other's best friend. Accordingly, each role would include those norms associated with behaviors of a best friend, for example, being supportive when the other is upset. Role 2 might be being the other's exclusive sexual partner and role 3 being the other's study partner.

The features or norms of these respective roles would include the eight social structures. As an example of boundary maintenance, both Sam and Barbara would avoid any activity that might pose a threat to their relationship, making it clear to an admirer that he or she is involved with somebody else and would not have any interest in having dinner with them.

On the far left in Figure 10.1 are the inputs that exist in the suprasystem. The primary inputs are the individuals in their respective group roles. Fundamental to the social group is the characteristic that those comprising the group are considered both signal/task and maintenance inputs. We will be developing this characteristic when we discuss the eight structural components of the social group.

The Structural Concepts

In Figure 10.2, we model the structural concepts comprising social systems theory. For purposes of illustration, the two persons comprising the social group are Barbara and Sam. The two occupy the status position of spouse in the Jones family. Our interest is to convey a generic presentation of the model. We will be using several different examples in modeling the social group, but will rely principally on the Joneses.

Boundary.   The outer, heavy broken line of Figure 10.2 is labeled *Boundary*. Those people inside the boundary comprise the system, Barbara and Sam. Those individuals, groups, agencies, and so on, that are external but that affect the system's output and input exchanges represent its suprasystem. Unlike the shell of a chicken's egg or the skin of a human, the boundaries of a social system cannot be seen, touched, heard, felt, or otherwise discerned by the human senses. This should remind us that, unlike the shell of an egg, groups and their boundaries do not have a physical existence. Boundary is a concept and pertains to patterned social behaviors, those that bind the members of the system together; boundaries also have the particular function of controlling input/output exchanges between the system and its suprasystem. The distinguishing feature of the social group's boundary is the informal, Gemeinschaft qualities of boundary-maintaining behaviors.

One way of conceptualizing boundaries is that the pattern of transactions that occurs within boundaries is different from the pattern

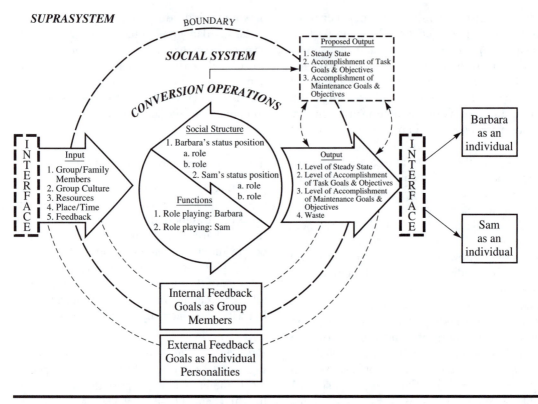

FIGURE 10.2   Modeling Social Systems Theory: The Social Group and Family

that occurs across boundaries. Thus, while the boundaries are invisible, they can be detected. For example, if you visit someone's home, the pattern of behavior in most cases is that you will be treated as a visitor, that is, differently from a family member. If someone asks if you would like something to drink, you know you are a guest. Over time, you are expected to go to the refrigerator and get something if you want it. In that case, you have crossed the boundary and are treated, in a limited way, as part of the family. For this reason, social work home visits, repeated over time, provide a much better insight into how a family really operates, since they incorporate the worker's presence into a more natural family maintenance pattern.

In our definition of a social group, we indicated that group members possessed a shared

sense of the group as a social entity. This shared sense of the group is essentially what we mean by boundary. It represents a state of consciousness of the other members of the group—their needs, their interests, and the importance of this association to all members.

Now to our example of the Joneses. Barbara and Sam are now married. One of the dilemmas faced by Barbara was whether or not to take Sam's family name of Jones rather than to keep her own family name of West. On the one hand, she was very proud of her family name; on the other, she wanted to share everything with Sam including his name. After discussing the matter at length with Sam and her parents, she decided to take Sam's family name.

This decision concerned boundary issues and how Barbara wished to deal with the newly created social system. While there were pros and cons, the couple decided they wanted to be known as Barbara and Sam Jones. Her adoption of Sam's family name was a clear social signal that they were now "one" as a family. Barbara's name change could be interpreted as the sign of a significant movement away from a family of origin to a new primary identity, thus in some ways blurring the role she now occupies in her family of origin.

It should also be noted that boundary maintenance can involve the use of a variety of physical structures, symbols, and actions as well as verbal and written forms of communication. The key is the social meaning attached to these. An example is the exchange of rings in a traditional marriage ceremony. The ring, an unending circle, conveys the notion of oneness, that a new family has been created. The ring is usually made of gold or some other precious metal. Symbolically, the preciousness of the ring stands for the preciousness of the new relationship that has been formed. Wedding rings, by reason of the cultural meanings attached, can be viewed in this model as serving a boundary function. When worn on the third finger of the left hand, it indicates to others that the person wearing the ring is married.

Is boundary something real? Is it important? How does the concept of boundary get linked to the socialization process and the notion described in an earlier chapter of in- and out-groups?

Think of a playground situation at the start of school. A young, mentally disabled child is being mainstreamed. That is, the child is attending regular classes as opposed to being in a special class with other children with similar disabilities. Our child, Art, approaches a group of children in his class, wanting to join their play. Noticing the approach, one youngster yells to his friends, "Hey, here comes the dummy!" Given this beginning definition of a situation, the chances are that Art will be taunted and otherwise excluded from this group—"he is not one of us" (Art is not an in-group member).

The behavior of the play group toward an outsider is an all-too-familiar but negative example of boundary maintenance. Is it important? We believe so; certainly if the social group is deemed to be fundamental in the development of selfhood, its dynamics need to be understood and its practice relevance considered.

Given this proposition, consider the impact over time on the development of a sense of self of this child who is being called dummy or worse in situation after situation. In this connection, the proposition associated with symbolic interaction theory takes on special meaning—"I am what I think you think I am." Many similar examples could be cited such as those involving racism, sexism, and other forms of discrimination. But the main point has been made: boundary is evident only in social behavior, and these behaviors distinguish insiders from outsiders. One difficulty with the above example should be emphasized: it deals with a negative set of behaviors. Boundary maintenance is crucial to the survival of any form of social organization; in short—no boundary, no organization. Therefore, every social system possesses a boundary and engages in boundary-maintenance behaviors.

In our earlier example, Barbara's name change could be seen as a positive step in establishing her married identity and creating new family boundaries—at the same time that it is a loss for the family of origin. The old saying, often repeated at weddings, is thus revealed in systems terms: "You are not losing a daughter, you are gaining a son." The multiple impacts on systems' boundaries, positive and negative, are apparent in the ambivalence of the axiom.

With the above as background, let us proceed with a discussion of boundary and its characteristics. Boundary should always be considered a form of social behavior basically aimed at preserving the integrity of the group. A social group's integrity or essential identity is maintained largely by controlling input and output exchanges. Every group has a normative structure that affects the behaviors of its members. That aspect of the normative structure that pertains to the control of input and output exchanges represents boundary. Earlier the point was made that every social organization develops its own subculture. One aspect of this subculture is how its boundaries are defined and maintained; that is, how the key relationships among its member units (individuals in the social group) are handled. This aspect of the normative structure in a social group is played out in the roles people enact both with respect to group and nongroup members, for example, children at play.

At a practical and applied level, almost every social organization has a name—the Joneses, the Rat Pack, the Trojans, or whatever. The specification of boundary in any application of the model usually starts with the group's name. Simply put, all people holding membership, formally or informally, in the group are insiders; all others are outsiders. Basically, the group-related behaviors that insiders have with or pertaining to outsiders are generally boundary-maintenance behaviors.

Suprasystem. Conceptually, the notion of suprasystem is used to operationalize the position that every social organization with system properties has vital and ongoing relationships with selected organizations, agencies, and individuals in its environment. The concept of suprasystem is used to operationalize the relevant open-system properties of the theory. It is roughly comparable to the notion of social environment, as in the phrase *human behavior and the social environment.*

Given that the member units of social groups are individuals (as opposed to groups of individuals), the suprasystem of the social group always includes other social groups to which the members belong, as well as the members in their nongroup member roles.

To illustrate this point, Barbara is a member of a number of other social groups, including her family of origin—her mother, father, a sister, and a brother. To understand the Joneses as a social group requires some understanding of how the Joneses relate to other social groups that include Barbara and Sam as members.

Since social groups tend to be informally organized (the legal state of marriage represents a formal contract, but even here the relationships among family members tend not to be formally specified), their suprasystem relationships also tend to be informal. For example, Barbara and Sam alternate spending Christmas with their respective families, Barbara's parents one year and Sam's parents the next. While such suprasystem relationships are not formally specified by a legal contract, they are no less firm and binding for the groups involved. For example, if Sam has a conflict between a planned overseas business trip and spending Christmas with Barbara and her family, the chances are that he is going to be confronted with a real dilemma.

In Figure 10.3, we present an **ecomap** depicting the suprasystem of the Joneses.[6] This figure builds from Figure 10.2 by specifying the system-suprasystem relationships of the Joneses beyond just Barbara and Sam as individuals. In the center is our system and surrounding it are the key people, groups, and organizations that include Barbara and Sam as individuals outside their spousal positions and that have an impact on the behavior of the Joneses. The thickness of the connecting line designates the relative importance to the lives of the Joneses at a given point in time. Arrows also move in both directions suggesting the mutual effects these systems have on each other.

The figure is a composite portrayal of the components of the Joneses' suprasystem. As will be noted in our next section, the influences of these other systems will vary depending on the cycle of activity being examined. For example, in one cycle perhaps only a few suprasystem influences will be operative. The remaining units of the suprasystem, in a sense, will be dormant.

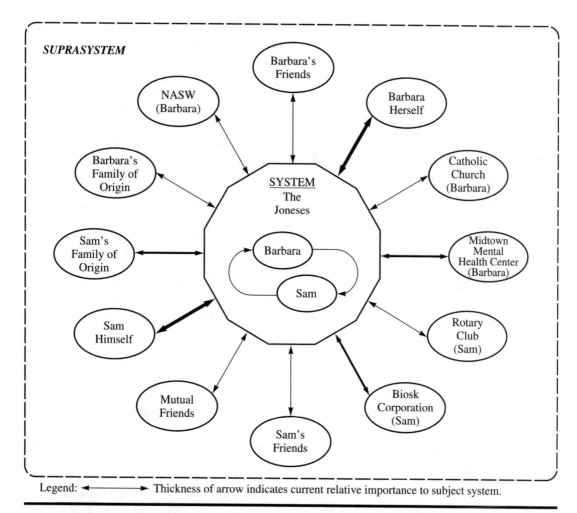

Legend: ◄─────► Thickness of arrow indicates current relative importance to subject system.

FIGURE 10.3   Ecomap: The Joneses

In our example involving the conflict between a Christmas trip to Barbara's parents and Sam's business trip, only two aspects of their suprasystem are directly involved. Here, leading in importance is Barbara's family of origin and the Biosk Corporation, Sam's employer. The remaining systems are essentially dormant in terms of their influence on the Joneses in this episode of their life.

Interface.   Technically, interface refers to a boundary segment that a system shares with another system comprising a portion of its suprasystem. Operationally, think of interface as representing a set of mutual understandings held by two or more systems that guide their interactions with one another. The social group is characterized by the dominance of Gemeinschaft over Gesellschaft relationships. Similarly, these Gemeinschaft qualities of relationships are evidenced in interface.

We will develop these features with our family the Joneses. Barbara's parents are June and Phil West, and Sam's, Verna and Todd

Jones. While the relationship among the three families has been cordial, Barbara has felt that she has never been fully accepted by Sam's parents, particularly by his mother, Verna. Sam and his mother have always been very close, and Barbara has surmised that Verna has felt that no woman was quite good enough for her Sam. The two sets of parents represent key parts of Barbara and Sam's suprasystem. Conceptually, the common understandings shared by Barbara and Sam as to their relationship with each of their parents is characterized by the term *interface*. These interfaces are distinctive, representative of the nature of the functional ties between the Joneses and their two sets of families. Using concepts drawn from symbolic interaction theory, the interface is evident in the particular spousal positions Barbara and Sam play when dealing with their two sets of parents.

Every other year, Barbara and Sam spend Christmas with Sam's folks; the alternate year it is with Barbara's parents. Since Sam's folks live some distance away, they usually spend two days together. For reasons stated earlier, Barbara feels that "two days are all I can take." Barbara and Sam have reached mutual agreement on alternating Christmas between the two sets of parents, a feature of the interface. They have also agreed on major aspects of their respective roles, especially as to how they are carried out when they visit Sam's parents. While Barbara would much prefer that she and Sam stay overnight at a local motel, she has agreed that they stay in his folks' spare room. Sam feels to do otherwise would hurt his parents' feelings. What Barbara finds particularly annoying during these visits is that Sam's mother waits on him hand and foot. She is convinced that Sam's lack of help to her in the kitchen is a direct result of the way his mother brought him up. To deal with some of these concerns, Sam has agreed that he will be particularly attentive to Barbara's feelings and needs during these visits. Barbara once observed to a friend, "The first time we visited I felt like an idiot; Sam spent most of his time with his mother, he acted like

I wasn't even there. I told him later he had better treat me like his wife or I would never darken their door again."

In this example, we have identified critical features of interface. The common boundary described was the one linking Barbara and Sam to his family. The interface is represented by selected features of the relationship between the two groups. Included would be the frequency of visits, living arrangements while they are there, and how the two families relate to each other. Both Sam and Barbara are close to their respective families and vice versa. The ties that they maintain with their respective families are intended to be supportive of these relationships on the one hand, but not so intense as to be disruptive of the relationship that Barbara and Sam have with each other. In a sense, the interface represents a kind of compromise, one that maintains and enhances their respective relationships with their families of origin, but also enhances their own relationship as husband and wife.

On one visit, in Barbara's presence, Sam posed the following question to his mother, "Look, Mom, next year why don't you and Dad spend Christmas with us? We will invite Barbara's folks and we can all have Christmas together. Our house has plenty of room and you and Dad have always enjoyed Barbara's parents. I think it would be a great idea." In this instance, and for quite different reasons, neither Barbara nor Verna thought it a great idea. While not mentioning it at the time, Barbara was furious that Sam had raised the issue without consulting her in advance. Simply put, Sam's idea presented a major change in the interface joining the Joneses with their respective families. Barbara was also quite sure her parents would not like the arrangement, but the day was saved when Verna replied, "Sammy, that is a good idea, but you know it really wouldn't be the same. When you're here, it's just like old times. You know, we have spent an awful lot of Christmases together in this old house!"

The above exchange highlights an important characteristic of an interface—the preservation of relationships both within and between the subject systems. In our example, it is clear that Sam's parents consider the Christmas visit by their son and his wife a special time and one they look forward to. Somehow a change in which they would share this visit with Barbara's parents in their son's home simply would not be the same.

Figure 10.4 charts the system-suprasystem relationships in this cycle. The large circle connected by an interface with the Joneses is the senior Jones family comprised of Sam's parents, Verna and Todd. In this episode, Barbara's parents, while not physically present, affected in part the outcome of this cycle, the decision to continue the alternating visits to the two sets of parents at Christmas.

In this section, we have attempted to highlight the Gemeinschaft nature of group behaviors and their meanings as evident in interface. Such behaviors are not to be understood in terms of their logic but by the emotional and

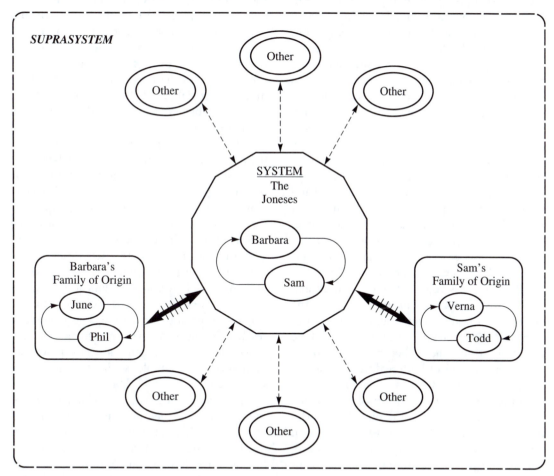

FIGURE 10.4   Ecomap Interface: The Joneses

personal meanings that they represent. The derivation of these behaviors is to be found in an underlying order; the behaviors are to be understood in terms of the related goals of the subject system.

Holon.   It is useful to review the concept of holon again in the context of group interfaces. Recall that holons are elements of a system that address inner and outer considerations. Each member of a group, including the social work facilitator, is constantly juggling internal group process and the client's roles in outside systems.

For example, think of a woman who goes to a support group to deal with issues about her husband's alcoholism. Inside the group, we hope and expect that she feels accepted, safe, and supported. Ideas and suggestions are offered, the experiences of others are shared and examined, and plans are made. As soon as the woman leaves the group, it is common to experience a rapid evaporation of the feelings of confidence and support. She returns home, finds that her husband is drunk, and the plans, confidence, and optimism she experienced in the group are gone. When she next returns to the group, she is disheartened. She begins to feel that she was kidding herself in her earlier optimism. Helplessness and hopelessness return. Each trip back and forth across the group interface confronts the client with the differences between the outer world of her marriage and the inner world of the group. In time, she either reconciles those worlds or exits one or both realities.

A worker who focuses on here and now group process to the exclusion of the outside world or who focuses on the outside world to the extent that the necessary trust and optimism never develop in the group will not succeed. The holonic perspective must remain a constant presence as we seek to accurately enter the world of our clients while creating a safe world to create and test solutions.

Input.   Inputs are always derived from the suprasystem and are classified in this model as being either maintenance or signal. Maintenance inputs are those that energize and operate the system, while signal inputs are processed by the system, resulting in its task output. The distinctive feature of input when applied to the social group is that group members always represent both maintenance and signal inputs. The reason is found in the Gemeinschaft nature of a relationship between group members; that is, the relationship serves as both a means and an end in itself. To restate the point, people become members of social groups because they enjoy one another's company, not just as a means to accomplish some other end. The group becomes the means by which members meet their social needs; the satisfaction of these needs then becomes the desired end state for group members.

Barbara and Sam met while in college, fell in love, and married. Barbara and Sam both represent input in the creation and continuance of the social group known as the Joneses. Conceptually, they represent maintenance inputs in their spousal positions because their spousal relationship constitutes the group. Their love, support, and attention to each other builds (maintains) the group. Similarly, in the absence of their mutual love, support, and attention, the group will weaken and perhaps dissolve, for example, in separation or divorce. The group represents the means by which Barbara and Sam satisfy many of each other's needs as well as their own, for example, social belonging and self-esteem.

Importantly, Barbara and Sam have an existence outside of their marriage as autonomous personalities. Recall that in symbolic interaction theory, selfhood is viewed as a lifelong process. In this sense, Barbara and Sam brought their own sense of selfhood into their marriage. Because of the importance of this relationship, their sense of selfhood is constantly being affected by their interactions with each other. Conceptually, think of the self as existing in large part outside of the group but being acted on by experiences within the group.

In using this way of modeling social systems theory, it is important to conceive of inputs occurring constantly, rather than at one point in time, for example, at the time of group formation. When systems are in an active mode, the concept of inputs represents the continuous process of infusion of information and resources from the suprasystem. Social organizations operate in cycles or through series of interconnected events; also, at times social organizations are dormant, for example when Barbara and Sam are in their work roles.

While developing the concept of interface, we described an episode in the lives of Barbara and Sam during which they were spending Christmas with Sam's parents. This episode was treated as a cycle in the life of this family. Utilizing symbolic interaction theory, both Barbara and Sam entered that cycle with a conception of themselves in their spousal role (a maintenance input). Recall Barbara's later remark to a friend, "The first time we visited I felt like an idiot; Sam spent most of his time with his mother, he acted like I wasn't even there. I told him later that he had better treat me like his wife or I would never darken their door again." Her description describes essentially a negative effect on her sense of selfhood attributed to that visit. This statement represents a task output of this cycle, an effect on her self-esteem. In this example, we are illustrating the reciprocal effects that the group has on the individuals as separate and distinct personalities. The reverse is also true as any person can attest who has had a bad day at work and comes home and takes it out on the family.

To develop this cyclical notion, consider the effect of paydays on family behavior. The money Barbara and Sam earn and apply jointly to meet family expenses would be treated as a mainte-

nance input (the money they retain for themselves would not). The so-called family money is used to purchase food, pay the rent, and for a host of other family purposes. Whether Barbara and Sam are paid weekly, bimonthly, or monthly, there is a cycle of activity associated with the receipt and dispersal of this money. The example of a paycheck is helpful because for most people it illustrates the concept of treating input as a resource that helps to energize and sustain a system during a cycle of activity. As with all forms of maintenance inputs, the amount of money devoted to the system is a critical determinant of system behaviors.

Suppose Barbara and Sam want to purchase their own home. As a consequence of adopting this goal, they will most likely budget their money so they can save a portion of their income in order to make the necessary down payment. The point is that there will always be a critical relationship between a system's inputs and its outputs. In the case of money, the Joneses will learn that they cannot pay out more than they take in without experiencing some difficulties. The systems model incorporates this point—there will always be a relative balance between a system's inputs and its outputs. If this balance is upset, a threat is posed to the performance of the four requisite functions and thus to steady state.

Earlier we made the point that in modeling the social group, the individual group members represent both maintenance and signal forms of input. If either Barbara or Sam fails in providing the maintenance inputs, their marriage will start experiencing difficulties. The familiar saying "You can't get something for nothing" is relevant when applied to any form of input. Exchange, field, and need theories can help in further developing this point.

For purposes of the example, let us say that both Barbara and Sam depend on each other primarily for satisfaction of their social belonging and love needs. Their marriage and their sense of relationship with each other is the means for achieving this satisfaction.

Barbara now finds herself being considered for a supervisory position at her agency. She is delighted at the prospects of this promotion, as is Sam. In the pursuit of the promotion, she spends increasing amounts of time on the job, brings work home, takes on more work-related committee assignments. From a field theory perspective,[7] her work-related activities have taken on greater importance vis-à-vis other activities as she pursues the goal of a promotion. Similarly, there is a reduction in the amount of time, energy, and related maintenance inputs that Barbara provides to her marriage (reduction in the relative importance of activities devoted to family goals). Unless there is a redefinition of what Barbara and Sam expect from each other in the marriage, problems will arise between the two. From an exchange theory perspective, both are providing something the other needs, and in so doing are satisfying their own needs. If the exchange becomes unbalanced, difficulties will arise. Here, the norm of distributive justice, as we employed the concept in our discussion of exchange theory, is useful.[8] If in their exchange relationship Sam believes that the unbalanced nature of the exchange is temporary and that in the longer term both he and Barbara will benefit (that is, Barbara's promotion will hasten the time when they can buy their home), their relationship will not be adversely affected.

The central point developed in this example is the assumed relationship between inputs and outputs. The example has also been developed to highlight the position that inputs are always derived from the suprasystem. The most complicated point has to do with the individuals comprising social groups representing both signal and maintenance forms of input. In this latter instance and in our example, if Sam continues not having his needs met by Barbara, it can be predicted that his contributions to the marriage will be diminished (reduced inputs).

There is a spiral-like phenomenon created between inputs and outputs that will pose a threat to the system. It should be noted that if Barbara and Sam have their needs fully satisfied (task outputs), they can be expected to put more of themselves into the marriage (increase in maintenance inputs).

Proposed Output. The concept of proposed output refers to the system's goal structure. It represents an approach to the operationalization of a system's purposes. We have already identified two of the most distinctive features of social groups: first, the Gemeinschaft nature of relationships among group members, and second, and linked to the first, that the individuals holding membership in the group comprise both its maintenance and its task inputs and outputs. More specifically, the individual's anticipated role performance within the group constitutes the maintenance input. The signal input is the individual as an autonomous personality. The proposed task output is the person's sense of self that is expected to result from the group experience. Proposed maintenance outputs are represented by an expected future state of the system itself.

We will develop an example using Barbara and Sam to help explain the notion of proposed output. When the couple was contemplating their future relationship, Sam said, "Barbara, marrying you would make me the happiest man on earth." Conceptually speaking, Sam is contemplating a future sense of selfhood, one that will result in part from his relationship with Barbara. This family, as viewed by this model, is a separate and distinct social entity. But so are Barbara and Sam separate and distinct human personalities. Only a part of their lives are spent in their respective family roles; each plays many other roles in many other systems, for example, Barbara in her role as a social worker. In everyday language and in everyday occurrences, we recognize and distinguish between ourselves and the various roles we play. In terms of means and ends, Sam's remark treated his relationship with Barbara as the means and the end state, his own happiness. Implicit in his remark would be the same end state for Barbara, to become the happiest woman on earth. In both instances, the means of becoming the happiest man and woman is represented by their relationship as husband and wife.

Proposed maintenance outputs pertain to the future status of their relationship as members of the Jones family. The marriage vows that Barbara and Sam took contain statements of proposed maintenance outcomes, for example, that they will remain married "until death do us part." Proposed is a lifetime relationship as husband and wife. While this is a proposed goal, it does not follow that proposed and actual outputs are always the same. Nevertheless, this mutually held goal should shape the kind of relationship that develops.

In the earlier sections dealing with input, reference was made to money as another form of maintenance input. The money earned by Barbara and Sam that was jointly held and used for family purposes would indeed be considered a maintenance input. If Barbara and Sam should establish an objective of buying a house, this would represent a proposed maintenance output. Here we make the assumption that the purchase of the home will serve to strengthen family relationships. The key to the classification is the purpose served by the money.

Before closing our discussion of proposed output and moving on to conversion operations, we remind you to keep in mind that proposed output always pertains to a cycle of activity. The cycle can be very short—a day, an hour, or less; the cycle can also be very long—a lifetime. Proposed output is always related to the end state of a cycle. Finally and because of their Gemeinschaft features, proposed outputs are not usually formalized as a hierarchy of outcomes. This does not mean that the people comprising a group may not mutually hold very specific objectives. An example would be a decision by Barbara and Sam to save enough money to buy their own home by their third wedding anniversary. This was a logically reasoned decision by the couple. In a sense, it was a businesslike decision based on income and tax considerations. Each payday they systematically deposit money in a savings account to be used for their down payment. Both the objective and the actions in pursuit of the objectives serve as an example of Gesellschaft features of a social relationship that is primarily Gemeinschaft in nature.

Conversion Operations.   In short, the concept of conversion operations designates how inputs are converted to outputs, no small task when you are theorizing about how social systems work. The approach we use involves two other concepts: structure and interactions (sometimes referred to as functions). The notion of structure merely implies the existence of an understandable order, the regularities characterizing the behaviors of all forms of social organization. As used in this model, structure is always anticipatory, it is never actual behavior. In contrast, interactions are the actual social behaviors of individuals acting as members of social organizations, for example, a family. Beyond the basic configurations and assumptions that comprise the model, it is the model user that selects appropriate narrower-range theories and related knowledge sources for specific applications.

Structure.   Roles are always the dominant structural feature in any application of systems theory. Given that social groups are characterized by Gemeinschaft relationships, the portrayal of these role relationships diagrammatically is difficult. However, important efforts have been made in measuring and depicting these social relationships. The general approach is known as **sociometry** and the actual graphical representation of these relationships is called a **sociogram**.[9]

Another useful approach for depicting structure in families is the **genogram.**[10] Here the focus is on kinship relationships both within the system and between the system and those kinship relations that comprise parts of what we designate as the suprasystem.

We can show these relationships by using the Joneses. To help develop this aspect of structure, we are going to pick up with the Joneses a little later in their marriage; now they have a daughter, Ann, who is three months old. Figure 10.5 displays a genogram of the Jones family. Our subject system is comprised of Sam, Barbara, and their daughter, Ann. Both sets of parents and grandparents are shown along with other family members.

As indicated by the legend, a square denotes a male, for example, Sam and a circle, a female, for example, Barbara. The horizontal line connecting a square and a circle indicates a marital relationship and the date of marriage, such as 6-15-84. The vertical line that descends from the couple indicates children of that marriage, for example, Ann. A crossed-out circle or a square indicates that the person named is deceased; an example is Todd's mother, Rose. The age shown, 73, was her age at death.

The genogram is not only a useful way of depicting the structural/kinship relationships within families, but it also has many helpful applications to social work practice by the generalist and the advanced practitioner working with families. In short, it presents a summary of important information on kinship relationships, ages, marital status, and so forth, to be used as a reference as well as a discussion guide for the practitioner and family members. It is important to note here that the structure implied by genograms may sometimes be illusory: the individuals who occupy roles are important, but at times in families, the various roles may be filled by other persons, either on a permanent or temporary basis. Likewise, the genogram suggests a stability not always evident in the dynamic flow of families; thus, more fluid models of family process may be useful in addition to this particular view of family structure.

This genogram provides much more information on the Joneses. With the birth of Ann, our social system has become more structurally differentiated. The system now has three subsystems: (1) Barbara and Sam in their spousal roles; (2) Barbara and Ann in the maternal parent and child roles; and (3) Sam and Ann in the paternal parent and child roles. To help to keep the structure from becoming unnecessarily complicated, we will consider Barbara's location in this social system as her status position. This position is made up of two major roles, wife and mother. Similarly, Sam's status position is comprised of two major roles, husband and father. For our immediate purposes, Ann's status position and role are one and the same, daughter. Figure 10.6 structurally portrays the Joneses as a social system with three associated subsystems.

We have stressed in our discussion that group-related experiences are fundamental in the development of selfhood. Similarly, one's sense of selfhood is constantly changing, constantly developing; selfhood is a process, and for most people vitally related to the family roles they play. Figure 10.6 is helpful in developing this point because it illustrates the evolving nature of the group. Until the birth of Ann, Barbara and Sam related to each other within their own family system only in their spousal roles. Now with the addition of the new family member, Ann, new family roles are taken. Life will not be the same for Barbara and Sam with the addition of their parenting roles. As a consequence, their own sense of selfhood will be different. Being a parent is now a vital part of their own sense of who they are and an important aspect of their interactions with each other in their family system.

In some ways, assuming a new role is like putting on a new suit of clothes, sometimes it takes a while to get used to oneself in this new outfit. For many, the transition is an easy and a natural one. For others, it is less so, and some

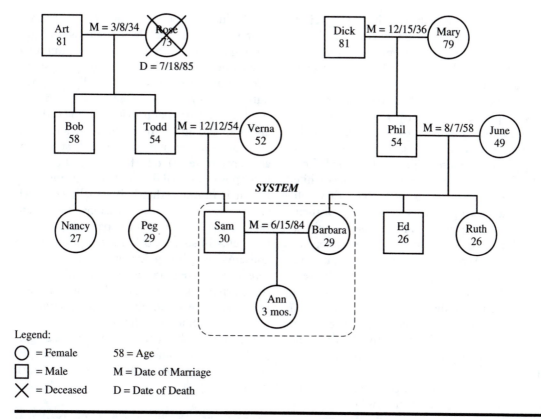

Legend:

◯ = Female   58 = Age
▢ = Male   M = Date of Marriage
✕ = Deceased   D = Date of Death

FIGURE 10.5   Genogram: The Joneses

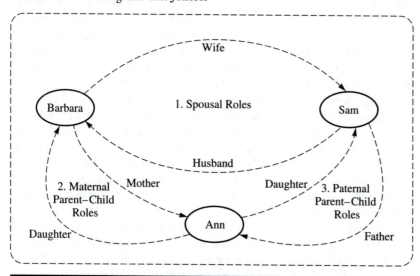

FIGURE 10.6   The Jones Family: Subsystems

are never able to make the transition; they reject the role. Roles exist independent of individuals. An example of this is the parental role. It is a societal role for which normative performance standards exist.

When Barbara and Sam became parents, they simply assumed their parental roles in relation to Ann. Both had their own ideas not only of their own parental roles, but of the parental role of their spouse. They had learned their roles from their own parents and others while growing up. In enacting these roles, they will judge their own performance and that of their spouse by these standards. For example, Barbara may think, "Sam is an awfully good father, he dearly loves Ann. We take turns getting up and feeding Ann and changing her diapers. It's a real partnership." Sam's sense of himself is going to be impacted not only by his own perceptions of his role performance but by the perceptions of those close to him who make their own judgments as to what kind of father he is, for example, Barbara.

Symbolic interaction theory, particularly its attention to the idea of situation, is helpful in understanding the structural features of the conversion operations. Recall that situation is the immediate social/environmental context in which role enactments take place. In our use of the term, the situation is essentially synonymous with what we mean by structure. Here *context* includes not only the other individuals in their respective roles, but time, space, and all of the environmental features that shape the perceptions of those who are enacting roles in a given interaction. For example, Barbara and Sam as human personalities will bring these parts (structural features) of themselves into any cycle of activity, say, having dinner together. Also shaping this situation is the amount of time they have for dinner, whether it is rushed or leisurely, whether it takes place in their own home or a restaurant, whether their dinner spaces are cramped or comfortable, clean or dirty, drab or attractive, and so on. All such situational features will affect role enactment.

Included in our conception of structure is proposed output. While for purposes of presenting the model we treat proposed output as a separate concept, it is a part of the system's conversion operations. Technically, proposed output or, more simply, goals are always the desired future state that provides for the ordering and sequencing of interactions in any given cycle of a social group. More simply stated, the assumption we make is that all social behavior is purposive or goal directed. This is not to say that it is rational, that it is socially acknowledged, or even that it is conscious. The intentional nature of social behavior is often denied by clients in social work practice, even as the consequences disrupt system balance. Therefore, every cycle of group activity will evidence this purposiveness. In turn, the purposiveness will shape the definition of the situation in which the interaction will take place. In our use of the Joneses, the goal of a cycle can be as simple as having breakfast together or as complicated and long term as living together "until death do us part."

Interactions.   Earlier we had observed that social structures cannot be seen, touched, heard, tasted, or smelled. These structures exist in the minds of people and represent their perceptions of how they are to act in any specific interactional situation. Interactions, on the other hand, are the functional behaviors that people engage in with one another. Interactions evidence structure and can be seen, heard, felt, tasted, and smelled. In other words, we see one another; we interpret gestures and body language; we hear what others say to us; we embrace, kiss, and touch one another. Through our senses we derive the meaning that shapes our development of self and our view of others.

The model user knows that the actual behavior of a social group via the behaviors of those who comprise it will never conform exactly to its structure. Why? In the first place, structure is retrospective; it exists in the minds of people and pertains to their perception of who they are, their sense of selfhood. This sense of self includes all the roles they are called on to play and how these roles are to be enacted. Second, the individual also holds in his or her own mind, expectations of how counter roles are to be played. In real life, most of this behavior is spontaneous and flows naturally like the waters of a stream following the contours of the stream bed. Importantly though, the stream bed (structure) is constantly changing as the water flows through it (interactions). The metaphor of the stream bed is also helpful in conveying the interaction between the channels that guide the flow of water and the water itself—each acts on the other, each is influenced by the other.

Conceptually it is helpful to equate interactions with symbolic interactions.[11] To develop the point, we will use our social group, the Joneses. A simple example would be the goal the Joneses have of buying a home (a proposed maintenance output of this system). Each payday, Barbara deposits $400 of her check into a joint savings account. This money will ultimately be used for a down payment on their house. This action on Barbara's part stems from the previously stated goal. Further, her role as wife now incorporates the expectation that she make this monthly deposit. The role change stems from the newly adopted goal and serves as a guide to her behavior as well as that of Sam, who may ask, for example, "Barbara, how much do we have in the bank now?" This statement incorporates the notion of symbolic interaction in the sense that Barbara and Sam have comparable meanings attached to such questions about the savings account. Another way of stating this shared meaning would be by saying, "How much money do we have toward the down payment on our home?"

A more complex set of interactions would be those directed toward their mutual goal of self-actualization. This goal, unlike the house, is likely to remain a goal as long as this social group (marriage) is intact. Earlier the point was made that Barbara and Sam are the most important people in each other's lives. As a consequence, each makes a contribution to the self-actualization of the other. Given their importance to each other, their actual interactions are likely to contribute to and distract from the goal.

An example of interactions associated with their mutual goal of self-actualization might be that Friday night Barbara and Sam set aside time just for each other (structure). One Friday, Sam arrives home with a dozen roses. Barbara is taken aback and asks, "What is the occasion?" His reply: "You are; it is just a reminder of what a wonderful wife and mother you are. I am probably the luckiest man in the world." The interaction includes the purchase and presentation of the roses to Barbara as well as her statement. For both Barbara and Sam, red roses are symbolic of their mutual love (Sam has been surprising Barbara with red roses throughout their marriage). The feelings engendered by this interaction make Barbara feel very good about herself, Sam, Ann, and their marriage.

This example can be useful when viewed as a social act, a cycle of activity occurring between Barbara and Sam. The goal of this cycle is the reaffirmation of their love for each other and their own sense of selfhood. The cycle is diagrammed in Figure 10.7.

Recall that in symbolic interaction theory, the social act is treated as the smallest interactional unit identifiable in an ongoing relationship. It will always involve at least two or more people, and although not necessarily made explicit, it will have a purpose, a beginning, and an end. The selection and the analysis of the social act is simply an approach to the study of the stream of human interaction that typifies the behavior of any given individual or social group. If the focus is on an individual, that person will be affected by a variety of different groups of which she or he is a member. If the focus is on the group, the group itself will change and develop over time as the relationships among its members change and develop.

Purpose: To reaffirm marital relationship

Beginning: Message sent by Sam

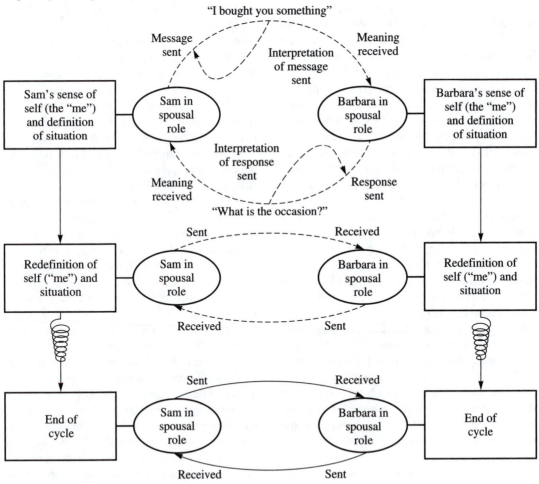

Ending Point: Sleep following sexual relations

FIGURE 10.7 The Social Act: The Joneses

This episode is about five hours in length and primarily involves Barbara and Sam. Ann is only incidentally involved but her involvement is shaped by the goal of the episode, the reaffirmation of the love that Barbara and Sam have for each other. The effects of this love are the esteem and support it provides for the development of their respective senses of selfhood.

The episode starts with Sam deciding to buy the roses. It is a pretty autumn day. Things have been going well for Sam in his job, it is Friday, and he is looking forward to the weekend. Sam is feeling quite good about himself and his family. As he is contemplating his situation, he decides to stop on the way home and pick up a dozen red roses for Barbara and a cuddly teddy bear for Ann. Here Sam is moving out of his work role and is in the process of taking on his husband and father roles. His actions in the purchase of the flowers and the teddy bear stem from the contemplation of these roles and how they should be enacted when he arrives home. With Sam, this contemplation is a cognitive process. His actions in buying the flowers and the teddy bear result from playing his role and that of both Barbara and Ann in his own mind. He anticipates both Barbara's response and that of Ann when he presents them with their respective gifts. It is their anticipated responses that cause him to stop and make the purchases. Even though she is present only in his mind, he starts feeling warmly toward Barbara and says to himself as he is driving home, "She is a fine woman," and he smiles.

In the foregoing description, the cognitive process that involves Sam thinking about himself and his family represents the evolution of structure. The structure is the imagined roles he plays out in his mind. These imagined interactions provide the guides to his behavior—structure always precedes and serves as the initial guide to social behaviors. The playing out of the role we label interactions. Using another term, it is social functioning within the framework provided by the role.

To return to our example, upon opening the door to the apartment, Sam greets Barbara with a loving smile and says, "I brought you something." In Figure 10.7, this represents the start of the interaction. We have, in the development of the example, alluded to Sam's own sense of selfhood (he is feeling very good about his family). This sense of selfhood is summarized in the rectangle on the left side of the figure. Sam's words of greeting stem from this sense of himself and his definition of the situation that is now unfolding. His words "I brought you something" represent the message sent. The intended meaning is further communicated by his smile, by his movement toward Barbara, and by the roses he is about to present. The moment Sam starts to speak, he hears what he is saying and renders a personal judgment as to whether this conforms to what he was intending to communicate. Here again, we have evidence of structure. Sam is judging what he actually hears himself saying (the meaning being transmitted to Barbara) against the meaning he was intending to convey. He mentally does this by playing his own spousal role and Barbara's spousal role simultaneously.

These imagined roles represent the structural determinants in this interaction. The looping back of the message as shown in the figure represents this comparison that is constantly going on in social interactions. As indicated above, Sam is taking the role of Barbara in this process even before she responds. In part, he does this by watching her face, her movements, and anything else that may provide clues to how she is receiving this message. This is a dynamic process and as a consequence, the actual words that Sam is using to convey his meaning to Barbara may be altered before he completes his part of the interaction and prior to the time Barbara actually responds.

Barbara will derive her own meanings from the message being sent in essentially the same way as described for Sam. She will process a sense of self, a definition of the immediate situation. She will do so in part by also playing her own role as well as Sam's. This occurs almost instantly (this is not a new situation for either Barbara or Sam) so their interactions will tend to play out in the way that they have before.

For purposes of this example let us assume that she responds in the way Sam has predicted. Her response, given with a smile, "What is the occasion?" is consistent with Sam's expectation. Just as with Sam, Barbara will not know exactly what her response is until she actually hears herself. Again, there is a looping back; she interprets her own words as soon as they are spoken and before a verbal response from Sam.

The interaction is now under way and both are defining the situation in essentially the same way. Here structure and interactions are flowing together—they are communicating. Sam's reply to Barbara's response is, "You are; it is just a reminder of what a wonderful wife and mother you are. I am probably the luckiest man in the world." This is the kind of response Barbara was expecting and it is confirming to her own sense of selfhood and their marriage. She smiles and the interaction continues. Sam gives the new teddy bear to Ann; she squeals with delight. Again, the response is consistent with what Sam has anticipated. For a few minutes Sam and Ann play peek-a-boo. The couple then decide to have dinner at their favorite restaurant. They call their babysitter for Ann. They have a fun evening with much small talk and return home quite late. Sam takes the babysitter home. When he returns, Barbara and Sam make love and go to sleep. The episode or cycle is now complete with Barbara and Sam both feeling good about each other and about themselves and their marriage. In Figure 10.7, the final interaction closes the cycle but it will reopen as they pick up their spousal roles in the morning.

This episode went in accord with the script. The couple is feeling good about themselves, each other, and the world in general. The system is in steady state. With a different scenario, the outcome could have been quite different. It could have ended with an argument and both parties sleeping in different rooms or worse. What if after Sam's initial greeting—the message sent—Barbara had responded suspiciously, "What have you done now?" (insinuating that he is trying to relieve his guilt by giving her the roses). Sam is now caught off guard, not having expected this response. His response would probably be a defensive one, reflecting also perhaps annoyance and emotional pain. Our interest here is not in the content but in the basic dynamics—the continuing interplay between the structure and interactions of what we call the system's conversion operations.

In our discussion of conversion operations, we have relied heavily on concepts drawn from symbolic interaction. In doing so, we have sought to offer an approach to the understanding of the behaviors of the social group, particularly the family. We find symbolic interaction theory useful because it deals effectively with behavior at the small group level. The theory, or at least the concepts from it, is fully consistent with systems theory and its basic assumptions. Also, what symbolic theory offers, with its focus on interpersonal communications, is especially helpful in terms of its application to social work practice.

While our focus is on the natural group, it is easy to apply the insights to the formed group. For example, the professional helping relationship is a social system. All the concepts comprising the theory and the way it is modeled can be identified in a helping relationship if that relationship exhibits the characteristics of interdependence and wholeness. The conversion operations will be comprised of a services plan and its associated tasks or activities. This is the structural aspect. The actual behavior of the social worker and client are the interactions, the functions being performed. Here the concepts of situation and social act as drawn from symbolic interaction can be very helpful. The social act (cycle) can be a single session or the entire process ending in the closure of the case.

Output.   Exchange theory is helpful in conceptualizing output. Output is what the system produces and exchanges for its inputs. These exchanges take place with organizations, groups, and individuals within its suprasystem. Also, just as there are various forms of inputs, so are there classes of output. In social systems theory, we identify three forms: task, maintenance, and waste. Task outputs are signal inputs that have been processed through the system; maintenance outputs are maintenance inputs following a processing cycle; waste represents a designation of inefficient and/or ineffective use of resources in providing both maintenance and task outputs. On a conceptual plane and over time, task and maintenance outputs should possess greater value than the original signal and maintenance inputs. In this sense, the system adds value—is functional. Under such a condition, the system would likely evidence negative entropy.

When applied to the social group, the concept of task output will always include the impact group members experience within the group on their own sense of selfhood. In this way, social systems theory seeks to explain the impact of the group on the socialization of its members and their own personal development.

In conceptualizing outcome for a social group, it is useful to do so both globally and for a specific cycle of activity. For example, on their tenth wedding anniversary, Barbara and Sam might reflect personally or with each other on what they expected from the marriage and what they have received. We would characterize this as a global assessment. On the other hand, an assessment of a cycle might be all of the activities that Barbara and Sam engage in to celebrate their tenth wedding anniversary. Suppose Sam was called away to an important business meeting and Barbara spent their anniversary evening alone. Both Barbara and Sam would probably assess the evening as disappointing. The emotional states attributable to this situation are im-portant. Let us say that Barbara was both angry and depressed over the situation. Barbara's emotional state would be considered a task outcome of this cycle of the group as would Sam's, that is, the effect on them as individuals.

The notion of selfhood as a primary outcome of the social group is a complicated notion. Barbara and Sam not only are married and thus constitute a social group in accord with our definition, but also they are the most important people in each other's lives. While obviously not constructed as a formal output statement, both Barbara and Sam derive important parts (definitions) of themselves from their relationship with the other. Not only do they rely on each other for meeting their belonging and love needs but for their self-esteem needs as well. Given the position taken in this theory that individual members of a social group constitute both maintenance and signal inputs, the so-called state of Barbara and Sam's marriage at any point in time would be considered a maintenance output. Similarly, the portion of Barbara and Sam's sense of selfhood derived from their marriage at any point would represent a task output of their marital relationship. Our position of treating the acquisition and support of selfhood as a system's output has its foundations in the theory of symbolic interaction. Recall the statement, I am what I think you think I am. In this example, Barbara and Sam have significance in each other's lives. The theory provides a way of operationalizing this position. While at times this may seem to be a cumbersome way to achieve this understanding, it provides a consistent language and schema for grounding observations of various systems in a framework suitable for practice interventions.

In concluding this section, we need to address the notion of waste. Conceptually, some waste is always associated with the conversion of inputs to outputs. We will be drawing particular attention to this point when we discuss feedback. But for the moment, we illustrate the concept of waste by Barbara's effort to secure a promotion. Let us say that Barbara did not receive the promotion. The time and effort she spent in the pursuit of the promotion, which came at the expense of her family, represent waste. Here we assume that no useful family outputs were achieved from this effort. Conceptually, waste is important because it becomes a means of accounting for a part of the discrepancy between a system's inputs and outputs. We can assume that both Barbara and Sam and their relationship suffered somewhat from the experience, that there was essentially a negative outcome to this experience. In systems terminology, we would consider the resources used in this effort as waste. In less technical terms, most people would agree that this was a wasted effort.

Feedback.   Technically, feedback is that feature of structure that possesses the function of gathering and reporting back into the system the progress (or lack thereof) toward goal achievement. All forms of social organization are characterized by efforts aimed at determining the extent to which their function is being performed satisfactorily. Here the notion of satisfactory functional performance pertains to relations within the organization (maintenance outcomes) as well as between the organization and other individuals, groups, and agencies in its suprasystem (task outcomes). As with other system features, the social group is distinguished by its informal feedback arrangements.

To develop the notion of external feedback, let us return to the Joneses. Recall that in our example Barbara and Sam have one child, Ann, and want to have a second, hopefully a son. Ann has two sets of grandparents who are both very proud of their granddaughter. Both sets of grandparents also hope that Barbara and Sam will have more children. In their case, gender is not an issue. They simply want more grandchildren. Let us also say, for purposes of developing the example, that at the time of their

marriage neither Barbara nor Sam wanted children; they both had strong career aspirations and felt that having children would interfere with their career goals. After their marriage and sometimes not too subtly, both Barbara's and Sam's parents inquired as to whether they had changed their minds about having children. In this instance, Barbara and Sam were receiving feedback regarding a goal that excluded having children; that is, their goal was not meeting suprasystem expectations.

Important from a conceptual position is that feedback is always information fed back into the system. At the point of reentry into the system, feedback becomes designated as maintenance input. To illustrate the notion of feedback as a maintenance input, we will provide a final example involving the Joneses. Recall that one goal of the Joneses was to purchase their own home. In pursuit of this goal, both Barbara and Sam decided on a savings plan in which they would deposit monthly into a savings account. Their savings would then be used for a down payment on a house. Now an action by Barbara of checking their savings account would not in itself constitute feedback to this system. Why? Because the information obtained was not shared with Sam and thus did not serve as a maintenance input. Recall that maintenance inputs serve to activate and drive the system. Feedback is always a vital maintenance input; its specific function is to help correct any imbalance that may be occurring in the system's pursuit of its goals. For example, if Barbara had found upon checking the savings balance that Sam had made an unexpected withdrawal, this would be positive feedback. Why? Because a baseline existed, a previous balance, and the amount in the account was moving in the direction opposite to the goal. There was less money to be used for their down payment.

In this situation, Barbara did check with Sam for an explanation. Since this information was fed back into the system, it served as a maintenance input for the next cycle of activity. Let us say that Sam offered a plausible explanation indicating that he had used the money to pay a bill because his bonus check hadn't come through yet, saying, "I thought I had mentioned this to you; I'll put the money back as soon as I get my check." A month later, Barbara makes her usual deposit and finds that another substantial withdrawal has been made. Given Sam's previous explanation and this new information, Barbara is now very upset. As a consequence, she confronts Sam and demands to know why he made the withdrawal. Barbara's confrontation of Sam would indeed be considered feedback, representing a major deviation from their goal (proposed output). Again, the feedback would represent a maintenance input, theoretically designed to get the system back on course. To extend the example, let us say that unknown to Barbara, Sam was on drugs and had started to use the money in their savings account to support his growing drug habit. Now let us suppose that after a series of heated exchanges over the withdrawal, Sam confesses to his wife that he is on drugs and used their down payment money to support his drug habit. Barbara is shocked, angry, bewildered, and at a loss as to what to do or say.

Given the nature of the problem, it appears as though the goal of purchasing their own home is no longer a realistic one, at least for the near future. Barbara and Sam will need to rethink the purpose of their relationship and establish some new goals; Sam may agree to seek treatment for his addiction and Barbara may agree to be supportive and to work toward meeting the cost of his treatment. Here we have a new goal structure and a new set of relationships between Barbara and Sam associated with the newly adopted family goal.

The adjustment that took place resulted from the feedback on the goal status of their down payment money. The feedback led to a major reworking of Barbara and Sam's relationship based on the establishment of new goals. Conceptually speaking, feedback, if not heeded, will lead to problems in the system's capacity to

function and, if serious enough, to the dissolution of the system itself. In short, if the system ceases to be functional, sooner or later it ceases to generate the inputs required for its continuance, resulting in a loss of steady state.

SUMMARY

In this chapter, we modeled the functional and structural features of social systems theory. Focusing on the distinctive features of the social group, we described the four functional and eight structural concepts comprising the theory, and through the use of examples, related them systemically to each other.

We have distinguished the formed from the natural group. In our use of these terms, the so-called natural group is essentially synonymous with our use of the term *social group*. These groups form naturally in the sense that their origins and their purposes are found in the distinctive qualities possessed by all human beings. Perhaps Maslow more than any other theorist identified these needs and labeled them as one of the basic needs in his theory of a hierarchy of human needs, that is, belongingness and love needs.[12] In our conceptualization of the social group, we also relied heavily on the contention made by Charles Horton Cooley that the distinctive qualities of humanness are socially acquired and supported through life by primary groups. What Cooley referred to as a primary group is very close to what we call the social group. We have sought to operationalize this contention by Cooley in the model by considering the individuals who comprise social groups as representing both the group's signal and maintenance inputs and the group's task outputs.

Our position is that a formed group, such as a therapeutic group or a helping relationship comprising the worker and the client, is distinguished from a social group by the type and purpose of the relationships utilized. Here we borrowed from the seminal works of Toennies and his use of the concepts of Gemeinschaft and Gesellschaft. In short, the professional relationship is essentially Gesellschaft in character, even though the social group is dominated by Gemeinschaft relationships. In a sense, the worker forms a group as a medium through which the helping process is to be conducted. We also contend that the professional helping person borrows on her or his knowledge of the dynamics of the natural/social group in fashioning this medium of intervention.

We used a number of different kinds of social groups to help identify the distinguishing features of the systems concepts. To help demonstrate the interrelationship or wholeness of these concepts, we made particular use of the Jones family. We could have used any other social group to serve this purpose. Our choice of a family as the principal example was intended to convey our belief that the family is the dominant form of social group and the one to which most of our readers can most easily relate.

We also used concepts from exchange, field, need, and symbolic interaction theories to extend the usefulness of the model when applied to the social group. In doing so, we have sought to show how existing theory can be used to further develop specific applications of the model.

GLOSSARY

Achievement goal A concept used by group theorists to identify a group's external goal. The equivalent term used by social systems theorists would be *task goal.*

Affiliative goal A goal structure used by group theorists characterized by a feeling of belonging by group members. In terms of systems theory, think of the affiliative goal structure as essentially the maintenance goal.

Deviance credit Deviance credit refers to a group's tolerance for deviation from expected behavior by members.

Ecomap As used here, a diagrammatic presentation of a system's suprasystem.

Genogram A graphic representation of family structure.

Individualistic A category of theories seeking to explain the behavior of the individual. The alternative category is labeled *situated.*

Ontogenetic The view that a person is understood in terms of a developmental process, which stresses the continuity of existence from birth to death. Such an approach emphasizes the themes and processes that make the person unique and identifiable to self and others. Often such models of individual development are organized as a series of stages, such as Erikson's psychosocial stages.

Situated A classification category of theories that focuses on the situation as one of the determinants of human and organizational behavior. The alternative category is labeled *individualistic.*

Sociogram A diametrical representation of social relationships in social groups. Special attention is given to the direction and intensity of these relationships.

Sociometry The study of the structure and function of small groups.

NOTES

1. See Part Two, The Individual, for a review of the various stage models.

2. William Kephart, "A Quantitative Analysis of Intergroup Relationships," *American Journal of Sociology,* vol. 55 (1950): 544–548.

3. See particularly Charles Horton Cooley, *Human Nature and the Social Order,* rev. ed. (New York: Charles Scribner's Sons, 1922).

4. For a review of the functional requisites as used here, see the discussion in Chapter 3, Social Systems Theory: General Features.

5. The review of Abraham H. Maslow's work is contained in Chapter 2, A Social Systems Perspective: The Foundations for Social Systems Theory. The original work is contained in Abraham H. Maslow, *Motivation and Personality*, 2nd ed. (New York: Harper and Row, 1970), 35–58.

6. An ecomap, or ecogram, as they are sometimes called, is a way of graphically depicting what we refer to as a system's suprasystem. For a discussion of the ecomap as it is sometimes used in social work, see Beulah Compton and Burt Galaway, *Social Work Processes*, 4th ed. (Belmont, CA: Wadsworth, 1989). For another representative family-centered presentation of this general approach to diagramming, see Evan Imber-Black, *Families and Larger Systems: A Family Therapist's Guide Through the Labyrinth* (New York: The Guilford Press, 1988), 9–13.

7. For a discussion, see Kurt Lewin, "Behavior and Development as a Function of the Total Situation," in *Manual of Child Psychology*, 2nd ed., Leonard Carmichael, ed. (New York: John Wiley & Sons, 1954), 918–948.

8. The norm *distributive justice* was discussed in Chapter 6. For a review of the concept, see Marvin Olsen, *The Process of Social Organization*, 2nd ed. (New York: Holt, Rinehart and Winston, 1975), 94–95.

9. See, for example, J. L. Moreno, *Who Shall Survive? Foundations of Sociometry, Group Psychotherapy and Sociodrama* (Beacon, NY: Beacon House, 1953).

10. For a useful summary of the genogram applied to social work practice, see Beulah R. Compton and Burt Galaway, *Social Work Process*, 4th ed. (Belmont, CA: Wadsworth, 1989), 168–173.

11. For a useful overview of symbolic interaction theory and the use of situation, see John P. Hewitt, *Self and Society: A Symbolic Interactionist Social Psychology*, 3rd ed. (Boston: Allyn and Bacon, 1984).

12. Maslow, *Motivation and Personality*.

PART FOUR

THE FORMAL ORGANIZATION

SUPRASYSTEM

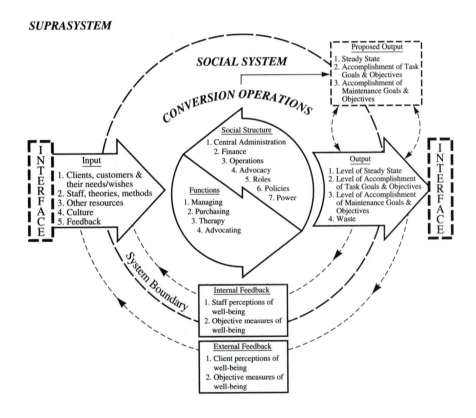

CHAPTER 11

THE FORMAL ORGANIZATION
AN INTRODUCTION

GEMEINSCHAFT AND GESELLSCHAFT
DEFINITION
ORGANIZATIONAL THEORY AND PRACTICE
AUTHORITY
THE WEBERIAN BUREAUCRACY—THE
   RATIONALIST POSITION

THE HUMAN RELATIONS POSITION
ORGANIZATIONAL THEORY AND SOCIAL
   WORK EDUCATION
SUMMARY
GLOSSARY
NOTES

The purpose of this chapter is to introduce the formal social organization. At this point, it is helpful to remember the distinction between so-called primary and secondary forms of social organization. The term *primary group* had its origins with Cooley[1] and pertains to relationships among group members that are personal in nature, carried out for their own sake, and usually face-to-face. Examples include the family and small friendship groups. Secondary groups, in contrast, are formally constituted, delimited in their functions, and do not require face-to-face contact among group members. In this chapter, the type of social organization described as a formal organization serves as a prototype of a secondary group and would include such diverse examples as a community mental health center, a state department of human services, a university, or General Motors.

Before proceeding further, it is important to note that we are treating the formal organization as a distinct social entity apart from the individuals who may comprise it at any given time. The reasoning that supports this position was identified in Chapter 2 and is contained in the assumptions comprising the social systems perspective. The separation between the organization and the particular individuals who comprise it is also one of the most fundamental distinctions between a primary group and a formal organization. For example, if the members of a friendship group should renounce their association with each other, the group would cease to exist, from a social systems perspective. In contrast, if all the staff of a local family service agency should simultaneously quit, the agency as a formal organization would not cease to exist as a legally constituted social entity. If such an event did occur, the board of directors could simply hire a new executive and have the person hire a new staff. While services would be temporarily disrupted, the act of all the staff leaving would not, in itself, affect the existence of the organization. In the study of formal organizations, the focus is on the organizational

roles that are enacted, not on the individuals enacting those roles.

GEMEINSCHAFT AND GESELLSCHAFT

Gemeinschaft and Gesellschaft are two useful concepts in distinguishing the formal organization from other forms of human association. Recall that it was Ferdinand Toennies who developed these concepts to contrast two basic types of social relationships.[2] While Toennies is not categorized as an organizational theorist, his work provides a useful starting place to develop our definition of a formal social organization and for tracking the development of organizational and **administrative** theory. His contrast of the Gesellschaft character of relationships within formal organizations with the Gemeinschaft nature of relationships among members of natural/primary groups is particularly useful:

> It [the formal organization] is never anything natural, neither can it be understood as a mere psychical phenomenon. It is completely and essentially a social phenomenon and must be considered as composed of several individuals. Capacity for unified volition and action, a capacity which is demonstrated most clearly as competency to pass resolutions, characterizes it. Just as the thinking individual is capable of making decisions, so is a group of several individuals when they continuously agree or agree to the extent that there prevails and is recognized as a definite will as the will of all or sufficient consensus to be the will of the social organization or corporate body [sic]. Thus, the volition of such a group can be represented by the will of a natural person behind whom the will of the whole social organization or corporate body stands.[3]

Toennies's position with respect to formal organizations is similar to the one we have adopted. The formal organization can be treated as a social entity and is essentially independent of those individuals who may comprise it at any one time. In this same sense, and like an individual, the social organization can and does enter into relationships with other social organizations and with individuals. Employment contracts with employees and contracts with clients are examples of such relationships.

Toennies says that a formal organization "is never anything natural." In this sense, the social organization is contrived, created as a means to achieve some specified end. It is a social tool used by its administrators and staff to accomplish some purpose, for example, to overcome a health problem, to protect children from abuse, or to build a car. It follows that the relationships these organizations enter into are Gesellschaft-like. These features are highlighted by the rationalist position in organizational theory, which will be addressed shortly. The point is that Gemeinschaft and Gesellschaft should generally be viewed as constituting dimensions of social relationships. These two concepts can be treated as representing the extreme points on a continuum, and, just as both features are found in personally based relationships, so also are they found in relationships entered into by formal organizations. So while the Gesellschaft-like relationship may appear to dominate in formal organizations, the Gemeinschaft dimension of these relationships helps overcome the unnatural (contrived) qualities of such organizations. These personally based (natural) relationships help bind people together so they are able to work collaboratively in order to achieve the goals of the formal organization. Later we will characterize these personally based feelings as an important part of the maintenance features of a formal organization.

DEFINITION

We noted a distinction between primary and secondary groups. Unfortunately, no consensus exists on a more detailed typology of organizations generally, or of formal organizations in particular.[4] This lack of a commonly agreed-on classification system characterizes the general state of development of organizational theory. Therefore, we begin by sharing our definition of a formal organization: A form of social organization deliberately and formally created to achieve relatively specific and delimited goals and in which logical actions dominate.

Further, establishment of a formal organization entails several activities. First, a deliberate action is taken to create the organization as a recognized social and legal entity. Usually the organization is created under state law as a public entity or through the filing of legal papers that register the organization under relevant laws as a nonpublic or private organization or corporation. Second, a written statement sets forth the general purposes and sphere of activity of the organization, for example, the private organization created as either for-profit or not-for-profit. In a publicly created organization, the statement of purpose will appear in the law, while in a nonpublic agency, it will usually be found in its constitution and bylaws and/or its articles of incorporation. Third, a governance structure is created. In this instance, the notion of formalization deals with the relationships among the organization's members in terms of how authority is exercised and how work is divided up and conducted. The governance structure will be specified in the law that creates the public organization; in the case of a nonpublic agency, it will be delineated in its legal charter.

In short, formal organizations represent one of the major ways in which people formally band together to perform functions or to solve problems that may not be accomplished or solved through individual efforts. Within the definition given, these organizations take many forms and sizes, ranging from the United Nations to city government, from General Motors to a local used car dealership, and from the federal Department of Health and Human Services to a local family and children's center. It is important to recognize the number of formal organizations that exist, their varied purposes, and the effects they have on all of our lives. In a complex postindustrialized society such as ours, people are immersed in webs of such organizations that vitally affect all aspects of life.

In understanding the importance that formal organizations have in people's daily lives, the question still arises as to why social workers and other human service professionals should study them in any direct way. The answer occurs at three levels. First, generalist practitioners must be able to practice competently with all size systems. This being the case, the understanding of and the ability to effect changes in formal organizations is a feature of practice. Most social workers conduct their work within a formally constituted organization, for example, a mental health center, hospital, or welfare department. As employees, they are members of a formal organization. This organization shapes how their professional practice is conducted and whom they will serve, for example, by applying program eligibility standards. Not only does the organization affect the client-worker relationship, it has direct effects on the worker. In this sense, the worker is immersed in a work environment that has multiple features, some positive, for example, providing a feeling of self-fulfillment, and some negative, such as having a potential for **burnout.**[5] Thus the worker needs to understand how organizations behave in order to organizationally participate in ways that advance both the direct practice with clients and the personal and professional development of staff.

Second, the organization is a human creation—a potentially powerful tool that can be differentially used for the relief of social problems and for the promotion of human well-being. The generalist practitioner will be working with clients who may be receiving services from a variety of agencies. Sometimes these agencies may be working at cross-purposes and actually providing a disservice to a client. The generalist must have some sense of organizational and interorganizational behaviors in order to practice competently. In other in-stances, the generalist may find that a badly needed service does not exist in the community. In such a situation, she or he needs to know how to go about establishing the need for such a service and creating an agency to offer such services.

Third, many social workers become administrators. Here, the social worker is still in a helping role but working as an administrator and/or manager rather than as a counselor. The social worker needs to understand organizations and how they are managed in order to practice competently as an administrator. Human service agencies (for instance, a community mental health center) are the chief means available to deal with large-scale social problems such as mental illness, or to assist people in realizing their potential by promoting mental health. The practice of social work administration offers unusual opportunities for professional practice.

ORGANIZATIONAL THEORY AND PRACTICE

The scientific study of formal organizations is a rather recent development. Commenting on this development, Scott observed, "It is safe to conclude that until the late 1940s, organizations did not exist as a distinct field of sociological inquiry."[6] Weber's works were translated into English during this period and probably were the single most important influence in the development of organizational theory as a distinct field of study.[7] This is not to say that there were not influential writings in this field prior to the 1940s, but these writings will be treated here as precursors to the development of modern organizational theory. (Here we are drawing a distinction between the development of organizational and administrative theory—the latter being an applied version of the former.)

Given the rather recent interest in the study of formal organizations, it is not surprising that no widely accepted agreement has been reached on a theory of organization. Similarly, no agreement has been reached on a theory in the applied area of administration, generally or specifically in social work administration.[8] However, intense activity in both the basic and applied areas is taking place. In this section, we will briefly review the main lines of theory development, but we will emphasize the developmental trends that build from a social systems perspective and contribute to a social systems conception of administrative practice. Our contention is that many of the earlier contributions to organizational theory can be viewed as part of a dialectical process in which the evolvement of the social systems theory can be treated as the synthesis.

The German sociologist Max Weber is generally recognized as the father of modern organizational sociology.[9] His writings also have formed important foundations to administrative theory (management of organizations). Weber's inquiries focused on the processes of formalization (based in law) and legitimization. Given our attention to formal organization in this chapter, the work of Weber in the area of the formalization and legitimization of organizations is particularly important.

AUTHORITY

Weber is perhaps best known for his writings about **bureaucracy.** Before describing these writings, it would be helpful to review his conception of the three forms of authority, since his notion of legal authority and the legitimacy attendant to this form of authority serve as a cornerstone to his model of a bureaucracy. **Authority** as defined by Weber is "the probability that a specific command will be obeyed."[10] The notion of authority is developed in the context of **legitimacy,** which means an acceptance on the part of those being commanded that the person commanding possesses that right. In other words, the person has the "legal" authority to tell a subordinate what to do.

It might be useful to stop for a moment and recognize that the term *command* as used by Weber has a troublesome and negative connotation when employed to describe a feature in social relationships. From our perspective, Weber identified and developed a very useful classification of ways in which human volition is exercised. His classification of types of authority also formed an important basis for the study of social power—the ability of one person to influence the actions of another. For the immediate purposes of this chapter, we will examine the exercise of authority (social power) in formal organizations.

Weber identified three pure types of authority: legal, traditional, and charismatic. These should be treated as distinct analytical models for examining authority as it pertains to organizational behavior. It should also be noted that each type of authority tends to be associated with different types of social structures.

Legal authority, according to Weber, is most clearly evident in the behaviors of bureaucracies. In this context, we are treating the notion of bureaucracy as a type of formal organization. Weber's concept of a bureaucracy will be developed later in this chapter. One characteristic of a bureaucracy is that the exercise of power is within the framework of established laws, rules, and other such formalized sources of governance. Earlier it was noted that formal organizations have a legal existence that establishes (sanctions) both their purpose and arrangements for governance. It is assumed that those who voluntarily accept membership in formal organizations are contractually bound by its formal arrangements for governance. The exercise of authority flows from these governance arrangements and the basis of legitimacy is established by contract (written or understood).

In order to understand the concept of legal authority and its relationship to legitimacy, it is important to grasp some of the more subtle features of Weber's reasoning. For example, while his writings focused on the importance of the assignment of authority to the office (position) as opposed to the individual, the assumption is that each office is occupied by a qualified person. A further assumption is that the person occupying a given office was appointed through known and objective procedures and was selected because of being the most qualified person available for the position.

Legitimacy, as noted earlier, pertains to the acceptance of orders, usually in the form of commands or requests, by those occupying a subordinate office to the one issuing the order. The exercise of legal authority rests on the right of the person occupying the office to give a particular order. The acceptance of the order by those affected legitimizes the authority—the person accepts the order because he or she believes the person issuing it has the right to do so and that he or she has the corresponding responsibility to accept and comply. A subtlety is involved that is important in terms of the administrative implications involved. While Weber focused on the legal source for this exercise of authority, there is another dimension to the acceptance of authority—the assumed qualifications or expertise of the person exercising the authority of the office. In essence, Weber combined the notions of the authority of position and the authority derived from expertise into his conception of legal authority.

An example of these two dimensions of authority is a decision by a casework supervisor to transfer a case from one worker to another (assuming the administrative authority and a professional judgment based on good cause). In the first instance, the worker might not necessarily agree with the decision, but would recognize the right of the supervisor to make it. By accepting the transfer decision based on the rights inherent in the position, the worker legitimizes the exercise of authority. On the other hand, if the worker believes the supervisor is incompetent or not qualified for the position (for example, the supervisor does not possess a pro-

fessional degree or was appointed through an assumed act of favoritism by the agency director), the exercise of authority might not be legitimized by the worker involved. In such an instance, the worker might contest the decision, not because the legal right to make the decision is not vested in the supervisor's office, but rather because the supervisor did not secure the position through established legal procedures or is not qualified to make the kind of decisions vested in that office. Similarly, the worker might accept the transfer only because to do otherwise would run the risk of the act being defined as **insubordination** and might result in the loss of the job. In such a situation, the supervisor's authority would not be legitimized. In any event, the conditions noted in the example are those that seriously affect the exercise of legal authority in a formal organization.

The second form of authority identified by Weber is derived from a belief in the sacredness of the social order, with compliance to expectations of behavior being rooted in piety. He labeled it **traditional authority.** Patriarchal authority represents its purest expression. Historically, the rule of estates by feudal lords and monarchs clearly represents this form of authority, a divinely given right. In its purest form, power is lodged in one person, with all others being dependent on that person in all matters. The constraints on the exercise of authority are rooted only in the sacredness of tradition. It should be noted that a person can occupy an organizational position in which legal authority is vested and still exert power based on traditional authority as well. The authority of the pope is an example; a portion of his power can be understood in terms of the position held, but the vastness of the power is most clearly understood in terms of traditional authority.

In a problem mode, the parent who physically abuses a child may feel justified in this behavior in terms of traditional authority. Here children are viewed as essentially without legal rights, and what takes place between the parent and child is a private family matter—"This is the way I was raised and this is the way I am going to raise my kid."Another example in a problem mode would include authority relationships in family-owned businesses. Here some exercises of authority can be explained best by traditional authority vested in property rights, not in legally based prerogatives—"It's my money so do it my way or get out." In such situations, personal loyalty based on tradition (or fear), not law, may be the controlling variable in the exercise of and acceptance of authority.

Charismatic authority is the third and final form of authority identified by Weber. Here authority is vested in a particular person because of the personal qualities possessed by that person, not because of the office or tradition. The war hero or human rights leader, the prophet, or the demagogue is each an example of a charismatic leader—Pericles, Joan of Arc, Napoleon, Gandhi, John Kennedy, Martin Luther King, Jane Addams, and others. The charismatic leader, as history has shown, can be very powerful. The tie between leader and followers is a personal one; the office held by such a leader is incidental; the tie is to the person—"I would follow him (or her) to the ends of the earth."

Weber made a significant contribution to the study of social organization with his identification of the sources of authority. His work has also served as a foundation for investigations into the more general area of social power and particularly the notion of leadership.[11] Formal organizations as we have defined them will always have some specified means for governance, or in Weber's terms, an authority structure. What he provided are three distinct models for examining this structure and its legitimizing features. Legal authority, according to Weber, is the most stable. Here the governing body is either elected or appointed, and the rule-making procedures are formalized; similarly, there are established procedures for the change or modification of rules.

In legal authority, the rules are assigned to an office for enactment, not to a person. In contrast, traditional authority is vested in the sacredness of the social order itself. Representatives of the social order are appointed or assume a recognized role in this order and their actions are vested in the sacredness of the order itself, for example, a king, a priest, a parent, and so forth. In charismatic authority, the power is vested in an individual and in this sense can be less stable than legal or traditional authority. In the case of legal authority, both the individual exercising the authority and the person being affected are bound by the same rule. Not so in the same sense with either traditional or charismatic authority; in each of these two forms, the person exercising the authority has much greater leeway for action and less personal accountability. Similarly, the loss of confidence in the legitimacy of the person is far more serious in traditional and charismatic authority than it is in legal authority. In the latter instance, the person can be removed from the office with relatively little effect on the office (as in the resignation of Richard Nixon from the presidency)—not so with traditional and charismatic leaders.

Several matters should be kept in mind when viewing Weber's contribution to the study of authority. Perhaps most important is that it is a presentation of pure types of authority. In any application, one form is likely to dominate, but this does not suggest that features of the other two might not be in evidence. For example, the willingness of a caseworker in a large public agency to follow the suggestions of her supervisor in the handling of a case may appear to be a clear expression of legal authority. However, in a given instance, this may represent only a part of the authority relationship between the two. The supervisor may be viewed as a great person in her own right as well as a skilled supervisor, and thus her authority over (her ability to influence) the worker is extended through the personally based charismatic qualities attributed to her by the worker. Similarly, the age and other characteristics of the association between the two might have qualities suggestive of a mother-daughter relationship. In such an instance, there might be a feature of traditional authority that would help explain the caseworker's reactions to suggestions made by her supervisor.

THE WEBERIAN BUREAUCRACY— THE RATIONALIST POSITION

With Weber's conception of authority as background, the following provides an overview of key features of the Weberian model of bureaucracy.[12] These features have served as foundations for the study of modern organizations and the subsequent development of organizational theory. Given the historical setting of his study, Germany in the year 1900, and its principal subject, the Prussian bureaucracy, it is not surprising that the model underscores the rational features of behavior to the point of suggesting machine-like qualities.

In introducing what we are labeling the rationalist position, it is important to note that authors vary in how they classify organizational theory. Sometimes what we call the rationalist position is known as bureaucratic theory, rational theory, or classical organizational theory. What we wish to identify is a line of theory development that emphasizes the rational nature and capacities of humans as they enact roles in formal organizations.

Because of the rational foundations of Weber's model of a bureaucracy, its key features are identified and described here as constituting the core of the rationalist position in organizational theory.[13] Weber also identifies characteristics of a bureaucracy that, in our judgment, are found in some form in every formal organization. For this reason, we use this opportunity to provide examples of how these characteristics are seen in human service agencies.

A Hierarchical Authority Structure

In his model of bureaucracy, Weber further developed his notion of legal authority. Legal authority becomes the chief means through which control is exercised over the organization's component parts. In other words, it is legal authority that formally links the parts of the organization together systematically. Through the use of legal authority, these parts are coordinated in the pursuit of the organization's goals.

According to Weber, legal authority is vested in a position, for example, the agency's executive director. From that position, authority is delegated downward, giving the organization its typical hierarchical and pyramidlike form. Utilizing Weber's concepts, structurally the bureaucracy can be viewed as organized around two axes—one vertical, the other horizontal. The vertical axis is the **hierarchical authority** structure; the horizontal axis represents a division of labor. Offices along the vertical axis are organized by levels of graded, legally based authority, with people located in higher offices exercising legal authority over the work of those located in lower offices. This gradient of authority is typically referred to as the **chain of command.** Within this chain of command, the number of positions (persons) being supervised by a given supervisor is generally referred to as the **span of control.**

In the hierarchical authority structure, there is a supervisor for every office (position). The top office in the pyramid, the agency director, typically reports to an elected or appointed board of directors or in some cases to an individual who is either elected or appointed. An example would be a state director of human services reporting to the state's governor. The central point here is the identification of a vertical chain of legally based authority that reaches from the top of the structure to its bottom and thereby affects every person employed in the agency. This authority structure connects every position with every other position in the organization, thereby coordinating the work of the organization's various parts.

The concept of **empowerment** is an important one in social work. Weber is helpful in understanding an aspect of empowerment that occurs in the delegation of legal authority from a higher level to a lower level position; in short, through delegation, the lower level position is empowered.

Division of Labor

The notion of **division of labor** as used by Weber has its clearest origins in the economic theory of Adam Smith and pertains to breaking down a given task or function into its component parts and then assigning persons to perform one or more of these subtasks as opposed to the total task. In Smith's celebrated analysis of pin making, he calculated that ten persons each performing a specialized part in the manufacturing of pins could produce 48,000 pins per day.[14] For example, one person would draw the wire, another would straighten the wire, another would cut it to the prescribed length, another would shape the head, another would solder the head to the shaft, and so on. If, on the other hand, each person had to perform all of these tasks, that person, according to Smith's analysis, would be lucky to produce twenty pins per day. A more familiar example of the notion of division of labor would be in building a house. Plans need to be made (architect), excavation must be performed (heavy machine operators), foundation laid (masons), utilities incorporated (plumbers and electricians), framing put up (carpenters), exterior walls and siding put in place (siding specialists and bricklayers), a roof put on (roofers), interior work completed (wallpaper hangers, painters, carpet layers, etc.), and so forth. While some individuals possess the knowledge, skill, and time to build a house themselves, most people would have the work done for them by a general contractor and a team of specialists as indicated.

Weber understood the vast potential for assembling specialists in the sense suggested by Adam Smith and coordinating their work organizationally. This functional division of work becomes the horizontal axis of the organization. Recall that every formal organization has been consciously created to perform some task(s) or function(s). On the horizontal axis, the functional link among the various parts of the organization accounts for the interdependence that characterizes the behavior of all formal organizations. To use our example of building a house, the carpenters are dependent on the cement masons for laying a foundation to which their wood framing can be attached. The roofers are dependent on the carpenters for walls on which they can construct the roof. The general contractor, through legal authority (a contract with the owner), provides the coordination necessary for all the specialists to work together toward the goal of building a house.

The breakdown of this overall organizational task into its component subtasks and the assignment of these subtasks to specific workers constitute the notion of division of labor. This process is sometimes referred to today as work simplification. The vertical axis or authority structure provides the means to coordinate the multiple subtasks so that the total function is performed. In effect then, each position in an organization is assigned some subtasks to perform (division of labor) and is allocated a specified amount of authority (hierarchical authority structure) that relates to the performance of those subtasks. In administrative theory literature, this is referred to as the organizing function.

According to Weber's position, assignment of the work to be performed (division of labor) and assignment of authority to see that the work is performed is always made to a position, not to an individual. In a bureaucracy, this process results in a specification of the knowledge, skills, and authority required to carry out each of the various organizational roles. This specification is then used to select those individuals with the qualifications needed to perform the duties required by the role. Weber's central notion is the separation of the position from the person. In other words, the organization can be viewed as a system of functionally interdependent roles.

Standardization of Role Performance

Not only are function and authority allocated to each office, but also role performance is standardized. This notion is perhaps most clearly seen in **job descriptions.** The rationalist position holds that everyone in the organization performing the same role should enact that role in essentially the same manner. The reasoning is that a best way exists for performing that role and if everyone performs that role the same way, the best results will be achieved.

The notion of **standardization of role performance** becomes the specification of method, or the precise way to perform a given task. Operationally, every person assigned to the same role would carry out that role essentially the same way—presumably producing a standardized outcome. A typical example is the person performing a job on an assembly line. Every person performing the specified job would do it essentially the same way. These highly prescribed procedures become one method of quality control—every product produced in a given classification is identical with every other product in that same classification. Why? Because precisely the same procedures are used. Such procedures can be helpful from your vantage point as the consumer, whether you are buying a new car (you don't want a lemon) or a McDonald's hamburger (a Big Mac will taste the same no matter where you buy it). As we will see later, the notions of standardization and the specific tasks associated with role performance and the division of labor can (and frequently do) create very boring types of work, and these create problems for both the worker and the employer (e.g., high job turnover rates).

For a role to be standardized, the function of that role (its outcome) must be clearly delineated. For that reason, many roles do not lend themselves to precise specification, for example, university professor, community organizer, family therapist, generalist practitioner. However, examples of standardization of role performances in the human services field abound. The role of the child protective services worker tends to be highly prescribed because it pertains to conducting an investigation for determining whether a child has been physically or sexually abused. The reasons for the levels of specification of role behaviors are quite clear—the overall function of the role is to protect the child from (subsequent) abuse and to determine whether abuse took place. Also, since court action may be involved, the worker must follow prescribed procedures in gathering and presenting evidence.

Inherent in the concept of standardization of role performance is the ability to match human capabilities with organizational requirements. In the rationally based logic employed by Weber, people looking for work are matched to the work requirements for each available position. Carried to its logical conclusion, if all the knowledge, skill, and personal features of job applicants were known and all the role requirements of jobs within an agency were known, it would be possible to design a perfect fit between the individual and the organizational role. Putting aside for the moment the desirability of such an approach, the intent here is to identify the underlying assumptions and key features of that logic employed in the rationalist position. The assumption in this view is that it is possible and desirable to get the best qualified person for the job.

At an organizational level, particularly in large agencies, personnel departments are formed, in part, to help carry out the function of standardizing role performance. This function includes preparing job (role) descriptions, recruiting and hiring, establishing work performance standards, and monitoring the regular evaluation of employees in accordance with established performance standards. Similarly, state licensure of professionals (including social workers) is related to this concept. Typically such laws specify the practice the person is being licensed for, the general methods employed, the qualifications necessary to practice in the profession, and the procedures to be employed to remove the license under specified conditions.

Depersonalization of Position

The notion expressed earlier that a formal organization can be characterized as a system of roles has its intellectual roots in the work of Weber. From his position, people are hired into jobs based on the related job requirements, not on personal characteristics. Weber also saw positions in bureaucracies as requiring the full-time attention of the individual in the work role. The combination of the depersonalization of office and viewing the position as needing the full-time attention and devotion of the officeholder has resulted in the professionalization of many work roles.

In Weber's model of a bureaucracy, all roles in the organization are depersonalized so that relationships pertaining to the authority structure as well as those related to the functional distribution of work are guided by work (Gesellschaft), not personal (Gemeinschaft) determinants. Weber used the notions of depersonalization and dehumanization in a different manner from the way these notions are currently used in the human services professions.

> When fully developed, bureaucracy also stands, in a specific sense, under the principle of *sine ira ac studio*. Its specific nature, which is welcomed by capitalism, develops the more perfectly the more the bureaucracy is "dehumanized," the more completely it succeeds in eliminating from official business love, hatred, and all purely personal, irrational and emotional elements which

escape calculation. This is the specific nature of bureaucracy and it is appraised as its special virtue.[15]

An example of **depersonalization of position** would be case assignments by a casework supervisor to workers. The assignment, based on this conceptualization, would be premised on objective criteria related to caseload standards and practice skills rather than personal features of the relationship; that is, the supervisor would not make preferential assignments because of personal feelings about a specific caseworker, for example, giving the more interesting cases to a favored worker.

The interrelationships among Weber's concepts should be clear by now. In his view, for an administrator to select the best qualified person for a given job, the specifications for the position should be standardized and the role depersonalized. The administrator must be free of all prejudices and other such personal biases so as to choose the person entirely based on objective and specified standards (obviously, the good old boy network would not thrive under such conditions).

As we will see later, some very serious questions arise when these concepts are put into action. For example, does the depersonalization of an office contribute to feelings of depersonalization in the officeholder? If so, under what sets of conditions and with what adverse effects to the officeholder and to the organization? More specifically, does the depersonalization of the position of caseworker in an agency tend to foster feelings of depersonalization on the part of the worker—losing a caring attitude toward clients and treating clients like impersonal objects? These are the conditions for burnout.[16]

Decision Making Guided by Rules Based in Law and/or Administrative Policy

The notion here is that decision making and related forms of organizational actions are based on legal (or quasi-legal) forms of authority. Weber's concept embodies the principle of fixed and official jurisdictional areas of responsibility. Authority is vested in the position, not in a person per se. The notion also includes the principle of the delimitation of authority and the right to appeal a decision to a higher authority. In this sense, the areas within the bureaucracy in which authority is exercised are not open ended but are limited to a given and known jurisdictional area. For example, a supervisor has the right to exercise authority over how agency cases are handled, but has no authority over actions by caseworkers after working hours, or matters not pertaining directly to agency interests, for instance, how these caseworkers handle their own family matters or conduct their own private practice.

One of the most powerful insights to be drawn from Weber's work comes from the recognition of the relative independence of the person and the position. Whereas the primary group is a form of social organization comprised of patterned behavior among specified individuals, the bureaucracy is a contrived pattern of behavior composed of vertically and horizontally linked offices, not persons—a system of roles, not individuals. In Weber's formulation, humans are the temporary occupants of roles, with the determinants of who should occupy a given role based on organizational, not personal, conditions. Following from this position, the life spans and development patterns of such formal organizations are not to be understood in human terms but from quite a different perspective—a social systems perspective. The Roman Catholic church, nearly 2,000 years old, is a familiar example of the independence of the organization from those who may comprise it at any given point in time.

Before proceeding further, it would be useful to stop a moment and examine Weber's model of a bureaucracy in terms of Toennies's concepts of Gemeinschaft and Gesellschaft. Viewing social life from an historical perspective, Toennies suggested that as social life becomes more complex, social relationships shift from possessing Gemeinschaft-like to possessing Gesellschaft-like features. It can be argued that Weber, observing the same shift, fashioned a model of organization embodying the Gesellschaft features described by Toennies. Weber's model of a bureaucracy is essentially a pure model of such relationships—one that systematically excludes the personally based Gemeinschaft relationships. The rationally conceived bureaucracy could thus be viewed as a potentially powerful social tool ideally suited for dealing with the ever-growing complexity of the modern world. It should also be noted that Weber foresaw both the power and the danger in this new creation—like Frankenstein's monster, it is a human creation that has the potential for harming its creator.[17]

In concluding this section, we remind you that Weber's writings have been used to develop the rationalist position in organizational theory. Weber was a scholar, and as such was primarily interested in the development of knowledge for its own sake. Writing at about the same time (but before Weber's works were translated) were other authors who, unlike Weber, were primarily interested in the application of knowledge to the problems faced by managers of industrial and business enterprises. These writings helped establish the beginnings of management theory, or what might be termed *applied organizational theory*. The views of some of these writers were very similar to those held by Weber, and so will be noted in this section. Best known among this group was Frederick W. Taylor.[18] Taylor, whose background was in engineering, is known as the father of scientific management. Taylor spent time with workers in the factory as they performed their duties. Just as an engineer might design a new machine, Taylor sought to design a worker–machine combination that would result in the most rational and scientific way of performing the job. His application of science to the study of management is perhaps most clearly reflected in time and motion studies. Using a stopwatch, the physical movements of the worker in performing a task were charted and timed in order to design the best possible way for accomplishing that task.

From a conceptual position, it is important to note that Taylor operated on the assumption that workers were motivated primarily by economic incentives, that is, earning wages that would be used to meet basic, survival-level needs. He reasoned that if production levels could be increased and costs reduced through worker-related actions, it would be possible for management to share the extra profits with workers. The task became one of precisely (rationally) designing the work environment so that workers would adopt new work procedures and work their hardest in order to make more money (assuming a "piece rate" basis for computing wages).

> Perhaps the most prominent single element in modern scientific management is the task idea. The work of every workman is fully planned out by the management at least one day in advance, and each man receives in most cases complete written instructions, describing in detail the task which he is to accomplish, as well as the means to be used in doing the work. And the work planned in advance in this way constitutes a task which is to be solved, as explained above, not by the workman alone, but in almost all cases by the joint effort of the workman and the management. This task specifies not only what is to be done but how it is to be done and the exact time allowed for doing it. And whenever the workman succeeds in doing his task right, and within the time limit specified, he receives an addition of from 30 percent to 100 percent to his ordinary wages.[19]

Given the assumptions and a rational model for viewing organizational and human behavior, Taylor's thinking became popular with administrators, owners, and many organizational theorists. Taylor's work is helpful in that it extends the line of reasoning about worker motivation associated with the rationalist position. In short, both workers and management can profit by optimizing working conditions, procedures, and incentives. This position is also predicated on the idea that no inherent conflict exists between organizational goals and the goals of workers. Many other writers in addition to Taylor made contributions to the rationalist perspective. These particular efforts will not be reviewed here, but include such well-known names as Henri Fayol, Henry Gantt, and Herbert Simon.[20]

We owe much to Weber and those who have contributed to the rationalist position. The principles comprising the rationalist position have contributed to economic development worldwide and the associated rise in the standard of living. In essence, the rationalists introduced science to the study of human social organization. The human was considered simply a component in a technical organization comprised of workers, materials, tools, machines, and a physical work space. These parts were configured in a manner to produce a product or service in the most efficient and effective way possible. This economic model of social organization was premised on the position that humans were logical in their behaviors and would act in their own self-interest. The logic was derived from a model borrowed largely from the physical sciences.

The rationalist position was most clearly dominant in the early development of administrative theory and its application to business and industrial enterprises. The basic principles of this position were also adopted in the management of public agencies and private, not-for-profit organizations. In this sense, the rationalist position is deemed to have application to all types of formal organizations. The rationalist position continues to be developed and refined and is still a major influence in the practice of management including that practiced by social workers.[21]

THE HUMAN RELATIONS POSITION

Criticisms of Weber's model of bureaucracy and of the rationalist position focused on its view of human actions being driven essentially by rational considerations. Critics argued that humans simply do not behave within formal organizations in the manner suggested. To borrow again from Toennies, the rationalists gave little consideration to the personal or Gemeinschaft features of social relationships and their effects on life within the organization. In introducing this criticism, it is important to recall that from Weber's perspective, the systematic exclusion of personal determinants in decision making was what gave the bureaucracy its superiority over other organizational forms.

> The decisive reason for the advancement of bureaucratic organization has always been its purely technical superiority over any other form of organization. The fully developed bureaucratic mechanism compares with other organizations exactly as does the machine with the non-mechanical modes of production.[22]

It is not surprising, given Weber's position and that of other writers holding the rationalist position, that it was sometimes referred to as the "machine school of organizational theory."[23] Nor is it surprising that these criticisms resulted in further investigations into the subject area. These inquiries led to the development of what became known as the human relations school. Elton Mayo is generally credited with the development of this school of thought.[24] Central to the establishment of the human relations position were findings from studies conducted at the Western Electric Company's Hawthorne plant in Chicago between 1927 and 1932. This research has come to be known as the Hawthorne studies. Initially the studies were aimed at testing hypotheses generated from the rationalist perspective. In a now famous study, the researchers were seeking an optimum level of illumination for workers assembling telephone relay equipment. The results were unexpected and confusing.

> The conditions of scientific experiment had apparently been fulfilled—experimental room, control room; changes introduced one at a time; all other conditions held steady. And the results were perplexing. . . . Lighting improved in the experimental room, production went up; but it rose also in the control room. The opposite of this; lighting diminished from 10 to 3 foot-candles in the experimental room and the production again went up; simultaneously in the control room, with illumination constant, production also rose.[25]

Left without a scientific explanation for their perplexing findings, the researchers turned to their subjects for help. It turned out that these employees had been so pleased with the interest shown in their work by the researchers and by the company that they had reciprocated by trying to do their best, thus creating what has come to be popularly referred to as the Hawthorne Effect. The findings from the study of illumination led to other studies dealing with key propositions of the rationalist position. One of the most famous is known as the Bank Wiring Room study. At issue was a fundamental proposition of the rationalist position that the individual was motivated by economic factors. Simply put, management assumed that the workers would, given an incentive structure, work hard and cooperate with fellow workers in order to maximize their pay. Etzioni summarized the findings:

> In practice, the men set a group norm of the "proper day's work" which was for each man to wire two complete sets of equipment each day. Workers who produced more were ridiculed as "speed kings" and criticized as "rate busters." Those who worked considerably less were labeled "chiselers." The actual production averages were, over the months, day in and day out, surprisingly close to the group's norms. There was much pressure not to reveal to the foreman and other management personnel that the work-

ers could produce much more. The workers firmly believed that if they produced a great deal more, their pay rate would be reduced or some of them would lose their jobs (the study took place during the Great Depression), and that if they produced considerably less, they would be unfair to management.[26]

Through the Hawthorne studies, researchers discovered the presence of an informal organization within the formal organization. For our purposes here, this informal organization can be thought of as comprised of loosely coupled social groups—natural as compared to contrived groups. Toennies can again be helpful in understanding the origins and the nature of such groups.[27] The relationships among members of the informal organization were personally based, essentially conducted face-to-face, and addressed the personal needs of members, particularly those needs associated with their work setting and actions by management. The relationships were primarily Gemeinschaft in nature and represented a kind of balancing of the formal or Gesellschaft relationships that typified the contrived structure of relationships within the formal organization.

Findings from the Hawthorne studies and related research posed serious questions about some of the assumptions associated with the rationalist position. Arising out of the questions were assumptions that became the foundations of the human relations perspective.

1. The level of production is set by social norms, not by physiological capacities;
2. Non-economic rewards and sanctions significantly affect the behavior of the workers and logically limit the effect of economic incentive plans;
3. Often workers do not act or react as individuals but as members of groups; and
4. Just as there is formal leadership in the formal organizational structure, so is there leadership in the informal organizational structure.[28]

The Hawthorne studies and related research challenged some of the key assumptions of the rationalists. The studies also were important in that they helped demonstrate the contribution that empirical research could make toward building a theory of organizational behavior.

As with the rationalist position, the human relations position was represented by a group of writers who shared similar, but by no means identical, views regarding the behavior of formal organizations. As previously noted, a central concern expressed by this collection of writers was the emphasis placed on the rational features of the organization; they felt that the rational model was both incomplete and misleading in its portrayal of organizational and human behavior. As suggested by their name, the human relationists focused on the individual as a member of a work group. These writers postulated as a central thesis that the social norms that developed within the work group were key determinants of individual behavior in the work environment. From this position, the work group took on critical importance in understanding the behavior of the total organization. This attention to the work group led in turn to explorations into worker motivation and the influence of leadership on a group's behavior.[29]

What the human relations position accomplished was a recognition of the social organization within the work site. Just as there is a formal organization and the related tools, machines, materials, and related features of the work site, so is there an informal social organization. The individuals and groups within formally constituted organizations have feelings about one another, their bosses, and their jobs. These feelings affect their work, which affects them as individuals. Through the research work of this group of writers, a social science perspective was added to the physical science orientation of the rationalist position.

The rationalist and human relations positions have both contributed significantly to the development of management theory and to the general development of organizational theory. At this point it would be useful to examine their similarities and their differences. In the most fundamental sense, both positions accepted an underlying rationality in seeking the kind of structural arrangements that would most efficiently and effectively produce the formal organization's goals. The rationalist position rested in part on an assumption that workers were primarily motivated by economic gain (as were their employers), so that the best structural arrangement would be the one that maximized economic returns for both management and labor.

The human relations argument was not against the thesis of organizational rationality in its most fundamental sense, but was against some of the assumptions pertaining to the role of humans. The argument was that the rationalist view of the worker and human motivation was incomplete and misleading. Workers were not motivated primarily by economic gain and did not relate to the work situation only as individuals, but rather as members of a work group as well. In this sense, the organization was seen as possessing both a formal administrative (rational) structure *and* an informal (natural) social structure. It was therefore deemed necessary to consider both structures and their respective needs to understand organizational behaviors and their outcomes. From the perspective of the human relationist, satisfaction of the worker's social as well as economic needs was necessary in order to create an optimum organizational environment. Simply put, satisfied (happy) workers would be productive workers.[30] Conceptually, the assumption was that worker and organizational needs were reconcilable and that an optimum balance could be struck. Finding and maintaining this balance was essentially a management function expressed through the leadership behavior of the manager.

Before leaving the discussion of the similarities and differences between these two positions, it would be useful to tie them to their historical antecedents. Earlier, we explored Toennies's two contrasting types of social relationships. Gemeinschaft characterizes those behaviors found in primary or natural groups. These relationships evolve informally, are based on sentiment, are spontaneous, and are engaged in for their own sake. The origins (motivation) for the development of these relationships are to be found in the nature of the person himself or herself. The human relations writers are in the tradition of such other social theorists as Rousseau, Proudhon, Burke, and Durkheim.[31] In contrast, Gesellschaft relationships are characterized by rationality and calculation and are means for achieving a specified end. The rationalists are clearly in this tradition. Here the intellectual roots go back to such social theorists as Hobbes, Lenin, and Saint-Simon.[32]

Some writers include a third major school of organizational theory in their reviews of theory development—the structuralists.[33] Typically, the **structuralist perspective** is treated as a view arising out of deficiencies in the human relations position and represents an attempt at synthesis of the rationalist and human relations perspectives. This synthesis is seen as occurring along three main lines: (1) recognition of the importance of both the formal and informal features of social structure; (2) the importance of the organizational environment as a variable that affects the organization's behavior; and (3) the role of conflict as a significant process employed in dealing with inter/intragroup differences. We have found the contributors to the structuralist position helpful, but treat the position as a precursor to the social systems position.[34]

ORGANIZATIONAL THEORY AND SOCIAL WORK EDUCATION

The early history of social work is essentially the history of casework, the dominant social work practice method. Other methods were eventually recognized, group work and community organization, but they were clearly "other methods."[35] As a consequence, organizational and administrative theory had little place in the social work curriculum during the profession's formative years.

In 1944, administration was recognized as one of the basic eight curriculum components of accredited schools by what was then called the American Association of Schools of Social Work.[36] As a result, some organizational content found its way into the curricula of schools of social work. In 1959, Boehm's Social Work Curriculum Study for the Council on Social Work Education recommended that administration be recognized as one of the five professional practice methods.[37] Administration and research were added to casework, group work, and community organization. It is of note that the recommendation called for community organization and administration to be combined in the academic curriculum.

Administration and the attendant theories supporting this method of practice have, until recently, had an uneven acceptance in schools of social work. Not only is the dominance of direct practice in social work a part of the explanation, but also the content of the theories supporting administration has been a factor. This is particularly true of the rationalist position in organizational theory with its emphasis on the use of legal authority and its "command and control" structures. Social work places high value on individual choice as the means for expressing self-determination. Much of the content of the rationalist position seemed antithetical to social work's emphasis on self-determination and personal development.

In contrast, the human relations position was seen as much more consistent with the value base of social work and a more suitable theoretical base on which to build the practice of administration.[38] A more recent factor affecting the role of organizational content in the curriculum has been the rapid growth in the size of human service programs both public and private and the need for social workers prepared to manage large and complex programs. Social work schools have not been well prepared to meet this new challenge. The demand has resulted in a renewed interest in the role of management and organizational theory in social work; but still, the majority of social workers entering management roles have not been academically prepared for those roles by their social work education.

The current emphasis on first preparing social workers as generalists capable of working at all system levels is likely to materially affect the amount of organizational and macro-level theory introduced in the curriculum. At issue is the relevance of the rationalist and human relations positions to the preparation of the generalist. Both are closed-system positions, having little relevance to practice at other system levels.

Spirituality in Organizations

Spirituality and religion present problems and opportunities in organizational life. Earlier we discussed learning theory and exchange theory, both of which deal with motivation in terms of benefits to the individual. There is another level of motivation. All organizations make an implicit appeal to the members on the basis of the mission of the system. We can expect that more spiritually developed workers might have a higher level of their motivation accounted for by transpersonal factors such as mission. Organizations as different as a combat unit and a surgical team have the ability to engage members in a transcendent cause, whether it be killing the enemy or saving a patient. One important issue that can arise is burnout, which may be largely understood as loss of faith or belief in the organization's mission.

When organizational mission is identified with religious institutional objectives, both problems and potential ensue. We have discussed at length the fact that the beliefs that define religious systems often divide as much as they unite. The schismatic and often violent history of religious conflicts suggests that one must be conscious of diverse views within an organization, even when those differences are submerged beneath superficial conformity. We recall a church-affiliated university whose CEO made frequent appeals to the members' dedication to the mission of the university but failed to observe the most basic church tenets about treating others with respect and consideration. Such incongruence can make appeals to institutionally shared beliefs a tricky motivational proposition.

SUMMARY

In this chapter, we established the foundations of organizational and administrative theory. Interest in organizational theory is largely a twentieth-century phenomenon and results in large part from the rapid industrialization that occurred in this country in the previous century.

Max Weber is identified as an early and perhaps the most influential organizational theorist.

We identified two distinct lines of theory development, the rationalist and human relations positions. Both stem from a closed-system view of the formal organization. In this sense, attention is to the internal operations of the system; little or no attention is given to the social environment or what we call the suprasystem.

Administration and the macro-level theories supporting this practice have had a cautious reception in social work. While significant numbers of social workers identify administration as their principal method, the majority have not been specifically prepared for this role by their social work education.

The need for generalist practitioners capable of practicing competently at all system levels is likely to materially increase the amount of organizational theory taught in schools of social work. At issue is the relevance of the rationalist and human relations positions in preparing social workers for generalist practice.

GLOSSARY

Administration   A form of professional practice involving the management of formal organizations. In short, the practice involves the coordination of the work of others and focuses on achieving the purposes of the organization in an efficient and effective manner.

Authority   An expression of social power; the ability of a person to influence the actions and thoughts of others.

Bureaucracy   A conceptualization of formal organizations from a rationalist position, for example, formal organizations characterized by a hierarchically organized social structure.

Burnout   A stress-related condition arising from the work situation evidenced by emotional exhaustion, detachment, and feelings of depersonalization.

Chain of command   The legally based and hierarchically arranged authority structure in bureaucratic types of formal organizations.

Charismatic authority   A form of social power identified by Weber derived from personal characteristics perceived to be possessed by the person exercising the power.

Depersonalization of position   The removal of personal considerations in the assignment of duties, work performance, and the evaluation of work performance—the rationalist position.

Division of labor   The breakdown of work or a function into its component parts and the assignment of this work to different people in work units—the rationalist position.

Empowerment   As used in this chapter, to invest a position and thus the person holding that position with specified legal authority.

Hierarchical authority   In the rationalist position, the concept corresponds to the organization of legal authority in formal organizations.

Human relations perspective A theorist holding the human relations position in organizational theory.

Insubordination An act of refusing to obey an order issued by one with the legal authority to issue that order.

Job description The specification of duties, performance standards, and qualifications needed to perform the work (also referred to as work role specification).

Legal authority A form of social power identified by Weber that derives from the legal foundations of formal organizations.

Legitimacy Acceptance of the exercise of authority by reason of the belief that those exercising authority have the right to do so. The acceptance of authority by those affected by it legitimizes the authority.

Span of control The number of positions supervised by a given supervisor.

Standardization of role performance A feature of a bureaucratic organization in which the specific features of each work position (role) are specified so that each person holding the position will perform the work the same way. *Job description* is a synonymous concept.

Structuralist perspective A school of management thought that arose out of criticisms of the rationalist and human relations perspectives. In this text, the structural perspective is viewed as the precursor to the systems perspective.

Traditional authority A form of social power identified by Weber in which the source of power is vested in the sacredness of the social order.

NOTES

1. Charles Horton Cooley, *Social Organization, A Study of the Larger Mind* (New York: Charles Scribner's Sons, 1910), 26–27.

2. Ferdinand Toennies, *Community and Society (Gemeinschaft and Gesellschaft)*, trans. and ed. Charles P. Loomis (1887; reprint, New York: Harper Torch Books, 1963).

3. Ibid., 258.

4. Marvin Olsen, *The Process of Social Organization* (New York: Holt, Rinehart and Winston, 1968), 57–69.

5. See Srinika Jayaratne and Wayne Chess, "Job Stress, Job Deficit, Emotional Support, and Competence: Their Relationship to Burnout," *The Journal of Applied Social Sciences*, 10 (Spring, Summer 1986): 135–155.

6. W. Richard Scott, *Organizations: Rational, Natural, and Open Systems* (Englewood Cliffs, NJ: Prentice Hall, 1981), 8.

7. Ibid.

8. Chor-fai Au, "The Status of Theory and Knowledge Development in Social Welfare Administration," *Administration in Social Work*, 11, 3 (1994): 27–57.

9. Scott, *Organizations*, 8–9.

10. Max Weber, "The Three Types of Legitimate Rule," trans. Hans Gerth, in *A Sociological Reader on Complex Organizations*, ed. Amitai Etzioni and Edward W. Lehman, 3rd ed. (New York: Holt, Rinehart and Winston, 1980), 6.

11. See David M. Austin, "Management Overview," *Encyclopedia of Social Work*, vol. 2, 19th ed. (Washington, DC: NASW, 1995), 1652–1654. For an overview of leadership theory and research from a social work perspective, see Barbara J. Friesen, "Administration: Interpersonal Aspects," in *Encyclopedia of Social Work*, vol. 1, 18th ed. (Silver Spring, MD: NASW, 1987), 17–27.

12. Max Weber, "Bureaucracy," in *Critical Studies in Organization and Bureaucracy*, ed. Frank Fischer and Carmen Sirianne (Philadelphia, PA: Temple University Press, 1984), 24–39.

13. Writers have classified organizational theories, particularly those pertaining to formal organizations, in a number of ways. The approach being taken here builds in part from the classification approach suggested by Scott in *Organizations*. For an example of alternative approaches, see Amitai Etzioni, *Modern Organizations* (Englewood Cliffs, NJ: Prentice Hall, 1964), 4; and Thomas P. Holland and Marcia K.

Petchers, "Organizations: Context for Social Service Delivery," in *Encyclopedia of Social Work*, vol. 2, 18th ed. (Silver Spring, MD: NASW, 1987), 204–217.

14. The example is found in Adam Smith, *An Inquiry into the Nature and Causes of the Wealth of Nations* (London: Strahan and Cadell, 1776). For a brief discussion, see Amitai Etzioni, *Modern Organizations*, 22.

15. Weber, "Bureaucracy," 32.

16. For a discussion of burnout within the general context suggested here, see Barry A. Farber, ed., *Stress and Burnout in the Human Service Professions* (New York: Pergamon Press, 1983). For a review of a model in which the authors discuss the relationship of depersonalization to burnout, see pp. 126–141.

17. Weber, "Bureaucracy," 35–39.

18. Frederick W. Taylor, *The Principles of Scientific Management* (New York: Harper, 1911).

19. Frederick W. Taylor, "Scientific Management," in *Critical Studies in Organizations and Bureaucracy*, Frank Fischer and Carmen Sirianni, eds. (Philadelphia, PA: Temple University Press, 1984), 72.

20. Henri Fayol, *General and Industrial Management*, trans. Constance Stours (1919; reprint, London: Pitman, 1949); Henry L. Gantt, *Industrial Leadership* (New Haven, CT: Yale University Press, 1916); Herbert A. Simon, *Administrative Behavior*, 2nd ed. (New York: Macmillan, 1957).

21. Skidmore, *Social Work Administration*, 45–69.

22. Weber, "Bureaucracy," 31.

23. Ibid.

24. Etzioni, *Modern Organizations*, 32. For additional information on the development of this line of reasoning, see F. J. Roethlisberger and W. J. Dickson, *Management and the Worker* (Cambridge, MA: Harvard University Press, 1939).

25. Elton Mayo, *The Social Problems of an Industrial Civilization* (Boston: Graduate School of Business Administration, Harvard University, 1945), 69.

26. Etzioni, *Modern Organizations*, 34.

27. Toennies, *Community and Society*.

28. Etzioni, *Modern Organizations*, 35–37.

29. Friesen, "Administration."

30. Etzioni, *Modern Organizations*, 39.

31. Scott, *Organizations*, 98–101.

32. Ibid.

33. See particularly Etzioni, *Modern Organizations*, 32–49.

34. For a discussion on the contributions made by the structuralists to systems theory, see particularly Scott, *Organizations*, 123–124.

35. Donald Brieland, "Social Work Practice: History and Evolution," *Encyclopedia of Social Work*, vol. 3, 19th ed. (Washington, DC: NASW, 1995), 2247–2257. Also see Carol H. Meyer, "Direct Practice in Social Work: Overview," *Encyclopedia of Social Work*, vol.1, 18th ed. (Silver Spring, MD: NASW, 1987), 410–414.

36. Brieland, "Social Work Practice: History and Evolution," 1646–1653.

37. Ibid.

38. Ibid., 1652.

CHAPTER 12

THE FORMAL ORGANIZATION
SOCIAL SYSTEMS THEORY

COMPARISONS WITH THE RATIONALIST AND
  HUMAN RELATIONS POSITIONS

THE DIALECTIC

SOCIAL SYSTEMS THEORY: EMERGENCE

SOCIAL SYSTEMS THEORY: THE FUNCTIONAL
  REQUISITES

SOCIAL SYSTEMS THEORY: THE STRUCTURAL
  COMPONENTS

SOCIAL SYSTEMS THEORY: DEVELOPMENTAL
  STAGES OF FORMAL ORGANIZATIONS

SOCIAL SYSTEMS THEORY: TOTAL QUALITY
  MANAGEMENT

THEORIES X, Y, AND Z

SUMMARY

GLOSSARY

NOTES

In this chapter, we will continue the development of social systems theory as an approach for connecting and unifying the knowledge base for the generalist practice of social work and for advanced practice in administration. In brief, we view social systems theory as a middle-range theory sufficiently flexible to accommodate the entire domain of generalist social work practice at its several levels of application—the individual, the social group, the family, the formal organization, and the geographic community. Social systems theory becomes a general theory through which the practitioner can employ more narrowly focused theories suited to specific practice situations. In terms of development, the theory is in its infancy. The merit in developing such a theory is that it provides a consistent language, set of concepts, and propositions that support the development of the generalist practice of social work.

Our approach to theory building utilizes the four-tier approach outlined in Part One. In summary, the tiers are as follows:

1. *Philosophy/Perspective.* Nine assumptions comprise the social systems perspective. These nine assumptions link the system levels together and provide the philosophy and values foundation on which social systems theory builds.
2. *Theory.* Social systems theory is comprised of two related sets of concepts. The four functional requisites operationalize well-being. The structural components identify the eight universal features that comprise all social systems and through which the functional processes take place.
3. *Technology.* A social systems model has been developed that illustrates the linkage of the two sets of concepts and how the theory can be differentially applied at all system levels.
4. *Practice.* At level 4, two models converge in a specific practice situation by a specific practitioner. At this point the social systems model is employed within the generalist practice model to the needs of a specific client system.

Our interest, in this chapter, is in dealing with those features of the theory that are distinctive to the social functioning of formal organizations and the individuals who comprise them. These features are captured in the definition of a formal organization: a form of social organization deliberately and formally created to achieve relatively specific and delimited goals in which logical actions dominate. The features

that distinguish this form of social organization can be characterized as follows: (1) the size and characteristics of the components comprising the system; (2) the type of relationships existing between the components; (3) the level of inclusiveness of the system; (4) the forms of power or authority employed; and (5) the explicitness of the goal structure.

First, at the social group and family level, the system components are always specific individuals enacting group or family roles—friend, mother, daughter, and so on. The individuals comprising the group or family in their non-group/nonfamily roles are always a key component of the system's suprasystem. In the formal organization, the components of the system are administrative units and work-related social groups. These administrative work units, while comprised of individuals, are not comprised of specific individuals as would be the case in a small group or family. The focus is on the work role, not the individual personality. In formal organizations, the individuals in work roles are interchangeable. For example, Ellen Hooper is a case manager at Midtown Family Service Center. She can quit her job or be transferred and another person can be hired into her role as case manager with little or no effect on the social system—it is still the Midtown Family Service Center.

The work units in formal organizations are of indeterminate size, typically running from five or six people, for example, the case management staff at Midtown Family Service Center, to hundreds or thousands, for example, the worldwide sales staff of IBM or a division in an army. Other formal organizations or administrative units of these organizations dominate the suprasystem; at this system level, seldom are individuals considered components of the suprasystem.

Second, Gemeinschaft relationships dominate at the group/family level. The relationships among the system components are thus personal, traditional, informal, and the relationship itself is both a means and an end.[1] Gesellschaft relationships dominate in formal organizations. These relationships are essentially contractual, formal, impersonal, and time limited. They serve as a means to obtain some end. The relationship is thus a selected means to some specified end state, for instance, the relationship of a seller to a customer. Gemeinschaft and Gesellschaft are pure types of relationships and some mixture of both forms will be found in all human relationships and thus in all social systems. We use them here to designate key characteristics of relationships found at each system level. Both forms will be found in formal organizations. Theorists from the rationalist position recognized the distinctive Gesellschaft relationships found in formal organizations, while theorists from the human relations position recognized the Gemeinschaft relationships that also existed in these organizations.

Third, the social group and family level is the least inclusive (least self-sufficient) of the several levels of social systems addressed in this text. The next most inclusive level is the formal organization. Formal organizations have specific arrangements by which they can become more inclusive. This is done by formally acquiring other social units in their suprasystem or by developing units that increase their inclusiveness. For example, an oil company can search and drill for oil, refine and distribute the oil products, as well as sell them in retail outlets. This is known as being vertically integrated. Or, an oil company can limit its operations to just the refining or any other such specialty. Human services agencies can do the same thing. An example would be a comprehensive mental health center. Such a center would be more inclusive than one offering only outpatient services.

This concept of inclusiveness is important as an organizational capacity. One of the characteristics of organizational behavior now evident is an increase in inclusiveness. An effect of health care reform is that facilities that previously had been called hospitals are now being labeled regional health centers. Not only are their programs becoming more geographically inclusive, but they are providing a broader range of health services. Further, what used to be labeled mental health services are now being called behavioral health care services or behavioral medicine. This development blurs the distinction between a social service and a health service.

In contrast, families and social groups are much more limited in their ability to become more inclusive. For example, a family can have more children and thereby become marginally more inclusive, but this capacity is very limited.

Fourth, traditional and charismatic forms of authority dominate in social groups/families.[2] Traditional authority is essentially historical and a feature of the social system itself (its value and normative structure). Charismatic authority is vested in the individual, in valued personal characteristics, for example, a woman who is a "spellbinder." Traditional authority in a family would be exemplified in a statement such as, She is your mother, you need to do what she says. In contrast, legal authority dominates in formal organization. The use of legal authority represents the centerpiece of the rationalist position. Coordination of the work of the various parts of the system in formal organizations is achieved primarily through the use of legal authority, as shown in the statement, She is the boss, she has the right to tell you how the job is to be done.

For comparison purposes, legal authority within a formal organization is contractual; as an employee (a member of the system) you are expected to abide by the conditions of the employment contract. Once you leave your employment, as a practical matter, you are no longer bound by its legal authority. Not so in a family or a social group. Here the authority is typically a blend of traditional and charismatic forms of authority. Compliance in a social group or family is essentially one of conforming to accepted group norms, not to a legally based employment contract.

Fifth, the goals of families and groups are implicit in the behaviors of participants. In contrast, the goal structure in formal organizations is explicit and specific. For Parsons, the specificity of the goal structure is the defining characteristic of the formal organization and the feature that distinguishes it from other social systems.[3]

COMPARISONS WITH THE RATIONALIST AND HUMAN RELATIONS POSITIONS

To develop our approach in presenting social systems theory, we will return to the contributions made by those associated with the rationalist and human relations positions. We will identify writers associated with these two lines of theory development who have contributed to social systems theory.

To introduce the social systems position, we will treat it as an overlay and apply it first to the rationalist position and then to the human relations position. This will provide a set of comparisons as to how each differs from the social systems position. We will then develop social systems theory as it applies to work with formal organizations.

Rationalist Position

When the system's overlay is applied to the rationalist position, three major differences appear. First is what we might refer to as the relative tightness of fit in the relationships connecting the social units. From the rationalist perspective, there is a tight fit, with every position being related to every other position in a specific and logical way. The logic of the fit is drawn from the legal charter of the formal organization and the product(s) or service(s) it is supposed to produce. Organizational positions are related to one another both vertically and horizontally in terms of the most efficient and effective means of achieving the organization's goals. The rationalists' portrayal of the formal organization suggests that it might have been designed by an engineer—it is precise, neat, and logical. The rationalists hold a unidimensional view of the formal organization. Based on a self-interest conception of human behavior, organizational goals and the goals of the individuals who comprise the organization are reconcilable. Under the guidance of management, work roles are constructed in such a way that individuals acting in accord with their own self-interest behave in a rational manner. Central to this position is the notion of financial incentives—by behaving in accord with management directions, the worker makes more money. And the harder the person works, the more money that person makes. If a problem exists between those advancing organizational goals and those advancing their individual goals, through problem solving, it can be resolved. Why? Because each side will act in accord with its self-interest and a position will exist at which their self-interests merge. The power in the form of legal authority is concentrated in the hands of management. It is in the self-interest of the individual worker to comply with management directives.

The social systems position holds an opposite view. The needs of the system and those individuals or social units who comprise the system are not reconcilable in any absolute sense. This is not a problem; it is simply a fact. Because these needs are not resolvable, a tension state between the two sets of needs is normal; it is not considered a problem state. Keep in mind that the function of goal attainment (an external function and an end state) deals with the necessity of the system to satisfy need states external to the system, that is, those external social units dependent on the product or service produced by the system. Internally, the integration function deals with the needs of the individuals who comprise the member parts of the system. These needs are different and are largely socially and personally based, for example, feeling good about oneself and those with whom one works. As a consequence of this inherent tension, the fit, or relationships linking member units, has much more slack than that in the rationalist position. In short, the fit between member units is not precise, neat, or logical. From the systems view, the fit is loose, sloppy, and frequently not logical; in other words, the fit among member units is humanlike rather than machinelike. This does not mean that periods of accommodation between these two functions and their related conflicting needs do not occur, they do. But, since the needs are inherently irreconcilable, these states of accommodation are always temporary. This characteristic of the social systems position establishes its dynamic quality—social systems are always in a state of change, always seeking steady state.

Second, the rationalist offers a closed-system view of social functioning. The focus is on the system itself; little attention is given to the social environment in which the system functions.

Social systems theory takes a much wider view and focuses on the formal organization in an environmental context, that is, the organization in relationship to its social environment. Stability and fixed relationships among member units is the desired normal state according to the rationalists; the social systems position is that change is the normal state.

From a closed-system view, there is little leakage into the system from outside sources. Such leakage, if it should occur, would be treated as a problem and efforts would be made to control it and thereby insulate the organization from it. The social systems position takes the opposite view. The formal organization must be viewed as an open system, one that is in constant interaction with its external environment. This openness is not to be viewed as a problem to be solved. Rather, it is simply a fact. Borrowing from ecological theory, this external environment is in constant change; this is

a given. If the organization is viewed as an open system, this means that the organization will be in a state of constant change as well. To push this idea one step further, the interaction between the organization and its environment is reciprocal; each influences the other in a cyclical manner. In the rationalist position, control by management of the system is assumed. Social systems theory holds that while management may attempt to adapt social units within the suprasystem in terms of goal attainment, the manager does not manage its suprasystem in the same sense that she or he manages internal operations, for example, the use of legal authority.

Third, the rationalist position relies heavily on the exercise of legal authority to secure the coordination of efforts necessary to produce a product or service.[4] This position arises, in part, from the closed-system view just noted. Legal authority, like all forms of social power, is a social process. Weber's use of the term *legitimacy* is helpful in understanding the social process involved.[5] Social systems theory, while recognizing the important contribution made by Weber in his formulation of authority, utilizes a wider framework, treating power as part of an exchange process.[6] By so doing, an explanation is offered for the external as well as the internal social relationships required for the coordination of efforts in seeking steady state. In other words, while the manager relies heavily on the use of legal authority in achieving the coordination of the internal parts of the system, the coordination of those social units that are external rely on a different incentive structure. An apt question might be, What do you have to offer in exchange for my cooperation?

In summary, rationalists have identified the characteristics of the system's formal or technical structure; by so doing, they have identified a new level of social organization. Through the application of their understanding, a new method of practice has emerged—administration, or what might be referred to as organizational management.

Human Relations Position

Now we will compare social systems theory with the human relations position. We will do this by again treating the social systems theory as an overlay. Writers holding the human relations position focus on the individuals who work in formal organizations, their needs, and their propensity to come together in social groups. The group is not only viewed as a medium through which individuals satisfy their social needs, but also as an avenue for dealing with organizational stresses and strains. In contrast to the focus on Gesellschaft relationships by the rationalist, the human relationist focuses on the Gemeinschaft—those relationships dominating social groups.

Viewed through the systems overlay, the human relationists tend to treat the formal organization more as a social group or a natural rather than a formed system. They suggest that the formal features identified by the rationalists to distinguish this type of organization from others are overstated. In turn, the human relationists hold that those features typifying social groups are understated in terms of their presence and influences in so-called formal organizations. Commenting on the perspective of viewing formal organizations as natural systems, Scott wrote the following:

> The whole thrust of the natural system view is that (formal) organizations are more than instruments for attaining narrowly defined goals; they are fundamentally, social groups attempting to adapt to and survive in their particular circumstances. Thus, formal organizations, like all other social groups, are governed by one overriding goal: survival.[7]

Scott's observations identify another major difference between the human relations view of the formal organization and the rationalist view. The human relationists note the tendency of formal organizations to change or modify their goals. This tendency is treated by the rationalists as a deviation or distortion of the basic nature of such organizations. In contrast, this tendency toward goal displacement, substitution, or modification is seen by the human relationists as strengthening their contention that the formal organization could be more appropriately treated as a special form of a social group rather than as a distinctive form of social organization. This argument reduces to a means–end or Gesellschaft–Gemeinschaft conception the distinction between these two organizational forms. In commenting on this argument, Gouldner noted:

> The organization according to this model [the natural systems view], strives to survive and to maintain its equilibrium, and this striving may persist even after its explicitly held goals have been successfully attained. This strain toward survival may even on occasion lead to the neglect or distortion of the organization's goals.[8]

From this position, survival is the most fundamental of all organizational goals and overrides all other considerations; given this position all organizations, including the formal ones, are self-serving and thus should be treated as means as opposed to ends. In other words, while formal organizations are constituted as means for achieving specified goals, fundamentally they are self-serving, and their continued existence is the ultimate goal to be served.

The argument by those holding the human relations position that formal organizations are self-serving and are concerned with survival is consistent with social systems theory; but, it is an incomplete explanation. In systems theory, survival as well as growth and development is dependent on meeting the needs of social systems external to the social system as well as the needs of the system itself. The human relations position focuses on the function of integration—satisfaction of the needs of the internal units of the system. In social systems theory, the goal-attainment function must also be adequately performed for the system to survive.

Both the rationalist and the human relations positions are based on a closed-system view of the formal organization. While the human relationists argue for greater attention to the needs of the workers and to the importance of social group formation within the work place, they treat organizational goals and purposes as essentially fixed; goal substitution, modification, or change are treated as distortions or deviations from the organization's main character, but are understandable in terms of the behaviors of social groups.

The social systems view of the organization in its environmental context would not consider goal modification or change as a deviation but simply as part of the constantly changing relationship that the organization has with its supporting environment; the system view is that change is the normal state.

THE DIALECTIC

It is useful to view the development of organizational theory as a dialectical process. Recall that in a dialectic process there will be a thesis, a proposed explanation. This thesis will be investigated, its deficiencies will be noted, and an antithesis will be advanced. These two competing positions will be resolved in a synthesis or a new thesis. In using a dialectical process to help understand the development of organizational theory, the rationalist position is the thesis. Simply put, this line of theory held that humans are rational and behave in what they perceive to be their own self-interest. Building on this position, a formal organization was understood as a rational set of relationships devoted to the achievement of specific goals. Under the guidance of management, work roles are constructed so that individuals will behave in a rational manner, being guided by their own self-interest.

From this rationalist position, it would be possible to configure human, material, and fiscal resources in a manner that would optimize efficiency. In short, the formal organization can operate like a well-engineered machine. This position is premised on a single dimension—that individuals in their organizational roles behave rationally.

This central thesis is challenged in the human relations position. The research findings conducted did not support many of the key propositions comprising the rationalist position. A counter position (the antithesis) was advanced. In formal organizations, members do not behave in their organizational roles as individuals, but rather as group members. The human relations position was premised on the discovery of social groups within the formal organization. Human relationists introduced a second dimension into organizational theory, the needs of the individuals who occupy roles within the organization. In a more fundamental sense, the human relationists questioned whether the formal organization (the bureaucracy in Weber's formulation) was truly a different form of organization. They argued that the so-called formal organization could be more usefully described as loosely coupled sets of social groups.

The organization from both the rationalist and the human relations positions was viewed essentially as a closed system. The state of well-being of the organization could then be viewed as homeostatic, a fixed equilibrium. Any deviation from this state of equilibrium represented a problem and through problem-solving activities, the equilibrium could be restored.

The synthesis introduced with the social systems position is based on an open-system view of the organization and its environment. Both the rationalist and the human relations positions relied on a homeostatic conception of social functioning, a fixed state of well-being. Social systems theory rejects the idea of a fixed state in favor of a dynamic state. Fundamental to the notion of a dynamic state is the proposition that the justification of every social system is found in its social environment; it is not found within the social system itself. This gives rise to the performance of the goal-attainment function and to the related requirement of conducting the adaptation function. As we have noted, the system's manager does not exercise administrative control over its suprasystem. A different dynamic is introduced in which the manager must negotiate with those units in its suprasystem by providing something of use to them. In this sense, an exchange process occurs.

Through performance of these two externally centered functions (goal attainment and adaptation), needs arise internally and thus the integration and pattern-maintenance functions emerge. When these internal functions stabilize and their linkage with the two external functions occurs, a social system will survive as long as those four functions are satisfactorily performed. Inadequate performance of any one of the functions will cause a disordering process to occur. Unless corrected, the disordering process leads to the loss of steady state, a loss of system status. An interdependent relationship no longer exists among the parts.

SOCIAL SYSTEMS THEORY: EMERGENCE

The concept of emergence is helpful in introducing the distinguishing features of social systems theory when applied to formal organizations.[9] It is also helpful in understanding the point in the dialectical process out of which a qualitatively different position is reached. Recall that the human relations position held that formal organizations could be viewed more usefully as confederations of social groups organized around the work setting. The concept of emergence holds that each higher level of social system develops from a precedent level and retains features of that level and is thus dependent on it. Further, the newer and higher system level develops properties that are not found in its antecedents. These new and distinctive features emerge in the higher-level system and thus require that it be considered as something different from its parts. The thinking behind this concept is antithetical to a reductionist logic that would hold that the higher-level entity can be explained through the disassembly and analysis of its component parts.

The oft-quoted "the whole is more than the sum of its parts" is premised on the assumptions underlying emergence. In seeking to explain what is meant by this phrase when applied to social groups, Buckley argued:

> Thus, if social groups are not "real entities" then neither are individuals, organisms, organs, cells, molecules or atoms, since they are all "nothing but" the constituents of which they are made But this "nothing but" hides the central key to modern thinking—the fact of *organization* of components into systemic relationships. When we say that "the whole is more than the sum of its parts," the meaning becomes ambiguous and loses its mystery: the "more than" points to the fact of *organization*, which imparts to the aggregate characteristics that are not only *different* from, but often *not found* in the components alone; and the "sum of the parts" must be taken to mean, not their numerical addition, but their unorganized aggregation.[10]

To recapitulate, all forms of social organization are created by the interactions of individuals enacting social roles. The ordered relationships that evolve and the meanings participants attach to these ongoing relationships constitute what is herein called *social organization*. At the social group level, the notion of emergence would hold that the characteristics of a specified group are derived from the particular individuals who comprise it, for example, the family comprised of Mary and John Smith. While the Smiths as a family unit are inseparable from the interacting individuals Mary and John, the behaviors of the family unit are not fully explainable based solely on their individual physical, social, and psychological characteristics. The explanation lies in the combining and the resulting unique organization of their respective characteristics.

A new whole or oneness is formed, providing a capacity to achieve ends not accomplishable or otherwise explainable in terms of the two individuals. In this sense, the relationships formed are assumed to possess synergic capacities, for example, a love (or hate) that transcends the initial individual's capacities for such feelings. It should also be noted that while Mary and John Smith comprise a special social group called the Smith family, the Smith family is not codeterminate with the respective personalities of Mary and John Smith; each has a separate and distinct existence as individual personalities while comprising a social entity called the Smith family. It is Mary and John in their respective family roles as husband and wife that constitute the social entity the Smith family, not Mary and John as total personalities.

Similarly, the formal organization is comprised of individuals. These individuals, in turn, are enacting functionally related roles that comprise the social structure of that organization. Earlier, we drew distinctions between primary and secondary groups (formal organizations). Three of these differences are important here: (1) formal organizations are consciously formed, they are not self-organizing; (2) they possess a legal authority structure; and (3) they pursue relatively specific and delimited goals. While both primary and secondary groups are comprised of individuals, the primary group is comprised of specific people, and each has a (direct) relationship with every other group member; this is not the case with formal organizations. Specific roles within formal organizations (e.g., case manager) are drawn from its formed or contrived nature (e.g., a mental health center), not from the personal needs of those who may work there. Therefore, the roles are independent of any particular person and thus are interchangeable. The depersonalized character of roles accounts for some of the formal organization's uniqueness.

Consistent with the notion of emergence, we hold that formal organizations are comprised, in part, of social groups which, in turn, are made up of individuals. This is not to argue that all individuals relate to the total organization only as group members; the position is that the formal organization is comprised of two or more social groups and its distinctive features have emerged from the social group level. From this position, we argue that the principal finding from the Hawthorne studies was the discovery of social groups embedded in formal organizations and the Gemeinschaft nature of the relationships among individuals who comprise social groups.[11] The difficulty that followed in the development of the human relations perspective was the lack of recognition of the distinctive qualities possessed by formal organizations; in other words, the formal organization was not to be understood as a "super" social group comprised of smaller, loosely coupled groups. It was more than the sum of its parts.

SOCIAL SYSTEMS THEORY: THE FUNCTIONAL REQUISITES

Figure 12.1 will help us introduce the distinctive features of social systems theory when applied to formal organizations. Starting on the far right side of the graphic is steady state, or at this level, the state of organizational well-being. Keep in mind that steady state/well-being is not a fixed or final state; it is a variable state that evidences negative entropy. This means that a process of ordering is evident and dominant. In social systems theory, this process operates as a cycle. Steady state can be assessed at any point in the cycle. To simplify the presentation, we will be using a budget cycle to examine how formal organizations seek to maintain steady state.

Moving to the left of steady state, we have the four functional requisites in their means-end and internal-external relationships. Pattern maintenance and integration are the internal variables while adaptation and goal attainment are the external variables. Pattern maintenance is the means on which achieving the end state

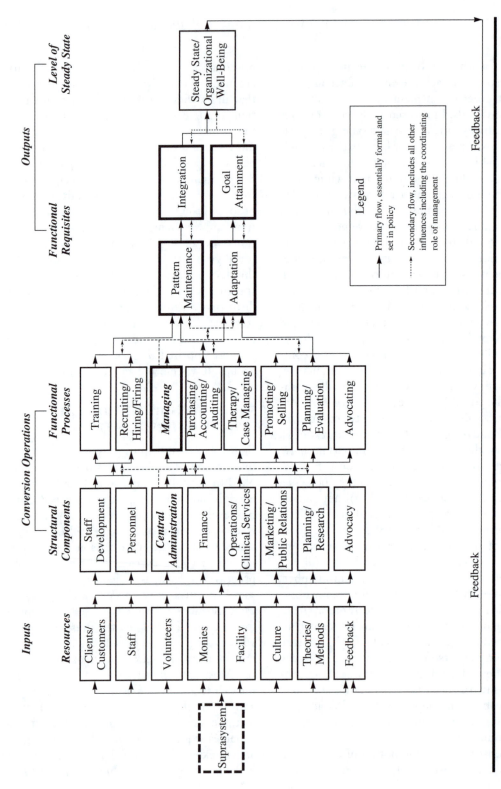

FIGURE 12.1 The Formal Organization: Modeling Steady State in a Human Service Agency

of integration largely depends. Similarly, adaptation is the means on which achieving the end state of goal attainment depends. As evidenced by this graphic, integration and goal attainment are the two independent variables used to explain the dependent variable steady state.

Minimal levels of successful outcomes in each of the four requisite functions are necessary for steady state to be achieved or maintained. If the minimal threshold is not achieved, steady state is threatened and a disordering rather than an ordering process becomes dominant.

To the left of the four functional requisites are the eight functional processes performed in every formal organization providing social services. The number and names assigned to these functional processes are arbitrary and should be considered illustrative. Some of the processes could be combined or further separated with different names assigned. For example, managing might be called administering or decision making by other authors. The point is that the underlying process illustrated by these eight functional processes will be evident in all formal organizations.

Again moving to the left, we find the system's structural components. Again for illustrative purposes, there are eight structures through which the functional processes are conducted. While the names assigned to the structures may vary depending on the application made, they are considered universals for this level of social system. For example, there will always be a structure within a system's conversion operations assigned the specific responsibility of converting task/signal inputs to task outputs. We have assigned the generic name *Operations* or *Clinical Services*. In a social service agency, it might be called the department of clinical services. Similarly there will always be supporting structures, for example, a personnel department that secures staff, that is, maintenance inputs. In small agencies, some of these structures are combined, for example, central administration

might be organized to handle finance, marketing, planning, and so on. Again, the point is that the structures will always be evident either formally or informally in all formal organizations. Why will they be evident? The functions conducted through these structures are necessary to maintain steady state.

For purposes of illustration, we have grouped the structural components and functional processes so that they are aligned with their respective functional requisites. Think of the unbroken lines and arrows as indicating primary flows. In social systems theory, all of the parts are linked functionally. This linkage is based on the use of legal authority and is basically under the control of management. The secondary flow is indicated by a lighter, broken line. This broken line is intended to include all the other forms of authority exercised to achieve coordination including the role played by management.

Every formal organization will have a structural feature labeled here as central administration, for example, the organization's **chief executive officer (CEO).** The most important management function performed by the CEO is the preservation and enhancement of those values that characterize his or her organization. The performance of this aspect of the management function links this functional process to pattern maintenance.

Certainly the CEO will be involved in management activities related to each of the other functions; but the most important and critical function has to do with pattern maintenance. We have tied three other functional processes directly to pattern maintenance, those associated with finance, staff development, and personnel. The department of finance is going to be responsible for the acquisition and certification of resources (purchasing, accounting/auditing). In systems terms, this function is associated with acquiring maintenance inputs. Closely linked is the recruitment and training of staff (departments of staff development and personnel). These functions are associated with the socialization of staff to the values of the organization and how these values are carried out within their specific organizational roles. The continuing socialization of staff in terms of the values of the organization and their respective roles ties these functions to pattern maintenance. They must be performed well; if not, steady state is at risk. In small agencies, these functions may be combined with the supervisory function. In large agencies, they may exist as separate administrative units.

It is the satisfactory performance of the pattern-maintenance function that establishes the conditions or means for accomplishing the integration function. In our structural presentation of social systems theory, the concept of maintenance output is used to designate the end state of the integration function. Recall that maintenance outputs are the effects that the social system has on itself. In accord with social systems theory, the system, in order to maintain steady state, must use some of its resources (inputs) to maintain and strengthen the system itself.

An example should help illustrate the means-end relationship between the pattern-maintenance and integration functions. If the staff of a social work agency felt that their executive director (CEO) did not support the social work code of ethics (a major component of the social work value system), then their ability to feel good about their job and their agency would be seriously affected and thus the performance of the integration function would be seriously impaired. To state the point another way, the staff could be given significant raises, improved benefits, praise for their work, and so forth, but the integration function would still be impaired. The reason is that the CEO did not support, as evidenced by his or her actions, social work's code of ethics. For example, he or she made derogatory remarks about clients who were minority of color, or was sexually harassing members of the staff. In short, the CEO was in

violation of a key pattern of behavior fundamental to the operation of this agency.

In accord with social systems theory, every social organization is purposive and to survive must satisfactorily perform the goal-attainment function. Not to do so is to risk losing steady state. In Figure 12.1, therapy and case management are identified as functional processes through which goal attainment, as a master and required function, is pursued. When we move left to the structural components column, we find the structural component labeled *Clinical Services*. The person who directs this unit in a social work agency is frequently called director of clinical services, program director, or director of social services. The more generic name is *operations*. Again, in every formal organization organized to perform social services, you will find the counterpart of this designation.

Goal attainment is an external function and an end state. Every formal organization will have the counterpart of an externally oriented goal structure. In an earlier presentation of the generalist practice model, we noted that the goals of every social system are derived from conditions that exist in the environment. Goals are no more than a statement by those who manage a formal organization as to how that organization intends to change relevant external conditions. An example in a social work agency would be to improve the well-being of a class of clients, for example, children who have been abused or neglected.

The relationship between the social system and its social environment is the content of social systems theory. In our structural presentation of social systems theory, the structural component corresponding to goal attainment is (task) output. The component pertaining to intended goal attainment is proposed (task) output.

Our final functional requisite variable is adaptation. While considered the least important of the four, it is nevertheless a required function to perform in order to maintain steady state. The concept embodies those role behaviors conducted by members of the social system that are designed to modify external conditions that facilitate goal attainment. It is in this sense both an external function and a means for accomplishing the goal-attainment function. Given a changing external environment, if the adaptation function is adequately performed, the goal-attainment function will be enhanced. Again moving to the left in Figure 12.1, three functional processes are identified as associated with performing the adaptation function—promoting/selling, planning/evaluation, and advocating. These functional processes are then linked to their respective structural components—marketing/public relations, planning/research, and advocacy.

Of the several functional processes, promoting/selling has the most obvious tie to adaptation. Selling seeks to create a need and thus motivates a person to acquire a product or service. The amount of advertising (selling) that we encounter every day attests to its importance and the implied means-end connection between the adaptation and goal-attainment functions. The connection of planning and evaluation processes and adaptation may be less obvious. Social systems theory holds that the external environment or suprasystem is in process, constantly changing. The interface that couples the system to its suprasystem causes reciprocating changes in both the system and suprasystem. Every social system, if it is to maintain steady state, will have structural components that seek to monitor the changes occurring in the suprasystem. The purpose of this function is to gather information that may suggest ways of modifying or adjusting to these changes. Again it becomes a way of seeking to adapt the suprasystem in ways that facilitate goal attainment.

The function of advocating has special meaning in social work and pertains to a modification of social structures in the suprasystem that will facilitate the advancement of well-being

of individuals, particularly of special populations and those who have been oppressed. Think of the function as the creation of a level playing field so that all people have equal access to resources and equal opportunities to advance their well-being. It is in this sense that the means-end relationship between adaptation and goal attainment is viewed in social systems theory.

In the previous paragraphs, we summarized the functional imperatives (variables) associated with a system's effort at achieving and maintaining steady state. Figure 12.1 was used to show the relationship between the structural components and functional variables in terms of the pursuit of steady state. The figure was intended to be illustrative of these relationships. Obviously, it is a massive simplification to reduce the multidimensional process covering all formal organizations to a single sheet of paper. Many of the structures and their associated functions relate to more than one functional outcome. Our intent was simply to illustrate the principal linkages. Now our focus moves from the functional processes to the structural components. While most of the structural components were included in Figure 12.1, the focus was on the functional processes and their outcome.

SOCIAL SYSTEMS THEORY: THE STRUCTURAL COMPONENTS

Figure 12.2 places the social system within the context of its suprasystem. Through modeling the relationships of the eight structural components, we establish the functional coupling of the system to its external environment and thereby operationalize the social work paradigm of human behavior and the social environment. Let us now distinguish between the structural components identified in Figure 12.1 and those to be presented here. In short, the structural components displayed in Figure 12.1 are those found in formal organizations and associated with conver-

SUPRASYSTEM

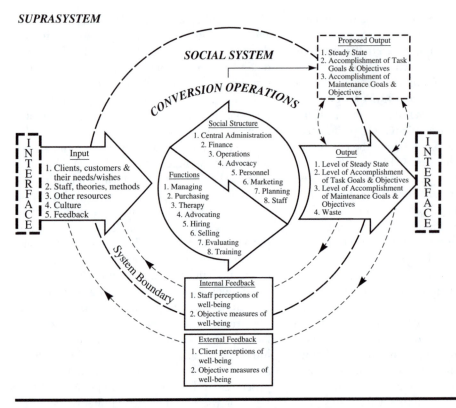

FIGURE 12.2 Formal Organization: Modeling the Structural Components

sion operations. You will find them summarized under *Social Structure* within *Conversion Operations* in Figure 12.2. In other words, the eight structural components are generic to all levels of social systems. Our interest in this chapter is in their specific application to formal organizations.

Boundary. All social systems will possess a formally designated boundary and expend energies in the maintenance of the boundary. Typically, this boundary will be referred to in the legal document that created the formal organization. Implicit in this designation is the area in which the system is sanctioned to operate. Boundary is always evident in the social (role) behaviors of those having a boundary-maintaining function. Physical structures may be

employed in performing the boundary-maintaining function, but these structures are not the system's boundary. A security guard would serve as an example of a person that would conduct a boundary-maintaining function, for example, checking IDs of those seeking admission to the offices of the organization.

Holon. In developing organizations, an important consideration is raised with regard to the concept of holons. Recall that holons are subsystems that are both complete systems on their own and also a functional part of the larger system. Many organizational theorists use varying language to make this basic point: each component subsystem should be as functionally self-contained as possible. Each component holon in a system should have its own system integrity and should also be efficiently integrated into the operation of the larger system. The basic premise is that each self-contained subunit becomes a module within the larger system.

We use the parable of the watchmakers to illustrate this point. It goes like this: There once were two watchmakers. The first watchmaker, the Craftsman, made each watch by hand, assembling the watch piece by piece until each was complete. The second watchmaker, the Holon, assembled his watches as subassemblies. He would put together the gears, the winding stem, the case, and so forth as parts. When he had a number of these subassemblies, he would put them together into finished watches. Two benefits lead to the Holon watchmaker running the Craftsman out of business. First, the Holon watchmaker was able to work more quickly and produce more watches. His watches were more reliable because he repeated each operation until it was familiar and efficient. Secondly, each time the Craftsman had to stop his assembly, he was forced to begin all over again. In addition, if he dropped a watch, it went to pieces and he had to start at the beginning. Even when Holon dropped a watch, it was relatively easy to put the finished subassemblies back together.

Holons can be understood as intermediate steady state components of a larger system. When possible, the preferred organizational principle is to design robust systems with stable and self-contained components that are both complete systems and a part of the larger system.

Suprasystem. This component identifies all social units external to the social system that influence the behavior of that system. These units are always specific and will tend to be those involved in input/output exchanges with the system. An example using a social work agency would be referral agencies, which are social units on the input side of the subject system. Structurally, there will be individuals performing extramural roles that manage

suprasystem relationships. An example would be those members of the social system engaged in marketing or in public relations.

Interface. Typically, the social units comprising the system's suprasystem will have specific and formalized arrangements through which they conduct their relationships. In formal organizations, this frequently takes the form of a contract. An example would be a contract that a youth-serving agency might have with a juvenile court. Those members of the agency involved in managing these contracts evidence social roles involved with the interface between the system and its suprasystem.

Input. All social systems acquire everything they need to operate from their suprasystems. The structure required in this procurement function is labeled input. An agency's outreach program would serve an input function as would the purchasing unit of that same agency. In social systems theory, we identify two classes of inputs. Task, or signal, inputs are those that are processed and become task outputs. This corresponds to the goal-attainment function. Maintenance inputs are those resources needed to convert task inputs to task outputs and correspond to performing the integration function.

Proposed Output. *Goal* is synonymous with our use of *proposed output* and all formal organizations by definition possess specific goals and objectives. A system's goal structure operationalizes its purpose and identifies its domain of operation. An example of a goal of an agency serving senior citizens might be to advance the health and well-being of senior citizens by providing daily home-delivered nutritious meals.

Conversion Operations. This component identifies the system's structural components and their associated functional processes that convert inputs to outputs. The ties between the structural components and these processes were also displayed in Figure 12.1. In that graphic, the focus was in identifying the functional processes associated with steady state.

Output.   This component identifies the results of the conversion of inputs to their final state. We identified two final states, maintenance and task, along with residuals labeled waste. Maintenance outputs deal with performing the integration function—satisfaction of the needs of the system's internal social units. Task outputs deal with the performance of the goal-attainment function. Waste refers to the inefficient use of all inputs. An example of a social structure involved with output would be a state hospital's discharge unit.

Feedback.   The final component, labeled feedback, describes the cyclical structures found in all social systems that link output back to inputs. Employing the generalist practice model, feedback measures the extent to which the original conditions were modified in accord with the system's intentions. A management information system (MIS) in a formal organization would serve as an example of a structure through which feedback occurs.

In discussing both functional requisites and structural components, our focus has been on the mature or fully operational social system. Now we turn our attention to how formal organizations form and develop.

SOCIAL SYSTEMS THEORY: DEVELOPMENTAL STAGES OF FORMAL ORGANIZATIONS

In earlier parts of this book, we identified authors who have made significant contributions to social systems theory. Now our special thanks go to Daniel Katz and Robert L. Kahn.[12] They have offered a way of examining what we are labeling the developmental stages of formal organizations.

These two theorists, like your authors, also owe much to the work of von Bertalanffy, Parsons, and Allport in the development of what they label open systems theory. In their words, "general systems theory should be open systems theory."[13] Katz and Kahn summarized their position as follows, "Our basic model of a social system is a structure that imports energy from the external world, transforms it, and exports a product to the environment that is the source for a reenergizing of the cycle."[14] In its essence, open systems theory develops from the notion of entropy, the disordering process that characterizes all matter. Open systems theory is a theory of negative entropy—the ordering process.[15] From this position, social organizations are, by their very nature, dependent on their environments for existence. Organizations, through input/output exchanges, have the capacity to resist the forces of entropy and to develop—to exhibit the characteristics of negative entropy.

We essentially hold the same basic position. Our interest is in the application of this position to the construction of a theory of social systems that will have relevance to the generalist practice of social work. We differ somewhat from Katz and Kahn around the notion of negative entropy. We believe that all social systems evidence both the processes of entropy and negative entropy. For us the concept of entropy is useful in thinking about the disordering process necessary for a system to adapt to a constantly changing environment. In other words, entropy as a social process is a useful way of thinking about social change. It is only when entropy becomes the dominant process that the system will lose steady state and cease to exist.

In the chapters dealing with the social group, we introduced you to exchange theory. Our interest at that point was to offer an explanation at the level of the social group of how groups form. Recall that a social group can be as small as two individuals enacting reciprocal roles, for example, husband to wife or friend to friend. Now we turn to open systems theory as developed by Katz and Kahn for assistance in describing the process by which formal organizations come into existence and develop.[16] Keep in mind our use of logic modeling (see Chapters 1 and 2). The origins of all social organizations are to be found in step 1 (conditions) and step 2 (assumptions about conditions).

Katz and Kahn identified three growth stages of formal organizations: stage 1—primitive collective responses to common problems; stage 2—insurance of stability of structure; and stage 3—elaborated supportive structures.[17] Through these three stages, they suggested it is possible to track the growth and development of formal organizations, with particular reference to the evolution of their specialized structures.

According to Katz and Kahn, two conditions set the stage for the initial development of formal organizations: (1) commonly defined environmental conditions and (2) the needs and abilities of the population. The position advanced by Katz and Kahn is very similar to the position we have taken with respect to how all social organizations come into existence. In short, there is a problem or opportunity that is commonly defined, the resolution of which is determined by those affected to be best addressed through some form of collective versus individual action. The functions to be performed generate the particular tasks to be accomplished. During stage 1, the continuing environmental pressure to solve the problem or to explore an opportunity maintains the conditions necessary for the pursuit of cooperative action; these same conditions facilitate the evolution of the social structure most advantageous for the accomplishment of the desired goal. An example of an environmental problem might be persistent vandalism and assaults on residents living in an apartment complex. Calls to the apartment owner and police have proved ineffective, so those living in the complex decide to organize and find ways of defending themselves and of protecting their property.

This collective action evidences evolvement of the goal-attainment function—dealing with a condition existing in the social environment.

In this first stage, the relationships are tenuous, and their continuance is understandable in terms of a commonly defined danger, both to property and to person. Here it is important to draw a distinction between the evolution of a primary (or natural) group and a secondary group (formal organization). The development of the social system is driven by external circumstances (the commonly defined threat), and the cooperative activities among members are functionally related to dealing with this threat. The evolving system has been consciously created as a means to accomplish an agreed-on end state—the control of vandalism and assaults. In contrast, recall that in the formation of a social group, the personal needs of participants act as the primary catalyst. The satisfaction of social needs by the group members represents the end state. In other words, the group exists principally to satisfy the needs of its members. Caution should be exercised here; all forms of social organization have both internally and externally oriented features. What is being illustrated are some differences in emphasis that affect the development patterns of formal organizations.

To return to the example, in this first stage, the members perceive their cooperative relationships to be effective vis-à-vis the external threat. This establishes the conditions for the second stage—insurance of stability of structure. As indicated by the name given to the second stage, the effort here is to control the variability of behaviors so that a required level of organizational stability is achieved—in other words, the creation of social structures. For example, if some rotation of watch by members of the concerned group is agreed on as a step toward mutual protection, and some people fail to take their turn, protection of person and property is again threatened. Katz and Kahn suggested that the bases for the development of the primitive cooperative structures are the shared values and normative expectations of task performance for those dealing with the common problem.[18] These features are not enough to assure the stability of the evolving social structure. Interfering at the individual level is a host of competing problems and time demands ("I can't watch tonight, this is my night to bowl."), and perceptions of how serious the current problem is and how successful the coping efforts have been. Arising out of these crude and tentative initial efforts at cooperation will be the beginnings of a formalized authority structure; its aim is the formulation and enforcement of rules to reduce the variability and instability of the behavior resulting from the emerging social structure. Examples would include the election of a chair, agreement on regular meeting times, publishing a roster of members, a dues structure, and so on. These actions give evidence of the evolution of social structures with which to perform the other three functional imperatives—adaptation, pattern maintenance, and integration. While initially focusing on establishing greater stability to internal structures associated with pattern maintenance, members will elaborate by also addressing external functions (the start of the marketing of the product or service—the adaptation function).

If the cooperative efforts continue to prove successful, and some level of stability of the emerging social structure is achieved, a decision might be made to further formalize the structure by creating a constitution and bylaws and having the organization registered as a not-for-profit or for-profit organization under state law. The development of a legal authority structure as the dominant form of authority further distinguishes this organization as a formal organization as opposed to a social group.

The point of special interest here is that if the fledgling organization survives, it is this primitive authority structure that becomes the basis of the organization's management subsystem, that is, the structure through which the work of the parts will be connected and coordinated. In social systems terms, the focus of the emerging legal form of authority is related to performing the goal-attainment function (task goals). The exercise of the authority structure diminishes in varying degrees the choices of actions available for those participating. Participants no longer are pitching in and helping out as they see fit. Rather, a series of organizational roles has evolved, and the individual is now being fitted into this system of roles. Further augmenting the normative expectations of role performance is a set of rules backed up by a legal authority structure—"If you don't pay your dues, your apartment will be dropped from those being watched." Here we have the emergence of the pattern-maintenance function and its associated value base.

If the primitive social organization is to survive, attention must be given to developing and maintaining the emerging social system. A new function emerges within the authority structure, that devoted to the maintenance of the structure itself. This growth feature is what will be referred to as part of the process of differentiation—the elaboration of specialized subsystems dealing with the special problems being confronted by the social system as it seeks to survive and then grow.

At this point in its development, the authority structure has two distinguishable functions—goal attainment and pattern maintenance. A third emerging function dealing with the needs of those individuals occupying roles within the social system also starts to become evident. In other words, a certain level of predictability and consistency is needed to pursue the goal-attainment function, but there is a growing need to be attentive to the individual and social needs of the members of the system. These needs give rise to the integration function, which is concerned with enhancing the social system itself. In our example we would expect the appointment of someone to be secretary. This person (also a part of the authority subsystem) would be responsible for taking minutes and otherwise recording decisions (rules) made by the group. Other maintenance functions would include such activities as holding workshops for the orientation (socialization) of new members, recognizing through awards the special contributions made by members, and so on.

The assumption is that the maintenance function within the formally constituted authority structure is never fully and continuously successful in meeting both the organization's needs and those of its members. This deficit gives rise to what is termed the organization's informal social structure. In social systems theory, the informal structure comprises an important part of any formal organization's maintenance function. This informal structure is comprised of a social group(s), or a natural system. A large formal organization may be comprised of any number of loosely coupled social groups. The communication linkage among such groups has frequently been termed the **grapevine** when contrasted with the organization's formal communication network.

Unlike the formal features of the organization's authority structure, which relate to members in their organizational roles, an informal structure emerges that helps to link people to each other as total personalities. The informal organization also tends to focus on tension points between organizational and human needs and thus can be very helpful in performing the integration function of the total organization. An example would be in the social support that members provide each other in dealing with work-related sources of stress, such as efforts at preventing or reducing burnout.

The focus of stage 2 is stabilizing the social structure, and this is accomplished largely through the development of its legal authority subsystem. In other words, rules and rule enforcement procedures are added to shared values and task requirements as the means through which the social structure becomes stabilized. In a more stable (predictable) environment, there is a tendency for additional elaboration of task-related structures to occur; this, in turn,

spurs further development of the related supportive structures. For purposes of illustration, let us assume that the organization originally formed for the protection of the apartment dwellers has proved quite successful. The organization became incorporated and now has a paid staff of twenty people. The organization and its paid staff are supported by a monthly fee paid by members who receive protection services. The structural elaboration is evident in the development of specially trained and paid personnel as opposed to the previous use of volunteers. Further, the paid staff not only provides security services for members but also checks daily on the well-being of the older residents.

According to the Katz and Kahn formulation, stage 3 focuses on the elaboration of the organization's supportive structure. Conceptually, the elaboration is related to the open-system nature of social organizations. The input/output relationship that the organization has with its suprasystem forms the basis for the elaboration of its various subsystems. On the input side is the tendency for subsystems to develop in order to procure needed resources. In social systems theory, this results in the creation of structures associated with acquiring the maintenance inputs. In very small organizations, this typically takes the form of expanded features of selected roles; for example, the executive of the agency assumes responsibility for fundraising activities. On the output side, the tendency is toward the development of subsystems concerned with the marketing/disposal of system outputs (adaptation function). Again, in small systems this is most likely to be evidenced by organizational members taking on additional duties related to the suprasystem's acceptance of the system's output.

To expand on the earlier example of the organization formed to provide security services, on the input side would be the evolution of specialized social structures associated with the screening and selection of new staff and new customers (the future personnel department). This effort will give rise to additional structures that will serve to help maintain the system's boundaries. Efforts will be made to obtain federal or state grants pertaining to the specialized security services being offered elderly residents, contacts will be negotiated with suppliers offering new technology in the area of security, and so on (interfaces will be formed with key social units in the system's suprasystem). Relative to output would be such efforts as marketing the security services to nearby apartment dwellers and local business establishments, and consulting with the police, courts, and other community agencies on the specialized functions of the security services. These actions would evidence the elaboration of the adaptation function.

To summarize, the contributions of Katz and Kahn have been particularly helpful in describing the developmental stages of formal organizations. More specifically, they have been helpful in suggesting linkages between the performance of the master functions (the four functional requisites) and the development of the eight structural components comprising social systems theory. Through the performance of these four functions, the eight structural components emerge and give rise to the social system itself. In terms of sequence, it is the goal-attainment function that initiates the process. This function gets regularized through the development of the adaptation function (marketing the product or service) and by attention to the pattern-maintenance function. The last to become stabilized is performance of the integration function. When all four master functions have become stabilized, we have, at this level, a social system.

SOCIAL SYSTEMS THEORY: TOTAL QUALITY MANAGEMENT

In Chapter 2 you were introduced to the social systems perspective and its nine assumptions. Two will be particularly relevant as we discuss Total Quality Management.

4. When fully developed, all forms of social organization display self-maintaining and development characteristics.
6. Well-being is the natural state of all humans and the various forms of social organization that humans join to form.

In the pages ahead, we will be examining the contribution made by those writing about **Total Quality Management** to our presentation of social systems theory and its application to formal organizations. While not synonymous, think of the notion of **quality** as being essentially comparable to our use of goal attainment as a requisite of all social systems.

We have indicated that there is no final steady state; there is no final state of well-being. Steady state is a variable and is evidenced by an ordering process. When we talk about a social system evidencing self-maintaining and development characteristics, we are talking about the presence of this ordering process. Authors writing about Total Quality Management build from this same assumption. In short, quality can be likened to a race without a finish line.

During the latter part of the decade of the 1980s and into the 1990s, the notion of quality began to take on special meaning in understanding the behavior of formal organizations. Our intent in this final section is to connect social systems theory to the growing interest in quality. The origin of this attention to quality is found in the work of W. Edwards Deming. As one writer put it, Deming is "the man who discovered quality."[19] Deming's contribution is in an approach to management known variously as Total Quality Management (TQM) or Continuous Quality Improvement (CQI).

In summarizing the implications of TQM to social work, Brannen and Streeter noted:

This introduction to TQM should provide enough information for social workers to recognize that TQM is clearly consistent with the foundations of social work practice. For example, TQM is based on a very humanistic philosophy. It begins with a belief that people are born good, they want to do a good job, and they deserve respect.

In addition, systems theory provides the conceptual framework for looking at the interrelationships that exist between parts of the organization. The key to TQM is that everyone in the organization must think in terms of systems rather than maintaining the focus on individuals working within the system. Continuing to focus on individual parts rather than relationships between the parts will preserve the practice of addressing the consequences rather than the root causes of problems.[20]

A statistician, W. Edwards Deming is generally recognized as the father of TQM. It is of consequence that the origins of his interest occurred during his work at Western Electric's Hawthorne plant in Chicago during the 1920s. This is the same plant and roughly the same time period in which the Hawthorne studies were conducted and that gave rise to what we have described as the human relations position on organizational theory.[21] Placing the origins of Deming's work in the 1920s is only to establish the point that this philosophy of management and its applications to practice are not new. What is new is the impact that his view of management is having on American business, health organizations, and most recently on human social service organizations and social work. Quality was the byword of the 1990s.

Largely ignored in this country until the early 1980s, Deming's approach to management was embraced by the Japanese. The comeback and success of Japanese business following World War II is credited in large part to the management philosophy and principles advanced by Deming and others who were focusing on the notion of quality.

Our interest in Deming's work is the contribution it makes to a theory of social systems. Several characteristics of quality offer a point of entry to a review of TQM and its systems features. First, quality is a characteristic of a system's output. It makes no difference whether the output is a product or a service; it needs to be perceived by those who receive it as possessing quality. Simply put, quality is defined by the customer or client, not by the person or persons who have produced the output. This position is entirely consistent with our presentation of social systems theory. The justification for every system is to be found in its suprasystem, not in the needs of the system itself. To link this position to the function of goal attainment, it is the customer or client who must be satisfied.

Social systems operate in cycles, and there are smaller cycles operating within larger cycles. In a human services agency, the condition of the client at case closure, that person's perception of the services received, and those held by the person's significant others defines quality. We refer to this person as the end recipient of the service. But there are internal customers or clients as well. For example, let us say that our end recipient was seen at intake and an assessment was conducted. Following that assessment, the end recipient was referred to a treatment worker. In this instance our end recipient was received by another, but internal, "customer," the treatment worker. The treatment worker will likewise assign a perception of quality or lack thereof to the service performed by the intake worker. In TQM, the quality of the product or service results from the process that produces that product or service. This process is never perfected; but efforts at improving the process are continuous. The implications are of consequence. In modeling social systems theory, we identify two types of feedback, process and outcome. The performance of the internal evaluation function monitors the process itself. Are we following the agreed-on services plan (step 5 in Figure 1.6, The Generalist Practice Model)—are we doing it this way? In other words, are we following the prescribed process? The two forms of feedback are linked in producing the immediate and final effects (steps 6 and 7 in the generalist practice model). This process evaluation provides the information necessary to continue the effort at improving the process itself.

Second, quality is a dynamic concept. It is constantly changing. Conceptually, the end recipient of a system's product or service is always in that system's suprasystem. The system's suprasystem is constantly changing. Therefore, the client's or customer's needs and wishes are changing and that person's definition of quality is changing. This characteristic of TQM helps explain the dynamic nature of social systems and the complexities involved in maintaining steady state. What a customer defined as quality yesterday may not be so defined today.

The final characteristic of quality to be mentioned here is that all those who hold roles in the organization must commit themselves to quality. This commitment to quality then becomes a key aspect of a shared organizational value—"we are number one in quality." The notion of a shared organizational value becomes part of the formal organization's culture. Here we establish a link between performance of the goal-attainment function, an external and consummatory function, and pattern maintenance, an internal and instrumental function. Through performing the pattern-maintenance function, this value is preserved and enhanced. Keeping in mind our earlier discussion of the pattern-maintenance function, central management must be committed to quality and arrangements must be made to socialize all system members to the importance of quality.[22] In other words, if the output of a system is to be perceived by the client or customer as representing quality, all members of the system must be committed to the notion of quality. Quality as used here is both a cause and an effect; it is a core pattern of the social system that must be maintained. Pattern maintenance, in social systems theory, is an internal function. It is also a means for dealing with the integration function.

From time to time in this book we have interrupted our discussion to suggest research questions drawn from social systems theory. We will again do so using the concept of quality as defined above and propose an hypothesis that derives from the means-end relationship between the performance of the pattern-maintenance and integration functions.

In all formal organizations, there will be the following:

1. a positive correlation between perception of job satisfaction among those holding organization roles and their perceptions of the quality of the system itself;
2. a negative correlation between the perception of the quality of the social system among those holding organizational roles and the level of burnout among these same members; and
3. a positive correlation between perceptions of job challenge and perceptions of the quality of the social system among those holding organizational positions.

Now we return to the contribution of TQM to social systems theory. Central in any discussion of TQM from the position held by Deming is the importance he attached to the principle of "constancy of purpose." To state this principle in social systems terms—a commitment to organizational purposes is the surest path to organizational well-being. Stated in the reverse, the surest path to social disorganization is the loss of organizational purpose. How do you stay on the path? If we were to pose this question to Deming, we believe he would answer—"you do it with data!" Recall that he was a statistician. This is the feedback loop in the social systems theory. Data systems can be created to monitor constantly the processes being followed in pursuit of organizational goals and the quest for quality.

Deming's mentor, Walter Shewhart, helped him in his applications of statistics to this monitoring function.[23] Shewhart was a physicist at Bell Laboratories during the 1930s. There he was interested in studying variations in manufacturing processes through statistical measures. Deming adopted the idea of using statistical measures as a means of reducing variance from an agreed-on process aimed at producing a quality product or service. Deming's approach is consistent with our use of positive and negative feedback when applied to the comparison of proposed and actual output. As formal organizations grow ever larger and technically more complex, feedback mechanisms also become more complex. The current use of statistical measures and computer programs to measure negative and positive feedback evidences this growing complexity.

Some social workers are uncomfortable with Deming's quantitative approach to the measurement of quality. We must remember that Deming's work was primarily focused on improvement in business practices. But his philosophy and his management principles have application to all formal organizations. We are interested in Deming's insights that have application to the development of social systems theory and to the generalist practice of social work.

Before leaving Deming's contributions, we wish to note his focus on the needs and wishes of the customer or client. In this sense, Deming's basic approach to management is entirely compatible with social work's focus on the client, starting where the client is and fully involving the client in every step of the helping process. Adherence to this approach produces quality. Finally, Deming was influenced not only by Shewhart but also by many others, including such experts on human motivation as Frederick Herzberg, Douglas McGregor, and Abraham Maslow.[24] Even the most casual reading of Deming's approach to TQM will evidence his beliefs in the inherent worth and strengths of humankind. A basic theme in his approach to TQM is a strengths perspective, one that links the commitment to quality to the opportunity that every individual seeks for self-development. In short, the role of management

is to create the organizational environment that will permit this to occur.

THEORIES X, Y, AND Z

One of the management perspectives most congenial to the social work viewpoint is found in the work of Douglas McGregor, a management professor at MIT. McGregor coined the terms "Theory X" and "Theory Y" to describe two views of human nature.

Theory X corresponded to the view identified with scientific management (and the behavioral learning perspective) that human beings are motivated by external factors, and need to be controlled and manipulated by rewards in order to perform. The Theory X perspective holds that people will avoid work where possible, and it is the role of the manager to be directive and controlling in managing the workforce.

Theory Y held that workers have intrinsic motivation, and that managers can tap the self-control of workers and harness it for the job. This latter view was more consistent with the human relations viewpoint of Mayo and others. While McGregor is often thought to be an advocate of Theory Y, in fact he wanted managers to consider both perspectives and try to develop new perspectives. In McGregor's view, the case on human motivation was not closed.[25]

One further development of which McGregor would likely have approved is Theory Z. This approach is based on a Japanese management model developed by William Ouchi. Theory Z emphasizes gaining employee loyalty by assuring lifetime employment. This implicitly encourages worker identification with the company, and promotes stable productivity and high morale.[26] The Theory Z approach was an indirect outgrowth of the work of Edward Deming in the Japanese industrial reconstruction, which we discussed earlier.

Theory X tends to regard the workers as outside the organizational system and to be used for conversion operations only. Theory Y treats workers as more an organic part of the system and regards their welfare as, in part, a system outcome. Theory Z is the most extreme view on treating workers as part of the integrative system function. Their welfare is to be considered as an internal factor rather than external.

SUMMARY

In this chapter, we developed our approach to a theory of social systems by distinguishing those features that are specific to formal organizations. This was accomplished by first distinguishing social systems theory from the rationalist and human relations theories. We employed the concept of emergence to help justify the categorization of the formal organization as a separate and distinct system level.

We then introduced the four functional variables in terms of their distinguishing characteristics within formal organizations, along with the eight structural features of social systems. We summarized Katz and Kahn's contributions to social systems theory with particular reference to their formulation of the stages of development found in all formal organizations. The chapter closed with a review of the contribution W. Edward Deming made to social systems theory and to the practice of management.

GLOSSARY

Chief executive officer (CEO)   The designation of the top administrator of a formal organization.

Grapevine   The slang expression for the informal information system found in formal organizations.

Quality   A perception of the client system as to the overall value of a service or product. As used in social systems theory, it is essentially equivalent to goal attainment, a variable in achieving steady state.

Total Quality Management (TQM)   A philosophy of management in which the concept of quality is deemed central.

NOTES

1. For a discussion of the concepts of Gemeinschaft and Gesellschaft, see Ferdinand Toennies, *Community and Society*, trans. and ed. Charles P. Loomis (Lansing, MI: Michigan State University Press, 1957).
2. Max Weber, "The Three Types of Legitimate Rule," trans. Hans Girth, in *A Sociological Reader on Complex Organization*, 3rd ed., eds. Amitai Etzioni and Edward W. Lehman (New York: Holt, Rinehart and Winston, 1980), 4–10.
3. See Talcott Parsons, "Suggestions for a Sociological Approach to Theory of Organizations," *A Sociological Reader on Complex Organizations*, 2nd ed., ed. Amitai Etzioni (New York: Holt, Rinehart and Winston, 1969), 32–46.
4. Weber, "The Three Types of Legitimate Rule."
5. Ibid.
6. Peter M. Blau, *Exchange and Power in Social Life* (New York: John Wiley & Sons, 1964).

7. W. Richard Scott, *Organizations: Rational, Natural and Open Systems* (Englewood Cliffs, NJ: Prentice Hall, 1981), 80–81.
8. Alvin W. Gouldner, "Organizational Analysis," in *Sociology Today*, eds. Robert K. Merton, Leonard Broom, and Leonard S. Cottrell, Jr. (New York: Basic Books, 1959), 405.
9. For a discussion of emergence, see Ludwig von Bertalanffy, *General Systems Theory* (New York: George Braziller, 1968), 55; F. Kenneth Berrien, *General and Social Systems* (New Brunswick, NJ: Rutgers University Press, 1968), 61–62; and Walter Buckley, *Sociology and Modern Systems Theory* (Englewood Cliffs, NJ: Prentice Hall, 1967), 143–145.
10. Walter Buckley, *Sociology and Modern Systems Theory* (Englewood Cliffs, NJ: Prentice Hall, 1967), 42.
11. For an interesting review, see Fritz J. Roethlisberger and William J. Dickson, "Human Relations

and the Informal Organization," in *Critical Studies in Organization and Bureaucracy*, eds. Frank Fischer and Carmen Sirianni (Philadelphia: Temple University Press), 86–95.

12. Daniel Katz and Robert Kahn, *The Social Psychology of Organizations*, 2nd ed. (New York: John Wiley & Sons, 1978), 8.

13. Ibid., 55.

14. Ibid., 25–26.

15. Ibid., 3–16.

16. Ibid., 69–119.

17. Ibid.

18. Ibid.

19. Andrea Gabor, *The Man Who Discovered Quality* (New York: Penguin Books, 1990).

20. Stephen J. Brannen and Calvin L. Streeter, "Total Quality Management: New Effectiveness Measures for Social Services," Unpublished paper presented at the Annual Program Meeting of the Council on Social Work Education, Kansas City, 1992.

21. Note the discussion in Chapter 11 under the heading, The Human Relations Position.

22. W. Edward Deming, "Out of Crises" (Cambridge, MA: Massachusetts Institute of Technology, Center for Advanced Engineering Study, 1986).

23. Walter Shewhart, *Statistical Method from the Viewpoint of Quality Control*, ed. W. Edward Deming (Washington, DC: Graduate School of the Department of Agriculture, 1939).

24. Gabor, *The Man Who Discovered Quality*, 12–13.

25. D. Pugh, D. Hickson, and C. Hinnings (Eds). *Writers on Organizations* (Beverly Hills, CA: Sage, 1985).

26. William Ouchi. *Theory Z* (New York: Avon Books, 1981).

CHAPTER 13

THE FORMAL ORGANIZATION AS A SOCIAL SYSTEM

BOUNDARY
SUPRASYSTEM
INTERFACE
INPUT
PROPOSED OUTPUT
CONVERSION OPERATIONS

OUTPUT
FEEDBACK
SUMMARY
GLOSSARY
NOTES

In this chapter, we will model the formal organization as a social system. The approach to model building derives from social systems theory and is designed for use by the generalist social work practitioner. The model also has application for the advanced practitioner planning a career in social work administration. The model is an assessment tool, providing the practitioner with a way of thinking about and working with formal organizations.

In our development of a theory of social systems, we hold that all social systems strive to maintain steady state through the performance of four required functions: goal attainment, adaptation, integration, and pattern maintenance. These functions are performed through the evolution of eight structural components. The distinctive features of these structures in formal organizations is that they are formalized; they are made explicit.

In earlier chapters, the social systems model was applied at the microscale level, a counseling relationship, or a family. In each instance, the subject system was comprised of specific individuals enacting reciprocal roles with others. The parts of the social system were specific individuals. Now we move to a more complex system, the formal organization. In so doing, the shift is away from specific individuals in specific roles to the formal organization itself. The parts of the system are administrative units, departments or divisions, for example, rather than individuals in specific work roles, such as a social worker. As we will show later, it is possible to move the level of analysis down to a specific work group and the individuals who comprise that work group. Like a microscope, one can pick up ever greater amounts of detail if we increase the power of the lens. For now, we will start with a low-power lens. Our interest is in understanding the relationships among the main parts comprising the formal social system, not the behaviors of specific individuals within the system. These parts, administrative units of the formal organization, can be viewed usefully as subsystems; they are the social structures that evolve to perform the four functions required to maintain steady state.

Many types of formal organizations are in existence. For example, it is possible for a lone social worker to incorporate for purposes of conducting a private practice. In such an instance, the organization might be comprised of the practitioner and a part-time secretary. Given its legal status under our definition, such an organization would constitute a formal organization. Our primary interest in this chapter, however, is with more complex social organizations such as

those public and private agencies that employ social workers and/or deliver social services. Given the absence of a generally accepted typology of formal organization, we offer two classes: type A and type B. Type A, the subject of this chapter, is characterized by (1) formal or legal existence, (2) a hierarchically organized legal authority structure, (3) functionally differentiated roles, and (4) a multigroup structure. Type B is comprised of all other forms of legally constituted social organizations.

Formal organizations categorized as type A can become quite large. Many such organizations have members numbering in the hundreds, thousands, or in some instances, the millions. Given the scale and scope of formal organizations, we have decided to use administrative units as the primary building blocks for the structural presentation of the model. Because of the relatively stable patterns that these roles take in formal organizations, it is possible to cluster them unit by unit and/or group by group for purposes of model construction and usage.

An example would be a large county welfare department employing a thousand people and made up of twenty different administrative units. One such unit, intake, might have thirty caseworkers performing the intake function for establishing eligibility of clients for the Temporary Assistance to Needy Families program. Given the federal and state regulations involved, it can be assumed that all thirty caseworkers will enact their work roles in essentially the same way. In this intake unit, there would be approximately six supervisors, each responsible for five workers and each carrying out his or her role in a similar manner. These six supervisors would be supervised by a program director. Given this administrative structure, if the model focused on the individual role (position) as its unit of analysis, there would be a thousand such units with thirty-seven professional roles in the intake unit alone. Such a size would render the model extremely complex and perhaps useless as a practice tool. For most applications, the intake unit itself could be treated as the unit of attention and a structural building block for purposes of modeling the total agency as a social system. This is possible because of the assumed comparability in the role behaviors of the thirty caseworkers, the six casework supervisors, and the one program supervisor. As indicated earlier, the focus of the model is on the common patterns characterizing role behaviors, not the individual features of the human personality. By focusing on the administrative units as sub-systems, the model can examine relationships among twenty subsystems rather than a thousand. In such an application, the role of the intake program supervisor is representative of the functions of the thirty caseworkers and six supervisors comprising that subsystem. Some detail is lost, but what is gained is an ability to grasp and better understand the larger and more complex patterns of the system as a whole.

If it became important to understand better what was happening within the intake unit, that unit would be designated as the system, with the remaining nineteen organizational units of the county welfare department becoming part of the intake unit's suprasystem. At this level of inquiry, the individual work roles would become the unit of study and thus the structural building block for the inquiry. In large formal organizations, the model assumes a nesting of systems within systems (subsystems), thus permitting inquiry at various levels of specificity.

Our discussion of concepts representing social structures of the model will focus on the special attributes of the formal social system that distinguish it from other levels of social systems. The single most important attribute is the degree of formality in relationships among its member units, that is, the Gesellschaft as distinguished from the Gemeinschaft nature of these relationships. For purposes of context, you should recall that the formal organization is

"formed"; that is, it is a social tool that has been formally created in order to respond to some social problem or social opportunity existing in its environment. The underlying assumption is that this problem or opportunity can be addressed most successfully through a formal type of collective action as opposed to individual action coordinated informally. The contrived nature of this type of social organization and its assumed relationship to a social problem or a social opportunity also provide an explanation of the functional interdependence that the system is assumed to have with its suprasystem.

Weber's contribution to organizational theory is very useful in understanding the behavior of formal organizations. Of special help are his concepts of legal authority and division of labor. The concept of legal authority helps one understand how the parts of formal organizations are coordinated. The concept of division of labor helps us understand the interdependence among these parts and the specific evolution of those social structures necessary to maintain steady state.

The paragraphs that follow are organized under the various structural components of social systems theory—boundary, suprasystem, interface, input, proposed output, output, conversion operations (structure and process), and feedback. Each is part of the overall structure of the system and contributes to the performance of one or more of the four functions necessary for the system to maintain steady state.

BOUNDARY

Boundary, like each of the concepts comprising the model, refers to a social structure(s) found in every social system. To start this discussion, we will refer to an assumption that serves as the foundation for all forms of social organization: No form of social organization is self-sufficient; each is dependent on its environment for survival as well as for development. Survival and development take place through input and output exchanges with its environment. We have referred to this as a holonic quality.

The notion of boundary is closely associated with the identity of the social system and, as such, is the logical starting place for any application of the model.

To illustrate the use of the model in this chapter, we will use a hypothetical community agency called the Midtown Mental Health Center. This agency provides a variety of mental health services for the residents of Midtown; one such service targets those designated as **seriously and persistently mentally ill (SPMI).** Midtown is comprised of some 300,000 residents. Based on national statistics, approximately 3,000 (1 percent) are estimated to be SPMI. The center receives public monies from the community, from the state department of mental health, and from the federal government in the form of Medicaid payments to provide services to its SPMI citizens. The center has adopted a policy that permits it to restrict its services to those citizens who are residents of Midtown. In this example, the center has evolved a set of formal **policies** that serve to distinguish those who are eligible for its SPMI services from those who are not. These policies will serve to guide the development of a social structure to administer these policies. We will refer to this social structure as the SPMI intake unit. This unit will conduct the boundary-maintaining function for the center's SPMI services.

In Figure 13.1, we graphically display a hypothetical boundary-maintaining function. We will refer to this figure to illustrate several other social structures as we attempt to convey their interdependent features. First, each structure will be linked to proposed output (the goal structure). Proposed output as you will recall is the concept that operationalizes the purposiveness or mission of the system. In Figure 13.1, we have noted the mission of the system and have identified a selected goal and objective. In

short, the logic of the boundary-maintaining function is to be understood in terms of the purpose of the system itself. In performing the boundary-maintaining function, applicants (signal inputs) are being screened in terms of characteristics deemed important to this particular center in performing its conversion operations.

SUPRASYSTEM

Once the system has been designated and its boundary identified, those individuals, groups, and agencies relevant to its input/output exchange that are external to the system are designated as the system's suprasystem. For purposes of this example, consider that a community **strengths/needs assessment** has been conducted and these data have been abstracted from that assessment. The conditions described exist in Midtown and are thus external to the Midtown Community Mental Health Center. These conditions start the process of identifying the center's suprasystem. The justification for every system's existence is found in its suprasystem. In this instance, the establishment of the center itself was premised on the mental health needs of the people of Midtown. Assuming that the SPMI have been underserved, this represents a justification for the development of a new specialized service within the center—a case management service.

To develop the example, let us assume the case management service is now operational so that we can identify those individuals, groups, and agencies that have become key components of the center's suprasystem. Keep in mind that the suprasystem is a conceptual designation; it is a way of thinking about the center as a whole and its interdependent relationships with the community and the people it serves.

First, and most important, those community citizens who are SPMI are a part of the center's suprasystem. As we will illustrate later, these citizens are a targeted population for the center's

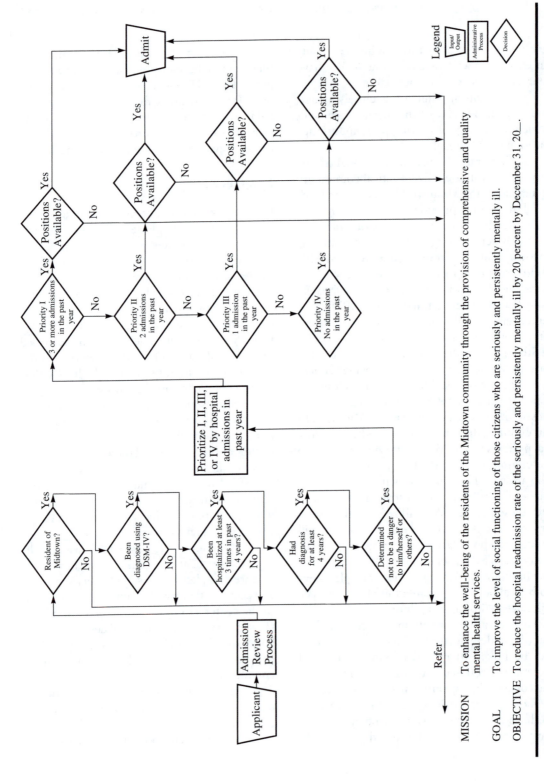

FIGURE 13.1   The Administration Process for the SPMI: The Boundary Maintenance Function

MISSION   To enhance the well-being of the residents of the Midtown community through the provision of comprehensive and quality mental health services.

GOAL   To improve the level of social functioning of those citizens who are seriously and persistently mentally ill.

OBJECTIVE   To reduce the hospital readmission rate of the seriously and persistently mentally ill by 20 percent by December 31, 20___.

services. Those that actually are admitted will be designated as signal inputs. Our strengths/needs assessment has indicated that 1.1 percent or 3,300 individuals (of the community's 300,000 population) have been defined as SPMI. The estimated SPMI population is above the state and national averages of 1.0 percent.

The hospital readmission rate of the SPMI in this community is 12 percent above the state's average. Immediately, these data indicate that those inpatient psychiatric units serving the SPMI are an important component of the center's suprasystem. Why? Because they suggest that the SPMI citizens of Midtown are utilizing inpatient services at a higher rate than those living elsewhere in the state. There may be a number of reasons for this high usage; one might be the lack of availability of community- and family-based alternatives to inpatient care. The center's case management service represents such an alternative.

Here we start to identify the systemic connections between the center, hospital inpatient units in the community, the SPMI and their families, and other agencies serving this population. In this sense, the center is part of a larger system that serves the SPMI in Midtown. Conceptually, what is the purpose of this larger system? As a practical matter, it is going to be very similar to the center's goal with respect to serving the SPMI: to enhance the well-being of the SPMI citizens of Midtown through the provision of quality mental health services. Suffice it to say at this point that community agencies serving the same population need to share some common goals for those they jointly serve. These common goals become the basis for working together.

INTERFACE

We have found the term *interface* to be useful to express the idea that formal social systems deal with each other both formally and specifically.

As used in this model, the system will have as many interfaces as it has components in its suprasystem. It is with the use of the concept of interface that we identify the specifics that occur in these exchanges.

It was noted that the SPMI population in Midtown was utilizing inpatient psychiatric services at a proportionately higher rate than the same population in other communities in the state. Let us now assume that those patients who are poor for the most part utilized the state mental hospital for their inpatient services. The hospital serving the region in which Midtown is located is one of several such mental health facilities operated by the state department of mental health. Both the department of mental health and the Midtown Mental Health Center share a goal of advancing the well-being of SPMI citizens by providing community-based mental health services in the least restrictive environment. To advance this goal, the department of mental health and the Midtown Mental Health Center entered into a contract that contained the following provisions:

1. The center's case management staff will participate with the hospital's social work staff in discharge planning for all SPMI clients residing in Midtown.
2. Upon discharge, the center's staff will personally contact all clients covered by the contract within forty-eight hours and offer case management services.
3. The center will provide quarterly progress reports to the director of the hospital's social work department on all SPMI citizens who have been referred to and have accepted the center's services.
4. The department's hospital will provide emergency inpatient services twenty-four hours a day for all of the center's SPMI clients deemed to be suicidal or at risk of harming others.
5. The department will reimburse the center for all out-of-hospital mental health services

not covered by Medicaid or related third-party payments at a mutually agreed-on rate.

Through this particular example we want to illustrate several features conveyed by interface. First, in formal organizations the interface frequently takes the form of a legal contract. Through the contract, the parties (there can be more than two) all agree to do something that has some perceived advantage to the other(s). In this way the contract advances the goal(s) of both the center and the state department of mental health.

Second, the concept of interface is helpful in conveying the idea that systems have input/output relationships with one another. In the example cited, the discharged client represents an output of the department's state hospital and an input to the center. This input/output relationship between systems is a universal characteristic incorporated into the systems model. Through this exchange, we get some sense of the ordering that exists in all societies and all communities.

Third, the example helps to demonstrate that no social system is self-sufficient; all are dependent on other social systems in order to accomplish their goals.

Now we will summarize some other interfaces that link the center to its suprasystem. The center does not own the building in which its offices are located. The building, the land, and certain maintenance services are leased from another community agency (social system), the Midtown Business Corporation (MBC). This is another of the center's many interfaces. In this instance, MBC has a goal of making money from property leases and the center has the goal of helping clients by providing its services in an accessible and efficient manner. The lease serves the interest of both systems.

The center does not employ its own pharmacist, technicians for laboratory work, or lawyers to handle its legal work. These services are contracted out and represent interfaces with other social systems that perform work required by the center. Two other interfaces illustrate the diversity and range of connections that the center has with its suprasystem. The center serves as a training center for a number of professional schools located at a nearby university. For example, the center has a practicum contract with the school of social work for both graduate and undergraduate students. This contract has specific provisions dealing with the number of students that can be accommodated, the stipends that will be paid to these students, their working hours, the amount and type of supervision they will receive, and so forth. Again, the contract serves the interest of both the center (by providing a source of new staff) and the school (by offering required practicum experiences for its students).

Finally, the center's service program, facilities, and administrative actions are monitored or accredited by a number of external agencies. For example, the state health department monitors the center to see that it conforms to the state's health and safety laws; the local fire marshal monitors to determine compliance with the local fire code; the center's service programs are reviewed periodically to determine compliance with accrediting standards; and the center's financial records are audited yearly to determine compliance with the rules of various external agencies that supply monies to the center, such as Medicaid monies. These are only a few of the agencies and groups that comprise the center's suprasystem. Each of these systems will expend resources in performing the boundary-maintenance function, maintaining their side of a shared boundary. These examples help establish the complexity and range of the external relationships that systems have and the administrative time required to manage these relationships. To understand how an agency works, it is not sufficient to simply understand its internal operations; its external relationships must be understood as well.

INPUT

The term *input* refers to all resources required from the suprasystem for the system to accomplish its purposes. What we wish to convey in this section is that social systems develop structures to acquire inputs from their suprasystems. Conceptually, every system has some specialized means for screening inputs to establish their relevance to system purposes. This screening has previously been described as associated with the boundary-maintenance function.

Inputs are classified as either signal or maintenance. In human service agencies, signal inputs are always clients or customers, though this is not necessarily so in other organizations. *Signal* is a generic term and simply means that the presence of such inputs activates the subject system. As used in this model, *signal inputs, task inputs,* and *throughputs* are synonymous terms used to distinguish those forms of input that are processed by the system as opposed to those that are employed in processing, that is, maintenance inputs.

We will develop the concept of input in the systems model through use of the Midtown Mental Health Center. The community strengths/needs assessment on which the logic model was based estimated that 1.1 percent of the 300,000 citizens of Midtown were SPMI. This suggests that 3,300 citizens would meet the definition of being SPMI and be eligible for case management services offered by the center. These people represent the center's potential customer base or client system for case management services.

Many readers find the idea of a client system being comprised of hundreds or thousands of people difficult to grasp. Most people are accustomed to thinking of a client as an individual, or at the most, a family. This is not so in generalist practice or in a social work administration or community practice. Just as a client system comprised of an individual or family possesses specific characteristics that are practice-relevant, so will a client system comprised of hundreds or thousands of people. In this illustration, these 3,300 citizens represent a key component of the center's suprasystem and many will become signal inputs for the center's case management service.

Maintenance inputs to the center include all resources to help clients and to maintain and develop the center as a social system. Its human resources include all of the mental health professionals, support and administrative staffs, and any others who directly help the center achieve its purposes.

In formal organizations, formal as well as informal means exist for tracking inputs as they progress through the system. In larger formal organizations, this tracking system is frequently referred to as a **management information system (MIS).** Through this feedback cycle, systems are able to maintain steady state. In the systems model, feedback is treated as a maintenance input, information that is critical for adjustments that may be necessary for the next processing cycle.

Recall that all forms of social organization develop a shared culture. This notion of a shared culture is particularly important in understanding the behavior of formal organizations. Culture is defined as a set of shared meanings that serve as the foundation for an organized way of life for people. Think of every formal organization as having a subculture that is derived from the larger culture. In this sense, its subculture is obtained from its suprasystem and treated as a maintenance input. Given that the larger culture is constantly changing, so is the system's own culture. Thus, every system is in process, is in a state of becoming.

PROPOSED OUTPUT

The importance of proposed output is highlighted in the definition of a formal organization: A form of social organization deliberately and formally created to achieve relatively specific and delimited goals.

Our approach to the formulation of proposed output builds from and extends the reasoning set forth in Chapter 3 and shown in Figures 3.3 and 3.4. There the notion of a hierarchy of outcomes was introduced as a way of formulating proposed output. In short, the hierarchy of outcomes represents a way of operationalizing the key feature of the definition of a formal organization.

The essential ideas of the hierarchy are set forth in Figure 13.2. The figure embodies the concept that every formal organization has its origins in some existing need or opportunity within the suprasystem and that the continued existence of the system depends to some degree on the satisfaction of these needs. In this presentation, the condition pertaining to the SPMI within the community of Midtown suggests that the population is underserved and the quality of their lives is being negatively impacted. As indicated in the *Conditions* column, it has been determined that a disproportionate number of the community's SPMI are being hospitalized. This is the condition that the center will seek to change.

Section II of Figure 13.2 diagrams the concept of a hierarchy of outcomes. Section III provides examples of proposed task outputs for each level of the hierarchy. The center's mission is "To enhance the well-being of the residents of the Midtown community through the provision of comprehensive and quality mental health services." Conceptually, the second or goal level of the hierarchy is formed by framing the mission statement as a question: How can this center enhance the well-being of the citizens of its community through the provision of comprehensive and quality mental health services? The answer to this question represents an operationalization of the mission statement and suggests areas of priority consistent with the community's needs and resources, and the center's capabilities. The structures that develop around producing the center's task output perform the goal-attainment and adaptation functions.

CONVERSION OPERATIONS

Conversion operations refer to a system's internal processes that transform its inputs into outputs. Our discussion will be organized around structure and interactions. In introducing the formal organization, we reviewed organizational and administrative theory.[1] Both the rationalist and human relations positions deal primarily with what we are describing as conversion operations—the internal operations of the system. The rationalist position assumes that, like a machine, the internal structures can be designed in a logical sequence that produces an output in an efficient and effective way. This position is premised on a closed-system view of the organization, one in which employees are motivated by economic incentives. Here the social structure of the system is Gesellschaft in its pure form.[2] Management, as a professional form of practice, is concerned with the design of these social structures and the motivation of employees to fully conform to those structures.

The human relations position accepts the closed-system view of the organization but rejects the premise that employees are guided primarily by economic incentives. They hold that employees behave as group members and are primarily motivated by social not economic incentives. The social structure of the system is defined in Gemeinschaft terms. The formal organization is not a new or higher-level system form; it is essentially a confederation of social groups organized around the work experience. The task of management is to design work structures that would satisfy the social needs of workers in their respective groups, but in a way that would get the work of the organization done as well—satisfied workers would be productive workers. Human relationists recognize

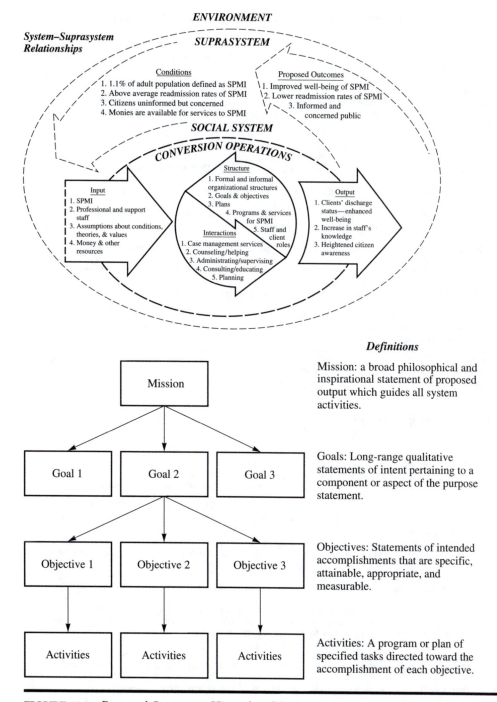

FIGURE 13.2   Proposed Output as a Hierarchy of Outcomes: The Formal Organization—Midtown Community Mental Health Center

THE HIERARCHY OF OUTCOMES—MIDTOWN MENTAL HEALTH CENTER

Section III
PROPOSED TASK OUTPUTS

MISSION: To enhance the well-being of the residents of the Midtown community through the provision of comprehensive and quality mental health services.

Goals

Goal 1: To reduce the incidence and prevalence of mental health problems among residents of Midtown.

Goal 2: To improve the level of social functioning of those citizens who are seriously and persistently mentally ill.

Goal 3: Through public education programs, to promote citizen-led efforts in improving the mental health of the citizens of Midtown.

Objectives

Objective 2.1: (Goal 2, Objective 1): To reduce the proportion of the adult population in the community who are seriously and persistently mentally ill from 1.1 to 1.0 percent by December 31, 20__.

Objective 2.2: To reduce hospital readmissions of the seriously and persistently mentally ill by 20 percent by December 31, 20__.

Objective 2.3: To increase the proportion of the seriously and persistently mentally ill who are working for pay from 5 percent to 10 percent by December 31, 20__.

Objective 2.4: To increase from 15 percent to 20 percent the number of those who are seriously and persistently mentally ill who live independently in their own home or apartment by December 31, 20__.

Activities

Activity 2.2.1 (Goal 2, Objective 2, Activity 1): By December 1, 20__ secure budget approval for implementing the Center's Readmission Reduction Program.

Activity 2.2.2: Effective January 1, 20__ to initiate a case finding program for those in the community who are seriously and persistently mentally ill.

Activity 2.2.3: Effective February 1, 20__ to add an additional half-time physician and a full-time nurse to the Center's medication clinic.

Activity 2.2.4: Effective February 15, 20__ to add one additional van and driver to the Center's Client Transportation Program.

Activity 2.2.5: Effective March 1, 20__ to add one additional social worker trained in medication compliance procedures to the Center's Supportive Counseling Service.

Activity 2.2.6: Effective April 1, 20__ to add one additional trainer to the Center's Daily Living Skills Program.

Activity 2.2.7: Effective April 15, 20__ to add two social workers to the Center's Case Management Program.

Activity 2.2.8: Monitor via monthly reports readmission of SPMI to inpatient care.

Activity 2.2.9: Prepare quarterly reports to executive staff on progress with Objective 2.2.

Section IV
PROPOSED MAINTENANCE OUTPUTS

MISSION: To enhance the well-being of the residents of the Midtown community through the provision of comprehensive and quality mental health services.

Goals

Goal 1: To develop a comprehensive range of quality mental health services.

Goal 2: To develop and maintain a professional staff dedicated to provision of quality mental health services.

Goal 3: Through programs of research, to increase the quality, efficiency, and effectiveness of the Center's mental health services.

Objectives

Objective 2.1 (Goal 2, Objective 1): To increase from 70 to 80 percent the proportion of the Center's current professional staff holding terminal degrees in their respective disciplines by December 31, 20__.

Objective 2.2: To employ and train ten case managers who possess professional degrees in social work by December 31, 20__.

Objective 2.3: to reduce the job turnover rate among the Center's professional staff from 26 percent to 20 percent by December 31, 20__.

Activities

Activity 2.2.1: (Goal 2, Objective 2, Activity 1): By January 12, 20__ to have obtained budgetary approval from the Center's board to hire 10 managers.

Activity 2.2.2: By January 27, 20__ to obtain administrative approval of the new case management job description.

Activity 2.2.3: By February 15, 20__ to advertise the case management positions in all of the state's major metropolitan papers.

Activity 2.2.4: By March 10, 20__ to have completed the training curriculum for case managers.

Activity 2.2.5: By March 30, 20__ to have hired five of the 10 case managers.

Activity 2.2.6: By May 15, 20__ the case managers will have completed training and developing their caseload.

Activity 2.2.7: By May 30, 20__ the evaluation of the training curriculum will have been completed and appropriate review made.

Activity 2.2.8: By December 31, 20__ ten case managers will have been hired, trained, and have full caseloads.

FIGURE 13.2 *(Continued)*

no inherent conflict between the organization's needs and those of its workers.

Structure

In accordance with social systems theory, social structures form as a consequence of performing the four required functions that produce steady state. While we identify eight such structures, conversion operations is the master concept; the remaining seven can be viewed as subconcepts. Within the concept of conversion operations, our focus is on those structures that are primarily concerned with the conversion of inputs to outputs, both task and maintenance.

This prescribed social structure is best evidenced by a formal organizational chart. Figure 13.3, Formal Administrative Structure—The Midtown Community Mental Health Center, incorporates all the basic features described by Weber and outlined in the rationalist position. In this sense, it is a useful tool to describe the internal features of what we call a system's conversion operations. Through this diagram, the following concepts are illustrated: (1) policy versus executive functions, (2) legal authority, and (3) division of labor.

Conceptually, every system is a subsystem of a larger system to which it is connected through input/output exchanges. In this example, the Midtown Mental Health Center is a formal organization whose function is to meet the mental health needs of the people residing in Midtown. It is one of many agencies in Midtown that has the purpose of responding to the needs and interests of its citizens. The center's **board of directors** is composed of representatives from the community and from other key segments of its suprasystem. It is useful to view the board as constituting a microcosm of the center's relevant suprasystem. Through use of the board generally and the individuals comprising the board particularly, the center possesses the capability of maintaining contact with relevant constituencies in the suprasystem, such

as the local medical society, politicians, the mental health society, industry, and human rights groups.

The board can be viewed as providing an oversight function, helping the center to pursue the purposes for which it was originally sanctioned. The board has a policy function, that of formulating agency goals and objectives and the general plans to be followed for achieving those goals, such as responding to the changing mental health needs of Midtown's citizens. The diagram shows how this board delegates its policy work to several subcommittees: community relations, personnel, finance, and nominating. The diagram also indicates that the board operates through an executive committee that deals regularly with the center's chief administrative officer, the executive director. The board has the overall responsibility of helping the center maintain steady state so that all four functions will be evident in the way it operates. For example, its community relations committee is largely concerned with performing the adaptation function while its personnel committee is largely concerned with performing the integration function.

At the operational level, the executive director usually recommends and otherwise assists the board in the development of the agency's statement of goals (hierarchy of outcomes); but it is the acceptance of these goals and related policies by the board that constitutes the sanction to operate under these policies. Central to Weber's rationalist position is his use of the concept of legal authority.[3] Through this formal administrative structure, the center's legal authority is exercised. Each of the boxes in this diagram refers to an organizational position. The name attached to the box, for instance, *Executive Director*, refers to the role that a person enacts within this system. These roles are linked through legal authority. The legal basis for this authority is found in the agency's constitution and bylaws. In its constitution, authority is first vested in the board of directors. Included in this

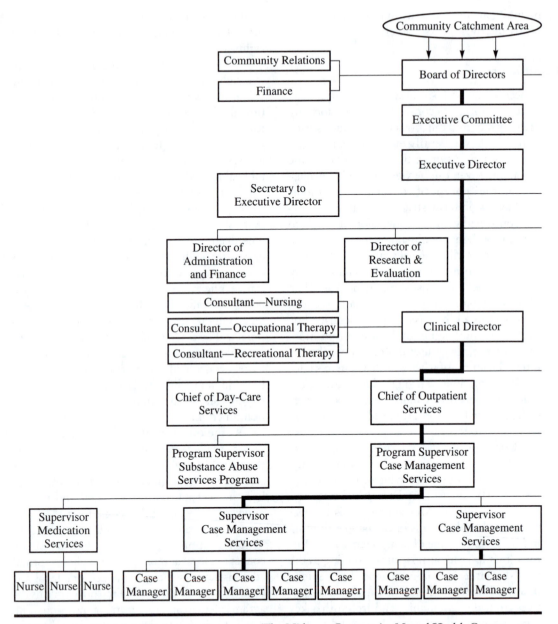

FIGURE 13.3   Formal Administrative Structure—The Midtown Community Mental Health Center

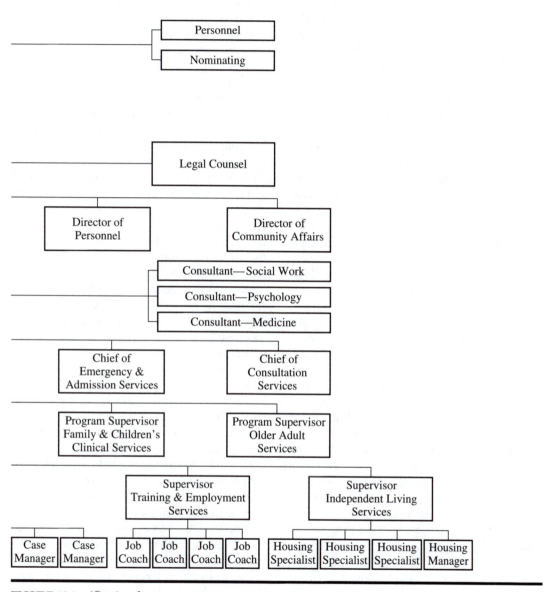

FIGURE 13.3   (*Continued*)

authority is the right to empower the executive director to carry out the board's policies. To do so, the executive director hires key staff (usually those reporting directly to him or her) and delegates authority to these respective positions. This delegation or empowerment process moves downward until it reaches the lowest-level positions. The authority structure thus connects all positions ultimately to that of the executive director. Both conceptually and practically, the person holding the position of executive director is responsible to the board of directors for everything that happens in the center. The decisions made by the executive director will have an effect on each of the four master functions relating to steady state. Of the four, pattern maintenance is the one most important to this position.

In the practice literature, this vertical axis of legal authority is known as the chain of command. For purposes of illustration, we have made bold this chain of command to show how it connects the board of directors to the program supervisor of case management services and finally down to a specific case manager.

You should be familiar with two other concepts that pertain to the exercise of legal authority in a formal organization—**line** versus **staff** and span of control. Line positions are those related to one another vertically along the chain of command. These positions are directly related to the conversion of signal inputs to task outputs. In the example, line positions are those with vertical lines connecting with the executive director, for example, the clinical director. In Figure 13.3, staff positions are connected horizontally to line positions; denoted by this horizontal line is a supportive relationship between line and staff members. Typically, persons in staff positions do not make administrative decisions or perform work directly related to task outcomes; frequently, staff positions are filled by specialists whose job is to advise people in line positions of the technical factors associated

with a given decision or action. This function is illustrated by the relationship the legal counsel has to the executive director. In such an organization, the role of counsel would be to advise the executive director of the legal implications for a given course of action. Technically, those in staff roles do not exercise legal authority. Their ability to exercise authority is found in the expert knowledge they possess.

Span of control refers to the extent of the horizontal administrative control, that is, how many positions a given administrator supervises. The concept pertains to the exercise of the legal authority by a specified administrator. The concept is illustrated by the number of people supervised by the executive director—five line and two staff positions. The clinical director in turn supervises four line and six staff positions. The chief of outpatient services supervises four line positions; the program supervisor of case management services supervises five line positions. The two supervisors of case management services each have line authority over five individual case managers.

In the rationalist's position, legal authority constitutes the vertical axis of the formal organization.[4] The horizontal axis is labeled the division of labor. As used here, *division of labor* and *departmentation* are synonymous. The total work of the organization is divided up into natural or logical units and then assigned to groupings of people to be performed. The grouping of these work activities and their assignment is given an organizational designation, for example, a department. This process proceeds downward, and at each administrative level the work is divided and assigned horizontally. Ultimately, all of the organization's work is assigned. These assignments become key attributes of all organizational roles. In this sense, the organization can be viewed as a functionally dependent system of roles. Each role represents a specialized aspect of a particular functional process, and each role becomes dependent in varying degrees on other roles performing that function. This process gives the system its chief feature, functional interdependence.

Figure 13.3 shows that the executive director has divided the work of the Midtown Mental Health Center into five functional areas and has placed a director in charge of each of these areas: administration and finance, research and evaluation, clinical services, personnel, and community affairs. Each of these social units is at the same level in the organization's authority structure, and therefore each director is presumed to possess roughly comparable amounts of authority. These five areas constitute the second level of administrative authority; the executive director occupies the top or first level.

The position of clinical director illustrates the second level in this agency's formal organizational structure. In accordance with social systems theory, the responsibility for the goal-attainment function is lodged with this position. For some, it is difficult to understand why a position within the agency should be considered as performing an external function. Remember the justification for this agency is external and pertains to the need for mental health services by the citizens of Midtown. Goal attainment is the satisfaction of those needs. Thus, all of the activities performed by the staff of this agency directly pertaining to the goal-attainment function are externally oriented. All staff reporting to the clinical director are primarily involved in performing the goal-attainment function. To perform the goal-attainment function, the center has organized this administrative unit by service, for example, day-care, outpatient, emergency, and consultation.

All of the center's clinical work is assumed to fall into one of these four service categories—that is how the board has operationalized the term *comprehensive* (see the mission statement in Figure 13.2). Again, a supervisor (chief) is placed in charge of each of the clinical programs, with that person reporting to the clinical

director. All of the positions vertically related to the clinical director are designated as line positions and constitute a part of the chain of command described earlier. (For purposes of further elaboration, the position of clinical director has been placed lower on the axis so that the staff positions could be illustrated.) In contrast, positions horizontally connected to the clinical director are staff positions. Persons occupying these roles advise the clinical director on matters pertaining to their particular areas of professional expertise. For example, the social work consultant would advise the clinical director on policy pertaining to the role of social work in the center's clinical program. It should be noted that these consultants have no line responsibility over the people in their professional discipline. Typically, such consultants, while administratively reporting to the clinical director, serve as consultants to people in their own discipline. They might also be responsible for holding workshops and other forms of in-service training for members of their discipline.

The position of chief of outpatient services is used to illustrate the third level of organization in this agency. This unit is also organized by service with a program supervisor responsible for each service. The fourth level is organized by clinical service. Here we have located those social units associated with performing the case management and related services associated with work with the community's SPMI citizens.

Figure 13.3 is also intended to illustrate how systems are embedded in other systems (as subsystems). For example, the clinical director is responsible for the center's clinical department, all clinical services. It would be possible to model this subsystem as a system, with the remaining administrative parts of the organization treated as key features of its suprasystem. Similarly, the chief of outpatient services heads another subsystem unit that could be examined as a social system, and so on. With each step down in the administrative hierarchy, the analysis can become more detailed. The open-system approach maintains the relationship of the system being examined to its environmental context (suprasystem). For example, modeling the outpatient department as a system would have limited value without reference to how its activities (input/output exchanges) relate to the rest of the center and to other relevant features of its suprasystem. Again recall the assumption that the whole is more than the sum of its parts; the center cannot be understood only by understanding each of its component parts.

Figure 13.3 has presented the overall formal social structure of the Midtown Mental Health Center. Every position shown on the organizational chart will have a job description, such as the one in Figure 13.4. In this instance, there are ten case management positions at the center. The job description will be identical for each of these positions. In the rationalist position, the notions of standardization of role performance and depersonalization of position were developed. In formal organizations, these concepts are operationalized through the use of job descriptions.

Earlier, the boundary-maintenance function was described. Through the use of job descriptions and related personnel policies, the boundary-maintenance function operates in the selection of personnel for a formal organization. For example, if the center had an opening for a case manager, the job description would serve as the guide for selecting this professional. The procedures can be quite specific. For example, the position calls for a person who has, as a minimum, a baccalaureate degree in social work from a program accredited by the Council on Social Work Education. If an applicant possesses such a degree, he or she meets the first test. If not, he or she is rejected. From all those who possess the minimum degree, interviewers seek the person who best fits the remaining specifications for this position. In this sense, the selection process is supposed to be objective, or depersonalized. While it is important to note the intent, we hasten to add that this intent is not always fulfilled in real life.

The final feature of the center's formal structure to be described is a line item budget, as illustrated in Figure 13.5. All formal organizations of the type illustrated will have a budget. A budget is a financial plan showing how the system intends to spend its fiscal inputs over the next program period, usually a year. For our immediate purposes, it is a way of showing how maintenance inputs are organized for purposes of achieving maintenance and task outcomes. We have shown an abbreviated organizational chart and a summary budget. If both were fully developed, every position on the organizational chart would be identified in the budget.

Budgets are prepared in a number of ways. The line item, or what is sometimes called the object classification, budget is the most common. The approach used in budget construction requires the use of a classification system that permits all costs to be assigned to mutually exclusive but interrelated categories or lines. In this sense, you can think of a budget as a system comprised of cost categories. These categories, when added together, represent the total cost of operating the agency for a period of time, usually a year. In this illustration, the bottom line, or the total cost for operating the Midtown Mental Health Center for one year, is $1,652,860. This money is obtained externally and represents a maintenance input. The budget is simply a way of structurally determining how much money the agency needs to operate for a year and how this money is to be divided.

The budget is also used to control costs. For example, the agency will probably spend about 1/12 of its money (1/12 of $1,652,860 = $137,738.33) each month. One job of the center's director of administration and finance is to make sure the center's staff is not over- or under-

MIDTOWN MENTAL HEALTH CENTER
Position Description

I.   Position Title: Case Manager I

II.   Salary: $22,500–$28,000

III.   Minimum Qualifications: A baccalaureate degree in social work from a program accredited by the Council on Social Work Education.

IV.   Position Description: This is an entry-level professional position in work with clients who are seriously and persistently mentally ill. The practitioner will work under the general direction of an agency-based supervisor. The focus of work is the enhancement of human well-being through an improvement of social functioning.

V.   Examples of Work Performed:
   1. Collects and assesses data to determine eligibility for services
   2. Conducts strengths assessments with client systems to determine capacity for improvement in level of social functioning
   3. Participates with client systems in formulating services goals and objectives
   4. Participates with client systems in developing and implementing services plan
   5. Participates with client systems in the evaluation of the effects of services
   6. Participates in staff conferences for purposes of overall case and program planning
   7. Inventories and assesses community resources for purposes of referral and resource development
   8. Participates in staff development
   9. Participates in staff conferences in which agency and public policies are analyzed in terms of improving client services

VI.   Knowledge and Skills
   1. Excellent communication skills, oral and writing
   2. Self-awareness and self-possession skills
   3. Interpersonal skills suitable for forming and conducting relationships with culturally and racially diverse client systems who are seriously and persistently mentally ill
   4. Understands and is able to utilize social systems theory in work with client systems of all sizes
   5. Familiarity with psychopharmacology
   6. Familiarity with DSM-IV
   7. Utilizes critical thinking skills in the conduct of practice

VII.   Personal Characteristics
   1. Good physical and mental health
   2. Commitment to practice that enhances human well-being and to the alleviation of poverty and oppression
   3. Behaviors consistent with the social work Code of Ethics

FIGURE 13.4   Position Description for a Case Manager

spending the budget. This example serves to illustrate how the requisite pattern-maintenance function would be performed by this agency in the area of finance. For most agencies, the budget evidences a proposed pattern of spending that must be controlled if steady state is to be maintained.

Up to this point, we have been primarily concerned with the formal structural features of a system's conversion operations. We

LINE ITEM		BUDGET TOTALS
1. Personnel		1,061,000
Executive Director	(1)	60,000
Director Professional Service	(1)	50,000
Business Manager	(1)	40,000
Secretaries	(4)	70,000
Clerk/Typist	(4)	52,000
Fiscal Analyst	(1)	22,000
Maintenance	(1)	17,000
Supervisor Aftercare Service	(1)	30,000
Supervisor Services—Family & Children	(1)	30,000
Supervisor Substance Abuse Services	(1)	30,000
Occupational Therapist	(1)	25,000
Caseworkers	(6)	120,000
Groupworkers	(4)	75,000
Case Managers	(10)	240,000
Recreational Therapist	(2)	40,000
Nurse	(2)	50,000
Education Specialist	(1)	25,000
Trainer	(1)	20,000
Research Director		40,000
Research Analyst	(1)	25,000
2. Fringe Benefits	@ 26%	275,860
3. Consultants		22,500
4. Equipment/Leases		90,500
5. Supplies		19,000
6. Travel/Subsistence		54,000
7. Space/Grounds		80,000
8. Utilities/Telephone		32,000
9. Contracts/Misc.		18,000
TOTAL		1,652,860

FIGURE 13.5   Midtown Mental Health Center Budget: 20__–20__

described a system's formal organizational chart and compared it with a formalized system of roles organized by function with the work being coordinated through a hierarchy of legal authority. We also provided an example of a position description noting that each position on an organizational chart is described with a similar level of specificity. We closed out this section dealing with the formal features of a system's conversion operations by describing a line item budget. For the most part, this con-tent on structure draws heavily from the ratio-nalist position.

Every formal organization will have a for-mal structure as well as an informal one. The system of roles are drawn from the human needs of those persons actually occupying roles in the formal structure. Assistance in developing this feature of structure is drawn from the work of the human relationists. Roles in the informal or-ganization are loosely linked; there is no formal functional and authority structure linking the roles. Here the relationship among people is Gemeinschaft in character. People relate to one another more as total personalities as opposed to in their formal role designations, such as case manager. While similar to what is generally referred to as a social group, there is the added dimension of the association being work related, that is, shaped by organizational variables in addition to personal ones. While the informal organization arises out of the personal needs of its members, one of the functions of this association is to mediate between members' needs and the demands of the organization. In this sense, the informal organization, irrespective of its location in the formal organization, is primarily dedicated to the performance of the integration function.

In modeling a formal organization as a social system, we consider its informal as well as its formal system of roles; the informal system is implicit, the formal is explicit. The two features of structure are treated as interactive, each operating on the other and thus collectively affecting outcome. No counterpart of the formal organizational chart exists in the informal system; it is discernible only by observation and by examination of its effects. The important point here is that, due to its contrived nature, the formal organization is unstable, and it is largely through the development of the informal organization that stability is maintained and the integration function performed.

We have identified the executive director's responsibility for the performance of each of the required functions and have highlighted the importance of pattern maintenance. We also noted the clinical director's responsibility for performing the goal-attainment function. Before moving on, we must consider those having primary responsibility for the integration and adaptation functions. Referring again to Figure 13.3, the director of community affairs will have lead responsibility for seeing that the adaptation function is successfully performed. Simply

stated, the person holding this position is responsible for marketing the center and its services. Adaptation is an external function and is the means by which goal attainment is facilitated.

The director of personnel has the lead responsibility for seeing that the integration function is successfully performed. This is the internal and consummatory function—employees feeling good about their jobs, their colleagues, and their agency—"This is a good place to work, we make a difference." As we have indicated earlier, the informal organization of the center is very important in the performance of the integration function.

Interactions

Interactions are the counterparts of structure. Only through the observation of people and the assignment of meaning to their interactions can the social structure of the system be discernible. The structure is evidenced by the ongoing and reciprocating interaction patterns of individuals carrying out their roles, each toward the other. In formal organizations, these same reciprocating interactions take place between the formally and informally constituted groups of which the system is composed. For example, just as there will be a discernable pattern of reciprocating behavior between a specific case manager and a specific client in a mental health center's case management service, so will there be an overall pattern in the interactions of all of the case managers and their respective SPMI clients. Here we are getting at the idea that a set of "best practices" exists on which case management at this center is based. Features of this best practice are found in the job description of the case manager, who "participates with client systems in formulating service goals and objectives" (item 3), and "participates with client systems in developing and implementing services plan" (item 4). This means that all case managers at the center are expected to fully involve their clients in the process of formulating the goals and objectives of the helping process and in developing and implementing the services plan. This is a structural feature of the role and has its origin in what is considered a component of best practice.

We need to be careful here not to convey a lockstep relationship between structure and interactions. Case managers are individuals and they will creatively carry out their roles and thereby give added richness and detail to them. Over time, if this pattern is continued, the role itself will change by incorporating selected features of these added details. If, on the other hand, the practices vary from case manager to case manager, you may not have a form of professional practice, but rather an "art form" peculiar to the needs and interests of each case manager. Such a development would prove troublesome to the administrator of the center. Why? Formal organizations seek, through the creation of structures, to reduce the variability of behavior in the system; they are always seeking those behaviors that will produce predictable outcomes. This is a part of performing the pattern-maintenance function.

At the department level, attention shifts from interactions among individuals to interactions among those who represent groups of people. For example, the interactions on a policy matter between the chief of the outpatient department and the chief of emergency and admission services can be viewed as representing the interests of all those people comprising their respective departments. Given the legal authority structure of a formal organization, the department head is administratively responsible for all that occurs within the department, which could, in this example, include the work of forty or more employees. In this role, the department head has particular responsibility for the input/output exchanges between the department and other administrative units comprising the center, as well as other components of its supra-system. In an application of the model to formal organizations, administrative units (subsystems) become the primary units of attention, not individuals in specific roles within the unit. Thus, the interactions of the administrative head of a unit with his or her counterparts can be treated as representative of all those members comprising the respective subsystems. Technically, the legal authority structure of the organization provides for this type of representation.

Certainly some of the richness and detail is lost by focusing on the interactions of larger social units via the behaviors of those who represent the members of these groups; what is sought, however, is an understanding of those organizational behaviors that help explain system outputs. To do this, one starts by seeking to explain or understand the interactions among the member units. As with the total system, there will be input/output exchanges, and the totality of these exchanges are functionally related to the outputs of the total system. The following example conveys the relationship between structure and interactions.

One objective of the center for the coming year is to reduce the readmission rate of the community's SPMI citizens by 20 percent. This objective (a feature of structure) was proposed to the board of directors by the center's executive director, Dr. Sara Shields (an interaction occurred between Dr. Shields in her role as executive director and members of the board of directors in their respective roles). Prior to bringing the recommendation to the board, Dr. Shields had held extensive discussions (interactions) on this matter with her various department heads and they in turn had discussed the issue with their respective staffs. In part, the objective pertaining to readmission had its origin in a community strengths/needs assessment that identified the SPMI as an underserved population in Midtown.

The discovery that the SPMI readmission rate was greater than the state average had been puzzling to Dr. Shields and her staff. It was also troublesome to the members of the center's board of directors. The finding suggested some breakdown in input/output exchanges between the center and its suprasystem. Discussions among her key staff and a subcommittee of the board identified two reasons for this increase in readmission among the SPMI. First, the state department of mental health had been forced to reduce its staff at the local state hospital because of state budgetary cutbacks. As a consequence, some SPMI were leaving the hospital prematurely. Because of staff shortages, there was less than adequate discharge planning.

Second, the center was admitting fewer SPMI clients to their adult aftercare service. Officially, the board asked Dr. Shields to look into the matter and report her findings back to them at their next meeting, again an interaction between the board and Dr. Shields acting in their respective organizational roles (structure).

Gradually over the last several years, the staff of the center's outpatient services began concentrating their services on those patients interested in and needing long-term psychotherapy. The chief of outpatient services, Dr. Fred Edwards, was aware of this trend and was informally supporting it because of his own conviction (a feature of structure) of the value of long-term psychotherapy versus other intervention methods. Dr. Edwards was also psychoanalytically oriented in his treatment of clients (theory also being a structural feature), and this approach was well suited to long-term treatment.

To make time available for clients in long-term psychotherapy, the outpatient services staff gradually reduced the time they were spending with the center's SPMI clients. As a consequence of this, the depleted state hospital staff found that many of their referrals to the center were not being admitted. According to the center's outpatient services staff, these clients were not following up on referrals or were not show-ing an interest in their services because, staff members explained, they lacked "motivation." Because of the pressure to discharge clients, the state hospital staff began to discharge many of their most vulnerable SPMI clients directly into the community rather than sending them to the center (an interaction). In this instance, a change in one part of the system (outpatient services) produced changes in other parts, another example of interaction. As a consequence of the growing practice of the staff of the state hospital of discharging those clients unable to profit from long-term psychotherapy directly into the community, various community agencies were increasingly concerned about the number of homeless people sleeping under bridges and in doorways, and eating out of garbage containers. Many of these people were known to be former state hospital patients.

This study by Dr. Shields led to a determination that a shift had occurred in the role played by the center's outpatient services in relation to other departments and to the state hospital. This role shift had occurred in the actual behaviors of the therapists comprising the outpatient services staff. There had been no formal structural change, in job descriptions, for example, or in the role expectations of these therapists by the center's clinical director, Dr. June Mason. This example shows how deviations can occur between structural expectations and role enactment. It was the effect of these changes in role behaviors evidenced in the center's behavior that brought the matter to the attention of its board.

Once the source of these changes had been identified by Dr. Shields and her staff, discussions (interactions) were held as to what should be done. It was agreed that during the coming year priority would be given to reducing the number of the center's SPMI clients who were being hospitalized. Once the objective had been agreed on and confirmed by the board (an interaction), a plan had to be agreed on and actions taken to implement this plan. Conceptually, the plan represents the set of activities that are always associated with the achievement of an objective—the means employed to achieve the proposed outcome. In this instance, several related plans were adopted. First, a meeting was held between Dr. Shields, the center's executive director, and the director of the state department of mental health. This meeting resulted in a contract between the department and the center for coordinating discharge planning involving SPMI citizens from Midtown (see the discussion under Interface). Second, the center reorganized its adult aftercare service and created a case management service devoted to working only with the community's SPMI. Third, a new professional position of case manger was created. This position required, as a minimum, that those hired possess a baccalaureate degree in social work.

OUTPUT

The results of a system's conversion operations are called output. In this section, we will be discussing three forms of output, task (signal), maintenance, and waste. In an earlier section, we discussed task and maintenance inputs and proposed task and maintenance outputs. We will be linking these concepts in our discussion of output.

Task Output

In human service agencies, the condition of the client system following completion of their services plan is what we designate as task output. Task output is also essentially equivalent to the results of the goal-attainment function. Keep in mind that in an application of the model to a formal organization, the output is not going to be the well-being of a specific client. The output will be the effects that the center had on all those who received services

during the budget period. Proposed output targets the specific populations to be served and the results expected. The concept of output is limited to the actual effects achieved during the time period specified in the statement on proposed output, as will be illustrated in the following example.

Sally Baker is the center's program supervisor of the case management service. That service and Ms. Baker particularly are responsible for helping the center reach the objective that reads: "To reduce hospital readmissions of the seriously and persistently mentally ill by 20 percent by December 31, 20__" (See Figure 13.2, Section III, objective 2.2).

Last year, 300 of Midtown's SPMI citizens were readmitted to local inpatient psychiatric units, the majority to the inpatient unit of the state mental hospital. In this example, 300 readmissions becomes the baseline. For the new program year, the center intends to reduce this number by 20 percent, or to 240 (300 - 60 = 240).

Ms. Baker and her program staff developed an intensive case management program for the community's SPMI citizens. By active case finding and by offering a variety of services focusing on maintaining SPMI clients in the community, she sought to accomplish her program objective.

Let's say the output as of December 31, 20__ was a 10 percent rather than a 20 percent reduction. The actual number of readmissions among the SPMI in Midtown dropped from 300 in the baseline year to 270 in our budget year (300 - 30 = 270). In short, for this objective, the system's output was 270 readmissions. While the objective was not fully achieved, a significant reduction in readmissions among this client system did occur. This reduction suggests that the initiation of the center's case management service had its intended effect.

Keep in mind that we are talking about the number of readmissions to a psychiatric unit of a hospital of a known SPMI population. We are not talking about individuals. A given person may be admitted to a hospital a number of times during a year. The strategy employed by Ms. Baker and her staff was to concentrate on those SPMI clients who were the heaviest users of in-patient services. This strategy was also evident in the center's admission policy for SPMI clients.

The staff and board of the center accepted these statistics on output as an indirect measure, through their agency's effort, of the improved level of social functioning of those citizens who are seriously and persistently mentally ill in Midtown. Further, they took these data as an indirect indication that the well-being of the residents of the Midtown community had been enhanced (see the mission statement of the Midtown Mental Health Center, Figure 13.2, Section III). While the objective had not been reached, the data suggested they were on the right track.

Maintenance Output

These outputs represent the center's efforts to improve the system itself. In accordance with social systems theory, maintenance outputs are essentially synonymous with the integration function. The importance of these efforts is illustrated by the human relations position developed in Chapter 12. The center's staff members must feel good about themselves, their agency, and the efforts they make to help their clients. They must also have sufficient supplies, equipment, time, and all of the other resources needed to do their jobs well. Just as the center's administrative staff and board must develop proposed task outcomes, so must they develop proposed maintenance outcomes if the integration function is to be successfully performed.

Here we will use two examples of maintenance outputs. Goal 2 of Figure 13.2, Section IV, reads: "To develop and maintain a professional staff dedicated to the provision of quality mental health services." Objective 2.2 reads: "To employ and train ten case managers who possess professional degrees in social work by December 31, 20__ (end of budget year)." The output for this objective would be the actual number hired and trained by the specified date. Let's say that ten were proposed and by the end of the budget year ten had been hired and trained. In this instance, the center reached 100 percent of its objective.

Objective 2.3 is a somewhat more complicated example: "To reduce the job turnover rate among the center's staff from 26 percent to 20 percent by December 31, 20__." The center's administrative staff and board use the turnover rate as an indirect measure of work satisfaction, work quality, and successful performance of the integration function. They further assume that both work satisfaction and turnover are indirect indications of the quality of the mental health services that their staff provides. In short, those staff members who feel satisfied with their jobs are going to provide a higher quality of service than those who are not satisfied; and the more experienced a staff member is, the higher the quality of the work she or he performs.

On a practical level, job turnover is expensive to the center. A staff member who leaves takes his or her experience with him or her. In addition, a new person must be hired and trained. This costs money and is thus a drain on the center's budget.

To keep the example simple, let us assume that for the baseline year the center had 100 employees, and during the year 26 of these people quit their job—a turnover rate of 26 percent. The center's objective was to reduce this from 26 people to 20 people during the budget year; the new rate would be 20 percent. Rather than 20 people leaving their jobs, only 18 left. The output then would be 18 percent. In this instance, the center exceeded its objective by two percentage points.

Waste

The final form of output addressed in this section is waste, which refers to negative or inappropriate outcomes. Our interest in the use of the concept of waste is to capture and account for all system outputs. Utilizing the notion of efficiency, the ratio of maintenance inputs to task outputs becomes a measure of **efficiency.** Assuming an organizational standard, a negative deviation from this standard would be treated as a measure of waste (an efficiency level not conforming to agency standards). A measure of **effectiveness** becomes the ratio that task outputs have to proposed task outputs. Since professional standards of effectiveness are in an early stage of development, most agencies evolve their own standards based, for example, on last year's performance.

Every agency is going to have waste; our intention is to measure the amount of waste that occurs during a budget period. For example, let us assume existence of a standard-setting body for mental health centers. This body indicates that a job turnover rate of 20 percent is a national standard. If an individual center has a turnover rate that is significantly higher than this standard, it may be an indicator that the agency is not successfully performing the integration function. If a center's board adopts this standard and finds that they have a turnover rate of 35 percent, they will probably accept this as an indirect measure of personnel-related problems and take steps to reduce the rate. To quantify the matter, the center might well treat the difference between the standard and its own higher rate as a measure of waste, and place a dollar value on the waste. To use another example, let us say that the board of the center has indicated that all of its clinical staff should spend 70 percent of their time in direct client contact. A more direct way of saying this same thing is to have an agency standard in which 70 percent of the time spent by clinical staff is represented by "billable hours," that is, charges are made to clients or their representatives for the clinician's time. If in a given instance only 50 percent of the time is billed, the difference between 50 percent and 70 percent is treated as waste, and a

dollar value is assigned. The old adage "time is money" is taking on new meaning in the practice of social work today. As a consequence, the idea of waste, and assigning a dollar value to it, is gaining momentum.

In summary, output is the actual performance of a system during a cycle of activity. Because of the importance of the budget cycle, usually one year, our examples have used this period to illustrate this feature of the model. In presenting our material, we have employed as a reference the center's proposed outputs, not the means for achieving these outputs. Many agencies will summarize their work by activity counts for the year. For example, 825 clients were served and 4,300 individual and group counseling sessions were provided. These are not outcome statements as we use the term in this model of a social system. They are activity counts or counts of system effort. These data do not tell us how many clients were actually helped—it is a measure of the means employed, for example, counseling sessions. What is needed is a statement of the client effects produced by these counseling sessions. In the systems model, the focus is on the end achieved, not the means employed in that achievement. This distinction is crucial in understanding the use of the model and the theory that it supports. We'll examine this point more closely in the next section.

FEEDBACK

The concept of feedback is at the heart of social systems theory and refers to the information needed by the system to maintain steady state—to survive and develop. We distinguish between process and outcome forms of feedback with both being considered in relation to the production of task and maintenance outputs. Feedback occurs both internally and externally. Through a system's feedback structure, we are informed of the extent to which the four functions necessary to maintain steady state are being conducted.

Social work practitioners have come to recognize the importance of feedback on the processes and outcomes of intervention. Feedback provides the direct practice worker with information about the impact of the intervention. For example, a worker helping a client deal with depression might use a validated measure of depression to assess the client's well-being.

As the intervention progresses, the worker takes repeated measures to assure that the client is making progress. One might use the Beck Depression Inventory, a standardized repeatable instrument that provides precise information on the level of depression. In addition, workers use clinical impressions to gain feedback on treatment efficacy. Does the client smile more now? Does the client report sleeping well? Has the client's appetite returned? Answers to these questions provide feedback that guides the worker in the ongoing helping process.

Through the planned use of clinical feedback, the worker can assess and adjust the treatment process. Information gained from the feedback can then be used to revise and improve the worker's understanding and application of treatment to other depressed clients.

In the same way, feedback data can inform program managers about processes and outcomes in an agency. Agency data can be aggregated for many clients. The manager may collect information about how long clients stay in treatment, which workers work best with which type of client, and which days are the busiest in order to schedule adequate staff. As obvious as it seems, it is essential that managers gather feedback on all crucial agency operations in order to make quality decisions.

Task Outputs

One of the proposed task outputs of the Midtown Mental Health Center was a 20 percent reduction in readmissions of its SPMI population during the budget year. In actual numbers, this meant a reduction from 300 readmissions,

which occurred during the baseline year, to a projected figure of 240 readmissions in the budget year. Actual output was a 10 percent decrease over the baseline; 270 readmissions occurred rather than the proposed 240. Feedback represents a comparison between immediate and final effects and the initial conditions.

Evaluation, as a component of practice, is premised on the assumption that the means (services plan) employed is responsible for the results achieved (output). This appears obvious enough, but the matter is more complicated than it appears. Social systems theory assumes constant exchanges between the system and its suprasystem. It is an open- versus closed-system formulation. Evaluation must in some manner consider the effects of external as well as internal influences in explaining outputs. This does not mean that the generalist or the administrator must be a researcher. What it does mean is that evaluation is an integral part of practice and some knowledge of research and evaluation methods is a requirement for competent practice.

The center's research and evaluation staff were using multiple measures in their work. Their analysis showed that while readmissions went up, there was a dramatic drop in the average length of hospital stay by the SPMI—from 63 to 18 days. The dollar savings achieved by the reduced stay were substantial. The center's staff reasoned that the new case management service and the new contract (interface) relationship with the department of mental health had resulted in much better discharge planning than had existed before. The center's case management staff were also much more alert to early signs of decompensation among their clients than the staff they replaced. As a consequence, these clients were hospitalized earlier and more frequently, but their stay was much shorter.

This new information was feedback and resulted in changes in how operations at the center were conducted. For example, changes were made in the center's day-care service so that

SPMI clients who were showing signs of decompensation could be accommodated. This was a more intensive form of care than was offered in outpatient but much less intensive (and less expensive) than was offered in the hospital's inpatient service. The feedback led to the adoption the following year of a new objective—a reduction in the average length of inpatient stay from 18 to 15 days.

Outcome evaluation does not occur at the end of a cycle. It is continuous and in this sense is like process evaluation, but the focus is on the proposed task output, not the process producing the task output. In our example, the director of research and evaluation would report monthly on the number of readmissions. The staff of the center could therefore be making continuous adjustments so that they could come as close as possible or even exceed their proposed task outputs.

Process evaluation focuses on the process employed to produce the proposed output. At the level of the formal organization, this is most clearly represented through its formal administrative structures (see Figure 13.3). In our example, the relevant structure is found starting with the program supervisor of case management services. Under that position are five other supervisors and their respective staffs. The work performed by this staff, particularly that being performed by the case manager, represents the center's approach for accomplishing its proposed output pertaining to the community's SPMI citizens. Other administrative units and services play a supportive role in this effort, as do other community agencies, but the lead responsibility for this effort lies with the program supervisor of case management services. Administratively, this person is responsible to the chief of outpatient services for making it work. The exact location for conducting the process evaluation represents an administrative decision and would be made by the executive director.

In our example, the responsibility for developing the methodology as well as monitoring the outcome and process components of the evaluation is assigned to the director of research and evaluation. Conceptually, the approach for conducting the process evaluation stems from the activities component of the hierarchy of objectives (see Figure 13.2, Section III, activities 2.2.1–2.2.9). The approach is illustrated in Figure 13.6, the mission, goals, objectives, and activities work plan form (MGOA form).

In reviewing the MGOA form, keep in mind that this work plan would be many pages in length and represents a level of detail that summarizes the center's conversion operations. In this sense, it would cover all of the center's goals, objectives, and activities to be conducted during the budget year. Copies of this form with appropriate updates would be circulated monthly to appropriate administrative and program staff. The form is a way for the center's staff and board to determine whether the services (work) plan was being executed in the agreed-on manner. The MGOA form is a component of "technology" used by the center generally in conducting the process component of their evaluation. Specifically, this form is designed for use by the center's supervisors of case management services. It is through the use of this form that they supervise the work of their case managers.

Maintenance Outputs

Just as there is a process form of evaluation with task outputs so there is a process form of evaluation used in tracking the activities aimed at accomplishing maintenance outputs. Both are necessary for the reasons previously described.

In closing this section, we should consider informal types of feedback. They pertain to each of the forms discussed and they are important. The only difference is that formal feedback is systematically created and used. It is also related to the system's other formal structures and is a part of the system's general management struc-

MISSION: To enhance the well-being of the residents of the Midtown community through the provision of comprehensive and quality mental health services.

Goal 2:   To improve the level of social functioning of those citizens who are seriously and persistently mentally ill.

Objective 2.2:   To reduce the hospital readmission rate of the seriously and persistently mentally ill by 20 percent by December 31, 20__.

Plan to Measure Objective:

Treat the readmission rate of SPMI as of 12-31-0_ as a baseline and compare the 12-31-0_ rate to the baseline. The necessary data are available from the department of mental health and the center's management information services' data bases.

	ACTIVITIES	RESPONSIBLE PARTY	TARGET DATE FOR COMPLETION	DATE COMPLETED	COMMENTS
2.2.1	Secure budget approval for RRP	Executive director	12-1-0_		
2.2.2	Initiate a case finding program for SPMI	Program supervisor, case management services	1-1-0_		
2.2.3	Hire an additional half-time physician and a full-time nurse to the center's medical clinic	Personnel director	2-1-0_		
2.2.4	Lease additional van and hire driver for the center's client transportation program	Director, administrative services and personnel services	2-15-0_		
2.2.5	Hire an additional social worker for the center's supportive counseling service	Personnel director	3-1-0_		
2.2.6	Hire trainer for the center's DLS program	Personnel director	4-1-0_		
2.2.7	Hire two social workers for the center's case management program	Personnel director	4-15-0_		
2.2.8	Monitor readmission of SPMI	Research director	Monthly 12-1-0_ to 1-31-0_		
2.2.9	Prepare quarterly progress reports	Research director	Quarterly		

FIGURE 13.6   Midtown Community Mental Health Center—Mission Goals, Objectives, and Activities 20__–20__ Work Plan

ture. Informal feedback is just that, informal. It takes the form of gossip and comments, written or oral, from those inside and outside the system. In short, informal feedback is represented by any information that is fed back into the system that pertains to the relationship between proposed and actual output. All else is noise!

It should be noted that feedback only pertains to information that compares output to proposed output and that is returned to the system as input. The fact that the information is fed back and becomes a form of input is the central point. There is no guarantee that feedback will be used or if used, used correctly. It is true, however, that feedback is how the system maintains steady state. If the feedback is not used or not used correctly, the system starts to lose steady state, to become disorganized.

SUMMARY

In this chapter, we used the social systems model as a feature of technology derived from social systems theory. Simply put, the theory holds that, once developed, social systems seek steady state, a state of well-being. Steady state is developed and maintained through the performance of four functions: goal attainment, adaptation, integration, and pattern maintenance. In the performance of these four functions, systems develop eight structural components. We have labeled these (1) boundary, (2) suprasystem, (3) interface, (4) input, (5) proposed output, (6) conversion operations, (7) output, and (8) feedback.

We use these eight concepts to model social systems. This model was used in this chapter to describe and analyze a hypothetical agency called the Midtown Mental Health Center. Every social system monitors its own behavior through feedback. The feedback channels provide information on the processes being performed with respect to proposed maintenance and task outputs. Through the feedback subsystem, organizations are constantly checking to see whether they are on course; if not, the feedback supplies information for corrective action.

GLOSSARY

Board of directors   The governing body of a formal organization, typically of a private as opposed to a public agency.

Effectiveness   The ratio of a system's task outputs to its proposed task outputs.

Efficiency   The ratio of a system's maintenance inputs to its task outputs.

Line   A position in a formal organization associated with the chain of command. All line positions utilize legal authority delegated to them from their supervisor to achieve the coordination of their work units.

Management information system (MIS)   The feedback structures used to secure, process, analyze, and disseminate information used by an agency's administrative staff to guide the work of the organization.

Policy   A general plan of action to achieve a system's goal(s); a guide to decision making in pursuit of a system's goals.

Seriously and persistently mentally ill (SPMI)   A designation of a class of patients or clients who have a long-term and disabling mental illness.

Staff   A position in a formal organization that provides support to a line position. Persons in staff positions do not usually utilize formal authority in performing their roles. Their contributions are typically in the form of expert knowledge or skills required by those in the line positions.

Strengths/needs assessment   A systematic appraisal of conditions affecting a client system. The appraisal typically includes both the strengths and problems having implications for the creation of a helping system.

NOTES

1. See Chapter 11, The Formal Organization: An Introduction.

2. The terms *Gesellschaft* and *Gemeinschaft* are contrasted in Chapter 11. For their origin, see Ferdinand Toennies, *Community and Society (Gemeinschaft and Gesellschaft)*, trans. and ed. Charles P. Loomis (1887; reprint, New York: Harper Torch Books, 1963).

3. See the discussion of legal authority in Chapter 10. For the origin, see Max Weber, "The Three Types of Legitimate Rule," trans. Hans Gerth, in *A Sociological Reader on Complex Organizations*, 3rd ed., eds. Amitai Etzioni and Edward W. Lehman (New York: Holt, Rinehart and Winston, 1980), 4.

4. Max Weber, "Bureaucracy," in *Critical Studies in Organization and Bureaucracy*, eds. Frank Fischer and Carmen Sirianne (Philadelphia, PA: Temple University Press, 1984), 24–39.

PART FIVE

THE COMMUNITY

SUPRASYSTEM

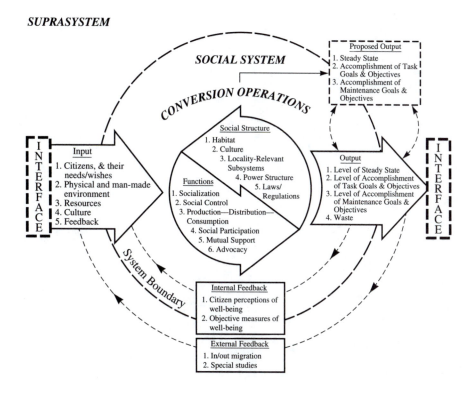

CHAPTER 14

THE COMMUNITY
AN INTRODUCTION

DEFINITIONS OF COMMUNITY

THE ECOLOGICAL POSITION: HUMAN
   ECOLOGY

THE COMMUNITY POWER POSITION

COMMUNITY POWER: THE ELITIST POSITION

COMMUNITY POWER: THE PLURALIST
   POSITION

THE CONFLICT POSITION

SUMMARY

GLOSSARY

NOTES

In this chapter, we introduce theory that helps support practice at the community level. Prior to a review of the main lines of development of community theory, we identify a problem that confronts community theorists, that of defining community. The problem is so severe that one leading scholar has questioned the use of the term *community* in social science research.[1] This problem of definition has affected the development of community theory. As will become evident later, the theoretical support for community practice in social work is quite thin.

Our position is that, while the multiple uses of the term *community* are troublesome, its level of familiarity and the common elements of its meaning are great assets and far outweigh the liabilities. In part, the many uses of the term can be viewed as attempts to capture the essence of a social phenomenon pertaining to human interdependence—the need people have for one another and for a "place" they can call home. What is needed is a renewed effort aimed at developing theory that will help inform community practice—one that recognizes and builds from the notion of interdependence and is based on the common needs and aspirations of those sharing the same habitat.

We will continue our overview by posing and then answering two questions. First, what is **community organization practice** in social work? Second, why should the generalist practitioner be required to be competent to work with communities?

In a well-known community practice book, Garvin and Cox have an article entitled "A History of Community Organizing Since the Civil War with Special Reference to Oppressed Communities."[2] They traced this form of practice starting in 1865. We cite this reference to make the point that community practice has a long and distinguished history in social work. In fact, community organizing is closely tied with the social reform movement of the past century that gave rise to the profession of social work itself.[3] Now to the question—what is community organization practice? The *Social Work Dictionary* offers the following definition:

> An intervention process used by social workers and other professionals to help individuals, groups, and collectives of people with common interests or from the same geographic areas to deal with social problems and to enhance social well-being through planned collective action. Methods include identifying problem areas, analyzing causes, formulating plans, developing strategies, mobilizing necessary resources, identifying and recruiting community leaders, and encouraging interrelationships between them to facilitate their efforts.[4]

Several important components of this definition are helpful in introducing this form of practice and the diverse forms it has taken. First,

the definition accommodates two quite different conceptions of practice by including both geographic and common interest communities. A geographic community is one based on people residing in a specific location, I am a New Yorker or I am from Denver. An example of a community of common interest would be all of the people who share that interest. Examples would include the business community, the medical community, the gay community, and the social work community. We will touch on this feature later, but in this text we limit our conception of the practice of community organization to geographic communities.

Second, the definition accommodates both efforts at the enhancement of well-being and problem solving. This twin focus is fully consistent with our conception of generalist practice. Third, the definition identifies the distinguishing feature of this form of practice—a collective response by those who are members of the community, which focuses on the encouragement (and strengthening) of the interrelationships among those comprising the community. In other words, community organization practice deals with organizing a community to accomplish a goal that advances that community's sense of well-being or deals with some identified community-scale problem. By *organizing* we mean the creation, addition, or modification of community social structures—the relationships among member parts. By so doing, interdependence among the parts is increased as efforts are shared to advance the well-being of those who reside in the community.

The definition of community organization practice used in this text is as follows:

COMMUNITY ORGANIZATION PRACTICE A form of social work practice in which the geographic community itself is designated as the client system and thus the beneficiary of its own helping efforts.

In some instances, the total community serves as the client system; in other instances, it is a community subsystem, for example, a neighborhood or its health care or educational institutions. When a community subsystem is designated as the subject system, the remaining parts of the community become components of its suprasystem.

Now to the second question—why should the generalist practitioner be required to be competent to work with communities? Most people have support networks of family and/or friends that reside in the same community. Further, they depend on the various organizations and institutions located in their community to help meet basic needs and to pursue efforts at enhancing their sense of well-being. At whatever system level the generalist is working—be it the individual, group, family, organization, or community—these levels are connected and interdependent; the levels represent the vertical axis of each other's suprasystem.

Recall the words of the English poet John Donne: "No man is an island, entire of itself; every man is a piece of the continent, a part of the main." The generalist must have an understanding of the practice implications of John Donne's verse, an ability to grasp the whole and the interrelationships among the parts. Most client systems seen by the generalist are going to have multiple needs and may require services from a number of different agencies. Every community will have a network of organizations and groups that serve the needs of those who reside in that community. The generalist must understand this network, and know where services are located and how they can be accessed. If a needed service is not available, the generalist needs to know how to establish that the need exists and how to mobilize the community to meet the need.

Individuals, groups, families, and organizations are constantly changing; so do communities change. In Chapter 2, you were introduced to ecological theory and the forces that bring about change at the macro level, for example, changes in population, environment, and social organization. These natural forces are at work in every community, but there are other forces at work in communities as well. Community groups join to

confront problems, for example, the abuse of alcohol and other drugs, or to deal with disasters, such as the bombing of the federal building in Oklahoma City or the terrorist attacks on the Twin Towers in New York City and the Pentagon in Washington, D.C. They also join to explore ways of making their community a better place to live and to raise children.

Many of today's problems are so massive and so destabilizing to society that intervention at any one level is insufficient, for example, the rising tide of violence. Intervention is required at all levels—the individual, group, family, organization, community, and the society itself. This does not mean that each generalist practitioner will, with each of her or his cases, be intervening at all levels. What it does mean is that she or he will function from a systems perspective and, depending on client system needs and agency sanction, be competent to function, if required, at all levels. In addition, some social workers will secure additional education and experience and will work as community organization practitioners.

DEFINITIONS OF COMMUNITY

The search for a definition of community offers a well-worn but intriguing path for writers. The dictionary, as is so frequently the case, offers a useful and convenient beginning point: "a group of people residing in the same locality."[5] Webster's definition does not restrict the concept of community to place; it also includes the notion of function or communities of common interest, "a group or class having common interest." It would appear that these definitions would accommodate such diverse community forms as people of the Roman Catholic faith, people residing in San Francisco, people visiting Disneyland, recipients of Temporary Assistance for Needy Families (TANF), and all of the nation's dentists. These diverse definitions help to illustrate the problem that must be solved if a social systems approach or any other approach is to be employed in work with the community—the lack of consensus on what is meant by the concept of community.

At a more technical level, the *Encyclopedic Dictionary of Sociology* offers an interesting and helpful approach to the definition of community:

Its major technical use in sociology refers to the spatial, or territorial, unit in social organization and, secondarily, to the psychological cohesion, or feeling of belonging, that is associated with such units.

It has been observed that there are only two truly universal units of human social organization, the family and the community. In evolutionary terms, the latter is the older. Animals do not have families (in the sense of symbolically recognized units), but nearly all animals do live in what the biological ecologist calls community or territorially based aggregates.

The fundamental reason that people live in communities is *convenience* based upon *interdependence*. Their multiple needs are better served if they live in clusters than if they are spatially scattered.[6]

Relative to the point made in the above definition regarding the two "universal" units of human social organization, it is curious how little attention has been given the community by social scientists and how much has been given the family. Hutchinson, in a paper dealing with community theory, suggested that the problem of defining the boundary of a community may have inhibited community theory development.[7] We agree.

In approaching our definition of community, it is useful to return again to two early scholars who have made substantial contributions to social theory, Toennies and Weber. Toennies offered a line of reasoning that is helpful in thinking about community. Earlier you were introduced to his concepts of Gemeinschaft and Gesellschaft. Gemeinschaft is translated as community and refers to personal relationships that are intimate, traditional, and informal—the kind of relationships associated with small towns in which everybody knows and cares about one another.[8] Gesellschaft translated means society and refers to relationships that are essentially the opposite of Gemeinschaft; they are impersonal, contractual, logical, and rational. Keep in mind that Toennies was describing "pure" relationships and contrasting types of relationships. He was also commenting on an historical trend in community relationships from Gemeinschaft to Gesellschaft.[9]

Weber, in his insightful and parsimonious approach, focused on the economic interdependence among people and viewed the community as a social organization that evolved to provide for the regular exchange of goods. In its essence, he saw the community as a marketplace.[10] From this perspective, the community can be viewed as a particular form of social organization, shaped in large part by common human needs and the increased interdependence of people caused by society's moving from agrarian to mercantile to industrial and now to service and information-based economies.

You will recall that the definition of community used in this text is as follows: A community is an inclusive form of social organization that is territorially based and through which most people satisfy their common needs and desires, deal with their common problems, seek means to advance their well-being, and relate to their society. The definition reflects the purposiveness that serves as the organizing scheme for social systems theory. It answers the question, What does a community do? There are also several distinctive features to the definition:

1. It is a form of social organization tied to a physical or geographic place. In this definition, the concept is not extended to groups of people sharing an interest or cause unless they also reside in the same locale.

2. It focuses on the people and their social organizations that reside in and/or are identified with a common place.

3. The community has as its highest purpose the improvement in the quality of life (well-being) for those who live there.

4. The components or subsystems of the community are the organizations and groups located in the community that, at least in part, serve those individuals who live there.

5. The interdependence that is inherent in the notion of social organization is linked to the presence of common needs, common problems, and opportunities for growth and development. In short, the community is viewed as a form of social organization that has come into existence in part because it provides comprehensive arrangements through which and by which people can meet their common needs, deal with their common problems, and advance their sense of well-being.

6. The assumption is made that the community is the dominant (but not the only) intermediate organization through which the individual relates to his or her society and through which society relates to the individual. In a conceptual sense, we view the community as a societal subsystem.

With the above definition of community as background, the remaining parts of this chapter will be devoted to an exploration of the various approaches to the construction of community theory. In short, we will explore the proposed explanations of how communities form or develop and how the work of the community gets done.[11] We will label these theories as positions, identify the principal theorist(s) for each position, and summarize the position's key features. Keep in mind that many theorists are identified with each line of theory development. Our task is one of identifying those who were most helpful in formulating a particular line of theory development, establishing the basic assumptions and key concepts undergirding the theory, and contributing to our development of a social systems theory applicable to generalist practice.

THE ECOLOGICAL POSITION: HUMAN ECOLOGY

You will recall that in Part One of this book you were introduced to ecology as a general theory. Our interest at this point is in human ecology and particularly in the contributions made by sociologists in the development of community theory. In terms of background, keep in mind that ecology is a branch of biology. Because of its subject matter, the interdependent relationship between the physical environment and living things, scientists from many disciplines are interested in ecology. In addition to sociology, there are, among others, ecological adherents in anthropology, geography, psychology, and social work.[12]

Human ecology had its beginnings in the 1920s and can be viewed usefully as a revival of biological determinism.[13] Here we have a link to the early development of sociology through the work of Herbert Spencer and his conception of Social Darwinism—the notion that Darwinian principles operate at the level of the individual.[14]

Assumptions

Key assumptions undergirding the ecological position applying to the development of community theory include the following:

1. The physical and social environments are part of a whole, and are thus interdependent. These environments are primarily influenced by natural, impersonal forces—population change and changes in the physical environment.

2. Competition for desirable space is a central process affecting all forms of life and all species of the animal kingdom including humans. Competition, as a social process, is the key in understanding the development of the human community.

3. Those life forms that are best adapted to an environment and those within the species that are the "fittest" become dominant and most successful in the competitive process.

4. There is a dynamic interplay between the organic and inorganic that seeks equilibrium or an ecological balance.

5. The social structure of the community is primarily formed and influenced by underlying natural (ecological) forces that pursue an equilibrium. In other words, social structure is an outcome resulting from the basic interplay of ecological forces. Culture, the shared meaning of those comprising the social structure, serves to maintain the ecologically induced equilibrium.

6. The natural (ecological) forces are evident in all human communities causing the development of the community to follow regular and recurring patterns.[15]

Several of the assumptions comprising the ecological position are similar to our social systems perspective. It would appear helpful at this point to contrast some of the differences. The social systems perspective focuses on human social organization, the purposiveness of human social behavior, and the exchange relationships between a social organization and those other social organizations that comprise its suprasystem.

From the social systems perspective, social structure can be understood as a result of the genetic adaptive capacities of the individual to the environment and to other forms of life (human and nonhuman) sharing the same habitat. Once formed, the social structure (the social system) takes on a separate and distinct existence. The social system at the level of a human society or culture becomes dominant; it shapes all of the other lower-level systems (subsystems)—communities, organizations, families, groups, and individuals. In lesser ways, it is shaped by these subsystems. All of these systems are shaped by their habitat. All are part of the whole, all are interdependent. In terms of a theory of social systems applicable to generalist practice, we do not find it instructive to consider

the habitat as dominant in shaping culture or in understanding social behavior. From our position, the habitat is a secondary or contextual variable.

In contrast to the social systems perspective, the ecological perspective gives primacy to natural (impersonal) forces that shape the relationships between all life forms and the habitat they share.[16] In the most fundamental sense, humans are treated like all other life forms. Here we have a clear tie between human ecology and the biological determinism associated with the work of Charles Darwin and as set forth in the latter part of the last century by theorists such as Herbert Spencer.[17]

Theorists

A useful place to start the tracking of the development of ecological theory applied to the community is with the work of Charles Galpin. He was interested in the social structure of rural communities. In his work entitled *The Social Anatomy of an Agrarian Community* (1915), Galpin studied the behaviors of families in rural Wisconsin.[18] He gathered data on where these families shopped, where they worshipped, and generally how they met basic needs. He plotted his findings on a map and thereby initiated an approach for the study of the geographic influences on human interaction.[19]

Perhaps the dominant figure in the application of ecological theory to the community was Robert Ezra Park, a sociologist at the University of Chicago (1864–1944). Park, along with Ernest W. Burgess and R. D. MacKenzie, exerted considerable influence in the early development of community theory. The central thesis of this group of ecologists was that cities evidenced a particular pattern of growth.[20] The notion of concentric zone theory enjoyed considerable interest during the 1920s and 1930s. In short, cities were viewed as evidencing circles of growth from a central core labeled the **central business district (CBD).** Around this

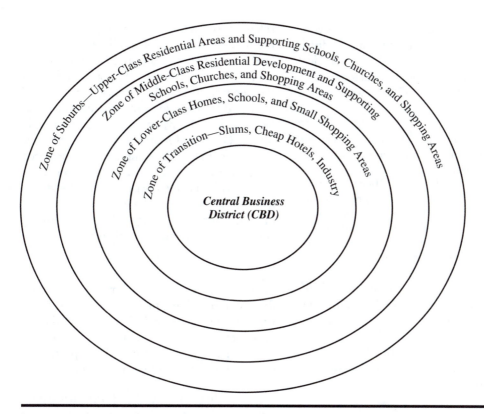

FIGURE 14.1   Urban Development Patterns: The Concentric Zone Theory

core were a series of circle-like developments extending to a commuter fringe. The basic notion is graphically displayed in Figure 14.1.

Each circle, starting with the central one and moving outward, represents a particular settlement pattern. Communities start with an initial core and grow in concentric patterns like growth rings in a tree. But unlike a tree, the growth rings change with the passage of time as the community grows and becomes more differentiated. The central ring (CBD) in large cities acts like a hub supporting the needs of those who reside in the surrounding rings. Within the first ring are located the large, expensive hotels; bus, rail, and other transportation facilities; governmental buildings; theaters; large department stores; and so forth. The second ring is the zone of transition. Here are industrial and related

businesses, slums and other lower-class residential housing, cheap hotels, and supporting services. The residences of the working class are located in zone III along with their schools and related service organizations. In zone IV we find more expensive homes and apartments. Zone V is the interface with the surrounding countryside. Here are some small satellite communities or suburbs of the central city.

Park and his colleagues at the University of Chicago led the way in developing a theory of community based on ecological principles. Many of the concepts we will identify later were identified by this group as they laid the framework to our approach for understanding how U.S. communities develop.

Amos H. Hawley was another significant contributor to the development of community theory from the ecological position.[21] His contribution served to widen the position set forth by Park and was an attempt to bring ecological theory more in line with general theory development in sociology. Hawley viewed human ecology as

> the study of the form and development of the human community. Community, in this connection is construed as a territorially localized system of relationships among functionally differentiated parts; human ecology, then, is concerned with the general problem of organization conceived as an attribute of a population—a point of view that has been shown to be consistent with a long-standing sociological tradition.[22]

While softening the central role of the physical habitat in shaping social organization, Hawley did elaborate usefully the general system properties of human social organization. His attention to what he described as the equilibrium assumption in human ecology was particularly helpful.[23]

> Morphological change is assumed to be a movement toward an equilibrium state, whether through a succession-like sequence of stages or through a process of continuous modification. Unlike the equilibrium notion in some of its other applications, such as functionalist theory, the ecological usage of the terms harbors no teleological overtones; on the contrary, this usage merely implies that as an organization attains completeness, it acquires the capacity for controlling change and for retaining its form through time, although the interval need not be specified. To put it differently, to the extent that an organization possesses unit character, an approximation to equilibrium obtains.[24]

The final two theorists to be named as influencing the ecological contribution to community theory are Jack P. Gibbs and Walter T. Martin. In their article "Towards a Theoretical System of Human Ecology" they argued that the concept of community is too limiting and in related ways not a "proper subject matter" of the field of human ecology. They suggested a broader approach to the study of human ecology, for example, society. The specific focus of their approach is on "sustenance organization," or the collective efforts of individuals to meet basic needs.[25] Our particular interest in the writings of Gibbs and Martin is in their argument for moving theory development in human ecology away from the community to the society or to the world itself. Consistent with this movement, there is little in the way of current writings in human ecology that are directly contributing to community theory.

Concepts

While human ecology has diminished as an influence in sociology, many concepts associated with this position remain important in the development of community theory. The following are considered particularly important in understanding the ecological position.

Biotic. This is a central and organizing concept in ecological theory. **Biotic** refers to the subsocial system that links all forms of life, plant and animal, to their habitats. This subsocial system evolves through impersonal and natural forces largely through the process of competition. Human social organization and culture evolves at the biotic level of organization. In this sense, culture is a secondary determination of social organization, the primary being at the biotic level. Importantly, much of the criticism of ecological theory within sociology evolved around the key role played by the biotic level and the secondary role played by the concept of culture.

Symbiosis. The term *symbiosis* is used to describe the impersonal patterns of relationships that exist at the biotic level. While competition exists, there is coexistence because those life forms sharing the same habitat need one another for their own existence. So while the flower needs the bee to pollinate and thus to survive, the bee needs the pollen for the creation of food by which it survives. The farmer, in turn, needs the bee to pollinate his or her orchards. And finally, we need the farmer in order to have fruits, vegetables, and related foods.

The point here is that the human ecologists introduced the concept of symbiosis, which helps to explain the form of interdependence at the community level among humans and their various forms of social organization. Examples would include everything from securing water and sanitary services from municipal government to buying food from a local grocery. Interdependence arises from impersonal forces.

Competition.   The concept of **competition** is central in human ecology and is used in essentially the same way as in ecology. Humans, as other forms of life—plant and animal—compete for space and for dominance in their habitats. Through competition, an ecological balance evolves and is maintained. Human ecology has its direct ties with the notion of biological determinism through the concept of competition.

Dominance.   Through competition, one form of life will become dominant over another. Similarly, within a species there will be those who will gain dominance over others. This same notion holds among humans and offers an explanation for the particular patterns of community development. The dominant members of the community will be found in the most desirable locations of the community. In other ways beyond geographic location, they will hold dominance over their fellow citizens, for example, they will have access to the best jobs.

Succession.   The concept of **succession** is used in ecology to describe the orderly pattern of change that can be discerned as a community develops. For example, as new poor people move into a community, they are likely to locate in the slums or least desirable locations. As those in the slums gain resources, they are likely to move to the more desirable areas of the community. This movement (succession) is viewed as a natural growth stage of a community.

Many other concepts used by human ecologists are important, but the above serve to introduce some of the basic ideas associated with the ecological position when applied to a theory of community.

A number of theorists have contributed to the development of a theory of community from the ecological position. Of special importance is a classical essay by Morton Long.[26] He likens the community to an "ecology of games." Using game playing as an analogy, he examines the interactions among people and their organizations in the community. Rather than a single game being played, Long suggests there are many, but all loosely related in a symbiotic manner. There is the political game, the school game, the business game, the social work game, the police game, and so on. Each game has its own set of rules, strategies, and tactics embedded in culture and in symbiotic relationships. As a consequence, the behavior of each game player is predictable (assuming you know which game is being played). In fact, knowledge of how other people play their games is crucial in how successfully a given player (or group of players) can play his or her own game. For example, the person playing the business game must be aware of how the banking, legal, and political games are played; because to play the business game well, the person will sometimes need the assistance of these other game players, or at least not their opposition. Similarly, for those other players to do well in their respective games, they will need the assistance of those playing the business game.

We found several features of Long's game-playing analogy especially useful in conceptualizing the community. First, nobody is in charge of the overall game—no central authority, in fact, no single overall game or overall winner exists. Second, the coordination that occurs between the games is more unconscious than conscious (reflecting the symbiotic relationship among units); and the results, while largely unplanned, are generally functional for the many games and game players. Third, the relationships of the games to one another differ from a natural ecology because of the existence of a territorially based general public. To some extent, the game players play their games with one eye on the scoreboard and the other on the general public (the fans). While the general public does not normally exert any direct formal control over how the game is conducted, the public does evaluate performance and thus has an influence. This influence is most clearly seen in the social game. Through the social game, social standing is obtained. Fourth, while territorially based, most games, except the newspaper game, have a specific rather than a general territorial interest and concern. This is important because the newspaper can alert and gain the attention of the general public. As a consequence, it is the one game that can set a community-wide agenda and to some extent influence how others play their respective games.

Long likened his view of the community as an ecology of games to Adam Smith's view of the behavior of a free market as the foundation for his general theory of economic activity.[27] As in the community, there is no one in charge of the free market. In short, the market would not be free if someone was in charge—being free is its most important characteristic. The notion of being free also identifies its principal social process—competition. The behavior of the market is likened to an ecological process in the sense that the forces are largely impersonal; like all systems, the free market seeks steady state.

The similarities between the behavior of the community and the behavior of a free market system as defined by Adam Smith can easily be overdrawn. Perhaps the analogy is most helpful in describing the business game within a community. Here games exist within games. For example, those involved in the banking

game are very dependent on how those in the real estate and industrial fields play their respective games and vice versa. In a sense, each of these smaller games can be thought of as part of a larger economic game played in every community. Similarly, this economic game is but a part of a larger community game which includes the education game, the political game, and the ecclesiastical game, along with many others. They are interdependent because they share the same playing field and they all are being watched by the same largely indifferent general public.

Building on Long's analogy, the community game is not without some rules and the means for insuring at least minimal compliance with those rules. These are provided by those who play the government game, who, along with their associates who play the political game, have the role of assuring a level playing field. This process is ongoing and agreement is never fully reached on what constitutes a level playing field. What is sought is some sort of ecological equilibrium. Finally, perhaps most important, Long's game-playing analogy helps in applying the ecological concept of symbiosis to the construction of community theory. In so doing, he introduces an approach for the study of the interdependence that characterizes the various organizations and groups that share a common habitat.

Carel B. Germain led the way in introducing ecological concepts in social work.[28] She found the ecological metaphor particularly helpful in operationalizing social work's historical commitment to the person-in-environment concept. In her earlier work, she was primarily interested in the application of the ecological perspective to direct practice. In her later work she developed the life model practice approach, which utilizes ecological concepts.[29] She did develop community applications. Her focus was on the use of ecological concepts and their applications to social work practice, not to ecological theory as such.

THE COMMUNITY POWER POSITION

While describing community power, we will address two contrasting positions—the elitist and the pluralist. These two views on the **community power position** are helpful in exploring the purpose of social work—the enhancement of human well-being and the alleviation of poverty and oppression.[30] In this chapter, we are interested in the community and community-scale efforts aimed at the enhancement of human well-being that build on strengths through **empowerment** strategies. We are also interested in the alleviation of poverty and oppression through community-based approaches. This is not to argue that poverty and oppression can successfully be dealt with at all system levels. Importantly though, poverty and oppression are manifested at the community level and must be specifically addressed at this level. This represents a major challenge to the profession and to the practitioner.

Now to the question, How can community power theory inform practice? Earlier we defined power simply as the ability of person A to get person B to do something he or she would not otherwise do. In short, it is a social process, a feature of a relationship. This definition provides a micro-level application of power, but what about a macro-level definition? Here Max Weber is again helpful.

> In general, we understand by "power" the chance of a man or of a number of men to realize their own will in a communal action even against the resistance of others who are participating in the action.[31]

Weber was careful in his wording so it is important to acknowledge his use of "even against." In other words, power can be exercised through the use of both cooperative and conflict-based "communal actions." This distinction will become important as we develop the community power position and later examine conflict theory.

Next, What is meant by empowerment? Here the *Social Work Dictionary* is helpful: "In community organization and social activist social work, the process of helping a group or community to achieve political influence or relevant legal authority."[32] This definition suggests that political influence or power and the attendant legal authority is one dimension of community power. Are there other dimensions?

In Chapter 11, we introduced Max Weber's conception of the various forms of authority and their application to the formal organization. We will again turn to Weber for a starting place in our development of the community power position. The concept of community from a systems perspective assumes an interdependence of parts, the existence of an underlying structure that connects the parts in some way. Weber's conception of power stems from the existence of a legal order to which those residing in the community adhere.[33] This legal order would be clearly represented in federal, state, county, and municipal law. According to Weber, this legal order directly influences the existence, form, and exercise of all types of power. However, he did not restrict his conception of power to that inherent in the law and the exercise of legal authority or power.

Weber identified three forms of ordering evident in a community, the first being the legal order. The second is the economic order and the third is the social order. All three forms are related and interdependent. The economic order is the way in which goods and services are produced, delivered, and consumed. The social order, according to Weber, is the means by which "social honor" (prestige) is distributed.[34] It is in this way that Weber identified a major component of a class system evident in every community or society. Those having the highest social honor (those at the top of the class structure) have attendant power. Frequently they also have great economic and legal power, but their social honor is not to be explained only by virtue of their economic or legal power. As we will see in exploring the community power position, both the elitist and pluralist assume the existence of a social class hierarchy in the community.

To summarize, Weber added economic power and power associated with one's perceived social position in the community to legal or politically based power. We find these three strands of community power useful in developing the community power position.

Assumptions

With the foregoing discussion of power as a context, we will now explore how the work of the community gets done. We will build on the following assumptions that we believe apply to the community power position:

1. No one is in charge of a community. Unlike a formal organization, the use of legal authority cannot account, in any fundamental way, for how the work of the community gets done.
2. While a symbiotic relationship among the member parts of a community is acknowledged, community growth and development evidences a level of purposiveness not explainable in terms of an ecological equilibrium model.
3. Communities do evince social structures and these structures can be modified by professionally directed efforts. To state the position otherwise, communities, like all social systems, are in process. This process is explainable through impersonal forces as well as through planned collective actions. The community power position is helpful in understanding how these planned collective actions take place.

In the sections to follow, the two contrasting positions on community power will be reviewed. Recall that the theorists selected are but two of many who hold similar positions.

COMMUNITY POWER: THE ELITIST POSITION

Perhaps more than any other writer, Floyd Hunter popularized the term *community power structure*.[35] He has been selected to illustrate the **elitist position.** Hunter was interested in how community decisions were made and implemented. His methodology is of particular interest. Simply put, he assumed that a community power structure existed. Acting from this position, he systematically asked people to identify the most influential people in the community and then sought to identify the relationships that existed among those who by consensus were identified as the most influential. His approach to the identification of the power people in the community became known as the reputational method. Simply stated, the method relied on the perceptions held by various people in the community who, by reason of their own positions, could be expected to know people by their reputation.[36]

Assumptions

The following assumptions are drawn from the work of Hunter. To some extent they extend some of the ideas noted in the general assumptions that introduced the community power position.

1. Policies that vitally affect community life appear suddenly, with the majority of citizens not knowing by whom they are sponsored.
2. Some community actions appear manipulated to the advantage of a privileged few.
3. In many instances, community actions appear not to square with democratic principles of decision making.
4. This nation's concept of democracy is in danger of losing its hold on citizens if the lines of communication between citizens and those who mold the development of communities are not broadened and strengthened.[37]

5. The differences between leaders and other people lie in the fact that within communities there exist informal social groupings who possess the power to give definite functions over to certain persons and not to others.[38]

Concepts

Following are some of the key concepts employed by Hunter.

Power. "Power is a word that will be used to describe the acts of men going about the business of moving other men to act in relation to themselves or in relation to organic or inorganic things."[39] With these words, Hunter described power as a social process. His words are reminiscent of the popular expression, "the movers and shakers" of the community.

Power Structure. The concept of a **power structure** is central in Hunter's work. In short, it is organized along a vertical axis with a relatively few "power people" at the top. As you move down the hierarchy, those at each lower level have less power than those at the next higher level. In a manner of speaking, one moves from those who decide to those who carry out the decisions. By reason of the numbers involved, the structure takes on the appearance of a pyramid.

Influence. Influence is conceived as a component of power but not synonymous with either power or its other component, authority. Influence is viewed as the ability to get another's attention and to be heard; based on being heard, one gains the ability to influence.

Authority. Authority is used in a way similar to its use in a formal organization, to command and expect the command to be followed (legal authority). In Hunter's study, he extended the concept beyond the source of legal authority. In this sense, Hunter's use of authority and power are very similar.

The Study

Hunter labeled his study community "Regional City." It was in fact Atlanta, Georgia, and the study took place in 1950–1951. Through his reputational method, he assembled a list of more than 175 persons. From this list, a group of judges identified the top forty. Twenty-seven members of this group were interviewed and the ten most influential were identified. According to Hunter, there was substantial agreement among the top twenty-seven as to who were the community's top leaders. One of those mentioned was identified by twenty-one of the twenty-seven raters. In answer to the question, Who is the "biggest" (most powerful) man in town? a specific individual ("Homer") was identified.[40]

The approach employed by Hunter produced a pyramid-shaped power structure with a relatively few men at the top who interacted informally on matters of personal and public interest. Dominating the group were businessmen, the CEOs of the major corporations located in Regional City. The perceived leaders of Regional City were, for the most part, leaders of its economic institutions.

There was no one leader who led all of the time. The leadership person(s) would depend on the policy issue and on a member's interest, for example, building a new community stadium, hospital, university, or highway system. Other members of this community elite would then play a supporting role to the person who agreed to accept the leadership role. The members of this informal elite group shared similar views on a wide variety of matters. In a more technical sense, they evidenced a normative group structure that held them together. Hunter identified a "face" that this leadership group presented to the public and to each other. It was termed the "patched pants theory" ("The biggest ones act like they have patches on their pants"). In other words, in their informal relationships, they act like common folks, not "big shots."[41]

In filling out his structural presentation of community power, Hunter identified four tiers to the pyramid of power.

First Rate: Industrial, commercial, financial owners and top executives of large enterprises.

Second Rate: Operations officials, bank vice-presidents, public-relations men, small businessmen (owners), top-ranking public officials, corporation attorneys, contractors.

Third Rate: Civic organization personnel, civic agency board personnel, newspaper columnists, radio commentators, petty public officials, selected organization executives.

Fourth Rate: Professionals such as ministers, teachers, social workers, personnel directors, and such persons as small business managers, higher paid accountants, and the like.[42]

At the first level, depending on the policy issue, might be a very few people, perhaps ten or twelve. These men and women would know each other and have a long history of working together. At each lower level the number of persons involved increases. Figure 14.2 is a graphic representation of the pyramid. In this presentation, there is a single power elite (first raters) but, depending on the issue involved, a somewhat different constituency at the second through fourth levels.

In thinking about Hunter's contribution to community power theory, it is important to view this pyramid as informal and fluid in terms of its structure. While in some ways it looks like the pyramid shape of a formal organization, the vertical axis is not comprised of legal authority. The power is informally and socially structured. The people at the top have power based on wealth and organizational and social status. Because of their power and their shared beliefs of what is right and good for the community, they can assure a level of compliance by those who carry out their wishes. The future power status of those in the lower ranks is controlled to some extent by those in the higher ranks.

Hunter's observation that the people in the top power positions are seldom seen is probably a useful notion for the "professional change agent" to keep in mind. Those in the second and third tiers are the visible leaders, but from Hunter's position, they are essentially carrying out the decisions reached essentially by consensus by the power brokers in the top positions.

Hunter's work served to establish what is frequently called the elitist conception of a community's power structure. In short, there are a relatively few men (white) who comprise a power elite and assume informally a stewardship responsibility for major community policy decisions. They disproportionately represent the principal economic enterprises located in the community. Like a small group, they share a similar value system and are guided by the group's normative structure. They are only concerned with major community initiatives in which they may have a personal, civic, or business interest. Depending on the issue, they rotate leadership responsibility with others of the group playing supporting roles. In this sense, Hunter argued, there does not appear to be a single power pyramid but pyramids of power (see Figure 14.2). These so-called pyramids are fluid and rudimentary when compared to the kind of power pyramid evidenced in a formal organization. Beneath the power elite are layers of those who implement and legitimatize the decisions made by the elite.

Government becomes not the policymaker itself but the implementor of major policy decisions informally made by the elite. While Hunter was primarily concerned with describing the power structure of the community, he also noted the influence local power people have at the state and national level. In this sense he

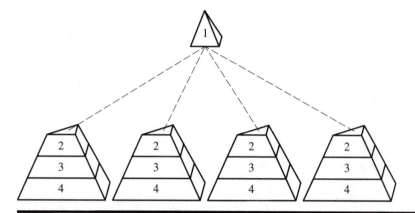

FIGURE 14.2   The Community Power Structure

described a vertical axis of power that connects the community with the state and federal government. Through this observation, Hunter has been helpful to us as we developed the concept of suprasystem within social systems theory.

> Interpersonal relationships have much to do with power-wielding, as all politicians seem to know. The personal connections between some of the men of power in Regional City and those in power in state offices are often quite close.[43]

In developing his point of the ties between community influentials and state government, Hunter noted that his study included questions to identify these relationships. Hunter's data suggest that these ties are sufficiently strong for local power figures to influence state legislation and to call on state officials for assistance to deal with community issues. It is in this sense that a community's suprasystem can be usefully thought of as including the state legislature and various offices of state government.

Reflective of the assumptions that undergirded his study, Hunter was concerned about his findings. In something of a warning, he noted the following:

> Power is structured socially, in the United States, into a dual relationship between govern-mental and economic authorities on national, state, and local levels. It is true that there is no formal tie between the economic interests and government, but the structure of policy-determining committees and their tie-in with the other powerful institutions and organizations of the Community make government subservient to the interests of these combined groups.[44]

While establishing the foundation for the elitist position in conceptualizing a community's power structure, Hunter's work was subject to considerable criticism. An important focus of criticism was his reputational method. At one level, the argument can be made that the method itself would produce a hierarchical power structure. At another level, the approach relied on perceptions and not objective data. Nevertheless, his work spurred interest in the development of community power theory while refining the methodology he pioneered. While his study is dated, many of Hunter's concepts have become part of everyday language holding much of their original meaning, for example, power structure. Similarly, many citizens as well as professional social workers still share Hunter's concern that community decision making may, in some instances, not be in accord with democratic principles and may have harsh effects on those with the least power.

COMMUNITY POWER: THE PLURALIST POSITION

Robert Dahl, in his classic study *Who Governs*, helped establish a position counter to the elitist position, the so-called **pluralist position**.[45] He selected New Haven, Connecticut, for his research, which got under way in 1955, some five years after Hunter's study of Atlanta. Dahl considered New Haven typical of other cities in this country while having the special advantage of being one of the country's oldest. New Haven was incorporated as a city in 1784 after nearly 150 years as an English colony. Dahl developed his study within an historical context, noting that the community, over a 200-year period, changed its governance from an oligarchic to a pluralistic structure. Initially, public office was in the hands of a few privileged families, then the newly rich, then the "E-plebes" (proletariat-common folks), and finally resting with the "new men"—an evolving group of bureaucrats and professional politicians. Simply stated, Dahl set the stage for his study by recognizing impersonal forces of change that affect governance, for example, population change (immigration) and industrialization.

Dahl introduced his problem statement as follows: "In a political system where nearly every adult may vote but where knowledge, wealth, social position, access to officials, and other resources are unequally distributed, who actually governs?"[46]

Assumptions

Dahl was a political scientist, not a sociologist like Hunter. He brought to his research certain assumptions about the workings of the political systems in this country. These assumptions, reflective of his discipline, fall most clearly under what he referred to as the democratic creed. This creed is comprised of a set of values and related societal norms.

1. The majority of American citizens possess a stable set of democratic beliefs pertaining to governance.

2. The majority of Americans believe that the nation's political system, in general, is consistent with this democratic creed.
3. Largely through our society's basic socialization process, e.g., our education system, the democratic creed is produced and maintained.
4. Governance is vitally affected by the American creed.[47]

As a practical matter, in our democracy, key offices are won by election—a vote of the people who by their actions consent to be governed, to act in conformity to the rules made by those who represent them. Dahl argued that most people in this country adhere to the doctrine of democracy. This doctrine constrains how those in office behave and how those "influentials" within the larger society behave. In this sense, not only do political and other influentials lead, they are also led by what they perceive their constituents want or will at least tolerate. This is not to say that great injustices do not exist in the system, but it is self-adjusting largely based on the social norms comprising the democratic creed.

It should be noted that Dahl did not define the above four items as assumptions. In fact, they are most clearly stated in his final chapter, yet they are organizing schemes found throughout his study.

Consistent with these assumptions built on a doctrine of democracy, Dahl proposed a series of hypotheses about how the political system of New Haven could work. These hypothesis can be summarized as follows:

1. Few citizens will have any substantial effect on initiating proposed community policies or in the defeat of those proposed by others.
2. Community leaders with direct influence on development of community policies will have a corps of subleaders to assist them.
3. The actions of community leaders and their subleaders will be clothed in rituals conveying the impression of democratic control. In other words, the intent will be to

convey to the public that the leaders are merely the spokespersons for their subleaders who in turn are representatives of the community at large.

4. Leaders need to win elections in order to develop and maintain their core support groups.

5. A leader's support groups are maintained by their memories of "past rewards." As a consequence, leaders will shape policies to maintain a flow of rewards to their key support groups.

6. Conflicts will occasionally occur between the overt policies of the leaders, which are aimed at their broad community constituents, and their "covert" policies, which are designed to benefit their core supporters. In stiff competition, the resolution will tend to "favor their overt commitments."[48]

To test these hypotheses, Dahl examined three "issue-areas" in which it was possible to determine how and by whom decisions were made—public education, urban redevelopment, and in the nomination process for local elective offices of the two major political parties. In the first two instances, a series of decisions by local government is required, for example, approval of budgets, new programs, acquisition of properties, and so forth.

Unlike Hunter, who essentially relied on a single measure of power or influence (reputation), Dahl decided on an eclectic measurement strategy. His approach to the study of community influence (Dahl apparently preferred the term *influence* to *power*) employed six approaches:

1. A longitudinal study of the demographic characteristics of office holders (Were there historical changes in the sources of leadership?)

2. Determine the type and extent of participation in local affairs by persons in a specific socioeconomic category

3. Determine "issue-areas" and study a set of decisions made in those areas (Who was in-

volved and what was the specific nature of their influence?)

4. Through random sampling procedures, survey participants in specific policy issue areas to determine their characteristics (What were the socioeconomic sources of the leaders' key support groups?)

5. Sample voters to determine the characteristics of those participating in local issues

6. Conduct longitudinal studies to chart changes in the patterns of voting by different socioeconomic levels[49]

In general, Dahl's hypotheses were supported. Like Hunter, he was able to identify a small group of leaders, a much larger group of subleaders, and a relatively large number of people with little or no direct but some indirect influence in how decisions were made and implemented. Unlike Hunter, he did not find a cohesive group of leaders who exercised influence (power) in a number of different areas of community life. Perhaps his most important finding was how specialized decision making was in New Haven. As might be expected, the mayor, by reason of his position, was able to exercise direct influence in a number of different areas of community life.

Dahl, in his study of political activity in New Haven, was particularly interested in the sources of leadership as it pertains to the issues examined. Unlike Hunter, Dahl found that leadership was not drawn from a business elite, but was specialized and largely found in the person of public officials. Also, leadership patterns changed over the years. Figure 14.3 is a way of graphically describing the power structure identified in Dahl's work. It stands in contrast to the monolithic pyramid form described by Hunter.

What the figure seeks to convey is that Dahl found multiple centers of power that were only loosely connected. There was not a single group of leaders operative in all centers. These centers were in specialized content areas, such as education, welfare, and transportation.

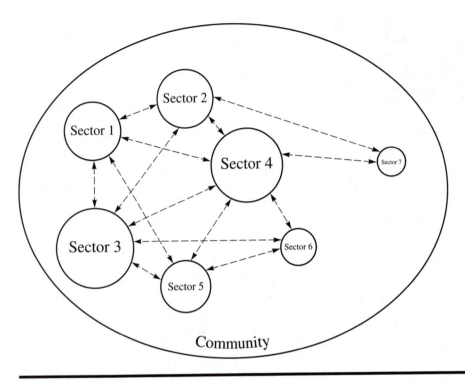

FIGURE 14.3   The Pluralist Concept of Community Power

Within these centers, like Hunter, he found pyramid-like structures. The vertical axis of the pyramid is power, the ability to influence a policy and determine its outcome. Relatively few men were at the top of the pyramid. As you move down the layers comprising the pyramid, you find groups of subleaders and followers having some level of interest in the content area. As in Hunter's study, the leaders and subleaders were primarily white men.

Concepts

While Dahl's theory of community power is not clearly constructed out of a series of specific concepts, two concepts are noteworthy for those interested in the applied aspects of his work: "slack in the system" and "political resources."

Slack in the System.   Dahl's concept of the **slack in the system** is useful, particularly to professional change agents. Most people in a community, in accord with the pluralist position, are not particularly concerned with attempting to influence community decision making. They use their time and resources in other and largely personal ways. A few community residents, particularly political professionals, concentrate their resources (time, money, influence) on community decision making. Importantly, this decision making is specialized so their influence does not tend to extend over several domains. In other words, these sectors or domains of influence are only loosely coupled and the key influential people are few in number and are concentrating their influence in their specialty area. An example would be a superintendent of schools. On matters of education, the superintendent might be very influential, but on matters pertaining to highway construction, she or he would have little interest or influence.

In contrast, large numbers of citizens have resources that can be converted from personal to political purposes. In this sense, there is considerable slack in the (political) system. In short, when mobilized, ordinary citizens can have considerable influence on community decision making. To extend the above example, the school superintendent concentrates her or his influence in the area of public education. When an issue comes up, her or his influence is already concentrated; there is not much to mobilize. On the other hand, if the ordinary citizen becomes acutely interested in the same issue, considerable slack in the system can be taken up and perhaps be critical in influencing the issue.

Political Resources.   The concept of (political) resource as used by Dahl pertains to anything a person can use to influence others. In other words, if social power is the ability of person A to get person B to do something that person B would not otherwise do, then a resource is anything that helps person A to get person B to act in accord with A's wishes. These resources could include, among others, person A's time, access to money, credit, and other things of value to person B, control over jobs, social status, control over information, and access to other people important to person B.

Dahl offered six observations about resources having relevance to influencing community decision making.

1. Many different kinds of resources for influencing officials are available to different citizens.
2. With few exceptions, these resources are unequally distributed.

3. Individuals best off in their access to one kind of resource are often badly off with respect to many other resources.
4. No one influence resource dominates all the others in all or even in most key decisions.
5. With some exceptions, an influence resource is effective in some issue-areas or in some specific decisions but not all.
6. Virtually no one, and certainly no group of more than a few individuals, is entirely lacking in some influence resources.[50]

The contribution of the power position to social work is evident in two major areas. First, the concept of power provides the community practitioner with an approach in understanding how community decision making works. In this sense, it becomes an assessment tool. If the worker is to be involved in a community change effort, the community power position becomes important in understanding how decisions are typically made in a particular community and what interests may have to be mobilized or at least neutralized for the change effort to be successful.[51]

Second, the concept of empowerment is central to the social work profession.[52] Most of social work's clients lack power and thus control over their lives. Whatever the problem clients may face, the helping effort will always focus on client strengths and ways of increasing the person's ability to manage his or her life. At the community level, the focus of the worker tends to be on a class or category of people who share some problem or opportunity status, for example, welfare recipients, those who are seriously and persistently mentally ill, or those who are physically disabled. The community power theorists have provided a way of thinking about power, the forms it takes, and how it is obtained and used. These theorists have informed community practice and particularly have helped social workers understand the process of advocacy and how it can be used to empower those without power.[53]

THE CONFLICT POSITION

The conflict position will be the final line of theory development summarized in this chapter. Perhaps more so than the other positions, conflict theory is difficult to categorize. **Conflict** among humans and their various forms of social organization is as old as human history. Perhaps the explanations (theories) of conflict are equally as old. In introducing this position, three features will be identified that contribute to the categorization problems. The first is definitional. What is meant by *conflict?* For example, is conflict a form of competition or are they separate and distinct social processes? What about the levels of human conflict—do they evidence a common core of determinants? For example, should the definition of social conflict include interpersonal conflict, for example, spousal or child abuse as well as international armed conflict?

Second, many psychological, psychosocial, as well as sociological theorists consider social conflict a secondary or tertiary issue within the framework of the theory. For example, Sigmund Freud wove instincts into his theory of psychoanalysis. In short, he postulated two opposing instincts, one aggressive, a self-destructive behavioral trend related to death; the other, a sexual instinct directed toward life. In accord with Freud's views, the death-related instinct is the seat of much of the conflict-related behaviors found in humans. Karl Menninger, a psychoanalyst, authored two important books related to this genetically based struggle between life and death: *Man Against Himself* and *Love Against Hate*.[54] Should theories such as psychoanalysis be included in the conflict position?

Finally, is there a general theory of conflict that has resolved these issues or should the position be comprised of a listing of the dominant specialized theories of conflict? The answer to this question is that, to date, there is no consensus as to a general theory of social conflict. It is important to note that many key social scientists are advocating that efforts be intensified to develop such a general theory.[55]

In this discussion, we will exclude theories in which social conflict is a secondary theoretical issue. With respect to the problem of definition, we will view social conflict as possessing the following characteristics:

1. It is a relational concept.
2. It always involves an overt struggle between at least two people with at least one seeking to dominate or subjugate the other.
3. It is an unregulated as opposed to a regulated contest of wills.
4. The struggle will always evidence incompatible objectives.

In part, our approach to the problem of definition has been shaped by this book's attention to generalist practice in social work. While we are including the conflict position in the community section of the book, it could just as well have been included as a general theory and introduced in the first section of the book. By placing it in the community section, we are seeking to emphasize the importance of social conflict as a major strategy of social change at the community level.

Our approach to the issue of definition has also been shaped by the profession's concerns with social justice, discrimination, and human oppression. The conflict position and its lines of theory development are helpful in conceptualizing these issues in ways that have practice relevance.

We will start the development of this position from an historical position. Here the writings of Marx and Simmel are critical. Both viewed social conflict as a basic social process, but the assumptions on which their positions were built differed greatly. Marx viewed social life from a macro-level perspective. Simply stated he believed the economic subsystem to be the fundamental determinant of the structure of society (the social system at the largest scale).[56] In social systems terms, the economic subsystem shapes all others—government, judicial, education, science, and morality itself.[57] Marx also held that the state is more important than the individual. As you will recall, this position is the antithesis of the democratic creed just discussed. Within the creed, the individual is supreme; the state is supposed to be a servant of the people.

Simmel, in contrast to Marx, sought an understanding of the social order by focusing on the individual and the patterns of human relationships. The explanation of conflict as a dominant social process is not to be found in a society's means of production, but in the genetic makeup of humans. For Simmel, conflict in the sense of gaining dominance over others is a vital life process. A central task of sociology is the discovery of the basic patterns of this life process.[58]

Karl Marx (1818–1883) was born in Germany of Jewish parents. He is best known for *The Communist Manifesto,*[59] a work that was co-authored with his colleague Friedrich Engels. Modern communism has its roots in the writings of these two social and political philosophers. In writing the introduction to *The Communist Manifesto,* Francis B. Randall observed that it has become the "most famous pamphlet in the history of the world."[60]

Marx might be categorized best as an activist philosopher and revolutionary as opposed to a dispassionate social theorist. He viewed himself as a scientific socialist possessing an evolutionary view of the world and humankind. The following assumptions appear central in this "theory."

1. There are fixed laws of nature that guide all development.
2. Economics is the fundamental structural determinant of society.
3. Social change occurs as a dialectic in three phases (a) a thesis (position 1), (b) an oppos-

ing thesis (position 2), and then (c) a new position (position 3). Social change is a cyclical process in the sense that position 3, the synthesis of positions 1 and 2, becomes the new position 1 and the process continues.
4. Violence is the final and necessary form that conflict will take to accomplish its social change ends.

There is little room in the position taken by Marx for independent human will or choice. The foundations of human behavior lie in the actions of the larger economic forces. He believed that through each successive wave of social change, human society was improved.[61]

Several key concepts are important in considering the contribution Marx made to the conflict position.

1. *Class Structure.*   In Marx's view, the **social class** system is determined by economics and is comprised of only two levels—the bourgeoisie (owners of the tools of production) and the proletariat (workers, the "common" people). As class consciousness occurs and the proletariat become aware of their exploitation by the bourgeoisie, violence results with the inevitable loss of power by the bourgeoisie and the gaining of power by the proletariat.

2. *Alienation (anomie).* The concept of **anomie** owes its importance to the "sociology" of Marx. Through exploitation by the bourgeoisie, the working class (proletariat) loses faith, is "ground down," and becomes disaffected from society. The task of the revolutionary is to help the disaffected to understand their plight, to join forces with others being exploited, and to overthrow their oppressors and establish a new state.

3. *Socialism/communism.* The concepts overlap and for our purposes can be considered synonymous. This is not to say that some writers do not attempt to clearly distinguish between the two. Important in the conflict position is the

contribution made by Marx in highlighting the societal form of governance (socialism/communism) in which wealth and power is shared by the community itself, for example, government ownership of the means of production.

In the first line of *The Communist Manifesto*, Marx established the foundation of his revolutionary social philosophy: "The history of all hitherto existing society is the history of class struggle."[62] In this simple statement, Marx summarized his philosophy of economic determinism and the role of social conflict in social change.

Governance, in the view of Marx, is under the control of the ruling class, or in his words, "The executive of the modern state is but a committee for managing the common affairs of the whole bourgeoisie."[63] This position is not too distant from the view that Hunter held in his elitist position of the exercise of community power in Regional City.

Earlier, we made the point that the economic subsystem of society was dominant and shaped all other institutions including the family and the individual. Marx in his rhetoric put it this way: "The bourgeoisie has torn away from the family its sentimental veil, and has reduced the family to a mere money relation."[64] The individual worker, within the operation of the economy, is dehumanized; work loses meaning and the person is treated as an appendage to his or her machine. It is interesting that while *The Communist Manifesto* was first published in early 1848, some of the same concerns about the effects of the economy on the individual and family are being voiced today, over 150 years later.

Marx's predictions of a class struggle failed to materialize. The Soviet Union, a society that tried to incorporate Marx's ideology, became, in systems terms, closed. Steady state was lost and the empire crumbled with a new and more open society emerging. What is of interest is that recent conflict on a national and internal scale has organized around ethnic and racial issues rather than class consciousness.

Georg Simmel (1858–1918) was a German sociologist who had a major influence in the development of sociology both in Europe and in this country. Simmel was a social scientist, Marx a social activist. The following assumptions are associated with Simmel's writings:

1. *Society, in its essence, is the psychological interaction among individuals.* In contrast to Marx, who started his exploration of human behavior at the societal level, Simmel started with the individual. In his words, "In a similar way, when we look at human life from a certain distance, we see each individual in his precise differentiation from all others. But, if we increase our distance, the single individual disappears and there emerges, instead, the picture of a 'society.'"[65]

2. *Humans have instinctual as well as acquired characteristics that provide the propensity to engage in certain behaviors, for example, aggressiveness.* Simmel put it as follows: "The whole category of hostilities that has its extreme development in the fight between brothers, draws its radically destructive character from the fact that experience and knowledge, as well as the instincts flowing from their common root, gives each of them the most deadly weapons precisely against their specific adversary."[66]

Simmel was a prolific writer covering the field of sociology as well as other subject areas. He is generally recognized as the founder of the formal school of sociology. Rather than attempt to identify the organizing concepts of his sociology, the remaining space will be focused on his contributions to the conflict position.

Simmel recognized other social processes underlying human interaction that have their origins in one's genetic structure, as well as those that are learned. So, unlike Marx who saw an increasing polarization that eventually leads to violent conflict and a restructuring of the social order, Simmel saw that conflict was frequently an interim social process that resulted in compromise and the resolution of conflict among the parties. In applied terms, Turner summarized a proposition based on Simmel's writings—the more conflict is a means to an end, the less likely the conflict is to be violent.[67]

Simmel's contribution to the conflict position in community organization is particularly helpful in understanding the effects of conflict on group members. Two points are particularly important; first, a conflictual relationship will tend to strengthen the boundaries of the groups engaged. In this sense, insiders will clearly be distinguished from outsiders. This is part of a polarization process. Second, the more group members are engaged in self-defense tactics, the greater the solidarity of group members will be.[68]

In thinking of the practice implications of Simmel's work, keep in mind that his quest was for the identification of basic patterns of human interactions. In other words, the same general patterns of conflict would be evident in the behavior of a small group, a family, and among nations (societies).

The other two conflict theorists whose views will be summarized are Ralf Dahrendorf and Lewis Coser. Dahrendorf is in the tradition of Marx while Coser's views run similar to those of Simmel. While in different traditions, both Dahrendorf and Coser have made substantial contributions to conflict theory.

Dahrendorf is of special interest because his construction of conflict theory places him in opposition to functionalism and other theories that recognize a basic ordering dynamic in social life.[69] In short, and in the worldview expressed by Marx, social life is inherently conflictual. All forms of social organization contain power differentials among members and thus by their very nature are conflictual. The tension state between the conflicting parties is not in itself negative. Rather, the conflict is the basis of social change. In this sense, conflict is adaptive and can at one level contribute to order; at another level, conflict contributes to a disordering process. In our construction of social systems theory, we build on this position by acknowledging the presence of entropic as well as negative entropic forces in the social functioning of all social systems.

Coser, like Simmel, was interested in the basic patterns of human interaction. Of particular interest to us is his attention to the relationship between social structure and social process.

> Nevertheless, I would like to show that structural analysis, like love, crucial though it is, is not enough. Exclusive concern with structural factors could lead intentionally or unwittingly, to a neglect of social process. Structural factors, I would like to show at the hand of a few concrete examples, do not operate directly upon social behaviors but are mediated through processes of social interaction among which social conflict is a major factor, though by no means the only one.[70]

In developing his point, Coser cited the civil rights and the women's liberation movements as examples. Using the women's movement, the massive structural changes in the nation's workforce brought about by war resulted in large numbers of women going into the workforce. Other structural changes brought about by technology included birth-control devices, which gave women control over reproduction. Coser argued that these structural changes in society, important as they were, do not fully account for the fundamental changes that have occurred between the roles occupied by men and women. In Coser's view, it was the use of conflict strategies by the women leaders of the women's liberation movement and others that helped account for these changes. He summarized his position on the relationship between structure and process as follows: "Structures and their differentiation set the stage and provide opportunities, but only specific interactive processes determine the outcome."[71]

We share this same position, which accounts for our separation of structure and function in a system's conversion operations. The recognition of conflict as a change strategy has a long and important history in the social work profession. In particular, the **settlement house** played an important role in the emergence of the social work profession. In the settlement house movement, social work was introduced to the use of conflict as a strategy of social change.[72] Leaders in this early movement were influenced by the conflict position in the sense that it provided a grounding in theory for the use of conflict as a change process.

A second tradition of growing importance in social work is what is usually referred to as conflict resolution. Here the social worker is not involved in the use of conflict but in the use of a mediation process to resolve conflict.[73] Whether using conflict as a change strategy or conflict resolution, theorists associated with the conflict position have provided the theoretical foundation for understanding this important social process.

SUMMARY

Three lines of theory development applicable to practice at the community level were introduced in this chapter. In recognition of the variations of each of these theories as defined by different authors, we have labeled them *positions*. Our attempt has not been to be comprehensive but to identify and distinguish them as different ways of thinking about communities in light of the professional practice of social work. The three positions are human ecology, community power (elitist and pluralist), and social conflict.

The human ecology and conflict positions view communities (all forms of human organization) as resulting from underlying processes. In the case of human ecology, the process is an impersonal, symbiotic process; with social conflict, the underlying process is conflict. In the case of the two community power positions, the presentation is essentially structural. From the elitist point of view, community power is primarily monolithic in nature and primarily lodged in the hands of those holding leadership roles in the economic subsystem of the community. In a structural sense, some similarity exists between this position and that held more generally by Karl Marx. Floyd Hunter made no reference to Marx in his research nor is his study embedded in a conflict ideology. Nevertheless, those holding key positions in the business and industrial sectors of the community are, according to the elitist position, those who appear to have the greatest influence in shaping its future.

Dahl, arguing from the pluralist position, viewed social power as decentralized and embedded in a value and normative structure based on democratic principles. His study of New Haven is of special interest when viewed from Marx's position that conflict is the medium of change. In Dahl's account of New Haven, power shifted peacefully over a period of 150 years through democratic processes from the control of the bourgeoisie to the proletariat to a group of professional politicians. The process was competitive but was essentially void of revolutionary and violent conflict. In this sense, Marx's thesis of violent conflict as the sole means of social change was not confirmed.

Each of the four positions summarized has contributed to our formulation of social systems theory, which will be summarized in the next chapter.

GLOSSARY _____

Anomie   A loss of connectedness, a feeling of being isolated and lacking purpose. A synonymous term would be *alienation*.

Biotic   The concept in ecological theory that refers to a subsocial system that links all forms of life, plant and animal, to their habitats.

Central business district (CBD) In ecological theory, the central core of a community around which the community develops. Comprising the core would be the hub of transportation, finance, government, and large commercial activities.

Community organization practice A form of social work practice in which the geographic community itself is designated as the client system and thus the beneficiary of its own helping efforts.

Community power position As used in this chapter, the community power position and community power perspective are synonymous. In short,power is viewed as the central organizing force in understanding the social functioning of communities.

Competition A central concept in ecological theory that pertains to the activities evident in all forms of life, plant and animal, undertaken to survive and to gain dominance in their habitats.

Conflict A social process in which defeat and subjugation of the adversary is the intended outcome. It differs from competition in that the intent is not only to prevail in a social process but also to subjugate the adversary.

Elitist position An approach to the study of community power based on a belief that e Very community has a small group of citizens who informally influence community decision making at the highest level. These citizens are able to do so by virtue of the economic and social positions they hold.

Empowerment The concept refers to a social process in which human well-being is enhanced through infusing the client system with a form of social power, for example, political power or power through the use of legal authority.

Pluralist position An approach to the study of community power that holds that power is decentralized, i.e., there is a plurality of power interest in a community.

Political resources A concept employed in the pluralist conception of community power that covers any resource that can be mobilized to influence a community outcome, for example, the reallocation of a person's time.

Power structure A concept used by the elitists to describe a hierarchy of social power evident in communities.

Settlement house These were neighborhood-based facilities typically established in large urban areas that served to bring people from different socioeconomic backgrounds together. The settlement movement began in England in 1884 at Toynbee Hall.

Slack in the system A concept in the pluralist conception of community power that identifies potential social power that can be mobilized around a community issue.

Social class In conflict theory, a social class structure exists and is essentially determined by economics. It is comprised of two levels—the bourgeoisie (owners of the tools of production) and the proletariat (workers).

Succession The concept employed in ecological theory that describes an orderly pattern of change in the relationships and positions of those sharing the same habitat.

Symbiosis A state in which different organisms form relationships that are mutually advantageous. The forces that produce these sets of relationships are impersonal.

NOTES

1. G. A. Hillery, Jr., "Villages, Cities, and Total Institutions," *American Sociological Review* (1963): 779–791.

2. Charles D. Garvin and Fred M. Cox, "A History of Community Organizing Since the Civil War with Special Reference to Oppressed Communities," in *Strategies of Community Intervention*, eds. Jack Rothman, John L. Erlich, and John E. Tropman, 5th ed. (Itasca, IL: F. E. Peacock, 1995), 64–99.

3. Philip R. Popple, "Social Work Profession: History," in *Encyclopedia of Social Work*, vol. 3, 19th ed. (Washington, DC: NASW Press, 1995), 2282–2292.

Also see Donald Brieland, "History and Evolution of Social Work Practice," in *Encyclopedia of Social Work*, vol. 1, 18th ed. (Silver Spring, MD: NASW, 1987), 739–754.

4. *Social Work Dictionary*, ed. Robert L. Barker (Silver Spring, MD: NASW, 1987), 29.

5. *Webster's II New Riverside University Dictionary* (Boston: Houghton Mifflin, 1988), 288.

6. *The Encyclopedic Dictionary of Sociology*, 3rd ed. (Guilford, CT: The Dushkin Publishing Group, 1986), 53–54.

7. Elizabeth D. Hutchinson, "Toward a Theory of Community: Enhancing the HBSE Curriculum," Paper presented at the Annual Program Meeting of the Council on Social Work Education, San Diego, February 1995.

8. Ferdinand Toennies, *Community and Society*, trans. and ed. Charles P. Loomis (Lansing, MI: Michigan State University Press, 1957), 252.

9. Ibid.

10. Max Weber, "The Nature of the City," in *Perspectives on the American Community*, ed. Roland Warren, 2nd ed. (New York: Rand McNally, 1973), 9–11.

11. For an alternative view to the one developed here, see Philip Fellin, "Understanding American Communities," in *Strategies of Community Intervention*, eds. Jack Rothman, John L. Erlich, and John E. Tropman, 5th ed. (Itasca, IL: F. E. Peacock, 1995), 114–128.

12. See, for example, Carel Bailey Germain, *Human Behavior in the Social Environment: An Ecological View* (New York: Columbia University Press, 1991). This book uses ecology as a metaphor for purposes of exploring the person-environment relationship.

13. The notion of biological determinism builds from the position that the human is first of all an animal and many of the characteristics of humans as well as human evolution can be understood in terms of the evolutionary development of animal life. The basic proposition was set forth by Charles Darwin in his book *On the Origin of Species by Means of Natural Selection* (New York: Modern Library, 1859). For example, see G. Jones, *Social Darwinism and English Thought: The Interaction Between Biological and Social Theory* (Atlantic Highlands, NJ: Humanities Press, 1980).

14. See *Herbert Spencer: Political Writings*, ed. J. Offer (Cambridge, England: Cambridge University Press, 1994).

15. Dennis E. Poplin, *Communities: A Survey of Theories and Methods of Research* (New York: Macmillan, 1972), 65–107.

16. *The Dictionary of Sociology*, eds. Nicholas Abercrombie, Steven Hill, and Bryan S. Turner (New York: The Penguin Group, 1994), 439–440.

17. For an interesting position on Social Darwinism, see T. Crippen, "Neo Darwinian Approaches Social Sciences: Unwanted Concern and Misconceptions," *Sociological Perspectives*, 37 (1994): 391–401.

18. For a review of the development of ecological theory in sociology and the works of Charles Gaplin, see Nicholas S. Timasheff, *Sociological Theory: Its Nature and Growth* (New York: Random House, 1967), 212–215.

19. Ibid.

20. Robert Ezra Park, "Human Ecology," in *Perspectives on the American Community*, ed. Roland Warren, 2nd ed. (New York: Rand McNally, 1973), 32–44. See also E. W. Burgess and Roderick D. McKenzie, *The City* (Chicago: University of Chicago, 1925).

21. For an overview of his position, see Amos H. Hawley, "Human Ecology," in *Population, Environment and Social Organization: Current Issues in Human Ecology*, ed. Michael Mecklin (Hinsdale, IL: The Dryden Press, 1973), 27–42.

22. Ibid., 29.

23. Ibid., 31.

24. Ibid.

25. Jack P. Gibbs and Walter T. Martin, "Toward a Theoretical System of Human Ecology," in *Population, Environment and Social Organization: Current Issues in Human Ecology*, ed. Michael Mecklin (Hinsdale, IL: The Dryden Press, 1973), 42–56.

26. Morton E. Long, "The Local Community as an Ecology of Games," *American Journal of Sociology*, 64 (November 1958): 251–261.

27. Ibid.

28. Germain first introduced the use of the ecological metaphor to the practice of casework in 1973. She has continued making contributions and now includes application at the community level. See, for example, Carel Bailey Germain, *Human Behavior in the Social Environment: An Ecological View* (New York: Columbia University Press, 1991). Also see Carel B. Germain and Alex Gutterman, "Ecological Perspective," *Encyclopedia of Social Work*, vol. 1, 19th ed. (Washington, DC: NASW Press, 1995), 816–824.

29. Ibid., "Ecological Perspective."

30. "Curriculum Policy Statement," M4.1. For a discussion, see Chapter 1.

31. See Max Weber, *From Max Weber: Essays in Sociology*, trans. and eds. H. H. Gerth and C. Wright Mills (New York: Oxford University Press, 1946), 180.

32. *Social Work Dictionary*, 49.

33. Max Weber, *From Max Weber*, 180–195.

34. Ibid.

35. Floyd Hunter, *Community Power Structure: A Study of Decision Makers* (Chapel Hill: University of North Carolina Press, 1953).

36. Ibid., 8–25.

37. Ibid., 151–170.

38. Ibid., 1–7.

39. Ibid., 2–3.

40. Ibid., 62.

41. Ibid., 105.

42. Ibid., 109.

43. Ibid., 161–162.

44. Ibid., 102.

45. Robert A. Dahl, *Who Governs? Democracy and Power in an American City* (New Haven: Yale University Press, 1961).

46. Ibid., 1.

47. Ibid., 311–325.

48. Robert Dahl, "Who Governs?" in *The Search for Community Power*, eds. Willis D. Hawley and Friedrich M. Wirt (Englewood Cliffs, NJ: Prentice Hall, 1968), 96.

49. Ibid., 94.

50. Ibid., 108–109.

51. For a general discussion, see Emilia E. Martinez-Brawley, "Community," in *Encyclopedia of Social Work*, vol. 1, 19th ed. (Washington, DC: NASW Press, 1995), 539–548.

52. B. L. Simon, "Rethinking Empowerment," *Journal of Progressive Human Services*, 1, 1 (1990): 27–39.

53. James S. Mickelson "Advocacy," *Encyclopedia of Social Work*, vol. 1, 19th ed. (Washington, DC: NASW Press, 1995), 95–100.

54. See particularly, Karl Menninger, *Love Against Hate* (New York: Harcourt, Brace, 1942). Also see Amitai Etzione, *Social Problems* (Englewood Cliffs, NJ: Prentice Hall, 1976).

55. For a useful overview of the arguments surrounding a general theory of social conflict, see Clifton F. Fink, "Some Conceptual Difficulties in the Theory of Social Conflict," *The Journal of Conflict Resolution*, *XII*, 4 (December 1968): 412–460.

56. For a useful discussion of the positions of Marx and Simmel, see Jonathan H. Turner, "Marx and Simmel Revisited: Reassessing the Foundations of Conflict Theory," *Social Forces*, *53*, 4 (June 1975): 618–627.

57. Timasheff, *Sociological Theory*, 49.

58. Ibid., 101–104.

59. Karl Marx and Friedrich Engels, *The Communist Manifesto*, trans. Samuel Moore and ed. Joseph Katz (New York: Washington Square Press, 1965). The book was originally printed in German and published in 1848.

60. Ibid., 7.

61. Timasheff, *Sociological Theory*, 48–51.

62. Marx and Engels, *The Communist Manifesto*, 57.

63. Ibid., 61.

64. Ibid., 62.

65. *The Sociology of Georg Simmel*, trans. and ed. Kurt H. Wolff (New York: The Free Press, 1950), 8.

66. Ibid., 168.

67. Turner, "Marx and Simmel Revisited," 624.

68. Ibid., 625.

69. For a review of Dahrendorf's position, see Ralf Dahrendorf, *Class and Class Conflict in Industrial Society* (Stanford, CA: Stanford University Press, 1959).

70. Lewis A. Coser, "Structure and Conflict," in *Approaches to the Study of Social Structure*, ed. Peter M. Blau (New York: The Free Press, 1975), 210.

71. Ibid., 217.

72. See, for example, Roland F. Smith, "Settlements and Neighborhood Centers," in *Encyclopedia of Social Work*, vol. 3, 19th ed. (Washington, DC: NASW Press, 1995), 2129–2135.

73. Bernard S. Mayer, "Conflict Resolution," in *Encyclopedia of Social Work*, vol. 1, 19th ed. (Washington DC: NASW Press, 1995), 613–622.

CHAPTER 15

THE COMMUNITY
SOCIAL SYSTEMS THEORY

COMPARISONS WITH ECOLOGICAL, POWER,
   AND CONFLICT POSITIONS
SOCIAL SYSTEMS THEORY
RURAL COMMUNITIES AS ADAPTING SYSTEMS

SUMMARY
GLOSSARY
NOTES

This chapter concludes the presentation of social systems theory as an undergirding to the generalist practice of social work. Here we examine the distinctive features of social systems theory when applied to the community. In earlier chapters, we described the special features of the theory at the group/family level and at the level of the formal organization. In introducing social systems theory at the community level, a summary of the features of the theory at each level should be helpful. The special features are categorized as follows: (1) the size and characteristics of the components comprising the system; (2) the types of relationships existing among the components; (3) the level of inclusiveness of the system; and (4) the forms of power or authority employed.

First, at the social group and the family level, the system components are individuals enacting social roles, such as friend, mother, daughter, and so on. The individuals comprising the group or family (in their nongroup or nonfamily roles) are always a key component of the system's suprasystem. In the formal organization, the components of the system are administrative units and work-related social groups. Individuals in work-related roles comprise these units and groups, but the system components are the larger functional work units, for example, the intake unit, the outpatient department, the case management service, and so on. Other formal organizations or administrative units of these organizations dominate the suprasystem; seldom are individuals considered components of the suprasystem at this system level.

At the community level, the components are typically groupings of formal organizations and groups performing similar community functions. A community's hospitals and related health care facilities would serve as an example of a component (a health care subsystem). In this example, it is reasoned that this subsystem would be utilized by community residents to meet their health-related needs. The community's suprasystem is typically comprised of regulatory and funding agencies at the county, state, and federal levels. As a general rule, the higher the system level, the larger the internal components become. The obvious reason for this is to keep the ability to analyze the behavior of these units manageable.

Second, Gemeinschaft relationships dominate at the group/family level. The relationships among the system components are thus personal, traditional, and informal, and the relationship itself is both a means and an end.[1] Gesellschaft relationships dominate in formal organizations. These relationships are essentially contractual, formal, impersonal, and time limited. They serve as a means to obtain some end. The relationship is thus a selected means to achieve some specified end state, for example, a relationship that a seller has to a customer. In contrast, the relationships among components in a community are essentially symbiotic. You will recall that symbiotic relationships are

impersonal but the relationships among the parts are to be understood in terms of conditions arising from sharing the same habitat. In this sense, the impersonal qualities of relationships are of a different order when contrasted with a Gesellschaft relationship. In the latter, those entering into the relationship are doing it purposively and as a means to an end. A symbiotic relationship, while impersonal, is not necessarily entered into knowingly. In many, if not most, instances, those involved may not even know each other personally. Keep in mind that Gemeinschaft and Gesellschaft are pure types of relationships and that some mixture of both forms will be found in all human relationships and thus in all social systems. We use them here to designate the key characteristics of relationships found at each system level. Both forms will be found in communities. What is distinctive about the community is the dominance of symbiotic relationships. What this implies is that most community change is not planned; it occurs as a consequence of symbiotic adjustments among parts. The larger the community, the more evident are the symbiotic adjustments.

Third, the social group and family level is the least inclusive of the three system levels. *Inclusive*, as used here, means self-sufficient in terms of the system's relationship to its suprasystem. The next least inclusive social system is the formal organization, and of the three, the community is the most inclusive, the most self-sufficient. To continue the notion of inclusiveness, the society is the most inclusive of all levels of social systems.

The fourth and final characteristic that distinguishes each system level is the form(s) of power that dominates. Consistent with prior usage, *power* and *authority* are considered synonymous. Traditional and charismatic forms of authority dominate in social groups and families.[2] Traditional authority is essentially historical and a feature of the social system itself (its value and normative structure). Charismatic authority is vested in the individual, stemming from a valued personal characteristic (we say, for example, "She is a born leader"). Traditional authority in a family would be exemplified by a statement such as, "She is your mother, you need to do what she says." Legal authority dominates in formal organization. It is primarily through the use of legal authority that coordination of the work of the various parts of the system in formal organizations is achieved ("She is the boss, she has the right to tell you how the job is to be done").

In contrast to the two preceding system levels, *power* appears to be the preferred term when discussing influence structures at the community level. While all forms of power will be evident, legal authority (power) is particularly important. However, the structure of legal authority in communities is evident in a way different from that in formal organizations. A judicial subsystem is evident in every community; it is comprised of courts, law enforcement agencies, and a variety of related agencies and professional groups that essentially perform the community's social control function. The laws enforced may be municipal, state, or federal, but the point is that these laws provide a comprehensive framework that constrains the social behaviors of those residing within the community.

For comparison purposes, legal authority within a formal organization is contractual; as an employee (a member of the system) you are expected to abide by the conditions of the employment contract. Once you leave your employment, as a practical matter, you are no longer bound by its "legal" authority. This is not the case in a community. In a community, there is no formal contract as such, but by residing in that community (and residing in that state and that society) there is an implicit contract that you will abide by its laws. If you do not, there are specified penalties. Again and as a practical matter, you can't quit a community except by physically moving to another community. You can quit a society by denouncing your citizenship, but even so, as long as you are phys-

ically located within that society (country) you must abide by its laws.

COMPARISONS WITH ECOLOGICAL, POWER, AND CONFLICT POSITIONS

In the previous chapter, we identified three distinct positions that have contributed to the development of community theory and have helped shape our construction of social systems theory. Within each position we summarized clusters of related theories. Our attempt has been to identify the principal theorist(s) within each position and the key features that distinguish this line of theory development. The three positions—ecological, power, and conflict—are essentially macro level in their orientation. This does not mean that some theorists have not attempted micro-level applications, but the central thrust of development of each has been macro. For the most part, the principal theorists have been sociologists and their application has largely been at the societal level.

In drawing comparisons among the three positions, our focus will be on the basic assumptions on which the position is built. We will contrast these assumptions with those contained within our social systems perspective.

The human ecology position builds from the assumption that the habitat (or physical environment) is the basic determinant of social structure. The fundamental processes of adaptation, for example, competition, are essentially the same for all forms of life. Consistent with the notion of adaptation, a strong link historically exists between the human ecology position and the notion of biological determinism set forth in the sociology of Herbert Spencer and other Social Darwinists.[3] In contrast, the social systems perspective treats culture (a feature of the social environment) and the genetic features that humans share as codeterminants of social structure. The habitat is a secondary determinant. From the social systems perspective, cooperation is the primary process by which development (ordering) takes place; competition and conflict are secondary processes. Both human ecology and social systems theory incorporate what generally may be labeled the concept of equilibrium, but in quite different ways. In ecological theory, the state of equilibrium incorporates the habitat centrally. In social systems theory, the equilibrium is labeled steady state and deals only with the subject system and those units comprising its social environment or suprasystem. In this sense, steady state is a more limited concept than its counterpart in human ecology.

The community power position represents a narrower theoretical position than ecological, conflict, or social systems theory. The power position focuses on human and organizational interactions as systems of influence. The basic assumption of the power position is that the sources (resources) of power are unequally distributed and employed to get the work of the community accomplished. Two basic conceptions have evolved within this position, the elitist and the pluralist. Both hold that a hierarchy of power exists in each community. They differ in their perceptions of this community power structure. The elitists hold that there is a dominant group that exercises a disproportionate influence over major decisions affecting community development. The members of this group know each other personally and in many ways possess characteristics of a social group, that is, they interact informally based on shared values and norms. The group members in the elitist conception represent disproportionately the interests of the economic subsystem of the community.

The pluralists, on the other hand, believe that multiple hierarchically arranged community power structures exist. These structures are fluid in the sense of being issue oriented. As a practical matter, they can be viewed as arranged around the subsystems of the community, for example, education, health, economic, and so forth. Unlike the elitists, pluralists view elected

officials and the citizens who elect them (those who hold a democratic ideology) as being dominant in community decision making.

There is nothing in the community power position that is fundamentally in opposition to the social systems perspective. In short, it is a narrower-range position that has applications at the community level for both the generalist and the advanced practitioner who use social systems theory. The variations evident in the elitist and pluralist positions are helpful to practitioners in the assessment phase of their work. The position informs practice by providing alternative ways of viewing the structural makeup of a community and how power is conceptualized and operationalized.

Theoretically, the conflict position and the social systems perspective have much in common. Both are limited to the study of social interaction. The fundamental difference between the two positions is in the assumptions held. The social systems perspective is based on an assumption of order—"There is an underlying intelligible general order in the world to which all matter relates and the existing social order is a subset of the general order" (Chapter 2, assumption 1). The various system levels addressed in this book—groups, families, organizations, and communities—are subsystems of this social order. From this perspective, order and the processes contributing to order are ubiquitous.

The conflict position focuses on social change, not order. Social conflict is ubiquitous, not ordering processes such as cooperation. Ralf Dahrendorf, a leading conflict theorist, was also a leading critic of the structural-functional position in sociology. In advancing his theory of social conflict, Dahrendorf observed:

> It is possible that the revival of the study of social conflict in the last decades appears to many not so much a continuation of traditional research paths as a new thematic discovery—an instance of dialectic irony in the development of science.[4]

The conflict position assumes conflict to be a principal system process, because, according to Dahrendorf, "Every society rests on constraint of some of its members by others."[5] Conflict theorists recognize other processes, but they are treated as secondary. Conflict is the means by which social change is accomplished. Both conflict and social systems theory hold that change is constant. They differ in their views of the fundamental process by which change is driven—conflict versus cooperation. The criticisms of each have their roots in the centrality of these two processes; social systems theory is viewed as unduly conservative, focusing on ordering or integration processes; conflict theory is seen as unduly negative, focusing on conflict and disordering processes.

SOCIAL SYSTEMS THEORY

Except for the early works of the human ecologists and the community power theorists, the community has not been a major focus in the development of theory in sociology. Nevertheless, a number of writers have made important contributions to community theory beyond those already named. We will not review their works here but their contributions should be considered precursors to social systems theory.[6]

Earlier we defined a community as an inclusive form of social organization that is territorially based and through which most people satisfy their common needs and desires, deal with their common problems, seek means to advance their well-being, and relate to their society. This definition incorporates community purpose in a manner consistent with the purpose of the social work profession. Simply put, the purpose of the community is to advance human well-being and to socialize its inhabitants into their societal roles. The community does so in a largely passive mode. This is inherent in the central role of symbiosis in community actions. As we indicated earlier, no one is in charge of the community; there is no board of directors, no executive committee. To put it another way, unlike a formal organization, the community does not actively seek to help a client/customer achieve a state of well-being. The individual is the active participant and through the roles played by the individual within the various social organizations located in the community, well-being is sought and socialization into a societal role occurs. The community provides the location and convenient access to those organizations that represent the resources needed to achieve well-being. Certainly there are both active and passive barriers that can limit access to and use of these resources. These barriers represent problem conditions. More important conceptually, the community must be seen in a positive light, as an arena of possibilities. The individual explores and makes use of these possibilities through the range of geographically accessible resources.

The function of community practice from a strengths perspective is to work toward enhancing community resources, to facilitate partnering among community agencies and groups, and to facilitate access to these resources by all. Communities, through collective actions, can also be oppressive to groups of individuals. When communities are hurtful either by passive neglect or active oppression, the practitioner has a problem-solving role—the client system in all instances is the community itself.

Contributing Theorists

Let us now briefly summarize the contributions made by two social systems theorists. One of the first major efforts in employing the notion of the social system to analyze the community was by Irwin T. Sanders.[7] He described the community as an arena of interaction with groups being the chief units of interaction.[8] He treated the social system as a metaphor for purposes of describing the interactions occurring within the community. Sanders saw the community as comprised functionally of interrelated parts or subsystems. The principal subsystems were (1) local government; (2) economy; (3) family, religion, and morality; (4) education; (5) health and social welfare; and (6) recreation.[9]

Sanders identified community behavior at two levels, processes and operations. Processes were the behaviors occurring between system components, for example, conflict and cooperation. Operations referred to higher-level behaviors involving the system as a whole, for example, socialization and social control.[10]

The best-known and most influential sociologist contributing to the development of social systems theory at the community level was Roland Warren.[11] More so than other community theorists, he applied functional theory in the tradition of Talcott Parsons to his study of the community. Roland Warren is also the theorist who has contributed most directly to our effort at identifying the distinctive features of social systems theory having application to social work practice at the community level.

Warren built his theory by employing two sets of interrelated concepts. With some modification, we have employed these same concepts in our social systems theory. The first set Warren labeled community-relevant functions. Through these five functions, Warren addressed the problem of defining a community. In his words, he considered a community "to be that combination of social units and systems that perform the major social functions having locality relevance."[12] The five functions are as follows:

1. Production–distribution–consumption
2. Socialization
3. Social control
4. Social participation
5. Mutual support

If these five functions are performed by a geographically identifiable social system, it is, according to Warren's definition, a community. These functions are interdependent and are performed by social units sharing the same habitat. In Warren's formulation, some social units located in the community may be involved to a greater or lesser degree in the performance of each of these locality relevant functions. In the next few paragraphs, we will summarize these functions and identify one or more social units associated with the performance of each. Keep in mind that this is being done for illustrative purposes and that some units, such as the family, will be involved in the performance of each function.

Production–Distribution–Consumption. In social systems theory, **production–distribution–consumption** represents designation of the community's economic subsystem plus the people and other subunits that hold jobs in this subsystem and consume its products. In thinking about Warren's usage, consider the community as, in part, a marketplace where goods are produced, distributed, and consumed. People living in a community need work; they also require goods and services to survive. This subsystem supplies both. The community's industries, businesses, and their various suppliers, among others, perform this function.

Socialization. This is the community function that, according to Warren, transmits the society's or community's values, knowledge, technology, and desired behaviors to the individuals and families who reside there. The educational, family, and spiritual subsystems represent the key social units that perform this function. Warren, like your authors, considered the **socialization** function as one that is operative from birth to death.

Social Control. In many ways, **social control** can be viewed as the flip side of the socialization function. The community's social control function seeks to assure minimum compliance with the community's values and normative behavioral expectations. It is performed both formally and informally by a wide variety of social units.

Formally, the community's judicial subsystem serves as an example of a unit that performs this community function. Informally, the family is critical in performing the social control function.

Social Participation.   Warren recognized that humans are, by their genetic nature, social. They require continuing opportunities for **social participation.** While the family and church are important, so are a wide variety of other community units such as civic and professional clubs and recreational and cultural outlets. The community serves as an arena offering opportunities for people to participate with one another for social purposes and for their own individual development.

Mutual Support.   **Mutual support** corresponds, in large part, to what we will later describe as the community's social welfare subsystem. The function has both formal and informal social units. The formal ones include hospitals, clinics, and welfare departments, along with a variety of social services. The family, neighbors, friends, and support groups serve as examples of informal or natural social units performing this function.

With respect to Warren's approach to definition, to the extent that these social functions have locality relevance, they pertain to and are part of the community.

The second set of concepts utilized by Warren are **horizontal** and **vertical patterns.** These two concepts are used to describe the interdependent features of the components comprising the community. The horizontal pattern refers to the interdependent features of the relationships the internal parts of the system have with one another. The vertical pattern refers to the interdependent relationship that these internal parts have with units outside the community.

For Warren, one of the most troublesome problems in applying social systems theory to the community was distinguishing the functions of the social systems located within the community from the functions performed by the community itself, for example, the community's locality relevant functions. A specific dimension of this problem was in clearly differentiating the internal and external patterns of families, groups, and formal organizations as freestanding social systems from the comparable patterns evidenced by these systems as they enacted a community role and participated in performing one or more community relevant functions.

Warren essentially bypassed this problem by employing his concepts of a community's vertical and horizontal patterns of behavior. In essence, Warren developed the concepts of horizontal and vertical patterns as alternative concepts to what other social systems theorists described as "internal and external patterns."[13] While not identical, a community's horizontal patterns would roughly correspond to the internal organization of its parts (subsystems). An example would be the role played by a community's chamber of commerce. This organization's members tend to be formal organizations, groups, and individuals who comprise the community's economic subsystem and help perform the production–distribution–consumption function. The chamber serves as a hub connecting the members of this subsystem horizontally. Simply stated, the local chamber's function is to advance the goals of this subsystem. Conceptually, these goals should also be viewed as advancing the community's economic goals. These goals might include increasing employment opportunities for local citizens and increasing the tax base of the community so that related community goals might be advanced, for instance, expanding library facilities. When chamber members are working together to advance these subsystem goals, they are helping to perform the community's production–distribution–consumption function. When they are back in their respective formal organizations enacting organizational roles, they are pursuing the goals of that organization, not community goals. The members of the local chamber are willing participants because by pursuing the community's economic goals, they are able to advance their own organization's goals as well. It is like the old saying of being able to kill two birds with one stone.

An example would be a local auto dealership anxious for economic expansion to take place in the community because more people having good-paying jobs means the opportunity for this car dealership to sell more cars (adaptation function). In game theory, this is known as **non zero sum** gaming. The basic idea is important in community planning. Simply put, the game is constructed so that every participant wins. The strategy employs cooperative versus competitive/conflict processes. In **zero sum** gaming, the gain of one side involves a corresponding loss to those on the other side. Here, competitive/conflict processes dominate, for example, a football game.

A non zero sum strategy is a useful way of thinking about how a community's horizontal pattern develops and operates. The social units comprising the horizontal pattern work together in a manner that advances each member's goals, but in doing so, the community's goals are also advanced. Other examples of such units would include the work of the local council of churches, a health and welfare planning council, and the local united appeal agency. Like the chamber, these organizations serve as a hub linking other members of the subsystem. In this sense, these units help develop the community's horizontal pattern and by so doing strengthen the community itself. The horizontal pattern would also include those relationships that link the various community subsystems. In each instance, these associations are voluntary. An example would be the convening by the mayor or other such person of a blue ribbon committee to determine how the community might be advanced, for instance, by being named an "All American City."

Warren's use of the vertical pattern corresponds somewhat to our use of suprasystem as

the system's external system. According to Warren, the vertical pattern links social units within a community to other units outside the community to which they are functionally linked. An example would be the link between a local subsidiary of a car dealership to its home office in another community. Other examples would include the chamber of commerce and its affiliation to the National Chamber of Commerce and the tie between a local Roman Catholic Church to the pope and the administration of the church in the Vatican.

The notion of a community's vertical pattern is a very important part of Warren's contribution to community theory. A basic proposition formulated from this position by Warren is that the vertical pattern in U.S. communities is continuing to strengthen and by so doing, it weakens the community's horizontal pattern. The position taken by Warren is very similar to the one taken by Toennies over 100 years ago. Simply put, Gesellschaft (societal) relationships are strengthening at the expense of Gemeinschaft (community) relationships.[14]

While not central in our construction of social systems theory, the society is the dominant and most inclusive of all social systems. In this sense, we find it useful to think of the community as a geographical subsystem of society. In terms of its functional processes and its internal social structures, the community can be viewed as a microcosm of society. We would also advance Warren's thinking by adding that the vertical patterns in each society are gaining strength to some extent at the expense of a society's horizontal pattern. This point is not central to the purposes of this book, but it does provide a larger context for viewing social systems theory and the efforts of larger forces of social change, for example, world economic competition.

The work of Warren has been particularly useful to us because he carefully ties his approach to other major theorists who have helped develop social systems theory, Charles

P. Loomis, Robert Bales, Edward A. Shils, Robert K. Merton, George C. Homans, and Talcott Parsons, among others.[15]

In the remaining pages of this chapter, we will summarize the distinctive features of social systems theory as applied to the community. This summary will be organized around the structural and functional concepts that provide the theory's framework. Recall that the four functional concepts are pattern maintenance, integration, goal attainment, and adaptation. The approach we use is graphically diagrammed in Figure 15.1, The Community as a Social System. This diagram is a structural-functional presentation of social systems theory as applied to the community.

As in all presentations of the theory, the proposed outcome is steady state or in this application, community well-being. In analyzing community behaviors, steady state is treated as the dependent variable (effect), a dynamic state which is constantly being acted on by two independent variables (causes)—integration and goal attainment. The other two requisite functions, pattern maintenance and adaptation, have a means-end link to the two independent variables.

Steady State

Recall that *steady state* is essentially synonymous with *well-being*. What we are seeking to explain through social systems theory is how a community seeks a state of well-being, and as a consequence, how the community can contribute to an individual's sense of well-being. Think of it this way: suppose you were answering a community's "quality of life survey" and there were questions such as:

1. All in all, how would you rate your own sense of well-being? Would you say that it was excellent, good, not so good, or not good at all?
2. To what extent has your community contributed to your own sense of well-being?

Would you say greatly, to some extent, not much, or not at all?

Your answers would represent a perceptual approach to the measurement of your well-being and the community's contribution to this state. When all such responses are aggregated, it would provide a perceptual measure of the sense of well-being of the residents of that community.

Another measurement approach is called objective. Here researchers and planners would agree on a set of objective indicators of a community's well-being or quality of life and then gather data on these social indicators, tracking them over a period of time. A couple of examples will help illustrate our point:

1. *Unemployment rate of citizens.* Here a high unemployment rate would be treated as an indirect, negative indicator of the community's well-being. Typically, planners would track this rate monthly or yearly to help determine trends. The reasoning behind the use of such an indicator is that people who have lost their jobs or their employment status are likely to have their sense of well-being negatively impacted.

2. *School years completed.* It is assumed that the greater the number of years of school completed, the better off a person is. This also would be treated as an indirect but positive measure of the well-being of the community. The reasoning behind the indicator is that there is an assumed relationship between educational achievement and achievement in other domains of community life such as employment.

We do not want to digress too far on how community well-being might be measured. What we do want to show is that well-being can be measured at the community level and that social systems theory offers an approach for understanding how communities work and a way of thinking about how social work practice might be conducted at this level and how

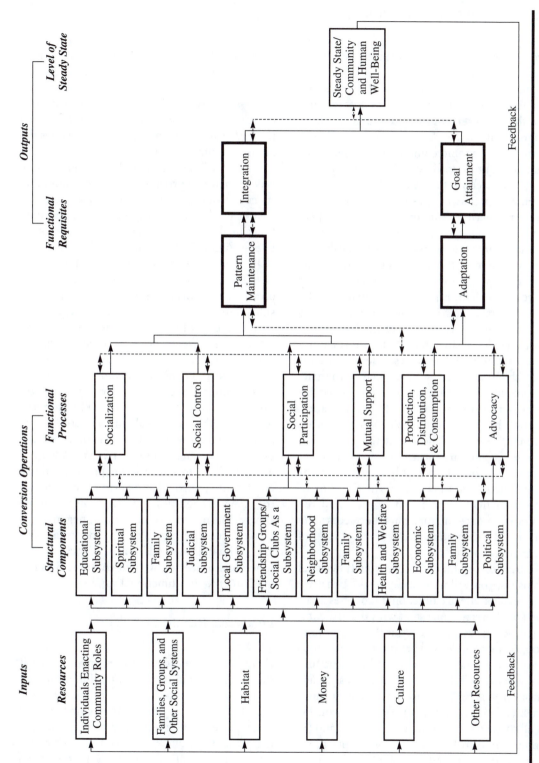

FIGURE 15.1 The Community as a Social System

407

research might be performed to measure the effects of practice.

Steady state is dynamic. While it can be measured at a point in time, it was different before the measurement was taken and it will be different afterward. A measurement is like a frame in an ongoing community movie. Now, what determines steady state? In social systems theory, we account for it in the behavior of the so-called functional requisites. These four constitute the master functions that must be performed if the system is going to achieve, maintain, or enhance its state of well-being. Steady state or well-being is equated with negative entropy or a state in which an ordering process is evident. Entropy is equated with the opposing state—a disordering process, the loss of steady state, a dying community. Figure 15.1 illustrates the means-end relationships among the four functional requisites. Each represents a variable state. The performance of the pattern-maintenance function is the primary determinant of how successfully the integration function has been performed (point of measurement). Similarly, how well the adaptation function is being performed is the primary determinant of how successfully the goal-attainment function has been performed (point of measurement). Both the integration and the goal-attainment functions must be successfully performed to maintain steady state (a state of negative entropy).

Prior to summarizing the four functional requisites, you will note in Figure 15.1 that we have retained the five functional processes identified by Warren. Consistent with the presentation of social systems theory at the levels of the group/family and formal organization, the conversion operations are comprised of structural components and (functional) processes. In addition to Warren's five locality relevant functions: (1) socialization; (2) social control; (3) social participation; (4) mutual support; and (5) production, distribution, and consumption, we have added a sixth—**advocacy.** One of the crit-

icisms of social systems theory is its assumed conservatism—it appears to describe the status quo. It does not clearly accommodate the processes of social change. We agree with this criticism, but you don't throw out the baby with the bath water. We argue that steady state is dynamic; adaptation is in our usage, the pattern variable dealing clearly with change. Needed was a functional process within the community specifically dealing with change processes. Our answer is advocacy. This, the sixth community functional process, is displayed with the other five in Figure 15.1. It refers to all of the social change processes evident in communities. The clearest structural component linked to advocacy is the political subsystem. Included in this subsystem, in addition to the major political parties, are all of the other groups and organizations that have advocacy as a recognized organizational function. It includes groups on the political far right and far left and all those in between; subprocesses include conflict, cooperation, competition, and so on. Through the process of advocacy, a realignment between system units is constantly taking place as is that between the system and its suprasystem. Advocacy will contribute to a disordering process within a community (entropy) and permit social change to occur, sometimes rapidly, typically more slowly. In this sense, entropic and negative entropic forces are always at play in a social system. With the above addition of advocacy to the functional processes, we will continue by summarizing the four functional variables.

Functional Requisites

Pattern Maintenance.   Pattern maintenance is the internal and instrumental function (see Figure 3.1). It is also the most important of the four functional requisites. It is comprised of those patterns of community behavior tied to the prevailing value system and the normative structures that build from these values. Here an example would be that all citizens acting in their community roles (reflected in the behaviors of the social units they comprise) would act as good citizens. The value is that it is right to act as a good citizen and wrong to act as a bad citizen. Built on this value would be a normative structure. An example would be that citizens should buy their goods from local businesses. Another community value might be that all citizens are valued equally, treated respectfully, and have the same rights, privileges, and responsibilities. This value would be important in accomplishing social justice. A community norm stemming from this value would be that all citizens should have the same access to jobs for which they qualify without consideration of gender, race, religion, age, or sexual preference.

As evident in Figure 15.1, four of the functional processes identified by Warren are linked to the pattern maintenance function: (1) socialization, (2) social control, (3) social participation, and (4) mutual support. Of these, socialization is the most important. Working our way back through this diagram, the educational subsystem (e.g., public schools), the spiritual subsystem (e.g., churches), and the family subsystem have a primary responsibility for this socialization process. These subsystems and their role in performing the pattern-maintenance function in a complementary way constitute the foundation on which performance of the remaining functions is built. On the input side, the individual is processed through this system and is socialized into relevant community roles. Socialization is a dynamic and lifelong process and so the community subsystems performing this function must be organized to recognize its changing and continuous nature. Also on the input side are the constraints and opportunities provided by the habitat, money, culture, and other resources. This function must be actively supported or steady state will be threatened. Certainly the other functional processes are important in contributing to the pattern-maintenance function, but should be

thought of as supportive and dependent on socialization.

As we move through this graphic, the lines and arrows suggest primary linkages. All of the parts are connected; we have used broken lines to convey the overall interdependence of the parts.

In the application of social systems theory, pattern maintenance, like the remaining functional requisites, would have to be operationalized through some scaling process. Variables change, so an index would need to be constructed that would permit a measurement of each of these variables. For example, a scale might be constructed that measures the extent to which family values contribute to the community's well-being. A series of scales would produce an index score that would be considered a measure of a component of pattern maintenance.

Religion is an important consideration in community pattern maintenance. Recall that Parsons originally referred to pattern maintenance as latency. He considered this function latent because it was not always evident in system functioning and often took a backseat to other functions.

Pattern maintenance is concerned with protection and transmission of a system's core structural patterns. Parsons maintained that these were commonly in the form of core values and beliefs. We have presented the idea that religion differs from spirituality in that it is more structured, codified, and dogmatic. A major concern of religious institutions is the transmission of core beliefs to new members.

The fit between the role of religion in the community and the functions that Parsons called pattern maintenance is like the proverbial hand in a glove. Unlike groups and organizations, communities have and nurture organizations that are manifestly religious, most often churches. The system function of churches is to support and transmit the values of the community, both material and nonmaterial. This overtly has to do with the nature of God, God's will, the nature of reality, guides for how we should conduct ourselves with respect to others (both within and outside the church), and so forth.

We have noted that material activities—such as aid to the poor, social services, medical care, and emergency assistance—are often assigned in whole or in part to religious organizations. Religious organizations may also transmit social norms and values that are distinctly material. An unhappy instance was often noted in the 1960s era of civil rights strife. As activists sought to end racial discrimination, oppression, and violence, the most segregated hour of the week was often noted to be eleven o'clock on Sunday morning. Churches had become pillars of a nonspiritual value having to do with race and racial equality. Today, churches have become a battleground for a new issue of oppression: gay rights. The evolving institution of the church will continue to transmit and enforce the pattern values of the community on matters of women's rights, gay rights, racial equality, and other issues. The positions the church accepts and communicates will evolve as the community adapts to changes within and without.

Integration.   Integration is an internal function. It is linked to the pattern-maintenance function in a means-end relationship. To state the relationship otherwise, minimum prerequisites must be met in the performance of pattern maintenance in order for the integration function to be adequately performed. An example would be, if the community's citizens who are minorities of color are not treated equally, in the workplace for instance, there will be tension among citizens based on color. This tension will affect all citizens in terms of their capacities to work together to accomplish or perform the integration function. This example assumes that the previously described community value of social justice had been institutionalized and that

a breakdown was occurring in the normative structure of the community—those in the economic subsystem were discriminating based on color.

Adaptation.   Adaptation is the external and instrumental function. The performance of this function is the means by which the goal-attainment function is pursued. Of the four variables, it is the least important in terms of its contribution to steady state. Goal attainment is critical to the survival of the system; it represents the export of products, which justifies the existence of the system. Through the export of valued products, the system secures the resources (money, goodwill) on which the receipt of all inputs is ultimately based. As long as this output/input exchange is in balance, steady state is not immediately threatened. The adaptation function can be viewed as establishing the conditions by which the goal-attainment function is enhanced. In our use of the term, adaptation is a proactive versus a passive function and includes all efforts at modifying or changing the system's suprasystem as it pursues its goal-attainment function. Here is an example:

> Spencer is a medium-sized community of about 500,000 residents. It has a diversified economic base, a well-developed highway system, a modern airport, and is located adjacent to a large waterway and interstate highway. The mayor, Ms. Jane Carter, is a competent and assertive woman who is well regarded by the governor and members of the state legislature. She has an enlightened and supportive city council. In addition, the legislators who represent the district in both the house and senate are politically competent and represent their district very well. They also hold the mayor in high regard.
>
> Mayor Carter serves on several state and national commissions dealing with economic development. She has been particularly active in supporting both state and federal legislation that would make monies available for highway and riverway construction. The mayor has a particular interest in two bills. The first is a bill in the

state legislature that would expand to four lanes two state routes that connect Spencer to the interstate system. The second bill is in Congress and would appropriate to the states monies for the expansion of waterways to accommodate barge traffic.

The community of Spencer has, as one of its goals, "the creation of more and better paying jobs through a program of economic development." In this example, Mayor Carter and those interested in working to see that these two bills are passed are participants in an advocacy process. They are seeking changes in the community's suprasystem (state and federal laws) that would create more favorable conditions for the community to realize its goal of economic development. Importantly, the passage of these bills would not in itself create economic development with "more and better paying jobs." What the change would do is create an environment that may serve as an inducement for companies to locate in Spencer. In this sense, adaptation is a means through which goal attainment is enhanced.

Think of the community as an arena of competing and conflicting interests. When these interests are focused on the performance of the goal-attainment function and pertain to changes in the community's suprasystem, they fall under what we label adaptation. The issue is not whether the changes are radical or conservative, but only whether they can be related to the facilitation of the community's goal-attainment efforts. In thinking about goal attainment, keep in mind that most communities do not have a formalized and unified goal structure. Communities, through the actions of their subsystems, tend to have many goals. Some of their goals will be in conflict, for example, economic expansion and the protection of the environment. These conflicting goals create conflicting arenas in which the process of adaptation takes place. While keeping in mind that adaptation is the least important of the four pattern variables in producing and maintaining

steady state, remember that a deficiency in the performance of any one of the four will affect all others and thus affect steady state.

Goal Attainment. Goal attainment is the external and output function. Specifically, it is through the performance of the goal-attainment function that the system is linked to its suprasystem; in this instance, it speaks to the linkage of the community with other communities and to society. As evident in Figure 15.1, it is through the performance of the production–distribution–consumption and advocacy functions that satisfaction of goal attainment is primarily pursued. The community's economic, family, and political subsystems are central in the performance of this function.

Treating goal attainment in the community as an external and output function is conceptually difficult. We must think about the community as a societal subsystem. Through the goal-attainment function, a system exports something of value to its suprasystem and by so doing establishes its interdependent relationship with the suprasystem. An example should help. If you live in a small community in Texas and go to buy a car, the chances are that the car was produced elsewhere (Detroit) and shipped to your community. In fact, many, if not most, of the material things you need have been produced (an output) by another community. Similarly, many of the products produced in your community will be shipped to other communities in this country and perhaps elsewhere in the world. In this sense, your community and you as a consumer are linked systemically to other communities in this nation and around the world. Warren labeled these linkages the community's external pattern. So far, so good. This example helps establish why goal attainment is an external pattern and output function.

We have retained Warren's use of the term *consumption* within the production-distribution framework. The individual is a consumer of all system functions and by being acted on and acting, the individual is socialized into a larger societal role. In the same sense, it is through this consumption role that the individual pursues his or her sense of well-being. Conceptually, the community is structured in a way similar to a social group. As a social system, the components are the group roles being enacted by group members. The other roles enacted by group members (within other groups) are external to the group and are typically included in the group's suprasystem. So it is with the community. The social units that comprise the community are only performing community relevant functions when they are enacting community roles, as are individuals who are enacting roles within those social units. When not enacting system roles, these individuals are always in the suprasystem. This is another example of the conceptual problem that confronted Warren and led to his "invention" of the community's internal and external patterns.

The following example should help: Linda Bailey is the manager of the community's Wal-Mart. She is also chairperson of the community's united appeal agency The united appeal agency is a key agency in performing the community's mutual support function. Wal-Mart is a key agency in the community's production–distribution– consumption function. Linda is enacting two important roles linked to the performance of the community's locality relevant functions. She is also an individual who plays many other roles, such as family member, church member, PTA member, and others.

These roles are embedded in a number of different social units performing locality relevant functions. Most important, Linda is an individual, and she exists as an independent personality apart from these roles. Like a social group, the community provides the opportunity to engage in a number of different roles and in a manner that offers an integrating experience. Through these roles, Linda is socialized into her societal role and pursues her own sense of selfhood.

Like Linda Bailey, all citizens are both signal inputs and task outputs of the community. In this sense, she is in the community's suprasystem and a consumer of the products and services produced by the system.

In this section, our focus was the relationship of community functions to the requisite variables. A logical question might be: What is the relationship between the requisite variables and the eight structural features of the community? The answer has to do with the relationship between structure and function. Let us start with our definition of a community as an inclusive form of social organization that is territorially based and through which most people satisfy their common needs and desires, deal with their common problems, seek means to advance their well-being, and relate to their society. In many ways, a community can be thought of as self-organizing in the same way as the social group. People have needs and face common problems. At a community level, collective actions are necessary to meet these needs and to deal with these problems. The four functional requisites describe the kinds of issues or problems that must be addressed for these collective actions to work. In short, through the performance of these four functions, social structures arise that regularize behaviors and through which these functions are conducted. An analogy would be water rushing down a hill. Soon channels are formed that move the water down more efficiently. The channels change and they deepen—they supply an order, so it is in the relationship between function and structure. Function determines structure but soon structure contains and determines function; they become interdependent if order is to be maintained and advanced.

Structural Components

With this as background, we will move to a presentation of the eight structural components that comprise all social systems. These features

SUPRASYSTEM

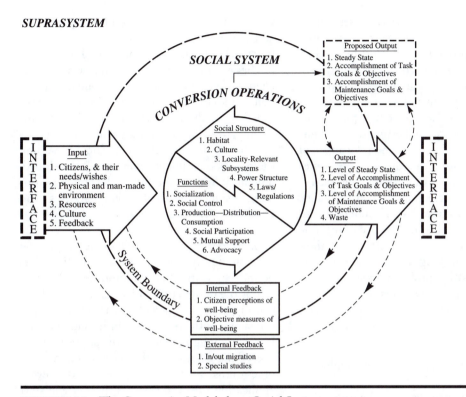

FIGURE 15.2   The Community Modeled as a Social System

are labeled (1) boundary, (2) suprasystem, (3) interface, (4) input, (5) proposed output, (6) conversion operations, (7) output, and (8) feedback. In Figure 15.2, these features are graphically displayed to show their relationships to one another.

In the paragraphs to follow, we will summarize each of the eight structural features found in social systems. From our position, if one or more of these structural features are missing in an analysis of a social organization, it is not a social system; the components are not sufficiently interdependent to seek and maintain steady state.

Boundary.   The concept of boundary is used to distinguish the border that separates the system from its suprasystem. Similarly, each of the eight structural features will have an associated

behavior; in this instance, it is boundary maintenance. Every social system will possess a boundary and will exert energies in performing the boundary-maintenance function.

Earlier we mentioned the special problem that has hindered the development of community theory—defining its border. Community theory development is not sufficiently developed to provide a clear guide for the designation of community boundaries. Our approach has focused on its application to practice. Until we establish better theoretical foundations, we have to be guided by the practical and professional judgments necessary to get the job done. For instance, many community initiatives require that a community needs assessment be performed to establish the existence of a community problem and to justify requests for monies to deal with the problem. The request may be for improved health services, services to the elderly, education services, or any number of other such programs. The problem confronting the practitioner is the determination of the actual community boundaries—what is to be placed in the system and what goes into the suprasystem. Needs assessment typically involves counts of people and estimates of conditions existing among specified groups of people.[16] Frequently the question becomes which existing boundary lines should be used—county lines, municipal lines, census tracts, united fund collection areas, mental health catchment areas, and so on. In any event, one cannot start counting people, measuring their needs, or inventorying resources until the boundary designation problem is solved.

Given these considerations, the following guides are applicable in designating a community boundary when employing social systems theory:

1. The boundary will always be geographically drawn.
2. The boundary will always be determined by the practice application involved.
3. The system will always include (but not necessarily be limited to) a politically drawn boundary, a municipality, a county, a township, or groupings of these. The test here is the presence of some political representation of the people residing in the area.
4. The boundary will include those groupings of populations for which data are routinely gathered and reported. Important here is the availability of census data, for example, the ability to group census tracts together in order to describe the residents of the community.
5. Finally, the boundary includes those social units that currently perform, or have the potential for performing, the six locality relevant functions.

To some, our approach to the designation of a community's boundary will appear cavalier.

Our own experiences in community practice and the application of social systems theory to practice has led us to this position. For us, both in theory and practice, you start where your client is. We would like to make one final point before moving on. Sometimes in this form of practice you do not start with an existing community. Instead, you start with the needs of people sharing the same habitat and by helping them work together, a community is developed. The notion of community or locality development is sometimes used to designate this form of community practice.[17]

Suprasystem.   The first step in the designation of a community is always the specification of its boundary. With this accomplished, the next step is the designation of its suprasystem. Universally, every system will have input and output exchanges with social units in its suprasystem. It is not enough to say that the suprasystem is everything external to the system. There is no practical use to such a designation. As in every application of social systems theory, you start with what you are seeking to accomplish. This decision becomes the filter for the designation of the suprasystem. Here Warren's proposition that the external pattern is becoming increasingly dominant in the behaviors of communities is helpful. We agree. The practice relevance of this observation is in identifying those external systems that are most influential in the performance of the locality-relevant functions of your subject community. You will have made an important step in determining those units when you have specified your community's boundary (see item 2 in the preceding list).

As an example, the municipality of Franklin has been designated as a community for purposes of securing grant funding to deal with the problem of substance abuse. Given the pervasiveness of the problem, all of the community's locality-relevant functions are deemed to be involved. The purpose of this grant-supported effort is the improvement of community well-being through a reduction in the incidence and prevalence of substance abuse. Clearly those funding sources external to the community would be included in the suprasystem. Assuming the strategy included both supply and demand reduction, the supply sources of the drugs would be included in the suprasystem as would those external units that promote demand, for example, media advertising. In this example, all five of the guidelines for establishing community boundaries are satisfied. The system's boundary and the municipal boundary are identical.

In conceptualizing the notion of suprasystem, it is useful to consider the community as a societal subsystem with multiple ties to society. Further, the community and society can be viewed as possessing many structural similarities (the internal pattern). The vertical ties between the community and its society can then be assumed to follow similar structural lines. For example, the economic system of the community tends to have its primary ties to the society's economic system. Some of the horizontal structures that serve to coordinate and integrate the activities of the community's economic system have their counterpart at the societal level (for instance, the local chamber of commerce and the National Chamber of Commerce and the local united fund and community welfare council and United Funds and Councils of America).

The final point to be made is that, unlike the other structural features, the concept of suprasystem refers to social units external to the subject system. These units will also tend to meet the definition of a social system. In reverse, the subject system itself will constitute a part of other systems' suprasystems.

Interface.   This concept labels the structural features that couple two social systems. It is the name given to a shared boundary that each maintains. Each system is dependent on the other and the two systems will relate to each

other in specific ways. These ways, or behaviors, will always be designed to advance their own well-being. The maintenance of these ways is labeled interface. The concept of interface helps describe features of this interdependence and the orderliness that results. The concept also helps explain how ever larger systems are created. At the highest level, it is the coupling of communities and other systems that comprises a society.

In introducing this chapter, we made the point that next to a society, the community is the most inclusive (self-sufficient) of all social systems. Conceptually, this means that the community will typically have more ties to its suprasystem than the group, family, or formal organization has to its respective suprasystem. The number of such ties is a rough measure of the complexity of the community. The number and complexity of these ties represent the most distinguishing feature of interface when applied to the community. The large numbers of these coupling arrangements and the disproportionate power wielded over the system by these external units operate as conservative forces on the system itself. The implication to the practitioner is the importance of being able to identify and systematically work with representatives of these external units in any community change effort. Not to do so is to miss the point of how influential these external units are to their community counterparts.

We restrict the use of the term *interface* to those arrangements that couple the system to external systems. In other words, we do not employ the term in describing the counterpart of this coupling arrangement internally. For us, the dynamics of the two are quite different. As displayed in Figure 15.2, the interface designation occurs on the input and on the output locations of the system. This is intended to illustrate the fact that the exchanges occur between the system and its suprasystem at these two locations. It is here that the boundary-maintenance function is concentrated.

Finally, interface is a specialized feature of a social relationship. The relationship may have either Gemeinschaft or Gesellschaft qualities. Earlier, the community of Franklin was used as an example to illustrate the concept of suprasystem. The community was seeking grant funding to help deal with the problem of substance abuse. The external funding agency would represent a key unit in its suprasystem. The funding contract and shared agreements it contains is an example of the interface between the two. The contract creates a Gesellschaft relationship between the two units. The mutual attention paid to the contract agreement by both systems would evidence their respective boundary-maintaining behaviors or interface.

An earlier example involving Mayor Carter and her personal relationship with the state's governor and members of the state legislature serves as an example of an interface that is essentially Gemeinschaft. In this example, the office of the mayor of Spencer is linked informally with the governor's office. In this case, the state government would be a key feature of the community's suprasystem.

Input.   All social systems come into being and survive through input/output exchanges with units or resources existing in their suprasystems. The input concept in social systems theory refers to all of the resources that exist in the suprasystem and are accepted by the system during a cycle of activity. In most applications of the theory, the time period of the cycle of activity corresponds to a budget or grant cycle, for example, January 1, 20__ through December 31, 20__. The start of the cycle always creates a baseline (statement of initial conditions); the end of the cycle provides the data to be compared with the baseline.

The categories of inputs are displayed in Figure 15.2. The feature that distinguishes the theory's application to the community is inclusion of the habitat. The habitat is treated as a contextual feature in applications of the theory

to the group, family, and formal organizations. This is not the case at the community level; the community by definition is tied to a specific habitat and the habitat will affect social behavior. It is at the community level of social systems theory that we are particularly indebted to those who have contributed to the development of ecological theory.

As mentioned earlier, the community has many similarities to the social group. In fact, some theorists have approached the study of the community as a group.[18] In a community, as in a social group, the individual is considered both a signal and a maintenance input. Social systems theory views communities as having effects on the people who comprise them. These effects can be either positive or negative. The processes causing these effects take place in what we designate as conversion operations; so, the concept of signal inputs is applied to the condition of people before they are affected by community processes during a cycle of activity. The behavior of social systems is always evident in cycles of activity. We incorporate this aspect of functioning in the way inputs are categorized. For example, the category "citizens" refers to all people residing in the community at the start of a cycle as well as those new people who move in or are born into the community during the cycle.

In our example of the community of Franklin, all citizens would be considered inputs at the start of the grant period; they would be considered at risk of being affected by the community's substance abuse problem. These citizens could be described demographically using census or similar data. Other baseline studies might be undertaken to describe this population and the problem of substance abuse at the start of a community intervention. These studies might include estimates of the abuse of drugs and alcohol by age, gender, race, and so on.

Maintenance inputs include relevant aspects of culture, money, material resources, information (particularly those pertaining to feedback), and so on. Every social organization incorporates aspects of culture, for example, values derived from the society of which it is a part. In the present application, the community is viewed as having a major responsibility for transmitting culture via its socialization function. This responsibility is seen most clearly in the operation of its educational system. By law, all of the community's children of a given age must attend school. It is through schooling that specific knowledge, skills, values, and other features of culture are transmitted to the community's youth. For the most part, these aspects of culture are not generated in the community; they are imported from the larger society and adopted in the community. It is important to view this process as dynamic, with changes constantly occurring in the larger society and fed into and acted on by the community. A cultural form of input related to the example involving the community of Franklin would be the values and norms associated with the use of drugs and alcohol. Is drinking morally wrong? Is the social use of cocaine considered OK? Grant monies received from outside the community to deal with its drug problem would be considered a maintenance input as would external consultation.

In an application of the theory, it is important to understand that a system is able to maintain steady state by importing resources from the suprasystem—thus the notion behind input. While communities are relatively self-sufficient when compared to most other forms of social organization (for example, they raise taxes to support some of their functions), they are modeled as open systems relying on substantial inputs from the suprasystem.

Proposed Output. Social systems theory is organized around purpose or, as used here, proposed output. Given our definition of community, the task becomes one of operationalizing community well-being. The inclusiveness of this system then represents the distinctive feature of proposed output. Consistent with its use

at other levels, the term *proposed output* will include both task and maintenance forms of proposed output.

Most communities do not have explicitly stated goals. Rather, their goals can be viewed as implicit in the definition of community. That is, a community's goal structure must pertain to the satisfaction of common human needs, the resolution of commonly held (community) problems, the advancement of the well-being of its citizens, and the socialization of citizens into their societal roles.

Perhaps the most relevant work on the problem of community goals or output has been done at the national level, particularly that body of work associated with the social indicator movement.[19] Here the effort was aimed at the construction and measurement of societal goals. During the 1960s, not only was there considerable scientific interest in societal goals but political interest as well. President Lyndon B. Johnson pledged his administration to the goal of building the Great Society. The question becomes What are the goals of a Great Society and what are the indicators that can be used to track progress in achieving those goals? We have taken the position that the community operates as a subsystem of society and may be considered a microcosm of society. Therefore, much of the work in the construction of social goals and indicators at the societal level has application at the community level as well. The above societal question can be rephrased: What are the goals of a Great Community and what are the indicators that can be used to track progress in achieving those goals?

The 1960s and 1970s was also a period when those in the field of human services gave considerable attention to the purposes of community services, their definition, their classification, their interrelationships, and their effectiveness. One such effort was the development of a taxonomy of social goals and human service programs called United Way of America Services Identification System (UWASIS).[20]

UWASIS was formulated in systems terms and sought to link collective human helping efforts to societal goals.

> UWASIS is a system for identifying, classifying and defining individual organized human endeavors in relation to major goals of society. It can be said that all organized human endeavors—characterized here as human service programs—can be traced to one ultimate purpose or goal overriding all others, and that is, to enable individuals to live a well-adjusted and satisfying existence and to enable them to realize their full potential.[21]

In keeping with that purpose, eight societal goals were established to which various programs pertain.

1. Optimal income security and economic opportunity
2. Optimal health
3. Optimal provision of basic material needs
4. Optimal opportunity for the acquisition of knowledge and skills
5. Optimal environmental quality
6. Optimal individual and collective safety
7. Optimal social functioning
8. Optimal assurance of the support and effectiveness of services through organized action

While these goals were formulated and treated as societal goals, the UWASIS authors created a framework that was designed for use by U.S. communities. As stated earlier, the intent was to develop a taxonomy of social goals to which human service programs could be related and evaluated. In effect then, these goals were treated as both societal and community goals.

The logic used in this chapter for operationalizing proposed output builds on the work associated with the social indicator movement and UWASIS, among others. The logic is also implicit in our definition of community—a territorially based social organization through which most people satisfy their common needs and desires, deal with their common problems, seek means to advance well-being, and relate to

their society. Based on this definition, output should pertain to the satisfaction of needs and desires, the level of progress made in dealing with common problems, and efforts made in seeking means to advance well-being.

With this background in mind, we have created the following community goal structure for use in social systems theory. As in other applications, a hierarchy of outcomes format is used.

Purpose

To improve the well-being of community members through the development and provision of facilities and services that contribute to the satisfaction of their needs and desires, and that help them cope with their common problems in ways that advance themselves, the community, and society.

Goals

1. *Work/employment.* To encourage the development of an economic system that will produce equal opportunities for all citizens to obtain healthy, safe, and satisfying remunerative work.
2. *Health.* To create and sustain those physical, social, and environmental arrangements that maximize the physical and mental health of all residents.
3. *Nutrition.* To assure that sufficient quantities and types of food, as well as required nutrients, are available and usable so that suitable nutritional standards are maintained for all residents.
4. *Safety and security.* To create the social conditions and the associated systems that satisfy the safety and security needs of community residents.
5. *Social welfare.* To provide a comprehensive and quality system of social welfare services that contributes to the strengthening of human resources and assures that the basic needs of all residents are satisfied.
6. *Education.* To provide a comprehensive range of educational programs and facilities

that assures that all people have access to educational opportunities consistent with their needs and potentials.

7. *Housing.*   Consistent with individual preferences and means, to encourage the provision of housing for all people that is aesthetically pleasing and meets standards of privacy, health, and safety.

8. *Social participation.*   To encourage the provision of programs and facilities that will offer all people opportunities for need satisfaction related to their psychological, social, and cultural development.

9. *Citizenship.*   To encourage the participation of all people in activities that promote a sense of community and societal citizenship.

Consistent with the definition of community, the goal structure is inclusive, thereby taking into consideration those functions required for the satisfaction of common needs and for the resolution of commonly held problems. While not shown, under each goal there would be a series of objectives and activities (see Figure 13.2). We make the assumption that, while communities share common goals, important differences would occur among communities in terms of how objectives would be formulated to achieve common goals and how goals and objectives would be prioritized. In using the model and consistent with community needs, the practitioner would develop the third level of the outcome hierarchy (statement of objectives). For example, under the work/employment goal there would be a series of objectives that would operationalize such concepts as "equal opportunity" and "healthy, safe, and satisfying." An objective aimed at operationalizing "equal" might read as follows: "By June 30, 20__, there will be a 25 percent increase in the number of employers who certify that all of their employees are paid in accordance with the principle of 'equal pay for equal work.'" Another example that would apply in our earlier use of the community of Franklin in their effort to deal with substance abuse might read: "To reduce by 20 percent during the next fiscal year the number of youth who are injured or killed in alcohol-related automobile accidents." This objective would fit under the community goal dealing with health (goal 2).

The substance abuse objective would be labeled a proposed task output—it is the individual that experiences the effect (fewer youth are drinking, driving, and having accidents). A proposed maintenance output might read: "In the next fiscal year, there will be a 15 percent increase in the number of agencies rendering substance abuse services who have resource-sharing contracts with one another." Maintenance outcomes are always directed toward strengthening the system. This objective would suggest more resource-related partnering efforts among agencies—a strengthening of the community's horizontal pattern.

The use of the Franklin community as an example has another value that needs emphasis. Most communities do not undertake comprehensive planning efforts. Rather they seek to deal with specific community problems like substance abuse, child abuse and neglect, poor housing, and so on. Even with these more narrowly conceived planning efforts, a comprehensive viewpoint is necessary and social systems theory can be helpful. Keep in mind that in a community, as in every other system, all the parts are connected. A change in one part of the community will affect other parts of the community as well.

A final form of output utilized in the theory is waste. Conceptually, the attempt is to account for all resources expended in converting inputs to outputs. Waste is the measure of the inefficient or inappropriate use of resources. This measure becomes incorporated as feedback and is channeled back into the system as a maintenance input—information that should result in improved (less wasteful) outputs in a subsequent cycle of the system. To cite an earlier community example, waste would include the loss of work because of the problem of alcohol and drug use. Not only is there a loss of income by the worker, but there is a loss of production by the community as well. These drug-related costs are significant for most communities.

Conversion Operations.   Conversion operations is the concept used to label the means by which social systems transform inputs to outputs. The two subconcepts used to describe how this transformation process takes place we call (social) structures and (social) functions. Structure refers to the recurring patterns in social life that provide stability and predictability to human interactions. The distinctive features of conversion operations at the community level are tied to the influences of the habitat on social behaviors and the size, diversity, and complexity of the social structures that share this common habitat.

The sociological concept of institution is helpful in thinking about a community's conversion operations. Let us take a moment to review this concept. In short, *institution* refers to regular and continuous patterns of behaviors evident in specific social systems. These behaviors are socially sanctioned and are integrated into a larger system of societal norms. The notions of institution and role are similar, but *institution* refers to a pattern having application at a higher level, such as a community or a society. For example, a specific school can be thought of as an institution to the extent that there is regularity in the way all of the roles applicable to schools in general are evidenced, for example, roles of students, teachers, administrators, parents, and so on. Another way of saying the same thing is to refer to education as an institution. A school can then be thought of as a specific organization through which the institution of education is evidenced in the behaviors of system members. Marriage is typically referred to as an institution. This means that there is regularity in the way the roles of husband and wife are enacted.

Institutionalization refers to the process by which social behaviors become patterned and regularized within a social system, such as a community. To institutionalize behaviors is to regularize those patterns that are functional to a system. In social systems theory, we recognize that some institutionalized behaviors are hurtful to citizens and can become dehumanizing. From a practice perspective, institutionalized behaviors should contribute to a state of well-being.

When institutionalized behaviors are hurtful and dehumanizing, a significant social problem exists. For example, racism can be institutionalized at the community level and be evident in the behavior of community institutions, for example, education, judicial, economic, and so on. Institutionalized behaviors that dehumanize a category of citizen, such as minorities of color, women, children, the elderly, the disabled, the mentally ill, homosexuals, and so on, will negatively affect the steady state of a community.

Societal institutions and their community counterparts are constantly changing—as is everything. Institutional practices that at one time were functional, at a different time can become dysfunctional, that is, dehumanizing. An example would be the institutionalization of the mentally ill, the practice of placing those who are mentally ill in specialized "mental hospitals." Starting in the 1960s, this practice was deemed to be dehumanizing for many. This started what is commonly referred to as the deinstitutionalization movement in mental health care, an institutional change process aimed at altering how communities care for their citizens who have severe mental health problems. This movement resulted in the development of community-based, less intensive, and alternative forms of care related to the clients' clinical needs. Here we have evidence of the advocacy function at the community level.

With this as an introduction, the remaining components of a system's conversion operations will be discussed as they relate to structure and functions. In Figure 15.2, we categorize the features affecting the social structure of the system. The community is the one system level in which we include the habitat. The habitat refers to the natural as well as the man-made environment. We will not be examining the habitat as such, but the influence of the habitat on social structure. In so doing, we are not accepting the assumption that the habitat is the primary determinant of social structure, only that at the community level, the habitat has a significant influence in shaping social structures. As an example, New York City is a huge community and the behavior of New Yorkers is in part shaped by its island location, the density of its population, its skyscrapers, its location by the sea, its forms of transportation, and so on. Every community is unusual or unique in some way. Our point is that the community is tied to its habitat and every community can be distinguished in part by its habitat—change key features of the habitat and the behavioral patterns of those who reside in the community will be changed. An example of such a change was the development of the River Walk in San Antonio. Not only has this changed the downtown area of the community, the River Walk has become a major tourist attraction. For many, these and related changes have made San Antonio a very liveable community.

Every community will have its own culture (a set of shared meanings serving as a foundation for an organized way of life); it follows that no two communities are identical. Certainly every U.S. community will have a distinguishable U.S. culture; it will also have a subculture that distinguishes it from other communities. New York will produce a New Yorker, somebody different from a Bostonian. Given the mobility of today's population, not everyone in a community will be significantly affected by the local culture. Nevertheless, treating culture as a feature of a community's social structure is useful in thinking about how the web of community groups and organizations is held together and how change takes place. These social units and the people who comprise them share a common culture that links them. As the culture changes so do the relationships among these so-

cial units. The sources of cultural change are largely external to the community and are related to larger societal changes such as urbanization, new developments in technology, and changes in the natural environment. But there are local effects on culture as well. Some of these changes are related to local social change efforts. In this sense, community organization can be thought of as an effort to effect changes in the community culture, that is, the way community members think about things and about each other.

In our example of the Franklin community, the change effort will target how people think about the use of alcohol and illegal drugs. Is it acceptable (a value and component of local culture) to smoke marijuana or use cocaine? Laws and regulations are codified features of culture and are thus a special form of social structure. Once a level of consensus is reached (something is politically "doable"), changes in law may be made that affect the use of alcohol or illicit drugs. An example would be changing the legal drinking age.

In Figure 15.1, the structural components of a community were graphically presented. These components correspond to what we are referring to here as locality relevant subsystems. Our intent has been to categorize all the social units to be found in a U.S. community. These subsystems perform the six locality relevant functions, and the relationships among the organizations and groups within each subsystem and between the subsystems comprise the internal pattern referred to earlier. A major focus of community practice is the strengthening of these patterns and the coordination of work in pursuit of community goals. This effort is the essence of what is meant by community organization in social work practice.

The six locality relevant functions were summarized earlier. These functions are conducted through the subsystems and in accord with social systems theory, which addresses how community well-being is pursued. What we have sought to do is to take a very complex set of relationships and reduce them to a few basic patterns common to all communities. How does it inform practice? Here we will build on our hypothetical community of Franklin.

Prior to submitting the grant to the Center for Substance Abuse Prevention (CSAP—a federal agency charged with the prevention of substance abuse), a number of concerned citizens conducted a need assessment. The assessment was supported by the Franklin Community Foundation, a private foundation focusing on community betterment. The need assessment indicated that a significant drug and alcohol abuse problem existed within the community. A comparison with national data suggested that the problem was more severe in Franklin than in most communities of similar size in the country (society). Responding to a CSAP **request for proposals (RFP),** the Franklin Community Foundation received a two-million-dollar, five-year grant to deal with this problem. The grant application specified the targeted community, data describing the community's problem, the results expected, and the means to be used to conduct the project and to achieve the intended results.

We will now stop and summarize how the theory has helped conceptualize this project. The boundary of the system coincides with the political boundaries of Franklin. Census data and a variety of need assessment data afforded a demographic description of the population, the incidence and prevalence of the substance abuse problem, and the resources needed to deal with the problem (inputs). These data established the baseline conditions for the planned community change effort. The funding agency, CSAP, became a critical part of Franklin's suprasystem as were a number of state agencies that provide funding for local organizations that either deal with or are affected by the substance abuse problem.

The specific contractual or relationship ties between agencies located within Franklin and these external agencies comprise important parts of the interface. These ties will affect the cooperative behaviors that take place during this project.

The Franklin Community Foundation established a nonprofit community agency to conduct the project—"Drugs Don't Work." Conceptually, the governing body (board of directors) of their new agency was formed to represent a microcosm of the locality-relevant subsystems of Franklin and its power structure (conversion operations). The board operates through a series of task forces that approximates the community subsystems, for example, education, judicial, and political (structure). What was being replicated was the internal pattern of Franklin that was relevant to its drug and alcohol problems. This project was designed to strengthen these internal patterns. A special task force was established comprised of representatives of the community's thirty-seven agencies that offered specific alcohol and drug abuse services. The intent was to strengthen the ties among these agencies, which would result in a strengthening of a key aspect of the community's internal pattern as it pertained to dealing with the community's drug and alcohol problems.

The logic of this comprehensive approach to the drug and alcohol problem in Franklin was based on an assumption that the problem permeated all community subsystems and that only a comprehensive approach would work. Based on this approach, the overall purpose was to improve community well-being (proposed output) by reducing the drug and alcohol problem.

Having presented this example of how theory can inform practice, we will move to a discussion of the final two system features, output and feedback.

Output. In systems theory, output is input following a processing cycle. Two forms of inputs and outputs are recognized, maintenance and task. The maintenance output is the status of the community itself, the task output would be the status of those people who reside in the community. Here our attention is to the whole person not to a specific role. The general question to be addressed is always whether the targeted members of the community are better, the same, or worse following a cycle of community action.

Given that some communities have citizens that number in the millions, answering the above questions may seem impossible and certainly far removed from the usual practice of social work. Not so. We routinely measure the well-being of our country using a variety of output measures. For example, the gross national product (GNP) is typically used as an indirect measure of our well-being as a nation (society). If it is increasing, that is usually considered good (more people are working and more goods are available for consumption). If it is declining, that is usually considered bad (people are losing their jobs and less money is available to buy things). There are many other such measures—new housing starts, new families being formed, birth and death rates, and so on.

Some of these measures not only can provide an indirect measure of the status of our nation's well-being compared to a previous benchmark, but also they can make predictions about the future. Most people have heard the term *Leading Economic Indicators (LEI)*. This is an index of selected economic indicators used to predict the economy six or so months in advance. It is a very helpful planning tool for those in business and in government. In short, nations, like communities, can be viewed as social systems. There is considerable stability to these patterns and the patterns have cyclical features that can suggest future movements. We do not want to push the analogy of a community and a nation too far, but they both can be viewed as social systems and some of the technology used in measuring the behavior of nations has application to their component communities as well.

In most instances, social work practice at the community level is focused on specific population groups rather than the total community. These "special population" groups may include the poor, the elderly, the mentally ill, abused children, and so on. The approaches to community practice are essentially the same whether for the entire community, a special population group, or for your own caseload—generalist practice is generalist practice.

A community's output is always measured against a baseline that specified the conditions that existed at the start of the cycle. The specific reference point is what we label proposed output, the proposed future state of the community following a cycle of activity. Two examples will be used from our community of Franklin. Keep in mind that in systems theory there is always a hierarchy of outcomes. We will only be using two specific ones. One objective was, "To reduce by 20 percent during the next fiscal year the number of youth who are injured or killed in alcohol-related automobile accidents." There would be a specific plan as to how to accomplish this objective. Output would represent the actual number of youth who were injured or killed in alcohol-related automobile accidents during the fiscal year. This would be labeled a task output. In research terms, tracking this output would be called outcome evaluation. The monitoring of the intervention plan being used to accomplish this output would be labeled process evaluation and would address the question, To what extent were the agreed-on procedures followed to lead to this output?

A maintenance output always deals with the status of the system following a processing cycle. A proposed maintenance output of the Franklin community's effort read as follows: "In the next fiscal year, there will be a 15 percent increase in the number of agencies rendering substance abuse services who have resource-sharing contracts with one another." Recall in the example that a task force comprised of community agencies providing drug- and alcohol-related services was formed. The intent was to strengthen the relationships among these agencies and to seek their cooperation with the rest of the community in dealing with this problem. The proposed maintenance output was accepted as an indirect measure of increased and focused cooperation among these agencies. Output would be represented by the actual increase in resource-sharing contracts among these agencies at the end of the fiscal year. In research terms, this measurement would be labeled outcome evaluation and along with other such measures would be a way of establishing the well-being of the system following a cycle of conversion operations. Similarly, the monitoring of the agreed-on tasks related to this outcome would be labeled process evaluation. Remember that the board of directors operated through a series of task forces and that these task forces were organized to represent a microcosm of the community's locality relevant subsystems. The reasoning behind this structuring was to replicate the community and by the work of this board, strengthen the community's real horizontal pattern.

Feedback. Feedback represents the information generated by the system and its suprasystem that results from comparing proposed and actual output. This information is then returned to the system as a maintenance input. Conceptually, it is through feedback that a system maintains steady state. The process is continuous and occurs both formally and informally as well as both externally and internally.

The symbiotic process characterizes the basic adaptive processes of communities. While these processes are not under any form of centralized control, the efforts of these adaptive processes can be charted and measured. This monitoring is feedback and is the basis of a great deal of community attention and planned adaptive responses to those unplanned changes. The feedback on the symbiotic adjustments occurring at the community level distinguishes this concept in systems theory.

There is constant movement in and out of communities (in- and out-migration). No one is in charge of this movement. It is simply a response to the personal decisions made by individuals and families. No one is in charge of the aging of the population, the spread of diseases, the amount and direction of the wind, the amount of rain that falls, the growth of weeds, the amount of drugs used, the amount and type of sexual activity that takes place, the number of new businesses formed, the level of unemployment, how many children drop out of school or choose to become social workers and go on to graduate schools. Again, no one is in charge.

Increasingly, various citizen groups are systematically monitoring what is happening to their communities believing that by understanding these changes they are better prepared to take collective action to control their future. In this sense, much community planning in the past can be thought of as a response to the primary determinants of change associated with symbiotic processes identified in ecological theory.

In the 1990s, there was evidence of a more proactive approach to community planning. For a number of years, the National Civic League sponsored competition for communities to be named an "All American City." This serves as a proactive example of how communities are seeking to become better places to live through comprehensive planning. In all such instances, the notion of feedback is critical because it seeks to answer the question, How can we make our community a better place to live?

RURAL COMMUNITIES AS ADAPTING SYSTEMS

In order to understand the system aspects of communities, we would like to consider the dynamics of rural communities. Rural communities in the United States have been the focus of concern for nearly half a century. Much of this concern has arisen from the tension between rural communities and the suprasystem, mainly the changing economic and technical environment that affects community activity. In the past half century, there has been a critical decline in the population of rural communities and in the general well-being of these communities. In order to understand this process, it is helpful to identify different types of rural communities.

The definition of *rural* varies widely. One way to define this is by saying any area is rural that has fewer than 1,000 people per square mile. Another definition is used by some government agencies, and it simply defines rural as any region that is outside a metropolitan area. Metropolitan areas are called Standard Metropolitan Statistical Areas (SMSAs), which are defined as population clusters in excess of 50,000 people. This ignores political boundaries like city and county divisions, and focuses on the proximity of the population. By this definition, about 20 percent of the United States population is rural. The rural 20 percent of the population occupies more than 80 percent of the physical territory of the United States.[22]

The classification of rural community types is based mainly on the economic dimension of the community. Most rural communities are more closed than their urban counterparts. In addition, rural communities tend to have more cohesive internal structure and less variation in operational style and in conversion processes. This uniformity in composition and process is one factor in the crisis confronting rural communities in the United States and elsewhere. Overall, rural communities lack the robustness of urban and suburban communities. There are other ways of classifying such systems, but this is the most common and, in general, the most valuable for assessing community viability.

Agrarian Communities. These communities are engaged in farming and ranching as the economic activity. This is the type of community most often thought of as "the country." Agrarian economies have a long history. They are rural due to the large areas of open land needed for farming and ranching. Such communities have the ability to establish a steady state, balancing raw materials, effort, and products over time. They do not deplete raw materials, and they produce an output that fulfills a universal human need. The social systems that accompany agrarian communities are family based and have generally produced regions of shared values and stable governance structures.

Destabilizing factors for agrarian communities include changing labor costs, agrarian technology changes that allow large-scale farming, the rise of global markets and competition from foreign farm and ranch products, and the rise of corporate agricultural systems that can use technology to farm larger areas more efficiently. A word here on vocabulary: In recent years, it has become fashionable to talk about agrarian communities as engaged in "agribusiness." In the past, such communities were called "agricultural." The change in language is telling.

What is being lost in small towns is not the business of farming; it is the culture of small towns and family-owned farms. The social stability, prosperity, and robustness of the system has compensated for the inefficiency of small-scale farming in an age of high-tech agrarian tools. The shift of agrarian production from small farms to corporate farming giants will change the nature of the farming and ranching business, and diminish the culture of agrarian America. In the end, the control of farm commodities by corporate giants will likely affect the nature and pricing of commodities as well. A single example: In the current political debate about illegal foreign workers, the illegal farm workers entering this country are largely in the employ of large agribusiness concerns, not family farmers. It is but one instance of the kind of cultural shift that we can anticipate as the erosion of rural community culture accelerates.

Extraction Communities. These are mining communities that rely on production of nonrenewable resources such as minerals (coal, gold, iron, oil, and so forth). Such communities are vulnerable to the boom and bust cycle. Alaska, for example, has had boom periods for gold and oil, alternating with bust periods characterized by poverty and entropy. Ghost towns are most often associated with extraction activities. Related to extraction are communities that rely on access to transportation arteries for income. Towns that grew up along the railroad right of way flourished until railroads were replaced by highways and air travel. Cattle towns flourished only so long as they were the rail head (the end of the line) and the terminus of the cattle drives. They were quickly rendered entropic as the railroads fanned out to serve the ranching regions of Texas and Oklahoma.

Extraction-based communities are in an inherently unstable relationship with their environment, since they deplete the supply of materials on which they rely for existence. In addition, many extraction-based communities (oil and mining, for example) are temporary, and thus are prone to serious degradation of the ecosystems in the areas where they exist. Third world countries are frequently exploited by extraction industries that create temporary communities, and then are left to cope with the environmental degradation after the extraction industries have moved on. As a consequence, many communities and countries seek to find sustainable economic foundations to continue the community after the inevitable depletion of the raw materials.

Exurbs. This is the term given to outer suburban areas. These communities appear rural because of the open spaces around them. They are not truly rural since the residents rely on urban centers for economic survival. Exurbs require highly developed transportation systems due to the travel needed from quasi-rural to urban areas. People living in these communities are often affluent, since the cost and time required for travel demand resources. The faux-rural nature of the exurbs is often an affectation,

which is inspired by the traditional notion of the landed wealthy whose capacious homes were symbols of their prosperity.

Exurban communities are vulnerable to the economics that affect the sustaining industry. For example, the crisis in the U.S. auto industry damaged many exurbs that had grown up around auto-producing centers such as Flint, Michigan. An economic downturn in the Silicon Valley would have a predictable effect on the exurbs around the San Francisco Bay area. In addition to the sustaining industry, exurbs are also vulnerable to the availability of efficient transportation. For instance, if an oil crisis caused the cost of commuting to quintuple, the attraction of exurbs might suffer. Another factor might be congestion, which would increase the travel time to the point that commuter existence would lose its appeal.

Area Trade Centers. These communities are the result of the depopulation of the rural areas. As the rural population declines, some small towns die, and the people in the region range further afield to find shopping, education, churches, and so forth. Over time, a county that once contained a dozen viable small towns may have only one or two. Services become concentrated in these cities, necessitating greater travel for the population. In addition, this process results in destabilization of the social structure and a loss of community identity. Many consolidated schools and churches have felt the sting of consolidation as a loss of history and social identity.

An interesting aspect of the area trade center phenomenon has been the rise of the so-called "Big Box" retail stores. As rural towns consolidated, some retailers began to develop retail stores modeled on the "five and dime stores" of the early twentieth century. These stores tended to locate in a central town in a dwindling rural area. The towns selected by the growing chain stores were given a stay of execution. The cost was that many of the traditional locally owned businesses could not compete with the chain retail monsters, so former store owners became employees, changing the nature of the small-town structure as well as its economics. This phenomenon has led to considerable debate about the impact of the large retail chains on rural America, while rural Americans tend to vote with their feet and patronize these stores to the detriment of local businesses.

Government Reservations.   These communities rely on the existence of large state or federal land holdings or enterprises. The primary examples are military reservations (bases), and Native American lands and reservations. Military and Native American reservations are distinctive social organizations, as different from local conditions as they are from each other.

Military reservations are by their nature an alien kind of social structure. Military culture is disconnected from most rural communities that depend on them. Decision and control lie outside the community, and the tensions between locals and the military can be considerable. Residents of a military base are temporary, creating some of the problems we see in extraction-based communities. On the other hand, the United States has a "citizen soldier" military model that reduces the tension to some degree.

Native American reservations are another story. These settings are some of the poorest in the United States. The populations of the reservations possess a culture and tradition that may be at a sharp variance with non-Indian locals. The continuing level of poverty, illness, oppression, and despair on Native American lands is a national disgrace, made possible in part because the mechanisms of participation and public awareness are so weak.

Recreational Communities.   Recreational communities rely on some attractive element in the local environment to draw in people from outside. Examples include national parks, eco-

tourism sites, theme parks, ski areas, and beach resorts.

Recreational communities require good transportation (in most cases, remoteness itself can be an attraction for some visitors). These communities are vulnerable to the larger economy, since recreation is often the first casualty of economic hard times. In addition, these communities produce a large proportion of temporary residents who may be indifferent to community values or local resources. There may be considerable friction between residents and visitors, as when the wave of Japanese tourists began visiting Hawaii in large numbers in the 1970s and 1980s.

Ideological/Religious Communities.   The United States has a long tradition of social experiments in rural communities, from the Oneida community, the Mormons, and many social Utopian groups based on various religious and ideological beliefs. Religious communities and retreats have a long tradition in the West, with many monasteries and communities locating in the countryside to practice their beliefs undisturbed. The United States also has noted the phenomenon of countercultural communities of survivalist groups and other types of separatist groups. Though not a large part of the rural community system, they are distinctive and often defy analysis on the same terms as the other types of communities. These communities are often defined less by their economic structure than by their internal governance and community mores.

Specialized Communities.   This category includes communities such as rural retirement communities consisting of an age group cross section. Academic communities based on the presence of universities, boarding schools, or industrial training centers in rural areas are also specialized communities. Such communities often rely on a population that is radically unlike the local residents, creating some tensions often referred to as "town and gown" conflicts in college towns. These tensions may be considerable and are also noted in other areas where a large economic entity moves to a rural area. The presence of large rural manufacturing concerns for products such as carpets or furniture creates a monolithic corporate presence that can distort local values and preferences. An extreme example was the creation of the communities at Oak Ridge, Tennessee, and Los Alamos, New Mexico, to create the atomic bomb. The secrecy and distinctive cultures of such specialized communities create potential breaches and tensions with locals, even while producing economic benefits.

The Community System Life Cycle

When viewed as a system, the community is likely to go through four stages of development. These stages vary considerably in duration and specifics based on the kind of community being discussed. A brief discussion of the phases follows, along with a consideration of the role of community development in trying to intervene in this cycle.

Morphogenesis.   In this phase, communities invest a great deal of energy into organizing community systems, securing needed inputs, developing relationships with the social and physical environment, and coping with conflicts. Applied to rural U.S. communities, the morphogenic state could be observed in the founding of the first communities by the original settlers.

A new community such as colonial Jamestown had to secure its economic means of survival (agriculture), defend the community from a hostile environment (both social and physical), and organize a system of self-regulation. Such communities had little energy left to deal with internal conflicts over issues of norms and mores. For that reason, many of the colonial settlements were made up of people who already shared significant religious, political, and moral beliefs. Even so, the expenditure of en-

ergy in the organizing phase was enormous, and many communities failed due to the hostile environment, internal conflicts, or starvation. In frontier town such as Deadwood, the vulnerability to the environment was less, but the internal conflicts were prodigious. Think of trying to organize a very disparate group of people into a community when they shared no values, mores, history, or language. They shared only a goal: to find gold and get rich. The potential for chaos was awesome.

Morphostasis.   If a developing community in an inhospitable environment gets up and running, the next phase is to get things settled down. Institutions need to be established for commerce, education, socialization, and other functions. This usually means, in this country, elections of government officials, development of courts and schools, orderly commerce, and social activities, such as worship. The pioneers begin to give way to the citizens. System creation gives way to system maintenance. In western frontier towns, the coming of law and order replaced the law of the gun. Relationship with Native Americans changed from conflict to coexistence. Links with the larger society were established, and towns became "respectable."

Metamorphosis.   When small towns had achieved a degree of economic, social, and cultural stability, they entered a state of relative well-being. They then had to adapt as external conditions evolved. Small southern towns had to adapt to the end of slavery, which challenged both the economic and cultural patterns on which the towns were built. Western "boom towns," like gold camps or rail heads, had to diversify when mines played out or railroads moved on. Towns based on sustainable activities such as farming fared better, since it was possible to achieve a stable relationship between the raw materials needed, the processes used, and the products of the community. Nonetheless, even farming towns were affected by weather, markets, and most of all, by revolutions in agricultural technology.

The metamorphosis in some towns took the form of reduced vitality, lowering the standard of living and becoming isolated. In others, alternate economic means were found: Failing farms and mines were replaced by new crops or by new industries—prisons became a favorite. A fortunate few benefited from gentrification, which occurs when a rural area becomes fashionable when affluent urban types choose to move there. These instances do not change the trend, but they allow some failing communities to hang on by changing an important aspect of their nature.

Entropy. The final phase for failing communities is breakdown and decay. If the community cannot sustain itself nor reinvent itself either alone or with outside help, it atrophies and dies. Even as communities die, there are a few survivors. As small towns disappear, the remaining towns consolidate the needs of people over a larger geographic area. Four of five failing towns cannot sustain a grocery store, but as each fails, people in a region begin to shop at one store, which then has a sufficient base to hold on. The same is true for schools and churches. These consolidated towns may experience some internal disruptions, since the homogeneity of the membership is reduced.

Those who travel rural America are familiar with the scene: small towns with businesses, schools, churches, and homes boarded up. The population moves on; one day, the last picture show closes. These are the visible indications of a community in the entropic phase.

There is a great deal of debate about how to cope with this state of affairs. The laissez-faire capitalist position is to let the obsolete communities fail. They no longer serve a purpose, and trying to preserve them merely postpones the inevitable.

A moderate position is that, although the towns are small, taken together the small town-

ers represent a lot of people, and it will be expensive and disruptive to move them to urban areas. It might be more feasible to infuse small towns with money and initiative to keep them in place. This represents a kind of welfare approach; external support will be offered to a system no longer able to support itself. The infusion model is the spirit that drives part of the community preservation movement. A more radical view is that small towns represent a resource in themselves and must be maintained. This is usually identified with the tradition that small towns represent the traditional value base for America.

Related to the restoration approach is the "public works" strategy. Taking a page from the New Deal, some advocate supporting inefficient farming practices by price supports, which allows a continuation of a system that is no longer viable on its own. Creating "make work" for agrarian communities might, for example, take the form of developing biofuels (like gasohol), which are at present not economical alternatives to fossil fuel sources.

By being cleaned up and restored, small towns become a kind of sociological zoo, where urban dwellers can come to see what the United States used to be like. The motives for those who advocate the restoration of the small town model vary from nostalgia to caution. It is clear, however, that over time if the small town as a system is not economically viable on its own, it is unlikely to receive infusion of resources and efforts from outside for an indefinite period.

SUMMARY

In this chapter, we summarized the application of social systems theory to the community. In introducing the chapter, we summarized the distinguishing features of systems theory applied to the community. To develop these distinguishing features, we compared systems theory with the ecological, power, and conflict positions. We then presented social systems theory in terms of its component concepts. This was displayed in Figure 15.1. In Figure 15.2, the theory was graphically modeled employing the eight concepts comprising the structural features of all social systems. Rural communities were introduced as adapting systems.

GLOSSARY

Advocacy   Active support of a cause or for a change in the way that things are done.

Horizontal patterns   The concept as used by Roland Warren is essentially synonymous with what we designate as a community's internal structuring. These horizontal relationships link functionally community-based groups and organizations to each other.

Mutual support   One of the locality-relevant functions identified by Roland Warren and roughly comparable to the notion of social welfare.

Non zero sum   A situation of contest in which no one loses, and everyone gains something. Participants in the contest experience a net gain.

Production–distribution–consumption   A locality-relevant function identified by Roland Warren and roughly comparable to a community's economic system.

Request for proposals (RFP)   An invitation or announcement given out by an organization that has available funds. Individuals and/or organizations that may be interested are invited to submit funding requests (proposals) to compete for these funds. An RFP usually will pertain to a social issue, such as substance abuse.

Social control   A locality-relevant function identified by Roland Warren. In short, the concept refers to the means utilized by a system to secure compliance with its rules (normative expectations). Conceptually, compliance is sought through socialization measures. When these measures are unsuccessful, they are, so to speak, backed up by social control measures.

Socialization   As used by Roland Warren, the process by which individuals acquire and internalize the values, knowledge, skills, and related matters necessary to function successfully as members of society.

Social participation   A locality-relevant function identified by Roland Warren. Reference is made to the community-based arrangements through which people are provided opportunities for social interaction.

Vertical patterns   The concept as used by Roland Warren is essentially synonymous with what we designate as a system's suprasystem. It refers to the interdependent relationships that a system has with units that exist outside of the system.

Zero sum   A situation in which the gain of one side involves a corresponding loss to those on the other side—there are winners and losers.

NOTES

1. Gemeinschaft and Gesellschaft are key concepts employed in social systems theory. Definitions are found at the conclusion of Chapter 7. See Ferdinand Toennies, *Community and Society*, ed. and trans. Charles P. Loomis (Lansing, MI: Michigan University Press, 1957), 247–259.

2. The concepts of power employed were introduced in Chapter 11. See particularly Max Weber, "The Three Types of Legitimate Rule," trans. Hans Girth, in *A Sociological Reader on Complex Organization*, eds. Amitai Etzioni and Edward W. Lehman, 3rd ed.

(New York: Holt, Rinehart and Winston, 1980), 6–15. For a more comprehensive review, see Max Weber, *Essays in Sociology*, ed. and trans. H. H. Girth and C. Wright Mills (New York: Oxford University Press, 1946), 159–179.

3. See Nicholas S. Timasheff, *Sociological Theory: Its Nature and Growth* (New York: Random House, 1967), 32–44.

4. Ralf Dahrendorf, "Toward a Theory of Social Conflict," *Conflict Resolution*, 11, no. 2 (June 1958): 170.

5. Ibid., 174.

6. See particularly Dennis E. Poplin, *Communities: A Survey of Theories and Methods of Research* (New York: Macmillan, 1972). Also see *Perspectives on the American Community*, ed. Roland Warren, 2nd ed. (Chicago: Rand McNally, 1973).

7. Irvin T. Sanders, *The Community: An Introduction to a Social System* (New York: The Ronald Press, 1958).

8. Ibid., 121.

9. Ibid., 204–341.

10. Ibid., 342–362.

11. Roland Warren, *The Community in America*, 3rd ed. (Chicago: Rand McNally, 1978), 137–169.

12. Ibid., 9.

13. Ibid., 140–147, 162–168, and 240–303.

14. Ibid., 52–136. Also see Emilia E. Martinez-Brawley, "Community," in *Encyclopedia of Social Work*, vol. 1, 19th ed. (Washington, DC: NASW Press, 1995), 539–548.

15. Warren, *The Community in America*, 137–169.

16. For an excellent overview of need assessment, see John E. Tropman, "Community Needs Assessment," *Encyclopedia of Social Work*, vol. 1, 19th ed. (Washington, DC: NASW Press, 1995), 563–569. Also see Sylvia Martí-Costa and Irma Serrano-García, "Needs Assessment and Community Development: An Ideological Perspective," in *Strategies of Community Intervention*, Jack Rothman et al., eds., 5th ed. (Itasca, IL: F. E. Peacock, 1995), 257–267.

17. Ram A. Cnaan and Jack Rothman, "Locality Development and the Building of Community," in *Strategies of Community Intervention*, Jack Rothman et al., eds. 5th ed. (Itasca, IL: F. E. Peacock, 1995), 241–257.

18. See particularly E. T. Hiller, "The Community as a Social Group," *American Sociological Review*, 6 (1941): 189–202.

19. For a review of the social indicator movement, see Robert J. Rossi and Kevin J. Gilmartin, *Handbook of Social Indicators* (New York: Garland STPM Press, 1980).

20. United Way of America. *UWASIS II* (Alexandria, VA: United Way of America, Planning and Allocations Division), November 1976.

21. Ibid., 7.

22. Fact Sheet: Rural renaissance. (2005) Rural Renaissance Network. Monroe, WI. www.ruralrenaissance.org

INDEX

academic communities, 427
accommodation, 112, 238
achieved roles, 219
achieved status, 78–79
achievement goals, 259–260
act, 131
action system, 23
activation response, 109
activities, 57, 58, 147
adaptation, 12–13, 34–35, 264–265, 324–325, 410–411
adaptive upgrading, 82
Adler, Alfred, 103
advocacy, 408
affect, 52
affiliative goals, 259–260
age, 87
agrarian communities, 425
alienation, 391
anal stage of development (Freud), 101
anomie, 391
area trade centers, 426–427
ascribed roles, 219
ascribed status, 78–79
assimilation, 112
attribution theory, 124
authority, 297–300, 315, 383, 399
autonomy versus shame and doubt, 154–155, 170

Bandura, Albert, 105, 109
Bank Wiring Room study, 306
baseline data, 63
basic trust versus mistrust, 151–152, 170
Bateson, Gregory, 251
behaviorism/learning theory, 104–110
    assumptions, 106–107
    concepts, 107–110
behavior modification, 106
belongingness and love needs (Maslow), 129
biotic subsocial system, 378
Blau, Peter, 206, 207, 208, 210–211
blended family, 241
boundaries, 14, 27, 49, 51–53, 188, 267–270, 326

and the community, 413–414
diffuse, 244
in families, 238, 241–245
in the formal organization, 340–341
lack of, within family, 248
maintenance, 35, 51–53, 57, 342
and social systems, 8
boundary effects, 71
and diversity, 74–76
Bowen, Murray, 245–246, 248, 249
Buber, Martin, 225
bureaucracy, 297, 300–305
burnout, 296

categories of people (versus social groups), 184–185
cathected relationships, 178
central business district (CBD), 376–377
chain of command, 300, 352
charismatic authority, 299, 399–400
Chess, Wayne, 131, 170
chief executive officer (CEO), 323–324
circular reaction (Piaget), 113–114
classical conditioning, 107
class structure, 391
closed system, 26–27, 317, 319
    and diversity, 74
coalition, 244–245
cognitive-behavioral theory, 124–125
cognitive development theory, 110–116
    assumptions, 111
    concepts, 112–116
    stages (Piaget), 113–116, 170
collections of people (versus social groups), 184
color, people of, 86–87
communications/interactive theory, 250–254
community, 22
    definition of, 45, 371–375
    life cycle, 428
    purpose of, 402
    rural, 424–428
    as a social system, 407
    and social systems theory, 398–430
    structural components, 411–424

community power position, 381–389, 401
  elitist position, 382–383
  pluralist position, 386–389
community power structure, 382, 385
competition, 379
complementary roles, 235
Comte, Auguste, 31
concentric zone theory, 377
concepts, definition of, 20
concrete operational thought (Piaget), 115–116
conditioned reflex (CR), 105
conditioned stimulus (CS), 105
conflict
  definition of, 390
  and religious diversity, 83–85
  theorists, 31
  theory, 81
conflict position, 390–394
  and the community, 400–402
conformity, 80–81
congruent communication, 251
consciousness, levels of (Freud), 98–99
Continuous Quality Improvement (CQI), 332
conventional morality, 119–120
conversation of gestures, 131
conversion operations, 14, 50, 51, 58–60, 327–328
  and the community, 420–422
  and the family, 277–280
  in the formal organization, 346, 349–360
Cooley, Charles Horton, 36, 39, 161, 178, 181–184,
    212, 216–217, 287
Coser, Lewis, 393–394
Council on Social Work Education (CSWE), 4–5
cultural diversity, 68–73
cultural infusion, 77
cultural relativity, 71
cultural stars, 71
culture
  definition of, 46, 70
  dominant, 72
  minority, 72

Dahl. Robert, 386–389
Dahrendorf, Ralf, 393, 401–402
death instinct (Freud), 98–99
defense mechanisms, 100
Deming, W. Edwards, 332–335
democracy, 68, 69
depersonalization of position, 303

determinism, 126
detouring, 245, 248
development, stages of
  psychoanalytic theory, 100–102
  psychosocial theory, 145–146, 151–169
  symbolic interaction theory, 131–137
developmental activities, 147
deviance credit, 260
dialectic, 183–184, 319–320
dialectical behavior therapy (DBT), 125
differentiation, 82, 207–209, 246–247
diffuse boundary, 244
directors, board of, 349
disability and diversity, 88–89
discrimination, 110
disengagement
  definition of, 244
  parent-child, 243
distortion, 242
diversity, 68
  conflict and consensus, 81–83
  ethical and cultural, 85–89
  and religion, 83–85
  and social systems theory, 73–78
division of labor, 301–302, 340, 352
divorce, 239
dominance, 379
dominant culture, 46, 72
double bind communication, 252–253
Dubos, Rene, 30
Durkheim, Emile, 6, 31, 32–33, 249
dynamics of social systems, 7, 56
dysfunction, 74

early adulthood life stage, 163–165
ecological perspective, 30–31, 50, 375–380
  and the community, 400–401
  ecology of games, 379–380
ecomap, 270–271, 273
ecosystem, 30
effectiveness, 362
efficiency, 362
ego (Freud), 99
ego integrity versus despair (Erikson), 167–168
Electra complex (Freud), 102
elitist position, 382–385
Ellis, Albert, 125
embeddedness, 8
emergence, 25–26, 320–321

emergent properties, 25
emotional cutoff, 249–250
empathy, 248
empowerment, 301, 381
enmeshment, 132, 244
entropy, 27–28, 328, 408, 429
environment, 30, 53
epigenesis, 150–151, 258
epiphenomenal structures, 236
equifinality, 29
equilibrium, 28
Erickson, Milton, 132
Erikson, Erik, 98, 132, 144–147, 151–152, 153–154,
    157–158, 161, 163–164, 165–170, 258
esteem needs (Maslow), 129
ethics
  definition of, 85
  NASW Code of Ethics, 85–89
ethnicity, 86
evaluative feedback, 10
evolution, 150
exchange theory, 200–211
  assumptions, 203–204
  differentiation, 207–209
  organization, 211
  stabilization, 209–211
extinction, 108, 109, 110
extraction-based communities, 425–426
exurbs, 426

family
  boundaries, 241–245
  communication/interactive theory, 250–254
  definition of, 45
  differentiation, 246–247
  as emergent structures, 230–232
  epiphenomenal structures, 236
  homeostasis, 253–254
  multigenerational structure, 248–249
  projection process, 248
  reciprocal and complementary roles, 235
  and the social group, 257–288, 262–287
  structural family theory, 232–245
  structure mapping, 243–245
  subsystems, 236–241
  as system of roles, 230–254
  systems theory, 245–250
  triangulation, 247–248
  universal and idiosyncratic constraints, 234–235

favorable balance, 28
feedback, 15–16, 50, 62–64, 328
  and the community, 424
  and the family, 286–287
  in the formal organization, 362–366
field theory, 195–200
focal system, 14
formal operational thought (Piaget), 116
formal organization
  authority, 297–300
  boundary, 340–341, 342
  conversion operations, 346, 349–360
  definition of, 45, 295–296
  developmental stages of, 328–332
  emergence, 320
  feedback, 362–366
  four functional requisites, 321–325
  input, 345
  interface, 343–344
  output, 360–361
  proposed output, 345–346
  as a social system, 338–366
  suprasystem, 341, 343
formal organizations, 293–369
  and spirituality, 309–310
  theory and practice, 296–297
  Weberian bureaucracy, 300–305
formed groups, 177, 185
  task and treatment groups, 186
four functional requisites, 321–325, 408–412
Four-Problem Matrix, 34, 48–49
Freud, Sigmund, 39, 96–104, 117, 133, 156, 158,
    170, 258
function, 59–60
functional theory, 31–36

Galpin, Charles, 376
game playing (ecological perspective), 379–380
game play stage (symbolic interaction theory),
    134–135
Gans, Herbert, 8
Gemeinschaft, 178–179, 200, 206, 209, 261, 267,
    271, 273, 288, 294–295, 303, 307, 308,
    314–315, 318, 416
  and the community, 399
  definition of, 178
gender, 87
generalist practice
  basic characteristics of, 7

generalist practice (*cont.*)
  definition of, 23
  model, 15, 58
generalization, 110
general systems theory, 23–30
generativity versus stagnation, 165–166
genital stage of development (Freud), 102
genogram, 249, 278–279
Germain, Carel B., 380
Gesellschaft, 178–180, 200, 209, 271, 288, 294–295,
    303, 307, 315, 318, 416
  and the community, 399
  definition of, 178
gestalt psychology, 195
Gibbs, Jack P., 378
goal attainment, 12–13, 34, 264, 324, 411–412
goals, 57, 58
  Lewin's meaning, 198
  structure of, 177, 259–260
Goffman, Erving, 38
government reservations, 427
grapevine, 331
groups
  development, stages of, 186–187
  identity, 260
  size, 259

Hawley, Amos H., 377–378
Hawthorne studies, 306–307, 333
Hegel, G. F. W., 183
helping system, 15
  example, 61
hierarchical authority, 300
hierarchy
  of needs (Maslow), 127, 130
  of outcomes, 57–58, 347
  of relationship patterns, 266
  of systems, 8–9
hodological space (Lewin), 197
holarchy, 9
holon, 29–30, 45, 242, 274, 326–327
Homans, George C., 203–204
homeostasis, 28, 253
horizontal patterns, 404–405
human ecology, 375–380
humanism, 69
  assumptions, 126–127
  concepts, 127–131
human relations position, 306–308

compared to social systems theory, 318–319
humor in metacommunication, 252
Hunter, Floyd, 382–385
hypotheses, 20

identity, 177
identity versus role confusion, 161–162
ideological/religious communities, 427
id (Freud), 39, 99
idiosyncratic constraints, 234
inclusion, 82, 399
inclusiveness, 315
incongruent communication, 251–252
individualism, 69
individualistic behavior, 257–258
industry versus inferiority, 158–159
infancy, 151–154
influence, 383, 387
information distortion, 188–189, 242
information loss, 242
in-groups, 187–190
initiative versus guilt, 157–158, 170
innovation, 80, 81
input, 14, 50, 56–57, 327
  and the community, 416–417
  and the family, 274–276
  in the formal organization, 345
institution, 420
insubordination, 298
integration, 12–13, 34, 35, 264, 324, 410
interactions, 54, 280–284, 357–360
interface, 14, 27, 49–50, 54–56, 327
  and the community, 415–416
  and the family, 271–274
  in the formal organization, 343–344
intimacy versus isolation, 163–164
involvement, 245
isophilia, 241
I-Thou relationship, 225–226

job descriptions, 302
Jung, Carl, 103

Kahn, Robert L., 328–332
Katz, Daniel, 328–332
Koestler, Arthur, 29–30, 242
Kohlberg, Lawrence, 117–124, 123, 132, 170,
    258
Kuhn, Thomas, 11

late adulthood life stage, 167–169
latency, 35
   stage of development (Freud), 102
latent affiliation, 190
latent functions, 73–74
learned helplessness, 124
legal authority, 297–298, 315, 340
   and the community, 400
legitimacy, 297, 298, 317
Lewin, Kurt, 195–200, 237
life space, 196–197, 198
life stages (psychosocial theory)
   adolescence, 161–163
   concepts, 145, 146
   early adulthood, 163–165
   infancy, 151–154
   late adulthood, 167–169
   middle adulthood, 165–167
   post infancy, 154–156
   preschool, 156–158
   school, 158–160
line positions, 352
logical actions, 45
Long, Morton, 379–380

maintenance inputs, 56
maintenance output, 14, 60, 361, 364, 366
manifest affiliation, 190
manifest functions, 73
marital status, 88
Martin, Walter T., 378
Marx, Karl, 31, 32, 390–392
Maslow, Abraham, 117, 126–130, 163–164, 165, 166, 335
Mayo, Elton, 306
McGregor, Douglas, 335
Mead, George Herbert, 36–37, 39, 132, 134, 212, 218
Menninger, Karl, 390
Merton, Robert, 20, 80–81
metacommunications, 251–252
metamorphosis, 428429
methodological behaviorism, 106
middle adulthood life stage, 165–167
minority culture, 72
   status as hollow, 76–78
model
   generalist practice, 15
   social systems, 13

modeling
   in behaviorism/learning theory, 109–110
   social systems theory, 50, 268
   steady state, 49, 263, 322
   structural components, 326
modernism, 68–69
moral development theory, 116–124
   assumptions, 118
   concepts, 118–121
   faith and spirituality, 122
   gender differences, 120–121
   stages, 119–120, 170
morphogenesis, 428
morphostasis, 428
multifinality, 29
Munition, Salvador, 232–234, 237, 246
mutuality, 181
mutual support, 404

NASW Code of Ethics, 85–89, 117
national origin, 86
natural groups, 177, 185
natural will, 179–181
needs, 127–130
   genuine (Lewin), 197–198
   hierarchy of (Maslow), 127, 130
   quasi (Lewin), 198
negative entropy, 27–28, 328
negative feedback, 63
negative reinforcement, 107, 108
non zero sum gaming, 405
norms, definition of, 46

objectives, 57, 58
Oedipal stage of development (Freud), 101–102
Olsen, Marvin E., 208, 209, 210, 211
ontogenetic perspective, 258
open system, 26–27
   and diversity, 74
operant conditioning, 107
oral stage of development (Freud), 100
organization
   in cognitive development theory, 112–113
   in exchange theory, 211
organizational theory, 296–297
   applied, 304–305
   and social work education, 308–310
Ouchi, William, 335
out-groups, 187–190

output, 14–15, 50, 60–62, 285–286, 328
    and the community, 422–424
    in the formal organization, 360–362
overinvolvement, 245

parental subsystem, 239–240, 240, 241
Park, Robert Ezra, 376–378
Parsons, Talcott, 13, 30, 33–36, 41, 48, 49, 82, 83,
        233, 262, 409
    four-problem matrix, 34
    and social stratification, 78
pathology, 126
pattern maintenance, 12–13, 34, 35–36, 48,
        265–266, 324
    and the community, 408–410
Pavlov, Ivan, 105, 106, 107
phallic stage of development (Freud), 101–102
Piaget, Jean, 110–116, 132, 135, 159, 170
pleasure principle (Freud), 102–103
pluralist position, 386–389
    and the community, 401
POET model, 33
polarity, 146
political belief, 88
political resources, 389
positive feedback, 63
positive reinforcement, 107, 108
postconventional morality, 120
postmodernism, 69–70
poverty, 89
power, 399
    and the community, 399, 400–401
    pyramids of, 384–385
    structure, 383
preconscious mind (Freud), 99
preconventional morality, 119
prelanguage stage (symbolic interaction theory),
        132–133
preoperational thought (Piaget), 114–115
prepotency principle (Maslow), 127–128
preschool life stage, 156–158
primary group, 39, 181–183, 295
production-distribution-consumption, 403, 404
proposed output, 14, 50, 51, 57–58, 276–277, 327
    and the community, 417–420
    in the formal organization, 345–346, 347–348
psychoanalytic/psychodynamic theory, 96–104
    assumptions, 97–98
    concepts, 98–103

and feminist theory, 104
and psychosocial crises, 146
and religion, 103–104
stages, 100–102, 170
psychosocial crisis, 145, 151, 154, 157, 158, 161,
        163, 165, 167
psychosocial stages, 170
psychosocial theory, 143–170
    assumptions, 145
    biological connection, 148–151
    concepts, 145–148
    focus, 144
    and spirituality, 169
punishment, 108–109
purpose, 57, 58
pyramids of power, 384–385

race, 86
radical behaviorism, 106
Rational Emotive Therapy, 125
rationalism, 69
    compared to social systems theory, 316–317
    and formal organizations, 300–305
rational will, 179–181
reality principle (Freud), 103
rebellion, 80, 81
reciprocal roles, 235
reciprocity, 210
recreational communities, 427
reductionism, 10, 126
reference groups, 39
reframing, 124
"Regional City" study, 383–384
reinforcement, 107–109
relationships, cathected, 178
religion, 88
    community pattern maintenance, 409–410
    definition of, 47
    and diversity, 83–85
    and formal organizations, 309–310
    in groups, 190–191
    role in social work, 6–7
religious communities, 427
repression (Freud), 99
request for proposals (RFP), 422
retreatism, 80, 81
ritualism, 80, 81
Robinson, Daniel, 105
role performance, standardization of, 302

role playing stage (symbolic interaction theory), 133
roles, 39
  definition of, 47
  and families, 230–254
  reciprocity, 47
  in symbolic interaction theory, 131
role theory, 36–40
rural communities, 424–428

safety and security needs (Maslow), 129
Sanders, Irwin T., 402–403
schema, 112
school life stage, 158–160
science, 68, 69
secondary group, 181, 295
self
  definition of, 45
  dramaturgy, 38
  measurement of, 37–38
  reflexive, 37, 39
  in symbolic interaction theory, 131, 215–220
self-actualization needs (Maslow), 128–129
self-efficacy, 146
selfhood, 146
  fulfillment (symbolic interaction theory), 136–137
  stabilization (symbolic interaction theory), 135
  stages of, 131–137, 170
"self-talk," 125
sensorimotor intelligence (Piaget), 113–114
seriously and persistently mentally ill (SPMI), 341
settlement house, 394
sexual orientation, 87
shaping, 110
sibling subsystem, 240–241
signal inputs, 56–57
Simmel, Georg, 189–190, 390–393
situated behavior, 257–258
situation, 220–223
Skinner, B. F., 105, 106, 117
slack in the system (Dahl), 388
Smith, Adam, 380
social act, 223–225, 281–282
social behaviorism, 212
social class, 391
social control, 403–404
social Darwinism, 375
social group, 46, 175–191

definition of, 45, 177, 259
effect on individual, 260–261
exclusiveness, 261
and the family, 258–261
identity, 260
natural versus formed group, 177
primary and secondary, 181–183
religion and spirituality, 190–191
theoretical support, 194–227
social interaction, 131
socialism/communism, 391–392
socialization, 32, 213–215
  and the community, 403
social organization, 320
  definition of, 45
social participation, 404
social relationships, 4, 22–23, 59
social systems
  assumptions, 21–23
  definition of, 4
  dynamics of, 7–8, 56
  function of, 12–13
  hierarchy, 8–9
  structure of, 8, 49–64, 349–357
social systems theory
  and the community, 398–430
  compared to human relations position, 318–319
  compared to rationalist position, 316–317
  comprehensiveness, 9
  construction of, 11–12, 21–23, 314
  and diversity, 73–78
  emergence, 320–321
  formal organizations, developmental stages of, 328–332
  foundations for, 19–41
  four requisite functions, 262–267, 321–325, 408–412
  general features, 44–64, 261–262
  and generalist practice, 7–10
  holistic perspective, 10
  interactivity, 9–10
  model, 13–16, 50
  structural concepts, 267–287, 325–328, 412–424
social work
  definition of, 3
  purpose of, 4–5
  and social systems theory, 11–12
  theory and practice, 5–6
society, definition of, 45

sociogram, 277
sociology, definition of, 31
sociometry, 277
span of control, 300, 352
Spencer, Herbert, 31, 32
spirituality
    definition of, 47
    in formal organizations, 309–310
    and group process, 225–226
    in groups, 190–191
    role in social work, 6–7
spousal subsystem, 237–239
stabilization, 209–211
staff positions, 352
stages, life (psychosocial theory), 146
stages in group development, 186–187
stages of selfhood (symbolic interaction theory),
        131–137
stage theories
    comparison chart, 170
    Piaget, 112
standardization of role performance, 302–303
status position, definition of, 47
steady state, 28–29, 31, 49, 64, 253–254, 262, 263
    and the community, 406, 408
    in formal organization, 321–325
stigma, 79
stimulus-organism-response (S-O-R) behaviorism,
        106
stimulus-response (S-R) behaviorism, 106
stratification, 73, 78–81
strengths/needs assessment, 341
strengths perspective, 11
structural family theory, 232–245
structural-functionalism, 31
structuralist perspective, 308
structure
    and the family, 233–234
    of social systems, 8, 12, 58–59, 60, 262, 349–357
        and the community, 411–424
subcultures, 46, 70
    cultural differentiation, 72–73
    cultural integration, 72
    definition of, 71
subject system, 14
subsystem, 14
succession, 379
superego (Freud), 99–100

suprasystem, 14, 26, 27, 29, 49, 53–54, 327
    and the community, 414–415
    and the family, 270–271
    in the formal organization, 341, 343
survival-level needs (Maslow), 128
symbiosis, 378–379
symbol, 131
symbolic interactionism, 36–37
symbolic interaction theory, 131–137, 211–225,
        280
    concepts, 131
    self, 215–220
    situation, 220–223
    social act, 223–225
symbols, 212–213
symmetrical relationships, 235
syntax and concepts, 20

task groups, 186
task output, 14, 60, 360–361, 363–364
Taylor, Frederick W., 304–305
technology, 12, 314
tension system (Lewin), 198–199
theory
    nature of, 19–21
    and practical applications, 5–6
Theory X, 335–336
Theory Y, 335–336
Theory Z, 335–336
Toennies, Ferdinand, 178, 180–181, 200, 294–295,
        307
Total Quality Management (TQM), 332–335
traditional authority, 298–299, 315
treatment groups, 186
triangulation, 247–248

unconditioned reflex (UR), 105
unconditioned stimulus (US), 105
unconscious mind (Freud), 98
universal constraints, 234

values, 82–83, 126
vertical patterns, 404–405
von Bertalanffy, Ludwig, 27, 29, 30

Warren, Roland, 403–405, 411
waste, 14, 60, 61, 361–362, 419–420
Watson, John, 105, 107

Weber, Max, 31, 32, 297–299, 300–305, 340,
    381–382
Weberian bureaucracy, 300–305
well-being, 22, 48, 123, 262
    and the community, 406, 408

and psychoanalytic theory, 102, 103
Wilber, Ken, 122, 124

Zeigarnik effect, 199
zero sum gaming, 405